# NEW IMMUNOLOGY RESEARCH DEVELOPMENTS

# New Immunology Research Developments

**Gunter V. Müller**
**Editor**

**Nova Science Publishers, Inc.**
*New York*

**Library of Congress Cataloging-in-Publication Data**

New immunology research developments / Gunter V. Müller (editor).
p. ; cm.
Includes bibliographical references and index.
ISBN-13: 978-1-60021-701-2 (hardcover)
ISBN-10: 1-60021-701-X (hardcover)
1. Immunology. I. Müller, Gunter V.
[DNLM: 1. Immune System. 2. Anti-Infective Agents--immunology. 3. Autoimmune Diseases--immunology. 4. Immunity. 5. Immunologic Factors. QW 504 N5316 2008]
QR181.N393 2008
616.07'9--dc22 2008013821

*Published by Nova Science Publishers, Inc. ✝ New York*

# Contents

# Preface

This new book focuses on new research advances in the field of immunology, which is the study of the body's protection from foreign macromolecules or invading organisms and the responses to them. These invaders include viruses, bacteria, protozoa or even larger parasites. In addition, immune responses are developed against our own proteins (and other molecules) in autoimmunity and against our own aberrant cells in tumor immunity. The first lines of defense against foreign organisms are barrier tissues, such as the skin, that stop the entry of organisms into our bodies. A second line of defense is the specific or adaptive immune system which may take days to respond to a primary invasion (that is, infection by an organism that has not hitherto been seen).

Short Communication - The specific and polyclonal immune response under the influence of T-independent antigens type 2 (TI-2 antigens) was studied. Mice BALB/c were immunized by different TI-2 antigens: Polyvinylpirrolidon, alpha (1→3) Dextran, Pneumococcal polysaccharide SIII and Ficoll) injected separately or together and by TI-2 antigen injected together with T-dependent (TD) antigen. On the $4^{th}$ day spleens were removed and the numbers of cells forming antibodies (AFC) and total Ig (IFC) were determined by ELISPOT. Splenocytes of unimmunized mice were used as control. The number of cells forming nonspecific Ig (nIFC) was calculated as the difference between IFC and AFC numbers. The number of nIFC induced by the antigens (inIFC) was calculated as the difference between the numbers of nIFC in immune and control splenocytes.

It was shown that TI-2 antigens lacking intrinsic mitogenic activity induced the appearance of AFC and the formation of inIFC (polyclonal activation) as well. Simultaneous injection of TI-2 and TD antigens resulted in summation of inIFC number, but unexpectedly, simultaneous injection of two TI-2 antigens did not. After combined injection of two TI-2 antigens the number of inIFC did not exceed that induced by the more potent of two TI-2 antigens used. This effect cannot be explained by unspecific immunosuppression since AFC formation did not decrease and sometimes even slightly increased.

It is suggested that T-dependent and TI-2 antigens involve in polyclonal activation different B cell subsets, whereas TI-2 antigens induce unspecific activation of cells belonging to the same restricted in size pool consisting either of bystander B-1/MZ-B cells or, more probable, of B cells in some definite stage of differentiation.

Chapter 1 - Polymorphonuclear leukocytes (PMNs or neutrophils) are the most abundant white cell in humans and an essential component of the innate immune system. PMNs are typically the first leukocyte recruited to sites of infection or areas of inflammation. Ingestion (phagocytosis) of microorganisms triggers production of reactive oxygen species (ROS) and fusion of granules with forming phagosomes. ROS and microbicides of granules are highly effective at killing ingested microorganisms. On the other hand, these cytotoxic molecules can cause non-specific damage to host tissues and thus it is critical that neutrophil turnover is tightly regulated. To that end, mature PMNs are short-lived cells programmed to undergo apoptosis as a means to facilitate immune system homeostasis. Our understanding of neutrophil apoptosis and its importance in the immune system has evolved over the past 18 years. Proinflammatory molecules, such as host-derived cytokines and chemokines or products of microorganisms, delay PMN apoptosis, thereby prolonging function. Phagocytosis of bacteria typically accelerates neutrophil apoptosis, a process involving production of ROS, which ultimately promotes resolution of infection. By comparison, some bacterial pathogens alter neutrophil apoptosis to survive and disseminate. This chapter provides a brief history of neutrophil apoptosis research and an overview of mechanisms of neutrophil apoptosis, phagocytosis of apoptotic PMNs, and ability of microorganisms to alter PMN apoptosis.

Chapter 2 – AD affects more than four million people in the United States and prevalence studies demonstrate an exponential rise of dementia with age (Katzman, 2001). The number of cases of dementia in the developed world is projected to rise from 13.5 million in 2000 to 21.2 million in 2025, and to 36.7 million in 2050 (Katzman and Fox, 1999). Currently the number of deaths caused by AD is similar to the number of deaths caused by stroke. AD and stroke together rank as the third most common causes of death (Ewbank, 1999).

The symptoms of typical AD begin with a loss of short-term memory that slowly progresses to affect all memory functions (Corey-Bloom et al., 1994). Initially, impaired short-term memory often manifests itself as losing objects or forgetfulness in conversations. Subsequently, other early cognitive deficits occur; they include difficulty in word-finding, problem solving and spatio-temporal awareness.

Identification of genetic mutations that cause early onset AD has helped to dramatically increase the understanding of the origins of AD. Although cases of familial AD are relatively rare, perhaps only 200 families identified to date, they represent identified molecular mutations that cause AD. The genes identified to be responsible for early onset familial AD code for the amyloid precursor protein (APP), presenilin-1 and presenilin-2; these are found on chromosomes 21, 14, and 1, respectively. In addition to these dominantly-transmitted disease-causing mutations in early onset AD, still other studies have identified over 25 genetic risk factors that influence the appearance of the more common sporadic late onset AD. Current research is actively using genetically-modified mice to determine how specific protein modifications lead to the pathology of AD.

AD is the most common form of elderly dementia and has no effective therapy. Pathological diagnosis is based on post-mortem neuropathology, defined by three hallmarks: senile plaque, NFT, and neuronal cell loss. Aβ is produced during the processing of APP by BACE and the γ-secretase complex that includes PS1. Both APP and PS1 are causative genes of AD, while apoE4 is a risk factor allele. The Aβ load in CNS is maintained by balancing its production and clearance, which is mediated by passive diffusion to blood stream, degradation by Aβ degrading enzymes (IDE and neprilysin), and microglial phagocytosis. Aβ production, deposition, and neurodegeneration are significantly regulated by astroglial and microglial activation via direct contact as well as secretion of a number of neurotoxicants. Specific pro-inflammatory cytokines, chemokines, and excitotoxins have been characterized as mediators of neuroinflammation and neurotoxicity. Pro-inflammatory cytokines, especially TNF-α and IFN-γ, are significantly involved in BACE expression and Aβ prodution from neurons and astrocytes. Those diverse studies are generating a large number of potential therapeutic targets for treating AD. Beneficial effects have been reported for anti-inflammatory drugs, such as NSAIDs, to treat glial inflammation and disease progression.

Chapter 3 - Acute phase proteins (APP) are serum proteins elevated in response to a variety of physiological injuries including infection and inflammation. These pathogen nonspecific proteins are predominantly synthesized in the liver and serve as a humoral component of innate immunity by way of recognizing and neutralizing pathogens, and facilitating tissue repair. The nature of APP and their physiological significance is not understood in sub mammalian species. In studying the avian acute phase response in experimental inflammation induced by endotoxin or croton oil, the authors identified serum transferrin as a major avian APP that was same as the ovotransferrin (OVT) present in the egg white. Using an enzyme-immunoassay, the results showed the serum OVT to be elevated during a variety of bacterial and viral infections. The ability of OVT to modulate avian macrophage and heterophil functions was evaluated using *in vitro* assays. The results showed that OVT activated both of these cell types as measured by nitric oxide, interleukin-6, matrix metalloproteinase, and reactive oxygen production. Additionally, OVT also stimulated heterophil degranulation. These results demonstrate that beyond its antibacterial effects, the OVT may act as a natural immunomodulator enhancing innate immune function.

Chapter 4 - It is now well established that dietary polyunsaturated fatty acids (PUFA) modulate immune function. There is less known about conjugated linoleic acid (CLA), a dietary PUFA that may also have immunomodulatory properties. CLA is a group of geometrical and positional isomers of linoleic acid (LA). Research has primarily focused on the cis9, trans11 (c9,t11) and trans10, cis12 (t10,c12) isomer singly or when fed in mixtures of isomers. The purpose of this review is to critically examine the *in vitro*, animal and human studies that have investigated the potential benefits of CLA on immune function. Although the area is in its infancy, there is evidence to support beneficial effects of feeding CLA isomers on immune-mediated catabolism, the ability to respond to bacterial and viral challenges, in allergic reactions, in inflammation and several aspects of the acquired immune system, including cytokine production, lymphocyte proliferation and immunoglobulin (Ig) production. To enable one to understand the potential significance of these studies, this review will include a background review of the immune system. Although the mechanistic pathway through which CLA acts on the immune system has yet to be determined, this review will propose candidate pathways through which CLA might modulate immune function.

Chapter 5 - Autoreactive T-cell responses directed to myelin proteins in the central nervous system (CNS) are widely believed to be fundamental in the pathology of multiple sclerosis (MS). This view has dominated the research field in MS for many years and led to the reliance on experimental models of neurological disease following immunisation with myelin antigens. Such experimental diseases have developed as the central paradigm to investigate underlying mechanisms operating in MS as well as the preclinical development of therapeutic strategies.

This long-standing concept has recently shifted and evidence is rapidly accumulating indicting a significance role of axonal damage and neurodegeneration in disease. Indeed, axonal damage is now considered to be the major cause of irreversible neurological disability in MS patients. One correlate of axonal damage in MS is the presence of antibodies against neurofilament light protein, a major component of the axonal cytoskeleton. Contrary to extensive literature on pathogenic myelin autoimmunity, the possible pathogenic role of autoimmunity to axonal antigens in MS has so far been ignored. The authors' recent experimental data indicate that autoimmunity to axonal antigens, as described in MS, is pathogenic rather than acting merely as a surrogate marker for axonal degeneration.

As validation of the concept that autoimmunity directed to neuronal antigens plays a role in disease, the authors define four criteria: first, that autoreactivity to neuronal antigens are consistently present in neurological disease in humans and experimental neurological disease in animals; secondly, that transfer of such neuronal reactive T cells and/or antibodies are pathogenic either *in vivo* or *in vitro* model systems; thirdly, that immunization with neuronal antigens induces pathogenic autoimmune responses and leads to neurological disease in experimental animals; and finally, that inhibition of such responses ameliorates neurological disease.

Using these criteria, the authors review the evidence for autoimmunity to neuronal antigens in several neurodegenerative disorders such as paraneoplastic disorders, and discuss how similar mechanisms may also operate in MS. Using the experimental models they describe their recent data to indicate that while clinical disease in MS models is due to autoimmune attack on myelin, neurons and axons can be also target for pathogenic autoimmunity. Understanding the factors leading to neuronal injury and neurodegenerative disorders is key to the development of effective therapies to prevent progression of disease and irreversible damage.

Chapter 6 - West Nile virus (WNV) infection is a zoonotic disease. The virus belongs to the family Flaviviridae. Wild birds serve as the reservoir of the virus in nature and mosquitoes mainly from the culex species serve as the vector for its replication cycle.

Humans as well as horses and other domestic animals are incidental hosts.

Until recently, WNV infections were traditionally considered to be a mild self-limited disease. When symptomatic it usually manifested with fever, headache, myalgia, generalized lymphadenopathy and rash. Central nervous system (CNS) involvement was infrequent. In the last decade several epidemics of WNV have occurred in several areas in Europe, in Israel, and for the first time in the Western Hemisphere, accounting for a large outbreak in New York. These epidemics were characterized by an exceptional high rate of neurological morbidity and mortality.

The most common neurological involvement are encephalitis/meningoencephalitis followed by aseptic meningitis and flaccid paralysis. Other less common neurological presentations include Guillain Barre syndrome, rhombencephalitis, optic neuritis and aphasia.

The cause for this clinical evolution from a mild flu-like illness to a severe neuroinvasive disease is not fully understood and is thought in part to be related to the emergence of more neurovirulent WNV strains.

This chapter discusses the wide range of neurologic manifestations of WNV infections, as well as the pathogenesis of WNV nervous system involvement and current and future therapeutic strategies.

Chapter 7 - Nerve growth factor (NGF) is a pleiotropic factor implicated in several physiological and pathological processes. Originally linked to the nervous system, NGF has been recently associated with many immune related disorders (chronic inflammatory, autoimmune allergy). NGF is produced by several cells belonging to the nervous, endocrine, immune and visual systems. In particular, NGF is produced by and acts on immune (T and B lymphocytes, mast cells (MCs), eosinophils (EOs), neutrophils, monocytes/macrophages) as well as structural cells (epithelial cells [ECs], fibroblast [FBs], and endothelial cells). The specific response to NGF is mediated by the expression of both tyrosin kinase trkA$^{NGFR}$ and pan-neurotrophin p75$^{NTR}$ receptors. Being constitutively expressed by structural and immune cells, NGF represents a molecule potentially responsible for modulating the crosstalk between the immune and peripheral nervous system.

Increased circulating and tissutal NGF levels have been reported in chronic allergic inflammatory condition such as allergic rhinitis, rhino-conjunctivitis and allergic asthma. The role of NGF during these process is actually controversial: NGF might exert pro-inflammatory or anti-inflammatory effect as well as acts as a "modulator" of the local immune and inflammatory responses.

Studies of the last decade suggest that NGF takes part in the development of allergic asthma. The process is characterized by a chronic Th2 mediated inflammation, airway hyper-responsiveness, goblet cell hyperplasia, mucus hyper-production and thickening of the sub-epithelial zone. Positively correlated with the severity of asthma, airway hyper-responsiveness appears to be mediated by multiple independent and additive pathways working in concert and leading to recurrent reversible bronco-obstruction. During chronic inflammatory responses, the up-regulation of Substance P (SP) has been reported, to be associated with increased NGF, indicating a link between NGF/SP and respiratory symptoms. Experimentally induced models of asthma indicate a clear role of NGF in chronic inflammatory response, though a number of unresolved questions regarding the mechanism(s) through which NGF exerts its action remains to be address. In this review, the authors will present and discuss findings and hypotheses indicating the neuroimmunododulatory contribution of NGF in airway inflammations.

Chapter 8 - Design of novel treatment options for chronic hepatitis B virus (HBV) infections is actually of particular importance, since current therapies based on IFNα and nucleoside analogues (lamivudine, adefovir) are limited by the emergence of drug–resistant mutants and the persistence of intranuclear covalently closed circular viral DNA (cccDNA) responsible for persistence of infection. Increasing number of recent data suggest that rationale therapy of hepatitis B may combine the use of antiviral drugs and immunotherapeutic approaches. In this regard, DNA-based immunization appears as a pertinent new approach, inducing rapid, potent and specific immune responses to hepadnavirus structural proteins as demonstrated in naïve chimpanzees, woodchuck and duck models. However, the therapeutic DNA vaccination against chronic hepatitis B was less investigated.

The authors' aim was to explore in the chronic duck HBV (DHBV) infection model, whether DNA vaccine-based immunotherapy in combination or not with an antiviral drug (adefovir, lamivudine) treatment is able to enhance cccDNA clearance and break humoral immune tolerance in chronic DHBV carriers. They first discuss a study associating adefovir with DNA vaccine against DHBV envelope and compare herein its therapeutic efficacy with their recent study combining lamivudine with DNA vaccine against viral envelope and/or core proteins.

In an adefovir-DNA study, a group of DHBV-infected ducks received adefovir treatment (weeks 6-10 p.i.) in combination or not with DNA immunization to DHBV preS/S protein (weeks 6, 9, 12 and 22). A marked drop in viremia titres (97%), reaching the limit of detection of the assay, was observed during the 4 weeks of drug administration in all adefovir-treated as compared with untreated ducks, although it was followed by a rebound of viral replication after drug withdrawal. At the end of follow-up, analysis of intrahepatic DHBV DNA revealed a more pronounced decrease in viral DNA in combination therapy group as compared with DNA or adefovir monotherapy groups, suggesting a trend to an additive effect of drug and DNA vaccine. However, only few animals eliminated liver viral DNA and no correlation with humoral anti-preS response restoration was observed.

In a lamivudine-DNA study, lamivudine was administrated alone or in combination with DNA vaccine to DHBV envelope and/or core proteins. DHBV-carrier ducks received lamivudine treatment earlier (weeks 1-8), with higher number of DNA immunizations (weeks 6,10,14,28,35), shorter overlap with DNA vaccination (2 weeks), larger amounts of plasmid and a longer follow-up in larger animal groups. A decrease in viremia titers (70%) was observed in all lamivudine-treated compared to untreated animals, although it was limited to only the first 3 weeks of lamivudine treatment and was followed by a rapid rebound in viral replication. Interestingly, about 30% of the animals, which received DNA vaccine alone or in association with lamivudine, had cccDNA levels that were at or under the lower real-time PCR detection limit and was associated for majority of them with restoration of anti-preS response.

In conclusion, our comparison of two combination therapy studies associating DNA vaccine-based immunotherapy with either adefovir or lamivudine indicates a better efficacy of the lamivudine-DNA protocol. In the adefovir-DNA study, only modest effect in term of viral cccDNA clearance and seroconversion was observed, in spite of the higher antiviral potency of the drug. By contrast, data obtained in lamivudine-DNA study provided a first demonstration that DNA vaccine alone and associated with drug treatment was able to induce drastic and sustained suppression of viremia and enhance viral cccDNA clearance in DHBV carriers, which was tightly associated with a break of immune tolerance. Because both studies differed not only by the choice of drug but, importantly, by the design of DNA immunization protocol, a number of factors known to determine the success of genetic vaccination such as plasmid construct, amount of plasmid DNA, number of DNA injections and immunization schedule may play an important role in better therapeutic efficacy of lamivudine-DNA study. Further investigations aiming to increase the potency of DNA vaccine–based immunotherapeutics need to be performed in animal models with the goal of acheiving a complete and sustained recovery from chronic hepatitis B.

Chapter 9 - Environmental changes over the last 40-50 years have been associated with an epidemic increase in many immune-mediated diseases, particularly allergic diseases. Changing dietary habits are among a number of Western lifestyle changes implicated in the increasing susceptibility to inflammatory disease, including a decline in omega-3 polyunsaturated fatty acids (n-3 PUFA), which have well described anti-inflammatory properties. There has been growing speculation that reduced exposure to these protective dietary factors may adversely influence patterns of immune responsiveness, particularly in during critical stages of "immune programming" in early life. This chapter reviews the anti-inflammatory properties of n-3 PUFA in the context of allergic disease. It also examines epidemiological links between dietary n-3 PUFA and the risk of inflammatory symptomatology, particularly in early life. Associations between immunomodulatory dietary nutrients and allergic disease may not only help define mechanisms of disease pathogenesis, but also offer avenues to prevent disease. Thus, the authors also review recent intervention studies that explore a potential role of n-3 fish oil supplementation in modifying immune development and reducing disease risk in early life. As escalating rates of allergic disease begin to also affect the developing world, these kinds of simple, cost-effective strategies are of growing relevance and enormous potential benefit.

Chapter 10 - Hemorrhagic cystitis, a common complication after bone marrow transplantation (BMT), has often been attributed to polyomavirus reactivation. However, this link is still being controversially discussed and needs to be further examined.

In a prospective study, 571 urine samples from 101 patients undergoing BMT were examined for the presence of human polyomaviruses BK (BKV) and JC (JCV) using electron microscopy, qualitative and quantitative PCR. The urine samples were also screened for adenoviruses, cytomegalovirus, and polyomavirus SV 40. The degree of hematuria as a marker for hemorrhagic cystitis was determined using semi-quantitative dipstick analysis.

Polyomaviruria was observed in 49 % of the patients. Thirty-three percent excreted only BKV, 9 % were found positive only for JCV, and in 7 % of the patients both viruses were detected. Hematuria occurred in 29 % of the patients. No urine was positive for other viral agents. Statistical analysis showed that neither sex, disease, conditioning, thrombocytopenia, nor acute graft-versus-host-disease correlated significantly with the development of polyomaviruria or hematuria. For patients undergoing *allogeneic* BMT, the incidence was significantly higher for both hematuria ($p = 0.002$) and BKV excretion ($p = 0.0002$), but not for JCV excretion. However, stratified analysis revealed no significant correlation between polyomaviruria and hematuria; for patients with parallel hematuria and viruria, the degree of hematuria did not correlate with the viral load anyway.

Based on this data, the authors presume that hemorrhagic cystitis after BMT cannot easily be linked to single episodes of polyomaviruria; it rather seems to depend on individually varying and independent factors.

Chapter 11 - The association of persistent presence of circulating antiphospholipid antibodies (aPL) and recurrent vascular thrombosis, pregnancy morbidity or a combination of these events is termed antiphospholipid syndrome (APS). The dominant antigenic targets in

APS are phospholipid (PL)-binding plasma proteins such as β2glycoprotein I (β2GPI) and prothrombin.

In the last few years, great interest has arisen concerning the binding of aPL to endothelial cells or other pro-coagulant cells, and how this binding mediates cell dysfunctions that potentially induce the clinical manifestations of APS. Pro-coagulant cells, exposed by aPL in the presence of PL -binding proteins, produce thrombophilic molecules such as tissue factor, adhesion molecules and tumor necrosis factor α. It is now recognized that the p38 mitogen activated protein kinase (MAPK) pathway plays an important role in aPL-mediated cell activation. Moreover, the role of annexin II as receptor for β2GPI and the interaction of β2GPI with different members of the low density lipoprotein receptor family have been reported.

In this chapter, the authors review the new research relating to the pathophysiological mechanisms that may contribute to the manifestations of APS, focusing on the pro-coagulant cell scenario.

Chapter 12 - Acetylcholine (ACh) plays an important role as a neurotransmitter of the central and peripheral nervous systems. Interestingly, this molecule and its synthesizing enzyme, choline acetyltransferase, are also present in lymphocytes. In addition, several types of nicotinic (nAChR) and muscarinic (mAChR) receptors have been identified in these blood cells. These findings have provided evidence that lymphocytes have most of the essential components needed to constitute a non neuronal cholinergic system. However, the precise role of this extraneuronal cholinergic system is poorly understood. ACh may act as an immunomodulator. Activated immune cells may use the released ACh in self-modulating autocrine and paracrine loops.

Upon phytohemagglutinin (PHA) stimulation of human lymphocytes, an increment in the synthesis of ACh occurs, suggesting that the neurotransmitter modulates T-cell activation. Different subtypes of mAChRs are present in lymphocytes. mAChRs are involved in lymphocyte activation by enhancing T cell antigen receptor/CD3-induced IL-2 production. Different nAChR subtypes have been reported in blood cells, although their patterns of expression and function remain unknown. α7 nAChR mRNA has been detected in peripheral human lymphocytes. Nicotine, probably acting through α7 nAChRs, elicits transient increases in $Ca^{2+}$ in mononuclear leukocytes and human leukemic cell lines. Nicotine and the antagonist α-bungarotoxin lead to up-regulation of α7 and to a concomitant protection of lymphocytes from cortisol-induced apoptosis, suggesting that α7 is involved in the modulation of this process. In summary, in addition to the recognized cytokine network, the extraneuronal cholinergic system plays a key role in the regulation of the immune function.

The extraneuronal cholinergic system could function independently or coordinated with the neural system. It is interesting to note that lymphocytes may reflect the metabolism of brain cells and this may be exploited as a neural and possible genetic probe in studies of psychiatric disorders.

In: New Immunology Research Developments
Editor: Gunter V. Müller
ISBN 978-1-60021-701-2


*Short Communication*

# T-Independent Antigens Type 2 as Polyclonal B Cell Activators

***I. N. Chernishova, M. V. Gavrilova and E. V. Sidorova***
Research Institute for Viral Preparations of Russian Academy of Medical Sciences, Moscow, Russia

## Abstract

The specific and polyclonal immune response under the influence of T-independent antigens type 2 (TI-2 antigens) was studied. Mice BALB/c were immunized by different TI-2 antigens: Polyvinylpirrolidon, alpha (1→3) Dextran, Pneumococcal polysaccharide SIII and Ficoll) injected separately or together and by TI-2 antigen injected together with T-dependent (TD) antigen. On the 4$^{th}$ day spleens were removed and the numbers of cells forming antibodies (AFC) and total Ig (IFC) were determined by ELISPOT. Splenocytes of unimmunized mice were used as control. The number of cells forming nonspecific Ig (nIFC) was calculated as the difference between IFC and AFC numbers. The number of nIFC induced by the antigens (inIFC) was calculated as the difference between the numbers of nIFC in immune and control splenocytes.

It was shown that TI-2 antigens lacking intrinsic mitogenic activity induced the appearance of AFC and the formation of inIFC (polyclonal activation) as well. Simultaneous injection of TI-2 and TD antigens resulted in summation of inIFC number, but unexpectedly, simultaneous injection of two TI-2 antigens did not. After combined injection of two TI-2 antigens the number of inIFC did not exceed that induced by the more potent of two TI-2 antigens used. This effect cannot be explained by unspecific immunosuppression since AFC formation did not decrease and sometimes even slightly increased.

It is suggested that T-dependent and TI-2 antigens involve in polyclonal activation different B cell subsets, whereas TI-2 antigens induce unspecific activation of cells belonging to the same restricted in size pool consisting either of bystander B-1/MZ-B cells or, more probable, of B cells in some definite stage of differentiation.

# Introduction

The injection of the antigens into animal induces not only the appearance of the antibody-forming cells (AFC) but the increase in the quantity of nonspecific Ig (nIg) and in the number of the nIg-forming cells (nIFC) [1]. The increase in nIFC number under the influence of T-dependent antigens (TD antigens) is due mainly to the action of unspecific stimulatory T-cell factors [2]. The increase in nIFC number under the influence of T-independent antigens (TI-antigens) type 1 depends on their mitoge-nic activity [3]. The increase in nIFC number under the influence of TI-antigens type 2 (TI-2 antigens) lacking mitogenic activity is unexplained until now. The role of different cell subsets in this process is not studied, and the mechanisms responsible for polyclonal activation are not yet defined.

Some years ago it was shown that simultaneous injection of two TD- or TD- and TI-2 antigens resulted in the summation of nIg content and the antigen-induced nIFC (inIFC) number [4, 5], and it was suggested that TD- and TI-2 antigens triggered unspecifically (as well as specifically) different B cell subsets (as if each of the antigens stimulated its "own" bystander B cell subset) [5]. Indirectly this suggestion is supported by the data on the dependence of polyclonal immune response to polyvinylpirrolidon (PVP), as well as specific one, not on B-2, but on CD5+ B-1 cells [6, 7].

Specific immune response to TI-2 antigens is due mainly to two B cell subpopulations – B-1 cells and B cells of marginal zone (MZ-B cells), responsible for the formation of antibodies to bacterial lipo- and polysaccharides [8, 9]. It was interest to study if different polysaccharide TI-2 antigens induced polyclonal B cell activation, and did they and PVP in this case stimulate different or same by-stander B cell subsets. It was assumed (by the analogy with the joint action of TD- and TI-2 antigens) that if PVP and polysaccharide antigens stimulate different B cell subsets simultaneous injection of two these TI-2 antigens should result in summation of inIFC number, in the opposite case no summation would be detected. To check it PVP and polysaccharide antigens were injected to BALB/c mice either separately or in pairs, and specific and polyclonal immune responses were studied.

# Materials and Methods

*Animals, antigens, immunization.* Female 18 g Balb/c mice were obtained from "Stolbovaya" breeding unit, Moscow, Russia).

Polyvinylpirrolidon 350 kDa (PVP), α (1→3) Dextran (Dex), Pneumococcal polysaccharide (SIII) and Ficoll (Fic) were used as TI-2 antigens. Water-soluble antigen of sheep erythrocytes (WSA) prepared according [10] was used as TD-antigen.

Mice were immunized intravenously by 2 μg of TI-2 antigens injected either separately or jointly or by 50 μg of WSA together with 2 μg of PVP. Spleens were removed on the $4^{th}$ day after immunization, monocellular suspensions were prepared, red blood cells were lysed, and AFC and IFC numbers per $10^6$ splenocytes were determined by ELISPOT [11].

*Determination of AFC, IFC, nIFC and inIFC.* To determine AFC number nitrocellulose plates (MAHAN4510, Millipore, USA) were coated by the antigens (10-50 μg/well) during 16 h at 4°C and blocked by bovine serum albumin (BSA) during 2.0 h at room temperature.

Splenocytes from unimmunized and immunized mice (100 x $10^3$ /well) were applied on the sensitized nitrocellulose and cultivated in RPMI 1640 medium with 1% of fetal calf serum and all necessary additives during 16 h at 37°C in $CO_2$ - incubator.

To determine IFC number nitrocellulose plates were coated by goat antibody to mouse Ig (ICN, USA) and blocked by BSA. Cells (10 x $10^3$ /well) were applied on the sensitized nitrocellulose and cultivated 16 h as described above. Cultivation being over cells were removed, mouse μ-specific rabbit antiserum (enhancing serum) was added, and AFC and IFC were detected using peroxidase conjugate of goat antibody to rabbit IgG (ICN, USA) and 1,4-Cl-Naphtol as substrate [11]. At least 3 cultures were run in parallel.

The number of nIFC per $10^6$ of cells was calculated as the difference between the numbers of IFC and AFC, and the number of the antigen-induced nIFC (inIFC) was calculated as the difference between the numbers of nIFC in immune and normal splenocytes.

# Results

The injection of TI-2 antigens induced the appearance of AFC, the increase in IFC number and, therefore, the formation of inIFC (Figure 1). The numbers of AFC induced by different TI-2 antigens variated from 82 to 580/$10^6$ splenocytes, and the numbers of inIFC – from 610 to 3965 /$10^6$ splenocytes, respectively. In total immune response to TI-2 antigens was much less than that to TD-antigen–WSA (Figure 2, A). PVP and Dex were more immunogenic than SIII and Fic.

The simultaneous injection of WSA and PVP resulted in the appearance of AFC to WSA and PVP and in summation of inIFC number (Figure.2, 1). The quantities of AFC and IFC after immunization by WSA were equal to 3808 and 14300 per $10^6$ splenocytes, respectively. Therefore, the number of nIFC was 10492/$10^6$ cells. After immunization by PVP the numbers of AFC, IFC and nIFC were 820, 5870 and 5050/$10^6$ cells, respectively. As the quantities of AFC, IFC and nIFC in normal splenocytes were 245, 3000 and 2755 per $10^6$ cells, respectively, the calculated number of new formed inIFC for WSA was 7692/$10^6$ cells and the number of inIFC fomed in response to PVP – 2295/$10^6$ cells. Therefore, the sum of inIFC number after simultaneous injection of WSA and PVP should be equal to 9987/$10^6$ cells. It is easy to see (Figure. 2,1) that simultaneous injection of both these antigens resulted in the appearance of 10536 inIFC /$10^6$ spleen cells, i.e. was almost equal to the theoretical value.

Very different picture was obtained in the experiments with simultaneous injection of two TI-2 antigens. As a rule, the number of inIFC appeared after immunization with two TI-2 antigens did not exceed that induced by the more potent (immunogenic) of two antigens (Figure 2, 2-5). Thus, for example, separate immunization by PVP and Dex resulted in the formation of 628 and 538 in IFC/$10^6$ cells, respectively, and simultaneous immunization by both antigens induced the appearance of 760 inIFC/$10^6$ splenocytes only instead of theoretical value 1166 in IFC/$10^6$ cells (Figure 2, 2). The separate immunization by PVP and Fic resulted in the formation of 1456 and 1065 inIFC per mln splenocytes, respectively, and simultaneous injection of both antigens induced the appearance of 1471 inIFC/$10^6$ cells instead of theoretical value 2521 inIFC/$10^6$ cells (not shown).

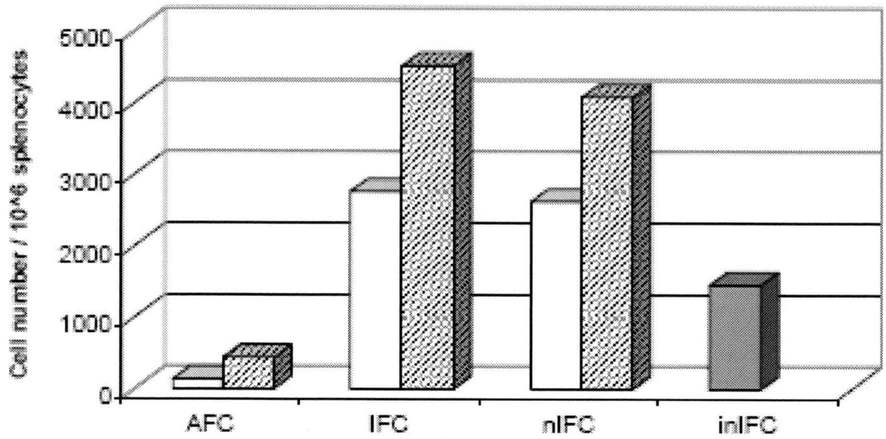


A

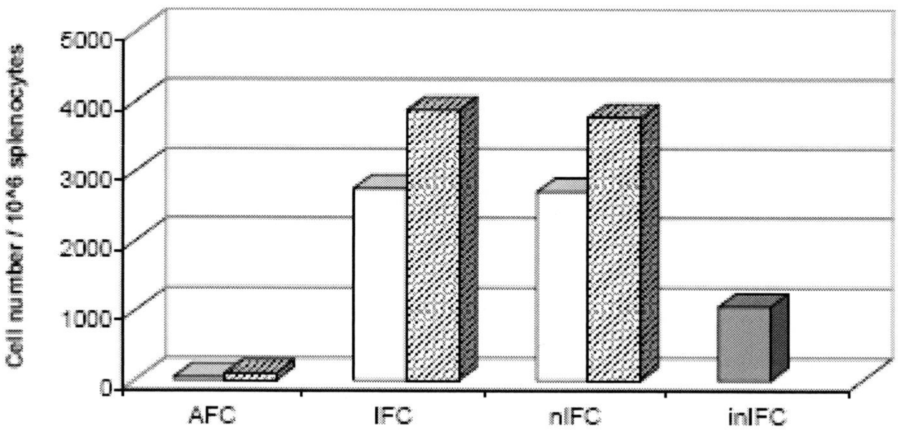


B

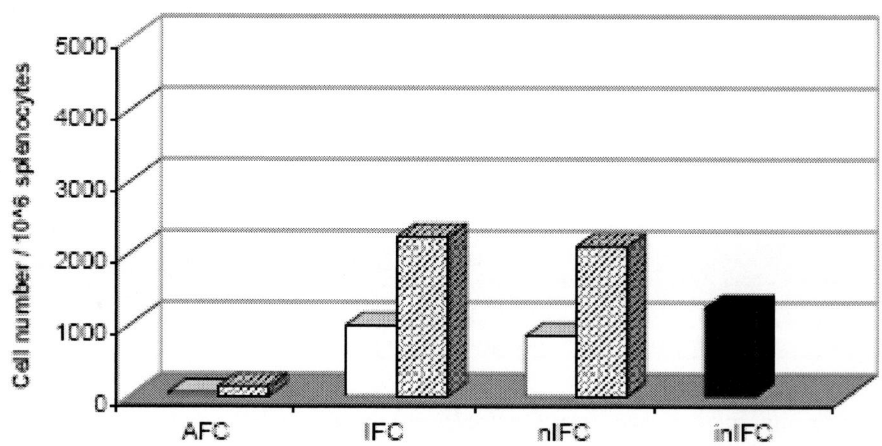


C

Figure 1. (Continued on the next page)

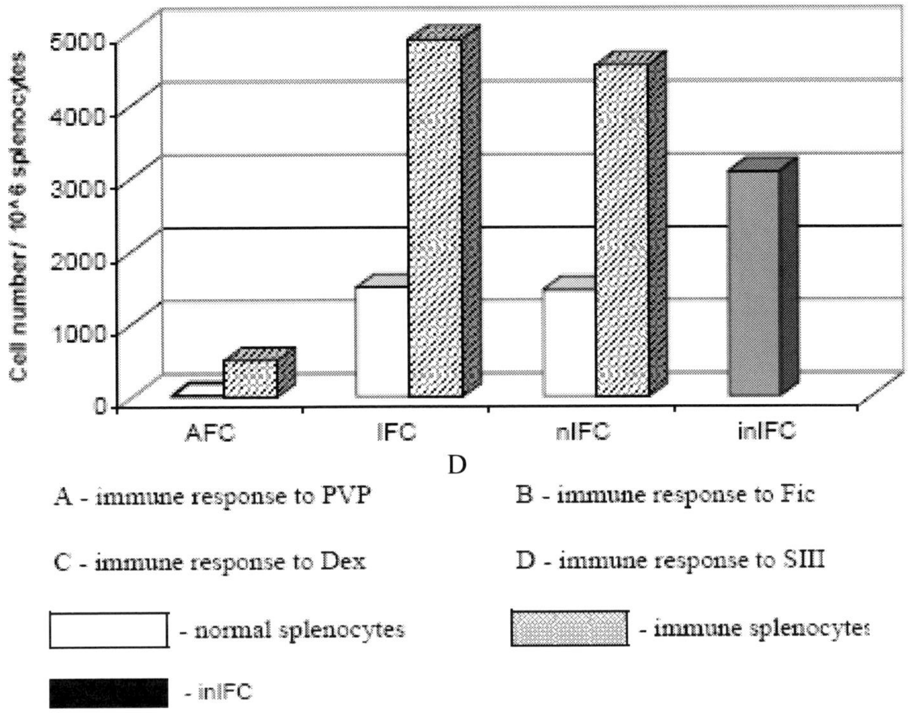


Figure 1. Immune response to TI-2 antigens.

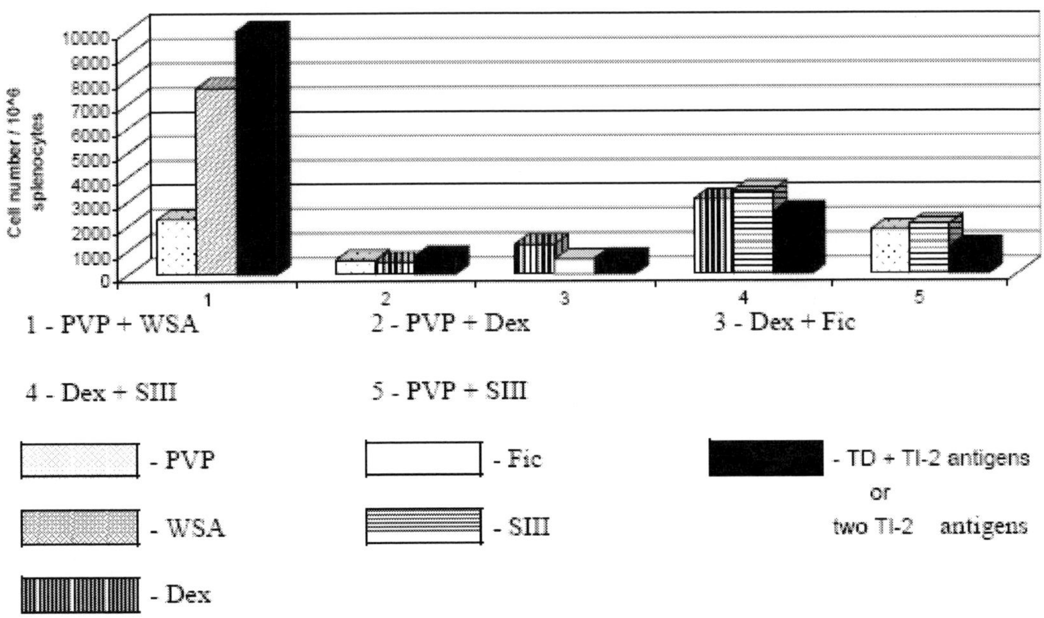


Figure 2. inIFC formation under the influence of TD + TI-2 or two TI-2 antigens.

Similar pattern was obtained with other TI-2 antigen pairs. In no case summation of inIFC number after simultaneous injection of two TI-2 antigens was observed (Figure 2).

It must be emphasized that combined injection of two TI-2 antigens practically did not disturb the specific immune response to any of them, and sometimes even slightly increased AFC number (Table).

**Table. AFC formation induced by separate and simultaneous injection of two TI-2 antigens**

| Antigen injected | AFC number/$10^6$ splenocytes | | | |
|---|---|---|---|---|
| | to PVP | to Fic | to Dex | to SIII |
| PVP | 437 | | | |
| Fic | | 102 | | |
| PVP+Fic | 560 | 143 | | |
| PVP | 421 | | | |
| Dex | | | 289 | |
| PVP+Dex | 520 | | 143 | |
| PVP | 421 | | | |
| SIII | | | | 82 |
| PVP+SIII | 310 | | | 103 |
| Dex | | | 134 | |
| Fic | | 107 | | |
| Dex+Fic | | 164 | 242 | |
| Dex | | | 510 | |
| SIII | | | | 220 |
| Dex+SIII | | | 580 | 180 |

# Discussion

Many years ago Boyd and Bernard have found that immunization by proteins (TD-antigens) apart the antibody formation induced the appearance of so-called nonspecific immunoglobulins (nIg), which did not react with the antigen injected [12]. Later it was shown that the increase in nIg quantity might be induced by very different TD-antigens (proteins, erythrocytes, viruses…) [1]. This phenomenon is usually explained by the action of unspecific stimulatory T factors arising under the influence of the antigens and activating bystander B cells in $G_1$ phase [2]. At the same time there are data pointing out that not only TD but also TI antigens which do not interact with T helpers can induce the increase in nIg formation [5, 6, 13].

Whereas polyclonal B cell activation by TI-1 antigens depend on their intrinsic mitogenicity, mechanism of triggering bystander B cells by TI-2 antigens lacking mitogenic activity remains unclear.

Many TI-2 antigens belong to bacterial polysaccharides. It may be useful to establish whether these antigens induce not only specific but also unspecific B cell activation. Thus, the formation of AFC and nonspecific Ig-forming cells (inIFC) in mouse splenocytes under the influence of four different TI-2 antigens (PVP and polysaccharides) was studied.

Intravenous injection of the TI-2 antigens resulted, as expected, in AFC formation and in the inIFC appearance, i.e. induced not only specific, but polyclonal B cell activation as well. Therefore, TI-2 antigens behave in this respect as TD antigens. It means that the capacity to induce polyclonal B cell activation like specific one is inherent for the antigens of very different nature (TD, TI-1 and TI-2). Unfortunately, the functions of these antigen-induced nIg remain unclear till now.

Immunogenicity of TI-2 antigens in total was lower than that of TD-antigens. Respectively, specific (AFC number) and unspecific (nIFC number) responses were much lower than these after TD antigen injection (Figure 2).

From the orthodox point of view, TI-2 antigens do not activate cells through Toll-like receptors [3]. Therefore, the increase of nIFC number detected in experiments can not be explained by the mitogenicity of antigens. Rather, it depends on the unspecific stimulatory B-cell factors similar, possibly, to T-cell factors released after TD-antigen injection, or to unspecific stimulatory factors provided by other cells – NK, macrophages or dendritic cells [14]. This question requires further investigation.

As was mentioned above, there are two B cell populations involved in the immune response to polysaccharides: B-1 and MZ-B cells. PVP was shown to be TI-2 antigen, which triggers mainly CD5+B-1 cells [8, 9]. Whether MZ-B cells can be polyclonally activated by PVP is not known. It might be assumed that PVP and polysaccharides unspecifically activate different bystander B cell subsets. In this case immunization by two TI-2 antigens with PVP as one of them may help to answer the question. Really, if PVP and polysaccharides polyclonally activate bystander B-1 cell subset the summation of inIFC number after simultaneous injection of both TI-2 antigens should be absent or diminished; on the contrary, if PVP and polysaccharides stimulate different B cell subsets such summation would take place. Thus, the numbers of inIFC were determined after joint injection of PVP with different polysaccharide TI-2 antigens. The action of joint injection of PVP and polysaccharides was compared with that of PVP and WSA, which as TD antigen activates mainly B-2 cell subset.

Simultaneous injection of TD- and TI-2 antigens resulted in summation of the number of cells producing antigen-induced nIg (Figure 2). Thus, previously obtained data [4] were confirmed. At the same time experiments with two TI-2 antigens injected together have given unexpected results. In contrast with the combined action of TD- and TI-2 antigens, the joint immunization neither by PVP with polysaccharide nor by two different polysaccharides did not result in summation of inIFC number (Figure 2). The number of inIFC in these cases did not exceed that induced by the more potent of two antigens injected. The same pattern was observed with all different combinations of TI-2 antigens under study. This absence of inIFC number summation could not be explained by unspecific suppression of immune response [15] dependent, for example, on the increase of TI-2 antigen dose, as previously we have found that 4 μg of polysaccharides/mouse were not suppressive (not shown). The absence of any suppression of specific immune response also testifies against this suggestion: as it may be seen from the Table, the numbers of AFC to each of simultaneously injected TI-2 antigens in most cases did not decrease and sometimes even slightly increased.

Although the results obtained point to that polyclonal response to simultaneously injected PVP and polysaccharides depends on the same CD5+ B cell pool, strictly speaking, they do not allow to state it unconditionally; rather they testify that polyclonal activation depends on the *same* cell pool, evidently, restricted in size. Such pool may be represented either by bystander B-1/MZ-B cells available for activation or by restricted in size pool of cells producing unspecific stimulatory factors common for B-1 and MZ-B cell subsets. It cannot be excluded that restriction in size depends on the number of cells in definite stage of activation: it is known, for example, that unspecific T-cell factors stimulate B-2 cells in G1, but not in G0 stage [2]. As these factors, evidently, arise under the influence of TI-2 antigens it is very probable that for their production are responsible B-1/MZ-B cells. Although the competition between cells for unspecific stimulatory factors cannot be excluded, it must be noted that such competition by unknown reasons affects only bystander B cells, while the formation of AFC to each of TI-2 antigens injected in pair remains undisturbed (Table).

Indirectly to the main role of namely CD5+ B cells in polyclonal B cell activation by TI-2 antigens point out data obtained previously in the experiments with xid-mice CBA/N. As it is known such mice do not respond to TI-2 antigens. We have shown that immunization of such animals by TI-2 antigens (PVP and DNP-Ficoll) almost did not increase the number of nIFC [16]. It means that in the absence of CD5+ B cells TI-2 injection does not induce the formation of unspecific stimulatory factors, therefore, in polyclonal activation by TI-2 antigens namely CD5+ B-1 cells play the main role.

Mechanism of bystander B cell activation by TI-2 antigens is not clear. Probably, it depends on the unknown factors produced by B cells, NK or macrophages which, by unclear reasons, activate only restricted cell pool, presumably, B-1 and MZ-B B cells. The nature of cells polyclonally stimulated by TI-2 antigens is now under investigation.

## Conclusion

1. T-independent antigens type 2 lacking intrinsic mitogenic activity induce the increase in the number of cells secreting nonspecific Ig (inIFC), i.e. activate B cells not only specifically but polyclonally as well.
2. Simultaneous injection of TD- and TI-2 antigens results in summation of inIFC number.
3. Simultaneous injection of two TI-2 antigens does not result in inIFC number summation. The number of inIFC in this case do not exceed that induced by the more potent of two TI-2 antigens used. It means that polyclonal B cell activation by TI-2 antigens is restricted. The restriction of activation may be due either to the small size of available effector bystander B cell pool, the same for different TI-2 antigens (presumably, B-1/MZ-B cells) or to the shortage of unspecific stimulatory factor(s) produced by restricted in size cell population (probably, by CD5+ B-1 cells).

## Acknowledgments

This work was supported by grant of Russian Foundation for Basic Researches.

## References

[1] Sidorova, EV. Antigen-dependent nonspecific immunoglobulins. Their nature and possible mechanisms of formation. *Uspekhi Sovr. Biol.* 1993. V 5. P. 20-30.

[2] Andersson, J; Schreier, M; Melchers, F. T-cell dependent B cell stimulation is H-2 restricted and antigen-dependent 0nly at the resting B-cell level. *Proc. Natl. Acad. Sci.*USA 1980. V. 77. P. 1612-1616.

[3] Gavin, A; Aït-Azzouzene, D; Mårtensson, A; Duong, B; Verkoczy, L; Nemazee, D. Peripheral B lymphocyte tolerance. *Kejo J. Med.* 2004. V. 53. P. 151-158.

[4] De Vos Cloetens, Ch; Minsart-Baleriaux, V; Urbain-Vansanten, G. Possible relationships between antibodies and non-specific immunoglobulins simultaneously induced after antigenic stimulation. *Immunology*. 1971. V. 20. P. 955-962.

[5] Agadzhanian, MG; Megrabian, TB; Sidorova, EV. Increase in the number of antibody-secreting cells and cells secreting non-specific immunoglobulins following mouse immunization with T-dependent and T-independent antigens. *Byull. Eksp. Biol. Med.* 1981. V. 92. P. 66-68.

[6] Sidorova, EV; Li-Sheng, Lu; Devlin, B; Chernishova, I; Gavrilova, M. Role of different B-cell subsets in the specific and polyclonal immune response to T-independent antigens type 2. *Immunol. Letts.* 2003; 88; 37-42.

[7] Whitmore, AC; Neely, HR; Diz, R; Flood, PM. Rapid induction of splenic and peritoneal B-1a cells in adult mice by thymus independent type 2 antigen. *J. Immunol.* 2004. V. 173. P. 5406-5414.

[8] Martin, F; Kearney, J. B-cell subsets and the mature preimmune repertoire. Marginal zone and B1 cells as part of a "natural immune memory". *Immunol. Rev.* 2000. V. 175. P. 70-79.

[9] Hardy, RR; Hayakawa, K. B cell development pathways. *Ann. Rev. Immunol.* 2001. V. 19. P. 595-621.

[10] Seman, M; Mazie, JC; Bussard, AE. Antigenic properties of a water soluble fraction of sheep erythrocytes. *Eur. J. Immunol.* 1972. V. 4. P. 387-388.

[11] Logunova, NN; Agadzhanian, MG; Sidorova, EV. Determination of cells secreting immunoglobulins and antibodies to influenza virus and polyvinylpirrolidon by immunoenzymatic method. *Immunology* (Russian) 1989. V. 2. P. 77-79.

[12] Boyd, WC; Bernard, H. Quantitative changes in antibodies and γ-globulin fraction in sera of rabbits injected with several antigens. *J. Immunol.* 1937. V. 33. P. 111-122.

[13] Kimura, S; Kiyono, H; Beagley, K; Torii, M; Eldridge, J; Hamada, S; Michalek, S; Koopman, W; McGhee, J. Streptococcal serotype carbohydrate represents a novel class of type 2 antigen which is T-independent. *J. Immunol.* 1987. V. 138. P. 4387-4394.

[14] Mond, JJ; Lees, A; Snapper, CM. T cell-independent antigens type 2. *Ann. Rev. Immunol.* 1995. V.13. P. 655-692.

[15] Baker, PJ; Stashak, PW; Amsbaugh, DF; Prescott, B. Regulation of the antibody response to type III pneumococcal polysaccharide. IV. Role of suppressor T cells in the development of low-dose paralysis. *J. Immunol.* 1974. V. 112. P. 2020-2027.

[16] Chernyshova, I; Borisova, T; Emelyanzeva, J; Sidorova, E. Role of different lymphocyte subpopulations in the formation of non-specific immunoglobulins induced by antigen injection. *Immunol. Letts.* 1999. V. 67. P. 113-116.

# Research and Review Studies

In: New Immunology Research Developments
Editor: Gunter V. Müller
ISBN 978-1-60021-701-2


*Chapter 1*

# Neutrophil Apoptosis and Innate Immunity

***Adam D. Kennedy, Amy M. Palazzolo-Balance and Frank R. DeLeo****
Laboratory of Human Bacterial Pathogenesis,
Rocky Mountain Laboratories,
National Institute of Allergy and Infectious Diseases,
National Institutes of Health, Hamilton, MT 59840

## Abstract

Polymorphonuclear leukocytes (PMNs or neutrophils) are the most abundant white cell in humans and an essential component of the innate immune system. PMNs are typically the first leukocyte recruited to sites of infection or areas of inflammation. Ingestion (phagocytosis) of microorganisms triggers production of reactive oxygen species (ROS) and fusion of granules with forming phagosomes. ROS and microbicides of granules are highly effective at killing ingested microorganisms. On the other hand, these cytotoxic molecules can cause non-specific damage to host tissues and thus it is critical that neutrophil turnover is tightly regulated. To that end, mature PMNs are short-lived cells programmed to undergo apoptosis as a means to facilitate immune system homeostasis. Our understanding of neutrophil apoptosis and its importance in the immune system has evolved over the past 18 years. Proinflammatory molecules, such as host-derived cytokines and chemokines or products of microorganisms, delay PMN apoptosis, thereby prolonging function. Phagocytosis of bacteria typically accelerates neutrophil apoptosis, a process involving production of ROS, which ultimately promotes resolution of infection. By comparison, some bacterial pathogens alter neutrophil apoptosis to survive and disseminate. This chapter provides a brief history of neutrophil apoptosis research and an overview of mechanisms of neutrophil apoptosis, phagocytosis of apoptotic PMNs, and ability of microorganisms to alter PMN apoptosis.

* Tel: 406-363-9448, Email: fdeleo@niaid.nih.gov

# Introduction

PMNs are the most abundant leukocyte in humans. In addition, neutrophils are typically the first type of white cell recruited to sites of infection, where they ingest microbes (*e.g.*, fungi or bacteria) by a process known as phagocytosis. Ingested microorganisms are destroyed by the combination of reactive oxygen species (ROS) and cytotoxic components of granules [1-4] (Figure 1). These tasks are facilitated by numerous receptors enriched on the cell surface by pro-inflammatory stimuli. In addition to playing a primary role in human host defense, surface molecules serve as a link between innate and adaptive immunity by modulating PMN function to coordinate lymphocytes and monocytes/macrophages at sites of inflammation [5;6]. These functions work collectively to provide a primary defense against bacterial and fungal infections.

On the other hand, PMNs contain or produce many cytotoxic molecules that can cause significant damage to host tissues/organs if the inflammatory response is not tightly regulated. Resolution of the inflammatory response is a complex process and includes production of host-derived anti-inflammatory mediators and apoptosis of PMNs. Specifically, PMN apoptosis and the ingestion of apoptotic PMNs by macrophages is a mechanism to clear effete neutrophils and ultimately facilitate the resolution of inflammation [7-10].

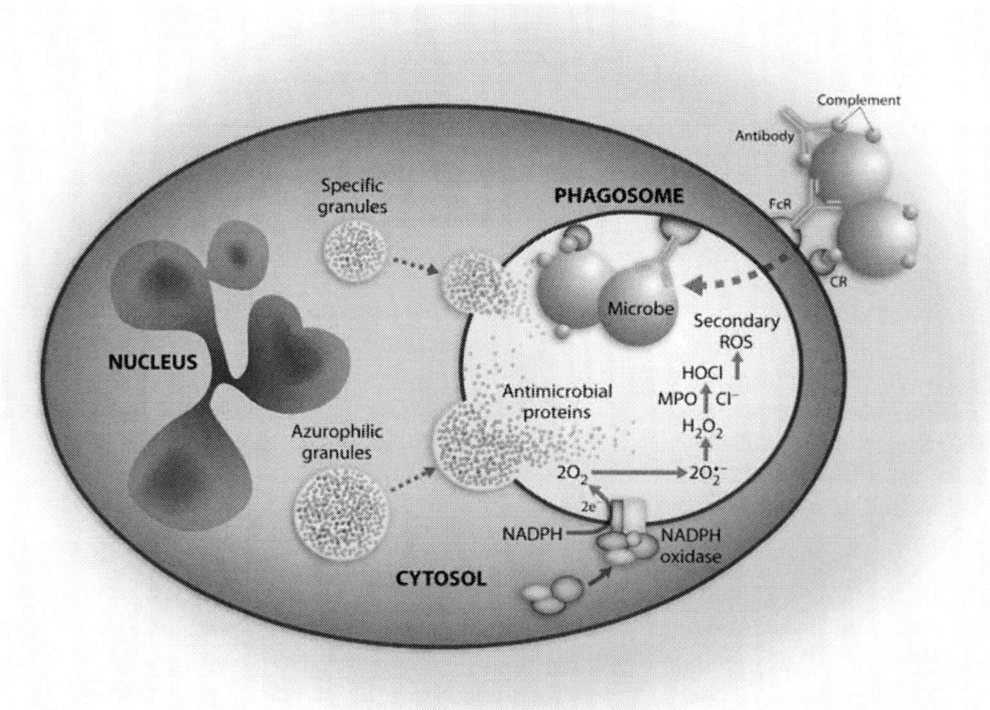


Figure 1. Neutrophil phagocytosis and microbicidal activity. Following phagocytosis, microbes are destroyed by NADPH oxidase-derived ROS and antimicrobial proteins released from granules. FCR, Fc receptor; CR, complement receptor; MPO, myeloperoxidase. Reproduced with permission, from M.T. Quinn, M.C.B. Ammons and F.R. DeLeo, 2006, *Clinical Science*, 111, 1-20. © the Biochemical Society.

This chapter highlights three areas of neutrophil biology related to homeostasis and the innate host defense; namely, granulopoiesis and myeloid development, mechanisms of PMN apoptosis and the ability of microbes to manipulate this process, and clearance of apoptotic cells by macrophages.

## Granulocytes, Granulopoiesis and the Development of Myeloid Cells

Granulocytes (basophils, eosinophils and neutrophils) can be differentiated from lymphocytes and other circulating leukocytes based on nuclear and cytoplasmic morphology, as illustrated by microscopy and flow cytometry (Figure 2). These differences include the presence of characteristic granules in the cytoplasm as well as multi-lobed nucleus. Development of granulocytes involves transcription factors distinct from those involved in lymphocyte maturation [11-15]. Many of these transcription factors are required for granule protein maturation, as different granules appear during separate stages of PMN development (reviewed in [16;17]).

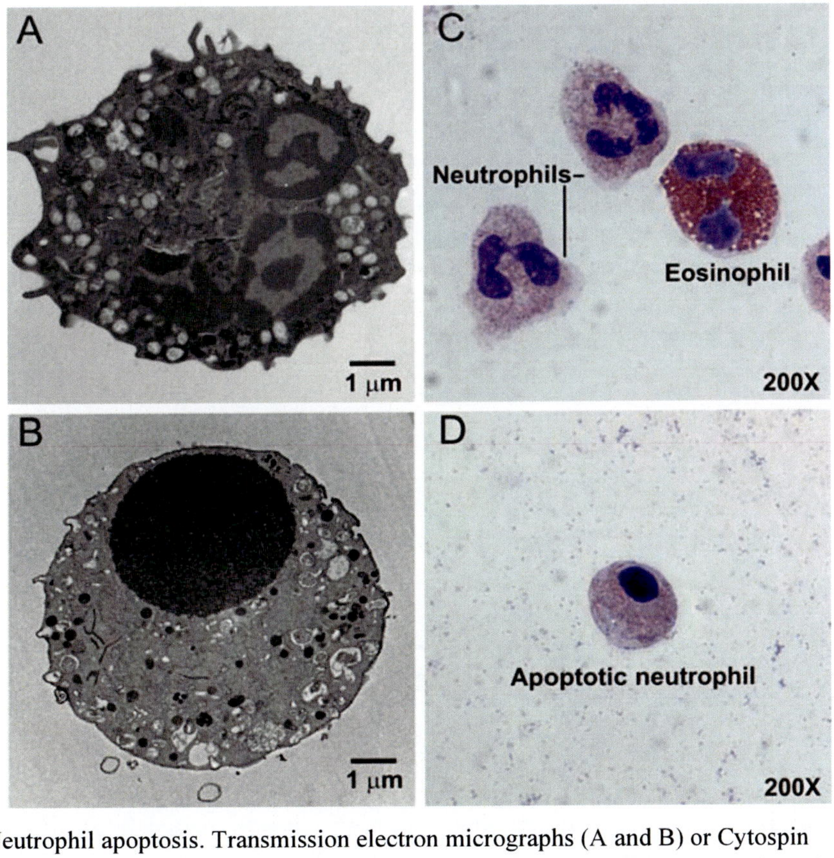


Figure 2. Neutrophil apoptosis. Transmission electron micrographs (A and B) or Cytospin (ThermoShandon) with modified Wright-Giemsa stain (C and D) of human neutrophils isolated fresh from peripheral blood (A and B) or a those having undergone spontaneous apoptosis after culture for 24 hours *in vitro* (C and D). Note the condensed chromatin/nucleus in apoptotic cells.

Circulating leukocytes and other cells of the immune system develop from pluripotent stem cells located in bone marrow [18-20]. Granulocytes develop in bone marrow for ~ 6.5 days before mature PMNs are released into the bloodstream [21]. This maturation and differentiation process is called granulopoiesis, *i.e.*, the formation of granulocytes. Although these cells have a relatively short life-span, the greatest percentage of hematopoiesis is committed to the production of neutrophils, as nearly 60% of all leukocytes in bone marrow are granulocyte precursors and PMN turnover is on the order of $10^{11}$ cells per day in the average adult human [22]. Differentiation of granulocyte precursors from hematopoietic stem cells happens early, as stem cells give rise to unipotent myeloblasts. These unipotent myeloblasts are "committed" stem cells, meaning that these myeloblasts will only develop into a cell of the myeloid lineage (*e.g.*, monocytes, neutrophils, eosinophils) [23]. Unipotent myeloblasts have a large oval nucleus with large nucleoli and no cytoplasmic granules. These cells differentiate into promyelocytes, which contain abundant azurophilic granules [21]. Azurophilic granules contain myeloperoxidase (MPO), defensins, proteinase 3, and azurocidin among other proteins, and form when immature transport vesicles bud from the Golgi apparatus [21]. The myelocyte stage of development can be differentiated from promyelocyte stage by the formation of specific (secondary) and gelatinase (tertiary) granules in the cytoplasm of myelocytes. Compared to azurophilic granules, specific granules contain neither lysosomal enzymes nor MPO; however, they do contain lactoferrin, collagenase, and a number of receptors and zymogens, including flavocytochrome $b_{558}$, CD11b, and hCAP-18 [21;24]. Gelatinase granules form at the band cell stage of neutrophil maturation and contain limited lactoferrin, high concentrations of gelatinase, and many receptors [25]. As myeloid cell differentiation proceeds into the postmitotic phase (~ 5 day process [21]), myelocytes develop sequentially into metamyelocytes, band cells, and finally mature PMNs. Mature PMNs are terminally differentiated cells, meaning that they do not undergo mitosis. These prominent host cells circulate in the bloodstream for 10-24 hours [22;26-28] before migrating into tissues, where they function for an additional 1-2 days before undergoing apoptosis [21;27] and are cleared by resident macrophages (reviewed in [29]). In mature neutrophils, specific granules predominate, as the relative number of azurophilic granules per cell decreases during neutrophil maturation [21]. Also, mature neutrophils contain secretory vesicles, a fourth readily mobilizable compartment, which contain multiple receptors, including CR3 (CD11b/CD18), CR1 (CD35) [30;31] and the N-formylmethionyl-leucylphenylalanine (fMLP) receptor [17].

# Recruitment of Neutrophils from the Bloodstream

## Neutrophil Recruitment, Priming, and Extravasation

Neutrophils survey venules and lymphatic organs for signs of invading microorganisms and are recruited to sites of infection by chemoattractants. Chemoattractants are host- (*e.g.*, cytokines and chemokines) or microorganism-derived (*e.g.*, fMLP, lipoteichoic acid, and peptidoglycan) molecules recognized by corresponding receptors on the cell surface (*e.g.*,

CXCR1, CXCR2, formyl peptide receptor, CD14, and toll-like receptors [TLRs]). Most chemoattractants, such as lipopolysaccharide (LPS) and N-formylated peptides, also prime neutrophils for enhanced function [32;33].

Neutrophil priming was first defined as the ability of primary agonists (*e.g.*, LPS or fMLP) to enhance superoxide production by a secondary stimulus [34]. Secretory vesicles, gelatinase-containing granules, and a limited population of specific granules fuse with the plasma membrane during priming, thereby enriching the cell surface with receptors important for host defense and the inflammatory response. Primed cells can be differentiated from unprimed cells in part by distinct cell morphology (*e.g.*, cell size and/or granularity by flow cytometry) or enhanced expression of key surface receptors, such as CD11b [35]. Some priming agents (reviewed in [5]) are agonists or ligands of TLR, and *in vitro* and *in vivo* experiments have shown that TLRs are critical for PMN priming as well as pathogen recognition [30].

Neutrophils enter sites of infection by exiting peripheral circulation through the endothelial wall in a process called extravasation. This process is initiated by the C-type lectin family of glycoproteins called selectins, which are expressed on activated endothelial cells (E- and P-selectin), platelets (P-selectin) and primed/activated PMNs (L-selectin). As part of the inflammatory response, E- and P-selectin become upregulated on endothelial cells and interact with CD62 (L-selectin) expressed on the surface of neutrophils. This initial interaction, called "tethering", facilitates subsequent rolling of PMNs along the surface of the endothelium. Rolling is followed by firm adhesion promoted by CD11b/CD18 [36] and CD54 [36], and transmigration is mediated in part by CD31 [37], CD54 [36], CD44 [38], and CD47 [39]. Following exstravasation, there are several possible fates for PMNs related to apoptosis and turnover, and these are discussed in detail below.

## PMN Apoptosis

Normal turnover of cells, regardless of type or tissue location, is governed by apoptosis and defects in apoptosis lead to profound and devastating conditions ranging from cancer to autoimmune diseases. Apoptosis can be initiated by extrinsic pathway stimuli (extracellular, *e.g.*, Fas ligand) or by intrinsic pathway stimuli (intracellular, *e.g.*, ROS and/or that mediated by mitochondria). Apoptosis is a non-inflammatory process characterized in part by cell shrinkage, membrane blebbing, cytoplasmic condensation, and condensation and fragmentation of nuclear heterochromatin (Figure 2). Neutrophils undergo constitutive or spontaneous apoptosis as a mechanism to maintain immune system homeostasis [40]. Importantly, PMN apoptosis is accompanied by a general decrease in function and pro-inflammatory capacity, which is key to non-inflammatory removal of effete cells [41;42]. PMNs also undergo apoptosis after phagocytosis and this process has been linked to production of ROS (see section below). Apoptotic neutrophils are subsequently ingested by macrophages in a manner that is non-inflammatory, thereby providing the means to resolve the inflammatory response without releasing cytotoxic molecules that would otherwise damage host tissues. Phagocytosis of apoptotic PMNs was first observed by Elie Metchnikoff in the 19th century, when his microscopy studies showed that granulocytes from infected tissues were removed from the sites of inflammation by macrophages [43].

## Spontaneous (Constitutive) PMN Apoptosis

PMN apoptosis can be induced through several mechanisms (Table 1). Spontaneous neutrophil apoptosis is an intrinsic process, meaning that the signal to initiate apoptosis originates from within the cell. Several mechanisms of consititutive PMN apoptosis have been elucidated [44-47]. Mechanisms of apoptosis rely on effector proteins called caspases, which trigger intracellular proteolytic cascades, ultimately resulting in the cellular apoptosis. For example, MCL-1 is key BCL2-family protein of human PMNs located in the nucleus and cytoplasm [45;46]. As senescent neutrophils undergo apoptosis, MCL-1 levels decline (presumably degraded by the proteosome and there is a concurrent decrease in *MCL1* mRNA). MCL-1 has also been shown to undergo rapid turnover, which suggests neutrophil survival is regulated by MCL-1 expression [48].

Another protein of importance for PMN survival is BCL2-A1. Like MCL-1, BCL2-A1 is a member of the BCL-2 family of proteins, and *BCL2A1* mRNA is constitutively expressed in human neutrophils [49]. PMN BCL2-A1 is upregulated by G-CSF or LPS, agonists known to promote neutrophil survival [49]. Promyelocytic HL-60 cells have increased *BCL2A1* mRNA after neutrophilic differentiation with all-trans retinoic acid [49], suggesting that the protein has an important role in mature neutrophils.

**Table 1. Mechanisms of neutrophil apoptosis**

| Type of Apoptosis | Receptor/ Organelle | Ligand | Intracellular Signalling Molecules | References |
|---|---|---|---|---|
| Constitutive (Spontaneous) | Mitochondria | BAX, BID, MCL-1, BCL2-A1 | ROS, Oxidative Stress, Redox | [29;40;44;58-62;83;127;133;144;252-254] |
| Fas-mediated | Fas (CD95) | Fas Ligand (CD95L) | Caspase-Dependent (Blocked by zVAD-fmk) | [50;88;255-259] |
| TNFα receptor-mediated | TNFα Receptor | TNFα | Caspase-Dependent and Independent (Not Blocked by zVAD-fmk) | [68-72;260-263] |
| ApoL (TRAIL)-mediated | One of five TRAIL-Receptors | TRAIL | Caspase-Dependent and Independent (Not Blocked by zVAD-fmk) | [73;74;76;80;81;264;265] |

MCL-1 and BCL2-A1 are important for regulating PMN survival, but several downstream proteins also participate. Many of these factors, including caspase 9, caspase 8, and caspase 3, trigger proteolytic cascades that result in the apoptotic death of human neutrophils [50]. The importance of neutrophil caspases in inflammation is illustrated clearly in a recent study by Tanejo *et al.* [51]. Those studies demonstrated that individuals with bacterial sepsis have significant reduction of caspase-9 and -3 activities and decreased neutrophil apoptosis [51]. BCL2-associated X protein (BAX) resides in the mitochondria, an intracellular organelle known to regulate PMN survival [52;53]. In contrast to BCL2-A1, BAX is a BCL2-family member that promotes neutrophil apoptotis. Upon translocation to the mitochondria, BAX is cleaved by calpain-1 to an 18-kDa fragment unable to interact with BCL2 family members, therby promoting apoptosis [54]. *In vivo*, inhibition of BAX cleavage leads to increased and prolonged inflammation, indicating that the protein is required for the resolution of acute inflammation [52]. Additional evidence by Maianski *et al.* and Altznauer *et al.* has shown that BAX is critical mediator of PMN apoptosis [55;56]. Macrophage migration inhibitory factor is a proinflammatory cytokine that delays cleavage of BAX and ultimately neutrophil apoptosis [57]. In addition to BAX activity, mitochondria regulate their transmembrane potential, which is critical for cell survival. As shown in Table 1, ROS production and oxidative stress can lead to PMN apoptosis through disruption of transmembrane potential [29;58-62]. Although human neutrophils express low levels of cytochrome *c*, it plays an important role in apoptosis [63]. As cytochrome *c* is released from the mitochondria (*e.g.*, during oxidative stress) it associates with apoptotic protease-activating factor 1 (APAF-1) and intiates apoptosis [53]. These are a few examples of known mechanisms of spontaneous neutrophil apoptosis and there exists overlap with extrinsic pathway stimuli as described below.

## Fas/Fas Ligand-Mediated Apoptosis

In contrast to spontaneous PMN apoptosis, Fas-mediated, tumor necrosis factor-alpha (TNFα)-mediated and TRAIL-mediated apoptosis procede by an extrinsic pathway, as an extracellular signal initiates apoptosis. Extrinsic pathway signals are usually soluble protein factors that bind to membrane-bound receptors on the cell surface and trigger apoptosis. Fas (CD95) is the nidus of the death-inducing signalling complex (DISC) and is expressed on the surface of neutrophils as well as on virtually all other cells in humans [50]. Neutrophils also express Fas ligand (FasL, CD95L) [64], and when FasL is bound to Fas, PMNs undergo apoptosis in a caspase-dependent manner. Because PMNs express Fas and soluble FasL, PMNs can cause apoptosis through autocrine and paracrine pathways. Fas-mediated PMN apoptosis can be suppressed by granulocyte-macrophage colony stimulating factor (GM-CSF), granulocyte-colony stimulating factor (G-CSF), interferon-gamma (IFNγ), TNFα, and the tyrosine kinase inhibitors herbimycin A and genistein [64], thus highlighting the complexity of signaling pathways involved in regulating neutrophil turnover.

Fas is a transmembrane protein containing a FasL-binding extracellular domain and Fas-associated death domain (FADD) on its intracellular region. Interaction of FasL with Fas leads to clustering of FADDs on the cytoplasmic side of the PMN plasma membrane, which in turn, leads to caspase activation and apoptosis. As with many other signalling receptor complexes (*e.g.*, T and B cell receptors), current evidence indicates Fas accumulates in cholesterol-rich membrane domains called lipid rafts and that clustering of these receptors leads to caspase 8 activation and ultimately, cell death [50]. Macrophages also express and secrete FasL in response to phagocytosis [65]. Secretion of FasL by macrophages induces leukocyte apoptosis in a paracrine manner and assists further with the resolution of inflammation [65]. The importance of Fas-induced PMN apoptosis was first reported by Jimenez *et al.*, who studied patients with systemic inflammatory response syndrome [66]. PMNs from these patients have decreased Fas-mediated apoptosis and accompanying tissue damage following bacterial infections, presumably from the accumulation of activated neutrophils that release tissue degrading enzymes [66].

## TNFα Receptor (TNFR)-Mediated Apoptosis

The TNFR is a transmembrane protein containing an extraclullar TNFα binding domain and a TNFR-associated death domain (TRADD) in the cytoplasmic region of the protein [67]. Neutrophils express two TNFRs, 55-R and 75-R, and each has a slightly different role in PMN apoptosis. 55-R is a 55 kDa TNFR also known as CD120a or TNFRI; 75-R is a 75 kDa TNFR known as CD120b or TNFRII. Gon *et al.* showed that TNFRI is required for TNFα-mediated PMN apoptosis and its ability to promote apoptosis is enhanced by TNFRII [68]. Blocking TNFRI but not TNFRII with specific antibodies inhibits neutrophil apoptosis [68]. Additional evidence has shown that TNFRI is dominant using TNFR-selective mutants [69]. As with FADDs, TRADDs cluster in lipid rafts during TNFR–TNFα binding. This clustering of signalling molecules leads to the recruitment of adaptor molecules and activation of transcription factors. Although similar to Fas/FasL-mediated apoptosis in many ways, one major difference is that TNFα receptor-mediated apoptosis does not depend solely on caspase activation [70].

TNFα can elicit inflammatory or anti-inflammatory effects depending on the type of cell with which it interacts. Notably, TNFα has been shown to have both pro-apoptotic and anti-apoptotic effects towards neutrophils. Van den Berg *et al.* showed that these effects are concentration dependent [71]. At low concentrations, TNFα delays PMN apoptosis and elicits production of pro-inflammatory cytokines. However, at higher concentrations (those that trigger production of ROS) TNFα initiates apoptosis [71]. It is interesting to note that high concentrations of TNFα (10-100 ng/mL) reverse the pro-survival effects of IFNγ and GM-CSF [71]. Moreover, the ability of TNFα to induce neutrophil apoptosis was linked to ROS production, since PMNs from chronic granulomatous disease (CGD, see section below) patients and PMN cytoplasts (PMNs without mitochondria) fail to undergo apoptosis in the presence of high concentrations of TNFα [70;71]. The importance of TNFR-mediated apoptosis is exemplified by patients with TNFR-associated periodic syndrome (TRAPS) [72]. These individuals have a defect in the TNF receptor, and therefore, diminished TNFα-induced PMN apoptosis [72].

## TNF-Related Apoptosis-Inducing Ligand (TRAIL)

Our understanding of TRAIL-induced PMN apoptosis is relatively recent compared to that of Fas- or TNF-receptor-mediated apoptosis. Five TRAIL receptors (TRAIL-R1, TRAIL-R2, TRAIL-R3, TRAIL-R4, and TRAIL-R5) have been identified and PMNs express TRAIL-R2 and TRAIL-R3 constitutively [73;74]. Of the five TRAIL receptors, only TRAIL-R1 and TRAIL-R2 have the ability to induce pro-apoptotic, caspase-dependent signalling, whereas TRAIL-R3 and TRAIL-R4 are decoy receptors that lack the ability to induce apoptosis [75]. TRAIL-induced apoptosis has been suggested to be important for senescent (non-activated) PMNs that preferentially home to bone marrow after circulating in peripheral blood [76]. TRAIL-/- mice have an enhanced susceptibility to autoimmune diseases [77] and TRAIL blocked experimentally in animal models exacerbates inflammation caused by type 1 diabetes [78] and autoimmune encephalomyelitis [79]. PMNs also express and secrete TRAIL, which has been implicated in host defense against virus-infected cells and tumor cells [80]. Komohara *et al.* showed that IFNγ upregulates PMN TRAIL expression and Cassatella *et al.* demonstrated that IFNγ-activated PMNs store TRAIL in an intracellular pool that is mobilizable following exposure to proinflammatory mediators [73;81]. TRAIL expressed and secreted by PMNs acts in an autocrine manner to induce PMN apoptosis [81].

## Factors that Prolong Neutrophil Survival

Although neutrophil apoptosis is critical for granulocyte homeostasis and the resolution of the inflammation, many pro-inflammatory molecules extend PMN survival during the initial stages of the inflammatory reponse. For example, neutrophils that migrate to sites of tissue inflammation have a prolonged lifespan and become resistant to both Fas- and TNF-induced apoptosis [82-84]. This delay in apoptosis likely promotes robust early response to infection or inflammatory insult and is important because it would increase the window of time during which neutrophils can be recruited to such sites and remain fully functional.

Host-derived factors as well as bacterial and fungal products serve to delay neutrophil apoptosis. Cytokines, such as IL-1β, TNFα, GM-CSF, G-CSF, and IFNγ, recruit PMNs to sites of infection and each of these molecules can delay PMN apoptosis [85-87]. For instance, GM-CSF interferes with the recruitment of FADDs to the Fas receptor and therefore, delays apoptosis [88]. Complement component C5 is cleaved to form C5b, a member of the membrane attack complex, and C5a is a power chemotactic agent for neutrophils. C5a dependent migration of PMNs is critical for the recruitment of neutrophils to the site of Gram-positive pneumonia in mouse models [89]. The mechanism by which C5a protects PMNs from apoptosis has been studied in human and is believed to involve BCL2-antagonist of cell death (BAD) and phosphoinositol-3 kinase [90]. Lastly, bacterial products, especially lipopolysacharride (LPS) and lipoteichoic acid (LTA), are potent inhibitors of PMN apoptosis [87]. PMNs exposed to LPS not only show a delay in constitutive apoptosis, but are primed for enhanced production of ROS in response to a second stimulus [87].

In addition to soluble factors, the extracellular environment can signal PMN apoptosis. Notably, acute hypoxia enhances the inflammatory response and causes a decrease in PMN apoptosis that has an additive effect with GM-CSF [91]. This effect is also BCL-2-independent, suggesting that another intracellular, pro-survival signalling molecule is involved in this process [92]. Hypoxia also increases TLR4 expression and enhances the pro-survival effects of LPS toward human PMNs (see TLR section) [93].

### Role of Toll-like Receptors (TLRs) in PMN Apoptosis

Toll-like receptors (TLRs) are a family of receptors known as pattern recognition receptors (PRRs). PRRs recognize and bind to molecules containing pathogen-associated molecular patterns (PAMPs) present on microorganisms. Because TLRs can discriminate between host and pathogens quickly, these molecules in combination with other receptors (*e.g.*, complement receptors) promote rapid and efficient recognition of pathogens by neutrophils. To date, ten TLRs are expressed in human tissues and all but TLR3 are expressed in neutrophils [94]. Ligands for TLRs include lipoproteins (TLR1/TLR2) LTA (TLR6), LPS (TLR4), flagellen (TLR5), double-stranded DNA (TLR3), single-stranded RNA (TLR7), unmethylated CpG DNA of bacteria and viruses (TLR9) [95]. TLR1, -2, -4, -5, and -6 are expressed on the surface of PMNs, whereas TLR7-9 are localized to intracellular compartments and are recruited to the plasma membrane during PMN priming/activation [95-98].

Although all TLRs play an important role in the innate immune response, only TLR2, -4, and -6 seem to modulate PMN apoptosis. Of these TLRs, TLR4 seems to be more tightly coupled to PMN survival than either TLR2 or TLR6. TLR4 binds to LPS and this interaction up-regulates PMN expression of IL-8 mRNA and leads to cell survival that involves monocytes [99]. This observation can be explained in part by the ability of monocyte CD14 to bind LPS, thereby signalling release of a factor that acts in a synergistic manner to prolong PMN survival [100]. The monocyte-dependent delay in PMN apoptosis can be reconstituted by adding peripheral blood mononuclear cells (PBMCs) to highly purified PMNs [101]. *Staphylococcus aureus* peptidoglycan and LTA, agonists for TLR2, also delay PMN apoptosis [102;103]. In PMN preparations that have been depleted of monocytes by magnetic bead isolation, TLR4 ligation to LPS is the principal TLR survival signal. However, the LPS-mediated delay in apoptosis (in the absence of monocytes) is relatively short (~ 4 hours), as opposed to the 22–hour delay observed in the presence of monocytes [45, 104].

## Resolution of Inflammation

### Down-Regulation of Proinflammatory Capacity

During phagocytosis of microbes, PMNs produce intraphagosomal ROS and cytoplasmic granules mobilize to fuse with forming phagocytic vacuoles [105]. In addition, PMNs produce/secrete numerous cytokines and chemokines, including TNFα and IL-8, which contribute to the inflammatory response [6;106;107]. Production of these molecules is regulated in part at the level of gene expression [108;109]. Microarray-based studies have shown that phagocytosis up-regulates neutrophil transcripts encoding proteins that play an important role in the inflammatory response, such as IL-1α, IL-1β, IL-1ε, IL-1RN, IL-6, IL-8, IL-10, IL-12β, IL-15, TNFα, vascular endothelial growth factor (VEGF), oncostatin M (OSM), IL-6, GROβ and GROγ [4-7;10;110]. Taken together, these processes are critical for defense against invading microorganisms. However, once phagocytosis is complete and microbes are destroyed, these PMN functions are down-regulated coincident with the induction of apoptosis [3;7;9;111-114]. For example, Walcheck *et al.* have shown recently that phagocytosis-induced neutrophil apoptosis is accompanied by shedding of L-selectin and concomitant increased surface expression of ADAM17, suggesting that ADAM17 may play a role in the down-regulation of neutrophil function [115]. Notably, key pro-inflammatory or signal transduction molecules, including CXCR1 and CXCR2, are down-regulated during the initial stages of apoptosis [10].

## Neutrophil Apoptosis Differentiation Program

Although a widely accepted view was that mature PMNs have little biosynthetic capacity, recent evidence indicates changes in PMN transcript levels (and associated protein synthesis) during phagocytosis are an important component to the resolution of the inflammatory response [3;6-8;108;109;116-121]. Futhermore, phagocytosis of bacterial pathogens, including *Burkholderia cepacia*, *Borrelia hermsii*, *Staphylococcus aureus*, *Streptococcus pyogenes*, and *Listeria monocytogenes,* is followed by global changes in neutrophil gene expression concurrent with induction of apoptosis [10]. These findings provide an explanation for the increased RNA synthesis in neutrophils following phagocytosis that was originally reported by Martin Cline decades ago [122]. Bacteria-induced neutrophil apoptosis correlates well with alterations in transcripts encoding factors that promote or repress apoptosis, influencing the fate of PMNs [10]. Furthermore, phagocytosis-induced neutrophil apoptosis is accompanied by down-regulation of genes encoding proinflammatory molecules [10]. Based on these findings, it was proposed that bacteria induce an apoptosis differentiation program in human PMNs that facilitates rapid neutrophil turnover during infection. As these processes are intimately associated with bacteria-induced PMN apoptosis, they are likely critical for the resolution of bacterial infections. The neutrophil apoptosis differentiation program represents the final stage of transcription-regulated neutrophil maturation and regulates multiple processes in human neutrophils, including apoptosis and associated decreased function [117].

## ROS and Neutrophil Apoptosis

ROS play a crucial role in neutrophil apoptosis [7;58-60;92;105;123-132]. For example, neutrophils from patients with chronic granulomatous disease (XCGD), in which ROS production is absent, have impaired constitutive-, death receptor-mediated-, and phagocytosis-induced apoptosis [60;61;127;129]. Additional links between ROS production and PMN apoptosis were identified in myeloperoxidase-deficient mice, which may involve generation of hypochlorous acid [62;133]. Work by Mayadas and co-workers has shown that ROS promote cleavage of caspases 3 and 8 following phagocytosis, thereby triggering apoptosis [58]. The importance of ROS in the resolution of infection is exemplified by studies in CGD mice, which revealed that neutrophils fail to undergo apoptosis after interaction with pathogens and are thus not removed from the site of infection [134]. Although data indicating ROS are important for neutrophil apoptosis are compelling, not all studies concur [10;59;135]. Inasmuch as pathogen-induced apoptosis is complex process involving a multitude of signalling molecules and bacterial components, the process is likely dictated by the specifc microbe and/or number of microbes ingested.

## Bacteria Induce Neutrophil Apoptosis

Phagocytosis-induced neutrophil apoptosis is a mechanism to clear tissues of spent neutrophils (including those containing dead microbes), thereby facilitating the resolution of inflammation and infection [10;132;136-138]. As with spontaneous neutrophil apoptosis, timely removal of neutrophils–although in this case after phagocytosis–would prevent release of cytotoxic molecules into surrounding host tissues, a phenomenon mediated by necrosis or lysis [139]. This process is important because neutrophils and neutrophil products are known to contribute to specific inflammatory diseases [129;140-143].

Watson *et al.* demonstrated that phagocytosis of *Escherichia coli* by PMNs accelerates apoptosis, a process mediated by ROS [144]. This work was the first to link the PMN ROS and apoptosis. Since that time, dozens of bacteria have been shown to trigger neutrophil apoptosis (Table 2). For instance, *Burkholderia cenocepacia* (a predominant species in the *Burkholderia cepacia* complex) is readily phagocytosed by human neutrophils and promotes apoptosis [145;146]. This proapoptotic effect is not due to a product of the microbe *per se*, such as secreted molecules, but is dependent on bacterial viability. Phagocytosis of *Burholderia cepacia* elicits normal NADPH oxidase-derived ROS, although this alone is insufficient to trigger PMN apoptosis [145].

Activation of neutrophils by *M. tuberculosis* also triggers apoptosis [137;147;148;148-150]. Remarkably, TNF$\alpha$, CD11b, CD14 or Fc$\gamma$ receptors are not involved in this process and apoptosis is induced by recognition of cell wall components via TLR2 and the p38 mitogen-activated protein kinase (MAPK) pathway [147]. This mechanism is independent of phagocytosis and may be important during the early stages of *M. tuberculosis* infection, when phagocytosis of the pathogen is limited due to the low bateria-to-PMN ratios [147;149]. Alternatively, a second mechanism was proposed to occur in sites with high bacterial burdens, such as in the lung of infected patients, where phagocytosis of *M. tuberculosis* could account for the enhanced neutrophil apoptosis [147].

Although most proinflammatory cytokines and many bacteria-derived factors delay apoptosis [87;103;151-154], a complex signalling system exists such that bacteria-induced apoptosis overrides any delay in apoptosis due to these factors [155;156].

**Table 2. Bacteria that modulate cell death in phagocytic leukocytes**

| Bacterial pathogen | Leukocyte affected | References |
|---|---|---|
| *Actinobacillus actinomycetemcomitans* | macrophages (J774.1), peripheral blood mononuclear cells | [266-275] |
| *Aeromonas hydrophila* | macrophages (RAW264.7) | [276;277] |
| *Anaplasma phagocytophilum* | neutrophils | [116;173-175;181;278] |
| *Bacilluis anthracis* | macrophages (J774.A1, RAW264.7), peripheral blood mononuclear cells | [279-283] |
| *Borrelia hermsii* | neutrophils | [10;112] |
| *Bordetella bronchiseptica* | macrophages | [284-286] |
| *Bordetella pertussis* | macrophages, neutrophils | [285;287-293] |
| *Brucella abortus* | macrophages (RAW264.7), monocytes | [294;295] |
| *Brucella melitensis* | monocytes | [296] |
| *Brucella suis* | monocytes | [297] |
| *Burkholderia cepacia* | macrophages (J774.2), neutrophils | [10;145;146;298;299] |
| *Chlamydia pneumoniae* | promyelocytic cells (U937, THP-1), neutrophils | [176;182;300-302] |
| *Chlamydia psittaci* | macrophages (J774) | [303] |
| *Chlamydia trachomatis* | macrophages, neutrophils | [304;305] |
| *Clostridium difficile* | macrophages, eosinophils | [306;307] |
| *Coxiella burnetii* | promyelocytic cells (THP-1) | [308] |
| *Escherichia coli* | macrophages, monocytes, neutrophils | [132;154;309-317] |
| *Francisella tularensis* | macrophages (J774) | [318;319] |
| *Fusobacterium necrophorium* | neutrophils | [320] |
| *Fusobacterium nucleatum* | neutrophils, peripheral blood mononuclear cells | [321] |
| *Haemophilus somnus* | neutrophils | [322] |
| *Helicobacter pylori* | macrophages, monocytes, neutrophils | [323-327] |
| *Legionella longbeachae* | promyelocytic cells (HL60) | [328] |
| *Legionella pneumophila* | monocytes, promyelocytic cells (U937, HL60) | [329-336] |
| *Leptospira interrogans* | macrophages (J774.A1) | [337] |
| *Listeria monocytogenes* | dendritic cells, macrophages, neutrophils | [338-340] |
| *Mannheimia (Pasteurella) haemolytica* | neutrophils | [341;342] |
| *Mycobacterium avium* | macrophages, monocytes | [343-349] |
| *Mycobacterium bovis-BCG* | macrophages, monocytes, neutrophils | [350-353] |
| *Mycobacterium kansasii* | macrophages, monocytes | [354] |

**Table 2. (Continued)**

| Bacterial pathogen | Leukocyte affected | References |
|---|---|---|
| *Mycobacterium leprae* | macrophages | [355] |
| *Mycobacterium tuberculosis* | macrophages, monocytes, neutrophils | [137;147;149; 150;356-374] |
| *Mycobacterium ulcerans* | macrophages (J774) | [375;376] |
| *Mycoplasma fermentans* | promyelocytic cells (U937, HL60) | [377-379] |
| *Parachlamydia acanthamoeba* | macrophages | [301] |
| *Photobacterium damselae subsp. Piscicida* | macrophages, neutrophils | [380] |
| *Porphyromonas gingivalis* | neutrophils, promyelocytic cells (THP-1) | [381;382] |
| *Pseudomonas aeruginosa* | dendritic cells, macrophages, neutrophils | [89;383-393] |
| *Orientia (Rickettsia) tsutsugamushi* | promyelocytic cells (THP-1) | [394] |
| *Salmonella choleraesuis* | macrophages | [395] |
| *Salmonella enterica* serovar Enteritidis | monocytes | [396-398] |
| *Salmonella enterica* serovar Dublin | macrophages | [399] |
| *Salmonella enterica* serovar Typhimurium | macrophages | [399-405] |
| *Salmonella enterica* serovar Typhi | macrophages | [406;407] |
| *Shigella dysenteriae* | macrophages, neutrophils | [408] |
| *Shigella flexneri* | macrophages, monocytes | [409-425] |
| *Sphingobacterium spiritivorum* | promyelocytic cells (HL60) | [426] |
| *Staphylococcus aureus* | neutrophils | [59;102;103;1 38;239;427] |
| *Streptococcus agalactiae* | monocytes, macrophages | [428-432] |
| *Streptococcus iniae* | pronephros phagocytes (fish) | [433] |
| *Streptococcus pneumoniae* | macrophages, neutrophils | [155;159;393; 434-437] |
| *Streptococcus pyogenes* | promyelocytic cells (U937), neutrophils | [169;172;438; 439] |
| *Yersinia enterocolitica* | macrophages | [440-447] |
| *Yersinia pestis* | macrophages | [448-451] |
| *Yersinia pseudotuberculosis* | macrophages | [441;452-454] |
| *Vibrio vulnificans* | macrophages | [455;456] |

This Table was reproduced in part from Springer and Kluwer Academic Publishers, Apoptosis, volume 9, 2004, pages 400-401, Modulation of phagocyte apoptosis by bacterial pathogens, F.R. DeLeo, Table 1, © 2004 Kluwer Academic Publishers, with kind permission from Springer Science and Business Media.

## Modulation of Neutrophil Apoptosis by Bacterial Pathogens

While phagocytosis-induced neutrophil apoptosis is desirable for the resolution of infection and prevention of excessive or chronic inflammation, many pathogens have devised mechanisms to alter apoptosis and promote pathogenesis [112]. Herein, we provide two examples of this phenomenon and refer the reader to recent reviews on the topic for a more comprehensive overview [112;157;158].

Community-associated methicillin-resistant *Staphylococcus aureus* (CA-MRSA) and *Streptococcus pyogenes* cause direct PMN lysis and/or accelerate bacteria-induced apoptosis to the point of secondary necrosis [10;112;149;152;159-161]. The most prominent CA-MRSA strains produce leukotoxins known to cause lysis of human neutrophils, thus leading to severe pathologic states such as necrotizing pneumonia or fatal sepsis [162-164]. Neutrophils are highly susceptible to several of these cytolytic toxins, and depletion of neutrophils is likely a key mechanism by which CA-MRSA causes disease [160;165-168]. *Streptococcus pyogenes* is a Gram-positive pathogen associated with human infections ranging from mild pharyngitis to life-threatening necrotizing fasciitis [169]. It is relatively resistant to neutrophil phagocytosis and circumvents killing by human PMNs [10]. Notably, *Streptococcus pyogenes* alters normal phagocytosis-induced neutrophil apoptosis, thereby causing necrosis [159;169-172]. Thus, as with CA-MRSA, *Streptococcus pyogenes* kills neutrophils to survive within the human host.

## Pathogens That Delay Apoptosis

In contrast to macrophages, there are few bacteria that survive and replicate within neutrophils. *Anaplasma phagocytophilum* and *Chlamydia pneumonia* are among the few pathogens that delay neutrophil apoptosis to survive and replicate within these host cells [116;173-177]. *A. phagocytophilum* is an obligate intracellular bacterium that survives and replicates within neutrophils; for this to occur, it must prolong the life of the PMN. These pathogens are taken up through caveolae-mediated endocytosis and survive within inclusions/vacuoles that do not fuse with specific granules or secretory vesicles. *A. phagocytophilum* actively modulates vesicular trafficking, protecting themselves from microbicides sequestered within granules [178]. *A. phagocytophilum* also prevents activation of NADPH oxidase and detoxifies superoxide anion, preventing accumulation of ROS [116;179;180]. Notably, the pathogen fails to induce neutrophil apoptosis and dysregulates neutrophil gene expression to maximize survival and dissemination within the mammalian host [173-175;181]. Although progress has been made, the mechanism(s) used by *A. phagocytophilum* to delay apoptosis are not well understood.

PMNs readily phagocytose *C. pneumonia*, and a small fraction of internalized bacteria remain viable for up to 90 h after uptake [176]. *C. pneumonia* can multiply within neutrophils and delay normal apoptosis [176;182]. Of note, both phases of the *Chlamydia* biphasic life cycle occur within PMN inclusions. Delay of neutrophil apoptosis by *C. pneumonia* can be as long as 3 days and is associated with a decrease in caspase-3 activity [176]. This delay in PMN apoptosis may be mediated by LPS and autocrine production of IL-8 [176].

Intracellular growth of *Chlamydia* is essential for pathogenisis, because the host cell supplies nutrients and shields the microbe from antimicrobial serum factors.

*A. phagocytophilum* and *C. pneumonia* are unusual and interesting pathogens that continue to provide fundamental insight into mechanisms of neutrophil apoptosis and bacterial pathogenesis.

## A Paradigm for the Resolution of Infection

Although it is difficult to fit all bacteria into a single, comprehensive model that illustrates how they each interact with human neutrophils, a schematic that takes into account much of the pulished data on the topic can be assembled (Figure 3). This model schematic suggests that there are two possible outcomes for neutrophil-bacteria interactions [112]. On one hand, phagocytosis and killing of bacteria culminate with induction of neutrophil apoptosis and subsequent removal by macrophages, ultimately resulting in the resolution of infection (Figure 3). Alternatively, pathogens such as *A. phagocytophilum*, *C. pneumoniae*, *Streptococcus pyogenes* and CA-MRSA alter neutrophil apoptosis to survive, and thereby disseminate and cause disease [116;170;171;173;174;176]. As we gain a better understanding of neutrophil-pathogen interactions, it is almost certain that this model will need to be modified/updated.

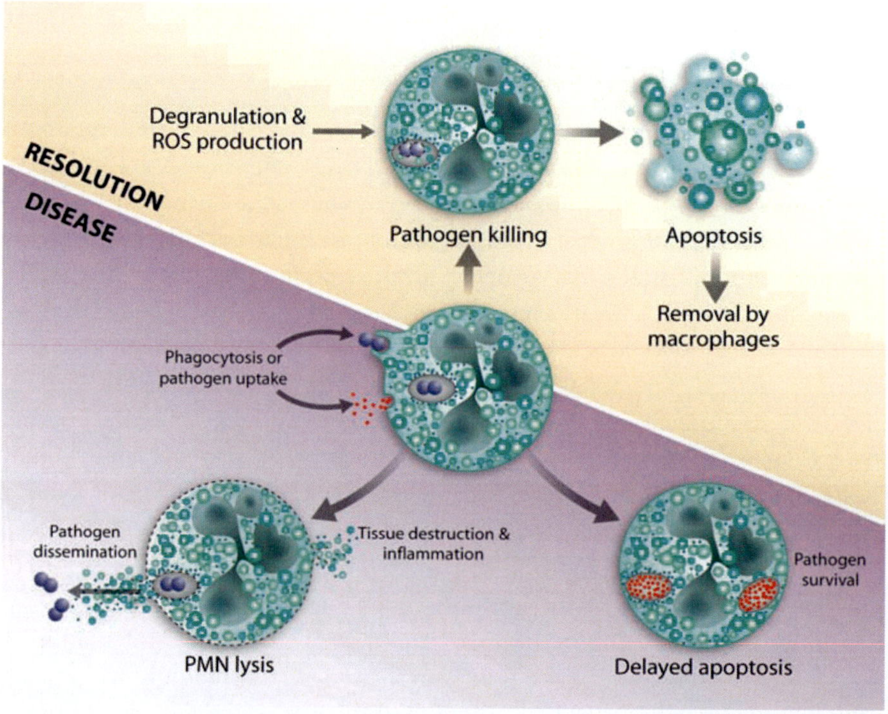


Figure 3. Neutrophil apoptosis. Transmission electron micrographs (A and B) or Cytospin (ThermoShandon) with modified Wright-Giemsa stain (C and D) of human neutrophils isolated fresh from peripheral blood (A and B) or a those having undergone spontaneous apoptosis after culture for 24 hours *in vitro* (C and D). Note the condensed chromatin/nucleus in apoptotic cells.

# Removal of Apoptotic PMNS by Macrophages

As with removal of undesirable, autoreactive T cells in the thymus, apoptosis is a mechanism to clear effete PMNs. Apoptotic cells maintain membrane integrity for a short period of time, but need to be cleared quickly to prevent secondary necrosis and release of cytotoxic molecules that would otherwise cause inflammation and/or damage to host tissues. Clearance of apoptotic neutrophils is mainly been studied with human monocyte-derived macrophages [183] and mouse alveolar macrophages [184]. Although clearance of apoptotic cells is not completely understood, several macrophage receptors have been implicated in this process. These receptors include the phosphatidylserine receptor [184;185], complement receptors [186], scavenger receptors and lectins [187], the $\alpha_v\beta_3$/CD36/thrombospondin recognition system [188;189], CD14 [190], and CD44 [191-193].

## Phosphatidylserine Receptor (PSR)

Transposition of the PSR from the inner leaflet of the plasma membrane to the outer leaflet is a major hallmark of cells undergoing apoptosis. The transcript for the PSR is expressed in several tissues in mice [194]. Human and mouse macrophages express the PSR and it is required for *in vitro* and *in vivo* clearance of apoptotic cells [194-196]. Consequently, mice genetically deficient in the PSR gene have accumulation of apoptotic cells in the lung and brain during embryogenesis and develop autoimmune diseases [194;197]. It is possible that the generation of autoimmune diseases in these models results from the pool of apoptotic cells that releases autoantigens over time.

## Complement Receptors

The human complement cascade can be activated by antibodies (classical pathway) or by oligosaccharide antigens on microbes or apoptotic cells (lectin and alternative pathways) (reviewed in [198]). Each of the complement cascades is a sequential, proteolytic cascade that results in opsonization of targets with C3b(i) and/or lysis of opsonized cell by the membrane attack complex (MAC). Complement proteins, specifically C3b and its breakdown products, bind to apoptotic cells, possibly through the exposure of PSR [186], and alter lipid and carbohydrate moieties. This process facilitates removal of apoptotic cells from tissues (reviewed in [199]). The majority of complement receptor phagocytosis is mediated through one of four receptors that bind to complement component C3; CR1 (CD35), CR2 (CD21), CR3 (CD11b/CD18), and CR4 (CD11c/CD18). Macrophages express CR3 and CR4 as well as the C1q receptor, which binds to the first component of the classical complement pathway. The importance of C3 and C1q have been shown in mice with targeted deletion of the genes encoding these receptors [197;200]. Mice with defective complement activation and reduced C3b(i) deposition have decreased clearance of apoptotic cells by macrophages [197;200]. Grevnik *et al.* illustrated that although systemic lupus erythematosus patients have reduced total complement hemolytic activity in their sera, complement-mediated phagocytosis of apoptotic cells remained unaffected [201]. This observation can be explained by differential depletion of specific complement components in the patients, *i.e.*, reduced levels of C9 and normal levels C3.

## Vitronectin ($\alpha_v\beta_3$)/CD36/Thrombospondin Recognition System

Vitronectin ($\alpha_v\beta_3$ integrin), CD36, and thrombospondin are believed to function in a complex on macrophages and promote binding and uptake of apoptotic cells. Cooperation among these three antigens was illustrated during recognition of apoptotic PMNs by human monocyte-derived macrophages [188] and murine bone marrow-derived macrophages [183]. Thrombospondin functions somewhat like C3b (see above) in that thrombospondin binds to an unknown ligand on apoptotic cells which then is recognized by the CD36/vitronectin complex expressed on macrophages. CD36 is an 88 kDa multifunctional glycoprotein (B-type scavenger receptor) expressed by several cell types including monocytes, endothelial cells, epithelial cells, and several tumor cell lines [202]. Macrophage CD36, along with $\alpha_v\beta_3$ integrin (vitronectin), is important for the removal of apoptotic cells during the resolution of viral infections [189]. The domain on CD36 that is critical for the removal of apoptotic cells has been localized to amino acids 155-183 [203].

## CD44

CD44 is a ~90 kDa protein expressed on hematopoietic and non-hematopoietic cells that binds to hyaluronic acid. CD44 cross-linking is associated with the generation of intracellular signals that specifically augment clearance of apoptotic PMNs. For example, blocking CD44 with anti-CD44 Fab' antibodies decreases macrophage mediated phagocytosis of apoptotic bodies [191]. Furthermore, CD44-deficient mice have reduced capacity to clear apoptotic PMNs post-inflammation [204].

## CD14

CD14 is a 53–55 kDa protein expressed on monocytes, macrophages, and at relatively low levels on granulocytes. Although CD14 is a receptor for LPS [205], recent evidence indicates CD14 also binds intercellular adhesion molecule-3 (ICAM-3) on leukocytes [206]. CD14 can be expressed in soluble form (sCD14) and may bind apoptotic cells and subsequently react with a sCD14 receptor on phagocytes [207]. Little is known about the role of CD14 in the removal of apoptotic PMNs; however, there is good evidence that CD14 is crucial for removal of apoptotic lymphocytes [208;209].

### Scavenger Receptors and Lectins

In addition to the flipping of phosphatidylserine from the inner leaflet to the outer leaflet of the plasma membrane, sugars and oxidized lipids that are exposed on the surface of apoptotic cells are modified and recognized as "non-self" by macrophages. These modifications are recognized by scavenger receptors and lectins expressed on the surface of macrophages and fibroblasts [210;211].

### Removal of Apoptotic PMNs: A Non-Inflammatory Process

Neutrophil apoptosis is a nonphlogistic (non-inflammatory) process. Phagocytosis of apoptotic cells by professional phagcocytes (macrophages, monocytes, or dendritic cells) causes these cell types to produce anti-inflammatory cytokines [212;213]. Lucas *et al.* demonstrated that macrophages exposed to apoptotic cells secrete TGF-β, which suppresses LPS-mediated release of inflammatory cytokines by infected cells [214]. Macrophages also secrete factors that contribute to PMN apoptosis (*e.g.*, soluble FasL [65]) and increase expression of anti-inflammatory factors [215]. For example, in the airway (bronchi and lungs), apoptotic PMNs are ingested by alveolar macrophages without release of inflammatory mediators (reviewed in [216]). Moreover, engagement of apoptotic cells by CD36 on macrophages inhibits production of proinflammatory cytokines TNFα, IL-1β, and IL-12, but increases secretion of TGF-β and IL-10 (anti-inflammatory cytokines) [217].

In addition to the autologous signals that contribute to the anti-inflammatory process, steroids–specifically glutocorticoids–promote a non-inflammatory environment during phagocytosis of apoptotic cells. Human and murine macrophages exposed to glucocorticoids for 24 hours have enhanced ability to phagocytose apoptotic leukocytes [218]. Compared to macrophages, peripheral blood monocytes have a much lower phagocytic capacity toward apoptotic cells, but incubation of human monocytes with glucocorticoids induces the phenotype of monocyte-derived macrophages much more competent to ingest apoptotic cells [40;219]. The ability of macrophages to phagocytose apoptotic leukocytes after incubation with glutocorticoids has been linked to 11β-hydroxysteroid dehydrogenase (11β-HSD), a molecule not present in monocytes [220;221]. Specifically, mice that are genetically deficient in 11β-HSD have delayed rate of clearance of apoptotic neutrophils [221]. Cytokines also dictate phagocytic capacity of macrophages. For example, IFNγ inhibits the glucocorticoid-induced ability of macrophages to clear apoptotic PMNs [222].

## Human Disease and Neutrophil Turnover

Although the cytotoxic components produced by neutrophils kill most ingested microorganisms efficiently, host tissue damage can occur inadvertently via degradative enzymes and ROS. PMN activation, unresolved inflammatory responses, and extracellular release of ROS and granule contents through neutrophil lysis can contribute to inflammatory disorders [223]. A few examples of such conditions are provided below.

### Rheumatoid Arthritis

Rheumatoid arthritis has been linked to the production of ROS by neutrophils following activation by immune complexes in the synovial fluid of joints [140;142;224]. This results in the release of cytotoxic ROS, which oxidize low-density lipoproteins (LDLs), contributing to the pathology of atherosclerosis [225-230]. Recognition of oxidized LDLs by resident macrophages and neutrophils activates these cells to generate ROS, thus contributing to atherosclerosis.

### Necrotizing Pneumonia

Host tissue damage caused by *Staphylococcus aureus* pneumonia (necrotizing pneumonia) is likely attributed in part to cytolytic toxins that lyse neutrophils [160;162;165-167;231-239]. This is underscored by the presence of multiple staphylococcal leukotoxins, which target neutrophils, in CA-MRSA strains associated with necrotizing pneumonia or fatal sepsis [240]. In addition to causing host tissue damage, lysis indirectly promotes recruitment of more leukocytes to the site of the infection, enhancing the inflammatory response. Thus, it is critical that neutrophil turnover and removal of apoptotic PMNs are highly regulated processes during infection and inflammation.

### Chronic Granulomatous Disease

Chronic granulomatous disease (CGD) is a hereditary disorder characterized by a defect in NADPH oxidase [143;241], and thus neutrophils from these patients are unable to generate ROS. As such, CGD patients are highly susceptible to bacterial and fungal infections [129;141;143;145;242;243;243-246]. These infections are often life-threatening, although relatively new treatments such as IFNγ or itraconazole therapries result in better prognoses [247;248]. One of the most prominent features of CGD is that patients develop granulomas in vital organs [129;143;246;249-251]. Recent studies have shown that neutrophils from CGD patients have increased expression of proinflammatory molecules and decreased expression of genes encoding anti-inflammation mediators compared to healthy PMNs [129]. This could contribute to the recruitment and activation of immune cells, prolonging the inflammatory response in CGD patients. Moreover, PMNs from patients with CGD have abnormal PMN turnover after phagocytosis [127;129], a phenomenon which may contribute directly to the formation of granulomas.

## Conclusion

Neutrophils are the most abundant leukocyte in humans and crucial defense against invading microorganisms. Neutrophil apoptosis is essential for maintaining normal immune system homeostasis and the process facilitates the resolution of inflammation. PMN apoptosis is mediated by both intrinsic and extrinsic mechanisms, and apoptotic cells are subsequently cleared by macrophages through multiple receptor-ligand interactions.

Bacterial pathogens can alter PMN apoptosis to survive and thereby cause disease. Pathogen survival is accomplished in part by inhibiting cell activation, blocking apoptosis, or causing PMN lysis. The use of genomics-based technologies has dramatically enhanced our discovery of mechanisms of bacterial virulence and fundamental immunlogy. A better understanding of innate host defense and bacterial pathogensis will likely provide information important for development of vaccines, treatments, and prophylactic agents designed to prevent and/or control infections.

## Acknowledgments

We thank Dr. David W. Dorward (Rocky Mountain Laboratories, Hamilton, MT) for performing transmission electron microscopy and Dr. Mark T. Quinn (Montana State University, Bozeman, MT) for critical review of the manuscript. This work was supported by the Intramural Research Program of the National Institute of Allergy and Infectious Diseases, National Institutes of Health.

## References

[1] Faurschou M, Borregaard N. Neutrophil granules and secretory vesicles in inflammation. *Microbes. Infect.* 2003;5:1317-27.

[2] Klebanoff SJ. Myeloperoxidase: friend and foe. *J. Leukoc. Biol.* 2005;77:598-625.

[3] Kobayashi SD, Voyich JM, DeLeo FR. Regulation of the neutrophil-mediated inflammatory response to infection. *Microbes. Infect.* 2003;5:1337-44.

[4] Quinn MT, Gauss KA. Structure and regulation of the neutrophil respiratory burst oxidase: comparison with non-phagocyte oxidases. *J. Leukoc. Biol.* 2004;76:760-81.

[5] Kobayashi SD, Voyich JM, Burlak C, DeLeo FD. Neutrophils in the innate immune response. *Arch. Immunol. Ther. Exp.* 2005;53:505-17.

[6] Scapini P, Lapinet-Vera JA, Gasperini S, Calzetti F, Bazzoni F, Cassatella MA. The neutrophil as a cellular source of chemokines. *Immunol. Rev.* 2000;177:195-203.

[7] Kobayashi SD, Voyich JM, Buhl CL, Stahl RM, DeLeo FR. Global changes in gene expression by human polymorphonuclear leukocytes during receptor-mediated phagocytosis: Cell fate is regulated at the level of gene expression. *Proc. Natl. Acad. Sci. USA* 2002;99:6901-6.

[8] Kobayashi SD, Voyich JM, Braughton KR, DeLeo FR. Down-regulation of proinflammatory capacity during apoptosis in human polymorphonuclear leukocytes. *J. Immunol.* 2003;170:3357-68.

[9] Kobayashi SD, Voyich JM, Somerville GA, Braughton KB, Malech HL, Musser JM, et al. An apoptosis-differentiation programme in human polymorphonuclear leukocytes facilitates resolution of inflammation. *J. Leukoc. Biol.* 2003;73:315-22.

[10] Kobayashi SD, Braughton KR, Whitney AR, Voyich JM, Schwan TG, Musser JM. Bacterial pathogens modulate an apoptosis differentiation program in human neutrophils. *Proc. Natl. Acad. Sci. USA* 2003;100:10948-53.

[11] Cowland JB, Borregaard N. Isolation of neutrophil precursors from bone marrow for biochemical and transcriptional analysts. *J. Immunol. Methods*. 1999;232:191-200.

[12] Ward AC, Loeb DM, Soede-Bobok AA, Touw IP, Friedman AD. Regulation of granulopoiesis by transcription factors and cytokine signals. *Leukemia* 2000;14:973-90.

[13] Bjerregaard MD, Jurlander J, Klausen P, Borregaard N, Cowland JB. The in vivo profile of transcription factors during neutrophil differentiation in human bone marrow. *Blood* 2003;101:4322-32.

[14] Friedman AD. Transcriptional regulation of myelopoiesis. *Int. J. Hematol.* 2002; 75:466-72.

[15] Friedman AD. Transcriptional regulation of granulocyte and monocyte development. *Oncogene* 2002; 21:3377-90.

[16] Faurschou M, Borregaard N. Neutrophil granules and secretory vesicles in inflammation. *Microbes. Infect*. 2003; 5:1317-27.

[17] Borregaard N, Theilgaard-Monch K, Sorensen OE, Cowland JB. Regulation of human neutrophil granule protein expression. *Curr. Opin. Hematol.* 2001;8:23-7.

[18] Baum CM, Weissman IL, Tsukamoto AS, Buckle AM, Peault B. Isolation of a candidate human hematopoietic stem-cell population. *Proc. Natl. Acad. Sci. USA* 1992;89:2804-8.

[19] Becker AJ, McCulloch EA, Till JE. Cytological demonstration of the clonal nature of spleen colonies derived from transplanted mouse marrow cells. *Nature* 1963;197:452-4.

[20] Cudkowicz G, Bennett M, Shearer GM. Pluripotent stem cell function of the mouse marrow "lymphocyte". *Science* 1964;144:866-8.

[21] Bainton DF, Ullyot JL, Farquhar MG. The development of neutrophilic polymorphonuclear leukocytes in human bone marrow. *J. Exp. Med.* 1971;134:907-34.

[22] Athens JW, Haab OP, Raab SO, Mauer AM, Ashenbrucker H, Cartwright GE, et al. Leukokinetic studies. IV. The total blood, circulating and marginal granulocytes pools and the granulocytes turnover rate in normal subjects. *J. Clin. Invest.* 1961;40:989-95.

[23] Killmann SA, Cronkite EP, Fliedner TM, Bond VP. Mitotic indices of human bone marrow cells. I. Number and cytologic distribution of mitoses. Blood 1962;19:743-50.

[24] Witko-Sarsat V, Rieu P, Descamps-Latscha B, Lesavre P, Halbwachs-Mecarelli L. Neutrophils: molecules, functions and pathophysiological aspects. *Lab. Invest.* 2000;80:617-53.

[25] Borregaard N, Sehested M, Nielsen BS, Sengelov H, Kjeldsen L. Biosynthesis of granule proteins in normal human bone marrow cells. Gelatinase is a marker of terminal neutrophil differentiation. *Blood* 1995;85:812-7.

[26] Cline MJ. Production, destruction, and distribution of neutrophilic granulocytes. The White Cell.Cambridge: Harvard University Press; 1975. p. 24-38.

[27] Cronkite EP, Fliedner TM. Granulocytopoiesis. *N. Engl. J. Med.* 1964; 270:1347-52.

[28] Fliedner TM, Cronkite EP, Robertson JS. Granulocytopoiesis. I. Senescence and random loss of neutrophilic granulocytes in human beings. *Blood* 1964; 24:402-14.

[29] Fadeel B, Kagan VE. Apoptosis and macrophage clearance of neutrophils: regulation by reactive oxygen species. *Redox Report* 2003;8:143150.

[30] Sengelov H, Kjeldsen L, Kroeze W, Berger M, Borregaard N. Secretory vesicles are the intracellular reservoir of complement receptor 1 in human neutrophils. *J. Immunol.* 1994;153:804-10.

[31] Faurschou M, Borregaard N. Neutrophil granules and secretory vesicles in inflammation. *Microbes. Infect.* 2003;5:1317-27.

[32] Schmeling DJ, Peterson PK, Hammerschmidt DE, Kim Y, Verhoef J, Wilkinson BJ, et al. Chemotaxigenesis by cell surface components of *Staphylococcus aureus*. *Infect. Immun.* 1979;26:57-63.

[33] Showell HJ, Freer RJ, Zigmond SH, Shiffmann E, Aswanikumar S, Corcoran B, et al. The structure-activity relations of synthetic peptides as chemotactic factors and inducers of lysosomal enzyme secretion for neutrophils. *J. Exp. Med.* 1976;143:1154-69.

[34] McPhail LC, Clayton CC, Snyderman R. The NADPH oxidase of human polymorphonuclear leukocytes. Evidence for regulation by multiple signals. *J. Biol. Chem.* 1984;259:5768-75.

[35] Sengelov H, Kjeldsen L, Diamond MS, Springer TA, Borregaard N. Subcellular localization and dynamics of Mac-1 ($\square_{m}\square_{2}$) in human neutrophils. *J. Clin. Invest.* 1993;92:1467-76.

[36] Diamond MS, Staunton DE, de Fougerolles AR, Stacker SA, Garcia-Aguilar J, Hibbs ML, et al. ICAM-1 (CD54): a counter-receptor for Mac-1 (CD11b/CD18). *J. Cell. Biol.* 1990;111:3129-39.

[37] Muller WA, Weigl SA, Deng X, Phillips DM. PECAM-1 is required for transendothelial migration of leukocytes. *J. Exp. Med.* 1993;178:449-60.

[38] Khan AI, Kerfoot SM, Heit B, Liu L, Andonegui G, Rufell B, et al. Role of CD44 and hyaluronan in neutrophil recruitment. *J. Immunol.* 2004;173:7594-601.

[39] Cooper D, Lindberg FP, Gamble JR, Brown EG, Vadas MA. Transendothelial migration of neutrophils involves integrin-associated protein (CD47). *Proc. Natl. Acad. Sci. USA* 1995;92:3978-82.

[40] Savill JS, Wyllie AH, Henson JE, Walport MJ, Henson PM, Haslett C. Macrophage phagocytosis of aging neutrophils in inflammation: programmed cell death in the neutrophil leads to its recognition by macrophages. *J. Clin. Invest* 1989;83:865-75.

[41] Nusbaum P, Laine C, Seveau S, Lesavre P, Halbwachs-Mecarelli L. Early membrane events in polymorphonuclear cell (PMN) apoptosis: membrane blebbing and vesicle release, CD43 and CD16 down-regulation and phosphatidylserine externalization. *Biochem. Soc. Trans.* 2004;32:477-9.

[42] Dransfield I, Buckle AM, Savill JS, McDowall A, Haslett C, Hogg N. Neutrophil apoptosis is associated with a reduction in CD16 (Fc gamma RIII) expression. *J. Immunol.* 1994;143:1254-63.

[43] Metchnikoff E. Lecture VII. Lectures on the comparative pathology of inflammation. In: Starling FA, Starling EH, editors.London: Kegan, Paul, Trench, *Trubner*; 1893. p. 107-31.

[44] Edwards SW, Derouet M, Howse M, Moots RJ. Regulation of neutrophil apoptosis by Mcl-1. *Biochem. Soc. Trans.* 2004;32:489-92.

[45] Leuenroth SJ, Grutkoski PS, Ayala A, Simms HH. The loss of Mcl-1 expression inhuman polymorphonuclear leukocytes promotes apoptosis. *J. Leukoc. Biol.* 2000;68:158-66.

[46] Moulding DA, Quayle JA, Hart CA, Edwards SW. Mcl-1 expression in human neutrophils: regulation by cytokines and correlation with cell survival. *Blood* 1998;92:2495-502.

[47] Kato T, Kutsuna H, Oshitani N, Kitagawa S. Cyclic AMP delays neutrophil apoptosis via stabilization of Mcl-1. *FEBS Lett.* 2006;580:4582-6.

[48] Moulding DA, .Akgul C, Derouet M, White MRH, Edwards SW. BCL-2 family expression in human neutrophils during delayed and accelerated apoptosis. *J. Leukoc. Biol. 2001*;70:783-92.

[49] Chuang PI, Yee E, Karsan A, Winn RK, Harlan JM. A1 is a constitutive and inducible Bcl-2 homologue in mature human neutrophils. *Biochem. Biophys. Res. Commun.* 1998;249:361-5.

[50] Scheel-Toellner D, Wang K, Assi LK, Webb PR, Craddock RM, Salmon M, et al. Clustering of death receptors in lipid rafts initiates neutrophil spontaneous apoptosis. *Biochem. Soc. Trans.* 2004;32:679-81.

[51] Taneja R, Parodo J, Jia SH, Kapus A, Rotstein OD, Marshall JC. Delayed neutrophil apoptosis in sepsis is associated with maintenance of mitochondrial transmembrane potential and reduced caspase-9 activity. *Crit. Care. Med.* 2004;32:1460-9.

[52] Sawatzky DA, Willoughby DA, Colville-Nash PR, Rossi AG. The involovement of the apoptosis-modulating proteins ERK 1/2, Bcl,$x_L$ and Bax in the resolution of acute inflammation *in vivo*. *Am. J. Pathol.* 2006;168:33-41.

[53] Murphy BM, O'Neill AJ, Adrain C, Watson RWG, Martin SJ. The apoptosome pathway to caspase activation in primary human neutrophils exhibits dramatically reduced requirements for cytochrome c. *J. Exp. Med.* 2003;197:625-32.

[54] Altznauer F, Conus S, Cavalli A, Folkers G, Simon H-U. Calpain regulates Bax and subsequent Smac-dependent Caspase-3 activation in neutrophil apoptosis. *J. Biol. Chem.* 2004;279:5947-57.

[55] Maianski NA, Mul FP, van Buul JD, Roos D, Kuijpers TW. Granulocyte colony-stimulating factor inhibits the mitochondria-dependent activation of caspase-3 in neutrophils. *Blood* 2002;99:672-9.

[56] Altznauer F, Conus S, Cavalli A, Folkers G, Simon H-U. Calpain regulates Bax and subsequent Smac-dependent Caspase-3 activation in neutrophil apoptosis. *J. Biol. Chem.* 2004;279:5947-57.

[57] Baumann R, Casaulta C, Simon D, Conus S, Yousefi S, Simon H-U. Macrophage migration inhibitory factor delays apoptosis in neutrophils by inhibiting the mitochondria-dependent death pathway. *FASEB J.* 2003;17:2221-30.

[58] Zhang B, Hiranhashi J, Cullere X, Mayadas TN. Elucidation of molecular events leading to neutrophil apoptosis following phagocytosis: Cross-talk between caspase 8, reactive oxygen species, and MAPK/ERK activation. *J. Biol. Chem.* 2003;278:28443-54.

[59] Yamamoto A, Taniuchi S, Tsuji S, Hasui M, Kobayashi Y. Role of reactive oxygen species in neutrophil apoptosis following ingestion of heat-killed *Staphylococcus aureus*. *Clin. Exp. Immunol.* 2002;129:479-84.

[60] Kasahara Y, Iwai K, Yachie A, Ohta K, Konno A, Seki H, et al. Involvement of reactive oxygen intermediates in spontaneous and CD95 (APO-1)-mediated apoptosis of neutrophils. *Blood* 1997;89:1748-53.

[61] Fadeel B, Ahlin A, Henter J-I, Orrenius S, Hampton MB. Involvement of caspases in neutrophil apoptosis: regulation by reactive oxygen species. *Blood* 1998;92:4808-18.

[62] Hampton MB, Kettle AJ, Winterbourn CC. Inside the neutrophil phagosome: oxidants, myeloperoxidase, and bacterial killing. *Blood* 1998;92:3007-17.

[63] Maianski NA, Geissler J, Srinivasula SM, Alnemri ES, Roos D, Kuijpers TW. Functional characterization of mitochondria in neutrophils: a role restricted to apoptosis. *Cell Death Differ.* 2004;11:143-53.

[64] Liles WC, Kiener PA, Ledbetter JA, Aruffo A, Klebanoff SJ. Differential expression of Fas (CD95) and Fas Ligand on normal human phagocytes: Implications for the regulation of apoptosis in neutrophils. *J. Exp. Med.* 1996;184:429-40.

[65] Brown SB, Savill J. Phagocytosis triggers macrophage release of Fas ligand and induces apoptosis of bystander leukocytes. *J. Immunol.* 1999;162:480-5.

[66] Jimenez MF, Watson RW, Parodo J, Evans D, Foster D, Steinberg M, et al. Dysregulated expression of neutrophil apoptosis in the systemic inflammatory response syndrome. *Arch. Surg.* 1997;132:480-5.

[67] Adam D, Adam-Klages S, Kronke M. Identification of p55 tumor necrosis factor receptor-associated proteins that couple to signaling pathways not initiated by the death domain. *J. Inflamm.* 1995;47:61-6.

[68] Gon S, Gatanaga T, Sendo F. Involvement of two types of TNF receptor in TNF-□ induced neutrophil apoptosis. *Microbiol. Immunol.* 1996;40:463-5.

[69] Murray J, Barbar JAJ, Dunkley SA, Lopez AF, Van Ostade X, Condliffe AM, et al. Regulation of neutrophil apoptosis by tumor necrosis factor-□: Requirement for TNFR55 and TNFR75 for induction of apoptosis in vitro. *Blood* 1997;90:2772-83.

[70] Maianski NA, Roos D, Kuijpers TW. Tumor necrosis factor a induces a caspase-independent death pathway in human neutrophils. *Blood* 2003;101:1987-95.

[71] van den Berg JM, Weyer S, Weening JJ, Roos D, Kuijpers TW. Divergent effects of tumor necrosis factor □ on apoptosis of human neutrophils. *J. Leukoc. Biol.* 2001;69:467-73.

[72] D'Osualdo A, Ferlito F, Prigione I, Obici L, Meini A, Zulian F, et al. Neutrophils from patients with TNFRSF1A mutations display resistance to tumor necrosis factor-induced apoptosis. *Arthritis. Rheum.* 2006;54:998-1008.

[73] Kamohara H, Matsuyama W, Shimozato O, Abe K, Galligan C, Hashimoto S-I, et al. Regulation of tumour necrosis factor-related apoptosis-inducing ligand (TRAIL) and TRAIL receptor expression in human neutrophils. *Immunology* 2004;111:186-94.

[74] Renshaw SA, Parmar JS, Singleton V, Rowe SJ, Dockrell DH, Dower SK, et al. Acceleration of human neutrophil apoptosis by TRAIL. J. Immunol. 2003;170:1027-33.

[75] Walczak H, Krammer PH. The CD95 (APO-1/Fas) and the TRAIL (APO-2L) apoptosis systems. *Exp. Cell Res.* 2000;256:58-66.

[76] Lum JJ, Bren G, McClure R, Badley AD. Elimination of senescent neutrophils by TNF-relating apoptosis-inducing ligand. *J. Immunol.* 2005;175:1232-8.

[77] Lamhamedi-Cherradi SE, Zheng SJ, Maguschak KA, Peschon J, Chen YH. Defective thymocyte apoptosis and accelerated autoimmune diseases in TRAIL$^{-/-}$ mice. *Nat. Immunol.* 2003;4:255-60.

[78] Lamhamedi-Cherradi SE, Zheng S, Tisch RM, Chen YH. Critical roles of tumor necrosis factor-related apoptosis-inducing ligand in type 1 diabetes. *Diabetes* 2003;52:2274-8.

[79] Hilliard B, Wilmen A, Seidel C, Liu TS, Goke R, Chen Y. Roles of TNF-related apoptosis-inducing ligand in experimental autoimmune encephalomyelitis. *J. Immunol.* 2001;166:1314-9.

[80] Koga Y, Matsuzaki A, Suminoe A, Hattori H, Hara T. Neutrophil-derived TNF-related apoptosis-inducing ligand (TRAIL): a novel mechanism of antitumor effect by neutrophils. *Cancer Res.* 2004;64:1037-43.

[81] Cassatella MA, Huber V, Calzetti F, Margotto D, Tamassia N, Peri G, et al. Interferon-activated neutrophils store a TNF-related apoptosis-inducing ligand (TRAIL/Apo-2 ligand) intracellular pool that is readily mobilizable following exposure to proinflammatory mediators. *J. Leukoc. Biol.* 2006;79:123-32.

[82] Simon HU. Neutrophil apoptosis pathways and their modifications in inflammation. *Immunol. Rev.* 2003;193:101-10.

[83] Akgul C, Moulding DA, Edwards SW. Molecular control of neutrophil apoptosis. *FEBS Lett.* 2001;487:318-22.

[84] Hotta K, Niwa M, Hara A, Ohno T, Wang X, Matsuno H, et al. The loss of susceptibility to apoptosis in exudated tissue neutrophils is associated with their nuclear factor-□B activation. *Eur. J. Pharmacol.* 2001;433:17-27.

[85] Daffern PJ, Jagels MA, Hugli TE. Multiple epithelial cell-derived factors enhance neutrophil survival; regulation by glucocorticoids and tumor necrosis factor-□. *Am. J. Respir. Cell Mol. Biol.* 1999;21:259-67.

[86] Kohl J, Bitter-Suermann D. Anaphylotoxins. In: Whaley K, Loos M, Weiler JM, editors. Complement in Health and Disease.Boston, MA: *Kluwer Academic Publishers*; 1993. p. 299-324.

[87] Colotta F, Re F, Polentarutti N, Sozzani S, Mantovani A. Modulation of granulocyte survival and programmed cell death by cytokines and bacterial products. *Blood* 1992;80:2012-20.

[88] Kotone-Miyahara Y, Yamashita K, Lee K-K, Yonehara S, Uchiyama T, Sasada M, et al. Short-term delay of Fas-stimulated apoptosis by GM-CSF as a result of temporary suppression of FADD recruitment in neutrophils: evidence implicating phosphatidylinositol 3-kinase and MEK1-ERK1/2 pathways downstream of classical protein kinase C. *J. Leukoc. Biol.* 2004;76:1047-56.

[89] Larsen GL, Mitchell BC, Harper TB, Henson PM. The pulmonary response of C5a deficient mice to *Pseudomonas aeruginosa*. *Am. Rev. Respir. Dis.* 1982;126:306-11.

[90] Perianayagam MC, Balakrishnan VS, Pereira BJ, Jaber BL. C5a delays apoptosis of human neutrophils via an extracellular signal-regulated kinase and Bad-mediated signalling pathway. *Eur. J. Clin. Invest.* 2004;34:50-6.

[91] Tamura DY, Moore EE, Partrick DA, Johnson JL, Offner PJ, Silliman CC. Acute hypoxemia in humans enhances the neutrophil imflammatory response. *Shock* 2002;17:269-73.

[92] Hannah S, Mecklenburgh K, Rahman I, Bellingan GJ, Greening A, Haslett C, et al. Hypoxia prolongs neutrophil survival in vitro. *FEBS Lett.* 1995;372:233-7.

[93] Molloy EJ, O'Neill AJ, Doyle BT, Grantham JJ, Taylor CT, Sheridan-Pereira M, et al. Effects of heat shock and hypoxia on neonatal neutrophil lipopolysaccharide responses: altered apoptosis, toll-like receptor-4 and CD11b expression compared with adults. *Biol. Neonate.* 2006;90:34-9.

[94] Hayashi F, Means TK, Luster AD. Toll-like receptors stimulate human neutrophil function. *Blood* 2003;102:2660-9.

[95] Takeda K, Akira S. Microbial recognition by toll-like receptors. *J. Dermatol. Sci.* 2004;34:73-82.

[96] Ahmad-Nejad P, Hacker H, Rutz M, Bauer S, Vabulas RM, Wagner H. Bacterial CpG-DNA and lipopolysaccharides activate toll-like receptors at distinct cellular compartments. *Eur. J. Immunol.* 2002;32:1958-68.

[97] Heil F, Ahmad-Nejad P, Hemmi H, Hochrein H, Ampenberger F, Gellert T, et al. The toll-like receptor 7 (TLR7)-specific stimulus loxoribine uncovers a strong relationship within the TLR7, 8, and 9 subfamily. *Eur. J. Immunol.* 2003;33:2987-97.

[98] Matsumoto M, Funami K, Tanabe M, Oshiumi H, Shingai M, Seto Y, et al. Subcellular localization of toll-like receptor 3 in human dendritic cells. *J. Immunol.* 2003;171:3154-62.

[99] Sabroe I, Jones EC, Usher LR, Whyte MKB, Dower SK. Toll-like receptor (TLR)2 and TLR4 in human peripheral blood granulocytes: A critical role for monocytes in leukocyte lipopolysaccharide responses. *J. Immunol.* 2002;168:4701-10.

[100] Sabroe I, Prince LR, Dower SK, Chilvers ER, Whyte MKB. What can we learn from highly purified neutrophils? *Biochem. Soc. Trans.* 2004;32:468-9.

[101] Watson RW, Rotstein OD, Parodo J, Bitar R, Marshall JC. The IL-1 beta-converting enzyme (caspase-1) inhibits apoptosis of inflammatory neutrophils through activation of IL-1 beta. *J. Immunol.* 1998;161:957-62.

[102] Sabroe I, Prince LR, Jones EC, Horsburgh MJ, Foster SJ, Vogel SN, et al. Selective roles for Toll-like receptor (TLR)2 and TLR4 in the regulation of neutrophil activation and life span. *J. Immunol.* 2003;170:5628-275.

[103] Lotz S, Aga E, Wilde I, van Zandbergen G, Hartung T, Solbach W, et al. Highly purified lipoteichoic acid activates neutrophil granulocytes and delays their spontaneous apoptosis via CD14 and TLR2. *J. Leukoc. Biol.* 2004;75:467-77.

[104] Feterowski C, Wieighardt H, Emmanuilidis K, Hartung T, Holzmann B. Immune protection against septic peritonitis in endotoxin-primed mice is related to reduced neutrophil apoptosis. *Eur. J. Immunol.* 2001;31:1268-77.

[105] Nauseef WM, Clark RA. Basic Principles in the Diagnosis and Management of Infectious Diseases. In: Mandell GL, Bennett JE, Dolin R, editors. *Granulocytes.*New York: Churchill Livingstone; 2000. p. 89-112.

[106] Cassatella MA. On the production of TNF-related apoptosis-inducing ligand (TRAIL/Apo-2L) by human neutrophils. *J. Leukoc. Biol.* 2006;79:1140-9.

[107] McDonald PP, Russo MP, Ferrini S, Cassatella MA. Interleukin-15 (IL-15) Induces NF-kappa B Activation and IL-8 Production in Human Neutrophils. *Blood* 1998;92:4828-35.

[108] Gasperini S, Marchi M, Calzetti F, Laudanna C, Vincentini L, Olsen H, et al. Gene expression and production of the monokine induced by IFN-□ (MIG), IFN-inducible T cell □ chemoattractant (I-TAC), and IFN-□-inducible protein-10 (IP-10) chemokines by human neutrophils. *J. Immunol.* 1999;162:4928-37.

[109] Lapinet JA, Scapini P, Calzetti F, Perez O, Cassatella MA. Gene expression and production of tumor necrosis factor alpha, interleukin 1-□, (IL-1□), IL-8, macrophage inflammatory potein 1□ (MIP-1□), MIP-1□, and gamma interferon-inducible protein 10 by human neutrophils stimulated with group b *meningococcal* outer membrane vesicles. *Infect. Immun.* 2000;68:6917-23.

[110] Gordon S. Development and distribution of mononuclear phagocytes: relevance to inflammation. In: Gallin JI, Snyderman R, editors. Inflammation, *Basic Principles and Clinical Correlates*.New York: Lippincott-Raven; 1999. p. 35-48.

[111] Cohen JJ, Duke RC, Fadok VA, Sellins KS. Apoptosis and Programmed Cell Death in Immunity. *Ann. Rev. Immunol.* 1992;10:267-93.

[112] DeLeo FR. Modulation of phagocyte apoptosis by bacterial pathogens. *Apoptosis* 2004;9:399-413.

[113] Ren Y, Savill J. Apoptosis: The importance of being eaten. *Cell Death Differ.* 1998;5:563-8.

[114] Savill J. Apoptosis in resolution of inflammation. *J. Leukoc. Biol.* 1997;61:375-80.

[115] Walcheck B, Herrera AH, St.Hill C, Mattila PE, Whiteney AR, DeLeo FR. ADAM17 activity during human neutrophil activation and apoptosis. *Eur. J. Immunol.* 2006;36:968-76.

[116] Borjesson DL, Kobayashi SD, Whitney AR, Voyich JM, Argue CM, DeLeo FR. Insights into pathogen immune evasion mechanisms: *Anaplasma phagocytophilum* fails to induce an apoptosis differentiation program in human neutrophils. *J. Immunol.* 2005;174:6364-72.

[117] Kobayashi SD, DeLeo FR. An apoptosis differentiation programme in human polymorphonuclear leucocytes. *Biochem. Soc. Trans.* 2004;32:474-6.

[118] McDonald P, Russo MP, Ferrini S, Cassatella MA. Interleukin-15 (IL-15) induces NF-κB activation and IL-8 production in human neutrophils. *Blood* 1998;92:4828-35.

[119] McDonald PP, Gasperini S, Calzetti F, Cassatella MA. Modulation of interferon-y of the production and gene expression of IL-1 receptor antagonist in human neutrophils. *Cell Immunol.* 1998;184:45-50.

[120] McDonald PP, Bald A, Cassatella MA. Activation of the NF-□B pathway by inflammatory stimuli in human neutrophils. *Blood* 1997;9:3421-33.

[121] Bovolenta C, Gasperini S, Cassatella MA. Granulocyte colony-stimulating factor induces the binding of STAT1 and STAT3 to the IFNγ response region within the promoter of the FcγRI/CD64 gene in human neutrophils. *FEBS Lett.* 1996;386:239-42.

[122] Cline MJ. Phagocytosis and synthesis of ribonucleic acid in human granulocytes. *Nature* 1966;212:1431-3.

[123] Quinn MT, Ammons MC, DeLeo FR. The expanding role of NADPH oxidases in health and disease: no longer just agents of death and destruction. *Clin. Sci.* (Lond) 2006;111:1-20.

[124] Gardai S, Whitlock BB, Helgason C, Ambruso D, Fadok V, Bratton D, et al. Activation of SHIP by NADPH oxidase-stimulated lyn leads to enhanced apoptosis in neutrophils. *J. Biol. Chem.* 2002;277:5236-46.

[125] Oishi K, Machida K. Inhibition of neutrophil apoptosis by antioxidants in culture medium. *Scand. J. Immunol.* 1997;45:21-7.

[126] Rollet-Labelle E, Grange MJ, Elbim C, Marquetty C, Gougerot-Pociadalo MA, Pasquier C. Hydroxyl radical as a potential intracellular mediator of polymorphonuclear neutrophil apoptosis. *Free Rad. Biol. Med.* 1998;24:563-72.

[127] Coxon A, Rieu P, Barkalow FJ, Askari S, Sharpe AH, von Andrian UH, et al. A novel role for the □2 integrin CD11b/CD18 in neutrophil apoptosis: A homeostatic mechanism in inflammation. *Immunity* 1996;5:653-66.

[128] Gamberale R, Giordano M, Trevani AS, Andonegui G, Geffner JR. Modulation of human neutrophil apoptosis by immune complexes. *J. Immunol.* 1998;161:3666-74.

[129] Kobayashi SD, Voyich JM, Braughton KR, Whitney AR, Nauseef WN, Malech HL, et al. Gene expression profiling provides insight into the pathophysiology of chronic granulomatous disease. *J. Immunol.* 2004;172:636-43.

[130] Ottonello L, Frumento G, Arduino N, Dapino P, Tortolina G, Dallegri F. Immune complex stimulation of neutrophil apoptosis: investigating the involvement of oxidative and nonoxidative pathways. *Free Rad. Biol. Med.* 2001;30:161-9.

[131] Schettini J, Salamone G, Trevani A, Raiden S, Gamberale R, Vermeulen M, et al. Stimulation of neutrophil apoptosis by immobilized IgA. *J. Leukoc. Biol.* 2002;72:685-91.

[132] Watson RW, Redmond HP, Wang JH, Condron C, Bouchier-Hayes D. Neutrophils undergo apoptosis following ingestion of *Escherichia coli*. *J. Immunol.* 1996;156:3986-92.

[133] Tsurubuchi T, Aratani Y, Maeda N, Koyama H. Retardation of early-onset PMA-induced apoptosis in mouse neutrophils deficient in myeloperoxidase. *J. Leukoc. Biol.* 2001;70:52-8.

[134] Hampton MB, Vissers MCM, Keenan JI, Winterbourn CC. Oxidant-mediated phosphatidylserine exposure and macrophage uptake of activated neutrophils: possible impairment in chronic granulomatous disease. *J. Leukoc. Biol.* 2002;71:775-81.

[135] Ottonello L, Frumento G, Arduino N, Bertolotto M, Dapino P, Mancini M, et al. Differential regulation of spontaneous and immune complex-induced neutrophil apoptosis by proinflammatory cytokines. Role of oxidants, Bax, and caspase-3. *J. Leukoc. Biol.* 2002;72:125-32.

[136] Matsuda T, Saito H, Inoue T. Ratio of bacteria to polymorphonuclear neutrophils (PMNs) determines PMN fate. *Shock* 1999;12:365-72.

[137] Perskvist N, Long M, Stendahl O, Zheng L. *Mycobacterium tuberculosis* promotes apoptosis in human neutrophils by activating caspase-3 and altering expression of Bax/Bcl-xL via an oxygen-dependent pathway. *J. Immunol.* 2002;168:6358-65.

[138] Lundqvist-Gustafsson H, Norman S, Nilsson J, Wilsson A. Involvement of p38-mitogen-activated protein kinase in *Staphylococcus aureus*-induced neutrophil apoptosis. *J. Leukoc. Biol.* 2001;70:642-8.

[139] Weiss JP. Tissue destruction by neutrophils. N. Engl. J. Med. 1989;320:365-76.

[140] Firestein GS. Immunologic mechanisms in the pathogenesis of rheumatoid arthritis. *J. Clin. Rheumatol.* 2005;11:39-44.

[141] Guide SV. Reinfection, rather than persistent infection, in patients with chronic granulomatous disease. *J. Infect. Dis.* 2003;187:845-53.

[142] Firestein GS. Inhibiting inflammation in rheumatoid arthritis. *N. Engl. J. Med.* 2006;354:80-2.

[143] Rosenzweig SD, Holland SM. Phagocyte immunodeficiencies and their infections. *J. Allergy Clin. Immunol.* 2004;113:620-6.

[144] William R, Watson G, Redmond PH, Wang JH, Condron C, Bouchier-Hayes D. Neutrophils undergo apoptosis following ingestion of *Escherichia coli*. *J. Immunol.* 1996;1996:3986-92.

[145] Bylund J, Campsall PA, Ma RC, Conway BA, Speert DP. *Burkholderia cenocepacia* induces neutrophil necrosis in chronic granulomatous disease. *J. Immunol.* 2005;174:3562-9.

[146] Hutchison ML, Poxton IR, Govan JR. *Burkholderia cepacia* produces a hemolysin that is capable of inducing apoptosis and degranulation of mammalian phagocytes. *Infect. Immun.* 1998;66:2033-9.

[147] Aleman M, Schierloh P, De La Barrera SS, Musella RM, Saab MA, Baldini M, et al. *Mycobacterium tuberculosis* triggers apoptosis in peripheral neutrophils involving toll-like receptor 2 and p38 mitogen protein kinase in tuberculosis patients. *Infection and Immunity* 2004;72:5150-8.

[148] Aleman M, De La Barrera SS, Schierloh PL, Alves L, Yokobori N, Baldini M, et al. In tuberculous pleural effusions, activated neutrophils undergo apoptosis and acquire a dendritic cell-like phenotype. *J. Infect. Dis.* 2005;192:399-409.

[149] Aleman M, Garcia A, Saab MA, De La Barrera SS, Finiasz M, Abbate E, et al. *Mycobacterium tuberculosis*-induced activation accelerates apoptosis in peripheral blood neutrophils from patients with active tuberculosis. *Am. J. Respir. Cell Mol. Biol.* 2002;27:583-92.

[150] Kasahara K, Sato I, Ogura K, Takeuchi H, Kobayashi K, Adachi M. Expression of chemokines and induction of rapid cell death in human blood neutrophils by *Mycobacterium tuberculosis*. *J. Infect. Dis.* 1998;178:127-37.

[151] Liles WC, Thomsen AR, O'Mahoney DS, Klebanoff SJ. Stimulation of human neutrophils and monocytes by staphylococcal phenol-soluble modulin. *J. Leukoc. Biol.* 2001;70:96-102.

[152] Moulding DA, Walter C, Hart CA, Edwards SW. Effects of staphylococcal enterotoxins on human neutrophil functions and apoptosis. *Infect. Immun.* 1999;67:2312-8.

[153] Hofman V, Ricci V, Mograbi B, Brest P, Luciano F, Boquet P, et al. *Helicobacter pylori* lipopolysaccharide hinders polymorphonuclear leucocyte apoptosis. *Lab. Invest.* 2001;81:375-84.

[154] Liu J, Akahoshi t, Sasahana T, Kitasato H, Namai R, Sasaki T, et al. Inhibition of neutrophil apoptosis by verotoxin 2 derived from *Escherichia coli* O157:H7. *Infect. Immun.* 1999;67:6203-5.

[155] Engelich G, White M, Hartshorn KL. Neutrophil survival is markedly reduced by incubation with influenza virus and *Streptococcus pneumoniae*: Role of respiratory burst. *J. Leukoc. Biol.* 2001;69:50-6.

[156] Watson RW, Redmond HP, Wang JH, Bouchier-Hayes D. Bacterial ingestion, tumor necrosis factor-alpha, and heat induce programmed cell death in activated neutrophils. *Shock* 1996;5:47-51.

[157] Urban CF, Lourido S, Zychlinsky A. How do microbes evade neutrophil killing? *Cell Micro* 2006;8:1687-96.

[158] Mayer-Scholl A, Averhoff P, Zychlinsky A. How do neutrophils and pathogens interact? *Curr. Opin. Cell Micro.biol.* 2004;7:62-6.

[159] Zysk G, Gejo L, Schneider-Wald BK, Nau R, Heinz H. Induction of necrosis and apoptosis of neutrophil granulocytes by *Streptococcus pneumoniae. Clin. Exp. Immunol.* 2000;122:61-6.

[160] Voyich JM, Braughton KR, Sturdevant DE, Whitney AR, Said-Salim B, Porcella SF, et al. Insights into mechanisms used by *Staphylococcus aureus* to avoid destruction by human neutrophils. *J. Immunol.* 2005;175:3907-19.

[161] Voyich JM, Otto M, Mathema B, Braughton KR, Whitney AR, Welty D, et al. Is Panton-Valentine Leukocidin the major virulence determinant in community-associated methicillin-resistant *Staphylococcus aureus* disease? *J. Infect. Dis.* 2006;194:1761-70.

[162] Francis JS, Doherty MC, Lopatin U, Johnston CP, Sinha G, Ross T, et al. Severe community-onset pneumonia in healthy adults caused by methicillin-resistant *Staphylococcus aureus* carrying the Panton-Valentine leukocidin genes. *Clin. Infect. Dis.* 2005;40:100-7.

[163] Gillet Y, Issartel B, Vanhems P, Fournet JC, Lina G, Bes M, et al. Association between *Staphylococcus aureus* strains carrying gene for Panton-Valentine leukocidin and highly lethal necrotising pneumonia in young immunocompetent patients. *Lancet* 2002;359:753-9.

[164] Adem PV, Montgomery CP, Husain AN, Koogler TK, Arangelovich V, Humilier M, et al. *Staphylococcus aureus* sepsis and the Waterhouse-Friderichsen syndrome in children. *N. Engl. J. Med.* 2005;353:1245-51.

[165] Drews TD. Community-associated methicillin-resistant *Staphylococcus aureus*: review of an emerging public health concern. *WMJ* 2006;105:52-7.

[166] Fridkin SK, Hageman JC, Morrison M, Sanza LT, Como-Sabetti K, Jernigan JA, et al. Methicillin-resistant *Staphylococcus aureus* disease in three communities. *N. Engl. J. Med.* 2005;352:1436-44.

[167] Maltezou HC, Giamarellou H. Community-acquired methicillin-resistant *Staphylococcus aureus* infections. *Int. J. of Antimicrobial Agents* 2006;27:87-96.

[168] Miller LG, Perdreau-Remington F, Rieg G, Mehdi S, Perlroth J, Bayer AS, et al. Necrotizing fasciitis caused by community-associated methicillin-resistant *staphylococcus aureus* in Los Angeles. *N. Engl. J. Med.* 2005;352:1445-53.

[169] Voyich JM, Musser JM, DeLeo FR. *Streptococcus pyogenes* and human neutrophils: a paradigm for evasion of innate host defense by bacterial pathogens. *Microbes. Infect.* 2004;6:1117-23.

[170] Musser JM, DeLeo FR. Toward a genome-wide systems biology analysis of host-pathogen interactions in group A *streptococcus*. *Am. J. Path.* 2005;167:1461-72.

[171] Voyich JM, Braughton KR, Sturdevant DE, Vuong C, Kobayashi SD, Porcella SF, et al. Engagement of the pathogen survival response used by group A *streptococcus* to avert destruction by innate host defense. *J. Immunol.* 2004;173:1194-201.

[172] Miyoshi-Akiyama T, Takamatsu D, Koyanagi M, Zhao J, Imanishi K, Uchiyama T. Cytocidal effect of *streptococcus pyogenes* on mouse neutrophils in vivo and the critical role of streptolysin S. *J. Infect. Dis.* 2005;192:107-16.

[173] Ge Y, Rikihisa Y. *Anaplasma phagocytophilum* delays spontaneous human neutrophil apoptosis by modulation of multiple apoptotic pathways. *Cell Micro.* 2006;8:1406-16.

[174] Lee HC, Goodman JL. *Anaplasma phagocytophilum* causes global induction of antiapoptosis in human neutrophils. *Genomics* 2006;88:496-503.

[175] Scaife H, Woldehiwet Z, Hart CA, Edwards SW. *Anaplasma phagocytophilum* reduces neutrophil apoptosis in vivo. *Infect. Immun.* 2003;71:1995-2001.

[176] van Zandbergen G, Gieffers J, Kothe H, Rupp J, Bollinger A, Aga E, et al. *Chlamydia pneumoniae* multiply in neutrophil granulocytes and delay their spontaneous apoptosis. *J. Immunol.* 2004;172:1768-76.

[177] Yoshiie K, Kim HY, Mott J, Rikihisa Y. Intracellular infection by the human granulocyte *ehrlichiosis* agent inhibits human neutrophil apoptosis. *Infect. Immun.* 2000;68:1125-33.

[178] Rikihisa Y. Ehrlichia subversion of host innate responses. *Current Opinion in Microbiology* 2006;9:95-101.

[179] Ijdo JW, Mueller AC. Neutrophil NADPH oxidase is reduced at the *anaplasma phagocyophilum* phagosome. *Infect. Immun.* 2004;72:5392-401.

[180] Mott J, Rikihisa Y, Tsunawaki S. Effects of *anaplasma phagocytophila* on NADPH oxidase components in human neutrophils and HL-60 cells. *Infect. Immun.* 2002;70:1359-66.

[181] Ge Y, Yoshiie K, Kuribayashi F, Lin M, Rikihisa Y. *Anaplasma phagocytophilum* inhibits human neutrophil apoptosis via upregulation of bfl-1, maintenance of mitochondrial membrane potential and prevention of caspase 3 activation. *Cell Microbiol.* 2005;7:29-38.

[182] Airenne S, Surcel HM, Tuukkanen J, Leinonen M, Saikku P. *Chlamydia pneumoniae* inhibits apoptosis in human epithelial and monocyte cell lines. *Scand J. Immunol.* 2002;55:390-8.

[183] Newman SL, Henson JE, Henson PM. Phagocytosis of senescent neutrophils by human monocyte-derived macrophages and rabbit inflammatory macrophages. *J. Exp. Med.* 1982;156:430-42.

[184] Yamaryo T, Oishi K, Yoshimine H, Tsuchihashi Y, Matsushima K, Nagatake T. Fourteen-member macrolides promote the phosphatidylserine receptor-dependent phagocytosis of apoptotic neutrophils by alveolar macrophages. *Antimicrob. Agents Chemother.* 2003;47:48-53.

[185] Fadok VA, Haslett JSC, Bratton DL, Doherty DE, Cambell PA, Henson PM. Different populations of macrophages use either the vitronectin receptor or the phosphatidylserine receptor to recognize and remove apoptotic cells. *J. Immunol.* 1992;149:4029-35.

[186] Mevorach D, Mascarenhas JO, Gershov D, Elkon KB. Complement-dependent clearance of apoptotic cells by human macrophages. *J. Exp. Med.* 1998;188:2313-20.

[187] Platt N, Suzuki H, Kurihara Y, Kodama T, Gordon S. Role of the class A macrophage scavenger receptor in the phagocytosis of apoptotic thymocytes *in vitro*. *Proc. Natl. Acad. Sci. USA* 1996;93:12456-60.

[188] Savill J, Dransfield I, Hogg N, Haslett C. Vitronectin receptor-mediated phagocytosis of cells undergoing apoptosis. *Nature* 1990;343:170-3.

[189] Savill J, Hogg N, Ren Y, Haslett C. Thrombospondin cooperates with CD36 and the vitronectin receptor in macrophage recognition of neutrophils undergoing apoptosis. *J. Clin. Invest.* 1992;90:1513-22.

[190] Devitt A, Moffatt OD, Raykundalia C, Capra JD, Simmonda DL, Gregory CD. Human CD14 mediates recognition and phagocytosis of apoptotic cells. *Nature* 1998;392:505-9.

[191] Hart SP, Dougherty GJ, Haslett C, Dransfield I. CD44 regulates phagocytosis of apoptotic neutrophil granulocytes, but not apoptotic lymphocytes, by human macrophages. *J. Immunol.* 1997;159:919-25.

[192] Vivers S, Heasman SJ, Hart SP, Dransfield I. Divalent cation-dependent and -independent augmentation of macrophage phagocytosis of apoptotic neutrophils by CD44 antibody. *Clin. Exp. Immunol.* 2004;138:447-52.

[193] Vivers S, Dransfield I, Hart SP. Role of macrophage CD44 in the disposal of inflammatory cell corpses. *Clin. Sci.* 2002;103:441-9.

[194] Li MO, Sarkisian MR, Mehal WZ, Rakic P, Flavell RA. Phosphatidylserine receptor is required for clearance of apoptotic cells. *Science* 2003;302:1560-3.

[195] Fadok VA, Bratton DL, Rose DM, Pearson A, Ezekewitz RAB, Henson PM. A receptor for phosphatidylserine-specific clearance of apoptotic cells. *Nature* 2000;405:85-90.

[196] Arur S, Uche UE, Rezaqul K, Fong M, Scranton V, Cowan AE, et al. Annexin I is an endogenous ligand that mediates apoptotic cell engulfment. *Dev. Cell* 2003;4:587-98.

[197] Botto M, Dell'Agnola C, Bygrave AE, Thompson EM, Cook HT, Petry F, et al. Homozygous C1q deficiency causes glomerulonephritis associated with multiple apoptotic bodies. *Nat. Genet.* 1998;19:56-9.

[198] Thielens NM, Tacnet-Delorme P, Arlaud GJ. Interaction of C1q and mannan-binding lectin with viruses. *Immunobiology* 2002;205:563-74.

[199] Ogden CA, Elkon KB. Role of complement and other innate immune mechanisms in the removal of apoptotic cells. *Curr. Dir. Autoimmun.* 2006;9:120-42.

[200] Taylor PR, Carugati A, Fadok VA, Cook HT, Andrews M, Carroll MC, et al. A hierarchical role for classical pathway complement proteins in the clearance of apoptotic cells in vivo. *J. Exp. Med.* 2000;192:359-66.

[201] Grevink ME, Horst G, Limburg PC, Kallenberg CGM, Bijl M. Levels of complement in sera from inactive SLE patients, although decreased, do not influence in vitro uptake of apoptotic cells. *J. Autoimmm.* 2005;24:329-36.

[202] Greenwalt DE, Lipsky RH, Ockenhouse CF, Ikeda H, Tandon NN, Jamieson GA. Membrane glycoprotein CD36: a review of its roles in adherence, signal transduction, and transfusion medicine. *Blood* 1992;80:1105-15.

[203] Navazo MDP, Daviet L, Savill J, Ren Y, Leung LLK, McGregor JL. Identification of a domain (155-183) on CD36 implicated in the phagocytosis of apoptotic neutrophils. *J. Biol. Chem.* 1996;271:15381-5.

[204] Teder P, Vandivier RW, Jiang D, Liang J, Cohn L, Pure E, et al. Resolution of lung inflammation by CD44. *Science* 2002;296:155-8.

[205] Schutt C, Schilling T, Grunwald U, Schonfeld W, Kruger C. Endotoxin-neutralizing capacity of soluble CD14. *Res. Immunol.* 1992;143:71-8.

[206] Moffat OD, Devitt A, Bell ED, Simmons DL, Gregory CD. Macrophage recognition of ICAM-3 on apoptotic leukocytes. *J. Immunol.* 1999;162:6800-10.

[207] Gregory CD. CD14-dependent clearance of apoptotic cells: relevance to the immune system. *Curr. Opin. Immunol.* 2000;12:27-34.

[208] Schlegel RA, Krahling S, Callahan MK, Williamson P. CD14 is a component of multiple recognition systems used by macrophages to phagocytose apoptotic lymphocytes. *Cell. Death Diff.* 1999;6:583-92.

[209] Bottcher A, Gaipl US, Furnrohr BG, Herrmann M, Girkontaite I, Kalden JR, et al. Involvement of phosphatidylserine, □v□3, CD14, CD36, and complement C1q in the phagocytosis of primary necrotic lymphocytes by macrophages. *Arth. Rheum.* 2006;54:927-38.

[210] Savill J, Fadok V. Corpse clearance defines the meaning of cell death. *Nature* 2000;407:784-8.

[211] Dransfield I. An appetite for apoptotic cells? Controversies and challenges. *Br. J. Haematol.* 2000;109:1-12.

[212] Huynh M-L, Fadok VA, Henson PM. Phosphatidylserine-dependent ingestion of apoptotic cells promotes TGF-□1 secretion and the resolution of inflammaiton. *J. Clin. Invest.* 2002;109:41-50.

[213] Fadok VA, Bratton DL, Konowal A, Freed PW, Westcott JY, Henson PM. Macrophages that have ingested apoptotic cells in vitro inhibit proinflammaotry cytokine production through autocrine-paracrine mechanisms involving TGF-□, $PGE_2$, and PAF. *J. Clin. Invest.* 1998;101:890-8.

[214] Lucas M, Stuart LM, Zhang A, Hodivala-Dilke K, Febbraio M, Silverstein R, et al. Requirements for apoptotic cell contact in regulation of macrophage responses. *J. Immunol.* 2006;177:4047-54.

[215] Xing L, Remick DG. Neutrophils as firemen, production of anti-inflammatory mediators by neutrophils in a mixed cell environment. *Cell Immunol.* 2004;231:126-32.

[216] Bianchi SM, Dockrell DH, Renshaw SA, Sabroe I, Whyte MKB. Granulocyte apoptosis in the pathogenesis and resolution of lung disease. *Clin. Sci.* 2006;110:293-304.

[217] Voll RE, Herrmann M, Roth EA, Stach C, Kalden JR, Girkontaite I. Immunosuppressive effects of apoptotic cells. *Nature* 1997;390:350-1.

[218] Liu Y, Cousin JM, Hughes J, Damme JV, Seckle JR, Haslette C, et al. Glucocorticoids promote nonphlogistic phagocytosis of apoptotic leukocytes. *J. Immunol.* 1999;162:3639-46.

[219] Giles KM, Ross K, Rossi AG, Hotchin NA, Haslett C, Dransfield I. Glucocorticoid augmentation of macrophage capacity for phagocytosis of apoptotic cells is associated with reduced p130$^{Cas}$ expression, loss of paxillin/pyk2 phosphorylation, and high levels of active Rac. *J. Immunol.* 2001;167:976-86.

[220] Thieringer R, Le Grand CB, Carbin L, Cai TQ, Wong B, Wright SD, et al. 11β-hydroxysteroid dehydrogenase type 1 is induced in human monocytes upon differentiation to macrophages. *J. Immunol.* 2001;167:30-5.

[221] Gilmour JS, Coutinho AE, Cailhier J-F, Man TY, Clay M, Thomas G, et al. Local amplification of glucocorticoids by 11β-hydroxysteroid dehydrogenase type 1 promotes macrophage phagocytosis of apoptotic leukocytes. *J. Immunol.* 2006;176:7605-11.

[222] Heasman SJ, Giles KM, Rossi AG, Allen JE, Haslett C, Dransfield I. Interferon γ suppresses glucocorticoid augmentation of macrophage clearance of apoptotic cells. *Eur. J. Immunol.* 2004;34:1752-61.

[223] Weiss SJ. Tissue destruction by neutrophils. *N. Engl. J. Med.* 1989;320:365-76.

[224] Verdrengh M, Tarkowski A. Role of neutrophils in experimental septicemia and septic arthritis induced by *Staphylococcus aureus*. *Infect. Immun.* 1997;65:2517-21.

[225] Boullier AG, Bird DA, Chang MK, Dennis EA, Friedman PE, Gillotte-Taylor KR, et al. Scavenger Receptors, Oxidized LDL, and Atherosclerosis. *Ann. NY Acad. Sci.* 2001;947:214-23.

[226] Heinecke JW. Oxidized amino acids: culprits in human atherosclerosis and indicators of oxidative stress. *Free Rad. Biol. Med.* 2002;32:1090-101.

[227] Malle E, Marsche G, Arnhold J, Davies MJ. Modification of low-density lipoprotein by myeloperoxidase-derived oxidants and reagent hypochlorous acid. *Biochim. Biophys. Acta.* 2006;1761:392-415.

[228] Kopprasch S, Leonhardt W, Pietzsch J, Kuhne H. Hypochlorite-modified low-density lipoprotein stimulates human polymorphonuclear leukocytes for enhanced production of reactive oxigen metabolites, enzymes secretion, and adhesion to endothelial cells. *Atherosclerosis* 1998;136:315-24.

[229] Ludwig PW, Hunninghake DB, Hoidal JR. Increased leukocyte oxidative metabolism in hyperlipoproteinaemia. *Lancet* 1982;2:348-50.

[230] Nicholls SJ, Zheng L, Hazen SL. Formation of dysfunctional high-density lipoprotein by myeloperoxidase. *Trends Card Med.* 2005;15:212-9.

[231] Dinges MM, Orwin PM, Schlievert PM. Exotoxins of *Staphylococcus aureus*. *Clin. Microbiol. Rev.* 2000;13:16-34.

[232] Ferry T. Virulence determinants in *Staphylococcus aureus* and their involvement in clinical syndromes. *Current infectious disease reports* 2005;7:420-8.

[233] Fitzgerald JR, Reid SD, Ruotsalainen E, Tripp TJ, Liu M, Cole R, et al. Genome Diversification in *Staphylococcus aureus*: molecular evolution of a highly variable chromosomal region encoding the staphylococcal exotoxin-like family of proteins. *Infection and Immunity* 2003;71:2827-38.

[234] Holden MTG, Feil EJ, Lindsay JA, Peacock SJ, Day NPJ, Enright MC, et al. Complete genomes of two clinical *staphylococcus aureus* strains: Evidence for the rapid evolution of virulence and drug resistance. *Proc. Natl. Acad. Sci. USA* 2004;101:9786-91.

[235] Kazakova SV, Hageman JC, Matava M, Srinivasan a, Phelan L, Garfinkel B, et al. A clone of methicillin-resistant *staphylococcus aureus* among professional football players. *N. Engl. J. Med.* 2005;352:468-75.

[236] Lindsay JA, Moore CE, Day NP, Peacock SJ, Witney AA, Stabler RA, et al. Microarrays reveal the each of the ten dominant lineages of *staphylococcus aureus* has a unique combination of surface-associated and regulatory genes. *J. Bacteriol.* 2006;188:669-76.

[237] Lowy FD. *Staphylococcus aureus* infections. *N. Engl. J. Med.* 1998;339:520-32.

[238] Lu D. Community-acquired methicillin-resistant *Staphylococcal aureus*, a new play in sports medicine. *Curr. Sports Med. Rep.* 2005;4:265-70.

[239] Nilsdotter-Augustinsson ASA, Wilsson ASA, Larsson JENN, Stendahl OLLE, Ohman LENA, Lundqvist-Gustafsson HELE. *Staphylococcus aureus*, but not *Staphylococcus epidermidis*, modulates the oxidative response and induces apoptosis in human neutrophils. *APMIS* 2004;112:109-18.

[240] Foster TJ. Immune evasion by staphylococci. *Nat. Rev. Micro.* 2005;3:948-58.

[241] Nauseef WM, Clark RA. Basic principles in the diagnosis and management of infectious diseases. In: Mandell GL, Bennett JE, Dolin R, editors. *Granulocytes*. New York: Churchill Livingstone; 2000. p. 89-112.

[242] Ellson CD, Davidson K, Ferguson GJ, O'Connor R, Stephens LR, Hawkins PT. Neutrophils from $p40^{phox-/-}$ mice exhibit severe defects in NADPH oxidase regulation and oxidant-dependent bacterial killing. *J. Exp. Med.* 2006;203:1927-837.

[243] Gerber CE, Bruchelt G, Falk UB, Kimpfler A, Hauschild O, Kuci S, et al. Reconstitution of bactericidal activity in chronic granulomatous disease cells by glucose-oxidase-containing liposomes. *Blood* 2001;98:3097-105.

[244] [244] Hampton MB, Vissers MCM, Keenan JI, Winterbourn CC. Oxidant-mediated phosphatidylserine exposure and macrophage uptake of activated neutrophils: possible impairment in chronic granulomatous disease. *J. Leukoc. Biol.* 2002;71:775-81.

[245] K□poszta R. Chronic neutropenia and defect in superoxide generation of granulocytes in two patients; enhancement of bactericidal capacity and respiratory burst activity by treatment with recombinant human granulocyte colony-stimulating factor. *Ped. Res.* 1995;37:50-5.

[246] Lekstrom-Himes JA, Kuhns DB, Alvord WG, Gallin JI. Inhibition of human neutrophil IL-8 production by hydrogen peroxide and dysregulation in chronic granulomatous disease. *J. Immunol.* 2005;174:411-7.

[247] Gallin JI, Alling DW, Malech HL, Wesley R, Koziol D, Marciano B, et al. Itraconazole to prevent fungal infections in chronic granulomatous disease. *N. Engl. J. Med.* 2003;348:2416-22.

[248] Jackson SH, Miller GF, Segal BH, Mardiney M3, Domachowske JB, Gallin JI, et al. IFN-gamma is effective in reducing infections in the mouse model of chronic granulomatous disease (CGD). *J. Interferon. Cytokine Res.* 2001;21:567-73.

[249] Brown JR, Goldblatt D, Buddle J, Morton L, Thrasher AJ. Diminished production of anti-inflammatory mediators during neutrophil apoptosis and macrophage phagocytosis in chronic granulomatous disease (CGD). *J. Leukoc. Biol.* 2003;73:591-9.

[250] Chin TW, Stiehm ER, Falloon J, Gallin JI. Corticosteroids in treatment of obstructive lesions of chronic granulomatous disease. *J. Pediatr.* 1987;111:349-52.

[251] Sanford AN, Suriano AR, Herche D, Dietzmann K, Sullivan KE. Abnormal apoptosis in chronic granulomatous disease and autoantibody prodution characteristic of lupus. *Rheumatology* 2006;45:178-81.

[252] Rotstein D, Parodo J, Taneja R, Marshall JC. Phagocytosis of *Candida albicans* induces apoptosis of human neutrophils. *Shock* 2000;14:278-83.

[253] Coakley RJ, Taggart C, McElvaney NG, O'Neill SJ. Cytosolic pH and the inflammatory microenvironment modulate cell death in human neutrophils after phagocytosis. *Blood* 2002;100:3383-91.

[254] Whyte MK, Meagher LC, MacDermot J, Haslett C. Impairment of function in aging neutrophils is associated with apoptosis. *J. Immunol.* 1993;150:5124-34.

[255] Leuenroth S, Lee C, Grutkoski P, Keeping H, Simms HH. Interleukin-8-induced suppression of polymorphonuclear leukocyte apoptosis is mediated by suppressing CD95 (Fas/Apo-1) Fas-1 interactions. *Surgery* 2004;124:409-17.

[256] Iwase M, Kondo G, Watanabe H, Takaoka S, Uchida M, Ohashi M, et al. Regulation of fas-mediated apoptosis in neutrophils after surgery-induced acute inflammation. *J. Surg. Res.* 2006;134:114-23.

[257] Akgul C, Edwards SW. Regulation of neutrophil apoptosis via death receptors. *Cell Mol. Life Sci.* 2003;60:2402-8.

[258] Scheel-Toellner D, Wang K, Craddock R, Webb PR, McGettrick HM, Assi LK, et al. Reactive oxygen species limit neutrophil life span by activating death receptor signaling. *Blood* 2004;104:2557-64.

[259] Liles WC, Klebanoff SJ. Regulation of apoptosis in neutrophils-Fas track to death? *J. Immunol.* 1995;155:3289-91.

[260] Allenbach C, Zufferey C, Perez C, Launois P, Mueller C, Tacchini-Cottier F. Macrophages induce neutrophil apoptosis through membrane TNF, a process amplified by *Leshmania major*. *J. Immunol.* 2006;176:6656-64.

[261] Chen H-C, Wang C-J, Chou C-L, Lin S-M, Huang C-D, Lin T-Y, et al. Tumor necrosis factor-□induces caspase-independent cell death in human neutrophils via reactive oxidants and associated with calpain activity. *J. Biomed. Sci.* 2006;13:261-73.

[262] Cowburn AS, Sobolewski A, Reed BJ, Deighton J, Murray J, Cadwallader KA, et al. Aminopeptidase N (CD13) regulates tumor necrosis factor-α-induced apoptosis in human neutrophils. *J. Biol. Chem.* 2006;281:12458-67.

[263] Walmsley SR, Cowburn AS, Sobolewski A, Murray J, Farahi N, Sabroe I, et al. Characterization of the survival effect of tumour necrosis factor-α in human neutrophils. *Biochem. Soc. Trans.* 2004;32:456-60.

[264] Li JH, Kirkiles-Smith NC, McNiff JM, Pober JS. TRAIL induces apoptosis and inflammatory gene expression in human endothelial cells. *J. Immunol.* 2003;171:1526-33.

[265] Matsuyama W, Yamamoto M, Higashimoto I, Oonakahara K-I, Watanabe M, Machida K, et al. TNF-related apoptosis-inducing ligand is involved in neutropenia of systemic lupus erythematosus. *Blood* 2004;104:184-91.

[266] Kato S, Muro M, Akifusa S, Hanada N, Semba I, Fujii T, et al. Evidence for apoptosis of murine macrophages by *Actinobacillus actinomycetemcomitans* infecttion. *Infect. Immun.* 1995;63:3914-9.

[267] Muro M, Koseki T, Akifusa S, Kato S, Kowashi Y, Ohasaki Y, et al. Role of CD14 molecules in internalization of *Actinobacillus actinomycetemcomitans* by macrophages and subsequent induction of apoptosis. *Infect. Immun.* 1997;65:1147-51.

[268] Muro M, Nakashima K, Tamioka J, Kato S, Nonaka K, Yoshida T, et al. Inhibitory effect of lipopolysaccharide on apoptotic cell death in macrophages infected with *Actinobacillus actinomycetemcomitans*. *FEMS Microbiol. Lett.* 1999;175:211-6.

[269] Nakashima K, Tomioka J, Kato S, Nishihara T, Kowashi Y. Nitric oxide-mediated protection of *Actinobacillus actinomycetemcomtans*-infected murine macrophages against apoptosis. *Nitric. Oxide* 2002;6:61-8.

[270] Nalbant A, Zadeh HH. *Actinobacillus actinomycetemcomtains* induces apoptosis of T lymphocytes by the Fas and Fas ligand pathway. *Oral Microbiol. Immunol.* 2002;17:277-84.

[271] Nonaka K, Ishisaki A, Muro M, Kato S, Oido M, Nakashima K, et al. Possible involvement of protein kinase C in apoptotic cell death of macrophages infected with *Actinobacillus actinomycetemcomitans*. *FEMS Mcrobiol. Lett.* 1998;159:247-54.

[272] Nonaka K, Ishisaki A, Okahashi N, Koseki T, Kato S, Muro M, et al. Involvement of caspases in apoptotic cell death of murine macrophages infected with *Actinobacillus actinomyetemcomitans*. *J. Periodontal. Res.* 2001;36:40-7.

[273] Permpanich P, Kowolik MJ, Galli DM. Resistance of fluorescent-labelled *Actinobacillus actinomycetemcomitans* strains to phagocytosis and killing by human neutrophils. *Cell Microbiol.* 2006;8:72-84.

[274] Shenker BJ, Denmuth DR, Zekavat A. Exposure of lymphocytes to high doses of *actinobacillus actinomycetemcomitans* cytolethal distending toxin induces rapid onset of apoptosis-mediated DNA fragmentation. *Infect. Immun.* 2006;74:2080-92.

[275] Shenker BJ, Besack D, McKay T, Pankoski L, Zekavat A, Demuth DR. Induction of cell cycle arrest in lymphocytes by *actinobacillus actinomycetemcomitans* cytolethal distending toxin requires three subunits for maximum activity. *J. Immunol.* 2005;174:2228-34.

[276] Galindo CL, Sha J, Ribardo DA, Fadl AA, Pillai L, Chopra AK. Identification of *Aeromonas hydrophila* cytotoxic enterotoxin-induced genes in macrophages using microarrays. *J. Biol. Chem.* 2003;278:40198-212.

[277] Galindo CL, Fadl AA, Sha J, Gutierrez C, Jr., Popov VL, Boldogh I, et al. *Aeromonas hydrophila* cytotoxic enterotoxin activates mitogen-activated protein kinases and induces apoptosis in murine macrophages and human intestinal epithelial cells. *J. Biol. Chem.* 2004;279:37597-612.

[278] Choi K-S, Park JT, Dumler JS. *Anaplasma phagocytophilum* delay of neutrophil apoptosis through the p38 mitogen-activated protein kinase signal pathway. *Infect. Immun.* 2005;73:8209-18.

[279] Artenstein AW, Opal SM, Cristofaro P, Palardy JE, Parejo NA, Green MD, et al. Chloroquine enhances survival in *Bacillus anthracis* intoxication. *J. Infect. Dis.* 2004;190:1655-60.

[280] Crawford MA, Aylott CV, Bourdeau RW, Bokoch GM. *Bacillus anthracis* toxins inhibit human neutrophil NADPH oxidase activity. *J. Immunol.* 2006;176:7557-65.

[281] Kau JH, Lin CG, Huang HH, Hsu HL, Chen KC, Wu YP, et al. Calyculin A sensitive protein phosphatase is required for *Bacillus anthracis* lethal toxin induced cytotoxicity. *Curr. Microbiol.* 2002;44:106-11.

[282] Popov SG, Villasmil R, Bernardi J, Grene E, Cardwell J, Wu A, et al. Lethal toxin of *Bacillus anthracis* causes apoptosis of macrophages. *Biochem. Biophys. Res. Commun.* 2002;293:349-55.

[283] Popov SG, Villasmil R, Bernardi J, Grene E, Cardwell J, Popova T, et al. Effect of *Bacillus anthracis* lethal toxin on human peripheral blood mononuclear cells. *FEBS Lett.* 2002;527:211-5.

[284] Forde CB, Shi X, Li J, Roberts M. *Bordetella bronchiseptica*-mediated cytotoxicity to macrophages is dependent on bvg-regulated factors, including pertactin. *Infect. Immun.* 1999;67:5972-8.

[285] Harvill ET, Cotter PA, Miller JF. Pregenomic comparative analysis between *Bordetella bronchiseptica* RB50 and *Bordetella pertussis* tohama I in murine models of respiratory tract infection. *Infect. Immun.* 1999;67:6109-18.

[286] Stockbauer KE, Foreman-Wykert AK, Miller JF. *Bordetella* type III secreton induces caspase1-independent necrosis. *Cell Microbiol.* 1999;5:123-32.

[287] Abramson T, Kedem H, Relman DA. Proinflammatory and proapoptotic activities associated with *Bordetella pertussis* filamentous hemaglutinin. *Infect. Immun.* 2001;69:2650-8.

[288] Basler M, Masin J, Osicka R, Sebo P. Pore-forming and enzymatic cativities of *Bordetella pertussis* adenylate cyclase toxin synergize in promoting lysis of monocytes. *Infect. Immun.* 2006;74:2207-14.

[289] Gueirard P, Druilhe A, Pretolani M, Guiso N. Role of adenylate cyclase-hemolysin in alveolar macrophage apoptosis during *Bordetella pertussis* infection in vivo. *Infect. Immun.* 1998;66:1718-25.

[290] Khelef N, Zychlinsky A, Guiso N. *Bordetella pertussis* induces apoptosis in macrophages: Role of adenylate cyclase hemolysin. *Infect. Immun.* 1993;61:4064-71.

[291] Khelef N, Guiso N. Induction of macrophage apoptosis by *Bordetella pertussis* adenylate cyclase-hemolysin. *FEMS Microbiol. Lett.* 1995;134:27-32.

[292] Khelef N, DeShazer D, Friedman RL, Guiso N. In vivo and in vitro analysis of *Bordetella pertussis* catalase and Fe-superoxide dismutase mutants. *FEMS Microbiol. Lett.* 1996;142:231-5.

[293] Khelef N, Gounon P, Guiso N. Internalization of *Bordetella pertussis* adenylate cyclase-hemolysin into endocytic vesicles contributes to macrophage cytotoxicity. *Cell Microbiol.* 2001;3:721-30.

[294] Gadiero E, Romano Carratelli C, Vitiello M, Nuzzo I, Del Vecchio E, Bentivoglio C, et al. HSP and apoptosis in leukocytes from infected or vaccinated animals by *Brucella abortus*. *New Microbiol.* 2000;23:271.

[295] Wang M, Qureshi N, Soeurt N, Splitter G. High levels of nitric oxide production decrease early but increase late survival or *Brucella abortus* in macrophages. *Microb. Pathog.* 2001;31:221-30.

[296] Fernandez-Prada CM, Zelazowska EB, Nikolich M, Hadfield TL, Roop RM2, Robertson GL, et al. Interactions between *Brucella melitensis* and human phagocytes: Bacterial surface O-polysaccharide inhibits phagocytosis, bacterial killing, and subsequent host cell apoptosis. *Infect. Immun.* 2003;71:2110-9.

[297] Gross A, Terraza A, Ouahrani-Bettache S, Liautard JP, Dornand J. *In vitro Brucella suis* infection prevents the programmed cell death of human monocytic cells. *Infect. Immun.* 2000;68:324-51.

[298] Punj V, Sharma R, Zaborina O, Chakrabarty AM. Energy-generating enzymes of *Burkholderia cepacia* and their interactions with macrophages. *J. Bacteriol.* 2003;185:3167-78.

[299] Sun GW, Lu J, Pervaiz S, Cao WP, Gan YH. Caspase-1 dependent macrophage death induced by *Burkholderia pseudomallei. Cell Microbiol.* 2005;7:1447-58.

[300] Carratelli CR, Rizzo A, Catania MR, Galle F, Losi E, Hasty DL, et al. *Chlamydia pneumoniae* infections prevent the programmed cell death of THP-1 cell line. *FEMS Microbiol. Lett.* 2002;215:69-74.

[301] Greub G, Mege JL, Raoult D. *Parachlamydia acanthamoeba* enters and multiplies within human macrophages and induces their apoptosis. *Infect. Immun.* 2003;71:5979-85.

[302] Miyairi I, Byrne GI. *Chlamydia* and programmed cell death. *Curr. Opin. Microbiol.* 2006;9:102-8.

[303] Ojcius DM, Souque P, Perfettini JL, Dautry-Varsat A. Apoptosis of epithelial cells and macrophages due to infection with the obligate intracellular pathogen *Chlamydia psittaci. J. Immunol.* 1998;1998:4220-6.

[304] Goth SR, Stephens RS. Rapid, transient phosphatidylserine externalization induced in host cells by infection with *Chlamydia* spp. *Infect. Immun.* 2001;69:1109-19.

[305] Ying S, Seiffert BM, Hacker G, Fischer SF. Broad degradation of proapoptotic proteins with the conserved Bcl-2 homology domain 3 during infection with *chlamydial trachomatis*. *Infect. Immun.* 2005;73:1399-403.

[306] Mahida YR, Galvin A, Makh S, Hyde S, Sanfilippo L, Borriello SP, et al. Effect of *Clostridium difficile* toxin A on human colonic lamina propria cells: Early loss of macrophages followed by T-cell apoptosis. *Infect. Immun.* 1998;66:5462-9.

[307] Solomon K, Webb J, Ali N, Robins RA, Mahida YR. Highly sensitive to *Clostridium difficile* toxin A-induced apoptotic and nonapoptotic cell death. *Infect. Immun.* 2005;73:1625-34.

[308] Dellacasagrande J, Capo C, Raoult D, Mege JL. IFN-gamma-mediated control of *Coxiella burneii* survival inmonocytes: The role of cell apoptosis and TNF. *J. Immunol.* 1999;162:2259-65.

[309] Brest P, Betis F, Cuburu N, Selva E, Herrant M, Servin A, et al. Increased rate of apoptosis and diminished phagocytic ability of human neutrophils infected with Afa/Dr diffusely adhering *escherichia coli* strains. *Infect. Immun.* 2004;72:5741-9.

[310] Savill JS, Henson PM, Haslett C. Phagocytosis of aged human neutrophils by macrophages is mediated by a novel "charge-sensitive" recognition mechanism. *J. Clin. Invest.* 1989;84:1518-27.

[311] Fernandez-Prada C, Tall BD, Elliott SE, Hoover DL, Nataro JP, Venkatesan MM. Hemolysin-positive enteroaggregative and cell-detaching *Escherichia coli* strains cause oncosis of human monocyte-derived macrophages and poptosis of murine J774 cells. *Infect. Immun.* 1998;66:3918-24.

[312] Hacker H, Furmann C, Wagner H, Hacker G. Caspase-9/-3 activation and apoptosis are induced in mouse macrophages upon ingestion and digestion of *Escherichia coli* bacteria. *J. Immunol.* 2002;169:3172-9.

[313] Lai XH, Arencibia I, Johansson A, Wai SN, Oscarsson J, Kalfas S, et al. Cytocidal and apoptotic effects of the ClyA protein from *Escherichia coli* on primary and cultured monocytes and macrophages. *Infect. Immun.* 2000;68:4363-7.

[314] Lai XH, Xu JG, Melgar S, Uhlin BE. An apoptotic response by J774 macrophage cells is common upon infection with diarrheagenic *Escherichia coli*. *FEMS Microbiol. Lett.* 2006;172:29-34.

[315] Rodrigues VS, Vidotto MC, Felipe I, Santos DS, Gaziri LC. Apoptosis of murine peritoneal macrophages induced by an avian pathogenic strain of *Escherichia coli*. *FEMS Microbiol. Lett.* 1999;179:73-8.

[316] Stravodimos KG, Singhal PC, Sharma S, Reddy K, Smith AD. *Escherichia coli* promotes macrophage apoptosis. *J. Endourol.* 1999;13:273-7.

[317] Yagi Y, Shiono H, Shibahara T, Chikayama Y, Makamura I, Ohnuma A. Increase in apoptotic polymorphonuclear neutrophils in peripheral blood after intramammary infusion of *Escherichia coli* lipopolysaccharide. *Vet. Immunol. Immunopathol.* 2002;89:115-25.

[318] Lai XH, Golovliov I, Sjostedt A. *Francisella tularensis* induces cytopathogenicity and apoptosis in murine macrophages via a mechanism that requires intracellular bacterial multiplication. *Infect. Immun.* 2001;69:4691-4.

[319] Lai XH, Sjostedt A. Delineation of the molecular mechanisms of *Francisella tularensis*-induced apoptosis in murine macrophages. *Infect. Immun.* 2003;71:4642-6.

[320] Narayanan S, Stewart GC, Chengappa MM. *Fusobacterium necrophorum* leukotoxin induces activation and apoptosis of bovine leukocytes. *Infect. Immun.* 2002;70:4609-20.

[321] Jewett A, Hume WR, Le H, Huynh TN, Han YW, Cheng G, et al. Induction of apoptotic cell death in peripheral blood mononuclear and polymorphonuclear cells by an oral bacterium, *Fusobacterium nucleatum*. *Infect. Immun.* 2000;68:1893-8.

[322] Yang YF, Sylte MJ, Czuprynski CJ. Apoptosis: A possible tactic of *Haemophilus somnus* for evasion of killing by bovine neutrophils? *Microb. Pathog.* 1998;24:351-9.

[323] Betten A, Bylund J, Cristophe T, Boulay F, Romero A, Hellstrand K, et al. A proinflammatory peptide from *Helicobacter pylori* activates monocytes to induce lymphocyte dysfunction and apoptosis. *J. Clin. Invest.* 2001;108:1221-8.

[324] Das S, Suarez G, Beswick EJ, Sierra JC, Graham DY, Reyes VE. Expression of B7-H1 on Gastric Epithelial Cells: Its Potential Role in Regulating T Cells during Helicobacter pylori Infection. *J. Immunol.* 2006;176:3000-9.

[325] Gobert aP, Cheng Y, Wang JY, Boucher JL, Iyer RK, Cederbaum SD, et al. *Helicobacter pylori* induces macrophage apoptosis by activation of arginase II. *J. Immunol.* 2002;168:4692-700.

[326] Hofman V, Ricci V, Mograbi B, Brest P, Luciano F, Boquet P, et al. *Helicobacter pylori* lipopolysaccharide hinders polymorphonuclear leukocyte apoptosis. *Lab. Invest.* 2001;81:375-84.

[327] Kim JS, Kim JM, Jung HC, Song IS, Kim CY. Inhibition of apoptosis in human neutrophils by *Helicobacter pylori* water-soluble surface proteins. *Scand. J. Gastroenterol.* 2001;36:589-600.

[328] Arakaki N, Higa F, Koide M, Tateyama M, Saito A. Induction of apoptosis of human macrophages in vitro by *Legionaella longbeachae* through activation of the caspase pathway. *J. Exp. Microbiol.* 2002;51:159-68.

[329] Alli OA, Gao LY, Pedersen LL, Zink S, Radulic M, Doric M, et al. Temporal pore formation-mediated egress from macrophages and alveolar epithelial cells by *Legionella pneumophila*. *Infect. Immun.* 2000;68:6431-40.

[330] Gao LY, Abu Kwaik Y. Apoptosis in macrophages and alveolar epithelial cells during early stages of infection by *Legionella pneumophila* and its role in cytopathogenicity. *Infect. Immun.* 1999;67:862-70.

[331] Gao LY, Abu Kwaik Y. Activation of caspase 3 during *Legionella pneumophila*-induced apoptosis. *Infect. Immun.* 1999;67:4886-94.

[332] Hagele S, Hacker J, Brand BC. *Legionella pneumophila* kills human phagocytes but not protozoan host cells by inducing apoptotic cell death. *FEMS Microbiol. Lett.* 1998;169:51-8.

[333] Muller A, Hacker J, Brand BC. Evidence for apoptosis of human macrophage-like HL-60 cells by Legionella pneumophila infection. *Infect. Immun.* 1996;64:4900-6.

[334] Neumeister B, Faigle M, Lauber K, Northoff H, Wesselborg S. *Legionella pneumophila* induces apoptosis via the mitochondrial death pathway. *Microbiology* 2002;148:3639-50.

[335] Walz JM, Gerhardt H, Faigle M, Wolburg H, Neumeister B. *Legionella* species of different human prevalence induce different rates of apoptosis in human monocytic cells. *APMIS* 2000;108:398-408.

[336] Zink SD, Pedersen L, Cianciotto NP, Abu-Kwaik Y. The Dot/Icm type IV secretion system of *Legionella pneumophila* is essential for the induction of apoptosis in human macrophages. *Infect. Immun.* 2002;70:1657-63.

[337] Merien f, Baranton g, Perolat P. Invasion of Vero cells and induction of apoptosis in macrophages by pathogenic *Leptospira interogans* are correlated with virulence. *Infect. Immun.* 1997;65:729-38.

[338] Barsig J, Kaufmann SH. The mechanism of cell death in *Listeria monocytogenes*-infected murine macrophages is distinct form apoptosis. *Infect. Immun.* 1997;65:4075-81.

[339] Guzman CA, Domann E, Rohde M, Bruder D, Darji A, Weiss S, et al. Apoptosis of mouse dendritic cells is triggered by listeriolysin, the major virulence determinant of *Listeria monocytogenes*. *Mol. Microbiol.* 1996;20:119-26.

[340] Vadyvaloo V, Arous S, Gravesen A, Hechard Y, Chauhan-Haubrock R, Hastings JW, et al. Cell-surace alteration in class IIa bacteriocin-resistant *Listeria monocytogenes* strains. *Microbiology* 2004;150:3025-33.

[341] Cudd LA, Ownby CL, Clarke CR, Sun Y, Clinkenbeard KD. Effects of *Mannheimia haemolytica* leukotoxin onapoptosis and oncosis of bovine neutrophils. *Am. J. Vet. Res.* 2001;62:136-41.

[342] Stevens PK, Czuprynski CJ. *Pasteurella haemolytica* leukotoxin induces bovine leukocytes to undergo morphologic changes consistent with apoptosis in vitro. *Infect. Immun.* 1996;64:2687-94.

[343] Balcewicz-Sablinska MK, Gan H, Remold HG. Interleukin 10 produced by macrophages inoculated with *Mycobacterium avium* attenuates mycobacteria-induced apoptosis by reduction of TNF-alpha activity. *J. Infect. Dis.* 1999;180:1230-7.

[344] Bermudez LE, Parker A, Petrofsky M. Apoptosis of *Mycobacterium avium*-infected macrophages is mediated by both tumor necrosis factor (TNF) and Fas, and involves the activation of caspases. *Clin. Exp. Immunol.* 1999;116:94-9.

[345] Bhattacharyya A, Pathak S, Basak C, Law S, Kundu M, Basu J. Execution of macrophage apoptosis by *Mycobacterium avium* through apoptosis signal-regulating kinase 1/p38 mitogen-activated protein kinase signaling and caspase 8 activation. *J. Biol. Chem.* 2003;278:26517-25.

[346] Feng CG, Kullberg MC, Jankovic D. Transgenic mice expressing human interleukin-10 in the antigen-presenting cell compartment showincreased susceptibility fo infection with *Mycobacterium avium* associated with decreased macrophage effector function and apoptosis. *Infect. Immun.* 2002;70:6672-9.

[347] Fratazzi C, Arbeit RD, Carini C, Remold HG. Programmed cell death of *mycobacterium avium* serovar 4-infected human macrophages prevents the mycobacteria from spreading and induces mycobacterial growth inhibition by freshly added, uninfected macrophages. *J. Immunol.* 1997;158:4320-7.

[348] Hayashi T, Catanazaro A, Rao SP. Apoptosis of human monocytes and macrophages by *Mycobacterium avium* sonicate. *Infect. Immun.* 1997;65:5262-71.

[349] Mohagheghpour N, van Vollenhoven A, Goodman J, Bermudez LE. Interaction of *Mycobacterium avium* with human monocyte-derived dedritic cells. *Infect. Immun.* 2000;68:5824-9.

[350] Ahmad A, Khan M, Raykundalia C, Catty D. Study of the mechanisms of killing of *Mycobacterium bovis* BCG by apoptosis in J774 murine macrophages. *J. Pak. Med. Assoc.* 1999;49:273-8.

[351] Gutierrez-Pabello JA, McMurray DN, Adams LG. Upregulation of thymosin beta-10 by *Mycobacterium bovis* infection of bovine macrophages is associated with apoptosis. *Infect. Immun.* 2002;70:2121-7.

[352] Kremer L, Estaquier J, Brandt E, Ameisen JC, Locht C. *Mycobacterium bovis* Bacillus Calmette Guerin infection prevents apoptosis of resting human monocytes. *Eur. J. Immunol.* 1997;27:2450-6.

[353] Suttmann H, Lehan N, Bohle A, Brandau S. Stimulation of neutrophil granulocytes with *Mycobacterium bovis* bacillus Calmette-Guerin induces changes in phenotype and gene expression and inhibits spontaneous apoptosis. *Infect. Immun.* 2003;71:4647-56.

[354] Guerardel Y, Maes E, Briken V, Chirat F, Leroy Y, Locht C, et al. Lipomannan and lipoarabinomannan from a clinical isolate of *Mycobacterium kansasii*: Novel structural features and apoptosis-inducing properties. *J. Biol. Chem.* 2003;278:36637-51.

[355] Hernandez MO, Neves I, Sales JS, Carvalho DS, Sarno EN, Sampaio EP. Induction of apoptosis in monocytes by *Mycobacterium leprae in vitro*: A possible role for tumour necrosis factor-alpha. *Immunology* 2003;109:156-64.

[356] Ciaramella A, Martino A, Cicconi R, Colizzi V, Fraziano M. Mycobacterial 19-kDa lipoprotein mediates *Mycobacterium tuberculosis*-induced apoptosis in monocytes/macrophages at early stages of infection. *Cell Death Diff.* 2000;7:1270-2.

[357] Ciaramella A, Cavone A, Santucci MB, Amicosante M, Martino A, Auricchio G, et al. Proinflammatory cytokines in the course of *Mycobacterium tuberculosis*-induced apoptosis in monocytes/macrophages. *J. Infect. Dis.* 2002;186:1277-82.

[358] Danelishvili L, McGarvey J, Li YJ, Bermudez LE. *Mycobacterium tuberculosis* infection causes different levels of apoptosis and necrosis in human macrophages and alveolar epithelial cells. *Cell Microbiol.* 2003;5:649-60.

[359] Duan L, Gan H, Arm J, Remold HG. Cytosolic phopholipase A2 participates with TNF-alpha in the induction of apoptosis of human macrophages infected with *Mycobacterium tuberculosis* H37Ra. *J. Immunol.* 2001;166:7469-76.

[360] Duan L, Gan H, Golan DE, Remold HG. Critical role of mitochondrial damage in determining outcome of macrophage infection with *Mycobacterium tuberculosis. J. Immunol.* 2002;169:5181-7.

[361] Durrbaum-Landmann I, Gercken J, Flad HD, Ernst M. Effect of in vitro infection of human monocytes with low numbers of *Mycobacterium tuberculosis* bacteria on monocytes apoptosis. *Infect. Immun.* 1996;64:5384-9.

[362] Keane J, Balcewicz-Sablinska MK, Remold HG, Chupp GL, Meek BB, Fenton MJ, et al. Infection by *Mycobacterium tuberculosis* promotes human alveolar macrophage apoptosis. *Infect. Immun.* 1997;65:298-304.

[363] Keane J, Remold HG, Kornfeld H. Virulent *Mycobacterium tuberculosis* strains evade apoptosis of infected alveolar macrophages. *J. Immunol.* 2000;164:2016-20.

[364] Keane J, Shurtleff B, Kornfeld H. TNF-dependent BALB/c murine macrophage apoptosis following *Mycobacterium tuberculosis* infection inhibits bacillary growth in an IFN-gamma independent manner. *Tuberculosis* 2002;82:55-61.

[365] Lopez M, Sly LM, Luu Y, Young D, Cooper H, Reiner NE. The 19-kDa *Mycobacterium tuberculosis* protein induces macrophage apoptosis through Toll-like receptor-2. *J. Immunol.* 2003;170:2409-16.

[366] Mustafa T, Phyu S, Nilsen R, Bjune G, Jonsson R. Increased expression of Fas ligand on *Mycobacterium tuberculosis* infected macrophages: A potential novel mechanism of immune evasion by *Mycobacterium tuberculosis*? *Inflammation* 1999;23:507-21.

[367] Oddo M, Renno T, Attinger A, Bakker T, MacDonald HR, Meylan PR. Fas ligand-induced apoptosis of infected human macrophages reduces the viability of intracellular *Mycobacterium tuberculosis. J. Immunol.* 1998;160:5448-54.

[368] Placido R, Mancino G, Amendola A, Mariani F, Vendetti S, Piacentini M, et al. Apoptosis of human monocytes/macrophages in *Mycobacterium tuberculosis* infection. *J. Pathol.* 1997;181:31-8.

[369] Rojas M, Barrera LF, Garcia LF. Induction of apoptosis in murine macrophages by *Mycobacterium tuberculosis* is reactive oxygen intermediates-independent. *Biochem. Biophys. Res. Commun.* 1998;247:436-42.

[370] Rojas M, Olivier M, Gros P, Barrera LF, Garcia LF. TNF-alpha and IL-10 modulate the induction of apoptosis by virulent *Mycobacterium tuberculosis* in murine macrophages. *J. Immunol.* 1999;162:6122-31.

[371] Rojas M, Garcia LF, Nigou J, Puzo G, Olivier M. Mannosylated lipoarabinomannan antagonizes *Mycobacterium tuberculosis*-induced macrophage apoptosis by altering $Ca^{2+}$-dependent cell signalling. *J. Infect. Dis.* 2000;182:240-51.

[372] Santucci MB, Amicosante M, Cicconi R, Montesano C, Casarini M, Giosue S, et al. *Mycobacterium tuberculosis*-induced apoptosis in monocytes/macrophages: Early membrane modifications and intracellular mycobacterial viability. *J. Infect. Dis.* 2000;181:1506-9.

[373] Sly LM, Hingley-Wilson SM, Reiner NE, McMaster WR. Survival of *Mycobacterium tuberculosis* in host macrophages involves resistance to apoptosis dependent upon induction of antiapoptotic Bcl-2 family member Mcl-1. *J. Immunol.* 2003;170:430-7.

[374] Spira A, Carroll JD, Liu G, Aziz Z, Shah V, Kornfeld H, et al. Apoptosis genes in human alveolar macrophages infected with virulent or attenuated *Mycobacterium tuberculosis*: A pivotal role for tumor necrosis factor. *Am. J. Respir. Cell Mol. Biol.* 2003;29:545-51.

[375] Adusumilli S, Mve-Obiang A, Sparer T, Meyers W, Hayman J, Small PLC. *Mycobacterium ulcerans* toxic macrolide, mycolactone modulates the host immune response and cellular location of *M. ulcerans* in vitro and in vivo. *Cell Micro.* 2005;7:1295-304.

[376] George KM, Pascopella L, Welty DM, Small PL. A *Mycobacterium ulcerans* toxin, mycolactone, causes apoptosis in guinea pig ulcers and tissue culture cells. *Infect. Immun.* 2000;68:877-83.

[377] Dedieu L, Chapey E, Balcer-Rodrigues V. *Mycoplasma mycoides* ssp. mycoides biotype small colony-secreted components induce apoptotic cell death in bovine leucocytes. *Scand. J. Immunol.* 2005;62:528-38.

[378] Hall RE, Agarwal S, Krestler DP. Induction of leukemia cell differentiation and apoptosis by recombinant P48, a modulin derived from *Mycoplasma fermentans*. *Biochem. Biophys. Res. Commun.* 2000;269:284-9.

[379] Into T, Nodasaka Y, Hasebe A, Okuzawa T, Nakamura J, Ohata N, et al. Mycoplasmal lipoproteins induce toll-like receptor 2- and caspases-mediated cell death in lymphocytes and monocytes. *Microbiol. Immunol.*2002;46:265-76.

[380] do Vale A, Marques F, Silva MT. Apoptosis of sea bass (Dicentrarchus labrax L.) neutrophils and macrophages induced by experimental infection with *Photobacterium damselae subsp. piscicida. Fish Shellfish Immunol.*2003;15:129-44.

[381] Ozaki K, Hanazawa S. *Porphyromonas ginigivalis* fimbraie inhibit caspase-3-mediated apoptosis of monocytic THP-1 cells under growth factor deprivation via exracellular signal-regulated kinase-dependent expression of p21 Cip/WAF1. *Infect. Immun.* 2001;69:4944-50.

[382] Preshaw PM, Schifferle RE, Walters JD. *Porphyromonas gingivalis* lipopolysaccharide delays human polymorphonuclear leukocyte apoptosis in vitro. *J. Periodontal Res.* 1999;34:197-202.

[383] Dacheux D, Goure J, Chabert J, Usson Y, Attree I. Pore-forming activity of type III system-secreted proteins leads to oncosis of *Pseudomonas aeruginosa*-infected macrophages. *Mol. Microbiol.* 2001;40:76-85.

[384] Dacheux D, Toussaint B, Richard M, Brochier G, Croize J, Attree I. *Pseudomonas aeruginosa* cystic fibrosis isolates induced rapid, type III secretion-dependent, but ExoU-independent, oncosis on marophages and polymorphonuclear neutrophils. *Infect. Immun.* 2000;68:2916-24.

[385] Dacheux D, Attree I, Schneider C, Toussaint B. Cell death of human polymorphonuclear neutrophils induced by a *Pseudomonas aeruginosa* cystic fibrosis isolate requires a functional type III secretion system. *Infect. Immun.* 1999;67:6164-7.

[386] Hauser aR, Engel JN. *Pseudomonas aeruginosa* induces type-III-secretion-mediated apoptosis of macrophages and epithelial cells. *Infect. Immun.* 1999;67:5530-7.

[387] Huang Yt, Jeng CR, Cheng CH, Chueh LL, Liu JJ, Pang VF. Morphological and immunological evidence of a unique selective production and endoplasmic reticular accumulation of interleukin-1alpha in rat peritoneal macrophages induced by *Pseudomonas aeruginosa* exotoxin A. *Cell Immunol.* 2003;221:143-56.

[388] Tateda K, Ishii Y, Horikawa M, Matsumoto T, Miyairi S, Pechere JC, et al. The *Pseudomonas aeruginosa* autoinducer N-3-oxododecanoyl homoserine lactone accelerates apoptosis in macrophages and neutrophils. *Infect. Immun.* 2003;71:5785-93.

[389] Usher LR, Lawson RA, Geary I, Taylor CJ, Bingle CD, Taylor GW, et al. Induction of neutrophil apoptosis by the *Pseudomonas aeruginosa* exotoxin pyocyanin: A potential mechanism of persistent infection. *J. Immunol.* 2002;168:1861-8.

[390] Worgall S, Martushova K, Busch A, Lande L, Crystal RG. Apoptosis induced by *Pseudomonas aeruginosa* in antigen presenting cells is diminished by genetic modification with CD40 ligand. *Pediatr. Res.* 2002;52:636-44.

[391] Zaborina O, Dhiman N, Ling Chen M, Kostal J, Holder IA, Chakrabarty AM. Secreted products of a nonmucoid *Pseudomonas aeruginosa* strain induce two modes of macrophage killing: external-ATP-dependent, P2Z-receptor-mediated necrosis and ATP-independent, caspase-mediated apoptosis. *Microbiology* 2000;146:2521-30.

[392] Zhang J, Takayama H, Matsuba T, Jiang R, Tanaka Y. Induction of apoptosis in macrophage cell line, J774, by the cell-free supernatant from *Pseudomonas aeruginosa. Microbiol. Immunol.* 2003;47:199-206.

[393] Dockrell DH, Lee M, Lynch DH, Read RC. Immune-mediated phagocytosis and killing of *Streptococcus pneumoniae* are associated with direct and bystander macrophage apoptosis. *J. Infect. Dis.* 2001;184:713-22.

[394] Kim MK, Seong SY, Seoh JY, Han TH, Song HJ, Lee JE, et al. *Orientia tsutsugamushi* inhibits apoptosis of macrophages by retarding intracellular calcium release. *Infect. Immun.* 2002;70:4692-6.

[395] Arai T, Hiromatsu K, Nishimura H, Kimura Y, Kobayashi N, Ishida H, et al. Endogneous interleukin-10 prevents apoptosis in macrophages during *Salmonella* infection. *Biochem. Biophys. Res. Commun.* 1995;213:600-7.

[396] Cerquetti MC, Goren NB, Ropolo AJ, Grasso D, Giacomodonato MN, Vaccaro MI. Nitric oxide and apoptosis induced in Peyer's patches by attenuated strains of *Salmonella enterica* serovar Enteritidis. *Infect. Immun*. 2002;70:964-9.
[397] Lehmann J, Springer S, Werner CE, Lindner T, Bellmann S, Straubinger RK, et al. Immunity induced with a Salmonella enterica serovar Enteritidis live vaccine is regulated by Th1-cell-dependent cellular and humoral effector mechanisms in susceptible BALB/c mice. *Vaccine* 2006;24:4779-93.
[398] Baran J, Guzik K, Hryniewicz W, Ernst M, Flad HD, Pryjma J. Apoptosis of monocytes and prolonged survival of granulocytes as a result of phagocytosis of bacteria. *Infect. Immun*. 1996;64:4242-8.
[399] Watson PR, Gautier AV, Paulin SM, Bland AP, Jones PW, Wallis TS. *Salmonella enterica* serovars Typhimurium and Dublin can lyse macrophages by a mechanism distinct from apoptosis. *Infect. Immun*. 2000;68:3744-7.
[400] Forsberg M, Bloomgran R, Lerm M, Sarndahl E, Sebti SM, Hamilton A, et al. Differential effects of invasion by and phagocysis of *Salmonella typhimurium* on apoptosis in human macrophages: potential role of Rho-GTPases and Akt. *J. Leukoc. Biol.* 2003;74:620-9.
[401] Monack DM, Raupach B, Hromockyj AE, Falkow S. *Salmonella typhimurium* invasion induces apoptosis in infected macrophages. *Proc. Natl. Acad. Sci. USA* 1996;93:9833-8.
[402] Richter-Dahlfors A, Buchan AM, Finlay BB. Murine salmonellosis studied by confocal microscopy: *Salmonella typhimurium* resides intracellularly inside macrophages and exerts a cytotoxic effect on phagocytes in vivo. *J. Exp. Med.* 1997;186:569-80.
[403] Santos RL, Tsolis RM, Baumler AJ, Smith R3, Adams LG. *Salmonella enterica* serovar Typhimurium induces cell death in bovine mnocyte-derived macrophages by early sipB-independent and delayed sipB-independent mechanisms. *Infect. Immun.* 2001;69:2293-301.
[404] van der Velden AW, Lindgren sW, Worley MJ, Heffron F. *Salmonella* pathogenicity island 1-independent induction of apoptosis in infected macrophages by *Salmonella enterica* serotype Typhimurium. *Infect. Immun*. 2000;68:5702-9.
[405] Zhou X, Mantis N, Zhang XR, Potoka DA, Watkins SC, Ford HR. *Salmonella typhimurium* induces apoptosis in human monocyte-derived macrophages. *Microbiol. Immunol.* 2000;44:987-95.
[406] Basso H, Rharbaoui F, Staendner LH, Medina E, Garcia-Del Portillo F. Characterization of a novel intracellularly activated gene from *Salmonella enterica* serovar Typhi. *Infect. Immun*. 2002;70:5404-11.
[407] Schwan WR, Huang XZ, Hu L, Kopecko DJ. Differential bacterial survival, replication, and apoptosis-inducing ability of *Salmonella* serovars within human and murine macrophages. *Infect. Immun*. 2000;68:1005-13.
[408] Raqib R, Ekberg C, Sharkar P, Bardhan PK, Zychlinsky A, Sansonetti PJ, et al. Apoptosis in acute shigellosis is associated with increased production of Fas/Fas ligand, perforin, caspase-1, and caspase-3 but reduced production of Bcl-2 and interleukin-2. *Infect. Immun*. 2002;70:3199-207.

[409] Fernandez-Prada CM, Hoover DL, Tall BD, Venkatesan MM. Human monocyte-derived macrophages infected with virulent *Shigella flexneri* in vitro undergo a rapid cytolytic event similar to oncosis but not apoptosis. *Infect. Immun.* 1997;65:1486-96.

[410] Fernandez-Prada CM, Hoover DL, Tall BD, Hartman AB, Kopelowitz J, Venkatesan MM. *Shigella flexneri* IpaH(7.8) facilitates escape of virulent bacteria from the endocytic vacuoles of mouse and human macrophages. *Infect. Immun.* 2000;68:3608-19.

[411] Francois M, Le Cabec V, Dupont MA, Sansonetti PJ, Maridonneau-Parini I. Induction of necrosis in human neutrophils by *Shigella flexneri* requires type III secretion, IpaB, and IpaC invasins, and actin polymerization. *Infect. Immun.* 2000;68:1289-96.

[412] Hathaway LJ, Griffin GE, Sansonetti PJ, Edgeworth JD. Human monocytes kill *Shigella flexneri* but then die by apoptosis associated with suppression of proinflammatory cytokine production. *Infect. Immun.* 2002;70:3833-42.

[413] Hilbi H, Chen Y, Thirumalai K, Zychlinsky A. The interleukin-1beta-converting enzyme, caspase 1, is activated during *Shigella flexneri*-induced apoptosis in human monocyte-derived macrophages. *Infect. Immun.* 1997;65:5165-70.

[414] Hilbi H, Moss JE, Hersh D, Chen Y, Arondel J, Banerjee S, et al. *Shigella*-induced apoptosis is dependent on caspase-1 which binds to IpaB. *J. Biol. Chem.* 1998;273:32895-900.

[415] Hilbi H, Puro RJ, Zychlinsky A. Tripeptidyl peptidase II promotes maturation of caspase-1 in *Shigella flexneri*-induced macrophage apoptosis. *Infect. Immun.* 2000;68:5502-8.

[416] Koterski JF, Nahvi M, Venkatesan MM, Haimovich B. Virulent *Shigella flexneri* causes damage to mitochondria and triggers necrosis in infected human monocyte-derived macrophages. *Infect. Immun.* 2005;73:504-13.

[417] Nonaka T, Kuwai A, Sasakawa C, Imajoh-Ohmi S. *Shigella flexneri* YSH6000 induces two types of cell death, apoptosis and oncosis, in the differentiated human monoblastic cell line U937. *FEMS Microbiol. Lett.* 1999;174:89-95.

[418] Sansonetti PJ, Phalipon A, Arondel J, Thirumalai K, Banerjee S, Akira S, et al. Caspase-1 activation of IL-1□ and IL-18 are essential for *Shigella flexneri*-induced inflamation. *Immunity* 2000;12:581-90.

[419] Yu J, Oragui EE, Stephens A, Kroll JS, Venkatesan MM. Inactivation of DsbA alters the behaviour of *Shigella flexneri* towards murine and human derived macrophage-like cells. *FEMS Microbiol. Lett.* 2001;204:88.

[420] Zychlinsky A, Prevost MC. *Shigella flexneri* induces apoptosis in infected macrophages. *Nature* 1992;358:167-9.

[421] Zychlinsky A, Kenny B, Menard R, Prevost MC. IpaB mediates macrophage apoptosis induced by *Shigella flexneri*. *Mol. Microbiol.* 1994;11:619-27.

[422] Zychlinsky A, Fitting C, Cavaillon JM, Sansonetti PJ. Interleukin-1 is released by murine macrophages during apoptosis induced by *Shigella flexneri*. *J. Clin. Invest.* 1994;94:1328-32.

[423] Zychlinsky A, Kenny B, Prevost MC, Holland IB, Sansonetti PJ. The ipaB gene of *Shigella flexneri* and macrophage-programmed cell death. *Infect. Agents Dis.* 1993;2:212-4.

[424] Zychlinsky A, Thirumalai K, Arondel J, Cantey JR, Aliprantis AO, Sansonetti PJ. In vivo apoptosis in *Shigella flexneri* infections. *Infect. Immun.* 1996;64:5357-65.

[425] Guichon A, Zychlinsky A. Clinical isolates of *Shigella* species induce apoptosis in macrophages. *J. Infect. Dis.* 1997;175:470-3.

[426] Minamino M, Sakaguchi I, Naka T, Ikeda N, Kato Y, Tomiyasu I, et al. Bacterial ceramides and sphinophospholipids induce apoptosis of human leukaemic cells. *Microbiology* 2003;149:2071-81.

[427] Genestier A-L, Michallet M-C, Prevost G, Bellot G, Chalabreysse L, Peyrol S, et al. *Staphylococcus aureus* panton-valentine leukocidin directly targets mitochondria and induced Bax-independent apoptosis of human neutrophils. *J. Clin. Invest.* 2005;115:3117-27.

[428] Buratta S, Fettucciari K, Manbrini R, Fetriconi I, Marconi P, Mozzi R. Group B *Streptococcus* (GBS) modifies macrophage phosphatidylserine metabolism during induction of apoptosis. *FEBS Lett.* 2002;520:68-72.

[429] Fettucciari K, Rosati E, Scaringi L, Cornacchione P, Migliorati G, Sabatini R, et al. Group B *Streptococcus* Induces Apoptosis in Macrophages. *J. Immunol.* 2000;165:3923-33.

[430] Fettucciari K, Fetriconi I, Mannucci R, Nicoletti I, Bartoli A, Coaccioli S, et al. Group B *Streptococcus* Induces Macrophage Apoptosis by Calpain Activation. *J. Immunol.* 2006;176:7542-56.

[431] Fettucciari K, Fetriconi I, Bartoli A, Rossi R, Marconi P. Involvement of mitogen-activated protein kinases in group B *Streptococcus*-induced macrophage apoptosis. *Pharmacological Research* 2003;47:355-62.

[432] Ulett GC, Bohnsack JF, Armstrong J, Adderson EE. Beta-hemolysin-independent induction of apoptosis of macrophages infected with serotype III group B *Streptococcus*. *J. Infect. Dis.* 2003;188:1049-53.

[433] Zlotkin A, Chilmonczyk S, Eyngor M, Hurvitz A, Ghittino C, Eldar A. Trojan horse effect: phagocyte-mediated *Streptococcus iniae* infection of fish. *Infect. Immun.* 2003;71:2318-25.

[434] Dockrell DH, Whyte MKB. Regulation of phagocyte lifespan in the lung during bacterial infection. *J. Leukoc. Biol.* 2006;79:904-8.

[435] Ali F, Lee ME, Iannelli F, Pozzi G, Mitchell TJ, Read RC, et al. *Streptococcus pneumoniae*-associated human macrophage apoptosis after bacterial internalization via complement and Fcgamma receptors correlates with intracellular bacterial load. *J. Infect. Dis.* 2003;188:1119-31.

[436] Kirby AC, Raynes JG, Kaye PM. The role played by tumor necrosis factor during localized systemic infection with *Streptococcus pneumoniae*. *J. Infect. Dis.* 2005;191:1538-47.

[437] Marriott HM, Dockrell DH. *Streptococcus pneumoniae*: The role of apoptosis in host defense and pathogenesis. *Int. J. Biochem. Cell. Biol.* 2006;38:1848-54.

[438] Staali L, Bauer S, Morgelin M, Bjorck L, Tapper H. *Streptococcus pyogenes* bacteria modulate membrane traffic in human neutrophils and selectively inhibit azurophilic granule fusion with phagosomes. *Microbiology* 2006;8:690-703.

[439] Medina E, Goldmann O, Toppel AW, Chhatwal GS. Survival of *streptococcus pyogenes* within host phagocytic cells: A pathogenic mechanism for persistence and systemic invasion. *J. Infect. Dis*. 2003;187:597-603.

[440] Denecker G, Declercq W, Geuijen CA, Boland A, Benabdillah R, van Gurp M, et al. *Yersinia enterocolitica* YopP-induced apoptosis of macrophages involves the apoptotic signaling cascade upstream of Bid. *J. Biol. Chem*. 2001;276:19706-14.

[441] Mills SD, Boland A, Sory MP, van der Smissen P, Kerbourch C, Finlay BB, et al. *Yersinia enterocolitica* induces apoptosis in macrophages by a process requiring functional type III secretion and translocation mechanisms and involving YopP, presumably acting as an effector protein. *Proc. Natl. Acad. Sci. USA* 1997;94:12638-43.

[442] Ruckdeschel K, Roggenkamp A, Lafont V, Mangeat P, Heesemann J, Rouot B. Interaction of *Yersinia enterocolitica* with macrophages leads to macrophage cell death through apoptosis. *Infect. Immun*. 1997;65:4813-21.

[443] Ruckdeschel K, Harb S, Roggenkamp A, Hornef M, Zumbihl R, Kohler S, et al. *Yersinia enterocolitica* impairs activation of transcription NF-kappaB: involvement in the induction of programmed cell death and in the suppression of the macrophage tumor necrosis factor alpha production. *J. Exp. Med*. 1998;187:1069-79.

[444] Ruckdeschel K, Mannel O, Richter K, Jacobi CA, Trulzsch K, Rouot B, et al. Yersinia outer protein P of *Yersinia enterocolitica* simultaneously blocks the nuclear factor-kappa B pathway and exploits lipopolysaccharide signaling to trigger apoptosis in macrophages. *J. Immunol*. 2001;166:1823-31.

[445] Ruckdeschel K, Richter K, Mannel O, Heesemann J. Arginine-143 of *Yersinia enterocolitica* YopP cruicially determines isotype-related NF-kappaB suppression and apoptosis induction in macrophages. *Infect. Immun*. 2001;69:7652-62.

[446] Ruckdeschel K, Richter K. Lipopolysaccharide desensitization of macrophages provides protection against *Yersinia enterocolitica*-induced apoptosis. *Infect. Immun*. 2002;70:5259-64.

[447] Haase R, Kirschning CJ, Sing A, Schrottner P, Fukase K, Kusumoto S, et al. A dominant role of Toll-like receptor 4 in the signaling of apoptosis in bacteria-faced macrophages. *J. Immunol*. 2003;171:4294-303.

[448] Jarrett CO, Deak E, Isherwood KE, Oyston PC, Fischer ER, Whitney AR, et al. Transmission of *Yersinia pestis* from an infectious biofilm in the flea vector. *J. Infect. Dis*. 2004;190:783-92.

[449] Ng LC, Forslund O, Koh S, Kuoppa K, Sjostedt A. The response of murine macrophages to infection with *Yersinia pestis* as revealed by DNA microarray analysis. *Adv. Exp. Med. Biol.* 2003;529:155-60.

[450] Vasil'eva GI, Kiseleva AK, Mishan'kin MB, Kozlovskii VN, Mishan'kin BN. Apoptosis of phagocytes as one of the probable mechanisms of the pathogenic *Yersinia pestis* "mouse" toxin. *Zh. Mikorbiol. Eidemil. Immunobiol.* 2002;2:49-52.

[451] Weeks S, Hill J, Friedlander A, Welkos S. Anti-V antigen antibody protects macropages from *Yersinia pestis*-induced cell death and promotes phagocytosis. *Microb. Pathog.* 2002;32:227-37.

[452] Monack DM, Mecsas J, Ghori N, Falkow S. *Yersinia* signals macrophages to undergo apoptosis and YopJ is necessary for this cell death. *Proc. Natl. Acad. Sci. USA* 1997;94:10385-90.

[453] Monack DM, Mecsas J, Bouley D, Falkow S. *Yersinia*-induced apoptosis in vivo aids in the establishment of a systemic infection of mice. *J. Exp. Med.* 1998;188:2127-37.

[454] Zhang Y, Bliska JB. Role of Toll-like receptor signaling in the apoptotic response of macrophages to *Yersinia* infection. *Infect. Immun.* 2003;71:1513-9.

[455] Kashimoto T, Ueno S, Hanajima M, Hayashi H, Akeda Y, Miyoshi S, et al. *Vibrio vulnificus* induces macrophage apoptosis in vitro and in vivo. *Infect. Immun.* 2003;71:533-5.

[456] Kashimoto T, Ueno S, Hayashi H, Hanajima M, Yoshioka K, Yoshida K, et al. Depletion of lymphocytes, but not neutrophils, via apoptosis in a murine model of *Vibrio vulnificus* infection. *J. Med. Microbiol.* 2005;54:15-22.

In: New Immunology Research Developments
Editor: Gunter V. Müller
ISBN 978-1-60021-701-2


*Chapter 2*

# Glial Regulation of Beta-Amyloid Deposition and Neurodegeneration in Alzheimer's Disease

***Tsuneya Ikezu***
Center for Neurovirology and Neurodegenerative Disorders, Department of Pharmacology and Experimental Neuroscience, University of Nebraska Medical Center, Omaha, Nebraska, USA

## Abbreviations

| | |
|---|---|
| AD | Alzheimer's disease |
| APP | Amyloid precursor protein |
| ApoE | Apolipoprotein E |
| Aβ | β-amyloid peptide |
| BACE | Beta-amyloid precursor protein converting enzyme |
| IDE | Insulin degrading enzyme |
| IFN-γ | Interfreon-γ |
| NFT | Neurofibrillary tangle |
| PS1 | Presenilin-1 |
| TNF-α | Tumor necrosis factor-α |

## 1. Epidemiology, Clinical Features and Pathology

AD affects more than four million people in the United States and prevalence studies demonstrate an exponential rise of dementia with age (Katzman, 2001). The number of cases of dementia in the developed world is projected to rise from 13.5 million in 2000 to 21.2 million in 2025, and to 36.7 million in 2050 (Katzman and Fox, 1999). Currently the number of deaths caused by AD is similar to the number of deaths caused by stroke. AD and stroke together rank as the third most common causes of death (Ewbank, 1999).

The symptoms of typical AD begin with a loss of short-term memory that slowly progresses to affect all memory functions (Corey-Bloom et al., 1994). Initially, impaired short-term memory often manifests itself as losing objects or forgetfulness in conversations. Subsequently, other early cognitive deficits occur; they include difficulty in word-finding, problem solving and spatio-temporal awareness.

Identification of genetic mutations that cause early onset AD has helped to dramatically increase the understanding of the origins of AD. Although cases of familial AD are relatively rare, perhaps only 200 families identified to date, they represent identified molecular mutations that cause AD. The genes identified to be responsible for early onset familial AD code for the amyloid precursor protein (APP), presenilin-1 and presenilin-2; these are found on chromosomes 21, 14, and 1, respectively. In addition to these dominantly-transmitted disease-causing mutations in early onset AD, still other studies have identified over 25 genetic risk factors that influence the appearance of the more common sporadic late onset AD. Current research is actively using genetically-modified mice to determine how specific protein modifications lead to the pathology of AD.

AD is characterized by an accumulation of senile plaques containing aggregated protein deposits of Aβ fibrils, numerous neurofibrillary tangles (NFTs), reactive astrocytes, and activated microglia in the neocortex and hippocampus (Alzheimer, 1907; Selkoe, 1997). Senile plaques can contain either a diffuse amyloid deposition (presumably early senile plaques) or a dense core of insoluble Aβ with neuritic structures (mature senile plaques). Although Aβ deposition and NFT are commonly observed in non-demented elderly 80 years and older, increased levels of senile plaques are seen in AD brains (Berg et al., 1993; Schmitt et al., 2000). The degree of both Aβ deposition and NFT formation are correlated with cognitive decline (Wilcock and Esiri, 1982; Berg et al., 1993; Braak and Braak, 1995; Naslund et al., 2000).

Although inflammation is a well-recognized phenomenon and intensively investigated, the precise definition of brain inflammation is not yet established (McGeer and McGeer, 2001). Clinically, AD patients exhibit few of the classic signs of inflammation. Histopathologically, the classical acute inflammatory response (neutrophil recruitment), immunoglobulin precipitation, and T-cell accumulation are not seen suggesting that humoral or classical cellular immune-mediated responses are not involved in AD progression (Eikelenboom et al., 1994). However, AD brains show an increase in activated microglial clusters on senile plaques surrounded by astrocytes, indicating focal glial inflammation (Eikelenboom et al., 2002; Wyss-Coray and Mucke, 2002). In particular, volume density of $CD68^+$ mononuclear phagocytes is correlated with volume density of congophilic compact plaque deposits (Arends et al., 2000). CD68+ cells are present from very early preclinical phases to terminal phases of AD and are involved in disease progression, which will be further described later (Akiyama et al., 2000; Fonseca et al., 2004b). Moreover, deactivation of microglia has implications for therapy since long-term treatment of affected patients with non-steroidal anti-inflammatory drugs (NSAID) has been shown to inactivate microglia and retard the development and progression of AD (in 't Veld et al., 2002).

# 2. Molecular Pathogenesis, Animal Models, and Neuroinflammation

The molecular pathogenesis of AD is centered around Aβ production and its clearance. Aβ is generated by the processing of APP by β and γ-processing enzymes, and cleared from brain by its diffusion, export to vascular system, phagocytosis, or degradation. The following molecules are essential for understanding the molecular mechanism of Aβ processing.

## 2.1. Amyloid Precursor Protein (APP)

APP is the first gene to be identified as a causative gene of familial AD (FAD) and has been a key molecule in the study of the molecular mechanism of AD. As shown in Figure 1, the APP molecule can be cleaved at different specific cleavage sites by various proteases to generate fragments of different sizes.

APP is primarily expressed in neurons and cleaved at the α, β,and γ sites by APP processing enzymes (called α,βand γ–secretases), producing Aβ (β-and γ-processing product), p3 (α-and γ-processing product), and other APP fragments (Selkoe, 1994). Aβ is composed of 39 to 43 amino acids, mainly 1-40 (Aβ40) and 1-42 (Aβ42). Aβ42 is more amyloidogenic (faster to be aggregated) than Aβ40, and early Aβ deposits are usually detectable with anti-Aβ42 antibodies, but not with anti-Aβ40 antibodies (Selkoe, 1994). FAD mutations on APP gene are all linked to abnormal APP processing (increase in Aβ42/Aβ40 ratio), Aβ aggregation, and Aβ deposition (Scheuner et al., 1996).

## 2.2. PS1 and γ-Processing Enzyme Complex

A combination of PS1, aph-1, pen-2, and nicastrin forms the γ-secretase complex (De Strooper, 2003). The γ-secretase complex cleaves not only APP but also other transmembrane molecules, such as Notch, ErbB-4, and sterol regulatory element binding proteins (SREBPs). PS1 and PS2 have been established as causative genes of early onset FAD (Levy-Lahad et al., 1995; Sherrington et al., 1995).

Transgene expression of PS1 FAD mutants enhances the Aβ42/Aβ40 ratio and accelerates Aβ aggregation and deposition in APP mice, which over-express Swedish FAD APP mutant in brains (Duff et al., 1996; Borchelt et al., 1997; Holcomb et al., 1998). PS2 FAD mutant over-expression converts Aβ40 to Aβ42, whereas PS2 wild type over-expression reduces both Aβ40 and Aβ42 (Mastrangelo et al., 2005). Taken together, these *in vivo* studies demonstrate the effect of PS1/2 FAD mutations on Aβ aggregation through transition of Aβ40 to Aβ42.

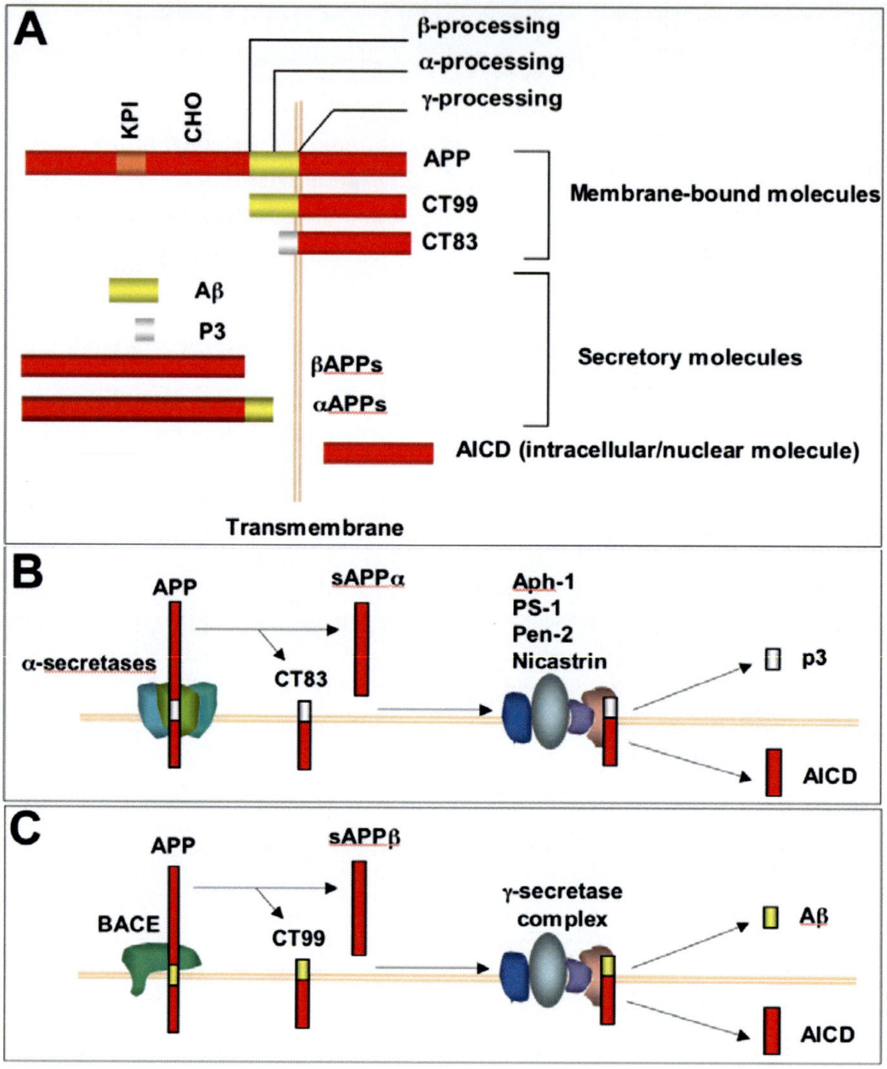


Figure 1. Scheme of APP processing. A, Cleavage sites and processing enzymes of APP. B, P3 and sAPPα production by α and γ-processing of APP. C, Aβ and sAPPβ production by β and γ-processing of APP.

## 2.3. APP and PS1 Animal Models

Several established AD mouse models have made significant contributions to the understanding of AD pathogenesis (Price et al., 1998; Spires and Hyman, 2005). Analyses of AD brain tissue obtained from autopsies provide only limited insight into the dynamic nature of the disease process. Currently, no AD mouse model has all of the characteristics of the human disease. However, several lines of transgenic mice expressing mutated APP, such as PDAPP (Games et al., 1995), Tg2576 (Hsiao et al., 1996), APP23 (Sturchler-Pierrat et al., 1997), TgCRND8 (Chishti et al., 2001), APPswe TgC3-3 (Borchelt et al., 1997), PSAPP (Holcomb et al., 1998), and 3xTg-AD mice (Oddo et al., 2003), simulate prominent behavioral and pathological features of AD. Phenotypes displayed by these mice include age-related impairments in learning and memory, electrophysiological abnormalities, neuronal loss, microgliosis, astrogliosis, neuritic changes, amyloid deposition, oxidative stress, and abnormal tau phosphorylation (Price et al., 1998; Smith et al., 1998) (Figure 2). Tg2576 mice, expressing Swedish familial AD mutant (K670N/M671L) of APP695 under a hamster prion promoter (Hsiao et al., 1996), show memory and learning impairments by 9 to 10 months, numerous Aβ plaques, dystrophic neurites, and microglial activation (Frautschy et al., 1998). Microglia in close proximity to fibrillar Aβ deposits are immunoreactive to interleukin (IL)-1β and TNF-α, whereas activated astrocytes are immunoreactive to IL-1β, transforming growth factor (TGF)-1β, and IL-10 in Tg2576 mice (Benzing et al., 1999; Apelt and Schliebs, 2001).

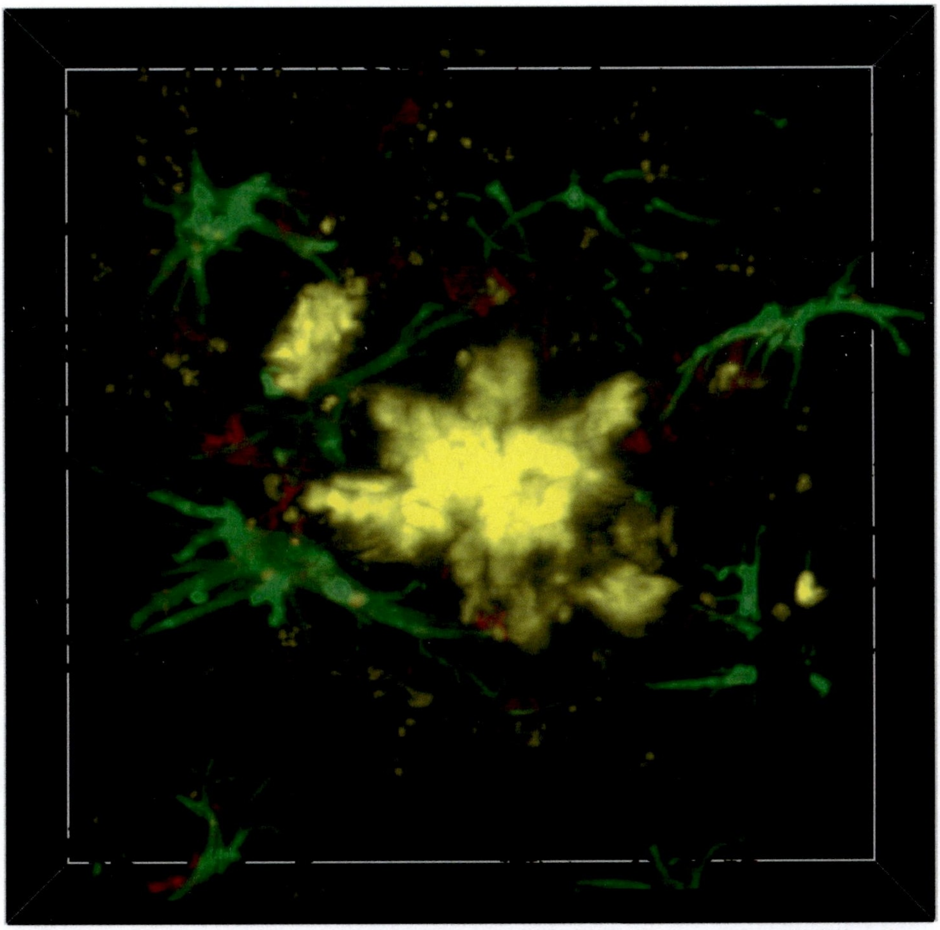

Figure 2. 3D reconstruction image of amyloid plaque deposition and glial accumulation in APP mouse brain. Cortical section of Tg2576 (14 months of age) was stained by thioflavin-S (compact amyloid plaque, yellow), anti-IBA1 rabbit polyclonal (microglia, red), and anti-GFAP mouse monoclonal (astrocytes, green), and imaged using a laser scanning confocal microscopy (Nikon SweptField). Z-stack images were deconvolved and 3D reconstructed using image processing software (AutoQuant).

## 2.4. β and α- Processing Enzymes

Beta-site APP-cleaving enzyme (BACE) is a β-secretase (Vassar et al., 1999); and most recently A Disintegrin And Metalloprotease (ADAM) 9, 10, and 17 have been identified as putative α-secretases (Asai et al., 2003). BACE expression enhances total Aβ production, deposition of both diffuse and compact Aβ plaques in brain parenchyma, and reduces cerebrovascular amyloid angiopathy in aged APP/BACE double transgenic mice (Mohajeri et al., 2004; Willem et al., 2004). However, this effect seems to be dose-dependent. Although modest over-expression of BACE enhances Aβ deposition, high BACE expression inhibits Aβ deposition (Lee et al., 2005). Thus, the effect of BACE upregulation in Aβ pathology *in vivo* is not conclusive. In addition, overexpression of ADAM10 prevents Aβ deposition and hippocampal defect in APP mice (Postina et al., 2004), suggesting its therapeutic application for enhancing α-processing of APP.

## 2.5. ApoE

ApoE is the most well characterized genetic risk factor of AD. Evidence indicates that endogenous apoE in mouse brain enhances Aβ deposition in APP animal models (Bales et al., 1999; Sadowski et al., 2004). Tg2576 mice lacking mouse apoE exhibit diminished compact plaque deposition, while diffuse plaque load remained unchanged (Bales et al., 1999). Mouse apoE is rather amyloidgenic since apoE disruption significantly reduces the compact plaque formation in APP mice (Bales et al., 1999). In contrast, human apoE3 enhances Aβ clearance in mouse brain, while apoE4 weakly promotes Aβ clearance (Holtzman et al., 1999; Holtzman et al., 2000; Fagan et al., 2002). Although many studies concluded that astrocytes are the main apoE-producing cell in brain (Danik et al., 1999), recent reports suggest that microglial cells are also significant source of apoE (Saura et al., 2003; Mori et al., 2004). Thus, both microglia and astrocytes are an abundant source of apoE in the CNS (Pitas et al., 1987; LaDu et al., 1998).

## 2.6. Aβ Degrading Enzymes

The current knowledge of Aβ degradation biology is limited since only a few of the molecules involved have been characterized, namely insulin degrading enzyme (IDE) and neprilysin, which is also known as enkephalinase, and neutral endopeptidase metalloendopeptidase (NEP) (Yamin et al., 1999; Iwata et al., 2000; Selkoe et al., 2001). IDE was originally identified as a microglia-secreted Aβ degrading enzyme (Qiu et al., 1998), and is also found in neurons (Vekrellis et al., 2000). Neprilysin protein level is downregulated during aging, but is locally upregulated in activated astrocytes surrounding Aβ plaques in APP mice (Apelt et al., 2003). Thus the amount of IDE and neprilysine can be altered by chronic inflammatory reaction. Neprilysin, a neutral zinc metallopeptidase, plays a role in degrading insoluble and/or aggregated Aβ42 (Iwata et al., 2000; Selkoe et al., 2001). Transgenic expression of both IDE and neprilysin show inhibition of Aβ accumulation in

APP mice (Leissring et al., 2003). In addition, endothelin converting enzyme and matrix metalloprotease-2 and 3 are also new candidates of Aβ degrading enzymes (Choi et al., 2006; White et al., 2006).

## 2.7. Neurotoxicity and Death

### *2.7.1. Direct Aβ-Mediated Neurotoxicity*

It has been widely accepted that toxicity of Aβ requires aggregation of native Aβ monomers (Hardy and Higgins, 1992; Pike et al., 1993). Aβ (Aβ40 or Aβ42) self-assemble to form low-n oligomers (dimers-hexamers), protofibrils, and fibrils (Roher et al., 1996; Harper et al., 1997; Walsh et al., 1997; Lambert et al., 1998). Since intermediates can further associate into higher-ordered aggregates, it is difficult to determine the oligomerization state of Aβ that causes pathogenicity. Nonetheless, several groups succeeded in isolating spherical non-fibrillar assemblies of synthetic Aβ (Aβ-derived diffusible ligands; ADDLs and amylospheroid; ASPD) (Lambert et al., 1998; Hoshi et al., 2003). Both ADDL and ASPD induce neuronal cell death *in vitro* and block hippocampal long-term potentiation (LTP) *ex vivo* at nanomolar concentrations. Neuronal cell death was mediated by activation of protein kinases, such as fyn tyrosine kinase and GSK3β (Lambert et al., 1998; Hoshi et al., 2003). *In vivo* applications of Aβ oligomers potently inhibit rat hippocampal LTP and cognitive function (Walsh et al., 2002; Cleary et al., 2005).

Thus, although the cell surface binding molecule and its signaling are yet to be characterized, Aβ oligomers are a likely therapeutic target, and several anti-amyloidogenic compounds have recently been reported (De Felice et al., 2004).

### *2.7.2. Indirect Aβ-Mediated Neurotoxicity*

Aβ can also potentially mediate neurotoxicity by activating microglia and glia and hereby promoting their secretion of a variety of neurotoxic factors. Aβ and secreted β-amyloid precursor protein (sAPP)-induce microglial activation and neurotoxicity (Giulian and Baker, 1986; Meda et al., 1995; Barger and Harmon, 1997; Ikezu et al., 2003). Neurotoxicity can be mediated through secretion of neurotoxic agents such as FasL, tumor necrosis factor (TNF)-α, reactive oxygen species (ROS), proteases, excitatory amino acids, and nitric oxides. Excitatory amino acids (glutamate, quinolinic acid, D-serine, among others) activate N-methyl-D-aspartate (NMDA) receptors, which are significantly involved in microglial-mediated neurotoxicity (Piani et al., 1992; Giulian et al., 1994).

Indeed, both Aβ and sAPP activated microglia increase glutamate secretion (Barger and Basile, 2001; Ikezu et al., 2003). Glutamate and ROS can exacerbate each other's neurotoxic effects due to their relationships with the cystine/glutamate exchange system ($Xc^-$) antiporter. Aβ/sAPP-induced microglial activation leads to ROS production and glutathione consumption, that in turn promotes cystine import to regenerate glutathione and, as a consequence, increased glutamate is exported in exchange through the $Xc^-$ antiporter (Ikezu et al., 2003).

# 3. Neuroimmunological Mechanism of AD

Neuronal loss, edema, and recruited mononuclear phagocytes (moving from blood to brain), are all classical hallmarks of brain inflammation in AD (Arvin et al., 1996). Gliosis, characterized by activation, proliferation, and hypertrophy of astrocytes and microglia, is one important feature of neuroinflammation. Amyloid plaques contain a number of proteins including complement proteins and pro-inflammatory cytokines and chemokines. Many of these proteins are secreted by activated microglia and reactive astrocytes. Activated microglia integrate deeply into neuritic plaques and express major histocompatibility complex type II (MHC-II), a marker for microglial activation. MHC-II expression is significantly upregulated in AD brains (Rogers et al., 1988; Styren et al., 1990).

Neurotoxicity can be mediated through secretion of various factors, ROS, proteases, excitatory amino acids, and nitric oxides. Pro-inflammatory cytokines and chemokines can inhibit fibrillar Aβ phagocytosis by a murine microglial cell line (Koenigsknecht-Talboo and Landreth, 2005). Such T-cell-mediated cytokines also inhibit post-phagocytosis intracellular Aβ degradation in human monocyte-derived macrophages. Aβ-microglia interaction results in two outputs: phagocytosis and signaling for priming and activation. Aβ binding to a complex of cell surface proteins (including CD36, integrin-associated protein (CD47), and $\alpha_6\beta_1$-integrin) leads to src-like tyrosine kinase activation and ROS production (Bamberger et al., 2003). CD36 is necessary for full Aβ-induced mononuclear phagocyte activation and chemotaxis (El Khoury et al., 2003). These findings strongly suggest that Aβ aggregates activates microglia by its binding to specific cell surface molecules, which activates src-like tyrosine kinases and other signaling for Aβ clearance and neuroinflammation in AD brains.

## 3.1. Microglia-Mediated Aβ Clearance

Our current knowledge of Aβ clearance is limited compared to the more detailed understanding of Aβ synthesis and aggregation mechanisms. It is well known that Aβ stimulation enhances microglial phagocytosis, *in vitro* (Kopec and Carroll, 1998). The internalized Aβ in phagosomes initially migrate to acid hydrolase-containing late endosomes and lysosomal compartments, and then moves into perinuclear vesicles, that are morphologically similar to lysosomes, where it stays up to 20 days (Paresce et al., 1997). In addition to microglia, astrocytes also contribute to the uptake and removal of Aβ in a manner enhanced by a CC-type chemokine, CCL2 (Wyss-Coray et al., 2003).

Microglia constantly take-up Aβ via potential Aβ receptors, including scavenger receptor type A (SR-A), CD36, and receptor for advanced glycation end product (RAGE) (El Khoury et al., 1996; Yan et al., 1996; El Khoury et al., 2003). Although SR-A was characterized as a major receptor for microglial phagocytosis of Aβ (Paresce et al., 1996), APP mice deficient in SR-A show no difference in amyloid plaque formation or synaptic degeneration (Huang et al., 1999). This suggests that other scavenger receptors or Aβ-binding molecules, such as CD36, CD47, and $\alpha_6\beta_1$-integrin, can compensate for the deficiency of SR-A. On the other hand, RAGE seems to enhance Aβ deposition. APP mice deficient in RAGE exhibit reduced Aβ deposition (unpublished observations), which is consistant with enhanced Aβ deposition in mice over-expressing RAGE (Arancio et al., 2004). Pgp is another molecule involved in Aβ clearance. Disruption of Pgp, encoded by both multidrug resistance-1 α and β, exhibits enhanced Aβ deposition, suggesting its role in endothelial clearance of Aβ (Cirrito et al., 2005).

## 3.2. Glial Inflammation and Innate Immunity

Innate immune responses in AD are mediated by a large number of inflammatory proteins, such as complement factors, acute-phase proteins, pro-inflammatory cytokines, and chemokines (Akiyama et al., 2000; McGeer and McGeer, 2001). Upregulation of the complement system includes activation of both classical and alternative pathways and enhanced secretion of cytokines and chemokines including, but not limited to, IFN-γ, IL-1α/β, IL-6, IL-8, IL-12, TGF-β1/2, TNF-α, CD40L, CCL2 (MCP-1), CCL3 (MIP-1α), CCL4 (MIP-1β), S100-β (for review, see (Akiyama et al., 2000)). The interplay between Aβ aggregates, microglia and astrocytes results in secretion of proinflammatory cytokines that, in turn, may affect local APP expression in nearby neurons. This process results in local upregulation of Aβ and seeding of "new" Aβ deposits, which may therefore be a potential mechanism for the plaque accumulation typically seen in AD brains.

### *3.2.1 Cytokines*

#### 3.2.1.1. IL-1

IL-1 upregulation seems to occur early in Aβ plaque formation since it is associated with diffuse plaques and also found in young children with Down's syndrome (Griffin et al., 1989; Griffin et al., 1995). IL-1 induces S100β, an astrocyte-derived neurite promoting cytokine (Kligman and Marshak, 1985), and α1-antichymotripsin (Das and Potter, 1995). IL-1 up-regulates APP synthesis in primary astrocytes (Rogers et al., 1999), and Aβ production when co-stimulated with IFN-γ *in vitro* (Blasko et al., 2000).

#### 3.2.1.2. IFN-γ

IFN-γ is predominantly made by $CD4^+$ T cells and natural killer cells (Young and Hardy, 1995), but is also produced by macrophages (Fultz et al., 1993), astrocytes, and microglia (DeSimone et al., 1998). IFN-γ affects both Aβ production and neurotoxicity. IFN-γ, in conjunction with TNF-α, has been shown to enhance APP mRNA transcription and Aβ production (Blasko et al., 1999), and indirectly induce neuronal loss by stimulating release of NO from microglia (Chao et al., 1995). In the Tg2576 mouse model, astrocytes significantly upregulate IFN-γ mRNA *in vivo* (Abbas et al., 2002). We have recently found that transgenic APP mice (Tg2576) lacking IFN-γ receptor type I show marked reduction of Aβ deposition, microgliosis, astrogliosis, and astrocytic BACE expression (Yamamoto et al., 2007). Thus, IFN-γ plays an important role for AD pathogenesis.

### 3.2.1.3. IL-6

A pleiotropic cytokine, which and its receptor complex, IL-6R and gp130/CD130, are all upregulated in AD brains in a region-specific manner (Hampel et al., 2005). IL-6 immunoreactivity is co-localized with diffuse plaques but not with compact plaques (Hull et al., 1996), suggesting its role in diffuse plaque reaction rather than compact plaque formation. Astrocyte-derived IL-6 induces expression of complement component C3, and may be involved in complement cascade activation in AD (Barnum et al., 1996).

### 3.2.1.4. TGF-β1/2/3

TGF-β1/2/3 are expressed in the CNS and are involved in development, homeostatis, and repair (Finch et al., 1993). TGF-β1 has been detected in plaques (van der Wal et al., 1993) and is elevated in cerebrospinal fluid and serum in AD (Chao et al., 1994b; Chao et al., 1994a). TGF-β2 has also been detected in reactive astrocytes, microglia, and in tangle-bearing neurons in AD brains (Wyss-Coray et al., 2000). TGF-β1 transgenic mice show cerebrovascular amyloid deposition (Wyss-Coray et al., 1997). Over-expression of TGF-β1 in APP mice accelerates vascular amyloid deposition although plaque burden was reduced in brain tissue (Wyss-Coray et al., 2001), suggesting its role in clearing Aβ from brain parenchyma. Since TGF-β1 increases APP expression in astrocytes and microglia (Gray and Patel, 1993; Monning et al., 1994; Harris-White et al., 1998), it may also be in involved in TGF-β1 glial Aβ production.

### 3.2.1.5. TNF-α

TNF-α, a pleiotropic pro-inflammatory cytokine, has been extensively investigated in AD. TNF-α is predominantly expressed by activated microglia, and to a lesser extent, astrocytes and neurons (Meda et al., 1995; Botchkina et al., 1997; Bezzi et al., 2001; Williams et al., 2005). In AD, TNF-α is upregulated in cerebrospinal fluid (Tarkowski et al., 1999), serum (Fillit et al., 1991), and cortex (Tarkowski et al., 1999). The effect of TNF-α on neurons is different dependent on the neuronal preparation and perhaps species; it is neurotrophic to rat cortical, hippocampal, and septal neurons (Cheng et al., 1994; Barger and Harmon, 1997), while directly neurotoxic (or enhances glutamate neurotoxicity) to human cortical neurons (Chao and Hu, 1994; D'Souza et al., 1995; Williams et al., 2005). This discrepancy could be due to the diverse signaling of two distinctly different TNF-α receptors, type I (p55 TNFR-1) and type II (p75 TNFR-2) (Botchkina et al., 1997; Dziewulska and Mossakowski, 2003). TNFR-1, but not TNFR-2, contains an intracellular death domain, common to proteins in the TNF receptor family. TNFR-1 mediates both apoptosis and NF-κB-mediated cell survival (Wallach et al., 1999; Gupta and Gollapudi, 2005). Importantly, primary cultured hippocampal neurons derived from TNFR-1 null mice were resistant to Aβ-mediated neurotoxicity (Li et al., 2004). Thus, TNF-α-mediated neurotoxicity is bidirectional and the outcomes of TNF signaling depends distinctly on cell type and species.

Our recent study shows that TNF-α significantly enhance Aβ production in primary cultured neurons and astrocytes (Yamamoto et al., 2007). This is partly mediated through upregulation of BACE and subsequent β-processing of APP. Since BACE is also upregulated in neurons and astrocytes surrounding Aβ plaques in vivo, this strongly implicates that pro-inflammatory cytokines, such as TNF-α and IFN-γ, regulate Aβ production in brains. This is a new paradigm to understand the role of neuroinflammation in disease progression, and potential therapeutic target in the future.

#### 3.2.1.6. CD40L

CD40L belongs to the TNF family and one of the most important T-cell mediated cytokines. CD40, the receptor of CD40L, is upregulated by Aβ-stimulation of primary cultured microglia *in vitro* (Tan et al., 1999) and is found to be expressed in reactive microglia in AD patient brain tissue (Togo et al., 2000). Transgenic APP (Tg2576) mice deficient in CD40L show reduced Aβ deposition, astro/microgliosis, and hyperphosphorylation of tau (Tan et al., 2002). In addition, chronic treatment of APP/PS1 bigenic mice with neutralizing anti-CD40L antibody reduces Aβ deposition and causes a modest improvement in cognitive performance (Tan et al., 2002; Todd Roach et al., 2004), suggesting its therapeutic application for AD.

### *3.2.2. Chemokines*

#### 3.2.2.1. CCL2 (MCP-1)

CCL2 (MCP-1) is a member of the β chemokine subfamily and a candidate molecule for stimulating monocyte chemotaxis into the CNS (Charo et al., 1994). Activated astrocytes and cells of monocytic origin (such as microglia and macrophages) have been shown to express CCL2 in the brain (Calvo et al., 1996; Glabinski et al., 1996). CCL2 has been detected in senile plaques, reactive microglia and microvessels in AD brains (Ishizuka et al., 1997; Xia and Hyman, 1999; Grammas and Ovase, 2001), and is upregulated in cerebrospinal fluid and serum of AD cases and AD animal models (Sun et al., 2003; Galimberti et al., 2005; Janelsins et al., 2005). Over-expression of CCL2 resulted in increased diffuse plaque deposition, microglial accumulation, and apoE expression in APP mice (Yamamoto et al., 2005), accompanied by cognitive impairment (Yamamoto, M et al., unpublished observations). These results show that CCL2/CCR2 signaling is critical in mononuclear phagocyte accumulation and Aβ deposition in CNS.

#### 3.2.2.2. CXCR Family

A number of other chemokines and their receptors have been identified in AD. CXCR2 is a member of the CXC chemokines receptor family and is a receptor for multiple ligands, including CXCL1/2/3 (GROα/β/δ) (Zlotnik and Yoshie, 2000). Both CXCR2 and CXCL1 have been detected in AD brains. In particular, CXCR2 expression has been identified in dystrophic neurites of senile plaques (Xia et al., 1997). CXCR3, another CXC receptor family, and its ligand CXCL10 (IP-10) have been found in both cortical and subcortical neurons in normal and AD brains. CXCL10 was significantly upregulated in AD brain (Xia et al., 2000). In addition, expression of CC chomokine receptors, such as CCR3 and CCR5, and their ligands, CCL4 (MIP-1β) and CCL5 (RANTES), is also enhanced on reactive microglia in AD brain (Xia et al., 1998). Although the exact physiological functions of these molecules have yet to be characterized in the context of AD pathogenesis, modulation of such chemokine signaling might be beneficial to correct the detrimental imbalance of metabolic homeostasis and neuroinflammation in brain.

### 3.2.3. Toll-like Receptors

One of the most important recent findings in the effort to understand innate immunity has been the identification of Toll-like receptors (TLRs). TLRs define a major class of pattern-recognition receptors critical to the initiation and tailoring of both innate and subsequent adaptive immune responses (Beutler, 2004; Iwasaki and Medzhitov, 2004). For example, bacterial cell wall components are recognized by TLR2, and lipopolysaccharide and viral envelope proteins are recognized by TLR4. Double strand RNA, single strand RNA, and unmethylated CpGs are recognized by TLR3, TLR7/8, and TLR9, respectively (for review, see (Akira et al., 2006)). Primary cultured human and mouse microglia express mRNA for TLR1-9, whereas human and mouse astrocytes express high levels of TLR3, and low-level TLR 1, 2, and 4-6(Olson and Miller, 2004; Jack et al., 2005) (Carpentier et al., 2005; McKimmie and Fazakerley, 2005).

The role of TLRs in neuroinflammation during AD is poorly characterized. However, recent reports indicate that TLR9 ligand (CpG-containing oligonucleotide) induced enhancement of Aβ updake by N9 microglia cell line (Iribarren et al., 2005), and Aβ stimulation modulates TLR-specific inflammation (NO and TFN-α release) in primary cultured mouse microglia (Lotz et al., 2005). These results suggest that there is crosstalk between Aβ and TLR signaling that may regulate glial inflammation and Aβ clearance in CNS.

### 3.2.4. Matrix Metalloprotease

Aβ stimulation induces robust expression of matrix metalloprotease (MMP) 1, 3, 10, 10, 12, 19, and disintegrin and metalloprotease (ADAM) 8 in primary cultured human microglia (Walker et al., 2005). Increased expression of MMP 1, 3 and 9 has been documented in AD brains (Backstrom et al., 1996; Leake et al., 2000; Yoshiyama et al., 2000) and may contribute to tissue damage (Cuzner and Opdenakker, 1999). These molecules may be involved in Aβ degradation, cytokine/chemokine processing, and shedding of cell adhesion molecules for enhancing glial motility.

### 3.2.5. Other Inflammatory Molecules: Complements and CD45

Complement C1q, the first complement of the classical complement pathway, is upregulated in AD brains and is found in senile plaques (Afagh et al., 1996). C1q binds to soluble Aβ and modulates its uptake by mononuclear phagocytes (Webster et al., 2000). C1q also directly induces neurotoxicity through its interaction with cell surface calreticulin, a C1q receptor (Luo et al., 2003). However, APP mice lacking C1q exhibited reduced glial and astroglial activation without changes in Aβ deposition (Fonseca et al., 2004a). Thus, C1q may be involved in AD pathogenesis by influencing neurotoxicity and glial inflammation, but its effect on Aβ metabolism is modest.

Complement C3 is upregulated in APP/TGF-β1 bigenic mice and AD brains (Wyss-Coray et al., 2001). Over-expression of soluble complement receptor-related protein y (sCrry), a complement C3 inhibitor, resulted in enhanced Aβ accumulation and hippocampal degeneration (Wyss-Coray et al., 2002). Since C3 is known to promote phagocytosis by binding to specific C3 receptor on specialized cells, C3 is likely to be positively involved in Aβ clearance.

CD45, a transmembrane protein tyrosine phosphatase critically involved in negative regulation of T- and B-cell activation, and an antagonizing partner of the TNF superfamily (Tan et al., 2000a), is also upregulated in AD brains (Masliah et al., 1991). APP mice deficient in CD45 have increased brain levels of TNF-α and NO, suggesting CD45 negative regulation of neuroinflammation in AD (Tan et al., 2000b).

## 3.3. Oxygen Free Radicals

Production of ROS, factors involved in the aging process (Finkel and Holbrook, 2000), is elevated in AD brain and may be an important cause of AD (Martins et al., 1986). Elevated levels of oxidized lipids (lipid peroxidation, malondialdehyde, 4-hydroxynonenal) (Markesbery and Carney, 1999), proteins (advanced glycation end product modifications, tyrosine nitration) (Good et al., 1996; Takeda et al., 1998), and nucleic acids (8-hydroxy-deoxyguanosine) have been documented in AD brains (Lyras et al., 1997). Mitochondria and nicotinamide adenine dinucleotide phosphate (NADPH) oxidase complex dysfunction can generate large amounts of ROS (Beal, 1998), and down regulation of mitochondrial NADPH 15-kD gene have been found in AD cases (Beal, 1998; Manczak et al., 2004). Markers of oxidative stress are elevated not only in the pathologic lesions in AD brain (Good et al., 1996), but also in cerebrospinal fluid of AD patients (Lovell et al., 1997). Aβ peptide can directly activate NADPH oxidase complex of mononuclear phagocytes (Bianca et al., 1999). ROS is also known to mediate Aβ-induced neurotoxicity (Behl et al., 1994; Ikezu et al., 2003). In addition to NADPH oxidase, myeloperoxidase (MPO) is expressed by microglia in close proximity to Aβ plaques, and surprisingly, in neurons of AD brains (Reynolds et al., 1999; Green et al., 2004). MPO can catalyze both apoE and Aβ, generating oxidated and fragmentated apoE (Jolivalt et al., 1996) and stable Aβ42 dimers through dityrosine bridge formation (Jolivalt et al., 1996; Galeazzi et al., 1999).

### *3.3.1. Oxidative DNA Damage*

DNA damage may also have a role in AD pathology. Recent studies indicate that aging-mediated DNA damage, including alterations in neuronal network and cognitive function-related gene expression profiles, is significantly increased after 40 years of age, (Lu et al., 2004). DNA damage induces cell cycle activation (Kruman et al., 2004), and cell cycle activation has been documented in AD brains (Nagy et al., 1998; Smith et al., 1999). DNA damage also potently induces p53, a tumor suppressor and transcriptional factor involved in neuronal apoptosis (Morrison et al., 2003; Kruman et al., 2004; Culmsee and Mattson, 2005). Neuronal expression of p53 is increased in AD brains (de la Monte et al., 1997) and in APP mouse brains (LaFerla et al., 1996). These data suggest that DNA damage is involved in neurodegeneration in AD brain, or the result of neurodegeneration.

# 4. Therapeutics Inventions

Epidemiological studies using non-steroidal anti-inflammatory drugs (NSAIDs) have led to the proposal that NSAIDs reduce the risk of AD (McGeer et al., 1996). These studies have been supported by data showing that treatment of APP mice with NSAIDs (such as ibuprofen and NO-flurbiprofen) *in vivo* results in reduced Aβ deposition and pro-inflammatory cytokine production (Lim et al., 2000; Jantzen et al., 2002; Yan et al., 2003). Microglial activation is suppressed by ibuprofen but rather enhanced by NO-flurbiprofen. Other studies have found that NSAID also affects γ-processing of APP through inhibition of the small GTP-binding protein Rho, which shifts Aβ processing from Aβ42 to Aβ40 both *in vitro* and *in vivo* (Weggen et al., 2001; Eriksen et al., 2003; Zhou et al., 2003). Based on these observations, a new series of drugs derived from NSAIDs having a more specific effect on γ-processing has been developed (Kukar et al., 2005).

Proliferator-activated receptor γ (PPARγ) agonists, such as the thiazolinedione family, are also NSAIDs and can efficiently clear Aβ deposition *in vitro* and *in vivo* (Camacho et al., 2004; Heneka et al., 2005). PPAR is a nuclear transcription factor and its effect is different from ibuprofen and its derivatives. PPARγ transcription factors play important physiological roles in the regulation of lipid metabolism (Mangelsdorf et al., 1995; Lemberger et al., 1996), suppression of inflammation (Heneka et al., 2000), and clinical treatment of diabetes type II (Dormandy et al., 2005). PPARγ agonists enhance Aβ degradation (Camacho et al., 2004), as well as suppress BACE expression and microglial activation (Heneka et al., 2005).

Other anti-inflammatory/anti-oxidant dietary applications include curcumin, the yellow pigment in turmeric that targets multiple AD pathogenic cascades (Lim et al., 2001; Yang et al., 2005). The dietary omega-3 fatty acid, docosahexaenoic acid (DHA), also reduced amyloid, oxidative damage and synaptic and cognitive deficits in a transgenic mouse model (Calon et al., 2004; Lim et al., 2005). Both DHA and curcumin have favorable safety profiles, epidemiology and efficacy, and may exert general anti-aging benefits (Cole et al., 2005).

# Summary

AD is the most common form of elderly dementia and has no effective therapy. Pathological diagnosis is based on post-mortem neuropathology, defined by three hallmarks: senile plaque, NFT, and neuronal cell loss. Aβ is produced during the processing of APP by BACE and the γ-secretase complex that includes PS1. Both APP and PS1 are causative genes of AD, while apoE4 is a risk factor allele. The Aβ load in CNS is maintained by balancing its production and clearance, which is mediated by passive diffusion to blood stream, degradation by Aβ degrading enzymes (IDE and neprilysin), and microglial phagocytosis. Aβ production, deposition, and neurodegeneration are significantly regulated by astroglial and microglial activation via direct contact as well as secretion of a number of neurotoxicants. Specific pro-inflammatory cytokines, chemokines, and excitotoxins have been characterized as mediators of neuroinflammation and neurotoxicity. Pro-inflammatory cytokines, especially TNF-α and IFN-γ, are significantly involved in BACE expression and Aβ prodution from neurons and astrocytes. Those diverse studies are generating a large number of potential therapeutic targets for treating AD. Beneficial effects have been reported for anti-inflammatory drugs, such as NSAIDs, to treat glial inflammation and disease progression.

# References


Abbas N, Bednar I, Mix E, Marie S, Paterson D, Ljungberg A, Morris C, Winblad B, Nordberg A, Zhu J (2002) Up-regulation of the inflammatory cytokines IFN-gamma and IL-12 and down-regulation of IL-4 in cerebral cortex regions of APP(SWE) transgenic mice. *J. Neuroimmunol.* 126:50-57.

Afagh A, Cummings BJ, Cribbs DH, Cotman CW, Tenner AJ (1996) Localization and cell association of C1q in Alzheimer's disease brain. *Exp. Neurol.* 138:22-32.

Akira S, Uematsu S, Takeuchi O (2006) Pathogen recognition and innate immunity. *Cell* 124:783-801.

Akiyama H, Barger S, Barnum S, Bradt B, Bauer J, Cole GM, Cooper NR, Eikelenboom P, Emmerling M, Fiebich BL, Finch CE, Frautschy S, Griffin WS, Hampel H, Hull M, Landreth G, Lue L, Mrak R, Mackenzie IR, McGeer PL, O'Banion MK, Pachter J, Pasinetti G, Plata-Salaman C, Rogers J, Rydel R, Shen Y, Streit W, Strohmeyer R, Tooyoma I, Van Muiswinkel FL, Veerhuis R, Walker D, Webster S, Wegrzyniak B, Wenk G, Wyss-Coray T (2000) Inflammation and Alzheimer's disease. *Neurobiol. Aging.* 21:383-421.

Alzheimer A (1907) Ueber eine eigenartige Erkrankung der Hirnrinde. *Allg. Z Psychiat.* 64:146-148.

Apelt J, Schliebs R (2001) Beta-amyloid-induced glial expression of both pro- and anti-inflammatory cytokines in cerebral cortex of aged transgenic Tg2576 mice with Alzheimer plaque pathology. *Brain Res.* 894:21-30.

Apelt J, Ach K, Schliebs R (2003) Aging-related down-regulation of neprilysin, a putative beta-amyloid-degrading enzyme, in transgenic Tg2576 Alzheimer-like mouse brain is accompanied by an astroglial upregulation in the vicinity of beta-amyloid plaques. *Neurosci. Lett.* 339:183-186.

Arancio O, Zhang HP, Chen X, Lin C, Trinchese F, Puzzo D, Liu S, Hegde A, Yan SF, Stern A, Luddy JS, Lue LF, Walker DG, Roher A, Buttini M, Mucke L, Li W, Schmidt AM, Kindy M, Hyslop PA, Stern DM, Du Yan SS (2004) RAGE potentiates Abeta-induced perturbation of neuronal function in transgenic mice. *Embo. J.* 23:4096-4105.

Arends YM, Duyckaerts C, Rozemuller JM, Eikelenboom P, Hauw JJ (2000) Microglia, amyloid and dementia in alzheimer disease. A correlative study. *Neurobiol. Aging.* 21:39-47.

Arvin B, Neville LF, Barone FC, Fewerstein GZ (1996) The Role of inflammation and cytokines in brain injury. *Neurosci. Biobehav. Rev.* 20:445-452.

Asai M, Hattori C, Szabo B, Sasagawa N, Maruyama K, Tanuma S, Ishiura S (2003) Putative function of ADAM9, ADAM10, and ADAM17 as APP alpha-secretase. *Biochem. Biophys. Res. Commun.* 301:231-235.

Backstrom JR, Lim GP, Cullen MJ, Tokes ZA (1996) Matrix metalloproteinase-9 (MMP-9) is synthesized in neurons of the human hippocampus and is capable of degrading the amyloid-beta peptide (1-40). *J. Neurosci.* 16:7910-7919.

Bales KR, Verina T, Cummins DJ, Du Y, Dodel RC, Saura J, Fishman CE, DeLong CA, Piccardo P, Petegnief V, Ghetti B, Paul SM (1999) Apolipoprotein E is essential for amyloid deposition in the APP(V717F) transgenic mouse model of Alzheimer's disease. *Proc. Natl. Acad. Sci. USA* 96:15233-15238.

Bamberger ME, Harris ME, McDonald DR, Husemann J, Landreth GE (2003) A cell surface receptor complex for fibrillar beta-amyloid mediates microglial activation. *J. Neurosci.* 23:2665-2674.

Barger S, Harmon A (1997) Microglial activation by Alzheimer amyloid precursor protein and modulation by apolipoprotein E. *Nature* 388:878-881.

Barger SW, Basile AS (2001) Activation of microglia by secreted amyloid precursor protein evokes release of glutamate by cystine exchange and attenuates synaptic function. *J. Neurochem.* 76:846-854.

Barnum SR, Jones JL, Muller-Ladner U, Samimi A, Campbell IL (1996) Chronic complement C3 gene expression in the CNS of transgenic mice with astrocyte-targeted interleukin-6 expression. *Glia* 18:107-117.

Beal MF (1998) Mitochondrial dysfunction in neurodegenerative diseases. *Biochim. Biophys. Acta.* 1366:211-223.

Behl C, Davis JB, Lesley R, Schubert D (1994) Hydrogen peroxide mediates amyloid beta protein toxicity. *Cell* 77:817-827.

Benzing WC, Wujek JR, Ward EK, Shaffer D, Ashe KH, Younkin SG, Brunden KR (1999) Evidence for glial-mediated inflammation in aged APP(SW) transgenic mice. *Neurobiol. Aging.* 20:581-589.

Berg L, McKeel DW, Jr., Miller JP, Baty J, Morris JC (1993) Neuropathological indexes of Alzheimer's disease in demented and nondemented persons aged 80 years and older. *Arch. Neurol.* 50:349-358.

Beutler B (2004) Inferences, questions and possibilities in Toll-like receptor signalling. *Nature* 430:257-263.

Bezzi P, Domercq M, Brambilla L, Galli R, Schols D, De Clercq E, Vescovi A, Bagetta G, Kollias G, Meldolesi J, Volterra A (2001) CXCR4-activated astrocyte glutamate release via TNFalpha: amplification by microglia triggers neurotoxicity. *Nat. Neurosci.* 4:702-710.

Bianca VD, Dusi S, Bianchini E, Dal Pra I, Rossi F (1999) beta-amyloid activates the O-2 forming NADPH oxidase in microglia, monocytes, and neutrophils. A possible inflammatory mechanism of neuronal damage in Alzheimer's disease. *J. Biol. Chem.* 274:15493-15499.

Blasko I, Marx F, Steiner E, Hartmann T, Grubeck-Loebenstein B (1999) TNFalpha plus IFNgamma induce the production of Alzheimer beta-amyloid peptides and decrease the secretion of APPs. *Faseb J.* 13:63-68.

Blasko I, Veerhuis R, Stampfer-Kountchev M, Saurwein-Teissl M, Eikelenboom P, Grubeck-Loebenstein B (2000) Costimulatory effects of interferon-gamma and interleukin-1beta or tumor necrosis factor alpha on the synthesis of Abeta1-40 and Abeta1-42 by human astrocytes. *Neurobiol. Dis.* 7:682-689.

Borchelt DR, Ratovitski T, van Lare J, Lee MK, Gonzales V, Jenkins NA, Copeland NG, Price DL, Sisodia SS (1997) Accelerated amyloid deposition in the brains of transgenic mice coexpressing mutant presenilin 1 and amyloid precursor proteins. *Neuron* 19:939-945.

Botchkina GI, Meistrell ME, 3rd, Botchkina IL, Tracey KJ (1997) Expression of TNF and TNF receptors (p55 and p75) in the rat brain after focal cerebral ischemia. *Mol. Med.* 3:765-781.

Braak H, Braak E (1995) Staging of Alzheimer's disease-related neurofibrillary changes. *Neurobiol. Aging.* 16:271-278; discussion 278-284.

Calon F, Lim GP, Yang F, Morihara T, Teter B, Ubeda O, Rostaing P, Triller A, Salem N, Jr., Ashe KH, Frautschy SA, Cole GM (2004) Docosahexaenoic acid protects from dendritic pathology in an Alzheimer's disease mouse model. *Neuron* 43:633-645.

Calvo CF, Yoshimura T, Gelman M, Mallat M (1996) Production of monocyte chemotactic protein-1 by rat brain macrophages. *Eur. J. Neurosci.* 8:1725-1734.

Camacho IE, Serneels L, Spittaels K, Merchiers P, Dominguez D, De Strooper B (2004) Peroxisome-proliferator-activated receptor gamma induces a clearance mechanism for the amyloid-beta peptide. *J. Neurosci.* 24:10908-10917.

Carpentier PA, Begolka WS, Olson JK, Elhofy A, Karpus WJ, Miller SD (2005) Differential activation of astrocytes by innate and adaptive immune stimuli. *Glia* 49:360-374.

Chao C, Hu S, Erlich L, Peterson P (1995) Interleukin-1 and tumor necrosis factor-alpha synergistically mediate neurotoxicity: involvement of nitric oxide and of N-methyl-D-aspartate receptors. *Brain Behav. Immun.* 9:355-365.

Chao CC, Hu S (1994) Tumor necrosis factor-alpha potentiates glutamate neurotoxicity in human fetal brain cell cultures. *Dev. Neurosci.* 16:172-179.

Chao CC, Hu S, Frey WH, 2nd, Ala TA, Tourtellotte WW, Peterson PK (1994a) Transforming growth factor beta in Alzheimer's disease. *Clin. Diagn. Lab. Immunol.* 1:109-110.

Chao CC, Ala TA, Hu S, Crossley KB, Sherman RE, Peterson PK, Frey WH, 2nd (1994b) Serum cytokine levels in patients with Alzheimer's disease. *Clin. Diagn. Lab. Immunol.* 1:433-436.

Charo IF, Myers SJ, Herman A, Franci C, Connolly AJ, Coughlin SR (1994) Molecular cloning and functional expression of two monocyte chemoattractant protein 1 receptors reveals alternative splicing of the carboxyl-terminal tails. *Proc. Natl. Acad. Sci. USA* 91:2752-2756.

Cheng B, Christakos S, Mattson MP (1994) Tumor necrosis factors protect neurons against metabolic-excitotoxic insults and promote maintenance of calcium homeostasis. *Neuron* 12:139-153.

Chishti MA, Yang DS, Janus C, Phinney AL, Horne P, Pearson J, Strome R, Zuker N, Loukides J, French J, Turner S, Lozza G, Grilli M, Kunicki S, Morissette C, Paquette J, Gervais F, Bergeron C, Fraser PE, Carlson GA, George-Hyslop PS, Westaway D (2001) Early-onset amyloid deposition and cognitive deficits in transgenic mice expressing a double mutant form of amyloid precursor protein 695. *J. Biol. Chem.* 276:21562-21570.

Choi DS, Wang D, Yu GQ, Zhu G, Kharazia VN, Paredes JP, Chang WS, Deitchman JK, Mucke L, Messing RO (2006) PKC{varepsilon} increases endothelin converting enzyme activity and reduces amyloid plaque pathology in transgenic mice. *Proc. Natl. Acad. Sci. U S A.*

Cirrito JR, Deane R, Fagan AM, Spinner ML, Parsadanian M, Finn MB, Jiang H, Prior JL, Sagare A, Bales KR, Paul SM, Zlokovic BV, Piwnica-Worms D, Holtzman DM (2005) P-glycoprotein deficiency at the blood-brain barrier increases amyloid-beta deposition in an Alzheimer disease mouse model. *J. Clin. Invest.* 115:3285-3290.

Cleary JP, Walsh DM, Hofmeister JJ, Shankar GM, Kuskowski MA, Selkoe DJ, Ashe KH (2005) Natural oligomers of the amyloid-beta protein specifically disrupt cognitive function. *Nat. Neurosci.* 8:79-84.

Cole GM, Lim GP, Yang F, Teter B, Begum A, Ma Q, Harris-White ME, Frautschy SA (2005) Prevention of Alzheimer's disease: Omega-3 fatty acid and phenolic anti-oxidant interventions. *Neurobiol. Aging.* 26:133-136.

Corey-Bloom J, Galasko D, Thal LJ (1994) Clinical features and natural history of Alzheimer's disease. Philadelphia: WB Saunders.

Culmsee C, Mattson MP (2005) p53 in neuronal apoptosis. *Biochem. Biophys. Res. Commun.* 331:761-777.

Cuzner ML, Opdenakker G (1999) Plasminogen activators and matrix metalloproteases, mediators of extracellular proteolysis in inflammatory demyelination of the central nervous system. *J. Neuroimmunol.* 94:1-14.

D'Souza S, Alinauskas K, McCrea E, Goodyer C, Antel JP (1995) Differential susceptibility of human CNS-derived cell populations to TNF-dependent and independent immune-mediated injury. *J. Neurosci.* 15:7293-7300.

Danik M, Chabot JG, Michel D, Quirion R, eds (1999) *Clusterin and apolipoprotein E gene expression in the adult brain.* Austin: RG Landes Company.

Das S, Potter H (1995) Expression of the Alzheimer amyloid-promoting factor antichymotrypsin is induced in human astrocytes by IL-1. *Neuron* 14:447-456.

De Felice FG, Vieira MN, Saraiva LM, Figueroa-Villar JD, Garcia-Abreu J, Liu R, Chang L, Klein WL, Ferreira ST (2004) Targeting the neurotoxic species in Alzheimer's disease: inhibitors of Abeta oligomerization. *Faseb J.* 18:1366-1372.

de la Monte SM, Sohn YK, Wands JR (1997) Correlates of p53- and Fas (CD95)-mediated apoptosis in Alzheimer's disease. *J. Neurol. Sci.* 152:73-83.

De Strooper B (2003) Aph-1, Pen-2, and Nicastrin with Presenilin Generate an Active gamma-Secretase Complex. *Neuron* 38:9-12.

DeSimone R, Levi G, Aloisi F (1998) Interferon-gamma gene expresion in rat central nervous system glial cells. *Cytokine* 10:418-422.

Dormandy JA, Charbonnel B, Eckland DJ, Erdmann E, Massi-Benedetti M, Moules IK, Skene AM, Tan MH, Lefebvre PJ, Murray GD, Standl E, Wilcox RG, Wilhelmsen L, Betteridge J, Birkeland K, Golay A, Heine RJ, Koranyi L, Laakso M, Mokan M, Norkus A, Pirags V, Podar T, Scheen A, Scherbaum W, Schernthaner G, Schmitz O, Skrha J, Smith U, Taton J (2005) Secondary prevention of macrovascular events in patients with type 2 diabetes in the PROactive Study (PROspective pioglitAzone Clinical Trial In macroVascular Events): a randomised controlled trial. *Lancet* 366:1279-1289.

Duff K, Eckman C, Zehr C, Yu X, Prada CM, Perez-tur J, Hutton M, Buee L, Harigaya Y, Yager D, Morgan D, Gordon MN, Holcomb L, Refolo L, Zenk B, Hardy J, Younkin S (1996) Increased amyloid-beta42(43) in brains of mice expressing mutant presenilin 1. *Nature* 383:710-713.

Dziewulska D, Mossakowski MJ (2003) Cellular expression of tumor necrosis factor a and its receptors in human ischemic stroke. *Clin. Neuropathol.* 22:35-40.

Eikelenboom P, Zhan SS, van Gool WA, Allsop D (1994) Inflammatory mechanisms in Alzheimer's disease. *Trends Pharmacol. Sci.* 15:447-450.

Eikelenboom P, Bate C, Van Gool WA, Hoozemans JJ, Rozemuller JM, Veerhuis R, Williams A (2002) Neuroinflammation in Alzheimer's disease and prion disease. *Glia* 40:232-239.

El Khoury J, Hickman SE, Thomas CA, Cao L, Silverstein SC, Loike JD (1996) Scavenger receptor-mediated adhesion of microglia to beta-amyloid fibrils. *Nature* 382:716-719.

El Khoury JB, Moore KJ, Means TK, Leung J, Terada K, Toft M, Freeman MW, Luster AD (2003) CD36 mediates the innate host response to beta-amyloid. *J. Exp. Med.* 197:1657-1666.

Eriksen JL, Sagi SA, Smith TE, Weggen S, Das P, McLendon DC, Ozols VV, Jessing KW, Zavitz KH, Koo EH, Golde TE (2003) NSAIDs and enantiomers of flurbiprofen target gamma-secretase and lower Abeta 42 in vivo. *J. Clin. Invest.* 112:440-449.

Ewbank DC (1999) Deaths attributable to Alzheimer's disease in the United States. *Am. J. Public. Health* 89:90-92.

Fagan AM, Watson M, Parsadanian M, Bales KR, Paul SM, Holtzman DM (2002) Human and murine ApoE markedly alters A beta metabolism before and after plaque formation in a mouse model of Alzheimer's disease. *Neurobiol. Dis.* 9:305-318.

Fillit H, Ding WH, Buee L, Kalman J, Altstiel L, Lawlor B, Wolf-Klein G (1991) Elevated circulating tumor necrosis factor levels in Alzheimer's disease. *Neurosci. Lett.* 129:318-320.

Finch CE, Laping NJ, Morgan TE, Nichols NR, Pasinetti GM (1993) TGF-beta 1 is an organizer of responses to neurodegeneration. *J. Cell Biochem.* 53:314-322.

Finkel T, Holbrook NJ (2000) Oxidants, oxidative stress and the biology of ageing. *Nature* 408:239-247.

Fonseca MI, Zhou J, Botto M, Tenner AJ (2004a) Absence of C1q leads to less neuropathology in transgenic mouse models of Alzheimer's disease. *J. Neurosci.* 24:6457-6465.

Fonseca MI, Kawas CH, Troncoso JC, Tenner AJ (2004b) Neuronal localization of C1q in preclinical Alzheimer's disease. *Neurobiol. Dis.* 15:40-46.

Frautschy SA, Yang F, Irrizarry M, Hyman B, Saido TC, Hsaio K, Cole GM (1998) Microglial Response to Amyloid Plaques in APPsw Transgenic Mice. *Am. J. Pathol.* 152:307-317.

Fultz M, Barber S, Dieffenbach C, Vogel S (1993) Induction of IFN-$\gamma$ in macrophages by lipopolysaccharide. *Int. Immunol.* 5:1383-1392.

Galeazzi L, Ronchi P, Franceschi C, Giunta S (1999) In vitro peroxidase oxidation induces stable dimers of beta-amyloid (1-42) through dityrosine bridge formation. *Amyloid* 6:7-13.

Galimberti D, Fenoglio C, Lovati C, Venturelli E, Guidi I, Corra B, Scalabrini D, Clerici F, Mariani C, Bresolin N, Scarpini E (2005) Serum MCP-1 levels are increased in mild cognitive impairment and mild Alzheimer's disease. *Neurobiol. Aging.*

Games D, Adams D, Alessandrini R, Barbour R, Berthelette P, Blackwell C, Carr T, Clemens J, Donaldson T, Gillespie F, et al. (1995) Alzheimer-type neuropathology in transgenic mice overexpressing V717F beta-amyloid precursor protein. *Nature* 373:523-527.

Giulian D, Baker TJ (1986) Characterization of ameboid microglia isolated from developing mammalian brain. *J. Neurosci.* 6:2163-2178.

Giulian D, Li J, Leara B, Keenen C (1994) Phagocytic microglia release cytokines and cytotoxins that regulate the survival of astrocytes and neurons in culture. *Neurochem. Int.* 25:227-233.

Glabinski AR, Balasingam V, Tani M, Kunkel SL, Strieter RM, Yong VW, Ransohoff RM (1996) Chemokine monocyte chemoattractant protein-1 is expressed by astrocytes after mechanical injury to the brain. *J. Immunol.* 156:4363-4368.

Good PF, Werner P, Hsu A, Olanow CW, Perl DP (1996) Evidence of neuronal oxidative damage in Alzheimer's disease. *Am. J. Pathol.* 149:21-28.

Grammas P, Ovase R (2001) Inflammatory factors are elevated in brain microvessels in Alzheimer's disease. *Neurobiol. Aging.* 22:837-842.

Gray CW, Patel AJ (1993) Regulation of beta-amyloid precursor protein isoform mRNAs by transforming growth factor-beta 1 and interleukin-1 beta in astrocytes. *Brain Res. Mol. Brain Res.* 19:251-256.

Green PS, Mendez AJ, Jacob JS, Crowley JR, Growdon W, Hyman BT, Heinecke JW (2004) Neuronal expression of myeloperoxidase is increased in Alzheimer's disease. *J. Neurochem.* 90:724-733.

Griffin W, Sheng J, Roberts G, Mrak R (1995) Interleukin-1 expression in different plaque types in Alzheimer's diseases: Significance in plaque evolution. *J. Neuropathol. Exp. Neurol.* 54:276-281.

Griffin WS, Stanley LC, Ling C, White L, MacLeod V, Perrot LJ, White CL, 3rd, Araoz C (1989) Brain interleukin 1 and S-100 immunoreactivity are elevated in Down syndrome and Alzheimer disease. *Proc. Natl. Acad. Sci. USA* 86:7611-7615.

Gupta S, Gollapudi S (2005) Molecular mechanisms of TNF-alpha-induced apoptosis in aging human T cell subsets. *Int. J. Biochem. Cell Biol.* 37:1034-1042.

Hampel H, Haslinger A, Scheloske M, Padberg F, Fischer P, Unger J, Teipel SJ, Neumann M, Rosenberg C, Oshida R, Hulette C, Pongratz D, Ewers M, Kretzschmar HA, Moller HJ (2005) Pattern of interleukin-6 receptor complex immunoreactivity between cortical regions of rapid autopsy normal and Alzheimer's disease brain. *Eur. Arch. Psychiatry Clin. Neurosci.* 255:269-278.

Hardy JA, Higgins GA (1992) Alzheimer's disease: the amyloid cascade hypothesis. *Science* 256:184-185.

Harper JD, Wong SS, Lieber CM, Lansbury PT (1997) Observation of metastable Abeta amyloid protofibrils by atomic force microscopy. *Chem. Biol.* 4:119-125.

Harris-White ME, Chu T, Balverde Z, Sigel JJ, Flanders KC, Frautschy SA (1998) Effects of transforming growth factor-beta (isoforms 1-3) on amyloid-beta deposition, inflammation, and cell targeting in organotypic hippocampal slice cultures. *J. Neurosci.* 18:10366-10374.

Heneka MT, Klockgether T, Feinstein DL (2000) Peroxisome proliferator-activated receptor-gamma ligands reduce neuronal inducible nitric oxide synthase expression and cell death in vivo. *J. Neurosci.* 20:6862-6867.

Heneka MT, Sastre M, Dumitrescu-Ozimek L, Hanke A, Dewachter I, Kuiperi C, O'Banion K, Klockgether T, Van Leuven F, Landreth GE (2005) Acute treatment with the PPARgamma agonist pioglitazone and ibuprofen reduces glial inflammation and Abeta1-42 levels in APPV717I transgenic mice. *Brain* 128:1442-1453.

Holcomb L, Gordon MN, McGowan E, Yu X, Benkovic S, Jantzen P, Wright K, Saad I, Mueller R, Morgan D, Sanders S, Zehr C, O'Campo K, Hardy J, Prada CM, Eckman C, Younkin S, Hsiao K, Duff K (1998) Accelerated Alzheimer-type phenotype in transgenic mice carrying both mutant amyloid precursor protein and presenilin 1 transgenes. *Nat. Med.* 4:97-100.

Holtzman DM, Bales KR, Wu S, Bhat P, Parsadanian M, Fagan AM, Chang LK, Sun Y, Paul SM (1999) Expression of human apolipoprotein E reduces amyloid-beta deposition in a mouse model of Alzheimer's disease. *J. Clin. Invest.* 103:R15-R21.

Holtzman DM, Bales KR, Tenkova T, Fagan AM, Parsadanian M, Sartorius LJ, Mackey B, Olney J, McKeel D, Wozniak D, Paul SM (2000) Apolipoprotein E isoform-dependent amyloid deposition and neuritic degeneration in a mouse model of Alzheimer's disease. *Proc. Natl. Acad. Sci. USA* 97:2892-2897.

Hoshi M, Sato M, Matsumoto S, Noguchi A, Yasutake K, Yoshida N, Sato K (2003) Spherical aggregates of beta-amyloid (amylospheroid) show high neurotoxicity and activate tau protein kinase I/glycogen synthase kinase-3beta. *Proc. Natl. Acad. Sci. USA* 100:6370-6375.

Hsiao K, Chapman P, Nilsen S, Eckman C, Harigaya Y, Younkin S, Yang F, Cole G (1996) Correlative memory deficits, Abeta elevation, and amyloid plaques in transgenic mice. *Science* 274:99-102.

Huang F, Buttini M, Wyss-Coray T, McConlogue L, Kodama T, Pitas RE, Mucke L (1999) Elimination of the class A scavenger receptor does not affect amyloid plaque formation or neurodegeneration in transgenic mice expressing human amyloid protein precursors. *Am. J. Pathol.* 155:1741-1747.

Hull M, Berger M, Volk B, Bauer J (1996) Occurrence of interleukin-6 in cortical plaques of Alzheimer's disease patients may precede transformation of diffuse into neuritic plaques. *Ann. NY Acad. Sci.* 777:205-212.

Ikezu T, Luo X, Weber GA, Zhao J, McCabe L, Buescher JL, Ghorpade A, Zheng J, Xiong H (2003) Amyloid precursor protein-processing products affect mononuclear phagocyte activation: pathways for sAPP- and Abeta-mediated neurotoxicity. *J. Neurochem.* 85:925-934.

in 't Veld BA, Launer LJ, Breteler MM, Hofman A, Stricker BH (2002) Pharmacologic agents associated with a preventive effect on Alzheimer's disease: a review of the epidemiologic evidence. *Epidemiol. Rev.* 24:248-268.

Iribarren P, Chen K, Hu J, Gong W, Cho EH, Lockett S, Uranchimeg B, Wang JM (2005) CpG-containing oligodeoxynucleotide promotes microglial cell uptake of amyloid beta

1-42 peptide by up-regulating the expression of the G-protein- coupled receptor mFPR2. *Faseb J.* 19:2032-2034.

Ishizuka K, Kimura T, Igata-yi R, Katsuragi S, Takamatsu J, Miyakawa T (1997) Identification of monocyte chemoattractant protein-1 in senile plaques and reactive microglia of Alzheimer's disease. *Psychiatry Clin. Neurosci.* 51:135-138.

Iwasaki A, Medzhitov R (2004) Toll-like receptor control of the adaptive immune responses. *Nat. Immunol.* 5:987-995.

Iwata N, Tsubuki S, Takaki Y, Watanabe K, Sekiguchi M, Hosoki E, Kawashima-Morishima M, Lee HJ, Hama E, Sekine-Aizawa Y, Saido TC (2000) Identification of the major Abeta1-42-degrading catabolic pathway in brain parenchyma: suppression leads to biochemical and pathological deposition. *Nat. Med.* 6:143-150.

Jack CS, Arbour N, Manusow J, Montgrain V, Blain M, McCrea E, Shapiro A, Antel JP (2005) TLR signaling tailors innate immune responses in human microglia and astrocytes. *J. Immunol.* 175:4320-4330.

Janelsins MC, Mastrangelo MA, Oddo S, LaFerla FM, Federoff HJ, Bowers WJ (2005) Early correlation of microglial activation with enhanced tumor necrosis factor-alpha and monocyte chemoattractant protein-1 expression specifically within the entorhinal cortex of triple transgenic Alzheimer's disease mice. *J. Neuroinflammation* 2:23.

Jantzen PT, Connor KE, DiCarlo G, Wenk GL, Wallace JL, Rojiani AM, Coppola D, Morgan D, Gordon MN (2002) Microglial activation and beta -amyloid deposit reduction caused by a nitric oxide-releasing nonsteroidal anti-inflammatory drug in amyloid precursor protein plus presenilin-1 transgenic mice. *J. Neurosci.* 22:2246-2254.

Jolivalt C, Leininger-Muller B, Drozdz R, Naskalski JW, Siest G (1996) Apolipoprotein E is highly susceptible to oxidation by myeloperoxidase, an enzyme present in the brain. *Neurosci. Lett.* 210:61-64.

Katzman R (2001) Epidemiology of Alzheimer's Disease and Dementia: Advances and Challenges. In: Alzheimer's Disease: Advances in Etiology, Pathogenesis, and Therapeutics (Iqbal K, Sisodia SS, Winblad B, eds), pp 11-21. West Sussex, UK: John Wiley and Sons Ltd.

Katzman R, Fox P (1999) The world wide impact of dementia in the next fifty years. In: Epidemiology of Alzheimer's Disease: From Gene to Prevention (Mayeux R, Christen Y, eds), pp 1-17. Berlin: *Springer*.

Kligman D, Marshak DR (1985) Purification and characterization of a neurite extension factor from bovine brain. *Proc. Natl. Acad. Sci. USA* 82:7136-7139.

Koenigsknecht-Talboo J, Landreth GE (2005) Microglial phagocytosis induced by fibrillar beta-amyloid and IgGs are differentially regulated by proinflammatory cytokines. *J. Neurosci.* 25:8240-8249.

Kopec KK, Carroll RT (1998) Alzheimer's beta-amyloid peptide 1-42 induces a phagocytic response in murine microglia. *J. Neurochem.* 71:2123-2131.

Kruman, II, Wersto RP, Cardozo-Pelaez F, Smilenov L, Chan SL, Chrest FJ, Emokpae R, Jr., Gorospe M, Mattson MP (2004) Cell cycle activation linked to neuronal cell death initiated by DNA damage. *Neuron* 41:549-561.

Kukar T, Murphy MP, Eriksen JL, Sagi SA, Weggen S, Smith TE, Ladd T, Khan MA, Kache R, Beard J, Dodson M, Merit S, Ozols VV, Anastasiadis PZ, Das P, Fauq A, Koo EH,

Golde TE (2005) Diverse compounds mimic Alzheimer disease-causing mutations by augmenting Abeta42 production. *Nat. Med.* 11:545-550.

LaDu MJ, Gilligan SM, Lukens JR, Cabana VG, Reardon CA, Van Eldik LJ, Holtzman DM (1998) Nascent astrocyte particles differ from lipoproteins in CSF. *J. Neurochem.* 70:2070-2081.

LaFerla FM, Hall CK, Ngo L, Jay G (1996) Extracellular deposition of beta-amyloid upon p53-dependent neuronal cell death in transgenic mice. *J. Clin. Invest.* 98:1626-1632.

Lambert MP, Barlow AK, Chromy BA, Edwards C, Freed R, Liosatos M, Morgan TE, Rozovsky I, Trommer B, Viola KL, Wals P, Zhang C, Finch CE, Krafft GA, Klein WL (1998) Diffusible, nonfibrillar ligands derived from Abeta1-42 are potent central nervous system neurotoxins. *Proc. Natl. Acad. Sci. USA* 95:6448-6453.

Leake A, Morris CM, Whateley J (2000) Brain matrix metalloproteinase 1 levels are elevated in Alzheimer's disease. *Neurosci. Lett.* 291:201-203.

Lee EB, Zhang B, Liu K, Greenbaum EA, Doms RW, Trojanowski JQ, Lee VM (2005) BACE overexpression alters the subcellular processing of APP and inhibits Abeta deposition in vivo. *J. Cell. Biol.* 168:291-302.

Leissring MA, Farris W, Chang AY, Walsh DM, Wu X, Sun X, Frosch MP, Selkoe DJ (2003) Enhanced proteolysis of beta-amyloid in APP transgenic mice prevents plaque formation, secondary pathology, and premature death. *Neuron* 40:1087-1093.

Lemberger T, Desvergne B, Wahli W (1996) Peroxisome proliferator-activated receptors: a nuclear receptor signaling pathway in lipid physiology. *Annu. Rev. Cell Dev. Biol.* 12:335-363.

Levy-Lahad E, Wasco W, Poorkaj P, Romano DM, Oshima J, Pettingell WH, Yu CE, Jondro PD, Schmidt SD, Wang K, et al. (1995) Candidate gene for the chromosome 1 familial Alzheimer's disease locus. Science 269:973-977.

Li R, Yang L, Lindholm K, Konishi Y, Yue X, Hampel H, Zhang D, Shen Y (2004) Tumor necrosis factor death receptor signaling cascade is required for amyloid-beta protein-induced neuron death. *J. Neurosci.* 24:1760-1771.

Lim GP, Chu T, Yang F, Beech W, Frautschy SA, Cole GM (2001) The curry spice curcumin reduces oxidative damage and amyloid pathology in an Alzheimer transgenic mouse. *J. Neurosci.* 21:8370-8377.

Lim GP, Calon F, Morihara T, Yang F, Teter B, Ubeda O, Salem N, Jr., Frautschy SA, Cole GM (2005) A diet enriched with the omega-3 fatty acid docosahexaenoic acid reduces amyloid burden in an aged Alzheimer mouse model. *J. Neurosci.* 25:3032-3040.

Lim GP, Yang F, Chu T, Chen P, Beech W, Teter B, Tran T, Ubeda O, Ashe KH, Frautschy SA, Cole GM (2000) Ibuprofen suppresses plaque pathology and inflammation in a mouse model for Alzheimer's disease. *J. Neurosci.* 20:5709-5714.

Lotz M, Ebert S, Esselmann H, Iliev AI, Prinz M, Wiazewicz N, Wiltfang J, Gerber J, Nau R (2005) Amyloid beta peptide 1-40 enhances the action of Toll-like receptor-2 and -4 agonists but antagonizes Toll-like receptor-9-induced inflammation in primary mouse microglial cell cultures. *J. Neurochem.* 94:289-298.

Lovell MA, Ehmann WD, Mattson MP, Markesbery WR (1997) Elevated 4-hydroxynonenal in ventricular fluid in Alzheimer's disease. *Neurobiol. Aging.* 18:457-461.

Lu T, Pan Y, Kao SY, Li C, Kohane I, Chan J, Yankner BA (2004) Gene regulation and DNA damage in the ageing human brain. *Nature* 429:883-891.

Luo X, Weber GA, Zheng J, Gendelman HE, Ikezu T (2003) C1q-calreticulin induced oxidative neurotoxicity: relevance for the neuropathogenesis of Alzheimer's disease. *J. Neuroimmunol.* 135:62-71.

Lyras L, Cairns NJ, Jenner A, Jenner P, Halliwell B (1997) An assessment of oxidative damage to proteins, lipids, and DNA in brain from patients with Alzheimer's disease. *J. Neurochem.* 68:2061-2069.

Manczak M, Park BS, Jung Y, Reddy PH (2004) Differential expression of oxidative phosphorylation genes in patients with Alzheimer's disease: implications for early mitochondrial dysfunction and oxidative damage. *Neuromolecular. Med.* 5:147-162.

Mangelsdorf DJ, Thummel C, Beato M, Herrlich P, Schutz G, Umesono K, Blumberg B, Kastner P, Mark M, Chambon P, Evans RM (1995) The nuclear receptor superfamily: the second decade. *Cell* 83:835-839.

Markesbery WR, Carney JM (1999) Oxidative alterations in Alzheimer's disease. *Brain Pathol.* 9:133-146.

Martins RN, Harper CG, Stokes GB, Masters CL (1986) Increased cerebral glucose-6-phosphate dehydrogenase activity in Alzheimer's disease may reflect oxidative stress. *J. Neurochem.* 46:1042-1045.

Masliah E, Mallory M, Hansen L, Alford M, Albright T, Terry R, Shapiro P, Sundsmo M, Saitoh T (1991) Immunoreactivity of CD45, a protein phosphotyrosine phosphatase, in Alzheimer's disease. *Acta. Neuropathol.* (Berl) 83:12-20.

Mastrangelo P, Mathews PM, Chishti MA, Schmidt SD, Gu Y, Yang J, Mazzella MJ, Coomaraswamy J, Horne P, Strome B, Pelly H, Levesque G, Ebeling C, Jiang Y, Nixon RA, Rozmahel R, Fraser PE, St George-Hyslop P, Carlson GA, Westaway D (2005) Dissociated phenotypes in presenilin transgenic mice define functionally distinct gamma-secretases. *Proc. Natl. Acad. Sci. USA* 102:8972-8977.

McGeer P, Schulzer M, McGeer E (1996) Arthritis and anti-inflammatory agents as possible protective factors for Alzheimer's disease: a review of 17 epidemiologic studies. *Neurology* 47:425-432.

McGeer PL, McGeer EG (2001) Inflammation, autotoxicity and Alzheimer disease. *Neurobiol. Aging.* 22:799-809.

McKimmie CS, Fazakerley JK (2005) In response to pathogens, glial cells dynamically and differentially regulate Toll-like receptor gene expression. *J. Neuroimmunol.* 169:116-125.

Meda L, Cassatella MA, Szendrei GI, Jr LO, Baron P, Villalba M, Ferrari D, Rossi F (1995) Activation of microglial cells by β–amyloid protein and interferon-γ. *Nature* 374:647-650.

Mohajeri MH, Saini KD, Nitsch RM (2004) Transgenic BACE expression in mouse neurons accelerates amyloid plaque pathology. *J. Neural. Transm.* 111:413-425.

Monning U, Sandbrink R, Banati RB, Masters CL, Beyreuther K (1994) Transforming growth factor beta mediates increase of mature transmembrane amyloid precursor protein in microglial cells. *FEBS Lett.* 342:267-272.

Mori K, Yokoyama A, Yang L, Maeda N, Mitsuda N, Tanaka J (2004) L-serine-mediated release of apolipoprotein E and lipids from microglial cells. Exp Neurol 185:220-231.

Morrison RS, Kinoshita Y, Johnson MD, Guo W, Garden GA (2003) p53-dependent cell death signaling in neurons. *Neurochem. Res.* 28:15-27.

Nagy Z, Esiri MM, Smith AD (1998) The cell division cycle and the pathophysiology of Alzheimer's disease. *Neuroscience* 87:731-739.

Naslund J, Haroutunian V, Mohs R, Davis KL, Davies P, Greengard P, Buxbaum JD (2000) Correlation between elevated levels of amyloid beta-peptide in the brain and cognitive decline. *Jama* 283:1571-1577.

Oddo S, Caccamo A, Shepherd JD, Murphy MP, Golde TE, Kayed R, Metherate R, Mattson MP, Akbari Y, LaFerla FM (2003) Triple-transgenic model of Alzheimer's disease with plaques and tangles: intracellular Abeta and synaptic dysfunction. Neuron 39:409-421.

Olson JK, Miller SD (2004) Microglia initiate central nervous system innate and adaptive immune responses through multiple TLRs. *J. Immunol.* 173:3916-3924.

Paresce DM, Ghosh RN, Maxfield FR (1996) Microglial cells internalize aggregates of the Alzheimer's disease amyloid beta-protein via a scavenger receptor. *Neuron* 17:553-565.

Paresce DM, Chung H, Maxfield FR (1997) Slow degradation of aggregates of the Alzheimer's disease amyloid beta-protein by microglial cells. *J. Biol. Chem.* 272:29390-29397.

Piani D, Spranger M, Frei K, Schaffner A, Fontana A (1992) Macrophage-induced cytotoxicity of N-methyl-D-aspartate receptor positive neurons involves excitatory amino acids rather than reactive oxygen intermediates and cytokines. *Eur. J. Immunol.* 22:2429-2436.

Pike CJ, Burdick D, Walencewicz AJ, Glabe CG, Cotman CW (1993) Neurodegeneration induced by beta-amyloid peptides in vitro: the role of peptide assembly state. *J. Neurosci.* 13:1676-1687.

Pitas RE, Boyles JK, Lee SH, Foss D, Mahley RW (1987) Astrocytes synthesize apolipoprotein E and metabolize apolipoprotein E-containing lipoproteins. *Biochim. Biophys. Acta.* 917:148-161.

Postina R, Schroeder A, Dewachter I, Bohl J, Schmitt U, Kojro E, Prinzen C, Endres K, Hiemke C, Blessing M, Flamez P, Dequenne A, Godaux E, van Leuven F, Fahrenholz F (2004) A disintegrin-metalloproteinase prevents amyloid plaque formation and hippocampal defects in an Alzheimer disease mouse model. J Clin Invest 113:1456-1464.

Price DL, Tanzi RE, Borchelt DR, Sisodia SS (1998) Alzheimer's disease: genetic studies and transgenic models. *Annu. Rev. Genet.* 32:461-493.

Qiu WQ, Walsh DM, Ye Z, Vekrellis K, Zhang J, Podlisny MB, Rosner MR, Safavi A, Hersh LB, Selkoe DJ (1998) Insulin-degrading enzyme regulates extracellular levels of amyloid beta-protein by degradation. *J. Biol. Chem.* 273:32730-32738.

Reynolds WF, Rhees J, Maciejewski D, Paladino T, Sieburg H, Maki RA, Masliah E (1999) Myeloperoxidase polymorphism is associated with gender specific risk for Alzheimer's disease. *Exp. Neurol.* 155:31-41.

Rogers J, Luber-Narod J, Styren SD, Civin WH (1988) Expression of immune system-associated antigens by cells of the human central nervous system: relationship to the pathology of Alzheimer's disease. *Neurobiol. Aging.* 9:339-349.

Rogers JT, Leiter LM, McPhee J, Cahill CM, Zhan SS, Potter H, Nilsson LN (1999) Translation of the alzheimer amyloid precursor protein mRNA is up-regulated by interleukin-1 through 5'-untranslated region sequences. *J. Biol. Chem.* 274:6421-6431.

Roher AE, Chaney MO, Kuo YM, Webster SD, Stine WB, Haverkamp LJ, Woods AS, Cotter RJ, Tuohy JM, Krafft GA, Bonnell BS, Emmerling MR (1996) Morphology and toxicity of Abeta-(1-42) dimer derived from neuritic and vascular amyloid deposits of Alzheimer's disease. *J. Biol. Chem.* 271:20631-20635.

Sadowski M, Pankiewicz J, Scholtzova H, Ripellino JA, Li Y, Schmidt SD, Mathews PM, Fryer JD, Holtzman DM, Sigurdsson EM, Wisniewski T (2004) A synthetic peptide blocking the apolipoprotein E/beta-amyloid binding mitigates beta-amyloid toxicity and fibril formation in vitro and reduces beta-amyloid plaques in transgenic mice. *Am. J. Pathol.* 165:937-948.

Saura J, Petegnief V, Wu X, Liang Y, Paul SM (2003) Microglial apolipoprotein E and astroglial apolipoprotein J expression in vitro: opposite effects of lipopolysaccharide. *J. Neurochem.* 85:1455-1467.

Scheuner D, Eckman C, Jensen M, Song X, Citron M, Suzuki N, Bird TD, Hardy J, Hutton M, Kukull W, Larson E, Levy-Lahad E, Viitanen M, Peskind E, Poorkaj P, Schellenberg G, Tanzi R, Wasco W, Lannfelt L, Selkoe D, Younkin S (1996) Secreted amyloid beta-protein similar to that in the senile plaques of Alzheimer's disease is increased in vivo by the presenilin 1 and 2 and APP mutations linked to familial Alzheimer's disease. *Nat. Med.* 2:864-870.

Schmitt FA, Davis DG, Wekstein DR, Smith CD, Ashford JW, Markesbery WR (2000) "Preclinical" AD revisited: neuropathology of cognitively normal older adults. *Neurology* 55:370-376.

Selkoe DJ (1994) Cell biology of the amyloid beta-protein precursor and the mechanism of Alzheimer's disease. *Annu. Rev. Cell. Biol.* 10:373-403.

Selkoe DJ (1997) Alzheimer's disease: genotypes, phenotypes, and treatments. *Science* 275:630-631.

Selkoe DJ, Xia W, Kimberly WT, Vekrellis K, Walsh D, Esler WP, Wolfe MS (2001) Mechanism of Abeta production and Abeta degradation: routes to the treatment of Alzheimer's disease. In: Alzheimer's disease: Advances in Ethology, Pathogenesis and Therapeutics (Iqbal K, Sisodia SS, Winblad B, eds), pp 421-432. New York: John Wiley and Sons Ltd.

Sherrington R, Rogaev EI, Liang Y, Rogaeva EA, Levesque G, Ikeda M, Chi H, Lin C, Li G, Holman K, et al. (1995) Cloning of a gene bearing missense mutations in early-onset familial Alzheimer's disease. *Nature* 375:754-760.

Smith MA, Hirai K, Hsiao K, Pappolla MA, Harris PL, Siedlak SL, Tabaton M, Perry G (1998) Amyloid-beta deposition in Alzheimer transgenic mice is associated with oxidative stress. *J. Neurochem.* 70:2212-2215.

Smith MZ, Nagy Z, Esiri MM (1999) Cell cycle-related protein expression in vascular dementia and Alzheimer's disease. *Neurosci. Lett.* 271:45-48.

Spires TL, Hyman BT (2005) Transgenic models of Alzheimer's disease: learning from animals. *NeuroRx* 2:423-437.

Sturchler-Pierrat C, Abramowski D, Duke M, Wiederhold KH, Mistl C, Rothacher S, Ledermann B, Burki K, Frey P, Paganetti PA, Waridel C, Calhoun ME, Jucker M, Probst A, Staufenbiel M, Sommer B (1997) Two amyloid precursor protein transgenic mouse models with Alzheimer disease-like pathology. *Proc. Natl. Acad. Sci. USA* 94:13287-13292.

Styren SD, Civin WH, Rogers J (1990) Molecular, cellular, and pathologic characterization of HLA-DR immunoreactivity in normal elderly and Alzheimer's disease brain. *Exp. Neurol.* 110:93-104.

Sun YX, Minthon L, Wallmark A, Warkentin S, Blennow K, Janciauskiene S (2003) Inflammatory markers in matched plasma and cerebrospinal fluid from patients with Alzheimer's disease. *Dement. Geriatr. Cogn. Disord.* 16:136-144.

Takeda A, Yasuda T, Miyata T, Goto Y, Wakai M, Watanabe M, Yasuda Y, Horie K, Inagaki T, Doyu M, Maeda K, Sobue G (1998) Advanced glycation end products co-localized with astrocytes and microglial cells in Alzheimer's disease brain. *Acta. Neuropathol.* (Berl) 95:555-558.

Tan J, Town T, Mullan M (2000a) CD45 inhibits CD40L-induced microglial activation via negative regulation of the Src/p44/42 MAPK pathway. *J. Biol. Chem.* 275:37224-37231.

Tan J, Town T, Mori T, Wu Y, Saxe M, Crawford F, Mullan M (2000b) CD45 opposes beta-amyloid peptide-induced microglial activation via inhibition of p44/42 mitogen-activated protein kinase. *J. Neurosci.* 20:7587-7594.

Tan J, Town T, Paris D, Mori T, Suo Z, Crawford F, Mattson MP, Flavell RA, Mullan M (1999) Microglial activation resulting from CD40-CD40L interaction after β-amyloid stimulation. *Science* 286:2352-2355.

Tan J, Town T, Crawford F, Mori T, DelleDonne A, Crescentini R, Obregon D, Flavell RA, Mullan MJ (2002) Role of CD40 ligand in amyloidosis in transgenic Alzheimer's mice. *Nat. Neurosci.* 5:1288-1293.

Tarkowski E, Blennow K, Wallin A, Tarkowski A (1999) Intracerebral production of tumor necrosis factor-alpha, a local neuroprotective agent, in Alzheimer disease and vascular dementia. *J. Clin. Immunol.* 19:223-230.

Todd Roach J, Volmar CH, Dwivedi S, Town T, Crescentini R, Crawford F, Tan J, Mullan M (2004) Behavioral effects of CD40-CD40L pathway disruption in aged PSAPP mice. *Brain Res.* 1015:161-168.

Togo T, Akiyama H, Kondo H, Ikeda K, Kato M, Iseki E, Kosaka K (2000) Expression of CD40 in the brain of Alzheimer's disease and other neurological diseases. *Brain Res.* 885:117-121.

van der Wal EA, Gomez-Pinilla F, Cotman CW (1993) Transforming growth factor-beta 1 is in plaques in Alzheimer and Down pathologies. *Neuroreport* 4:69-72.

Vassar R, Bennett BD, Babu-Khan S, Kahn S, Mendiaz EA, Denis P, Teplow DB, Ross S, Amarante P, Loeloff R, Luo Y, Fisher S, Fuller J, Edenson S, Lile J, Jarosinski MA, Biere AL, Curran E, Burgess T, Louis JC, Collins F, Treanor J, Rogers G, Citron M (1999) Beta-secretase cleavage of Alzheimer's amyloid precursor protein by the transmembrane aspartic protease BACE. *Science* 286:735-741.

Vekrellis K, Ye Z, Qiu WQ, Walsh D, Hartley D, Chesneau V, Rosner MR, Selkoe DJ (2000) Neurons regulate extracellular levels of amyloid beta-protein via proteolysis by insulin-degrading enzyme. *J. Neurosci.* 20:1657-1665.

Walker DG, Link J, Lue LF, Dalsing-Hernandez JE, Boyes BE (2005) Gene expression changes by amyloid {beta} peptide-stimulated human postmortem brain microglia identify activation of multiple inflammatory processes. *J. Leukoc. Biol.*

Wallach D, Varfolomeev EE, Malinin NL, Goltsev YV, Kovalenko AV, Boldin MP (1999) Tumor necrosis factor receptor and Fas signaling mechanisms. *Annu. Rev. Immunol.* 17:331-367.

Walsh DM, Lomakin A, Benedek GB, Condron MM, Teplow DB (1997) Amyloid beta-protein fibrillogenesis. Detection of a protofibrillar intermediate. *J. Biol. Chem.* 272:22364-22372.

Walsh DM, Klyubin I, Fadeeva JV, Cullen WK, Anwyl R, Wolfe MS, Rowan MJ, Selkoe DJ (2002) Naturally secreted oligomers of amyloid beta protein potently inhibit hippocampal long-term potentiation in vivo. *Nature* 416:535-539.

Webster SD, Yang AJ, Margol L, Garzon-Rodriguez W, Glabe CG, Tenner AJ (2000) Complement component C1q modulates the phagocytosis of Abeta by microglia. *Exp. Neurol.* 161:127-138.

Weggen S, Eriksen JL, Das P, Sagi SA, Wang R, Pietrzik CU, Findlay KA, Smith TE, Murphy MP, Bulter T, Kang DE, Marquez-Sterling N, Golde TE, Koo EH (2001) A subset of NSAIDs lower amyloidogenic Abeta42 independently of cyclooxygenase activity. *Nature* 414:212-216.

White AR, Du T, Laughton KM, Volitakis I, Sharples RA, Hoke DE, Holsinger RM, Evin G, Cherny RA, Hill AF, Barnham KJ, Li QX, Bush AI, Masters CL (2006) Degradation of the Alzheimer's disease amyloid beta peptide by metal-dependent up-regulation of metalloprotease activity. *J. Biol. Chem.*

Wilcock GK, Esiri MM (1982) Plaques, tangles and dementia. A quantitative study. *J. Neurol. Sci.* 56:343-356.

Willem M, Dewachter I, Smyth N, Van Dooren T, Borghgraef P, Haass C, Van Leuven F (2004) beta-site amyloid precursor protein cleaving enzyme 1 increases amyloid deposition in brain parenchyma but reduces cerebrovascular amyloid angiopathy in aging BACE x APP[V717I] double-transgenic mice. *Am. J. Pathol.* 165:1621-1631.

Williams MA, Turchan J, Lu Y, Nath A, Drachman DB (2005) Protection of human cerebral neurons from neurodegenerative insults by gene delivery of soluble tumor necrosis factor p75 receptor. *Exp. Brain Res.* 165:383-391.

Wyss-Coray T, Mucke L (2002) Inflammation in neurodegenerative disease--a double-edged sword. *Neuron* 35:419-432.

Wyss-Coray T, Lin C, von Euw D, Masliah E, Mucke L, Lacombe P (2000) Alzheimer's disease-like cerebrovascular pathology in transforming growth factor-beta 1 transgenic mice and functional metabolic correlates. *Ann. NY Acad. Sci.* 903:317-323.

Wyss-Coray T, Masliah E, Mallory M, McConlogue L, Johnson-Wood K, Lin C, Mucke L (1997) Amyloidogenic role of cytokine TGF-beta1 in transgenic mice and in Alzheimer's disease. *Nature* 389:603-606.

Wyss-Coray T, Yan F, Lin AH, Lambris JD, Alexander JJ, Quigg RJ, Masliah E (2002) Prominent neurodegeneration and increased plaque formation in complement-inhibited Alzheimer's mice. *Proc. Natl. Acad. Sci. USA* 99:10837-10842.

Wyss-Coray T, Lin C, Yan F, Yu GQ, Rohde M, McConlogue L, Masliah E, Mucke L (2001) TGF-beta1 promotes microglial amyloid-beta clearance and reduces plaque burden in transgenic mice. *Nat. Med.* 7:612-618.

Wyss-Coray T, Loike JD, Brionne TC, Lu E, Anankov R, Yan F, Silverstein SC, Husemann J (2003) Adult mouse astrocytes degrade amyloid-beta in vitro and in situ. *Nat. Med.* 9:453-457.

Xia M, Qin S, McNamara M, Mackay C, Hyman BT (1997) Interleukin-8 receptor B immunoreactivity in brain and neuritic plaques of Alzheimer's disease. *Am. J. Pathol.* 150:1267-1274.

Xia MQ, Hyman BT (1999) Chemokines/chemokine receptors in the central nervous system and Alzheimer's disease. *J. Neurovirol.* 5:32-41.

Xia MQ, Qin SX, Wu LJ, Mackay CR, Hyman BT (1998) Immunohistochemical study of the beta-chemokine receptors CCR3 and CCR5 and their ligands in normal and Alzheimer's disease brains. *Am. J. Pathol.* 153:31-37.

Xia MQ, Bacskai BJ, Knowles RB, Qin SX, Hyman BT (2000) Expression of the chemokine receptor CXCR3 on neurons and the elevated expression of its ligand IP-10 in reactive astrocytes: in vitro ERK1/2 activation and role in Alzheimer's disease. *J. Neuroimmunol.* 108:227-235.

Yamamoto M, Horiba M, Buescher JL, Huang D, Gendelman HE, Ransohoff RM, Ikezu T (2005) Overexpression of monocyte chemotactic protein-1/CCL2 in beta-amyloid precursor protein transgenic mice show accelerated diffuse beta-amyloid deposition. *Am. J. Pathol.* 166:1475-1485.

Yamamoto M, Kiyota T, Horiba M, Buescher JL, Walsh SM, Gendelman HE, Ikezu T (2007) Interferon-gamma and tumor necrosis factor-alpha regulate amyloid-beta plaque deposition and beta-secretase expression in Swedish mutant APP transgenic mice. *Am. J. Path.* in press.

Yamin R, Malgeri EG, Sloane JA, McGraw WT, Abraham CR (1999) Metalloendopeptidase EC 3.4.24.15 is necessary for Alzheimer's amyloid-beta peptide degradation. *J. Biol. Chem.* 274:18777-18784.

Yan Q, Zhang J, Liu H, Babu-Khan S, Vassar R, Biere AL, Citron M, Landreth G (2003) Anti-inflammatory drug therapy alters beta-amyloid processing and deposition in an animal model of Alzheimer's disease. *J. Neurosci.* 23:7504-7509.

Yan SD, Chen X, Fu J, Chen M, Zhu H, Roher A, Slattery T, Zhao L, Nagashima M, Morser J, Migheli A, Nawroth P, Stern D, Schmidt AM (1996) RAGE and amyloid-beta peptide neurotoxicity in Alzheimer's disease. *Nature* 382:685-691.

Yang F, Lim GP, Begum AN, Ubeda OJ, Simmons MR, Ambegaokar SS, Chen PP, Kayed R, Glabe CG, Frautschy SA, Cole GM (2005) Curcumin inhibits formation of amyloid beta oligomers and fibrils, binds plaques, and reduces amyloid in vivo. J. *Biol. Chem.* 280:5892-5901.

Yoshiyama Y, Asahina M, Hattori T (2000) Selective distribution of matrix metalloproteinase-3 (MMP-3) in Alzheimer's disease brain. *Acta. Neuropathol.* (Berl) 99:91-95.

Young H, Hardy K (1995) Role of interferon-gamma in immune cell regulation. *J. Leukoc. Biol.* 58:373-381.

Zhou Y, Su Y, Li B, Liu F, Ryder JW, Wu X, Gonzalez-DeWhitt PA, Gelfanova V, Hale JE, May PC, Paul SM, Ni B (2003) Nonsteroidal anti-inflammatory drugs can lower amyloidogenic Abeta42 by inhibiting Rho. *Science* 302:1215-1217.

Zlotnik A, Yoshie O (2000) Chemokines: a new classification system and their role in immunity. *Immunity* 12:121-127.

In: New Immunology Research Developments
Editor: Gunter V. Müller
ISBN 978-1-60021-701-2


*Chapter 3*

# Avian Acute Phase Protein Ovotransferrin Modulates Phagocyte Function

***Narayan C. Rath, H. Xie, W. E. Huff and G. R. Huff***
Agricultural Research Service, USDA, Poultry Science Center,
University of Arkansas, Fayetteville, Arkansas 72701, USA

## Abstract

Acute phase proteins (APP) are serum proteins elevated in response to a variety of physiological injuries including infection and inflammation. These pathogen nonspecific proteins are predominantly synthesized in the liver and serve as a humoral component of innate immunity by way of recognizing and neutralizing pathogens, and facilitating tissue repair. The nature of APP and their physiological significance is not understood in sub mammalian species. In studying the avian acute phase response in experimental inflammation induced by endotoxin or croton oil, we identified serum transferrin as a major avian APP that was same as the ovotransferrin (OVT) present in the egg white. Using an enzyme-immunoassay, the results showed the serum OVT to be elevated during a variety of bacterial and viral infections. The ability of OVT to modulate avian macrophage and heterophil functions was evaluated using *in vitro* assays. The results showed that OVT activated both of these cell types as measured by nitric oxide, interleukin-6, matrix metalloproteinase, and reactive oxygen production. Additionally, OVT also stimulated heterophil degranulation. These results demonstrate that beyond its antibacterial effects, the OVT may act as a natural immunomodulator enhancing innate immune function.

## Introduction

Innate or natural immunity is an interactive network of cellular and humoral defense mechanisms that recognize and protect the organism against invading pathogens (Fearon and

Locksley, 1996; Magor and Magor, 2001; Janeway and Medzhitov, 2002; Beutler, 2004). The 'acute phase proteins (APP)' are the humoral components of this defense system which are elicited in response to inflammation caused by physical, chemical, or infection-induced physiological trauma (Gabay and Kushner, 1999; Suffredini et al., 1999). Most APP are constitutive plasma proteins, the concentrations of some of which increase or decrease by few to a several hundred folds qualifying them to be either a positive or a negative acute phase protein. These pathogen nonspecific proteins are synthesized in the liver and to a lesser extent in tissues such as fibroblasts, and endothelium, by the action of proinflammatory cytokines such as interleukin-1, interlekin-6, and tumor necrosis factor alpha. The APP response has been shown in a wide variety of species of animals including many invertebrates and vertebrates (Ellis, 2001; Magor and Magor, 2001; Bayne and Gerwick, 2001; Law 2002). Over 40 APP have been identified in mammals which include several well known proteins such as C-reactive protein, mannose binding protein, $\alpha$1-acid glycoprotein, and haptoglobin, and the list continue to grow. Because the levels of these proteins generally remain altered as long as the inflammation persists, some positive APP has been used as diagnostic markers of infection and inflammation both in clinical and veterinary medicine (Gabay and Kushner, 1999; Peterson et al., 2004; Murata et al., 2004). Whereas the knowledge of APP is limited to a handful of mammalian proteins, there is a great deal of diversity in APP response among different species of animals that include the extent, and the duration of their response. However, the functional significance of most APP in relation to health and disease are not well understood which can be as diverse as the proteins themselves. These proteins are presumed to recognize and neutralize pathogens, activate tissue repair processes, and restore physiological homeostasis (Gabay and Kushner, 1999; Suffredini et al., 1999; Minchinton et al., 2004). Compared to mammals, the acute phase response, the APP, and their function in sub mammalian species such as poultry are much less understood although their potential in monitoring of flock health, wellbeing, and pre harvest food safety has been proposed (Peterson et al., 2004; Eckersall, 2004). This review is based on studies on acute phase response in poultry using experimentally induced inflammation and the identification of ovotransferrin (OVT) as a major avian APP, and its immunomodulatory effects on phagocytes.

## Experimental Inflammation and the Identification of OVT as a Major APP in Chickens

Experimental inflammation was induced in four week-old male broiler chickens by a single intramuscular injection of 5 mg *Salmonella typhimurium* lipopolysacharide (LPS) in 0.2ml saline or 0.5ml of 50% croton oil in olive oil. Control birds were treated with appropriate vehicle solutions saline or olive oil, or received no treatment. The serum protein profiles of birds treated for different time durations 0 through 48h were compared using 10% SDS gel electrophoresis under non reducing conditions (Xie et al., 2000; 2001). Densitometric analysis of corresponding protein bands indicated quantitative changes in 4-5 different proteins of which a band corresponding to MW approximately 65kD showed a significant increase at 24h-48h post treatment in birds that were administered either LPS or croton oil (Figure 1). Because of the uniformity and the robustness of response, the characterization of the 65kD band protein was carried out using sera from chickens that were subjected to treatment with croton oil for 48h (Xie et al., 2002a).

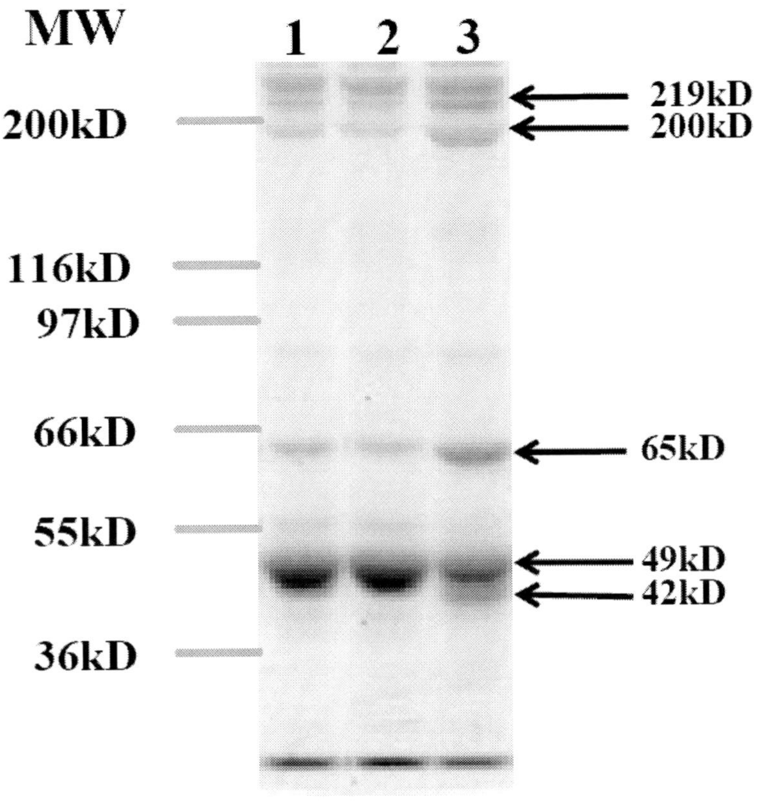


Figure 1. A typical serum protein profiles of a (1) normal, untreated, (2) an olive oil-treated control, and (3) a croton oil–treated chicken after 48h of treatment.

Two-dimensional gel electrophoresis was performed with sera from croton oil inflamed chickens using commercial gel kits from Invitrogen (Carlsbad, CA) to characterize the 65kD band protein. Serum samples from three individual birds were subjected to isoelectrofocusing (IEF) using pH 3-10 IEF gels then subjected to separation in 2$^{nd}$ dimension over 4-20% tris-glycine gels under non-reducing condition. The proteins were electrophoretically transferred to polyvinylidene difluoride (PVDF) membrane using a Transblot apparatus, stained with Coomassie blue, destained, and the spots corresponding to 65kD were excised, and subjected to N-terminal sequence analysis using a protein sequence analyzer (Model 473A, Applied Biosystem, Foster City, CA) for 30 cycles. Serum samples from three experimental birds were subjected to similar procedures yielding consensus sequence information. A Genbank data search using the first 22 amino acids showed a complete sequence homology of the protein with chicken ovotransferrin (OVT) also, called conalbumin. The identity of the protein was further verified using a western blot analysis of the 65kD band with a rabbit anti-chicken serum transferrin antibody and a monoclonal anti-chicken OVT antibody both of which separately identified the same band of proteins (Xie et al., 2002a). Besides, the anti-chicken serum transferrin antibody also recognized the chicken egg white OVT implying that both chicken serotransferrin and OVT are the same protein.

The serum transferrin is a glycoprotein which has a MW approximately 78-80kD although it migrated as a 65kD band under nonreducing conditions. Both oviductal OVT and the serum transferrin have been shown to be encoded by the same gene (Thibodeau et al., 1978; Schaeffer et al., 1987; Spik et al., 1988; Awade et al., 1994) except that the serum transferrin is synthesized in the liver. The transferrins are to a family of phylogenetically conserved iron binding proteins most of which are molecularly homologous and have similar tertiary structures (Metz-Boutigue et al., 1984; Schaeffer et al., 1987; Welch, 1990; Yun et al., 1999; Qian et al., 2002). Most transferrins including serotransferrin and lactoferrin transport $Fe^{3+}$ into the cells and bind to their appropriate receptors on the cell surface (Baker et al., 2002; Qian et al., 2002). The antibacterial efficacy of transferrin is attributed to their iron binding property by which they withhold iron, an essential nutrient for bacterial growth (Bezkorovainy, 1981; Valenti et al., 1983; Singh et al., 2002; Ardehali et al., 2003; Weinberg, 2004; Orsi, 2004). In insects, transferrin acts as a positive acute phase protein which is elevated in response to bacterial infection (Yoshiga et al., 1997) but in vertebrates it behaves both, as a positive or a negative APP depending upon the species. In several species of fish and birds serotransferrin is a positive APP (Hallquist and Klasing, 1994; Chamanza et al., 1999; Stafford and Belosevic, 2003) whereas in most mammals including humans it is a negative APP (Gabay and Kushner, 1999; Murata et al., 2004). However, the lactoferrin that occurs in the secretion of neutrophils and other body fluids such as tears, milk, and saliva is a potent antibacterial protein (Gahr et al., 1991; Crouch et al., 1992; Vorland et al., 1999; Edde et al., 2001; Ward, 2002;). The protease cleavage products of both lactoferrin and OVT have also been shown to have substantial anti-bacterial properties (Ibrahim et al., 2000; Orsi, 2004) and both lactoferrin and OVT also exhibit certain anti-viral efficacy (Vorland, 1999; Giansanti et al., 2002, 2005; Tanaka et al., 2003; Beljaars et al., 2004). Chicken fibroblasts infected with an oncogenic strain of Marek's disease virus, has been shown to upregulate OVT gene induction (Morgan et al., 2001).

## Serum OVT Levels During Infection and Inflammation

To measure the time course changes in serum OVT concentrations in chickens with croton oil-induced inflammation, we used a competitive enzyme immunoassay (Xie et al., 2002b). Affinity purified rabbit anti-chicken transferrin immunoglobulin (Accurate Chemicals, Westbury, NY) was coated to the wells of microtiter plates as the capture antibody which was then blocked with gelatin/ bovine serum albumin. Unlabelled serially diluted OVT standards or diluted serum samples were added to the wells along with a fixed concentration of biotin labeled OVT to bind to the capture antibody. After at least 2h of incubation and several successive washing steps, the residual biotinylated OVT was probed with a peroxidase conjugated streptavidin followed by its colorimetric determination. The change in optical density with increasing concentrations of unlabeled OVT was calculated as percent relative to the wells that did not receive unlabeled OVT. Using those data a standard curve was generated which was used to calculate the concentrations of OVT in serum samples (Xie et al., 2002b). Measured by this method, the croton oil-induced inflammation showed an increase in the serum OVT levels between 12-16h post-injection that remained elevated through 120h before reaching back to its control level at 240h. These changes were not evident in birds that were treated identically with olive oil. Also, the serum OVT concentrations of specific pathogen free (SPF) chickens challenged with and *Escherichia coli* or several pathognomic poultry viruses were significantly elevated compared with the untreated, control birds (Figure 2).

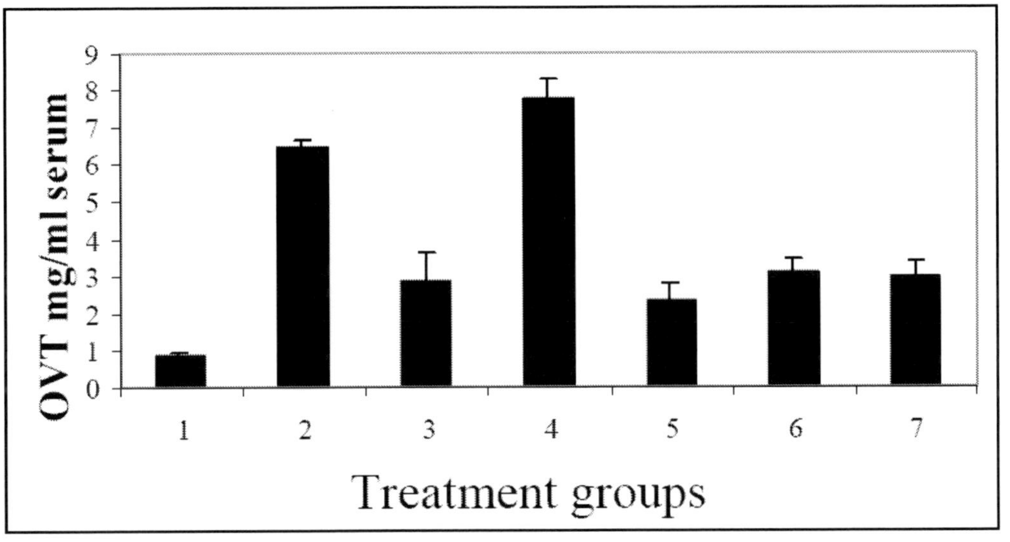


Figure 2. Serum OVT concentration of specific pathogen free chickens either non challenged (1) or challenged with *Escherichia coli* (2), infectious laryngotracheitis virus (3), reovirus (4), Fowl pox virus (5), Infectious bursal disease virus (6), or Infectious bronchitis virus (7) after seven days of infection (Xie et al., 2002b).

## Immunomodulatory Effect of OVT on Macrophage and Heterophil Function

The immunomodulatory potential of OVT was tested using a transformed chicken macrophage cell line HD11 (Beug et al., 1979) and the avian neutrophils, the heterophils, as the responding cells. Whereas the HD11 cells were continuously propagated in culture, the heterophils were freshly isolated from EDTA anti-coagulated peripheral blood of 2-3 week-old chickens with density gradient centrifugation medium Polymorphprep (Accurate Chemicals, Westbury, NY) (Rath et al, 1998). The cells were cultured at concentrations of 1X $10^6$ cells/ ml RPMI-1640 medium containing antibiotics, 10% fetal bovine serum, and 0-1,000μg of substantially iron free and endotoxin free OVT. Except for the studies using respiratory burst activity assay that was done within 3h of the addition of OVT, all other assays were done following 24h of treatment with OVT. The results were normalized with respect to the culture medium that contained no cells but was identically treated (Xie et al., 2002c).

## Interleukin-6 Production

Interleukin-6 is a pleotropic cytokine produced by different cell types including activated macrophages and neutrophils (Hirano et al., 1990; Taga and Kishimoto, 1997). It regulates a variety of immunological processes including B cell proliferation, T cell activation, and inflammation (COPE, 2003). Although it is predominantly a pro inflammatory cytokine, it has also been shown to act as an anti-inflammatory cytokine by down regulating other proinflammatory factors (Xing et al., 1998). IL-6 reduces the secretion of IL-1 and TNF-α, up regulates the expression of IL-1 receptor antagonists (IL-1ra), and soluble TNF receptor (TNFR) levels (Steinmetz et al., 1995; Jordan et al., 1995). Both macrophages and heterophils produce IL-6 in response to LPS stimulation (Rath et al., 1998; Xie et al., 2001). Whereas neither the culture medium alone with maximal concentration of OVT (1mg /ml) nor the conditioned medium from HD11 cells treated with up to 10μg OVT/ ml showed any detectable IL-6 activity, at concentrations of 100μg and above the change was significant. By contrast, the heterophils produced IL-6 with an OVT concentration of 10μg/ ml which increased further in a concentration dependent manner with 100 and 1,000μg OVT per ml of medium (Xie et al., 2002c).

## Nitrite Production

Nitrite is an end product of nitric oxide (NO) metabolism which is an important signaling molecule that regulates a diverse range of physiological processes such as inflammation, immune activation, and cell death (Clancy et al., 1998; Bogdan et al., 2000). It is synthesized from arginine by nitric oxide synthase. In macrophages and granulocytes nitric oxide is synthesized by an inducible form of nitric oxide synthase (iNOS) which is upregulated by the action of endotoxins, cytokines, and other proinflammatory factors. NO is important in killing bacteria, parasites, and tumor cells. Because of its ability to interact with oxygen radicals, metalloproteins, thiols, and protein tyrosine, NO also causes enzyme inactivation, lipid per oxidation, and cell death (Clancy et al., 1998; Bogdan et al., 2000; Fang, 2004). It is reported that nitric oxide also inhibits neutrophil migration, causes their deformity, and apoptosis (Secco et al., 2003) which may be a way of the resolution of inflammation. Measurement of nitrite level in the conditioned medium is indicative of macrophage and neutrophil activation although the neutrophils apparently, are less efficient producers of NO (Nathan and Shiloh, 2000). However, LPS induces production of nitrite by the heterophils (Rath et al., 1998). Nevertheless, OVT at any concentration was not able to induce nitrite production by the heterophils but it stimulated nitrite production by the HD11 cells albeit at a relatively high concentration of 100μg per ml of culture medium that increased further with 1,000μg per ml (Xie et al., 2002c).

## Respiratory Burst

A major feature of the phagocytic process is the activation of 'respiratory burst' which is caused by an increased oxygen uptake by the phagocytes cells resulting in the production of several reactive oxygen intermediates such as superoxides ($O_2.^-$), hydroxyl radicals, and their end product hydrogen peroxide (Condliffe et al., 1998; Dahlgren and Karlsson, 1999; Babior, 2000). Microbial products and inflammatory cytokines stimulate respiratory burst in macrophages and granulocytes by activating the NADPH oxidase system that causes production of superoxide ($O_2.^-$). Superoxide is converted to hydrogen peroxide ($H_2O_2$) by the action of superoxide dismutase. Some of the products of oxidative burst such as superoxides in conjunction with nitric oxide lead to the formation of peroxynitrite ($ONOO^-$), a powerful toxic intermediate that has potentiality to kill both bacteria and eukaryotic cells (Bogdan et al., 2000; Fang, 2004). Though most of these products are toxic to pathogens, their persistent release can be harmful to the producing cells themselves because they can react with various cellular components and cause cellular injuries committing the cells to die (Edwards et al., 2003). These mechanisms could be important in the resolution of inflammation by reducing the inflammatory cell population. In granulocytes such as heterophils and eosinophils, the enzyme myeloperoxidase catalyzes the formation of chlorination products such as hypochlorous acid (HOCl) from $H_2O_2$ that is a potent antimicrobial agent (Babior, 2000). Employing 2'7' dichlorofluorescein diacetate (DCF-DA) oxidation to measure the end products of oxidative burst hydrogen peroxide (Curtin et al., 2002), the effect of OVT on macrophage and heterophil respiratory burst activities were evaluated over a period of 2h. OVT by itself stimulated $H_2O_2$ production in the heterophils but not in the macrophages. However, in the presence of a suboptimal concentration (0.1µg /ml) of phorbol myristate acetate (PMA), a protein kinase C activator, OVT stimulated DCF-DA oxidation suggesting that OVT can play a supportive role in stimulating phagocytic activities in macrophages. Although a precise function of OVT-induced production of reactive oxygen and nitrogen metabolites during the inflammatory process is not known it is likely that modulating the function of phagocytes during acute phase response may not only provide a continued protection of host against pathogens but also facilitate resolution of inflammation.

## Metalloproteinases

Matrix metalloproteinases (MMP) are zinc-dependent endopeptidases that function extracellularly at neutral pH. The MMP family consists of many related but distinct enzymes that occur as secreted and membrane anchored proteins (Massova et al., 1998). MMP are implicated in tissue remodeling and angiogenesis by breaking down structural connective tissue matrix proteins such as collagens and proteoglycans also, activate growth factors, enzymes, chemokines, and antimicrobial peptides by releasing them from their respective binding proteins or converting from their inactive forms (Fowlkes et al., 2002; Opdenakker and Van Damme, 2004). MMP play many important roles in inflammation, immunity, cell-cell interactions, and angiogenesis (Goetzl et al., 1996; Parks et al., 2004). Uncontrolled productions of MMP lead to undesirable effects such as sustained tissue damage and inflammation. Both macrophages and granulocytes produce different MMP which are critical in tissue remodeling, wound healing, and angiogenesis that follow tissue damage (Sternlicht and Werb, 2001). Using gelatin zymography to detect MMP, the chicken macrophages have been shown to produce several types of MMP corresponding to approximate MW of 68kD and 75kD (Rath et al., 1998; 2003; Hahn-Dantona et al., 2000). The heterophils on the other hand, not only produce the 68-75kD forms but also some high MW forms corresponding to ~150-200kD. OVT enhanced the production of both forms of these enzymes in a concentration dependent manner in their respective cell types with macrophages predominantly producing the 68-75kD forms whereas the heterophils produced the 150-200kD forms of MMP (Xie et al., 2002c). It is possible that an enhanced production of MMP by phagocytes may help with post-inflammatory release of stored growth factors, chemokines facilitating recruitment of appropriate cells to the site of inflammation, remodeling, and repair of tissues including angiogenesis. Also, the OVT has also been shown to act as angiogenic molecule that promotes endothelial cell migration (Carlevaro et al., 1997).

## Heterophil Degranulation

Degranulation is a critical event in neutrophil activation which leads to the discharge of preformed enzymes, antibacterial peptides, proteins, adhesion, and chemotactic molecules (Berton, 1999). These factors facilitate microbial killing, cellular adhesion and transmigration of the leukocytes, and finally tissue remodeling (Condliffe et al., 1998). The avian heterophils contain spindle shaped granules which consist of a variety of enzymes, proteins, and antimicrobial peptides (Harmon, 1998).

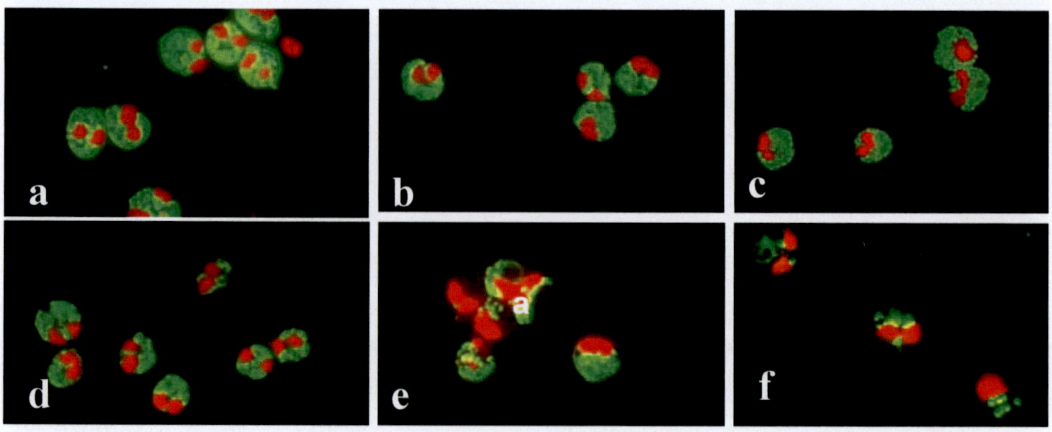


Figure 3. Effect of OVT on heterophil degranulation. Heterophils were cultured with OVT for 24h, cytocentrifuged and treated with fluorescein isothiocynate and propidium iodide to stain cytoplasmic granules (green) and nucleus (red). (a) Freshly prepared heterophils (b-f), cultured for 24h with no OVT (b) or OVT 1μg (c), 10μg (d), 100μg (e), and 1,000μg (f) per ml of culture.

The heterophil granules bind fluorescein isothiocyanate (FITC) that are depleted when the cells are activated (Rath et al., 1998). Using cytopspin preparation after treatment of cells with OVT and staining the cells with FITC to identify intracellular granules, the degranulation of heterophils by OVT was evaluated. Heterophils cultured with OVT at concentrations of 100 and 1,000μg showed distinct depletion of FITC binding granules as compared to untreated control cultures or the cells at the onset of culture (Figure 3). It also caused a concentration dependent release of peroxidase into the culture medium measured by tetramethylbenzidine hydrochloride method according to Madersbacher and Berger (2000) (Figure 4).

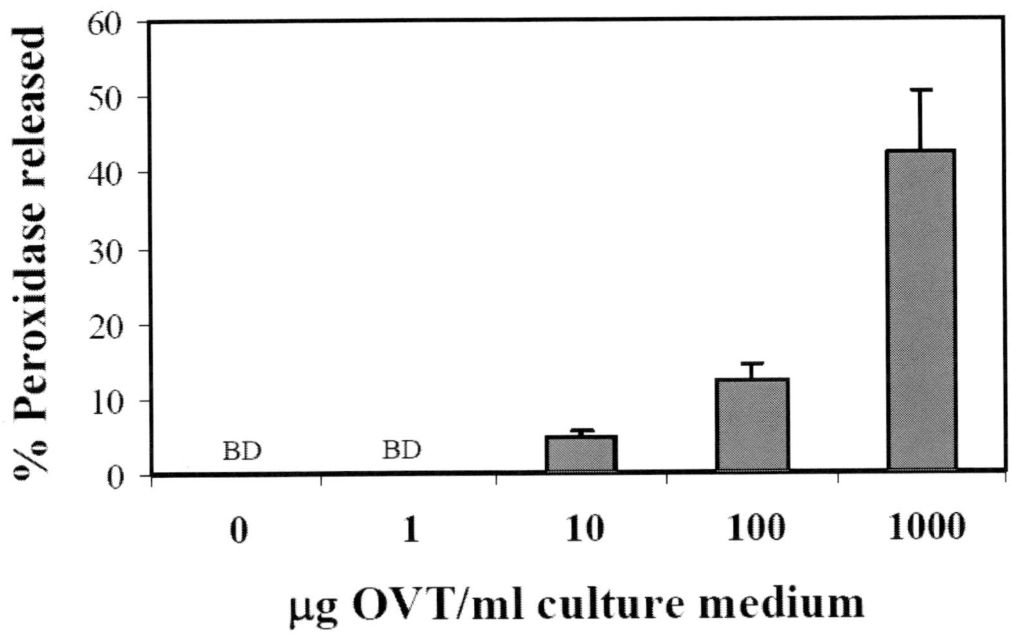


Figure 4. Peroxidase release into the culture medium by the heterophils at 24h following treatment with OVT. BD= below detection.

## Discussion and Conclusion

From the foregoing discussions it is evident that OVT is an acute phase protein in chickens, the serum levels of which is elevated under infection and inflammation. Besides its ability to act as an antibacterial protein, OVT is also capable of up regulating macrophage and heterophil metabolism thus fortifying innate immune function. While this is a novel finding for the role of OVT, the mammalian lactoferrin has been shown to modulate respiratory burst activities of neutrophils and induce cytokine production by these cells (Miyauchi et al., 1998; Vorland, 1999; Thomas et al., 2002; Son et al., 2002). However, such studies have not been done using macrophages.

We propose that an elevated level of serum OVT during acute phase response acts as a natural agonist sustaining the production of cytokines and growth factors that possibly help maturation of lymphocytes responsible for the development of adaptive immunity. From our studies it is evident that OVT concentration needed to activate phagocyte cell functions is in the order of 100μg/ml or more that appears far above the concentrations of conventional cytokines which normally elicit biological responses in nanogram ranges. However, the normal physiological concentration serum OVT being in the range of ≥1 mg/ml it may not be of any biological advantage if the cells were to elicit biological response under normal physiological conditions. But under physiological emergencies such as infection, inflammation, and stress when the level of OVT is elevated, it is able to upregulate their biological responses. In localized inflammation, the OVT in inflammatory exudates may also help regulate immune function causing the resolution of inflammation. Unlike cytokines that have short half lives and the release of which may be episodic, the OVT remains elevated during the course of inflammation providing continuous defense against pathogens at the same time, facilitating restoration of homeostasis and the resolution of inflammation.

# References


Ardehali, R; Shi, L; Janatova, J; Mohammad, SF; Burns, GL. The inhibitory activity of serum to prevent bacterial adhesion is mainly due to apo-transferrin. *Journal of Biomedical Material Research*, 2003, 66A:21-28.

Awade, AC; Moreau, S; Molle, D; Brule, G; Maubois, JL. Two-step chromatographic procedure for the purification of hen egg white ovomucin, lysozyme, ovotransferrin and ovalbumin and characterization of purified proteins. *Journal of Chromatography* A, 1994, 677:279-288.

Babior, BM. Phagocytes and oxidative stress. *American Journal of Medicine*, 2000, 109:33-44.

Baker, E; Baker, HM; Kidd, RD. Lactoferrin and transferrin: functional variations on a common structural framework. *Biochemistry and Cell Biology*, 2002, 80:27-34.

Bayne, CJ; Gerwick, L. The acute phase response and innate immunity of fish. *Developmental and Comparative Immunology*, 2001, 25:725-743.

Bogdan, C; Rollinghoff, M.; Diefenbach, A. Reactive oxygen and reactive nitrogen intermediates in innate and specific immunity. *Current Opinions on Immunology*, 2000, 12:64-76.

Berton, G. Degranulation. In: Galin, JI; Snyderman, R, editors, Inflammation: basic principles and clinical correlates. 3rd ed. Philadelphia, PA: Lippincott Williams and Wilkins; 1999.703-719.

Beljaars L, van der Strate BW, Bakker HI, Reker-Smit C, van Loenen-Weemaes AM, Wiegmans FC, Harmsen MC, Molema G, Meijer DK. Inhibition of cytomegalovirus infection by lactoferrin in vitro and in vivo. *Antiviral Res*. 2004, 63:197-208.

Beutler, B. Innate immunity: an overview. *Molecular Immunology*, 2004, 40:845-859.

Bezkorovainy, A. Antimicrobial properties of iron-binding proteins. *Advances in Experimental Medicine and Biology*, 1981, 135:139-154.

Beug, H; von Kirchbach, A; Doderlein, G; Conscience, JF; Graf, T. Chicken hematopoietic cells transformed by seven strains of defective avian leukemia viruses display three distinct phenotypes of differentiation. *Cell,* 1979, 18:375-390.

Bogdan, C; Rollinghoff, M; Diefenbach, A. Reactive oxygen and reactive nitrogen intermediates in innate and specific immunity. *Current Opinions in Immunology*, 2000, 12:64-76.

Carlevaro, MF; Albini, A; Ribatti, D; Gentili, C; Benelli, R;Cermelli, S; Cancedda, R; Cancedda, FD. Transferrin promotes endothelial cell migration and invasion: implication in cartilage neovscularization. *Journal of Cell Biology*, 1997, 136:1375-1384.

Chamanza, R; Van Veen, L; Tivapasi, MT; Tousssaint; MJM. Acute phase proteins in domestic fowl. *World's Poultry Science Journal*, 1999, 55:61-72.

Clancy, RM; Amin, AR; Abramson, SB. The role of nitric oxide in inflammation and immunity. *Arthritis Rheumatism*, 1998, 41:1141-1151.

Condliffe, AM; Kitchen; Chilvers, ER. Neutrophil priming: pathophysiological consequences and underlying mechanisms. *Clinical Science* (London), 1998, 94:461-471.

COPE, 2003. http://www.copewithcytokines.de/cope.cgi?005108

Crouch, SPM; Slater, KJ; Fletcher, J. Regulation of cytokine release from mononuclear cells by the iron-binding protein lactoferrin. *Blood*, 1992, 80:235-240.

Curtin, JF; Donovan, M; Cotter, TG. Regulation and measurement of oxidative stress in apoptosis. *Journal of Immunological Methods*, 2002, 265:49-72.

Dahlgren, C; Karlsson, A. Respiratory burst in human neutrophils. *Journal of Immunological Methods*, 1999, 232:3-14.

Eckersall, PD. The time is right for acute phase protein assays. *The Veterinary Journal*, 2004, 168:3-5.

Edde, L; Hipolito, RB; Hwang, FF; Heado, DR; Shalwitz, RA; Sherman, MP. Lactoferrin protects neonatal rats from gut-related systemic infection. *American Journal of Physiology*, 2001 281:G1140-1150.

Edwards, SW; Moulding, DA; Derouet, M; Moots, RJ. Regulation of neutrophil apoptosis. *Chemical Immunology and Allergy*. 2003, 83:204-224.

Ellis, AE. Innate host defense mechanisms of fish against viruses and bacteria. *Developmental and Comparative Immunology*, 2001, 25:827-839.

Fang, FC. Antimicrobial reactive oxygen and nitrogen species: concepts and controversies. *Nature Reviews Microbiology*, 2004, 2:820-832.

Fearon, DT; Locksley, RM. The instructive role of innate immunity in the acquired immune response. *Science*, 1996, 272:50-54.

Fowlkes, JL; Winkler, MK. Exploring the interface between metallo-proteinase activity and growth factor and cytokine bioavailability. *Cytokine Growth Factor Review*, 2002 13:277-287.

Gabay, C; Kushner, I. Acute phase proteins and other systemic response to inflammation. *New England Journal of Medicine*, 1999, 340:448-454.

Gahr, M; Speer, C; Damerau, B; Sawatzki, G. Influence of lactoferrin on the function of human polymorphonuclear leukocytes and monocytes. *Journal of Leukocyte Biology*, 1991, 49:427-433.

Giansanti, F; Rossi, P, Massucci; MT; Botti, D; Antonini, G; Valenti, P; Seganti, L. Antiviral activity of ovotransferrin discloses an evolutionary strategy for the defensive activities of lactoferrin. *Biochemistry and Cell Biology*, 2002, 80:125-130.

Giansanti F, Massucci MT, Giardi MF, Nozza F, Pulsinelli E, Nicolini C, Botti D, Antonini G. Antiviral activity of ovotransferrin derived peptides. *Biochemical and Biophysical Research Communications*. 2005, 331:69-73.

Goetzl, EJ; Banda, M; Leppert, D. Matrix metalloproteinases in immunity. *Journal of Immunology*, 1996, 156:1-4.

Hallquist, NA; Klasing, KC. Serotransferrin, ovotransferrin and metallothionein levels during an immune response in chickens. *Comparative Biochemistry and Physiology*, 1994, 108:375-384.

Hahn-Dantona, EA; Aimes, RT; Quigley, JP. The isolation, characterization, and molecular cloning of a 75-kDa gelatinase B-like enzyme, a member of the matrix metalloproteinase (MMP) family. An avian enzyme that is MMP-9-like in its cell expression pattern but diverges from mammalian gelatinase B in sequence and biochemical properties. *Journal of Biological Chemistry*, 2000, 275:40827-40838.

Harmon, BG. Avian heterophils in inflammation and disease resistance. *Poultry Science*, 1998, 77:972-977.

Hirano, T; Akira, S; Taga, T; Kishimoto, T. Biological and Clinical Aspects of Interleukin-6. *Immunology Today*, 1990, 11:443-449.

Ibrahim, HR; Sugimoto, Y; Aoki, T. Ovotransferrin antimicrobial peptide (OTAP-92) kills bacteria through a membrane damage mechanism. *Biochimica et Biophysica Acta*. 2000, 1523:196-205.

Janeway, CA Jr; Medzhitov, R. Innate immune recognition. *Annual Review of Immunology*, 2002; 20:197-216.

Jordan, M; Otterness, IG; Ng, R; Gessner, A; Rollinghoff, M; Beuscher, HU. Neutralization of endogenous IL-6 suppresses induction of IL-1 receptor antagonist. *Journal of Immunology*, 1995, 154:4081-4090.

Law, JH. 2002. Insects, oxygen, and iron. *Biochemical and Biophysical Research Communication*, 292:1191-1195.

Madersbacher, S; Berger, P. Antibodies and immunoassays. *Methods*, 2000, 21:41-50.

Magor, BG; Magor, KE. Evolution of effectors and receptors of innate immunity. *Developmental and Comparative Immunology*, 2001, 25:651-682.

Massova, I; Kotra, LP; Fridman, R; Mobashery, S. Matrix metalloproteinases: structures, evolution, and diversification. *FASEB Journal*, 1998, 12:1075-1095.

Metz-Boutigue, MH; Jolles, J; Mazurier, J; Schoentge, F; Legrand, D; Spik, G; Montreuil, J; Jolles, P. Human lactotransferrin: amino acid sequence and structural comparisons with other transferrins. *European Journal of Biochemistry*, 1984, 145:659-676.

Minchinton, RM; Liley, H; Eise, DP. The body as fortress: innate immune surveillance. *Vox Sanguinis*, 2004, 87 (Suppl 1):30-34.

Miyauchi H, Hashimoto S, Nakajima M, Shinoda I, Fukuwatari Y, Hayasawa H. Bovine lactoferrin stimulates the phagocytic activity of human neutrophils: identification of its active domain, *Cellular Immunology*, 1998, 187, 34-37.

Morgan, RW; Sofer, L; Anderson, AS; Bernberg, EL; Cui, J; Burnsid, J. Induction of host gene expression following infection of chicken embryo fibroblasts with oncogenic Marek's disease virus. *Journal of Virology*, 2001, 75:533-539.

Murata, H; Shimad, N; Yoshioka, M. Current research on acute phase proteins in veterinary diagnosis: an overview. *The Veterinary Journal*. 2004, 168:28-40.

Nathan, C; Shiloh, MU. Reactive oxygen and nitrogen intermediates in relationship between mammalian hosts and microbial pathogens. *Proceedings of the National Academy of Science USA*, 2000, 97:8841-8848.

Opdenakker, G; Van Damme, J. The countercurrent principle in invasion and metastasis of cancer cells. Recent insights on the roles of chemokines. *International Journal of Developmental Biology*, 2004, 48:519-527.

Orsi, N. The antimicrobial activity of lactoferrin: current status and perspectives. *Biometals*, 2004, 17:189-196.

Parks WC, Wilson CL, Lopez-Boado YS. Matrix metalloproteinases as modulators of inflammation and innate immunity. *Nature Review Immunology*, 2004, 4: 617-629.

Petersen, HH; Nielsen, JP; Heegard, PMH. Application of acute phase protein measurements in veterinary clinical chemistry. *Veterinary Research*, 2004, 35:163-187.

Qian, ZM; Li, H; Sun, H; Ho, K. Targeted drug delivery via the transferrin receptor-mediated endocytosis pathway, *Pharmacological Reviews*, 2002, 54:561-587.

Rath, NC; Huff, GR; Balog, JM; Huff, WE. Fluorescein isothiocyanate staining and characterization of avian heterophils. *Veterinary Immunology and Immunopathology*, 1998, 64:83-95.

Rath, NC; Parcells, MS; Xie, H; Santin, E. Characterization of a spontaneously transformed chicken mononuclear cell line. *Veterinary Immunology and Immunopathology*, 2003, 96:93-104.

Schaeffer, E; Lucero, MA; Jeltsch, JM; Py, MC; Levin, MJ; Chambon, P; Cohen, GN; Zakin, MM. Complete structure of the human transferrin gene. Comparison with analogous chicken gene and human pseudogene. *Gene*, 1987, 56:109-116.

Secco, DD; Paron, JA; de Oliveira, SH; Ferreira, SH; Silva, JS; Cunha, Fde Q. Neutrophil migration in inflammation: nitric oxide inhibits rolling, adhesion and induces apoptosis. *Nitric Oxide*. 2003, 9:153-164.

Singh, PK; Parsek, MR; Greenberg, EP; Welsh, MJ. A component of innate immunity prevents bacterial biofilm development. *Nature*. 2002, 417:552-555.

Son, KN; Park, J; Chung, CK; Chung , DK; Yu, DY; Lee, KK; Kim, J. Human lactoferrin activates transcription of IL-1beta gene in mammalian cells. *Biochemical and Biophysical Research Communication*, 2002, 290:236-241.

Spik, G; Coddeville, B; Montreuil, J. Comparative study of the primary structures of sero-, lacto- and ovotransferrin glycans from different species. *Biochimie*, 1988,70:1459-1469.

Stafford, JL; Belosevic, M. Transferrin and the innate immune response of fish: identification of a novel mechanism of macrophage activation. *Developmental and Comparative Immunology*, 2003, 27:539-554.

Steinmetz, HT; Herbertz, A; Bertram, M; Diehl, V. Increase in interleukin-6 serum level preceding fever in granulocytopenia and correlation with death from sepsis. *Journal of Infectious Disease*, 1995, 171:225-228.

Sternlicht, MD; Werb, Z How matrix metalloproteinases regulate cell behavior. *Annual Review of Cell and Developmental Biology*, 2001, 17:463-516.

Suffredini, AF; Fantuzzi, G; Badolato, R; Oppenheim, JJ; O'Grady, NP. New insights into the biology of the acute phase response. Journal of Clinical Immunology, 1999, 19:203-214.

Taga, T; Kishimoto, T. Gp130 and the interleukin-6 family of cytokines. *Annual Review of Immunology*, 1997, 15:797-819.

Tanaka, T; Nakatani, S; Xuan, X; Kumura, H; Igarash, I; Shimazaki, K. Antiviral activity of lactoferrin against canine herpesvirus. *Antiviral Research*, 2003, 60:193-199.

Thibodeau, SN; Lee, DC; Palmiter, RD. Identical precursors for serum transferrin and egg white conalbumin. *Journal of Biological Chemistry*, 1978, 253:3771-3774.

Thomas, LL; Xu, W; Ardon, TT. Immobilized lactoferrin is a stimulus for eosinophil activation. *Journal of Immunology*, 2002, 169:993-999.

Valenti, P; Antonini, G; Von Hunolstein, C; Visca, P; Orsi, N; Antonini, F. Studies on the antimicrobial activity of ovotransferrin. *International Journal of Tissue Reaction*, 1983, 5: 97-105.

Vorland, LH. Lactoferrin: a multifunctional glycoprotein, 1999, *APMIS*, 107: 971-981.

Ward, PP. Lactoferrin and host defense. *Biochemistry and Cell Biology*, 2002, 80: 95-102.

Welch, SA. Comparison of the structure and properties of serum transferrin from 17 animal species. *Comparative Biochemistry and Physiology B*. 1990, 97:417-427.

Weinberg, ED. Suppression of bacterial biofilm formation by iron limitation. *Medical Hypotheses*, 2004, 63: 863-865.

Xie, H; Huff, GR; Huff, WE; Balog, JM; Holt, P; Rath, NC. Identification of ovotransferrin as an acute phase protein in chickens. *Poultry Science*, 2002a, 81:112-20.

Xie, H; Newberry, L; Clark, FD; Huff, WE; Huff, GR; Balog, JM; Rath, NC. Changes in serum ovotransferrin levels in chickens with experimentally induced inflammation and diseases. *Avian Disease*, 2002b, 46:122-131.

Xie, H; Huff, GR; Huff, WE; Balog, JM; Rath, NC. Effects of ovotransferrin on chicken macrophages and heterophil-granulocytes. *Developmental and Comparative Immunology*, 2002c, 26: 805-815.

Xie, H; Rath, NC; Huff, GR; Balog, JM; Huff, WE. Inflammation-induced changes in serum modulate chicken macrophage function. *Veterinary Immunology and Immunopathology*, 2001, 80:225-235.

Xie, H; Rath, NC; Huff, GR; Huff, WE; Balog, JM. Effects of Salmonella typhimurium lipopolysaccharide on broiler chickens. *Poultry Science*, 2000, 79: 33-40.

Xing, Z; Gauldie, J; Cox, G; Baumann, H; Jordana, M; Lei, XF; Achong, MK. IL-6 is an anti-inflammatory cytokine required for controlling local or systemic acute inflammatory responses. *Journal of Clinical Investigation*, 1998, 101:311-320.

Yoshiga, T; Hernandez, VP; Fallon, AM; Law, JH. Mosquito transferrin, an acute-phase protein that is up-regulated upon infection. *Proceedings of the National Academy of Science, U S A*, 1997, 94:12337-12342.

Yun, EY; Kang, SW; Hwang, JS; Goo, TW; Kim, SH; Jin, BR; Kwon, OY; Kim, KY. Molecular cloning and characterization of a cDNA encoding a transferrin homolog from Bombyx mori. *Biology and Chemistry*, 1999, 380:1455-1459.

In: New Immunology Research Developments
Editor: Gunter V. Müller
ISBN 978-1-60021-701-2


*Chapter 4*

# The Impact of Conjugated Linoleic Acid on Immunity

***Megan R. Ruth, Kate A. Hanneman and Catherine J. Field****
Department of Agricultural, Food and Nutritional Sciences
University of Alberta, Edmonton, Alberta, Canada

## Abstract

It is now well established that dietary polyunsaturated fatty acids (PUFA) ability to modulate immune function. There is less known about conjugated linoleic acid (CLA), a dietary PUFA that may also have immunomodulatory properties. CLA is a group of geometrical and positional isomers of linoleic acid (LA). Research has primarily focused on the cis9, trans11 (c9,t11) and trans10, cis12 (t10,c12) isomer singly or when fed in mixtures of isomers. The purpose of this review is to critically examine the *in vitro*, animal and human studies that have investigated the potential benefits of CLA on immune function. Although the area is in its infancy, there is evidence to support beneficial effects of feeding CLA isomers on immune-mediated catabolism, the ability to respond to bacterial and viral challenges, in allergic reactions, in inflammation and several aspects of the acquired immune system, including cytokine production, lymphocyte proliferation and immunoglobulin (Ig) production. To enable one to understand the potential significance of these studies, this review will include a background review of the immune system. Although the mechanistic pathway through which CLA acts on the immune system has yet to be determined, this review will propose candidate pathways through which CLA might modulate immune function.

**Keywords:** lipids, immunology, inflammation, cytokines, allergy, virus, bacteria, nutrition, conjugated linoleic acid, immunoglobulin, prostaglandins, leukotrienes

* Catherine.field@ualberta.ca

## Abbreviations

| | |
|---|---|
| AA | Arachadonic acid |
| Ab | Antibody |
| Ag | Antigen |
| APC | Antigen presenting cell |
| BALT | Bronchiole associated lymphoid tissue |
| BCR | B cell receptor |
| c9t11 | Cis9, trans11 |
| CLA | Conjugated linoleic acid |
| ConA | Concanavalin A |
| COX | Cyclo-oxygenase |
| CRP | C-reactive protein |
| DTH | Delyed-type hypersensitivity |
| EILN | Extra inguinal lymph nodes |
| EPA | eicosapentanoic acid |
| GALT | Gut associated lymphoid tissue |
| IFN-γ | Interferon-gamma |
| Ig | Immunoglobulin |
| IL | Interleukin |
| iNOS | Inducible nitric oxide synthase |
| IP | Intraperitoneal |
| LA | Linoleic acid |
| MLN | mesenteric lymph nodes |
| NFκβ | Nuclear factor- kappa β |
| NK | Natural killer |
| NO | Nitric oxide |
| PBMC | Peripheral blood mononuclear cells |
| PCV2 | Type 2 porcine circovirus |
| PG | Prostaglandins |
| $PGI_2$ | Prostacyclin |
| PHA | Phytohemagglutinin |
| PLA | Phospholipase A |
| PPAR | Peroxisome proliferator-activated receptor |
| PUFA | Polyunsaturated fatty acids |
| PWM | Pokeweed mitogen |
| ROI | Reactive oxygen intermediates |
| t9t11 | Trans9, trans11 |
| t10c12 | Trans10, cis12 |
| TCR | T cell receptor |
| TGF-β | Transforming growth factor-β |
| Th | T helper |
| TNF-α | Tumor necrosis factor-α |
| Ts | T suppressor |

| | |
|---|---|
| TX | Thromboxane |
| WBC | White blood cells |

# Introduction

The immune system defends our body from the invasion of foreign pathogens and prevents the survival and spread of altered self-cells. There are two branches of this complex system, the innate and adaptive or acquired, each providing unique functions but are inextricably linked. The innate system serves as the first line of defence against invading pathogens and tissue damage and key mediators involved in this non-specific branch are macrophages/monocytes, dendritic cells, and natural killer (NK) cells. The acquired immune system, consisting of T and B cells, develops over one's lifetime and maintains a memory of all of the foreign substances previously recognized enabling a more efficient response in future encounters. It is now well established that dietary polyunsaturated fatty acids (PUFA) have the ability to modulate immune function. Conjugated linoleic acid (CLA) is a group of geometrical and positional isomers of linoleic acid (LA), found in small amounts in the diet, which is reported to have immunomodulatory properties. The main dietary source of CLA is that produced by the bacteria *Butyrivibrio fibrisolvens* in the rumen and is therefore found in dairy and beef products. CLA can also be produced synthetically from various oils that are rich in LA, resulting in mixtures of many isomers of CLA. Research has focused on the cis9,trans11 (c9,t11) and trans10,cis12 (t10,c12) isomers, or a mixture of isomers in which the predominant species are a combination of these two isomers. The primary focus of this review is to critically examine the *in vitro*, animal and human studies that have investigated the potential benefits of CLA on immune function. To enable one to understand the potential significance of these studies, this paper will briefly review the various cells and molecules involved in immunity. Although the area is in its infancy, there is evidence to support immunomodulatory affects of feeding CLA isomers on immune-mediated catabolism, the ability to respond to bacterial and viral challenges, in allergic reactions, in inflammation and several aspects of the acquired immune system, including cytokine production, lymphocyte proliferation and immunoglobulin (Ig) production. Although the mechanistic pathways through which CLA acts on the immune system have yet to be determined, this review will attempt to purpose candidate pathways, including alteration of membrane composition and function, gene regulation or through the modification of lipid-derived mediators, such as prostaglandins (PG) and leukotrienes. The following sections will comprehensively review studies which have investigated CLA's role in immune-mediated catabolism, bacterial and viral challenges, allergy, inflammation, and various functions of the acquired immune system.

# Overview of Immunology

Immunology is the study of the immune system – a defence mechanism which includes not only resistance to disease, but also processes leading to allergy, graft rejection, autoimmune disease and inflammatory problems. An immune system is responsible for three tasks. The presence of a pathogen must be sensed. Upon recognition, the pathogen must be killed or contained. Less obvious is the requirement that a host's tissue must be spared in the process of accomplishing these first two processes [1]. The mammalian immune system can be loosely divided into two arms, innate (Figure 1) and adaptive (Figure 2). These branches are cooperative and it is difficult to clearly divide where innate responses end and adaptive ones begin. The innate system is generally regarded as the first line of defense and is present in all metazoan organisms [1]. This response is non-specific, meaning that it does not rely on previous memory of an antigen (Ag) nor does it need to have Ag presented to it. The innate immune system acts to quickly resist or control microbial invasion that might otherwise harm or kill the host. The innate response to a pathogen does not change with repeated exposure to a pathogen or other stimulants. The adaptive system has evolved only in vertebrates and acts in a very specific manner. This arm is dependent on the innate immune system and takes longer to generate but results in lifelong immunity or memory to a specific insult. This response involves the proliferation of lymphocytes, which are specialized cells of this arm, the secretion of antibodies (Ab) and other mediators (i.e. cytokines). A specific molecule that can initiate these responses, whether soluble or surface-bound, is referred to as an Ag, because it can stimulate the generation of Ab. Ag binds to receptors on the surface of lymphocytes and trigger their proliferation and the stimulation of an adaptive response.

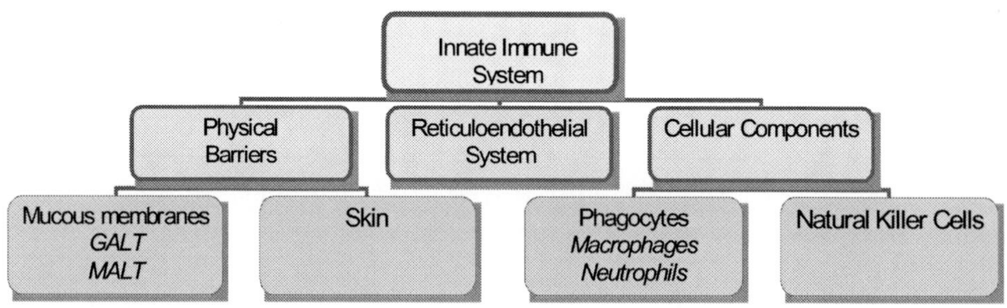


Figure 1. The Innate Immune System.

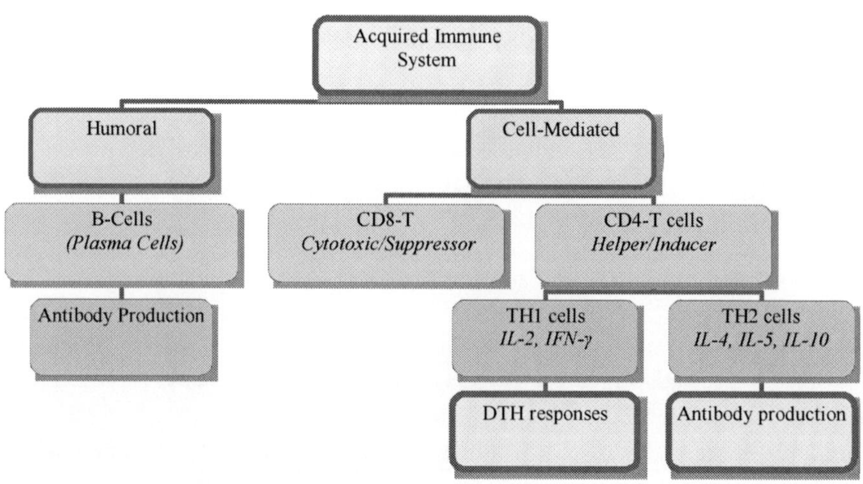


Figure 2. The Acquired Immune System.

# Organs of the Immune System

Lymphoid organs are organized tissues containing lymphocytes within a framework of non-immune cells. These organs are divided into primary or central lymphoid organs and peripheral or secondary lymphoid organs (Table 1). Primary organs are the sites of lymphocyte production and maturation. Secondary organs are the locations where lymphocytes migrate to and are first exposed to Ag. Lymphocytes are continuously circulating through peripheral organs, sites where Ag are transported to and presented by antigen presenting cells (APCs), such as macrophages or dendritic cells. Mucosal associated lymphoid tissue is a specialized subset of secondary organs and includes BALT (Bronchiole associated lymphoid tissues) and Gut associated lymphoid tissues (GALT) where lymphocytes act to protect the epithelium of the respiratory tract and the intestine respectively. Tonsils, adenoids, the appendix and Peyer's patches (located along the small intestine) are all components of GALT. Of the studies that examine the impact of nutrients on immune function, those in humans generally study blood derived immune cells and those conducted in animals examine blood, spleen or lymph node derived cells. Considerable differences exist in the composition and function of immune cells isolated from different tissues/organs and thus particular attention must be drawn to this when interpreting the literature.

**Table 1. Function of Human Lymphoid Organs**

| Organ | Function |
|---|---|
| *Primary* | • Lymphocytes are generated |
| Bone Marrow | • B and T cells originate<br>• B cells mature |
| Thymus | • T cells mature |
| *Secondary* | • Lymphocytes maintained<br>• Adaptive processes initiate: Lymphocytes and Ag meet |
| Lymph Nodes | • Convergence point of Ag and lymphocytes carried in the lymph |
| Spleen | • Convergence point of Ag and lymphocytes carried in the blood<br>• Trap and dispose of red blood cells |
| Mucosal Associated lymphoid tissue | • Protection of epithelial surfaces in frequent contact with pathogens |
| GALT | • Protection of gut epithelium |
| BALT | • Protection of respiratory epithelium |

# Innate Immunity

## Cells of the Innate Immune System

Cells involved in immunity (Table 2) are continuously generated in the bone marrow. The precursor is a pluripotent hematopoetic stem cell from which all cellular elements in the blood are derived. This gives rise to either a myeloid or lymphocyte progenitor. The myeloid line generates platelets and red blood cells in addition to several immune cells which are important in innate immunity (Table 2).

**Table 2. Cells Involved in Immunity**

| CELL | Location | Function |
|---|---|---|
| Myeloid | | |
| Monocyte | Blood | Differentiate into macrophage upon migration to tissue |
| Macrophage | Tissue (throughout body) | Phagocytosis: engulf and kill microbes<br>Secretion of chemotactic cytokines: recruit polymorphonuclear cells<br>Initiation of adaptive response: present Ag to T cells |
| Dendritic cell | Tissue/Lymph Node | Initiation of adaptive response: present Ag to T cells<br>Phagocytosis in tissue |
| Mast cell | Tissue | Release of granule contents: affect vascular permeability<br>Mediator of allergic responses |
| Polymorphonuclear cells | | Containment of infection |
| Neutrophils | Blood | Phagocytosis, important in defense against bacteria<br>Kill microbes |
| Eosinophils | Blood | Production of inflammatory mediators<br>Kill Ab-coated parasites |
| Basophils | Blood | Production of inflammatory mediators |
| Lymphoid | Bone Marrow | |
| NK cells | | Lyse cells: release cytotoxic contents of granules |
| B lymphocyte | | Secrete Ab |
| T lymphocyte | | Central to adaptive response |
| CD8+ | | Lyse cells: release cytotoxic contents of granules |
| CD4+ | | Activate other immune cells |
| Th1 | | Aid cell mediated response |
| Th2 | | Aid humoral (Ab) response |

Monocytes, derived from the myeloid lineage, circulate in the blood and differentiate into macrophages upon migration to tissues. Macrophages engulf pathogens by the process of phagocytosis and degrade them in intracellular vesicles. When immature, dendritic cells are also capable of phagocytosis, but become specialized to display Ag to lymphocytes upon activation. Following engulfment of a microbe, dendritic cells mature and migrate to lymph nodes where they efficiently initiate an adaptive immune response by presenting Ag to CD4+ T lymphocytes via major histocompatability complex (MHC) class II molecules. Mast cells, also of myeloid lineage, differentiate in the tissue and once activated release substances that affect vascular permeability. They function primarily in allergic responses by releasing histamine. Granulocytes or polymorphonuclear cells are a category of cells with dense staining granules in the cytoplasm and odd shaped nuclei. They include neutrophils, which are important phagocytising cells in the innate defense; eosinophils, which are important in parasitic infection; and basophils, which are similar to mast cells and eosinophils and play a role in allergy. Myeloid cells have specialized effector mechanisms and can act on their independently; however, they function optimally when acting in conjunction with elements of the adaptive arm. NK cells respond to an Ag non-specifically and thus are commonly categorized as mediators of the innate branch. NK cells are capable of killing abnormal cells directly, including those infected by viruses or those that have undergone nuclear modifications (i.e tumors) by releasing the lytic contents of their granules.

## Detection

Physical barriers, including skin and the gastrointestinal track, mucus and cilia, act to protect the host from the external environment and are composed of epithelial cells (tight junctions). If these barriers are breached then the host must depend on the next line of defence, the innate immune system. This major defence system is a simple, non-specific detection system, which depends on a limited number of receptors to recognize microbial constituents that are highly conserved among pathogenic organisms. These must not bind to or recognize molecules of host origin. These receptors have been termed pattern recognition receptors, and the molecules they recognize are referred to as pathogen associated molecular patterns [1]. It is now accepted that specific molecules are recognized and not necessarily a pattern, and that all microbes, not only pathogens, are identified through this system. Microbial molecules that have been identified to date include: LPS (lipopolysaccaride) of gram negative bacteria, peptidoglycan present in the cell walls of gram positive bacteria, unmethylated DNA, double stranded RNA, flagella and lipoteichoic acid [1].

## Response

One of the first reactions initiated in response to a recognized pathogen is the release of vasoactive, antimicrobial and chemotactic factors. Phagocytic cells are recruited to sites of injury or infection via a chemotactic gradient and the increased permeability of the endothelium allows them to move to the site of infection. These signals are amplified further when phagocytosis commences, promoting further release of inflammatory and antimicrobial mediators. The last step in the activation of the adaptive response is the transport of microbes and other antigenic material to the regional lymph nodes via the lymphatic system. This response occurs rapidly but is relatively non-specific.

## Inflammation

Inflammation is a physiological response to stimuli such as injury or infection and includes classic symptoms of swelling, redness, heat and pain. This process results in three main events. Autocoids, such as histamine and bradykinin, cause vasodilation resulting in increased blood flow to the area and a reduction in blood flow velocity. These vasoactive amines are classic mediators of immediate vascular permeability, which promotes tissue swelling (oedema) along with the influx of cells and proteins. The movement of phagocytes into infected or damaged areas is facilitated by the upregulation of adhesion molecules on capillaries, such as E-selectin and VCAM-1. A group of plasma proteins, complement, is also activated in cascades by tissue damage. Complement is involved in three main functions: the direct killing of microbes via the membrane attack complex (C5b, C6, C7, C8, C9); promoting phagocytosis by opsonizing pathogens (C3b); and promoting influx of immune cells through chemotactic factors (C3a, C5a). The damage imposed to the epithelium results in the release of several proteins including specific cytokines, which are small proteins that generally function locally in cell to cell communication (Table 3). Chemokines are compounds that function to effectively recruit cells with the appropriate receptor to move up the gradient toward the site of injury. Reactive oxygen intermediates (ROI) are produced within the phagosomes of neutrophils and macrophages to kill microbes. One of the most important ROI is nitric oxide (NO). NO is a lysosomal constituent that dilates blood vessels and acts to kill bacteria. Neutrophils also release the contents of their granules during inflammation. C-reactive protein (CRP) is an acute phase protein produced in the liver that is another marker of inflammation. One of its major roles is to trigger the complement cascade and its release from hepatocytes is initiated by the proinflammatory cytokines IL-1 and IL-6 [2]. Elevated levels of CRP are indicative of an inflammatory response and are observed during states of acute infection or chronic inflammatory conditions such as rheumatoid arthritis [3]. More recently, serum levels of CRP have been recognized as predictors of cardiovascular disease in patients who are at increased risk and elevated levels have been correlated with reduced endothelial function [4].

Unfortunately, host tissues are not resistant to these pro-inflammatory and reactive molecules and thus, are normally released in small, controlled amounts to prevent serious damage to the host. There are several enzymes, which are essential in the cascade leading to the generation of inflammatory lipid mediators or eicosanoids. Phospholipase $A_2$ ($PLA_2$) catalyzes the release of arachidonic acid (AA) from the sn2 position of cell membrane phospholipids to initiate the cascade of events leading to eicosanoid production [5]. Downstream of $PLA_2$, cyclo-oxygenase (COX) converts AA into PG; and 5-lipo-oxygenase catalyzes leukotriene (LT) production. Important PG are thromboxane $(TX)A_2$ which promotes platelet aggregation and constricts blood vessels; prostacyclin ($PGI_2$) which prevents platelet aggregation and dilates blood vessels; and PGE which is an important vasodilator and potentates the action of bradykinin and chemotactic mediators. LTs that are important in inflammation include $LTC_4$ (and its products $D_4$ and $E_4$) which promotes vascular permeability and smooth muscle contraction and $LTB_4$ which is a chemotactic agent. In addition to the lipid mediators produced by COX enzymatic action, there is a group of prostaglandin-like compounds generated from AA independent of COX activity. Isoprostanes are produced by the peroxidation of AA in presence of free radicals and contain the prostane ring structure present in prostaglandins [6]. Several isomers of $F_2$-isoprostane are generated during this lipid peroxidation of AA, as well as other isoprostanes including $E_2$, $D_2$, $A_2$, $J_2$ [6]. $F_2$-isoprostane is now considered a reliable and accurate in vivo marker of oxidative stress [6].

The inflammatory response to infection is generally a necessary life-preserving response. However, should the same mechanisms that function to contain small infections generalize to a systemic response, the general health of the host may be compromised. Persistent inflammation can also result in unwanted tissue damage and is considered a risk factor for some cancers and more recently for cardiovascular disease. There are many checkpoints and regulatory processes involved in the generation and resolution of the inflammatory response to protect host tissue. Cytokines (Table 3) are involved in the inflammatory response. The proinflammatory cytokines are interleukin (IL)-1β, tumor necrosis factor (TNF)-α, IL-6, interferon-gamma (IFN-γ), and IL-12. Other proinflammatory mediators include LT, some of the PG and NO. The anti-inflammatory cytokines are IL-4, IL-10 and transforming growth factor (TGF)-β.

## Adaptive/Acquired Immunity

### Cells of the Adaptive/Acquired Immune System

The adaptive or acquired immune response develops over the lifetime of an individual in response to environmental challenges (pathogens/Ag). Cells of the adaptive immune system (Table 2), lymphoid cells, are dependent upon innate mediators. Lymphoid cells include T (differentiate in thymus) and B (differentiate in the bone marrow) lymphocytes. Naïve lymphocytes are mature cells that have not yet encountered Ag via their Ag-specific receptors. They circulate in the blood and lymphatic system where they proliferate and differentiate into effector cells upon recognizing an Ag. The two arms of the acquired immune system are cell-mediated (T-cells) and humoral (B-cells).

### T Cell Function

T lymphocytes are divided into two main subsets based on the presence of surface markers, CD4+ (helper/inducer) and CD8+ (cytotoxic/suppressor) cells. T cells are activated by a signal they receive through their T cell receptor (TCR) when Ag is presented in association with the major histocompatibility complex (MHC) molecules on the surface of an APC, such as dendritic cells or macrophages. A single lymphocyte has receptors capable of identifying only one specific component (epitope) of a given Ag.

**Table 3. Cytokines and Chemokines Involved in Immunity**

| Cytokine | Production | Action | Involvement |
|---|---|---|---|
| Hepatopoietins | | | |
| IL-2 | T cells | • T-cell proliferation | |
| IL-4 | T cells, mast cells | • B cell activation<br>• IgE switch Suppresses<br>• Th1 cells | Th2 responses |
| IL-5 | T cells, mast cells | • Eosinophil growth and differentiation | Th2 responses |
| IL-6 | T cells, macrophages, endothelial cells | • T and B cell growth and differentiation<br>• Acute phase protein production<br>• Fever | Inflammation |
| IL-9 | T cells | • Enhances mast cell activity<br>• Stimulates Th2 | Th2 responses |
| IL-13 | T cells | • B cell growth and differentiation<br>• Inhibits production of inflammatory cytokines Inhibits Th1 cells | Th2 responses |
| GM-CSF | Macrophages, T cells | • Dendritic cells growth and differentiation | |
| Interferons | | | |
| IFN-α | Leukocytes | • Increases MHC class I expression<br>• Induces resistance to viral replication<br>• Activates NK cells | Antiviral, antitumor |
| IFN-β | Fibroblasts | • Increases MHC class I expression<br>• Induces resistance to viral replication<br>• Activates NK cells | Antiviral |
| IFN-γ | Macrophages T cells, NK cells | • Regulates macrophage maturation<br>• Classical macrophage activation<br>• Increases MHC class I and II expression<br>• Ig class switching<br>• Suppresses Th2 | Inflammation Th1 responses |
| TNF Family | | | |
| TNF-α | Macrophages, T cells, NK cells, mast cells | • Upregulate adhesion molecules on endothelium<br>• Stimulates polymorphonucelar cells, activates macrophages<br>• Promotes Lymphocyte proliferation | Acute inflammatory response |
| TNF-β | T cells, B cells | • Killing<br>• Endothelial activation | |
| Unassigned | | | |
| TGF-β | Monocytes, T cells | • Inhibits cell growth<br>• IgA switch<br>• Late in response, down regulates classically activated macrophages | Anti-inflammatory |
| IL-1α | Macrophages, epithelial cells | • Fever<br>• T cell and macrophage activation<br>• Upregulate adhesion molecules on endothelium | Acute inflammatory response |
| IL-1β | Macrophages, epithelial cells | • Fever<br>• T cell and macrophage activation | |
| IL-10 | T cells, macrophages | • Suppresses macrophage function | Th2 responses |
| IL-12 | B cells, macrophages | • Activates NK cells<br>• Stimulates Th1 | Th1 responses |
| Chemokines | | | |
| IL-8 | | • Attracts Neutrophils | |

However, there are millions of different B and T cells creating a huge repertoire of Ag specificities so that potentially any Ag can be recognized by the acquired immune system. CD4+ cells are activated by exogenous Ag presented on MHC class II molecule and function to activate other immune cells such as B cells and macrophages. Macrophages are activated to produce IL-1, which stimulates T helper (Th) cells to generate IL-2, which consequently activates both T and B lymphocyte populations and recruits other cells to the site. Cytokines produced and secreted by lymphocytes can also be used to identify immune cells. For example, the CD4+ subset is subdivided into classes of immune cells based on the cytokines they produce and secrete. Th-1 cells produce IL-2 and IFN-γ, which generally promote a cell-mediated inflammatory response. Th2 cells produce IL-4, IL-5, IL-10 and IL-13, which support a humoral Ab response. More recently a cytokine pattern to describe a Th0 (produces both Th1 and Th2 cytokines) and Th3 (produces TGF-β) response by T cells has been described. Although Th1 and Th2 cytokine profiles are not as clearly defined in humans as they are in rodents, it has been hypothesized that the balance between these two responses may explain how the immune system can respond appropriately to a specific type of infection.

Cytotoxic CD8+ T-cells are activated via endogenous Ag presented on MHC class I molecules. Once activated, these T-lymphocytes can directly kill target cells. These cells contain granules that contain perforin, a substance that creates 'pores' on target cell membranes and allows for the entry of lytic substances into the cells. Destruction of infected cells can also be carried out through apoptosis, a process that is thought to be mediated by cytokines secreted by the CD8+ cells. Cytotoxic CD8+ T-cells, like CD4+ cells, can be identified by the cytokines they produce and similar to Th cells they have been separated into T (suppressor)-0, Ts-1 and Ts-2.

## B Cell Function and Ig

The humoral branch is comprised of B cells, which are the Ab producing cells effective against soluble proteins generated from pathogens such as bacteria and fungi. B lymphocytes can modulate the function of other immune cells or can directly destroy cells infected with intracellular pathogens. With the help of Th cells, B lymphocytes can respond to soluble protein Ags. In contrast, B cells can respond directly to bacterial wall components, such as LPS, without the aid of Th cells. Similar to the TCR, B-cells express a B-cell receptor (BCR), composed of a membrane Ig and two Igα and Igβ heterodimers [7], which enables these lymphocytes to directly recognize a specific Ag. Bacterial polysaccharides, such as LPS, are highly effective at cross-linking the BCR, thereby directly activating B cells [7]. Ag with weaker affinity for the BCR can be internalized and processed for binding to MHC II molecules for presentation to CD4+ T-cells. Once activated, CD4+ cells serve to trigger a B cell response specific to the Ag presented. Direct or indirect activation of mature B cells induces B cells to become memory or Ab-secreting plasma cells specific to the Ag encountered.

Plasma cells secrete a variety of Ab isotypes including IgM, IgE, IgA, IgG and IgD. Collectively, Abs act to neutralize toxins, prevent bacterial and viral invasion of host cells, facilitate phagocytosis by coating target cells (opsonization) and activate complement [7]. During a primary response (first encounter with a specific Ag), plasma cells initially secrete IgM, followed by increasing class-switch to IgG [8]. IgM constitutes approximately 5% of serum Ab levels [9]. Membrane-bound IgM is in monomeric form, whereas, plasma cells secrete a pentameric form of IgM, which due to its higher valency, can bind more readily to larger, multidimensional Ag compared to other Ig s [8]. IgG subclasses are the predominant Abs found in human serum, accounting for approximately 85% of the total Igs [9]. There are four subclasses of IgG, IgG1, IgG2, IgG3 and IgG4 and they function to activate complement, to protect fetal development (cross placental barrier), and to facilitate opsonization [8]. IgA accounts for 7-15% of total serum Ab and exists primarily as a monomer. Production of secretory IgA (dimer or tetramer) surpasses that of all other Abs and is secreted at mucous membrane surfaces, including the small intestine and the respiratory tract [8]. IgE composes less than 1% of the total Igs in human serum [9] and is involved primarily in type I hypersensitivity responses and to a lesser extent is involved in parasitic infections [8]. IgD also accounts for less than 1% of total serum Ab and next to IgM it is the major membrane-bound Ig on B cells [9]. Presently, little is known about its functional role in its secreted form [10]. Similar to T lymphocytes, B lymphocytes can also be subdivided into two different subsets, B1 and B2 type B cells. B1 cells are defined by the cell surface expression of IgM and IgD and are mainly involved in Ab production, which is independent of T-cells, whereas, B2 cells are responsible for T-cell dependent responses to Ag [7].

# CLA and Immune Function

## Introduction

It is widely accepted that nutrients are fundamental to development and homeostasis of the immune system. Researchers in the field of nutritional immunology have identified several macro and micronutrients, which are particularly important to immune health. Lipids, particularly PUFA, can modulate lymphocyte proliferation, cytokine and Ig production, or phagocytic activity [11, 12]. Many different mechanisms have been identified to explain the influence of lipids, predominantly PUFA, on immune function (Figure 3).

Via Changes in:

- Gene Expression
- Immune/Tissue Development
- Membrane Structure and Composition
- Membrane-mediates Functions and Signals
  - Membrane Lipids
  - Membrane Proteins

Figure 3. Mechanisms by which fatty acids can influence immune function.

One of the best-characterized mechanism by which dietary lipids modulate these immune parameters is through incorporation into the plasma membrane of immune cells. These changes in lipid composition have been reported to alter membrane-mediated signal transduction and/or protein composition on the cell surface, which influence the subsequent pathways and ultimate function of the cells.

In addition, other methods may exist by which lipids alter immune function, including changes to gene expression. Several transcription factors, such as peroxisome proliferator-activated receptor (PPAR) and nuclear factor kappa B (NFκB), have been identified as direct targets for PUFA [11]. Several groups have provided evidence that manipulating dietary intake of specific PUFAs can alter levels and activity of these and other transcription factors [11, 13].

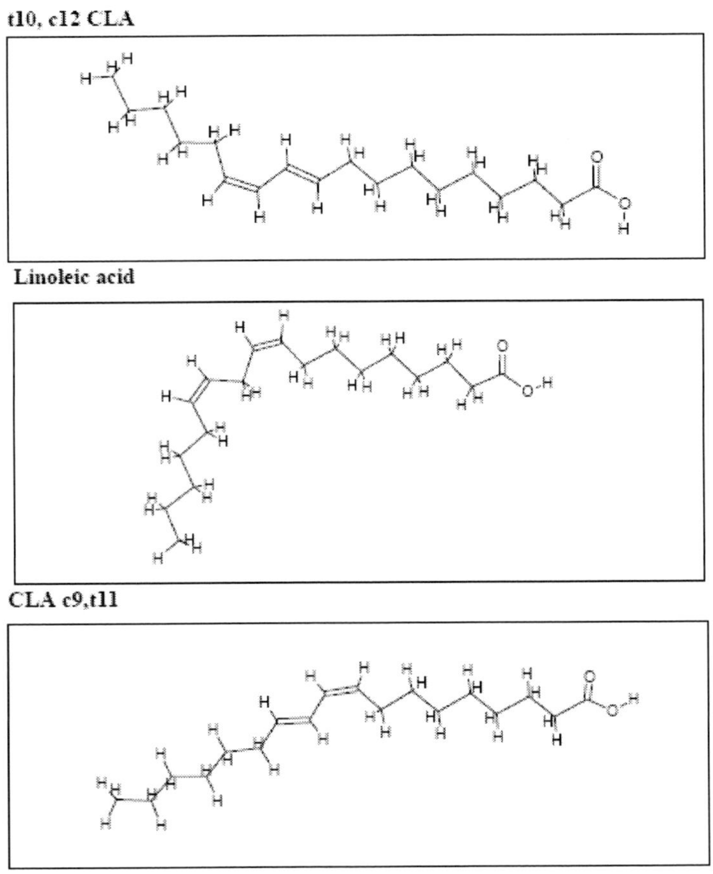


Figure 4. Linoleic acid and the major isomers of CLA.

In addition to plasma membrane incorporation, emerging research has identified specialized membrane components, termed lipid rafts, which may be fundamental to immune cell signalling [14, 15]. Research in this area has focused primarily on n-3 fatty acids, particularly eicosapentanoic acid (EPA) and docosahexanoic acid, and their role in altering lipid raft composition of T-cells.

A dietary lipid that has been of particular interest to scientists more recently, is CLA. CLA is a collective term that refers to a class of positional and geometric conjugated dienoic isomers of linoleic acid (LA) (Figure 4). The most abundant, naturally occurring isomer is the cis-9, trans-11 (c9t11) isomer [16]. It is formed from LA as an intermediate species in the biohydrogenation of LA to vaccenic acid in the rumen [16], making dairy and beef products the main source of this isomer in the diet [16].

CLA can also be produced synthetically from various oils that are rich in LA (e.g. safflower oil, canola oil, soy oil) by alkaline isomerization reactions [17]. Synthetically prepared CLA mixtures are composed of many isomers, but c9t11 and trans-10, cis-12 (t10c12) usually comprise the majority of isomers [16]. There are many studies that have investigated the effects of CLA in cell culture, animal models and human trials. From animal studies, many potential beneficial health effects for CLA have been reported (Table 4). Experimental evidence indicates that the various CLA isomers have favourable effects (albeit not necessarily the same effects) on atherosclerosis, body composition and systemic inflammation [18, 19].Both isomers have been reported to have potent anti-carcinogenic properties [12]. Although, evidence collected from animal models and cell culture work is convincing, there has been little research conducted to elucidate the isomer-specific effects in humans. Since the discovery that this fatty acid has anti-carcinogenic properties in 1979 [20], several investigators have attempted to identify CLA's role in immune function as well as the molecular pathways utilized by this fatty acid. Despite a growing body of literature in support of CLA's activity in modification of immune function, inconsistencies persist and the mechanistic pathway(s) through which immunomodulation occurs has yet to be identified. The remainder of this chapter will thoroughly review the current literature investigating CLA's role in inflammation and various aspects of immune function.

**Table 4. Reported Potential Beneficial Effects of CLA on Health in Animal Models**

| Putative Effect | Reference |
|---|---|
| Positively affects body composition | [21] |
| Decreases incidence of diabetes | [19] |
| Bone Health | [22] |
| Preserves muscle mass | [23] |
| Decreases subcutaneous fat | [24] |
| Reduces body fat | [25] |
| Suppresses the development of hypertension | [26] |

# Immune-Mediated Catabolism

## Animal Feeding Studies

Exploration into the effects of CLA on immune-mediated catabolism is limited to animal studies, but preliminary evidence suggests a beneficial effect. Miller et al (1994) [27] induced immune-mediated catabolism in mice by intraperitoneal (IP) injections of LPS. Mice consuming a 0.5% w/w CLA mixture of isomers for 15 days prior to LPS injections lost less body weight and recovered faster to pre-injection weight. It was suggested by these authors that decreased $PGE_2$ production might have contributed to this slower rate of catabolism [27].

Furthermore, splenocytes isolated from these mice had an increased proliferative response following ex vivo phytohemaglutinin (PHA) stimulation [27]. This same group reported that feeding the same mixture of CLA to rats for 14 days and chicks for 7 days allowed animals that received LPS injections to gain weight similar to animals that were not treated with LPS [27]. Yang and Cook (2003) [28] examined the effects of immune-mediated catabolism in mice. Mice were fed nutritionally complete diets with or without 0.5% w/w synthetic CLA mixture for 6 weeks and received IP injections at the end of this feeding period to induce cachexia. There was a decrease in LPS-induced weight loss and anorexia in mice fed CLA [28]. Furthermore, plasma levels of TNF-α were lower when CLA was supplemented in the diet and the authors suggested that this may have contributed to the improved weight loss and anorexia [28]. Resident peritoneal macrophages were also examined in this study and despite the in vivo decrease in the plasma, TNF-α level was unchanged with ex vivo LPS treatment [28]. There was, however, a reduction in NO levels in IFN-γ and LPS stimulated cells. These animal studies suggest that feeding a mixture of CLA isomers is beneficial when animals are challenged with catabolic cytokines or bacterial products. In addition to the benefits on reducing weight loss, CLA also lowered plasma levels of the inflammatory-catabolic cytokine TNF-α. As suggested by Yang and Cook (2003), this may partially contribute to protecting the host against weight loss and anorexia. However, Turini et al (2003) [29] explored the effects of CLA supplementation in dexamethasone treated rats and concluded that this fatty acid has little effect on immune function. Following IP dexamethasone injections, animals were fed a 0.5%w/w synthetic CLA isomer mixture for 4 days. Contrary to previous reports, CLA supplementation did not alter unstimulated or PHA-stimulated splenocyte proliferative response. There was, however, an observed increase in the number of blood monocytes, while other white blood cells (WBC) were unaffected by CLA treatment. This study suggests that supplementation with a CLA mixture may not influence steroid-induced immune catabolism or that 4 days of feeding CLA is an insufficient period of time to impact immune or muscle metabolism. Clearly, differences exist in the methods employed to induce immune-catabolism between studies and also in the immune parameters measured and the mixtures of isomers of CLA that were fed.

Further to these studies designed specifically to address immune-mediated catabolism, Changhua et al (2005) [30] conducted a study to explore the impact of CLA supplementation during states of acute inflammation induced by LPS injections. When pigs were fed a 2% w/w CLA mixture (1:1) for 28 days, decreased levels of $PGE_2$, TNF-α, IL-1β and IL-6 and increased levels of IL-10 were observed in plasma of the LPS injected animals [30]. Feeding CLA isomers also suppressed mRNA expression of TNF-α and IL-6 and elevated expression of IL-10 and PPAR-γ in spleen and thymus tissue of LPS challenged pigs. CLA supplementation, however, did not alter IL-1β mRNA expression in either tissue. This report supports the earlier studies of Miller and Yang that suggested that feeding mixtures of CLA isomers is beneficial during acute episodes of inflammation. In summary, in vivo studies in general support that feeding mixtures of CLA isomers prior to the induction of immune-mediated catabolism is beneficial. Additional research is necessary to isolate the isomer-specific role of CLA in preventing or diminishing the damage caused by induction of immune-mediated catabolism. Specific detail should also be paid to the duration of the feeding studies.

### *In Vitro* Studies of the Response to LPS

*In vitro* studies using LPS as a mitogen, have also been utilized to explore the role that CLA has on bacterial Ag. Yang (2003) [28] examined the impact of individual CLA isomers on a murine macrophage cell line, RAW264.7, stimulated with LPS. TNF-α production by this macrophage cell line was reduced by incubation with 50μM and 100μM of the *c*9,*t*11 isomer in a dose-dependent manner [28]. The *t*10,*c*12 isomer did not have this effect [28]. This finding is supported by two other studies conducted in RAW macrophages. Both Iwakiri et al (2002) [31] and Cheng et al [32] reported that incubation with a CLA isomer mixtures suppressed LPS-induced NO and $PGE_2$ production and reduced inducible nitric oxide synthase (iNOS) and COX 2 mRNA. Iwakiri's group incubated with a low dose of CLA of only 30μM; whereas Cheng's group found significant differences at all studied concentrations of CLA (20μM, 100μM or 200μM) for $PGE_2$ and iNOS, but only at 100μM and 200μM for NO and COX2. Furthermore, Cheng (2004) [32] shows that CLA's suppressive activity may be mediated via the NF-κB pathway as CLA decreased phosphorylated IκBα, thus reducing NF-κB DNA binding activity. In support of this finding, Changhua et al (2005) [30] reported that porcine peripheral blood mononuclear cells (PBMC) treated with 100μM of c9t11, t10c12 or a CLA mixture (1:1) reduced the production and mRNA expression of TNF-α, IL-1β and IL-6. Examination of the individual isomers revealed that the t10c12 isomer had greater suppressive activity than the c9t11 isomer [33]. Collectively, *in vitro* work strongly supports a role for both of the major CLA isomers together or individually in suppressing the secretion and activity of pro-inflammatory mediators after LPS stimulation and is further strengthened by Cheng's work that provides a possible mechanism through inhibition of the NF-κB pathway of inflammation. Future *in vitro* work should be directed at clarifying the mechanistic pathways utilized by the individual CLA isomers to exert this potentially immuno-protective response.

## Bacterial and Viral Challenges

### Bacterial Challenges

For ethical reasons, animals are used to establish the efficacy of a dietary supplement on the response to a bacterial or viral challenge. In the case of CLA, pigs have been used as the model to determine the impact of bacterial challenges. Hontecillas et al (2002) [34] explored the role that a 1.33% w/w synthetically-derived CLA mixture had in weanling pigs challenged with *B. hyodysenteriae*, a bacteria that induces swine dysentery [34]. Feeding CLA for 49 days prior to intramuscular inoculation prevented the bacterial-induced enlargement of colonic mucosa and minimized epithelial damage [34]. Furthermore, CLA appeared to have preserved the number of CD4+ and CD8α+ cells in colonic tissue at concentrations similar to uninfected pigs [34]. In the same paper, Hontecillas reported that supplementation with the identical CLA isomer mixture for 72 days prior to induction of colitis with *B. hyodysenteriae* maintained IL-10 and IFN-γ mRNA expression similar to non-infected pigs. The mRNA expression of PPAR-γ was also enhanced in CLA-supplemented pigs following infection compared to pigs that received the non-supplemented control diet. Additionally, the inflammation-mediated damage induced by *B. hyodysenteriae* to colonic tissue was prevented when pigs consumed this CLA mixture. In both experiments, CLA minimized the bacterial induced growth suppression compared to the control diet, suggesting that supplementing pigs during development may help pigs to thrive in face of immune challenge. These experiments propose that CLA could participate in preserving the integrity of colonic tissue and colonic immune function in cases of acute inflammation, such as ulcerative colitis. The authors also provide a possible mechanism through which CLA mediates the beneficial effects on colonic immune function.

## Viral Challenges

To date, only one research group has explored the immunomodulatory capacity of CLA in virally challenged animals. Bassaganya-Riera et al (2003) [35] investigated the effects of CLA supplementation on the immune system's response to type 2 porcine circovirus (PCV2), a single-stranded DNA *Circoviridae* virus. Pigs were supplemented with 1.33% w/w CLA mixture for 63 days. On day 42, the lysate obtained from PCV2-infected PK-15 cells was injected into the extra inguinal lymph nodes. Regardless of whether or not pigs were infected with PCV2, feeding CLA increased the percentage of CD4+CD8+ and CD8+ cells in the thymus and expanded the proportion of CD8+CD45RC+ in the peripheral blood [35]. The proportion of CD8+CD29$^{low}$ and CD8+CD25+ cells were also augmented in blood of uninfected and infected pigs, respectively, by CLA dietary treatment [35]. Additionally, CLA diminished the depletion of B-cells in EILN following the viral challenge; however, the proliferative response of B-cells to either a PCV2 Ag or the mitogen ConA was not affected by dietary treatment [35]. PCV2-induced IFN-γ production (ex vivo) was also suppressed by dietary CLA in CD4+ cells, but this change was not observed in CD8+ T-cells. The proliferative response of CD8+ T-cells was increased at day 56 and 63 in infected pigs only. Even though the authors indicate that CLA decreased the intracellular levels of IFN-γ and mRNA expression of IL-12 in infected pigs and IL-18 in uninfected animals, there was no significant ($p>0.05$) main effect of diet on these outcomes, nor was there a dietary effect on IL-2mRNA expression. Further to the direct effects CLA had on immune cells, CLA-fed infected pigs gained weight similar to uninfected pigs [35], possibly due to increased food intake. Post-mortem examination revealed that PCV2 DNA was recovered from the (EILN) of 25% of CLA-fed pigs as compared to 50% of pigs fed the control diet. In summary, it is difficult to draw any conclusive remarks regarding the effectiveness of dietary CLA treatment on immune function during in vivo viral challenge. This single study provides some preliminary evidence that CLA can influence the host's immune response when a virus is introduced in vivo. These effects appear to be positive, as evidenced by greater expansion and proliferative response of CD8+ T-cells, preservation of B-cell population, better growth performance and feed intake and reduced viral infection. However, it is necessary to clearly identify the role that single isomers have in viral infections, including the biological mechanisms involved.

## Vaccine Responses in Animals

Bassaganya-Riera (2001) [36] examined the effect of supplementing pigs with a 1.33% w/w CLA mixture for 72 days during which animals were intramuscularly vaccinated with a proteinase digested *B. hyodysenteriae* bacterin; animals in the control group received intramuscular injections of squalene adjuvant preparation. The authors reported that in both vaccinated and unvaccinated animals, CLA enhanced the expansion of TCRγδCD8αα cells, an NK cell subset ($CD3^{-}$CD16+ CD8αα+) and TCRαβ+CD8αβ+ cells in peripheral blood [36]. Feeding CLA, however, did not influence the proportion of CD4 single-positive T cells in blood. Thymocyte phenotypes were influenced by CLA supplementation. On day 35, the proportion of CD8αβ+ and CD4-CD8- thymocytes was greater in pigs that consumed CLA [36]. Granzyme activity in PBMC was increased regardless of whether or not pigs were vaccinated and this increase was positively correlated with the greater proportion of CD8αβ+ T-cells [36]. Furthermore, the proliferative response of TCRγδ+CD8αα+ cells and CD4+ single-positive T-cells (B. *hyodysenteriae* bacterin-stimulated) was greater in pigs fed CLA [36]. Overall, the authors concluded that CLA improved cellular immunity due to expansion of the CD8+ cell population and thus supplemented pigs may fare better when their immune systems are challenged during growth. Further evidence (such as Ab titres or re-challenging animals with the Ag) are required to confirm that animals feed CLA increases the ability of animals to respond to immune challenges after their immune systems have been primed.

## Vaccine Responses in Humans

A robust immune response must be generated in response to a vaccine to achieve sufficient immune memory to a pathogen. The impact of feeding CLA isomers on vaccination response in humans has been explored in two studies. The effect of feeding CLA was tested in human females, it was reported in one study that there was no effect on the titre response to influenza virus [37]. Women were acclimatized to a basal diet for 30 days and then fed 3.9 g/day of a synthetic CLA mixture for 63 days. At day 65, women received a trivalent influenza (1997-1998) vaccination and PBMC were used to assess several immune parameters. The authors reported that consuming CLA did not influence circulating WBC counts, lymphocyte proliferative response to phytohemaglutinin (PHA), delayed-type hypersensitivity (DTH) response or serum Ab titres [37]. More recently, the outcome of vaccination against hepatitis B virus in healthy male subjects supplemented with 1.7 g/day of a 1:1 (c9t11:t10c12) or 1.6 g/day of an 80:20 (c9t11:t10c12) CLA mixture has been reported [38]. On day 43, 57 and 71 volunteers were injected with a recombinant DNA hepatitis B surface Ag. Although the authors of this study claimed that feeding the 50:50 CLA mixture may have improved the human immune response to hepatitis B vaccination, none of their results reached statistical significance (i.e. $P \leq 0.05$ was not reached). Further to this finding, there was no difference in NK cell target lysis, DTH response, PBMC proliferative response to LPS or PHA or the production of IL-2, IL4 and IFN-γ (PHA-stimulated) or TNF-α, IL-6, IL-1β and PGE2 (LPS-stimulated). Despite the positive results on bacterial vaccinations in piglets, both of these human clinical studies do not support that consuming a mixture of CLA isomers prior to influenza or hepatitis B virus vaccination will improve the titre response. Specie-specific differences could account for these discrepancies; however, age may also have been an important factor. In pigs, CLA was supplemented to growing animals, which may partly explain why significant findings were observed in this study, as opposed to the clinical trials that examined adult humans. Thus, further research is necessary to identify the isomer-specific role of CLA on vaccination response in humans.

## Allergy

Allergy or a type I hypersensitivity reaction is an immune response to an innocuous substance, defined as an allergen. Animal studies feeding CLA have provided some promising results. Whigham et al. (2001) [39] reported that feeding a 0.25% w/w CLA mixture to guinea pigs for 25 days suppressed type I hypersensitivity responses. After consuming the experimental diets for one week, animals were primed with IP injections of chicken egg ovalbumin (OVA). The animals continued to consume CLA for two more weeks and were then challenged with subcutaneous injections of OVA. The subsequent type I hypersensitivity response was examined. Tracheal contractions were reduced in animals that consumed CLA as reported as a percent of maximal carbachol-induced contraction [39]. Tracheal release of histamine was also suppressed in CLA fed animals, although total histamine release did not differ between the treatment and control groups [39]. Finally, total $PGE_2$ release from tracheal tissue and superfusates was also down-regulated in guinea pigs that consumed CLA suggesting an effect on PG synthesis [39]. Although it appears that CLA suppressed the type I hypersensitivity response, dietary treatment did not affect weight gain or feed intake [39]. In a second study, this group reported that guinea pigs fed a diet supplemented with 0.25% w/w CLA mixture for 32 days compared to animals that consumed 0.25% w/w corn oil or LA had a lower inflammatory response to OVA [40]. Fourteen days after consuming the experimental diets, animals were primed with IP injections of OVA and then challenged subcutaneously on day 28. Ex vivo release of eicosanoids were measured in several tissues after stimulation with OVA. It was reported that CLA reduced $TXB_2$, 6-keto-$PGF_{1\alpha}$, $PGF_{2\alpha}$, $PGD_2$ and $LTC_4/D_4/E_4$ release in lung, decreased $TXB_2$, 6-keto-$PGF_{1\alpha}$, $PGF_{2\alpha}$, $PGE_2$, and $PGD_2$ release in trachea and suppressed $PGD_2$ release in the bladder in response to OVA challenge [40]. There was, however, no significant difference in basal levels of these inflammatory mediators. Furthermore, protein levels of COX-2 were unaffected by dietary CLA treatment in ex-vivo stimulated or unstimulated lung tissue, suggesting that CLA does not suppress eicosanoid production by inhibiting this enzyme. Whigham's studies provide evidence in an animal model that supplementation with a synthetic CLA mixture may be beneficial during type I hypersensitivity responses. The mechanisms directing this suppressive response, however, have yet to be defined. Although these findings suggest that CLA may mediate its effects through a COX-2 independent pathway.

The effect of oral and topical CLA (mixed isomer) supplementation on reducing type I hypersensitivity reactions has also been explored in mice and rats [41]. During an anaphylactic response to hen egg lysosome, mice that consumed a 0.1% w/w synthetic CLA mixture maintained blood pressure and blood flow to a greater extent than animals that did not receive dietary CLA [41]. Furthermore, both oral (0.1 or 0.2% w/w) and topical (2.5 mg/30 µl/d, respectively) administration of CLA resulted reduced scratching behaviour and vasodilation after challenge with a chemical compound that stimulated histamine release [41]. These results suggest that both oral administration and topical application of CLA mixtures of isomers can reduce allergen-induced anaphylaxis and pruritus, common type 1 hypersensitivity clinical responses, in rodents [41]. There is no data at present defining the isomer-specific effects of CLA. Future studies should also be aimed at examining dose-response relationships and defining the potential role in prevention and treatment of allergy.

# Inflammation

## *In Vitro* Studies on Endothelial Cells

There are a few *in vitro* studies examining the potential efficacy of CLA on the inflammatory process in cardiovascular disease. The data is quite contradictory. In a study conducted using bovine aortic endothelial cells, incubating cells with 0 to 10 µM of a CLA isomer mixture lowered levels of 6k-$PGF_{1\alpha}$, a breakdown product of $PGI_2$, and potentiated bradykinin (BK) stimulated nitrite release [42]. However, CLA isomers did not significantly influence endothelial nitric oxide synthase (eNOS), COX-I or COX-II protein or mRNA levels, nor on levels of nitrite released by bovine aortic endothelial cells [42]. The authors suggest that CLA is beneficial to endothelial health mediated through its ability to suppress the production of inflammatory mediators, while increasing the levels of a vasodilating mediator [42]. Contrary to these results, incubation of human aortic endothelial cells with c9t11 and t10c12 CLA isomers resulted in less favourable effects on endothelial function [43]. In this study at a concentration of 50µM of each single isomer, c9,t11 and t10,c12 produced less 6k-$PGF_{1\alpha}$, $TXB_2$ (product of $TXA_2$), $PGE_2$ and NO and had a lower mRNA expression of COX II than cells cultured in media alone[43]. In contrast to the effects of c9t11 observed at 50µM, at a lower 5µM concentration incubation with c9t11 resulted in a higher mRNA expression of COX I. Lower mRNA expression of $sPLA_2$ was also observed in endothelial cells incubated with 50µM of either isomer [43]. The activity of this enzyme, however, was reduced only by the c9t11 isomer at both concentrations [43]. It is suggested by the authors that lower production of NO and $PGE_2$, which occurred at the higher CLA concentrations, could have an adverse influence on human endothelium by inhibiting vasodilatation and anti-aggregation, however further in vivo research is needed to test this hypothesis. These results also suggest that the c9t11 isomer may be more biologically active in the endothelium and that its activity varies depending on the specific dose administered.

In another study, unstimulated and calcium ionophore-stimulated human saphenous vein endothelial cells were cultured with a CLA mixture (1:1) or c9t11 and t10c12 single isomers for 72 hours [44]. All CLA treatments inhibited resting production of $^{14}C$-$PGF_2$ [44]. A dose-dependent inhibition of prostacyclin (as measured by $PGI_2$), $TXB_2$, $PGE_2$, $PGD_2$ and $PGF_{2\alpha}$ occurred in cells that were treated with the CLA mixture. Both the c9t11 and t10c12 isomers resulted in lower calcium ionophore-stimulated eicosanoid production ($PGI_2$, $TXB_2$, $PGF_{2\alpha}$, $PGE_2$ and $PGD_2$) when provided at a concentration of 50µM. Although the inhibitory effect of the c9t11 isomer remained at concentration, 100μM of the t10c12 induced greater production of these eicosanoids [44]. None of the CLA treatments significantly altered the mRNA expression of COX-I [44], suggesting that this was not the mechanism to explain the effects on eicosanoid production. Taken altogether, these results imply that both CLA isomers are capable of inhibiting several of the 2-series eicosanoids, independent of COX-I, which could have a beneficial impact on endothelial health. Again, it appears that the dose of CLA administered is an important factor. When examining the effects of CLA on human osteoarthritic chondrocytes isolated from osteoarthritis patients, it was reported that LPS- and IL-1β–stimulated $PGE_2$ production was reduced when cells were cultured for 6 days with 20μM CLA (1:1) mixture [45]. These suppressive effects were augmented when cells were treated with a combination of CLA and eicosapentanoic acid (EPA) [45]. In addition, LPS- and IL-1β-stimulated NO production were reduced with CLA treatment alone, increased with CLA+EPA mixture and was not changed when treated with CLA in combination with AA [45]. Incubation of the HEL-30 murine epidermal cell line, with or without 1, 4, or 16 ug/ml of an unspecified CLA mixture of isomers for 12 h resulted in lower TPA (12-O-tetradecanoyl-phorbol-13-acetate, a mitogen)-induced $PGE_2$ synthesis without altering arachidonic acid (AA) release [46].

Collectively, these studies suggest that CLA, including the two major individual isomers, can influence the *in vitro* production and/or expression of eicosanoids, NO and proinflammatory cytokines in endothelial cells. This does not appear to be due to alterations in AA levels or AA metabolism. Although one study suggests that COX-I is not the enzyme involved in mediating CLA's suppressive effects on eicosanoid production, the physiological implications of these effects are not clear nor are the underlying mechanisms understood. However, alterations in production of pro-inflammatory mediators by endothelial cells would be expected to impact on the immune system, particularly mediators of innate immunity, such as macrophages.

## *In Vitro* Studies on Immune Cells

The inflammatory response in immune cells has also been examined *in vitro*. In the RAW264.7 murine macrophage cell line, incubation with 25, 100 or 200μM of CLA (c9t11, c9c11, t9t11 or t10c12) or a mixture of isomers for 24 hours affected the production and expression of key inflammatory mediators [47]. At 200μM all CLA treatments decreased IFN-γ stimulated mRNA expression of COX-2, iNOS and TNF-α and reduced IFN-γ–induced production of TNF-α and NO [47]. The c9t11 in a dose-dependent manner reduced COX-2 and iNOS promoter activity and suppressed $NO_2$ (a measurement of NO) and $PGE_2$ production in IFN-γ treated cells [47]. When a dominant negative form of PPAR-γ was transfected into RAW cells, the ability of CLA to regulate the iNOS reporter construct was eliminated [47], suggesting that the anti-inflammatory properties of CLA are mediated, at least in part, by this nuclear hormone receptor. More recently, Changhua et al. [30] investigated the effect of CLA on LPS-induced cytokine mRNA expression and production. Using isolated porcine PBMCs they examined the effects of 100 μM of c9t11 or t10c12 CLA, singly or in combination, on IL-1β, TNF-α and IL-6. Culturing these cells for 24 hours with the isomers reduced mRNA expression and production of IL-1β, TNF-α and IL-6 in response to 3 hour incubation with LPS [30]. In this protocol, the t10c12 isomer appeared to have a greater suppressive effect on these inflammatory mediators than the c9t11 isomer [30], supporting the hypothesis that the different CLA isomers have different degrees (or use different pathways) of anti-inflammatory properties. It is too early to apply this *in vitro* evidence of the anti-inflammatory properties of the two major CLA isomers to clinical conditions, but the findings are promising.

## Functional Assays on Immune Cells from CLA-Fed Rodents

There have been a number of studies examining the effect of feeding CLA on immune function. The first studies that will be reviewed are those that isolated cells from the CLA-fed rodents and examined immune function ex vivo. Rats fed a 0.5% or 1%w/w CLA mixture for 3 weeks had altered tissue eicosanoid release [48]. In this study there was a dietary dose-response decrease in splenic $LTB_4$ levels, and a reduction in lung $LTC_4$ and serum $PGE_2$ levels in rats fed either 0.5% or 1% w/w CLA [48]. There was, however, no difference in the release of histamine or $LTB_4$ from stimulated or unstimulated peritoneal exudate cells. In another rodent study that investigated the effects of feeding a mixture of CLA isomers (1% w/w) in diets varying in the amount of n-6 and n-3 PUFA, it was reported that at both high n-6:n-3 (7.28) and low n-6:n-3 (1.85) dietary PUFA ratios there was reduced basal macrophage TNF-α production. There was also a significant reduction in basal and LPS-stimulated production of IL-6 from isolated macrophages, but this suppressive effect was observed only in the lower n6:n3 PUFA diet. IL-1 production, was not significantly altered by feeding CLA [49]. Feeding 0.5% w/w c9t11 and t10c12 CLA isomers for 56 days to mice resulted in greater splenocyte TNF-α and IL-6 production and lower IL-4 production after stimulation with T (Con A) or B (LPS) cell mitogens [50]. These reductions in pro-inflammatory cytokines occurred without a change in splenocyte numbers or phenotype. Furthermore the production of IL-2 and $PGE_2$ in response to these two mitogens was not altered [50]. The ex vivo immune studies in rodents are suggestive that feeding CLA isomers can both reduce and increase the production of some pro-inflammatory cytokines and mediators from tissues and immune cells. The mediators which are most influenced by feeding CLA are not clear at this time as different combinations of CLA isomers were fed, the length of feeding differed between studies and the assays used to assess the ability to produce inflammatory mediators differed.

## Inflammation Studies *in Vivo*

Consistent with an inflammatory response, it was reported that following two weeks of dietary supplementation with 1% w/w commercial CLA mixture there was a lower $PGE_2$ levels in the serum of rats [51]. The epidermis of mice fed diets containing 0.5, 1 or 1.5% w/w CLA isomer mixture showed a dose-dependent increase of CLA into phospholipids and neutral lipids after consuming the diets for 6 weeks [52]. When these mice were topically treated with TPA, feeding CLA (1.5% w/w) significantly reduced $PGE_2$ synthesis. Vascular permeability was unaffected by dietary manipulation in this study. Supplementation during gestation and 25 days or 8 weeks following birth with a 3%w/w CLA mixture to ddy mice resulted in decreased $PGE_2$ production but increased COX-I (significant) and COX-II (not significant) mRNA levels in the brain [53]. Although food intake was unaltered by supplementation, the body weights of offspring fed CLA were reduced compared to those that did not receive supplementation. These results imply that brain $PGE_2$ production can be reduced by dietary CLA without inhibition of COX gene expression in mice. The implications of this in healthy animals, however, are unclear at this time.

The Han: SPRD-cy rat model of polycystic kidney disease (PKD), which features prominent renal interstitial inflammation and fibrosis, was used to assess the effect of CLA supplementation in the modification of inflammatory outcomes. Feeding CLA (1%w/w) for 8 weeks reduced interstitial inflammation, fibrosis, and renal $PGE_2$ release suggesting that CLA may be beneficial in the treatment of renal disease [54]. Resting and phorbol myristate acetate (PMA)-activated macrophages and heterophils from brown hens fed a control or CLA (1% w/w) supplemented diet for 18 weeks were assayed for total cell-associated urokinase plasminogen activator (u-PA), membrane-bound u-PA, free u-PA binding sites and superoxide production [55]. These parameters were not altered by dietary manipulation in unstimulated macrophages and heterophils. However, activated heterophils and macrophages isolated from CLA-fed hens had higher membrane-bound u-PA activity and lower superoxide production. These results suggest that in stimulated cells, CLA has both pro-inflammatory (increased membrane-bound u-PA activity) and anti-inflammatory properties (decreased superoxide production).

Further work is needed to explore the isomer-specific role of CLA in the inflammatory process. Preliminary work in animal models has provided mixed information regarding the precise actions of CLA on mediators of inflammation. Obviously, many discrepancies exist among the aforementioned studies. Several possibilities can explain these differences including the species studied, the tissue examined, the duration of feeding and the assays used to determine inflammatory status.

# Acquired Immune System

## Cytokine Production *In Vitro*

*In vitro* work investigating the impact of CLA on acquired immune function is very limited and little conclusive evidence has been drawn from these experiments. Two separate groups have examined the effect of CLA on the T-cell proliferation cytokine, IL-2. Chew et al (1997) [56] isolated lymphocytes from porcine blood and incubated them with one of the following concentrations of a synthetic CLA isomer mixture: 0, 17.8, 35.7 or 71.4 μM. Cells were stimulated with ConA during this 24hr incubation. The authors observed that this CLA mixture inhibited IL-2 production in a dose-dependent manner. Contrary to this earlier report, Luongo et al. (2003) [57] reported that IL-2 mRNA expression was increased by CLA, in a dose-dependent manner. In this study, Jurkat T-cells were incubated with 0, 50, 100 or 200 uL of CLA for 72 hours in the presence or absence of PMAI+αCD3. In stimulated cells, mRNA expression of IL-2 was increased by CLA in a dose-dependent manner [57]. The apparent differences observed between these two studies could arise for multiple reasons. First, the authors used very distinct cells to study the effects of CLA; Chew et al. (1997) [56] used primary cell culture isolated from pigs consisting of blood lymphocytes, whereas Luongo's group [57] utilized a human T-cell line. Furthermore, cells were incubated for significantly different periods and a different mitogen was employed by each group. Finally, the authors employed two distinct methods to determine the effects of a synthetic CLA mixture on IL-2; one group measured IL-2 production, the other IL-2 mRNA levels. Taken together, it appears that CLA has an effect on the proliferative hormone IL-2; however, further research is required to generate consisting findings and to establish the true influence of CLA on this cytokine.

*In vitro* experiments have also explored the impact of CLA treatment on IFN-γ. Luongo et al. (2003) [57] measured IFN-γ mRNA expression in the above-mentioned experiment and reported that at 200 μM, incubation with the mixture of CLA isomers resulted in a higher expression in stimulated cells compared to cells incubated without CLA. This is the only report of the effects of CLA on IFN-γ *in vitro* and they did not investigate the isomer-specific influence on IFN-γ. At present there is insufficient evidence to draw a clear conclusion as to the overall effects of CLA on IFN-γ, however, Luongo's results indicate that CLA might influence mRNA expression.

## Lymphocyte Proliferation *In Vitro*

The proliferative response of lymphocytes has been examined in two distinct cell culture experiments. Chew et al. (1997) [56] examined the effects of a synthetic CLA isomer mixture on the proliferative response of porcine blood lymphocytes. Cells were stimulated with ConA, PHA or pokeweed mitogen (PWM) for 48 hours and then cells were pulsed with [$^3$H]-thymidine for 24 hours. They reported a dose-dependent increase in proliferative response to PWM in cells treated with CLA [56]. For both ConA and PHA-stimulated cells, 71.4μM of CLA increased the proliferation of lymphocytes [56]. Luongo et al. (2003) [57] examined the proliferation of unstimulated Jurkat T-cells the CLA. In their experiments, unstimulated cells were incubated for 48 hours with 50μM synthetic CLA isomer mixture and then pulsed with [$^3$H]-thymidine for 18hr. Unlike the finding of Chew with porcine immune cells, treatment of Jurkat cells with CLA inhibited the proliferation of cells [57]. The discrepancies in results may be partly due to comparing a mixture of cells in a primary culture to a transformed T cell line. Further work is needed to establish the impact of single and mixtures of CLA isomers on T cell function.

## Ig Production *In Vitro*

The effect of CLA on Ig production has also been explored *in vitro* in one study. Yamasaki et al. (2000) [58] incubated rat splenocytes with 0, 1, 10 and 100 μL of c9t11, t10c12, trans9, trans11 (t9t11) or a mixture of CLA isomers for 24 hours. They reported (contrary to their in vivo studies) that the c9t11, t10c12 and the CLA mixture suppressed the production of IgA, IgM and IgG in unstimulated immune cells [58]. The production of IgA was inhibited to the greatest extent [58] with the mixture of isomers having the greatest effect, followed by the t10c12 isomer with the c9t11 isomer inhibiting IgA production the least [58]. IgG and IgA production was only altered by t9t11 at 10μM and IgM production was not affected by this isomer [58]. Although this is the only *in vitro* study published, it support that individual CLA isomers may influence humoral immunity differently. Clearly, further research is required to conclusively elucidate the isomer-specific effects of CLA on these immune parameters and to determine their mechanisms.

## Animal Studies

### *Cytokine Production*

#### TNF-α

Examination into the effects of CLA supplementation on TNF-α production or levels in healthy animals is limited to only two groups. Of these studies, only one group has examined blood levels of TNF-α following CLA supplementation in healthy animals. Akahoshi et al.[59] supplemented mice with a 1%w/w CLA mixture for 8 weeks and reported decreased levels of serum TNF-α. Contrary to these findings, Yamasaki et al. (2003) [60] reported that TNF-α production was increased in ConA-stimulated spleen lymphocytes of mice consuming a single isomer or a 1:1 mix for 3 weeks. These effects were found only in animals that consumed the c9t11 CLA isomer (0.5%w/w), while t10c12 and the 1:1 mix had no effect on TNF-α splenocyte production [60]. The varied results reported in these studies may be due to the length of feeding (ie shorter duration), supplementation with a single isomer as compared to a mixture, or ex vivo stimulation with ConA, a T-cell mitogen. Another obvious difference between Yamasaki's (2003) experimental design and Akahoshi's is that a polycolonal T-cell mitogen was used to stimulate immune cells ex vivo. This suggests that the effect of feeding CLA on the TNF-α response is different when examining the unstimulated basal state compared to T cell stimulation.

#### IL-1

Only one research group has examined CLA's influence on IL-1 production ex vivo. When mice were fed a 1%w/w CLA mixture (1:1) for 8 weeks, supplementation had did not alter basal or LPS-stimulated splenocyte production of IL-1 [61].

#### IL-6

The effect of feeding CLA on IL-6 has also been limited one study. Yamasaki et al (2004) [62] reported that feeding 1%w/w synthetic CLA (~1:1, c9t11:t10c12) for 3 weeks in the form of triglycerides (TGs) reduced IL-6 production by murine splenocytes stimulated ex vivo with LPS. This report suggests that supplementation with a synthetic CLA mixture may have suppressive effects on IL-6 production when the innate and B-cell immune systems are stimulated.

## IL-2

The impact of CLA supplementation on the production of IL-2 has been measured by several research groups, although results are limited to the murine models. Of the five studies conducted in mice, four have reported an increase in IL-2 production in stimulated splenocytes [62]; [28]; [61]; [63] and one study reported that CLA did not alter splenic lymphocyte production [60]. The studies that reported an increase in IL-2 production used synthetically prepared CLA mixtures ranging in concentration from 0.1%-1%w/w of c9t11:t10c12 (approximately 1:1 ratio) containing only minimal amounts of other CLA isomers. Whereas, Yamasaki (2003) [60] fed 0.5%w/w of pure c9t11, t10c12 or a 1:1 mixture of these isomers and found that neither the single isomers or the mixture had an effect on IL-2 production in ConA-stimulated splenocytes. Four groups stimulated their cells with ConA [63];[61];[28];[60] and one group stimulated with LPS [62]. There was also variation in the duration of these feeding trials. Yang (2003) and Hayek (1999) fed their animals for six and eight weeks respectively, whereas Wong (1997), Yamasaki (2003) and Yamasaki (2004) had shorter supplementation periods of three weeks. Collectively, these studies suggest that feeding a mixture of CLA isomers to mice increases the ability of T-lymphocytes to respond to ex vivo stimulation (both T and B-cell mitogens) by producing more IL-2. However, the sole study addressing isomer-specific actions of CLA does not agree with this conclusion and thus further research is necessary to clearly define the activity of individual isomers on ex vivo IL-2 production.

## IL-4

To date investigations into the activity of CLA on the production of IL-4 have been limited to two groups. After 6 weeks of supplementing a 0.5% w/w CLA isomer mixture to mice, Yang (2003) [28] reported that IL-4 production was reduced in ConA stimulated splenocytes. In contrast to this finding, Yamasaki (2004) [62] reported that a 1% w/w CLA mixture supplemented for 3 weeks to mice increased production of this Th2 cytokine. These results were obtained when splenocytes were stimulated ex vivo with LPS. The conflicting results generated from these two studies may have arisen from differences in the amount and duration of CLA supplementation. However, it is most plausible that the differences are due to differences in the action of the difference mitogens used to stimulate the cells ex vivo, suggesting that that CLA affects IL-4 production differently depending on whether B-cells or T-cells are stimulated.

## IL-10

IL-10 is considered an anti-inflammatory cytokine secreted by T-lymphocytes and mediates resolution of the inflammatory immune response. A single study conducted in mice revealed that a 1% w/w synthetic CLA mixture administered for 3 weeks increased IL-10 production in splenic lymphocytes stimulated with LPS [62]. Although this study is suggestive that CLA may increase production of IL-10, this work is limited to only one species. Furthermore, the isomer-specific effects on IL-10 levels have yet to be explored, but are necessary to clearly elucidate CLA's impact on this anti-inflammatory cytokine.

## IFN-γ

IFN-γ is secreted by CD4+ and CD8+ T-lymphocytes and mediates important aspects of both the innate and adaptive immune system. One of its hallmark functions is to act as a potent stimulator of macrophages [64]. Despite its important role in both branches of the immune system, investigations into only two studies conducted in animals have examined the effects of CLA supplementation on IFN-γ production. The single study conducted in mice reported that feeding 1% w/w CLA (TG or FFA) resulted in increased production of IFN-γ in splenic lymphocytes after LPS stimulation [62].

## IL-12

IL-12 is a Th1 cytokine which acts to induce IFN-γ production and is considered an important mediator of the inflammatory response. Only one group has reported the influence of CLA supplementation of IL-12 production. Mice that consumed a 1%w/w synthetic CLA mixture had reduced production of IL-12p40 and IL-12p70 in isolated splenic lymphocytes stimulated with LPS [62].

### *Other Cytokines and Immune Mediators*

The above-mentioned cytokines warranted separate discussion for two reasons: i) these cytokines are used often in the literature to describe experimental immune function and ii) these cytokines were measured in at least two different studies with the exception of IL-18. Only one study conducted in animals has examined other cytokines that have not been typically measured when assessing immune function in experimental animals. Yamasaki et al. (2004) [62] used protein array analysis to detect various cytokines and other immune mediators produced from splenocytes stimulated with LPS. Mice supplemented with a 1%w/w synthetic CLA mixture in TG form for 3 weeks produced higher levels of MCP-5 (monocyte chemoattactant protein), GM-CSF (granulocyte-macrophage colony stimulating factor), IL-9, sTNFr1 (soluble tumour necrosis factor receptor 1) and MIP (macrophage inflammatory protein)-1α. In addition, the TG from of CLA decreased the production of IL-3, IL-5, and RANTES. Supplementation with 1%w/w CLA in FFA form resulted in increased production of IL-9, MCP-5 GM-CSF, sTNFr1, KC, IL-13, IL-5, MIP-3β, Eotaxin, GCSF (granulocye colony stimulating factor) and SCF (stem cell factor) [62].

### *Immunoglobulins*

## IgG

The impact of CLA supplementation on IgG production and levels has been widely investigated in animal models relative to other immune markers. Serum levels of IgG following CLA supplementation have been measured in rat, mouse and pig models in five separate experiments. All of these groups reported that feeding synthetic CLA isomers ranging in amounts from 0.05%-1%w/w increased serum levels of IgG, regardless of the species examined [48, 65-68]. The production of IgG has also been examined in lymphocytes isolated from spleen tissue. Yamasaki et al. (2000) [58] fed CLA mixtures to rats ranging in amounts from 0.05-0.5% w/w for three weeks and reported that IgG production in unstimulated splenocytes was increased. In another experiment conducted in mice,

Yamasaki's group [62] reported that a 1% (free fatty acid or triglyceride form) CLA mixture also increased production of IgG in unstimulated splenocytes. CLA supplementation, however, does not appear to have the same impact on stimulated splenocytes. Yamasaki et al (2003) [60] reported that LPS or ConA-stimulated splenic lymphocyte production of IgG was unaffected when CLA mixtures or single isomers were fed to mice. Regardless of the species, tissue examined or type and amount of CLA supplemented, the level of IgG in plasma was higher in CLA-fed animals in 7 out of the 8 studies conducted. Splenocyte IgG production was enhanced in unstimulated immune cells, however, when lymphocytes are stimulated with either a T-cell or a B-cell mitogen, IgG production does not differ.

### IgA

The impact of CLA supplementation on IgA has also been examined to a greater extent than most other immune parameters in animal models. Five different studies have reported that CLA supplementation increases IgA levels in pig, rat and mouse models. Three of these studies have reported that feeding a synthetic CLA mixture ranging in amounts from 0.5 – 1.5% w/w resulted in increased serum levels of IgA [48], [65], [66]. The production of IgA has also been examined in immune cells isolated from spleen and mesenteric lymph nodes (MLN). Sugano et al. (1998) [48] reported that production of IgA was higher in unstimulated and LPS-stimulated MLN in rats fed either a 0.5% or 1% synthetic CLA mixture for three weeks. CLA, however, did not influence IgA production in splenocytes (unstimulated or LPS-stimulated). Contrary to the results reported on spleen tissue by Sugano's group [48], Yamasaki et al. (2000) [58] reported that unstimulated rat splenocytes produced more IgA after consuming a CLA mixture ranging in amounts from 0.05-0.5%w/w for three weeks. Another study produced by Yamasaki's group [60] reported that 0.5% w/w t10c12 CLA fed for three weeks increased IgA production in ConA-stimulated splenocytes [60]. These results were not observed in unstimulated spleen cells or in mice fed the c9t11 isomer or 1:1 (c9t11:t10c12) mixture of CLA [60]. More recently, Yamasaki et al (2004) [62] reported that a 0.1 or 1% CLA mixture (either triglyceride or free fatty acid) to mice for three weeks had no effect on IgA production in unstimulated splenocytes from mice [62]. Overall, it appears that IgA levels in serum are increased by CLA supplementation regardless of the type and percentage of CLA given or the species examined. There are, however, inconsistencies related to the production of IgA in spleen tissue. It appears that when splenocytes are stimulated with a T-cell mitogen (ConA), but not by a B-cell mitogen (LPS), feeding CLA increases IgA production. Furthermore, this effect was only observed when mice were given the t10c12 isomer, suggesting these effects are limited to a single isomer and may influence IgA production indirectly by targeting T-lymphocytes.

### IgM

Serum levels and immune cell production of IgM have also been examined in rats, mice and pigs following CLA supplementation. It has been reported that serum concentrations of IgM were increased in rats fed a 1% w/w CLA mixture for 3 weeks[48] and in piglets fed a 0.5% w/w CLA mixture for 7 days (pre-partum until weaning ) [66]. Production of IgM in immune cells has also been investigated in spleen and MLN. Sugano et al. (1998) [48] reported that LPS-stimulated splenocytes produced more IgM when rats were fed a 0.5% or

1% w/w CLA mixture for 3 weeks. This group also reported that LPS-stimulated MLN produced more IgM when rats were fed a 1% w/w CLA mixture. There was no difference in IgM production in either tissue when immune cells were not stimulated [48]. Yamasaki et al. (2000) [58] also reported the splenic IgM production was increased after rats were fed 0.05, 0.1, 0.25 or 0.5% w/w CLA mixture, however, this was observed in unstimulated immune cells. In a more recent study conducted in mice, Yamasaki et al. (2003) [60] examined the isomer-specific effects of CLA on IgM production in unstimulated or ConA-stimulated splenocytes. It was reported that IgM production was increased when mice were fed 0.5% w/w t10c12 CLA isomer, but the authors did not observe any difference when the c9t11 CLA isomer or an equal mixture of both isomers was fed to the animals [60]. This group, however, reported in a later study in mice that neither a 0.1% nor a 1% w/w CLA mixture (triglyceride or free fatty acid form) had an effect on IgM production in unstimulated spleen cells [60]. Animals were fed for 3 weeks in both experiments and the most obvious difference between these two studies is that when CLA was examined as single isomers, a difference was observed in IgM. Again, this emphasizes the importance of studying CLA as single isomers, as opposed to a grouping of mixed isomers. In summary, the effect of feeding CLA on IgM levels in serum has only been examined in two separate studies. Regardless of the animal model and the amount and length of time that CLA was administered, both studies reported that a mixture of CLA increased serum levels of IgM. It appears that when mixed isomers are fed to animals, IgM production is increased when either a T-cell mitogen or a B-cell/innate immunity mitogen are used to stimulate immune cells. There is, however, inconsistency in reports on the production of IgM in unstimulated immune cells. Two separate groups have reported increased production in spleen cells when animals were fed either a CLA mixture or the t10c12 CLA isomer. Again, only one study measured isomer-specific effects; however results from that study were similar to those that used mixed isomers.

### *Lymphocytes: Concentrations and Phenotypes*

Many of the studies investigating the impact of CLA supplementation on the proportion of immune cells have focused on the acquired branch of the immune system, particularly T-lymphocytes. Only two studies conducted in healthy animals have investigated the impact of CLA supplementation on immune cell phenotypes. The sole study conducted in mice investigated the isomer-specific effects of CLA on both T and B-lymphocyte populations. Yamasaki (2003) [60] reported that both t10c12 and a 1:1 mix of t10c12:c9t11 CLA isomers increased the proportion of B cells in splenic lymphocytes; however supplementation with the c9t11 CLA isomer decreased the proportion of B cells. The proportions of CD4+ T cells were decreased when mice were fed the t10c12 isomer and CD8+ T cells were increased in the c9t11 and mixed isomer dietary groups. This study also investigated the ratio of CD4:CD8 T cells and concluded that all three dietary treatments increased this ratio [60]. Phenotype analysis from this experiment, again highlight the importance of designing isomer-specific feeding trials. Bassaganya-Riera et al (2001) [36] fed a 0.67, 1.33 or 2% w/w CLA mixture for 7 weeks to weanling piglets and examined T-cell phenotypes in whole blood. The proportion of $CD4^-CD8^+$ and $TCR\alpha\beta CD4^+CD8\alpha\alpha$ T lymphocytes linearly increased with increasing levels of CLA while the proportion of $TCR\alpha\beta CD4^+$ T lymphocytes decreased [36]. The physiological significance of this is not clear but the increase in the CD4+CD8+

population (that is unique to swine peripheral blood cells) suggests an effect of CLA on T maturation.

### *Lymphocyte Proliferation*

In healthy animals, the proliferative response of lymphocytes to mitogen stimulation has been limited to three studies and the findings are not consistent. Wong et al (1997) [63] fed mice either 0.1, 0.3 or 0.9% w/w CLA mixture for 3 weeks and found that PHA-stimulated proliferative response was greater in splenocytes of supplemented animals. There was, however, no difference after 6 weeks of supplementation or when immune cells were stimulated with LPS or ConA. Hayek et al. (1999) [61] also reported that feeding CLA isomers increases the proliferative response of splenocytes. In their studies splenocytes from mice fed a 1% w/w CLA mixture for 8 weeks had a higher proliferative response to ConA (old mice only) and PHA compared to mice that did not consume CLA [61]. There was, however, no effect of feeding CLA when splenocytes were stimulated with LPS [61]. Only one study has examined the influence of feeding CLA on swine lymphocyte proliferative Bassaganya-Riera et al (2001) [36] fed a 0.67, 1.33 or 2% w/w CLA mixture for 7 weeks and measured the proliferative response of unstimulated and ConA-stimulated immune cells in whole blood. The authors reported that unstimulated cells collected from pigs fed CLA had a greater proliferative response after 14 days of feeding than animals that did not consume CLA [36]. There was no significant difference in proliferative response after 14d of feeding or when immune cells were stimulated with ConA [36]. The data collected on the proliferative response of healthy animals fed CLA is inconsistent. The variation in reports could have stemmed from the duration of feeding, the amount of CLA supplemented or the species examined. The results do suggest that when immune cells are stimulated with different mitogens (i.e. a T-cell mitogen as compared to a B-cell mitogen) or unstimulated, mixtures of CLA isomers may have different effects.

## Human Studies

To date, cell culture work and animal studies have dominated the literature, providing much stronger and more convincing evidence than human intervention trials. Collectively, feeding studies, primarily done in healthy individuals, have not provided convincing evidence that feeding CLA can influence immune function. Kelley et al. (2001) [69] examined the effects of feeding a synthetic CLA mixture on immune function in healthy women on immune parameters in blood. In brief, subjects were acclimatized to identical diets for 30 days and then given a total of 3.9g/d of CLA (total 6g of supplement) or a placebo supplement (6g of sunflower oil) for 63 days. The reported composition of CLA isomers was as follows: 22.6% t10c12, 23.6% c11t13, 17.6% c9t11, 16.6% trans8, cis12 CLA and the remainder being a mixture of other isomers. It was reported that supplementation had no effect eicosanoid production ($PGE_2$, $LTB_4$), IL-1β, TNF-α and IL-2 production or intracellular concentrations of IFN-γ, TNF-α and IL-2 [69]. Although this study does not allow for separation of isomer specific effects it suggests that feeding 3.9g of CLA per day for 2 months to healthy women has a limited effect on commonly assessed measures of immunity.

Kreider et al. (2002) [70] examined the effects of CLA supplementation in resistance-trained, young men in a double-blind, placebo-controlled, randomized study design. Subjects were given either 9 g of olive oil (placebo) or 6 g of CLA with an additional 3 g of fatty acids per day for 28 days and the effect on immune cell populations in blood. The source of CLA consumed was identical to the CLA provided by Kelley's groups [37, 69]. In agreement with the earlier studies there was no significant effect of supplementation with CLA on WBC, immune or immune cell phenotype in blood [70]. No functional measures of immune function were made.

In a randomized, double-blind, placebo-controlled trial, Riserus et al. (2002) [71] examined the effects of CLA on inflammatory markers in men with metabolic syndrome. For 12 weeks subjects were supplemented with one of three dietary treatments: 3.4 g/day CLA mixture (c9t11:t10c12, 1:1), 3.4 g/day t10c12 CLA or 3.4g/day olive oil (placebo control). Plasma levels of TNF-α and IL-6 were not influenced by dietary treatment [71]. Feeding the t10c12 CLA isomer significantly increased a marker of lipid peroxidation (8-iso-$PGF_{2\alpha}$) and inflammation (15-K-DH-$PGF_{2\alpha}$.) in urine [71]. Feeding the t10c12 isomer increased the levels of the inflammatory marker CRP from baseline values, compared to the placebo group [71]. The level of CRP was also significantly higher from the baseline in the CLA mixture group, but the comparison to the placebo groups was not made. There was no association compared to the placebo group [71]. A second randomized, double-blind, placebo-controlled trial was conducted by this group aimed at examining the effects of supplementing the c9t11 CLA isomer to men with abdominal obesity [72]. Twenty-five subjects received 3g of c9t11 CLA daily for 3 months. Similar to the results of the earlier study where they fed the t10c12 isomer, feeding the c9t11 CLA isomer significantly increased 8-iso-$PGF_{2\alpha}$ (marker of in vivo oxidative stress) and 15-keto-dihydro-$PGF_{2\alpha}$ (marker of inflammation) excretion in urine. These studies suggest that feeding the major CLA isomers to individuals with a chronic inflammatory condition (obesity) impacts negatively on at least one marker of oxidative stress and inflammation. The results of this study cannot be translated to healthy individuals or other patient populations. Further work is needed to determine the physiological implications of consuming CLA in this patient population.

More recently, Tricon et al. (2004) [73] investigated the influence of single CLA isomers on blood immune parameters in healthy men. In this randomized, double-blind, cross-over trial subjects received increasing amounts (0, 0.59, 1.19, 2.38 g/d) of either c9t11 or t10c12 CLA for the first 8 week period and then consumed the other isomer for an additional 8 weeks following a wash-out period. Contrary to what was previously reported by Albers et al [38], both isomers decreased in a dose-dependent manner the proliferative response of PBMC to a T-cell mitogen [73]. Feeding CLA isomers did not significantly affect lymphocyte phenotypes or TNF-α, IFN-γ, IL-2, IL-4, IL-5 or IL-10 production following LPS or ConA stimulation. This work suggests that the supplementation with c9t11 or t10c12 CLA can reduce the proliferative response of immune cells isolated from healthy, male subjects [73]. Despite a difference in proliferative response there was no difference in cytokine production, including the proliferative cytokine IL-2, raising questions as to the physiological implications of a decreased proliferative response.

Collectively, human intervention studies offer little evidence that CLA beneficially modulates immune function in healthy individuals. Findings from healthy individuals can not be directly translated to those with chronic inflammatory conditions and there is some evidence that further work is required to determine the immune effects of supplementing single and mixtures of isomers to men with metabolic syndrome or abdominal obesity. Several clinical trials have suggested safety concerns of supplementing CLA isomers to individuals with insulin resistance or metabolic syndrome [71]. The animal and *in vitro* studies are quite convincing that there is an effect of CLA on immune function. More carefully designed studies are required in healthy individuals to determine if CLA influences immunity in humans.

**Table 5. Summary of Immune Benefits of CLA**

| Immune Functions | Reference |
|---|---|
| Reduce immune-mediated catabolism | [27-30] |
| Improve response to bacterial Ag | [28, 31, 32, 34, 36] |
| Improve the response to viral challenges | [35, 38] |
| Reduce allergen-induced immune responses | [40, 41] |
| Reduce the production of pro-inflammatory mediators | [42-48, 51, 53, 54] |
| Increase the production of anti-inflammatory cytokines | [49] |
| Potential benefits to acquired immune system | [56, 58] |

## Summary and Conclusions

Although research on the effects of CLA isomers on immunity is primarily limited to *in vitro* and animal models, there is convincing data that feeding the major isomers of CLA can impact on important immunological functions (Table 5). The published studies, available at the time of this review, are summarized in Table 6. Although the mechanisms for the potential benefits of feeding CLA isomers are yet to be identified, there is data to support many of the same mechanisms through which other dietary lipids influence the function of immune cells.

## Acknowledgments

The authors would like to acknowledge the excellent work by Tara Martin in preparing this chapter. M.R. Ruth received the Muttart/Collip Diabetes Studentship from the Muttart Diabetes Research and Training Centre. We acknowledge the funding of the Alberta Agriculture Funding Consortium for a grant to fund the Human Health Module of the CLA Network.

## Table 6. Summary of Studies on the Effects of CLA on Immune Function

| Species | Study Description | Tissue or Organ Studied | CLA Isomer and Content | Outcome Measure | Major Findings |
|---|---|---|---|---|---|
| IMMUNE MEDIATED CATABOLISM | | | | | |
| Outbred mice [27] | 15d feeding trial; 2 dietary treatments + control group; then IP LPS injection (1mg/kg body weight) | spleen | 0.5% CLA | Weight loss and feed intake | -↓ body weight loss<br>- faster return to pre-injection weight<br>- ↑ feed intake<br>- ↑ PHA-P induced spleen lymphocyte blastogenesis |
| Harlan Sprague-Dawley rats [27] | 14d feeding trial; dietary treatments + control group; then IP LPS injection | | 0.5% CLA | Body weight loss | -↓ reduction in body weight gain |
| Leghorn New Hampshire Chicks [27] | 7d feeding trial; dietary treatments + control group; then IP LPS injection | | 0.5% CLA | Body weight loss | -↓ reduction in body weight gain |
| Weanling BALB/c mice [28] | 6 wk feeing trial; 1 dietary treatment + control (corn oil); half injected IP with LPS (0.1 mg/ml PBS), half with PBS | Plasma, peritoneal fluid, spleen | 0.5%w/w synthetic CLA isomer mixture | LPS-induced cachexia, plasma cytokine levels, cytokine and NO production | -↓ LPS-induced anorexia and body weight loss<br>-↓ plasma TNF-α levels after LPS injection<br>- no effect on LPS-induced release of TNF-α in peritoneal resident macrophage<br>-↓ IFN-γ and LPS-induced release of NO in peritoneal resident macrophage |
| Sprague-Dawley rats [29] | 4d feeding trial following dexamethasone injection with 4 dietary treatments 20% protein with or without 0.5% CLA or 10% protein with or without 0.5% CLA | Blood, spleen | 0.5% synthetic mixture | Lymphocyte proliferation (PHA, $^{3}$H-thymidine), WBC | -↑ monocytes (blood)<br>-no effect on lymphocyte proliferation (unstimulated or PHA, splenocytes) |
| Pigs [30] | 28d feeding trial with one dietary treatment + control group; 50% of pigs were injected with LPS at day 14 | Plasma, thymus, spleen | 2% w/w CLA; 1:1 (c9t11:t10c12) synthetic mixture | Cytokines (LPS) and PPARγ mRNA expression | -↓ $PGE_2$, IL-1β, IL-6 and TNF-α (LPS injected, plasma)<br>-↑IL-10 (LPS-injected, plasma)<br>-↑IL-10 mRNA expression (LPS-injected, spleen and thymus)<br>-↓IL-6 and TNF-α mRNA expression (LPS-injected, spleen and thymus)<br>-↑PPAR-γ mRNA expression (LPS-injected, spleen and thymus) |

**Table 6. (Continued)**

| Species | Study Description | Tissue or Organ Studied | CLA Isomer and Content | Outcome Measure | Major Findings |
|---|---|---|---|---|---|
| ***IN VITRO RESPONSE TO LPS*** | | | | | |
| RAW 264.7 macrophage cell line [28] | Cells plated, 24hrs later FA containing media added, 24 hrs later changed to LPS and F.A. containing media for 16 hrs; 1 treatment group + control | | 50μM or 100μM of c9t11 or t10c12 | TNF-α | -↓ TNF-α production with c9t11 (LPS)<br>-no effect on TNF-α production with t10c12 (LPS) |
| RAW264.7 macrophages [31] | Cells incubated in medium containing no added lipid (control), 30 μM AA, or 30 μM CLA for 24 h followed by activation with LPS (100 ng/ml) for 9 h | Supernatant and cells (RNA and DNA) | 30 μM synthetic CLA isomer mixture | $PGE_2$ and NO production, enzyme mRNA expression | -↓ $PGE_2$ and NO production (LPS)<br>-↓ COX-2 and iNOS mRNA expression (LPS) |
| RAW 264.7 macrophages [32] | Cells plated, incubated until 90% confluence was reached; treated with or without LPS (1 μg/mL) plus methanol vehicle control or 20-200 μM CLA for 18 h or treated with methanol or 20-200 μM CLA for 12 h prior to addition of LPS (1μg/mL) | Cells, supernatant | 20, 100 or 200 μM synthetic CLA isomer mixture | LPS-induced inflammatory responses | -no adverse effects on growth in the presence of LPS (concentration of CLA up to 200 μM)<br>-↓ LPS-induced nitrite and $PGE_2$ production (not due to ↓ cell viability)<br>-↓ LPS-induced expression of iNOS and COX2 mRNA<br>-no affect on basal level of iNOS and COX2 protein expression<br>-↓ LPS-induced iNOS and COX2 protein<br>-↓ LPS-induced phosphorylated IκBα protein expression<br>-↓ LPS-induced NF-κB nuclear protein-DNA binding activity |
| ***BACTERIAL AND VIRAL CHALLENGES*** | | | | | |
| Pigs [34] | Pigs were fed for 72d (experiment 1) before colitis induction with Brachyspira hyodysenteriae (an enteric bateria) or for 49d (experiment 2) with or without CLA before immunization (proteinase –digested *Brachyspira hyodysenteriae* bacterin) | Colonic lymph nodes and tissue | 1.33% w/w synthetic isomer mixture | Cytokine mRNA expression and PPARγ, and phenotype | -↓ colitis-induced growth suppression and mucosal damage caused by inflammation<br>-CD4+ and CD8α+ cells same as uninfected pigs (colon, experiment 2)<br>-↑ PPARγ expression (colonic lymph nodes, experiment 1)<br>-IFNγ and IL-10 mRNA expression comparable to non-infected pigs (colonic lymph nodes, experiment 1) |

| Species | Study Description | Tissue or Organ Studied | CLA Isomer and Content | Outcome Measure | Major Findings |
|---|---|---|---|---|---|
| ***BACTERIAL AND VIRAL CHALLENGES*** | | | | | |
| Pigs [35] | 63d feeding trial; at day 42 pigs were inoculated with type 2 porcine circovirus (PCV2) or a placebo | Serum, PBMC, extra inguinal lymph nodes (EILN), thymus | 2.21% w/w 60% pure synthetic mixture (represents 1.33% dietary CLA) | Lymphocyte proliferation (ConA or PCV2 Ag), cytokine mRNA expression (PCV2 Ag and PMAI), lymphocyte phenotype analysis | -weight gain in infected pigs similar to uninfected pigs<br>-↓ B-cell depletion following PCV2 infection (EILN)<br>-B-cell proliferative response unaffected (ConA or PCV2 Ag)<br>-↑ CD8+ and CD4+CD8+ cells (thymus, infected and uninfected)<br>-↑CD8+CD45RC+ (PBMC, infected and uninfected)<br>-↑ CD8+CD29$^{low}$ (PBMC, uninfected)<br>- CD8+CD25+ (PBMC, infected)<br>-attenuated decrease in Bcl-xl expression due to virus<br>-↓IFN-γ production in CD4+ T-cells (PBMC, PCV2 stimulated)<br>-↑ CD8+ T lymphocyte proliferation (PBMC, PCV2 stimulated, d56 and d63) |
| Pigs [36] | 72d feeding trial; pigs were fed either control diet or CLA diet and inoculated with or without *Brachyspira hyodysenteriae* bacterin | PBMC, thymus | 2.21% w/w 60% pure synthetic mixture (represents 1.33% dietary CLA) | Lymphocyte proliferation (ConA or B. hyodysenteriae B204), lymphocyte phenotype analysis, granzyme activity | -↑ expansion of TCRγδCD8αα cells, CD3-CD16+ CD8αα and TCRαβCD8αβ (PBMC, infected and uninfected)<br>-↑ CD8+ granzyme activity<br>-↑ TCRγδCD8αα lymphocyte proliferative response (UNS PBMC, d63 and d72)<br>-no effect on CD4+ (PBMC) |

**Table 6. (Continued)**

| Species | Study Description | Tissue or Organ Studied | CLA Isomer and Content | Outcome Measure | Major Findings |
|---|---|---|---|---|---|
| ***BACTERIAL AND VIRAL CHALLENGES*** | | | | | |
| Healthy women, aged 20-41 yrs [37] | 93 day feeding trial with 1 dietary treatmet; basal diet for 30d, 3.9g Tonalin/day for next 63 days, day 65 immunized with influenza vaccine | Blood, serum | 3.9g/day synthetic CLA isomer mixture (Tonalin/) | Number and proliferation of WBC, DTH response, Ab | -no effect on total number of circulating WBCs or their subsets<br>-no effect on proliferation of T or B lymphocytes<br>-no effect on DTH skin resonse<br>-no effect on serum Ab titres after vaccination |
| Healthy males, aged 31-69 yars [38] | 12 wk feeding trial; 2 dietary treatments + control group; soft gel capsule supplements given daily; vaccinated to HepB during trial; | Blood, intradermal (DTH) | c9t11:t10c12 1.7g (1:1) FA or 1.6g (4:1) glyceride synthetic CLA mixture | NK activity, humoral and cellular resp to HepB vaccination, cytokines | -no effect on NK cell target lysis, DHT, lymphocyte proliferation, or TNF-α, IL-1β, IL-6, IFN-γ, IL-2, IL-4 or PGE2 production (stimulated with PHA or LPS) |
| ***ALLERGY*** | | | | | |
| Hartley (Harlan Sprague Dawley) guinea pigs [39] | 25 d feeding trial; 1 dietary treatment + control; IP injection 50 µg OVA at 1 wk, wk 3 subcutaneous injection 200 µg OVA w/ iFA | Trachea | 0.25%w/w synthetic CLA isomer mixture | Smooth muscle contraction, histamine, PGE2 | -↓ tracheal contraction (type I hypersensitivity)<br>-↓ early histamine release<br>-no effect on total histamine release or tissue levels<br>-↓ PGE2 release |
| Hartley (Harlan Sprague Dawley) guinea pigs [40] | 32 d feeding trial; 1 dietary treatment + contol; IP injection 50 µg OVA (ovalbumin) at day 14, day 28 subcutaneous injection 200 µg OVA w/ iFA | Lungs, trachea, bladder | 0.25%w/w synthetic CLA isomer mixture | Ex vivo eicosanoid release (type I hyper-sensitivity model) | -↓ $TXB_2$, 6-keto-$PGF_{1\alpha}$, $PGF_{2\alpha}$, $PGE_2$, and $PGD_2$ in lung and trachea in response to OVA challenge<br>-↓ $LTC_4/D_4/E_4$ release (lungs)<br>-↓ $PGD_2$ (bladder)<br>-no change in basal release in all tissues<br>-no effect on COX-2 protein levels before or after OVA challenge |

| Species | Study Description | Tissue or Organ Studied | CLA Isomer and Content | Outcome Measure | Major Findings |
|---|---|---|---|---|---|
| ***ALLERGY*** | | | | | |
| ddY mice and Wistar ST rats [41] | Hen egg-white lysozyme (HEL)-anaphylactic reaction; CLA orally administered and painted onto skin; scratching behaviour induced by compound 48/80 (COM) – histamine release agent | | 0.1% or 0.2% w/w Synthetic CLA mixture (75% pure) administered orally for 2 wks; synthetic CLA mixture (0.625, 1.25, or 2.5 mg/30μl/d) applied topically for 5d | Type 1 hypersensitivity | - suppressed decrease in BP and blood flow due to anaphylaxis in mice (0.1% CLA)<br>- antipruritic activity, with significant inhibition of scratching behaviour when administered orally (0.2%w/w 24hr prior to COM administration and 0.1% in mice) or topically (2.5mg/30μl/d, mice)<br>-↓ COM induced vasodilation in rats (topical administration, unspecified concentration) |
| ***INFLAMMATION*** | | | | | |
| Bovine Aortic Endothelial cells (Corriell Cell Repository) [42] | Cells seeded, at 80% confluency, treated with CLA (0 to 10 μg/mL, 0 to 24 h); additional pharmacological treatments included 10 μM A23187 and 5 μM BK (braykinin) | Cells and supernatant | 0 to 10 μg/mL synthetic CLA isomer mixture (50:50, c9t11+t9c11:t10c12) | Eicosanoids, COX expression | - no effect on eNOS protein or mRNA expression<br>-no effect released nitrite over 3 h<br>- Pretreatment with 10 μg/mL CLA for 3 h or 24 h potentiated BK-stimulated nitrite release<br>- no effect on COX-I protein expression or COX-I or COX-II mRNA expression<br>-↓ 6k-$PGF_{1\alpha}$ release |

**Table 6. (Continued)**

| Species | Study Description | Tissue or Organ Studied | CLA Isomer and Content | Outcome Measure | Major Findings |
|---|---|---|---|---|---|
| ***INFLAMMATION*** | | | | | |
| Human aortic endothelial cells, obtained from a 38-y-old female donor [43] | After reaching 70–80% confluence, cells incubated for 24 h at 37°C with fresh medium alone (control), or with medium supplemented with either *cis*-9, *trans*-11 CLA or *trans*-10, *cis*-12 CLA at final concentrations of 5 or 50 µmol/L | | 5 or 50 µmol/L of c9t11 or t10c12 or synthetic CLA isomer mixture | Eicosanoids, inflammation | - no effect on growth and viability of the cells<br>- no effect on δ5-desaturase mRNA<br>-↓ δ6-desaturase mRNA (50 µM)<br>-↓ 6-keto-$PGF_1\alpha$, $TXB_2$ and $PGE_2$ (50 µM, c9t11 and t10c12)<br>- no effect on 6-keto-$PGF_1\alpha$ to $TXB_2$ ratio<br>-↓ relative $sPLA_2$ mRNA (50 µM, c9t11 and t10c12)<br>-↓ activity of $sPLA_2$ (5 or 50 µM, c9t11)<br>-↓ COX-1 mRNA (50 µM, c9t11)<br>- ↑ COX-1 mRNA (5µM, c9t11)<br>-↓ COX-2 mRNA (50 µM, c9t11 and t10c12)<br>-↓ NO release with 5 or 50 µM c9t11 and 50 µM t10c12<br>- no effect on eNOS mRNA |
| Human saphenous veins endothelial cells [44] | After 60% confluence, medium containing the CLA, DHA, EPA, LA or DMSO vehicle were added for 72 h, at 69 h medium changed to allow 3 h co-incubation with $^{14}$C-AA (1 µCi); medium removed and serum free medium containing calcium chloride (2mM) and calcium ionophore A23187 (3µM) added for 30 min | | CLA mixture (100µM), c9t11-CLA (93% purity, 50µM) or t10c12-CLA (98% purity, 50µM) isomers | $^{14}$C-eicosanoids ($PGI_2$, $TXB_2$, $PGF_{2a}$, $PGE_2$ and $PGD_2$) | -↓ of all stimulated $^{14}$C-eicosanoids (CLA mixture)<br>-↓ calcium ionophore -stimulated $^{14}$C-eicosanoids (50µM, c9t11and t10c12; 100µM c9t11)<br>-↑ stimulated $^{14}$C-eicosanoids (100µM, t10c12)<br>-↓ resting production of $^{14}$C-$PGF_2\alpha$<br>- no effect on expression of COX-I under basal or stimulate conditions |

| Species | Study Description | Tissue or Organ Studied | CLA Isomer and Content | Outcome Measure | Major Findings |
| --- | --- | --- | --- | --- | --- |
| ***INFLAMMATION*** | | | | | |
| Osteoarthritic chondrocytes (OC) isolated from osteoarthritis patients (osteoarthritic articular cartilage) [45] | Human OC treated with (1:1w/w): CLA, CLA/AA, CLA/EPA, LA, LA/AA, LA/EPA, or ethanol (as a vehicle control) at 10 and 20 mM for 6 d in the presence of LPS (10μg/ml) and IL-1β (5ng/mL) | Culture media and cell morphology | 20μM synthetic CLA isomer mixture (1:1) | $PGE_2$ and NO | -↓ $PGE_2$ production (CLA, LA and CLA/EPA, LA/EPA); lowest with CLA/EPA<br>-↓ NO production (CLA, LA/EPA and LA/AA); lowest with LA/AA<br>-↑ NO production (LA and CLA/EPA)<br>-no effect with CLA/AA |
| Murine epidermal cell line, HEL-30 [46] | Confluent cells incubated for 12 h with $^{14}$C-AA at 0.2 μCi and methanol vehicle, LA or CLA (16 μg/ml); media changed, containing acetone (0.1%) or TPA (12-*O*-tetradecanoyl-phorbol-13-acetate) dissolved in acetone (1.6 μM) and incubated for 3 h | | 1, 4 or 16 μg/ml synthetic CLA isomer mixture | $PGE_2$, $^{14}$C-AA release | -↓ TPA-induced $^{14}$C-$PGE_2$ synthesis<br>- no effect on TPA-induced $^{14}$C-AA release |

**Table 6. (Continued)**

| Species | Study Description | Tissue or Organ Studied | CLA Isomer and Content | Outcome Measure | Major Findings |
|---|---|---|---|---|---|
| ***INFLAMMATION*** | | | | | |
| Murine macrophage RAW264.7, HL-60 (myeloid precursor cell line) and COS-1 cells [47] | RAW cells transfected with the PPRE containing reporter gene (PGJ3TK) and treated with various CLA isomers (200 μM); HL-60 cells cultured for 5 days with CLA, LA (150 μM) or 15dPGJ$_2$ (10 μM) then assessed by flow cytometry for CD14 (LPS receptor) expression. | Cells and supernatants | 15, 100 or 200 μM of synthetic CLA individual (c9t11, c9c11, t9t11, t10c12) or mixed isomers | Eicosanoids, cytokines, cell surface expression, PPARγ, | - ↓ IFNγ-induced COX2, iNOS, and TNF-α mRNA and TNF-α and NO production (200μM, all isomers)<br>- all CLA isomers activated endogenously expressed PPARγ<br>- ↓ COX-2 and iNOS promoter activity and IFN-γ-dependent $NO_2$ production (c9t11, dose-dependent)<br>- ↓ $PGE_2$ (c9t11, dose-dependent, IFN-γ induced)<br>-↑ CD14 expression of HL-60 cells (monocytic differentiation)<br>-↑ CD36 mRNA levels (monocyte/macrophage differentiation into foam cells)<br>-↓ iNOS reporter activity and ↑ PGJ3TK activity in a PPARγ-dependent manner in COS1 cells<br>-dn (dominant negative) PPARγ ↓ the effects of the CLA isomers on iNOS promoter and PPRE reporter activity (RAW) |
| Rat [48] | 3 wk feeding trial; 2 dietary treatments + control | peritoneal exudate cells, serum, spleen and lung | 0.5 or 1.0% w/w CLA | Eicosanoid release | -↓ in peritoneal exudate<br>- no effect on histamine or $LTB_4$ release in peritoneal exudate<br>-↓ splenic $LTB_4$ (dose-dependent), lung $LTC_4$ and serum $PGE_4$ |
| Sprague-Dawley rats [49] | 42 d feeding trial; 70g/day extra fat; 4 dietary treatments, SBO (n-6:n-3 7.3:1) or MSO (n-6:n-3 1.8:1) and CLA (0% or 1%) | Liver, resident peritoneal macrophages | 1% or 10g/kg diet synthetic CLA isomer mixture | $PGE_2$ and cytokines | -↓ basal and LPS-induced levels of IL-6 (resident peritoneal macrophages, MSO)<br>-↓ basal levels of TNF-α production (resident peritoneal macrophages, MSO and SBO)<br>-no effect on IL-1 production |

| Species | Study Description | Tissue or Organ Studied | CLA Isomer and Content | Outcome Measure | Major Findings |
|---|---|---|---|---|---|
| ***INFLAMMATION*** | | | | | |
| C57BL/6J Mice [50] | 56 d feeding trail; 2 dietary treatments + control group | Blood, spleen | 0.5%w/w c9t11 or t10c12 synthetic CLA isomer mixture (FFA) | Numbers of cells, cytokine and eicosanoid secretion | - no change in circulating WBCs (number or phenotype)<br>-no change in splenocyte proliferation in response to ConA or to LPS<br>-no change PGE2 or IL-2 (spleen, LPS and ConA)<br>-↑ TNF-α and IL-6 production (spleen, LPS and ConA)<br>-↓ IL-4 production (spleen, LPS and ConA) |
| Sprague-Dawley rats [51] | 2 wk feeding trial; dietary treatment + control | Lymph, serum, liver, spleen | 1%w/w Synthetic mixture | Lymphatic recovery, weight, PGE2 | -↓ lymphatic recovery rate<br>-no effect on food intake or weight gain<br>-↓ serum and spleen PGE2 |
| Female CD-1 mice or Sencar mice [52] | 6 wk feeding trial with 3 dietary treatments + control group; after 6 wk treated with TPA or acetone control; sacrificed 6 hrs later | Dorsal skin epidermis | 0.5%, 1.0%, or 1.5% w/w synthetic CLA isomer mixture | $PGE_2$ and vascular permeability | -↓ TPA-induced $PGE_2$ (1.5% dietary CLA)<br>-no effect on TPA-induced vascular permeability |
| Sea: ddY strain mice [53] | 1 dietary treatment + control;<br>Feeding trial, at 9 weeks old, female mice mated with male mice given the same diet; after weaning, the offspring were fed the same diet as their dams; killed at weaning, 25 days old or 8 weeks old | Cerebrum of brain | 30 g/kg diet synthetic CLA isomer mixture | cerebral prostaglandin $E_2$ ($PGE_2$) levels and cyclooxygenase (COX)-1 and COX-2 mRNA expression | -↑ body weight in offspring, but no increase in feed intake<br>-↓ cerebral $PGE_2$ concentration<br>-↑ COX-1 mRNA expression<br>-COX-2 mRNA expression not significantly affected |

**Table 6. (Continued)**

| Species | Study Description | Tissue or Organ Studied | CLA Isomer and Content | Outcome Measure | Major Findings |
|---|---|---|---|---|---|
| ***INFLAMMATION*** | | | | | |
| Male offspring of known Han:SPRD-*cy* heterozygotes [54] | 8 wk feeding trial; 1 dietary treatment + control | kidney | ~1% of diet by weight synthetic CLA isomer mixture | Inflammation and $PGE_2$ | -↓ interstitial inflammation, macrophage infiltration, fibrosis, and renal $PGE_2$ release |
| ISA brown hens [55] | 18 wk feeding trial; 1 dietary treatment + control, Blood samples were collected from 6 hens per diet group every 3 weeks and macrophages and heterophils were isolated | Blood | 1% w/w CLA mixture | Urokinase plasminogen activator and superoxidce production (UNS or PMA) | -↑ quantity of u-PA on the membrane of macrophages and heterophils isolated (PMA-activated)<br>-↓ superoxide production by activated (PMA) macrophages and heterophils during last 9 weeks<br>-no affect on basal levels |
| ***ACQUIRED IMMUNE SYSTEM IN VITRO AND ANIMAL MODELS*** | | | | | |
| Porcine [56] | Isolated blood lymphocytes were co-cultured with or without different concentrations of CLA | Blood lymphocytes | 0,17.8, 35.7 and 71.4μM; 46% c9t11 and/or t9c11 and 50% t10c12 synthetic mixture | Lymphocyte proliferation, cytotoxicity, and IL-2 production | -↑ proliferation (PWM (dose-dependent), ConA and PMAI)<br>-no significant effect on cytotoxicity ($p<0.05$)<br>-↓ IL-2 production (dose-dependent) |
| Jurkat T-cells [57] | Jurkat cells were incubated in culture media with different concentrations of CLA for 72hr | n/a | 0, 50, 100 or 200 μM CLA; 50% c9t11, 40% t10c12 synthetic mixture | Cytokine mRNA expression (PMAI + αCD3) and lymphocyte proliferation (UNS) | -↑ IL-2 mRNA expression at all concentrations of CLA (dose-dependent, PMAI+αCD3)<br>-↑ IFN-γ mRNA expression at 200μM CLA (PMAI+αCD3)<br>-↓ proliferation at 50μM CLA (UNS) |
| Piglets [74] | 28 day feeding trial with 2 dietary treatments and control group | Serum | 0.5% and 1% CLA synthetic mixture (65% purity of CLA isomers) | IgG | -↑IgG |

| Species | Study Description | Tissue or Organ Studied | CLA Isomer and Content | Outcome Measure | Major Findings |
|---|---|---|---|---|---|
| ***ACQUIRED IMMUNE SYSTEM IN VITRO AND ANIMAL MODELS*** | | | | | |
| Balb/c mice [63] | 3 or 6 wk feeding trial with 3 dietary treatment groups and one control | Spleen | 0.1%, 0.3%, 0.9% w/w synthetic mixture (unknown composition) | Lymphocyte proliferation ($^{3}$H-thymidine, ConA, PHA or LPS) and cytotoxicity and IL-2 production (ConA) | -↑ IL-2 (3wk group, ConA)<br>-↑lymphocyte proliferation (PHA, 3wk group, but not 6wk group)<br>-no effect on ConA or LPS-stimulated splenocyte proliferative response<br>-no effect on lymphocyte cytotoxicity |
| Sprague-Dawley rats [48] | 3 wk feeding trial; 2 dietary treatments + control group | Spleen, serum, peritoneal exudates cells (PEC) and MLN[1] | 0.5% and 1%w/w synthetic CLA isomer mixture | Igs (LPS), phenotype analysis | -↑ IgA, G (0.5 and 1% w/w) and M (serum, 1%w/w)<br>-↑ IgA, G and M (MLN, LPS)<br>-↑IgM (spleen, LPS, 0.5 and 1% w/w)<br>-no effect on IgG or IgA (spleen)<br>-↓ IgE (serum and MLN, LPS)<br>-no effect CD4/CD8 ratio |
| Young and Old C57BL/6NCrl BR Mice [61] | 8wk feeding trial with one dietary treatment + control group | Spleen | 1%w/w c9t11:t10c12, 1:1 synthetic mixture | Cytokines (ConA or LPS), DTH, lymphocyte proliferation ($^{3}$H-thymidine, ConA, PHA or LPS) | -↑ proliferation (old mice, Con A and young mice w/ConA or PHA)<br>-↑IL-2 (UNS and ConA)<br>-no effect on IL-1 (UNS or LPS), NK cell activity or DTH response |
| Sprague-Dawley Rats [75] | 3wk feeding trial with 4 dietary treatments and control group | Spleen | 0.05, 0.10, 0.25 and 0.50% w/w; (50:50 c9t11:t10c12) synthetic isomer mixture | Igs (UNS) | -↑IgG, M and A (dose-dependent, but plateau at 0.25% for IgG and M - UNS) |
| Piglets [68] | 28 day feeding trial with 2 dietary treatments and control group | Serum | 0.5% and 1% CLA synthetic mixture (65% purity of CLA isomers) | IgG | -↑IgG |
| Piglets [36] | 72 day feeding trial with 3 dietary treatments and control group | Blood | Mixed Isomers (60% purity); 0.67, 1.33 or 2%w/w CLA | Lymphocyte proliferation ($^{3}$H-thymidine, ConA) and phenotype | -↑$CD4^{-}CD8^{+}$, $TCR\alpha\beta CD4^{+}CD8\alpha\alpha$ T lymphocytes<br>-↓ $TCR\alpha\beta CD4^{+}$ T lymphocytes<br>-↑ proliferation (UNS, day 14)<br>-no effect on ConA-stimulated proliferative response |

**Table 6. (Continued)**

| Species | Study Description | Tissue or Organ Studied | CLA Isomer and Content | Outcome Measure | Major Findings |
|---|---|---|---|---|---|
| ***ACQUIRED IMMUNE SYSTEM IN VITRO AND ANIMAL MODELS*** | | | | | |
| Crj:CD-1 (ICR) Mice [59] | 8wk feeding trial | Serum | 1%w/w synthetic mixture | Cytokines | -↓ TNF-α level |
| C57BL/6J Mice [60] | 3 wk feeding trial | Spleen | 0.5%w/w t10c12, c9t11 or 1:1 mix CLA | Igs (ConA), Cytokines (ConA) and Lymphocyte Phenotype | -↑ IgA (ConA, t10c12) and IgM (UNS and ConA, t10c12)<br>-IgG and IgE unaffected<br>-↑TNF-α (c9t11, ConA)<br>-IL-2,3,5 and IFN-γ production unaffected<br>-↑B cells (1:1 mixand t10c12)<br>-↓CD4+ (t10c12)<br>-↓B cells (c9t11)<br>-↓ CD4/CD8 (all)<br>-↑ CD8+ (c9t11 and 1:1 mix) |
| Weanling BALB/c mice [28] | 6 wk feeding trial; 1 dietary treatment + control (corn oil) group | Spleen | 0.5% w/w synthetic CLA isomer mixture | Cytokine production | -↑ IL-2 (ConA)<br>-↓ IL-4 (ConA) |
| Balb/c mice [65] | 3wk feeding trial with 2 CLA dietary treatments + control group | MLN, serum | 0.5% or 1.5% w/w<br>76% pure synthetic mixture | Igs (LPS) | -↑ secretory IgA (serum and MLN, LPS)<br>-↑ IgG (serum, 0.5% CLA)<br>-no effect on IgE |
| Pigs [66] | Sows fed CLA 7 days pre and post-partum (D1) or 7d pre-partum until weaning (D2) | Serum | 0.5% w/w CLA; 50% pure synthetic mixture | Igs | -↑IgG (piglets D1)<br>-↑IgG, M and A (piglets D2) |
| C57Bl/6N Mice [62] | 3wk feeding trial with 4 dietary treatments + control group | Spleen | 0.1% and 1% FFA<br>CLA and 0.1% and 1% TG CLA synthetically prepared (1:1, c9t11:t10c12) | Igs (unstimulated) and Cytokines (LPS-stimulated) | -↑IgG (1% FFA and 1% TG CLA)<br>-IgM and IgA unaffected<br>-↑IL-9, MCP-5, GM-CSF, IL-10, sTNFri, IFN-γ, KC, IL-13, IL-2 IL-5, MIP-3β, Eotaxin, GCSF, SCF (1%FFA)<br>-↑MCP-5, GM-CSF, IFN-γ, IL-10, IL-9, sTNFri, MIP-1α (1%TG)<br>- ↓IL-3, IL-12p70, IL-6, IL-5, IL-12p40, RANTES and IL-4 (1%TG) |

| Species | Study Description | Tissue or Organ Studied | CLA Isomer and Content | Outcome Measure | Major Findings |
|---|---|---|---|---|---|
| ***HUMAN STUDIES*** | | | | | |
| Healthywomen, aged 20-41 yrs [69] | 93 day feeding trial with 1 dietary treatment; basal diet for 30d, 3.9g Tonalin/day for next 63 days | Blood, serum | 3.9g/day synthetic CLA isomer mixture | PBMC function | - no effect on $PGE_2$, $LTB_4$, IL-1β or TNF-α secretion after PHA stimulation<br>-no change in % T cells producing IL-2 or IFN-γ or in monocytes producing TNF-α<br>-no change in intracellular concentration of cytokines |
| Resistance-trained men, mean, aged 23yrs [70] | Double-blind randomized Clinical Trial; subjects were given a placebo (olive oil) or CLA for 28d | PBMC | Subjects received 9g/d of olive oil (placebo) or 6g/d of CLA (65% pure synthetic mixture) with 3g/d fatty acids | WBC count and phenotype | -no effect on WBC count<br>-no effect on lymphocyte phenotypes |
| Men with metabolic syndrome aged 35–65yrs [71] | 3 months feeding trial; 2 dietary treatments + control; baseline and endpoint samples collected | Urine and plasma | Subjects received 3.4g of olive oil (placebo), t10c12 CLA, or a CLA mixture (1 :1) | Eicosanoids, in vivo lipid peroxidation (determined as urinary 8-iso-$PGF_{2\alpha}$ [F2-isoprostanes]), 15-ketodihydro $PGF_{2\alpha}$, CRP, IL-6 and TNF-α | -↑ CRP (t10c12)<br>-↑ CRP (mix, compared to baseline levels)<br>-↑ 8-iso-$PGF_{2\alpha}$ (↑ lipid peroxidation)<br>-↑15-K-DH-$PGF_{2\alpha}$<br>-no effect on TNF-α and IL-6 levels (plasma) |
| Healthy men, aged 20–47 yrs [73] | 13 month feeding trial; 2 treatment groups; one isomer for 24 wks, 6 wk washout, other isomer for 24 wks | Blood, serum, PBMC, | c9t11 (0.59, 1.19, and 2.38 g/d) or t10c12 (0.63, 1.26, and 2.52 g/d) | Mitogen-induced activation of lymphocytes | -no consistent effect on PBMC subsets<br>-↓ mitogen-induced T lymphocyte activation<br>-no effect on serum CRP concentrations<br>-no consistent effects on ex vivo cytokine production (TNF-α, IL-10, IL-6, IL-1β, IL-8, IFN-α, TNF-α, IL-10, IL-5, IL-4, and IL-2) |
| Abdominally obese men, aged 35–65 y old [72] | 3 month feeding trial; 1 dietary treatment + control; | Urine | 3 g c9,t11 CLA/d | Eicosanoids, 8-iso-$PGF_{2\alpha}$ (urine) and 15-*keto*-dihydro-$PGF_{2\alpha}$ (marker of inflammation) | -↑ 8-*iso*-prostaglandin $F_{2\alpha}$ and 15-*keto*-dihydro-prostaglandin $F_{2\alpha}$ excretion |

# References


[1] Beutler, B. Science review: key inflammatory and stress pathways in critical illness - the central role of the Toll-like receptors. *Crit. Care,* 2003, 39-46.

[2] Lind, L. Circulating markers of inflammation and atherosclerosis. *Atherosclerosis,* 2003, 203-14.

[3] Koenig, W. Predicting risk and treatment benefit in atherosclerosis: the role of C-reactive protein. *Int. J. Cardiol,* 2005, 199-206.

[4] Gonzalez, MA; Selwyn, AP. Endothelial function, inflammation, and prognosis in cardiovascular disease. *Am. J. Med.,* 2003, 99S-106S.

[5] Diaz, BL; Arm, JP. Phospholipase A(2). *Prost. Leukot. Essent. Fatty Acids,* 2003, 87-97.

[6] Montuschi, P; Barnes, PJ; Roberts, LJ. Isoprostanes: markers and mediators of oxidative stress. *FASEB J.,* 2004, 1791-800.

[7] Ollila, J; Vihinen, M. B cells. *Int. J. Biochem. Cell Biol.,* 2005, 518-23.

[8] Goldsby, RA, Kindt, TJ, Osborne, BA. Immunoglobulins: Structure and Function. In: Goldsby, RA, Kindt, TJ, Osborne, BA, editors. *Kuby Immunology ed 4.* New York: W.H. Freeman and Company; 2000; 83-113.

[9] Manz, RA; Hauser, AE; Hiepe, F; Radbruch, A. Maintenance of serum antibody levels. *Annu. Rev. Immunol,* 2005, 367-86.

[10] Preud'homme, JL; Petit, I; Barra, A; Morel, F; Lecron, JC; Lelievre, E. Structural and functional properties of membrane and secreted IgD. *Mol. Immunol.,* 2000, 871-87.

[11] Yaqoob, P. Lipids and the immune response: from molecular mechanisms to clinical applications. *Curr. Opin. Clin. Nutr. Metab. Care,* 2003, 133-50.

[12] Field, CJ; Schley, PD. Evidence for potential mechanisms for the effect of conjugated linoleic acid on tumor metabolism and immune function: lessons from n-3 fatty acids. *Am. J. Clin. Nutr.,* 2004, 1190S-8S.

[13] Wahle, KW; Rotondo, D; Heys, SD. Polyunsaturated fatty acids and gene expression in mammalian systems. *Proc. Nutr. Soc.,* 2003, 349-60.

[14] Dykstra, ML; Cherukuri, A; Pierce, SK. Floating the raft hypothesis for immune receptors: access to rafts controls receptor signaling and trafficking. *Traffic,* 2001, 160-6.

[15] Ma, DW; Seo, J; Switzer, KC; Fan, YY; McMurray, DN; Lupton, JR; Chapkin, RS. n-3 PUFA and membrane microdomains: a new frontier in bioactive lipid research. *J. Nutr. Biochem.,* 2004, 700-6.

[16] Ma, DW; Wierzbicki, AA; Field, CJ; Clandinin, MT. Conjugated linoleic acid in canadian dairy and beef products. *J. Agric. Food Chem.,* 1999, 1956-60.

[17] Ma, DW; Wierzbicki, AA; Field, CJ; Clandinin, MT. Preparation of conjugated linoleic acid from safflower oil. *J. Am. Oil. Chem. Soc.,* 1999, 729-30.

[18] Pariza, MW. Perspective on the safety and effectiveness of conjugated linoleic acid. *Am J. Clin. Nutr.,* 2004, 1132S-6S.

[19] Belury, MA. Dietary conjugated linoleic acid in health: physiological effects and mechanisms of action. *Annu. Rev. Nutr.,* 2002, 505-31.

[20] Pariza, MW; Loretz, LJ; Storkson, JM; Holland, NC. Mutagens and modulator of mutagenesis in fried ground beef. *Cancer Res.,* 1983, 2444s-6s.

[21] Choi, JS; Jung, MH; Park, HS; Song, J. Effect of conjugated linoleic acid isomers on insulin resistance and mRNA levels of genes regulating energy metabolism in high-fat-fed rats. *Nutrition,* 2004, 1008-17.

[22] Watkins, BA; Li, Y; Lippman, HE; Reinwald, S; Seifert, MF. A test of Ockham's razor: implications of conjugated linoleic acid in bone biology. *Am. J. Clin. Nutr.,* 2004, 1175S-85S.

[23] Graves, E; Hitt, A; Pariza, MW; Cook, ME; McCarthy, DO. Conjugated linoleic acid preserves gastrocnemius muscle mass in mice bearing the colon-26 adenocarcinoma. *Res. Nurs. Health,* 2005, 48-55.

[24] Wiegand, BR; Parrish, FC, Jr.; Swan, JE; Larsen, ST; Baas, TJ. Conjugated linoleic acid improves feed efficiency, decreases subcutaneous fat, and improves certain aspects of meat quality in stress-genotype pigs. *J. Anim. Sci.,* 2001, 2187-95.

[25] Javadi, M; Beynen, AC; Hovenier, R; Lankhorst, A; Lemmens, AG; Terpstra, AH; Geelen, MJ. Prolonged feeding of mice with conjugated linoleic acid increases hepatic fatty acid synthesis relative to oxidation. *J. Nutr. Biochem.,* 2004, 680-7.

[26] Inoue, N; Nagao, K; Hirata, J; Wang, YM; Yanagita, T. Conjugated linoleic acid prevents the development of essential hypertension in spontaneously hypertensive rats. *Biochem. Biophys. Res. Commun.,* 2004, 679-84.

[27] Miller, CC; Park, Y; Pariza, MW; Cook, ME. Feeding conjugated linoleic acid to animals partially overcomes catabolic responses due to endotoxin injection. *Biochem. Biophys. Res. Commun.,* 1994, 1107-12.

[28] Yang, M; Cook, ME. Dietary conjugated linoleic acid decreased cachexia, macrophage tumor necrosis factor-alpha production, and modifies splenocyte cytokines production. *Exp. Biol. Med.,* 2003, 51-8.

[29] Turini, ME; Boza, JJ; Gueissaz, N; Moennoz, D; Montigon, F; Vuichoud, J; Gremaud, G; Pouteau, E; Piguet, C; Perrin, I; Verguet, C; Finot, PA; German, B. Short-term dietary conjugated linoleic acid supplementation does not enhance the recovery of immunodepleted dexamethasone-treated rats. *Eur. J. Nutr.,* 2003, 171-9.

[30] Changhua, L; Jindong, Y; Defa, L; Lidan, Z; Shiyan, Q; Jianjun, X. Conjugated linoleic acid attenuates the production and gene expression of proinflammatory cytokines in weaned pigs challenged with lipopolysaccharide. *J. Nutr.,* 2005, 239-44.

[31] Iwakiri, Y; Sampson, DA; Allen, KG. Suppression of cyclooxygenase-2 and inducible nitric oxide synthase expression by conjugated linoleic acid in murine macrophages. *Prost. Leukot. Essent. Fatty Acids,* 2002, 435-43.

[32] Cheng, WL; Lii, CK; Chen, HW; Lin, TH; Liu, KL. Contribution of conjugated linoleic acid to the suppression of inflammatory responses through the regulation of the NF-kappaB pathway. *J. Agric. Food Chem.,* 2004, 71-8.

[33] Lai, C; Yin, J; Li, D; Zhao, L; Chen, X. Effects of dietary conjugated linoleic acid supplementation on performance and immune function of weaned pigs. *Arch. Anim. Nutr.,* 2005, 41-51.

[34] Hontecillas, R; Wannemeulher, MJ; Zimmerman, DR; Hutto, DL; Wilson, JH; Ahn, DU; Bassaganya-Riera, J. Nutritional regulation of porcine bacterial-induced colitis by conjugated linoleic acid. *J. Nutr.,* 2002, 2019-27.

[35] Bassaganya-Riera, J; Pogranichniy, RM; Jobgen, SC; Halbur, PG; Yoon, KJ; O'Shea, M; Mohede, I; Hontecillas, R. Conjugated linoleic acid ameliorates viral infectivity in a pig model of virally induced immunosuppression. *J. Nutr.,* 2003, 3204-14.

[36] Bassaganya-Riera, J; Hontecillas-Magarzo, R; Bregendahl, K; Wannemuehler, MJ; Zimmerman, DR. Effects of dietary conjugated linoleic acid in nursery pigs of dirty and clean environments on growth, empty body composition, and immune competence. *J. Anim. Sci.,* 2001, 714-21.

[37] Kelley, DS; Taylor, PC; Rudolph, IL; Benito, P; Nelson, GJ; Mackey, BE; Erickson, KL. Dietary conjugated linoleic acid did not alter immune status in young healthy women. *Lipids,* 2000, 1065-71.

[38] Albers, R; van der Wielen, RP; Brink, EJ; Hendriks, HF; Dorovska-Taran, VN; Mohede, IC. Effects of cis-9, trans-11 and trans-10, cis-12 conjugated linoleic acid (CLA) isomers on immune function in healthy men. *Eur. J. Clin. Nutr.,* 2003, 595-603.

[39] Whigham, LD; Cook, EB; Stahl, JL; Saban, R; Bjorling, DE; Pariza, MW; Cook, ME. CLA reduces antigen-induced histamine and PGE(2) release from sensitized guinea pig tracheae. *Am. J. Physiol. Regul. Integr. Comp. Physiol.,* 2001, R908-R912.

[40] Whigham, LD; Higbee, A; Bjorling, DE; Park, Y; Pariza, MW; Cook, ME. Decreased antigen-induced eicosanoid release in conjugated linoleic acid-fed guinea pigs. *Am. J. Physiol.,* 2002, R1104-R1112.

[41] Ishiguro, K; Oku, H; Suitani, A; Yamamoto, Y. Effects of conjugated linoleic acid on anaphylaxis and allergic pruritus. *Biol. Pharm. Bull,* 2002, 1655-7.

[42] Coen, P; Cummins, P; Birney, Y; Devery, R; Cahill, P. Modulation of nitric oxide and 6-keto-prostaglandin F(1alpha) production in bovine aortic endothelial cells by conjugated linoleic acid. *Endothelium,* 2004, 211-20.

[43] Eder, K; Schleser, S; Becker, K; Korting, R. Conjugated linoleic acids lower the release of eicosanoids and nitric oxide from human aortic endothelial cells. *J. Nutr.,* 2003, 4083-9.

[44] Urquhart, P; Parkin, SM; Rogers, JS; Bosley, JA; Nicolaou, A. The effect of conjugated linoleic acid on arachidonic acid metabolism and eicosanoid production in human saphenous vein endothelial cells. *Biochim. Biophys. Acta.,* 2002, 150-60.

[45] Shen, CL; Dunn, DM; Henry, JH; Li, Y; Watkins, BA. Decreased production of inflammatory mediators in human osteoarthritic chondrocytes by conjugated linoleic acids. *Lipids,* 2004, 161-6.

[46] Liu, KL; Belury, MA. Conjugated linoleic acid reduces arachidonic acid content and PGE2 synthesis in murine keratinocytes. *Cancer Lett.,* 1998, 15-22.

[47] Yu, Y; Correll, PH; Vanden Heuvel, JP. Conjugated linoleic acid decreases production of pro-inflammatory products in macrophages: evidence for a PPAR gamma-dependent mechanism. *Biochim. Biophys. Acta.,* 2002, 89-99.

[48] Sugano, M; Tsujita, A; Yamasaki, M; Noguchi, M; Yamada, K. Conjugated linoleic acid modulates tissue levels of chemical mediators and immunoglobulins in rats. *Lipids,* 1998, 521-7.

[49] Turek, JJ; Li, Y; Schoenlein, IA; Allen, KGD; Watkins, BA. Modulation of macrophage cytokine production by conjugated linoleic acids is influenced by the dietary n-6:n-3 fatty acid ratio. *J Nutr Biochem,* 1998, 258-66.

[50] Kelley, DS; Warren, JM; Simon, VA; Bartolini, G; Mackey, BE; Erickson, KL. Similar effects of c9,t11-CLA and t10,c12-CLA on immune cell functions in mice. *Lipids,* 2002, 725-8.

[51] Sugano MA; Tsujita M; Yamasaki K; Ikeda I; Kritchevsky D. Lymphatic recovery, tissue distribution, and metabolic effects of conjugated linoleic acid in rats. *J. Nutr. Biochem.,* 1997, 987-93.

[52] Kavanaugh, CJ; Liu, KL; Belury, MA. Effect of dietary conjugated linoleic acid on phorbol ester-induced PGE2 production and hyperplasia in mouse epidermis. *Nutr. Cancer,* 1999, 132-8.

[53] Nakanishi, T; Koutoku, T; Kawahara, S; Murai, A; Furuse, M. Dietary conjugated linoleic acid reduces cerebral prostaglandin E(2) in mice. *Neurosci. Lett.,* 2003, 135-8.

[54] Ogborn, MR; Nitschmann, E; Bankovic-Calic, N; Weiler, HA; Fitzpatrick-Wong, S; Aukema, HM. Dietary conjugated linoleic acid reduces PGE2 release and interstitial injury in rat polycystic kidney disease. *Kidney Int.,* 2003, 1214-21.

[55] Politis, I; Dimopoulou, M; Voudouri, A; Noikokyris, P; Feggeros, K. Effects of dietary conjugated linoleic acid isomers on several functional properties of macrophages and heterophils in laying hens. *Br. Poult. Sci.,* 2003, 203-10.

[56] Chew, BP; Wong, TS; Shultz, TD; Magnuson, NS. Effects of conjugated dienoic derivatives of linoleic acid and beta-carotene in modulating lymphocyte and macrophage function. *Anticancer Res.,* 1997, 1099-106.

[57] Luongo, D; Bergamo, P; Rossi, M. Effects of conjugated linoleic acid on growth and cytokine expression in Jurkat T cells. *Immunol. Lett.,* 2003, 195-201.

[58] Yamasaki, M; Kishihara, K; Mansho, K; Ogino, Y; Kasai, M; Sugano, M; Tachibana, H; Yamada, K. Dietary conjugated linoleic acid increases immunoglobulin productivity of Sprague-Dawley rat spleen lymphocytes. *Biosci Biotechnol Biochem,* 2000, 2159-64.

[59] Akahoshi, A; Goto, Y; Murao, K; Miyazaki, T; Yamasaki, M; Nonaka, M; Yamada, K; Sugano, M. Conjugated linoleic acid reduces body fats and cytokine levels of mice. *Biosci. Biotechnol. Biochem.,* 2002, 916-20.

[60] Yamasaki, M; Chujo, H; Hirao, A; Koyanagi, N; Okamoto, T; Tojo, N; Oishi, A; Iwata, T; Yamauchi-Sato, Y; Yamamoto, T; Tsutsumi, K; Tachibana, H; Yamada, K. Immunoglobulin and cytokine production from spleen lymphocytes is modulated in C57BL/6J mice by dietary cis-9, trans-11 and trans-10, cis-12 conjugated linoleic acid. *J. Nutr.,* 2003, 784-8.

[61] Hayek, MG; Han, SN; Wu, D; Watkins, BA; Meydani, M; Dorsey, JL; Smith, DE; Meydani, SN. Dietary conjugated linoleic acid influences the immune response of young and old C57BL/6NCrlBR mice. *J. Nutr.,* 1999, 32-8.

[62] Yamasaki, M; Kitagawa, T; Chujo, H; Koyanagi, N; Nishida, E; Nakaya, M; Yoshimi, K; Maeda, H; Nou, S; Iwata, T; Ogita, K; Tachibana, H; Yamada, K. Physiological difference between free and triglyceride-type conjugated linoleic acid on the immune function of C57BL/6N mice. *J. Agric. Food Chem.,* 2004, 3644-8.

[63] Wong, MW; Chew, BP; Wong, TS; Hosick, HL; Boylston, TD; Shultz, TD. Effects of dietary conjugated linoleic acid on lymphocyte function and growth of mammary tumors in mice. *Anticancer Res.,* 1997, 987-93.

[64] Muhl, H; Pfeilschifter, J. Anti-inflammatory properties of pro-inflammatory interferon-gamma. *Int. Immunopharmacol.,* 2003, 1247-55.

[65] Kim, JY; Chung, BH. Effects of combination dietary conjugated linoleic acid with vitamin A (retinol) and selenium on the response of the immunoglobulin production in mice. *J. Vet. Sci.,* 2003, 103-8.

[66] Rossi, R; Pastorelli, G; Bontempo, V; Corino, C. Effects of dietary conjugated linoleic acid (CLA) on immunoglobulin concentration in sow colostrum and piglet serum. *Vet. Res. Commun.,* 2004, 241-4.

[67] Bontempo, V; Sciannimanico, D; Pastorelli, G; Rossi, R; Rosi, F; Corino, C. Dietary conjugated linoleic acid positively affects immunologic variables in lactating sows and piglets. *J. Nutr.,* 2004, 817-24.

[68] Corino, C; Bjorling, DE; Sciannimanico, D. Effects of dietary conjugated linoleic acid on some aspecific immune parameters and acute phase proteins in waned piglets. *Can. J. Anim. Sci.,* 2001, 115-7.

[69] Kelley, DS; Simon, VA; Taylor, PC; Rudolph, IL; Benito, P; Nelson, GJ; Mackey, BE; Erickson, KL. Dietary supplementation with conjugated linoleic acid increased its concentration in human peripheral blood mononuclear cells, but did not alter their function. *Lipids,* 2001, 669-74.

[70] Kreider, RB; Ferreira, MP; Greenwood, M; Wilson, M; Almada, AL. Effects of conjugated linoleic acid supplementation during resistance training on body composition, bone density, strength, and selected hematological markers. *J Strength Cond. Res.,* 2002, 325-34.

[71] Riserus, U; Basu, S; Jovinge, S; Fredrikson, GN; Arnlov, J; Vessby, B. Supplementation with conjugated linoleic acid causes isomer-dependent oxidative stress and elevated C-reactive protein: a potential link to fatty acid-induced insulin resistance. *Circulation,* 2002, 1925-9.

[72] Riserus, U; Vessby, B; Arnlov, J; Basu, S. Effects of cis-9,trans-11 conjugated linoleic acid supplementation on insulin sensitivity, lipid peroxidation, and proinflammatory markers in obese men. *Am. J. Clin. Nutr.,* 2004, 279-83.

[73] Tricon, S; Burdge, GC; Kew, S; Banerjee, T; Russell, JJ; Grimble, RF; Williams, CM; Calder, PC; Yaqoob, P. Effects of cis-9,trans-11 and trans-10,cis-12 conjugated linoleic acid on immune cell function in healthy humans. *Am. J. Clin. Nutr.,* 2004, 1626-33.

[74] Corino, CBVaSD. Effects of dietary conjugated linoleic acid on some a specific immune parameters and acute phase protein inweaned piglets. *Can. J. Anim. Sci.,* 2002, 115-7.

[75] Yamasaki, M; Kishihara, K; Mansho, K; Ogino, Y; Kasai, M; Sugano, M; Tachibana, H; Yamada, K. Dietary conjugated linoleic acid increases immunoglobulin productivity of Sprague-Dawley rat spleen lymphocytes. *Biosci. Biotechnol. Biochem.,* 2000, 2159-64.

In: New Immunology Research Developments
Editor: Gunter V. Müller
ISBN 978-1-60021-701-2


*Chapter 5*

# Autoimmunity to Neuronal Proteins in Neurological Disorders

***Ruth Huizinga and Sandra Amor****
Department of Immunobiology, Biomedical Primate Research Centre,
P.O. Box 3306, 2280 GH Rijswijk, The Netherlands

## Abstract

Autoreactive T-cell responses directed to myelin proteins in the central nervous system (CNS) are widely believed to be fundamental in the pathology of multiple sclerosis (MS). This view has dominated the research field in MS for many years and led to the reliance on experimental models of neurological disease following immunisation with myelin antigens. Such experimental diseases have developed as the central paradigm to investigate underlying mechanisms operating in MS as well as the preclinical development of therapeutic strategies.

This long-standing concept has recently shifted and evidence is rapidly accumulating indicting a significance role of axonal damage and neurodegeneration in disease. Indeed, axonal damage is now considered to be the major cause of irreversible neurological disability in MS patients. One correlate of axonal damage in MS is the presence of antibodies against neurofilament light protein, a major component of the axonal cytoskeleton. Contrary to extensive literature on pathogenic myelin autoimmunity, the possible pathogenic role of autoimmunity to axonal antigens in MS has so far been ignored. Our recent experimental data indicate that autoimmunity to axonal antigens, as described in MS, is pathogenic rather than acting merely as a surrogate marker for axonal degeneration.

As validation of the concept that autoimmunity directed to neuronal antigens plays a role in disease, we define four criteria: first, that autoreactivity to neuronal antigens are consistently present in neurological disease in humans and experimental neurological disease in animals; secondly, that transfer of such neuronal reactive T

* Tel: +31 15 284 2732, Fax: +31 15 284 2600, Email: amor@bprc.nl

cells and/or antibodies are pathogenic either *in vivo* or *in vitro* model systems; thirdly, that immunization with neuronal antigens induces pathogenic autoimmune responses and leads to neurological disease in experimental animals; and finally, that inhibition of such responses ameliorates neurological disease.

Using these criteria we review the evidence for autoimmunity to neuronal antigens in several neurodegenerative disorders such as paraneoplastic disorders, and discuss how similar mechanisms may also operate in MS. Using the experimental models we describe our recent data to indicate that while clinical disease in MS models is due to autoimmune attack on myelin, neurons and axons can be also target for pathogenic autoimmunity. Understanding the factors leading to neuronal injury and neurodegenerative disorders is key to the development of effective therapies to prevent progression of disease and irreversible damage.

## Introduction

In this chapter we will review the evidence for autoimmunity to neurons and axons in neurological diseases and suggest how this may also be relevant in the pathogenesis of MS.

The view that autoreactive T-cells directed to myelin proteins in the CNS are fundamental in the pathology of demyelinating disorders such as MS has dominated neuroimmunology research for many years. This has led to the reliance on experimental models of paralytic neurological disease, namely experimental autoimmune encephalomyelitis (EAE), induced in susceptible animals by immunisation of myelin proteins. EAE has developed as the central paradigm to investigate the underlying mechanisms operating in MS in humans and heavily influenced the preclinical development of therapeutic strategies. In particular such approaches have focused on the role of $CD4^+$ helper T cells since several lines of evidence support the held notion that $CD4^+$ T cells play a crucial role in mediating the development of inflammatory lesions in both MS and EAE. Furthermore, histopathology of actively developing MS lesions has revealed the presence of many activated $CD4^+$ T cells in such lesions, and therapeutic intervention that targets helper T-cell functions in MS patients has at least partly positive clinical effects. More recently the long-standing concept that pathogenic autoreactive T cells are critical for myelin damage and disease in MS has shifted. Evidence is now rapidly accumulating indicating a significant role of axonal damage and neurodegeneration in disease (Trapp et al., 1998). Indeed axonal damage is now considered to be the major cause of irreversible neurological disability in MS patients. One correlate of axonal damage in MS is the presence of antibodies against neurofilament light protein, a major component of the axonal cytoskeleton (Eikelenboom et al., 2003). Contrary to extensive literature on pathogenic myelin autoimmunity the possible pathogenic role of autoimmunity to axonal antigens in MS has so far been ignored. Recent experimental data indicate that immunity to axonal antigens, as described in MS, is pathogenic rather than acting merely as a surrogate marker for axonal degeneration.

That autoimmune responses to neuronal antigens occur in neurodegenerative disorders other than MS is well documented (for an overview refer to Table 1). For example many paraneoplastic neurological disorders (PND) are thought to be caused by an autoimmune reaction directed against 'onconeural' antigens expressed by neurons and tumour cells (summarised in Table 2).

**Table 1. Distribution of neuronal antigens, immune responses and disease association**

| Antigens | Expression and Role | Disease Association with Antineuronal Antigens | Reference |
|---|---|---|---|
| Neurofilament-light | Axons – intracellular. Control of axonal calibre and axonal transport | ALS; Axonal neuropathy, MS | Couratier et al 1998 Grady et al 1993 Silber et al 2002 |
| Neurofilament-heavy | Axons - intracellular Control of axonal calibre and axonal transport | Alzheimer's disease, GBS | Soussan et al 1994 Terryberry et al 1998 |
| GluR3 | Glutamate subunit on postsynaptic cell surface protein | Rasmussen's encephalitis | Levite and Hermelin 1999 |
| aldolase C; monomeric γ-gamma-enolase; pyruvate kinase; dimeric γ-enolase | 40, 45, 60 and 98 kDa proteins of neurons | Basal ganglion disease, Encephalitis lethargica. Sydenham's Chorea Tourette's syndrome | Martino and Giovannoni 2004 Church et al 2002; Church et al 2003 Hallet et al 2000 |
| Tau | Microtubule-associated protein that stabilizes neuronal microtubules | Alzheimer's disease | Rosenman et al 2006 |
| NR2A and NR2B | Neurons in hippocampus, amygdale and hypothalamus Subunits of NMDA receptor | SLE | Huerta et al 2006 Sakic 2005 DeGiorgio et al 2001 |
| Beta-III-tubulin | Neuronal cytoskeleton | Brain trauma, CIDP | Skoda et al 2006 |
| Gangliosides GM1; GQ1b GD1b GD1a GalNAc-GD1a | Cell membranes – enriched in neurons | ALS MFS; cerebellar ataxia Ataxic sensory neuropathy GD1a GalNAc-GD1a | Hughes and Cornblath 2005 Willison 2005 |
| GAD | synapses Nerve terminals GABAnergic neurons | Stiff person syndrome in association with diabetes | Schloot et al 1999 |

In Lambert-Eaton myasthenic syndrome (LEMS) and neuromyotonia there are indications that disease is mediated by autoantibodies to antigens within the nervous system. Likewise, in other neurodegenerative diseases such as ALS, Parkinson's disease and Alzheimer's disease antibodies to neuronal proteins are present in patients and may contribute to disease. It is probably that, like myelin autoimmunity, pathogenic immunity to neuronal antigens is more common than originally thought and may be an important mechanism underlying neuronal damage and axonal damage observed in many neurological diseases including neurodegenerative disease such as MS.

## Table 2. Paraneoplastic neurological disorders

| Antigens | Antibody | Expression Distribution and Role | Tumor | Tumor and neurological Disease Association | Reference |
|---|---|---|---|---|---|
| Munc-18 | Anti-Munc-18 | Intracellular protein presynaptic terminals | | Rasmussen's encephalitis | Yang et al. 2000 |
| Hu antigens encoded by genes HuB, HuC, and HuD (Hel-N1), | Anti-Hu (ANNA-1) | 35-40 kDa Neuron specific RNA binding proteins | small cell lung carcinoma | Hu encephalopathy;<br>Subacute sensory neuronopathy;<br>Paraneoplastic brainstem encephalomyelitis<br>Limbic encephalitis | Tanaka 2004<br>Rousseau et al. 2005 |
| Yo (PCA-1)<br>Cdr62/<br>Cdr34 | Anti-YO | Purkinje cells<br>62 kDa Intracellular binds to myc | Ovarian and breast carcinomas | Cerebellar ataxia | Tanaka 2004 |
| Ri<br>(genes Nova-1 and NOVA 2 ) | anti-Ri<br>(ANNA-2) | Neuronal nuclei 55 and 80kDa<br>Neuron specific RNA binding protein | Small cell carcinoma, breast carcinoma | Paraneoplastic opsoclonus myoclonus ataxia (POMA) [NOVA-2] | Fadare and Hart 2004 |
| Ma antigens<br>Ma1 (PNMA-1)<br>Ma2 (Ta) (PNMA-2)<br>Ma3 (PNMA-3) | Anti-Ma1<br><br>Anti-Ma2<br>Anti-Ma3 | Ma-1 37kDa neuron and testis<br>Ma-2 40 kDa neurons of limbic system<br>Ma-1 37kDa neuron and testis | Testisicular, tumors small cell carcinoma of lungrs | Limbic encephalitis | Gultekin et al. 2000 |
| ANNA-3 | ANNA 3 | 170 kDa in nuclei of Purkinje cells and renal glomerular podocytes. | | cerebellum and small-cell carcinoma sensory/sensorimotor neuropathies, cerebellar ataxia, myelopathy, brain stem and limbic | Chan et al. 2001 |
| Tr | Tr cell location, cytosol and outer surface of ER | Purkinje cells | Hodgkin's lymphoma | Tr syndrome | Bernal et al. 2003 |
| Amphiphysin | Anti-amphiphysin | 128kDa Pre-synaptic Nerve terminals | Lung and thymoma | Stiff person syndrome and breast cancer .<br>SPS in association with diabetes | Folli et al. 1993 |
| AChr | Anti-AChR<br>Anti-striational | Motor endplates transmembrane | thymoma | Myasthenia Gravis | Vincent et al. 1999 |
| Voltage gated calcium channels (VGCC) | Anti-VGCC | | Small cell lung | Lambert Eaton syndromes<br>RA and SLE. ALS | Vincent et al. 1999;<br>Vincent 2006. |
| Voltage gated potassium channels | Anti-VGKC | | | Limbic encephalitis | Kleopa 2006 |
| mGluR1 | Anti-mGluR1 | Cerebellum purkinje cells, cerebellar cortex | Hodgkin's lymphoma | Ataxia | Coesmans et al. 2003 |

The question now is whether there is also evidence for involvement of autoimmunity to neuronal antigens in CNS disorders such as MS as well as other neurodegenerative disorders. Clearly this is of fundamental importance to the perspective of therapy in neurological disorders by targeting the pathogenic anti-neuronal responses. In MS several concepts have suggested how autoimmunity to myelin antigens may arise. For example the idea that similar structures on viruses and myelin antigens – so called molecular mimicry. Yet another idea suggests that the progression of neurological disease is due to the phenomenon of determinant spreading. In this view the repertoire of the anti-myelin T cell responses that drives the disease becomes increasing dynamic with the generation of new reactivities recognising antigens released with each new wave of disease. With these ideas in mind we discuss how autoimmunity to neuronal antigens may arise and, rather than focus on the role of pathogenic T cells, as is common in MS, we will discuss the evidence for autoantibodies in neurodegenerative disorders. Understanding the mechanisms by which autoimmunity to neuronal antigens leads to neuronal injury and neurodegenerative disorders is key to the development of effective therapies to prevent progression of disease and irreversible damage.

## Neurons and Axons as Targets of the Immune Response

The immune responses must maximise the removal of harmful microorganisms while protecting the healthy tissues and cells. In the CNS this protection is exemplified in part by the presence of the blood brain barrier (BBB) and low level expression of molecules on neurons required for immune activation as well as expression of molecules crucial for tissue protection and repair.

To exert a pathogenic effect on neurons and axons T cells need to recognise antigenic peptides presented by the major histocompatibility complex (MHC) molecules. Antigens derived from endogenously synthesised proteins are bound to MHC class I molecules and are recognised by CD8 positive (CD8+) T cells whereas antigens derived from proteins, internalised by endocytosis and processed in vesicles, are bound to MHC class II molecules and recognised by CD4 positive (CD4+) T cells. However, in health the CNS and in particular neurons are protected in part from pathogenic immunity by the blood brain barrier but also by expression of low levels of MHC molecules. The situation is different in disease where the expression of MHC molecules is dependent in the type of tissue injury. In MS lesions neurons and axons express Class I but not MHC class II molecules (Neumann et al. 1995; Hoftberger et al. 2004) and thus may be target for Class I restricted killing. Indeed CD8+ cytotoxic T cell induced neuronal damage in dorsal root ganglia is a prominent feature in viral infections such as lentivirus infections (Zhu et al. 2006) although the exact role of T cells in neurodegenerative disorders is unknown.

# Evidence for Autoimmunity to Axonal Antigens in Neurological Disorders

The precise role of pathogenic autoimmunity to self antigens including myelin antigens, as has been described in MS or indeed neuronal antigens in human neurological disorders is difficult to establish. The mere presence of antibodies and T cell responses to CNS antigens in human disease is clearly insufficient to assume that autoimmunity is relevant to disease or damage in the CNS. Firm evidence for the role of autoimmunity to axonal antigens in neurological disorders heavily relies on the pathogenic effect of autoreactive T cells and antibodies in cell culture and *in vivo* or following immunisation of experimental animals with neuronal proteins. Nevertheless many neuronal antigens and immune responses to neuronal antigens have been associated with human disorders (Table 1) in particular with the PND (Table 2).

To rationally examine the evidence for a pathogenic effect of autoimmunity to axonal antigens in neurological disorders we believe that the evidence should fulfil Witebsky's criteria (Rose and Bona 1993). These include *indirect* (circumstantial) evidence from clinical clues in patients i.e. a) the autoantibody or T cell should be present in the patient with disease; b) the autoantibody and/or T cells recognises the specific antigen, and *direct* evidence in which c) antibodies or T cells from patients are pathogenic to neuronal cells *in vitro* or induce neurological disease in laboratory animals and d) immunisation of the animal with the antigen should mimic the disease in humans.

Most of the direct evidence for a pathogenic role of anti-neuronal autoimmunity in humans comes from studying the effects of antibodies and T cells from patients with neurological disease *in vitro* on neuronal cell cultures. Adoptive transfer of T cells and antibodies *in vivo* has proven to be more difficult probably due to the difficulty in directing antibodies into the PNS or CNS due to the blood nerve barrier or BBB. Furthermore the pathogenic action of antibodies may rely on uptake by or entry into neurons via species specific pathways e.g. FcR receptors. In the case of FcR mouse Fc receptors are known to have different functions than those of humans and moreover the Fc portion of human immunoglobulins may not be recognised by rodents FcR. Likewise, activated T cells from humans may not recognise antigen due to sequence differences or due to inadequate presentation by murine antigen presenting cells. Thus transferring immunoglobulin or T cells from patients to mice or other animals must be viewed with caution.

Despite these limitations, animal models can be crucial tools in defining the pathogenesis of human diseases and are essential to develop and examine the safety of therapeutic interventions for patients with complex neuroimmunological syndromes. For example, the autoimmune basis of MS is well-accepted due to rodent and primate models which replicate many but not all of the pathological features (Brok et al. 2001; Amor et al. 2005). It is worth noting that animal models themselves must also be viewed with caution as being an analogue rather than the exact copy of the human counterpart, because they invariably differ to some degree from the human disease.

**Table 3. Neurological disease in animals induced by immunization with neuronal antigens**

| Human disease | Animal strain | Immunisation/procedure | reference |
|---|---|---|---|
| Myasthenia Gravis | mouse | Torpedo AChR in CFA | Drachman et al. 1998<br>Christadoss et al. 2000 |
| | mouse | MuSK extracellular domain | Jha et al. 2006 |
| | rabbits | MuSK extracellular domain | Shigemoto 2006 |
| | rhesus monkeys | Torpedo AChR | Toro-Goyco et al. 1986 |
| LEMS | rats mice | Synaptotagmin peptides | Takamori |
| GBS | mice | lipooligosaccharide of B. melitensis | Watanabe et al. 2005 |
| | rabbits | ganglioside or galactocerebrosides | Caporale et al. 2006; Saida et al. 1981 |
| | guinea pigs | C jujuni LOS | Shu et al 2006 |
| Paraneoplastic neurodegenerative disorders e.g. HuD PNMA1 (Ma1) | mice<br>rats | Immunization with plasmid coding HuD and implantation with neuroblastoma cell line<br>Immunisation and transfer of Ma specific T cells | Carpentier et al. 1998<br>Pellkofer et al. 2004 |
| SPS | rats | *Passive transfer SPS patients Ig to amphiphysin' | Sommer et al. 2005 |
| Diabetes neuropathy | mice, rats | Neuropathy in diabetic mice and following T cell transfer | Calcutt 2002; Schmidt et al 2003; Bour-Jordan et al. 2005 |
| Movement disorders Sydenhamn's Chorea Tourette's syndrome | SJL/J mice | Homogenate of group A beta-haemolytic streptococcal bacteria in CFA. | Hoffman et al. 2004 |
| Amyotrophic lateral sclerosis | guinea pigs | bovine spinal motor neurons<br>spinal cord ventral horn homogenate<br>choline acetyltransferase | Engelhardt 1990 |
| Alzheimer's disease | rats<br>rats<br>mice<br>rats<br>rats<br>guinea pigs | cholinergic neurons.<br>peptides of B-sunuclein<br>recombinant human tau protein<br>cholinergic Torpedo neurons.<br>with NF-H protein of cholinergic neurons<br>with septal cholinergic neurons | Chapman et al. 1989<br>Mor et al. 2003.<br>Rosenmann et al. 2006b.<br>Michaelson et al. 1990<br>Oron et al. 1997<br>Kalman et al. 1997 |
| Parkinson's Disease | guinea pigs | homogenates of bovine mesencephalon dopaminergic MES 23.5 cells | Appel et al. 1992;<br>Le et al. 1995 |
| Brain Trauma | rats | brain trauma<br>fluid percussion injury | Hoshino et al. 1996<br>Rudehill et al. 2006 |
| Epilepsy; Rasmussen's syndrome | mice<br>rabbits | Glu3RB peptide aa 372-395<br>Glu3R fragment aa residues 245-457 | Levite and Hermelin 1999<br>Twyman et al. 1995 |
| SLE | MRL/lpr mouse | spontaneous | Hikawa et al. 1997; Ballok et al. 2004; Sidor et 2005 |

AChR - acetylcholine receptors. CFA – complete Freund's adjuvant. * only passive transfer of antibodies.

Due to the wide variety of biological tools available, rodent models are the most widely used system to probe the mechanisms underlying human disorders. Moreover, the extensive numbers of mutant mice deficient in specific immune factors allow detailed investigation of the disease models. These include mice deficient in FcR, B cells or TCR, or SCID mice which can be reconstituted to examine individual components of the immune response or indeed 'humanised' by reconstituting with human cells. For several neurodegenerative diseases models in non-human primates such as Parkinson's disease (Eslamboli 2005) may be more relevant since behavioural studies such as cognitive changes can be better investigated in higher species (Philippens et al. 2000).

Taking these factors into account here we discuss the evidence for pathogenic responses of T cells and antibodies to neuronal antigens from patients with neurological disease *in vitro*. In addition, we will outline the major models of diseases in which autoimmunity to neuronal structures have been demonstrated (summarised in Table 3). These experimental models provide evidence that autoimmunity to neuronal antigens may contribute to the disease process rather than act as markers of neuronal damage, or are secondary to neuronal damage, or being an epiphenomenon.

## Disorders of the Neuromuscular Junction

Autoimmunity to antigens of the neuromuscular junction is observed in several neurological disorders such as the well-known disorder myasthenia gravis (MG) in which antibodies to acetycholine receptor (AChR), an important neurotransmitter receptor results in weakness and fatigue (Vincent et al. 1999; Vincent 2006). In many cases MG is associated with thymomas and therefore considered to belong to the group of diseases known as paraneoplastic disorders (see below). That antibodies to AChR may be pathogenic comes from indirect evidence in patients. Anti-AchR antibodies are observed in over 80% of MG patients where increasing levels of autoantibody correlate with deterioration in disease. In addition, MG patients respond to intravenous immunoglobulin (IVIg) which is thought to block the pathogenic antibodies. In mothers with MG anti-AChR antibodies cross the placenta or via the mother's milk enter the baby resulting in antibody-mediated arthrogryposis multiplex congenital (AMC) providing more direct evidence of autoimmunity in disease. However firm evidence for a pathogenic role of autoantibodies was first observed following passive transfer of serum from MG patients to mice (Toyka et al. 1975). Following injection of the serum, mice developed neuromuscular defects associated with a reduction in the numbers of ACh receptors. In a follow up study the active fraction in the serum was identified as IgG and the effect was enhanced by complement component (C3) (Toyka et al. 1977). To address the role of autoreactive T cells in MG Wang et al. (1999) transferred lymphocytes from MG patients to SCID mice. In this study lymphocytes, activated to AChR epitopes, were depleted of either CD4+ or CD8+ T cells and the depleted population transferred to mice. Here it was clearly shown that CD4+ T cells were crucial for the induction of experimental MG by providing 'help' to B cells in the production of pathogenic anti-AChR antibodies.

As well as autoimmunity to AChR MG is also associated with muscle atrophy in which antibodies to the muscle-specific kinase (MuSK) are observed and the LEMS associated with antibodies to voltage-gated calcium channels (VGCC). The role of antibodies and T cells to another autoantigen in MG, MuSK a muscle specific kinase, using approaches as described for AChR is unknown. In contrast, antibodies to ligand- and voltage-gated ion channels have been associated with a variety of clinical disorders in which defects in neuronal signalling and synaptic transmission are observed (Vincent 2006). For example autoantibodies to the Shaker type (Kv1) K+ channels are associated with peripheral nerve excitability, neuromyotonia and limbic encephalitis (Kleopa et al. 2006). In LEMS the pathogenic role for antibodies to nerve terminal voltage-gated calcium channels (VGCCs) has been demonstrated in animals following chronic administration of plasma, serum or immunoglobulin G to mice. Following transfer, electrophysiological and ultrastructural findings similar to those seen in patients are observed (Flink and Atchison 2003). These studies also showed a reduction in amplitude of Ca2+ currents through P/Q-type channels. In addition, transfer of antibodies to the presynaptic VGKC, the autoantigen in neuromyotonia, into mice also results in defects in neuromuscular transmission.

Animal models of experimental autoimmune myasthenia gravis (EAMG) can be induced in many rodents by immunization with AChR from *Torpedo california* neurons or mouse AChR in complete Freund's adjuvant (review Christadoss et al. 2000). As with many models in mice (Drachman et al. 1998) the MHC class II genes influence autoimmunity to AChR since MHC class II-restricted CD4 cells are crucial for induction of anti-AChR antibodies. Moreover tolerance to AChR or dominant peptide epitopes prevents EAMG by blocking the action of these pathogenic T cells.

Immunisation with peptides of synaptotagmin, one of the functionally VGCC-associated proteins, induced electrophysiological changes following repeated injections of Lewis rats (Takamori et al. 1994). Whether active immunization with VGKC in experimental animals will mimic channelopathies in humans is unknown.

EAMG may also be induced following immunization of H-2(a), H-2(b), H-2(bm12) and H-2(d) mice with recombinant rat-MuSK extracellular domain (Jha et al. 2006) although variations in clinical signs are observed. In rabbits immunization with the MuSK ectodomain protein induces MG-like muscle weakness with a reduction of AChR clustering at the NMJs (Shigemoto 2006) which more closely mimics the human disease.

Experimental models in higher species have also been developed, which are crucial for development of novel therapies as well as the study of effects of the disease on higher functions not possible in rodents. EAMG in rhesus monkeys may be induced with purified AChR from *Torpedo california* (Toro-Goyco et al. 1986). Rhesus monkeys immunised with three doses of 80 mg protein at two-week intervals developed antibodies and clinical signs of disease correlating with the levels of antibodies induced. Histological examination revealed muscular atrophy, fibrous degeneration and lymphocyte infiltration in the lesions characteristic of MG.

In summary, MG serves as the prototypic disease fulfilling many criteria demonstrating a role for autoimmunity to neuronal antigens in disease. Not only do antibodies to MG correlate with disease but *in utero* transfer of antibodies in MG patients and transfer of human antibodies to AChR to animals mimics MG in humans. Evidence is also observed following immunisation of animals with purified AChR thus fulfilling Witebsky's criteria for pathogenic autoimmunity to axonal antigens in MG.

# Guillain-Barré Syndrome

Guillain-Barré syndrome (GBS) consists of several subtypes of monophasic disorders associated with inflammation and demyelination of the peripheral nervous system. GBS and related syndromes, such as Miller Fisher syndrome (MFS) are related to bacterial and viral infections and thought to be due to antibody responses to gangliosides such as GM1 and GQ1b. In approximately 25% of patients with GBS, particularly the axonal form, disease occurs after infection with *Campylobacter jejuni* which contains ganglioside-like structures similar to those of peripheral nerves. It has therefore been suggested that disease is induced via the mechanism of molecular mimicry. That antibodies to neuronal proteins in GBS may also involve the CNS was reported by Bae and Kim (2005) who reported that serum antibodies to GD1b and GM1 were elevated in a patient with GBS presenting with cerebellar ataxia. Further evidence is observed in Bickerstaff's encephalitis, a rare condition related to MFS involving the CNS in which antibodies to GQ1b gangliosides are thought to play a pathogenic role.

The pathogenicity of antibodies to gangliosides in GBS is proven by studies whereby transfer of serum and immunoglobulin from GBS patients induces neurodegenerative changes *in vivo* and physiological and pathological effects in culture. For example GBS sera containing anti-ganglioside antibodies as well as monoclonal antibodies raised against gangliosides induce neuronal cell lysis in culture by targeting specific cell surface gangliosides and this effect is complement dependent (Zhang et al. 2004). Furthermore purified IgG from GBS patients' sera induces postsynaptic block of mouse myotubes expressing native embryonic-type nAChR channels or HEK 293 cells transfected with recombinant nAChR channels (Krampfl et al. 2003; for review see Willison 2005). The GBS variant, acute motor axonal neuropathy (AMAN) has also been associated with anti-GM1, anti-GM1b, anti-GD1a, and anti-GalNAc-GD1a antibodies. The evidence for this is suggested by the finding that ntibodies from patients have been shown to damage motor terminal endplates in vitro suggesting a pathogenic role in disease (Hughes and Cornblath 2005).

In vivo monoclonal antibodies against gangliosides, transferred to mice as hybridomas induced axonal neuropathy affecting a small proportion of nerve fibres whereas purified anti-ganglioside antibodies had no effect despite high titre circulating antibodies (Sheikh et al. 2004). It was suggested that this effect was due to properties of the hybridoma on the blood nerve barrier eg by allowing direct access of immunoglobulin to the nerve.

Purified IgG from Miller-Fisher syndrome patients induced muscle weakness in adult mice due to inhibition of postsynaptic channels (Buchwald et al. 1998). This effect was also seen with anti-GQ1b antibodies in conjunction with activated complement at the NMJ (Plom JJ 1999) while motor nerve terminal injury was associated with antibodies specific for disialoside epitopes on gangliosides GT1a (Halstead et al. 2004).

The variant of GBS, AMAN, is modelled in rabbits following immunization with the lipo-oligosaccharide of *Campylobacter jejuni,* which as mentioned above may be involved in disease by inducing antibodies that cross-react with peripheral nerve antigens. Watanabe et al. (2005) also demonstrated that the lipo-oligosaccharide of *Brucella melitensis* may also play a role in GBS since this is also expressing a GM1 ganglioside-like structure that induces strong anti-GM1 ganglioside antibody responses in BALB/c mice resulting in flaccid limb weakness.

As discussed anti-GM1, anti-GM1b, anti-GD1a, and anti-GalNAc-GD1a IgG antibodies are associated with AMAN in humans and have been shown to augment experimental autoimmune neuritis (EAN) in rabbits as well as induce disease following immunization of rabbits with galactocerebrosides or GM1 ganglioside (Saida et al. 1981; Caporale et al. 2006). Paralyzed rabbits developed pathological changes in their peripheral nerves identical to changes seen in human GBS. The pathogenicity of ganglioside structures of lipo-oligosaccharide of *C jejuni* were also demonstrated following immunization of guinea pigs using the *C jejuni* strain HB9313, which resulted in neuropathy and axonal degeneration (Shu et al. 2006). Thus evidence for autoimmunity to neuronal structures comes from the finding of autoantibodies in patients, passive transfer of antibodies to laboratory animals as well as experimental disease induced following active immunisation with neuronal antigens.

## Paraneoplastic Neurological Disorders

The paraneoplastic neurological disorders (PND) are observed in patients who have cancer along with abnormal neurological symptoms despite the absence of tumours in the nervous system. Common tumours of the breast, ovary and lung express some proteins generally restricted to the nervous system and the patients generate immune responses to these 'nervous system specific' proteins. While autoimmune responses to these neuronal antigens help to suppress the growth of the tumour they also cause damage in the nervous system leading to neurological symptoms (for review see Roberts and Darnell 2004; Table 2). PND are thus considered to be due to autoimmune attack on neurons expressing the antigens abnormally expressed by the tumour. The clinical syndromes are very heterogeneous due to the many different regions of the nervous system that may be involved, as a summary please refer to Table 2 although it should be noted that for many PND the neuronal antigen expressed by the tumour is unknown. In many of these disorders antibodies against the tumour and the neurons are detected in the patient's serum and cerebrospinal fluid (Posner 2003).

The majority of the PND antigens are intracellular and, are thus, not readily available for recognition by antibodies although, as demonstrated in other pathological conditions, antibodies do gain access to intracellular proteins. Indeed PND antibodies enter neurons and may trigger responses in the neuron such as apoptosis. Alternatively it has been suggested that tumour cells taken up by dendritic cells in the periphery present not only tumour antigens but also the neuronal antigens present on tumours. In this way the immune response may be activated to respond not only to the tumour but could also elicit CD8+ cytotoxic cells that subsequently target neurons.

Evidence of the pathogenicity of the antineuronal antibodies is limited to a few cases such as Lambert Eaton syndrome where antibodies to VGKC induce Lambert-Eaton myasthenia syndrome and are involved in peripheral nerve hyperexcitability (Hart et al. 2002). In others the pathogenic role of autoimmune responses requires further study. The antigen Ri encoded by the gene *Nova* is expressed in the brain stem, cortex and motor neurons, and also by neuroblastomas (in children) and lung and ovarian tumors. Autoimmunity to Ri is associated with the disorder Paraneoplastic Opsoclonus Myoclonus (dancing eyes) Ataxia where unlike most PND this disease can be relapsing remitting. In adults Opsoclonus Myoclonus may follow a viral infection but has, similar to basal ganglia disease, also been reported following pharyngitis due to streptococcal infection in which the antigen was identified as neuroleukin (Candler et al. 2006). In another PND - Paraneoplastic Cerebellar Degeneration autoimmune responses to antigens of cerebellar Purkinje neurons are expressed by breast or ovarian tumour. Subacute Sensory Neuronopathy and Hu Encephalopathy are associated with responses to the Hu antigens expressed by small cell lung cancer or breast cancer which induce disease in which many regions of the CNS and PNS may be involved. In this disease symptoms include memory loss, dorsal root ganglionopathy or more destructive multifocal neurological degeneration. Limbic encephalitis occurs in conjunction with small cell carcinomas of the lung and testicular tumours in which the anti-Ta (anti-Ma2) antibodies are present. Paraneoplastic syndromes also affect the lower motor neurons as described in a patient with breast cancer with antibodies directed against axons and nodes of Ranvier. More detailed studies showed that these antibodies were directed to isoforms of βIV spectrin – a protein enriched in axonal initial segments and nodes of Ranvier (Berghs et al. 2001). The antigen Tr expressed in the cerebellum is also a target for anti-Tr antibodies in Hodgkin's disease that react with the cytoplasm of Purkinje cells (Bernal et al 2003).

Compared to MG and LEMS, most neoplastic antigens are intracellular antigens and thus considered unlikely to be targeted by the antibody directly. It is probably for this reason that development of models or demonstration for a direct pathogenic effect of antibodies has been difficult.

Although antibodies to recoverin have been shown to induce apoptosis of cells in cancer associated retinopathy (Adamus 2003), for others this effect has not be demonstrated. For example, application of anti-Yo or anti-Hu antibodies on primary mouse-brain-derived neurons did not kill neurons, but instead induced the expression of cell adhesion molecules and accelerated neuronal differentiation. Similar effects of serum IgG fractions from patients containing the anti-Yo or the anti-Hu antibody on the cultured neurons were observed, suggesting that their effects were not through the binding of the antibody to specific antigens, but to some other factors contained in IgG fractions (Tanaka 2004).

IgG purified from the serum of patients with Hodgkin's disease paraneoplastic cerebellar ataxia in which the number of Purkinje cells is severely reduced was shown to affect the basal activity of Purkinje cells in mouse brain slice cultures (Coesmans et al. 2003). The number of studies demonstrating the pathogenic effects of antibodies to intracellular paraneoplastic neuroantigens is scare however earlier studies by Greenlee et al. (1995) show that microinjection of anti-Yo antibodies from humans in rats reach the CNS. While anti-Yo antibodies were identified on the dendrites and within the cell body of Purkinje cells, animals did not develop ataxia or cerebellar injury. Additional studies to determine the mechanism of action are required to provide clues to their effect in human disease.

Immunization of mice with a plasmid coding HuD induced a strong and specific anti-Hu response. To model the human disease mice were challenged by implantation of a neuroblastoma cell line that constitutively expresses HuD. In the presence of secreted HuD and subsequent immunity to Hu significant inhibition of tumour growth was observed however the animals did not develop neurological deficits or neuropathological evidence of nervous system pathology (Sillevis-Smitt et al. 1996; Carpentier et al. 1998). Likewise it has not been possible to induce experimental disease following passive transfer of anti-Yo antibody and immunization with recombinant Yo protein, does not induce damage to Purkinje cells (Tanaka et al. 1995). In humans paraneoplastic cerebellar degeneration is also associated with immune responses to PCD17/cdr2 on Purkinje cells. Sakai et al. (2001) demonstrated that while mice immunised with naked pcd17 cDNA developed autoantibodies against Purkinje cells and CTLs from these mice lysed cells pulsed with H-2K-restricted PCD17 peptide, clinical or pathological changes in the cerebellum were absent.

Development of animal models for PND has focussed on induction of antibodies to onconeuroantigens and as such has been problematic. As a step to study the involvement of T cells in PND, Pellkofer et al. (2004) show that following immunisation of rats with Pnma1 (Ma1), transfer of T-cell blasts specific from the rats into naïve animals induced encephalitis indicating a role for T cells in PND. However, animals did not develop clinical disease.

## Stiff Person Syndrome

The "Stiff person syndrome"(SPS) is a rare chronic neurological disorder characterized by progressive stiffness, painful persistent or spasmodic muscle contractions, mostly involving spine and lower extremities. In 60 to 90% of cases, non-paraneoplastic forms are associated with the presence of autoantibodies against glutamic acid decarboxylase (GAD), an enzyme that converts the excitatory neurotransmitter glutamate to gamma-aminobutyric acid (GABA), a major inhibitory neurotransmitter of the CNS. The syndrome often occurs spontaneously and in association with type I (insulin-dependent) diabetes mellitus. In contrast SPS associated with antibodies to amphiphysin, a protein involved in clathrin-mediated endocytosis, are frequently associated with the paraneoplastic types. The relevant treatment for SPS is to alter the inhibitory processes controlling muscle activity, control of the immune response and removal of associated neoplasia. High-dose intravenous immunoglobulin (IVIg) has been shown to be effective suggesting an involvement of humoral immunity in disease.

While antibodies to GAD were first recognised in an SPS patient they are also observed in patients with chronic cerebellar ataxia, drug-resistant epilepsy and myoclonus, Batten disease (Ramirez-Montealegre et al. 2005) as well juvenile ceroid lipofuscinosis, a fatal paediatric neurological disorder. The serum from patients with juvenile ceroid lipofuscinosis reacted with GAD-positive GABAergic neurons but also with other cell populations (Lim et al. 2006) distinguishing the responses from sera from Stiff-persons syndrome and type-1 diabetes. The role of anti-GAD antibodies is still unclear although decreased GABA synthesis in nerve terminals as a result of antibody interference with exocytosis of GABA may be crucial to disease expression. This is suggested from *in vitro* studies whereby GAD autoantibodies or purified IgG from the CSF, or serum from people with SPS were observed to reduce GABA production in crude rat cerebellar extracts (Dinkel et al 1998). Likewise, Raju et al. (2006) showed that patients with SPS had a decrease in the level of GABA(A)-receptor-associated protein (GABARAP), responsible for stability and expression of the

GABA(A)-receptor. Furthermore sera from SPS patients immunoprecipitated GABARAP and significantly reduced GABA(A)-receptor expression *in vitro* suggesting that these antibodies may play a role in disease.

In addition to GAD antibodies, IgG antibodies to the intracellular synaptic protein amphiphysin purified from patients not only recognised rat CNS tissue but when injected intraperitoneally, induced stiffness with spasms in rats (Sommer et al. 2005). It is important to mention that in this particular study, MBP reactive T cells were co-transferred to open the blood brain barrier and that high and repeated doses of antibodies were required to induce the clinical signs. Nevertheless these studies elegantly show that in SPS patients antibodies to neuronal antigens not only induced physiological changes in vitro but also mimic the human disease in experimental animals. It remains to be seen whether immunization of experimental animals with amphiphysin leads to clinical disease as observed in patients.

## Diabetes and Rheumatoid Arthritis Complicated by Neuropathy

In other autoimmune disorders such as diabetes and rheumatoid arthritis (RA) antibodies to neuronal structures have also been described and are associated with peripheral neuropathies. Nearly 60% of all people with diabetes suffer from peripheral neuropathy in which the underlying mechanisms are unknown although autoimmune responses to neuronal structures may play a key role. Neurons and pancreatic Beta-cells share common determinants such as GAD. In early diabetes GAD specific antibodies are present and patients with high levels of GAD-65 antibodies were more likely to develop neuropathological complications. Although there is not a clear association between the presence GAD65 antibodies and diabetic neuropathy autoantibodies were associated with worse peripheral nerve function (Hoeldtke et al. 2000). Serum from diabetic type-1 patients react with neuroblastoma cells in culture and exert apoptotic effects on neurons in culture (Vinik et al. 2005).

Using whole-cell recording of rat cerebellar slices Mitoma et al. (2003) showed that Ig in CSF from ataxic patients with anti-GAD antibodies reduced gamma-aminobutyric acid (GABA) release in vitro. More specifically the pathogenic role of anti-GAD Ig in the CSF in a patient with progressive cerebellar ataxia associated with insulin-dependent diabetes was clearly demonstrated by a selective suppression of the inhibitory postsynaptic currents in Purkinje cells (Ishida et al. 2007). As well as anti-GAD antibodies anti-neurofilament antibodies are present in patients with RA complicated by peripheral neuropathy and may correlate with extent of neuropathological disease activity (Salih et al. 1998). While the mechanism of neuronal damage is unclear, Towns et al. (2005) showed that serum from diabetic patients with neuropathy induced autophagy, a lysosome-dependent degradation pathway of cytoplasmic contents, in the neuronal SH-SY5Y cells. The effect was abolished when serum was incubated with Protein L beads, which bind immunoglobulin, suggesting that autophagy was induced by autoantibodies present in the patients' serum.

Mechanisms underlying the neurological complications in diabetic patients have been studied in the experimental models of diabetes namely non-obese diabetic (NOD), streptozotocin (STZ)-induced diabetic mice (type 1 diabetes), db/db mouse (type 2 diabetes) and diabetic BBW rats (Calcutt 2002; Schmidt et al. 2003). As well as diabetes these animals also develop neuropathy similar to diabetic patients providing a model to study mechanism of disease. While the role of antibodies in neuropathy is unknown autoreactive T cells are observed in the peripheral nerves although neuropathy is not dependent perforin or fas pathways (Bour-Jordan et al. 2005). To date similar studies on the mechanisms underlying neuropathy in patients with RA have not been studied in experimental rheumatoid arthritis in animals.

## Movement Disorders, Encephalitis Lethargica and Infections

The question of whether autoimmunity to neuronal antigens plays a role in these neurological disorders is undisputable. The question is ''how do such responses arise? In 1916 von Economo described a neurological disease characterized by a sleep associated with basal ganglia signs and neuropsychiatric sequele. While there was speculation that Encephalitis lethargica (EL) was associated with the 1918 influenza pandemic investigators found no evidence of influenza RNA. More recently Dale et al. (2004) have described patients with similar characteristics as von Ecomos EL patients which similarly developed sequele following pharyngitis. Rather than viral aetiology, antibodies to streptolysin-O were elevated in 65% of the patients. As in Sydenham's chorea (Church et al. 2003), EL patients develop antibodies against cells within the basal ganglia and respond well to steroids suggesting a role for autoimmunity in disease in particular anti-basal ganglia (neuronal) antibodies. Sydenham's chorea occurs after infection with group Aß haemolytic streptococcal infection and is characterized by involuntary, purposeless movements of the limbs. Neurological diseases occurring after such infections also include tics, and dystonia, emotional disorders such as Tourette's syndrome, obsessive-compulsive disorder, anxiety and depression. However, experimental models of these disorders are lacking and the pathological relevance of antibodies is unclear.

Antibodies to basal ganglia antigens in patients with movement disorders probably arise due to cross-reactivity with streptococcal infections although their pathogenicity remains unknown (reviewed by Martino and Giovannoni 2004). Serum from patients with Syndenham's chorea, but not other streptococcal disorders, bound to the surface of human neuronal cells and recognised the neuronal glycolytic enzymes aldolase C, $\gamma$-gamma-enolase, and pyruvate kinase (Dale 2006). Subsequent studies showed that such antibodies were also present in other patients with post-streptococcal infection presenting with a spectrum of movement and psychiatric disorders. The association of the antibodies with the disease was examined *in vitro* whereby serum from patients with Syndenham's Chorea were found to induce calcium/calmodulin-dependent protein (CaM) kinase activity that leads to dopamine release (Kirvan et al. 2006). While further studies are necessary to define the mode of action of antineuronal antibodies in Syndenham's chorea itself, Dale et al. (2006) demonstrated that commercial antibodies to neuronal glycolytic enzymes induced apoptosis in cultured neurons.

The relevance of anti-brain antibodies in the movement disorder Tourette's syndrome was examined in rats infused with serum or purified IgG from patients. The antibodies induced involuntary movements in the animals similar to that seen in patients and examination of the CNS demonstrated antibodies bound to the striatal neurons (Hallett et al. 2000). It remains to be determined if this observation occurs in other disorders or if there is a pathogenic role for cell mediated immune response to basal ganglia antigens.

To establish a model of these disorders SJL/J mice were immunized with homogenates of the group A beta-haemolytic streptococcal bacteria in CFA (Hoffman et al. 2004). Mice developed behavioural changes and autoantibodies in the serum that reacted histologically against neurons within the deep cerebellar nuclei, globus pallidus, and thalamus. In addition IgG deposits were observed in the neurons suggesting that anti-GABHS antibodies cross-reactive with brain components may play a role in disease.

In spongiform encephalopathy neurofibrillary tangles similar to those observed in AD are observed particularly in Guamanians with Parkinson's disease. Scrapie associated fibrils of Kuru and CJD and has been suggested to be related to changes in ALS (Gajdusek 1985). In all these diseases antibodies to neurofilaments are present and may have a common origin.

Autoimmunity to the neuronal antigen heterogeneous nuclear ribonuclear protein – A1 (hnRNP-A1) has been demonstrated in patients with human T-lymphotropic virus type 1 (HTLV-1) associated tropical spastic paraparesis (HAM/TSP). IgG isolated from HAM/TSP patients contains antibodies to neurons as determined by western blot studies on neuronal homogenates and more specifically to proteins identified as hnRNP-A1. A functional significance of such IgG in patients was confirmed using patch clamp recording of neurons from rat brain sections where infusion of IgG inhibited neuronal firing (Levin et al. 2002).

# Amyotrophic Lateral Sclerosis

Amyotrophic lateral sclerosis (ALS) is the most common form of motor neurone disease affecting adults. Research on mechanisms of neurodegeneration has focussed on oxidative stress, glutaminergic excitotoxicity and aberrant protein aggregation, such as NF, in the neurons although ALS has also been suggested to be an unconventional autoimmune disease (Drachman and Kuncl, 1989). This is supported by findings of autoimmunity to neuronal antigens since immunoglobulin is present in the motor neurons of ALS patients more frequently than serum from controls (Fishman and Drachman 1995). IgG and IgM to spinal cord proteins and gangliosides (GM-1 is located on the outer surface of motor neurons) are present in the serum and CSF of ALS patients (Annunziata et al. 1995; Niebroj-Dobosz et al. 2004; 2006;) and responses to NF associated with the slow evolution of disease in a subgroup of patients (Couratier et al. 1998). In a more extensive study high frequency of antibodies to tubulin and NF-H were observed in ALS patients but also observed in patients with other neurological disorders (Terryberry et al. 1998). In culture IgG from ALS patients recognises L-type VGCC resulting in an inhibition of dopamine mediated by L-type calcium channels in cultured PC12 cells (Offen et al 1998) and induces calcium dependent motor neuron cell death that is prevented by preincubating IgG with purified intact L-type VGCC (Smith et al. 1994). That ALS Ig may have a pathogenic effect in vivo was demonstrated following injection of mice with IgG from ALS patients. IgG form ALS patients (but not from people without ALS) was observed in motor neurons and at the neuromuscular junction of mice (Appel et al. 1991). These mice had increased miniature end-plate potential frequency, with normal amplitude and time course and normal resting membrane potential, indicating an increased resting quantal release of acetylcholine from the nerve terminal. Similar studies were reported by Pullen and Humphreys (2000) in which Ig from ALS patients was present in the cell bodies of lumbar motor neurons and EM studies revealed histological abnormalities including abnormal formation of Nissle bodies and fragmented Golgi and ER.

Several models of ALS have been developed and have contributed to the understanding of ALS. For example the pathogenic role for autoimmune responses to neuronal antigens was demonstrated in guinea pigs immunised with purified bovine spinal motor neurons or with bovine spinal cord ventral horn homogenate (Engelhardt et al. 1989; 1990). Immunisation with purified bovine spinal motor neurons caused signs of lower motor neuron deficits. In comparison guinea pigs immunised with bovine spinal cord ventral horn homogenate developed acute muscle weakness and paresis concomitant with inflammation in the CNS and both upper and lower motor neuron degeneration. As with the human disorder, IgG deposits at the motor end plate and within the motor neurons were observed. Passive transfer with immunoglobulin from guinea pigs with disease into naive mice demonstrated the presence of IgG in motor neurons and at the neuromuscular junction. Similar to the finding following injection of Ig from an ALS patient the mice showed an increase in miniature end-plate potential frequency providing evidence for autoimmune mechanisms in the pathogenesis of both the animal models and human ALS (Appel et al. 1991). Immunisation of guinea pigs with choline acetyltransferase was shown to induce lower motoneuron destruction and striated muscle atrophy. As with the other models IgG was detected in lower motoneurons and at the motor end-plate and transfer of antibodies into mice induced selective lower motoneuron damage (Engelhardt et al. 1997).

## Alzheimer's Disease

Alzheimer's disease (AD) is the most common human neurodegenerative disease leading to progressive cognitive decline and death. The conventional paradigm is that abnormally folded proteins accumulate in neurons leading to neuronal death via apoptosis. However, inflammatory processes, and possibly autoimmunity, may also play a role in disease since antibodies, complement components and T cells (CD4+ and CD8+) are observed in the brains of AD patients. Moreover, the presence of antibodies in sera of AD patients targeting specific neuronal antigens such as NF-H has lead to the suggestion that AD should be classified as an autoimmune disorder (D'Andrea 2005). That immune responses may play a role in AD is supported by the finding that anti-inflammatory approaches reduce disease severity.I In an attempt to remove the accumulations of amyloid-β (Aβ) in the brains of AD patients, vaccinations with Aβ protein were unexpectedly resulting in severe meningoencephalitis, inflammation and worsening of the disease possibility due to autoimmune responses. Aβ is also recognised by T cells from AD patients although many reports are those on antibody responses such as those directed to glial fibrillary protein (GFAP). In the search for autoantigens antibodies to spectrin (Fernandez-Shaw et al. 1997), choline acetyltransferase (Engelhardt et al. 2005), tau protein (Rosenmann et al. 2006a) and aldolase A (Mor et al. 2005) have been reported in AD. Autoimmunity to neuronal antigens is significantly higher in older (aged 70-79) than in younger (aged 40-59) subjects that may explain why neurodegenerative disorders generally occur at a later age. More specifically while the sera of older people recognised both bovine ventral root and dorsal root NF-H and their NF-H specificity was unchanged during aging the sera of AD patients contain IgG antibodies that bind more to ventral root cholinergic neurons which is enriched in phosphorylated NF-H, an observation that distinguished normal aged persons and those with AD (Soussan et al. 1994). IgG responses to NF-H that binds specifically to epitopes highly enriched in Torpedo cholinergic neurons are also observed in older people with Down's syndrome that develop AD in later life (Hassin-Baer et al. 1992).

Also in patients with AD antibodies to the extracellular domain of beta-amyloid precursor protein (APP) induced morphological changes in neuronal cultures consistent with apoptosis and may be the mechanism by which neuronal death in AD occurs (Rohn et al. 2000). Of relevance to disease was the report that injection of purified IgG from AD patients into rat basal forebrain decreased the numbers of cholinergic neurons four weeks after injection of AD IgG. Injection of IgG from control patients had no effect, suggesting that autoimmunity may play a major role in neurodegeneration in AD patients (Engelhardt et al. 2000).

To examine the pathogenic potential of antibodies to cholinergic neurons Chapman et al. (1989) immunised rats with cholinergic neurons. Repeated immunizations induced antibody responses and immunoglobulin was detected in neurons and the animals displayed behavioural deficits involving spatial awareness and memory. In another study, Michaelson et al. (1990) also showed that repeated immunisation with cholinergic Torpedo neurons induced memory impairment in rats. Hippocampal neurons contained IgG and tangle-like structures. Experimental AD was also induced following prolonged immunisation of rats with NF-H protein of cholinergic neurons and again revealed IgG in neurons and cognitive deficits (Oron et al 1997) or immunisation of guinea pigs with septal cholinergic neurons (Kalman et al.1997).

Amyloid precursor protein (APP) and B-synuclein are neuronal proteins that accumulate in plaques in AD and PD. Immunisation with APP or B-synuclein was proposed as a therapy for reducing accumulation in the brain. Contrary to the expectations, some treated patients as well as mice immunised with APP peptide developed encephalitis (Nicoll et al. 2003; Furlan et al. 2003). Similarly, immunisation of rats with peptides of B-synuclein was shown to induce pathogenic T cells that resulted in acute paralytic encephalitis and uveitis following adoptive transfer (Mor et al. 2003). In another study mice, immunised with recombinant human tau protein developed neurological deficits and histopathological features of AD and tauopathies, such as the presence of neurofibrillary tangle-like structures, axonal damage, gliosis and inflammation in the CNS (Rosenmann et al. 2006b). Although the clinical signs of immunised mice do not mimic the symptoms observed in human AD, these data suggests that autoimmunity to neuronal antigens leads not only to neuronal deficits but also cognitive changes suggesting that autoimmunity may also play a role in human disease.

## Parkinson's Disease

Idiopathic Parkinson's disease (PD) is a progressive neurological disorder characterised by loss of motor control as observed by for example rigidity of muscles and gait dysfunction. The pathology of PD is predominantly the degeneration of dopaminergic (DA) neurons within the substantial nigra and intracytoplasmic inclusions known as Lewy bodies which contain accumulated alpha-synuclein fibrillar aggregates. The cause of PD is unknown although mutations in e.g. alpha-synuclein have been implicated in susceptibility to disease. While alpha-synuclein can form several different aggregate morphologies including oligomers, protofibrils and fibrils, the role of these morphologies in the progression of PD is not known.

It is clear that immune responses play a crucial role in disease since substantia nigra degeneration is associated with microglia activation and anti-inflammatory approaches appear to control disease. Gamma delta+ T cells are increased in patients with PD (Fiszer et al. 1994) and more recently Orr et al. (2005) describe the presence of immunoglobulin on DA neurons and Lewy bodies in PD patients while FcR were expressed by adjacent microglia. Whether the elevated gamma delta+ T cell population in Parkinson's disease reflects previously unrecognized inflammation or may occur also in non-inflammatory disorders remains to be elucidated. The strongest evidence that autoimmunity to DA neurons may play a role in disease comes from studies showing that the CSF of patients is toxic to DA cells in culture (Dahlstrom et al. 1990) via complement-dependent mechanisms (Defazio et al. 1994). Furthermore microinjection of IgG from the sera of PD patients in the substantia nigra of rats induced severe neuronal loss concomitant with microglia activation. That microglia, activated by lipopolysaccharide, induced injury to dopaminergic neurons in cultures (Le et al. 2001) suggests that activated microglia could also induce neurological disease in vivo. The role for Fcgamma receptors on microglia in the autoimmune attack on nigral neurones is reflected by the lack of neuronal damage in mice lacking Fcgamma receptors following injection of IgG from PD patients (He et al. 2002). More recently Huber et al (2006) showed that antibodies in the sera of PD patients bind to DA neurons and reduce dopamine production suggesting the potential for autoimmunity in disease.

To investigate a pathogenic role for autoimmune mechanisms in PD guinea pigs were immunized with homogenates of bovine mesencephalon (containing neurons of the substantia nigra). While no overt clinical signs of basal ganglia dysfunction were observed animals showed evidence of neuronal damage in the substantia nigra concomitant with a decrease in tyrosine hydroxylase activity and dopamine content. IgG was observed in neurons in the substantia nigra (Appel et al. 1992). In a follow-up study Le et al 1995 immunized guinea pigs with dopaminergic MES 23.5 cells which resulted in hypokinesia in over 50% of the animals. Severe loss of substantia nigra neurons, decreased tyrosine hydroxylase activity and dopamine content as well as IgG deposition within neurons in the substantial nigra was observed. These data suggest that a similar mechanism in which autoimmunity to substantia nigra neurons induces neurodegeneration in animals may operate in Parkinson's disease in humans.

## Brain Trauma

During injury of the nervous system for example as a result of mechanical stress, antigens may become exposed to the immune system and may provoke an autoimmune response.

In general autoimmunity is considered harmful to the host but more recent studies suggest that such responses may be protective following brain trauma (Stein et al. 2002). Despite massive release of brain antigens and early expansion of myelin specific T cells in local lymph nodes, animals do not develop autoimmune neurological disease (Kwidzinski et al. 2003). Brain trauma typically leads to neuronal damage and loss and while T cells reactive against myelin antigens are observed in 40% patients with traumatic brain injury (Cox et al. 2006) few studies have examined the impact of anti-neuronal responses. Furthermore little is known about the impact of autoantibodies to neuronal antigens following brain trauma despite increased levels of NF-L in the CSF following cerebrovascular accidents, subacute haemorrhage and severe brain traumas (van Geel et al. 2005). While these may reflect the degree of axonal damage these antigens may also trigger a pathogenic immune response.

Antibodies to self antigens help remove dead cells by enhancing phagocytosis although, as discussed above antibodies do not generally reach the CNS due to an intact BBB. During mechanical injury to the brain the BBB is compromised and serum antibodies may reach the CNS. A probable necessary step to repair, however this may also lead to the activation of the immune response as brain antigens are removed to local lymph nodes such as the cervical lymph nodes.

IgG and IgM antibodies to β-tubulin class III (βTcIII), which is almost exclusively found in neuronal cytoskeletons is present in the serum of people shortly after brain trauma (Škoda et al. 2006). That these responses may be involved in the diseases is suggested by mouse studies (Ankeny et al. 2006).

To investigate the relevance of autoantibodies in patients with brain trauma serum from blood draining the CNS or systemic blood was applied to human leukemia cell lines and apoptosis assessed with annexin V and propidium iodide staining. Serum draining the brain lesions and less so from systemic blood, induced cell death in vitro (Lopez-Escribano et al. 2002). However, the effect of autoimmunity to neuronal cells is unknown and so far has only been studied in experimental models of brain trauma. More research is required to fully determine the pathogenic role of autoimmune responses in patients with brain trauma. Extensive literature on brain injury is available not only in humans but also in the many animal models (Morales et al. 2005, Duhaime 2006). In adult rats in which brain trauma was induced, circulating IgG autoantibodies were also observed in degenerating neurons suggesting that anti-brain antibodies in trauma may be epiphenomenal (Rudehill et al. 2006) or play a role in the phagocytosis and removal of injured neurons (Stein et al. 2002). Alternatively such responses may contribute to axonal damage following prolonged exposure of the CNS to protein extravasation in severe fluid percussion injury in the rat brain (Hoshino et al. 1996). In experimental spinal cord injury organ-specific and systemic autoimmune response is observed in mice and sera from the mice recognise CNS proteins and bind to DNA and RNA (Ankeny et al. 2006). These data indicate that trauma to the CNS does evoke autoimmunity to CNS components and could induce disease although the evidence is weighted to such responses having a protective effect.

## Epilepsy

Rasmussen's syndrome (RS) is a rare slowly progressive neurological childhood illness characterized by frequent and severe seizures, loss of motor skills and speech and paralysis on one side of the body. The encephalitis observed is suggested to result from autoimmunity following CMV and EBV infection although this is still controversial. The idea that neuronal damage is due to autoimmunity is reflected by serum antibodies and T cell responses to anti-glutamate receptor (GluR3) receptors in RS patients (Takahashi Y et al. 2005). The pathogenic effect of antibodies to glutamate receptors (GluR), implicated in epilepsy and Rasmussen's syndrome, is reflected by their association with the frequency of seizures. In addition, plasma exchange and IVIg and immunosuppressive therapies have been shown to be effective in controlling disease in some patients. In cultured neuronal cells, antibodies to GluR3 act as ligands for AMPA subtype of glutamate receptors and evoke glutamate-like ion currents (Twyman et al. 1995) which may explain the clinical phenotype in humans. The pathogenic potential of the AMPA receptor subunit GluR3 in RE was reported by Levite and Hermelin (1999) who immunised four strains of mice with the Glu3RB peptide (aa 372-395). The mice developed antibodies and T cells to the peptide and behavioural abnormalities but not epilepsy. The murine antibodies bound to neurons in vitro and evoked GluR channel activity, mimicking the pathophysiological effects of excess of glutamate inducing neuronal death (Levite et al. 1999).

In another study rabbits immunised with peptides of the receptor developed anti-GluR3 antibodies that bound to neuronal cultures and induced apoptosis (Twyman et al. 1995). More relevant was the finding that the rabbits exhibited recurrent episodes of seizures as well as inflammatory lesions in the CNS resembling human RE. Taken together, these studies demonstrate that antibodies to a specific peptide of the GluR can kill neurons by an excitotoxic mechanism, and induce clinical features resembling the human disease RE.

## Other Neurological Disorders

Antibodies to neurofilaments proteins have been associated with a variety of disorders including neuropathy with monoclonal gammaopathy of undetermined significance (MGUS). In these patients antibodies to NF-heavy in the serum bind to neuronal antigens (Stubbs et al. 2003). The pathogenic potential of serum containing NF antibodies was demonstrated following injection of rat sciatic nerve. Serum containing antibodies to NF but not control serum altered the axonal calibre and induced vesiculation and ovoid formation leading to peripheral nerve conduction block (Stubbs et al 2003). Furthermore patients with slowly progressive sensory motor axonal neuropathology have a monoclonal IgG-kappa that bound to NF protein (Nemni et al 1990).

Growing evidence also demonstrates the presence of autoantibodies to neurons in psychiatric disorders such as schizophrenia (Margutti et al. 2006) and in autistic disorders in which patients display impaired socialisation and abnormal patterns of behaviour. While the exact cause of the disorder is unknown, genetic, biochemical and environmental causes have been suggested to play a role. One factor may be abnormal immune responses since patients with autism come from families in which autoimmune disorders cluster. In the autistic person, autoantibodies to myelin proteins and neuronal antigens such as NF are observed (Cohly and Panja 2005) and altered T cell functions and cytokine levels (Zimmerman 2005) have been reported. In a an extensive study examining responses to human brain proteins serum antibodies in autistic subjects more frequently and intensely responded to antigens in caudate, putamen and prefrontal cortex as well as cerebella and cingulated gyrus antigens than aged matched controls (Singer et al. 2006).

The role of gangliosides in neurological disease is evident form the induction of experimental sensory neuropathy in rabbits immunized with ganglioside GD1b (Kusunoki et al. 1996; 1999). Animals developed experimental sensory ataxic neuropathy with severe axonal degeneration in the dorsal column, dorsal roots and sciatic nerve. Antibodies to GD1b bound to large primary sensory neurons and were considered the underlying cause of disease. Neurophysiological studies show that anti-GM-1 antibodies derived from immunised rabbits alter K- and Na-channels and disrupt the membrane at nodes of Ranvier (Takigawa et al. 1995) (also see GBS and channelopathies above).

## Systemic Lupus Erythematosus

SLE is a multi-organ autoimmune disorder in which the CNS may be involved and in which a significant loss of central neurons may occur. In some cases SLE patients present with Parkinsonian-like deficits, changes to the basal ganglia and axonal dysfunction although the underlying mechanisms of such damage are unknown. Antibodies to double stranded DNA (dsDNA), present in the serum of SLE patients, are known to deposit in the kidney and skin contributing to disease. DeGiorgio et al (2001) demonstrated that a subset of the dsDNA antibodies, present in the CSF and serum of SLE patients also recognised NR2A and NR2B subunits of the NMDA receptor and reduced the viability of brain cells which proliferate *in vitro* (Sakic 2005). Responses to microtubule-associated protein 2 (MAP-2), a cellular protein restricted to neurons and important in the control of cytoskeletal, is also a common finding in neuropsychiatric systemic lupus erythematosus (Williams et al. 2004).

The suggestion that intrathecally synthesized IgG autoantibodies in SLE patients with neuropyschiatric disorder patient may be pathogenic is demonstrated by the finding that CSF IgG of SLE patients reduces the viability of a neural stem cell line in vitro (Sakic et al. 2005). In a further study, anti-NMDAR antibodies in serum and cerebrospinal fluid from SLE patients induced cognitive impairment in mice injected with LPS to compromise the BBB integrity. Mice also exhibited neuron damage and memory impairment. Moreover immunoglobulin eluted from the brains of SLE patients, bound to DNA and NMDAR and caused neuronal apoptosis in mouse brains. Despite these findings further studies are necessary to reveal the mechanism of autoimmunity to NMDAR in neuropsychiatric lupus and the approaches by which such patients may be treated (Kowal et al. 2006).

Spontaneous development of lupus-like disease in the MRL/lpr mouse model has been invaluable to study mechanism underlying neuropsychiatric SLE. SLE in the MRL/lpr mouse is accompanied by impaired dopamine catabolism and degenerating axon terminals in the mesencephalon (Hikawa et al. 1997). Mice show behavioural dysfunction similar with progression of SLE in humans. The neurodegeneration in MRL/lpr mice (Ballok 2007) is associated with the cytotoxicity of the IgG fraction CSF on neurons (Sidor et al. 2005) which was attenuated by the immunosuppressive drug cyclophosphamide (Ballok et al. 2004). Although the specificity of the mediators in the CSF is unknown, it is probable that autoimmunity to neurons contributes to pathology in the MRL/lpr mouse.

In a subset of SLE patients antibodies to NR2A and NR2B subunits of the NMDA receptor are present. The effect of antibodies to NR2 was studied in BALB/C mice in which epinephrine was used to compromise the BBB. These mice shown a decrease in neurons in the lateral amygdala and develop cognitive and emotional behaviour changes (Huerta et al. 2006).

## Neuronal and Axonal Reactive T Cells

Many neurological disorders discussed so far have been associated with antibodies to neuronal antigens however in some case cellular responses are also observed. Evidence that T cells may be involved in the pathogenicity of neurodegenerative disorders comes from the observation of T cells in the nervous system as well as the CSF and blood both in the PNS and CNS disorders. T -cells are present in the spinal cord from patients with ALS, MS, GBS as well as patients with paraneoplastic cerebellar degeneration. In many cases it is unclear what these T cells recognise and indeed whether they are pathogenic. The paucity of evidence comes from studies of paraneoplastic disorders. Autoreactive cytotoxic T lymphocytes (CTLs) specific for a cytoplasmic protein of Purkinje cells PCD17/cdr2 are present in the blood of patients (Sakai 2001) suggesting that they may play a role in the ensuing neuronal damage. Likewise T cells responses to Hu-D peptides are present in patients with neuronal and axonal injury particularly those with the common paraneoplastic neurologic syndrome anti-Hu syndrome (Rousseau et al. 2005). The pathological significance of such responses were demonstrated by Tanaka et al. 1999, whereby activated CD8+ T cells from a patient lysed autologous fibroblasts following induced expression of HLA class I and HuD protein. These authors also demonstrated cytotoxic T cell activity to Yo protein expressed by autologous dendritic cells suggesting that cytotoxic T cells could be involved in Purkinje cell loss in paraneoplastic cerebellar degeneration (Tanaka 1998).

Conversely culture of human neurons with activated T cells leads to neuronal death through contact-dependent non-MHC class I mechanisms (Giuliani et al. 2003). Neuronal structures may be key targets in disease as demonstrated by elegant studies using two-photon microscopy in living brain tissues (Nitsch et al. 2004). However while these studies provide compelling evidence for a role of T cells in neurodegeneration whether this is the result of an autoimmune phenomenon is unclear. In some disorders such as following facial nerve axotomy while T cells are observed close to injured nerves they appear to confer neuroprotection to injured motor neurons (Ha et al. 2006). This protective role for CNS specific T cells may be why patients with brain injury that developed reactivity to myelin had a much more favourable outcome. However, such a 'protective' role for antibodies is unknown. Likewise CNS trauma following spinal cord injury induces activation of T cells and enhances macrophage activity but this may be concomitant with increased functional impairment (Jones et al. 2005).

## Evidence for Autoimmunity to Axonal Antigens in Multiple Sclerosis

Multiple Sclerosis (MS) is considered an autoimmune disease of the CNS and is characterised by demyelination and axonal loss. While research in MS has focussed on pathogenic T cells targeting myelin antigens relatively few studies have described the role for pathogenic antibodies to myelin antigens or indeed other CNS antigens such as neuronal proteins. Moreover despite Charcot's detailed description of the pathology of MS in a lecture in 1868 on the extent of inflammation and axon loss it has only been recently that researchers returned to examine the mechanism of axonal and neuronal loss in MS. Undoubtedly the development of magnetic resonance spectroscopy has allowed a unique view of the progression of the disease in patients with time. Such approaches have helped clarify the relationship of axonal damage and atrophy of the brain to the irreversible neurological disability. Nevertheless the cause of axonal damage remains unclear. As explained above the role for autoimmunity, in particular autoantibodies to neuronal antigens has been clearly demonstrated in other neurodegenerative disorders. The realisation that MS may also be classified as a neurodegenerative disorder in which autoantibodies to neuronal antigens may also play a role may help to not only uncover the pathogenic role for such autoimmune responses but may also lead to novel therapeutic strategies.

Before completely dismissing the role of neuronal specific T cells in MS it is pertinent to mention a study in which T cells recognising synapsin - a highly conserved neuronal protein – were detected in MS patients (Polak et al. 2001). However, in the animal model at least, T cells recognising the myelin protein MBP also recognised synapsin (de Santis et al. 1992) indicating that myelin specific T cells could also induce neuronal damage via cross-reactivity with neuronal antigens. So far T-cell reactions to other neuronal or axonal proteins have not been described.

Recognition of neurons and thus T cell activation leading to neurological damage requires the expression of key molecules for antigen presentation, such as major histocompatibility complex (MHC) and co-stimulatory molecules. For direct attack on neurons this requires neurons and axons to express MHC class I molecules for recognition and killing by CD8 specific T cells. Although it has become clear that CD8 T cells outnumber CD4 T cells in MS lesions, very little information is available to show whether or how T cells may kill neurons. In the normal brain, neurons express negligible levels of MHC-class I probably to avoid such lethal consequences. However during inflammation neurons and axons may upregulate MHC class I (Neumann et al. 1995 Redwine et al. 2001). Correspondingly, in MS lesions axons have been found positive for MHC class I (Hoftberger et al. 2001). In vitro, it has been shown that axons upregulate MHC class I after IFN-γ and tetrodotoxin treatment, resulting in transection of neurites by cytotoxic T-cells (Medana et al. 2001). More evidence for the impact of T cells on neurons comes from studying interactions of PLP-specific T cells in brain slice cultures. While not specific for neurons, activated PLP-specific T cells induced calcium changes in neurons leading to neuronal damage (Nitsch et al. 2004). Likewise MBP-specific T cells are more effective in activating microglia that have axon-damaging ability as observed in organotypic CNS cultures (Gimsa et al. 2000) suggesting that in some way CNS specific T cells augment the CNS damage.

To study the possible involvement of autoimmunity to neuronal antigens in MS several studies have used the experimental model – experimental autoimmune encephalomyelitis (EAE). In EAE in rats depletion of synaptic terminals during acute disease has been described suggesting that neuronal structures may also be target for immune responses. This may also be due to inflammation Similar to several of the neurodegenerative diseases in humans and the experimental models rats immunised with bovine myelin, immunoglobulin deposits are observed in the spinal cord neurons (Slavin et al. 1996). This staining may however be due to the cross-reactivity of immunity to myelin proteins with neuronal proteins since T cells to MBP also recognise synapsin (de Santis et al. 1992).

The evidence for the presence of anti-neuronal antibodies in MS is far more compelling. Antibodies have been found to be present inside axons in MS lesions and in neurons in EAE (Slavin et al. 1996). In addition it was shown that axon-reactive B-cells can be detected in MS lesions and isolated from CSF from patients and immunoglobulin was found attached to axons in the lesions (Zhang et al. 2005a; Zhang et al. 2005b). These B-cells were recently shown to be directed against the glycolytic enzymes triosephosphate isomerase (TPI) and GAPDH (Kolln et al. 2006). However, these enzymes are ubiquitously expressed and this does not seem to correspond with the specific central nervous system involvement in MS. In a review by DeVries (2004) evidence is described whereby antibodies to axolemma-enriched fractions may play a role in axonal destruction. Indeed such antiserum has been shown to induce neuronal changes in vitro like destruction of neurites and inhibition neurite outgrowth.

Another neuronal protein proposed as an autoimmune target in MS is neurofilament light (NF-L), a cytoskeletal protein expressed in neuronal cells. The protein has been used as a biomarker in the CSF to measure the amount of neuronal damage in MS patients and in animals with EAE (Semra et al. 2002; Norgren et al. 2005). However antibodies to NF-L have been described in both serum and CSF of MS patients (Silber et al. 2002; Eikelenboom et al. 2003; Ehling et al. 2004) and in SCH induced EAE in Biozzi ABH mice (our unpublished observations). Among all subgroups in MS, patients with progressive disease seem to have elevated levels of antibodies to NF-L. In one study, patients with primary progressive MS had higher levels of antibodies to NF-L in the serum, but not in the CSF, than patients with secondary progressive MS (Ehling et al. 2004). In another study, patients with primary progressive-MS or secondary progressive MS had higher levels of Abs to NF-L than patients with relapsing remitting-MS (Silber et al. 2002). Significant differences in levels of NF-L Abs between different MS subtypes, however, have not been found in other studies (Eikelenboom et al.2003), possibly due to differences in the selection of patients.

An important question is whether the antibody levels to NF-L in MS patients are reflecting disease progression. To address this, anti-NF-L indices have been correlated with

MRI measures of tissue damage. It appears that the anti-NF-L index in MS patients, especially in the relapsing remitting subgroup, correlates with MRI measures for axonal loss (Eikelenboom et al. 2003). However, in that study there were no adjustments made for possible confounding factors, such as age which is known to influence both NF-L antibody levels and cerebral atrophy (Ehling et al 2004; Resnick et al 2003).

NF-L – among others – was also identified as an antigenic protein in MS, using serological proteome analysis i.e., 2D SDS-PAGE, followed by immunoblotting and mass spectrometry (Almeras et al. 2004). In another paper from that same group, NF-L was identified as a discriminate antigen between MS and healthy controls or Sjögren syndrome patients (Lefranc et al. 2004). In fact, the frequency sera positive for NF-L was lower in MS patients compared to healthy controls or Sjögren syndrome patients. This finding is in contrast with other studies that describe that antibodies to NF-L are more frequently found in MS patients than in healthy controls (Newcombe et al. 1985). To examine the pathogenicity of anti-NF-L immune responses, we have demonstrated that immunisation of Biozzi mice with NF-L leads to axonal damage and paralysis and spasticity (Huizinga et al. 2007), debilitating clinical features of MS. In this novel model of axonal damage, which may mimic several features observed in MS, immunoglobulin was observed in the axons in the spinal cord of animals with disease but not in immunised mice that did not exhibit overt clinical signs.

## Mechanisms of Immune-Mediated Damage and Perspectives for Therapy

How autoimmunity to neuronal structures develops is debateable. Evidence for cross-reactive immune responses between infectious agents and self-antigens i.e. molecular mimicry has been suggested but is nevertheless controversial. Exposure to environmental agents such as neurotoxic agents has also been suggested since autoantibodies to neuronal specific antigens such as neurofilaments were prevalent in people exposed to lead or mercury and correlated with degree of exposure. In rats such exposure related to the pathology in the nervous system and antibodies purified from humans and rats exposed to this environmental chemical interfered with neuromuscular function following injection in experimental animals (El-Fawal et al. 1999).

One question is how, following such exposure to infectious agents or environmental neurotoxic agents and neurological damage, does release of neuronal antigens induce autoimmune responses? The CNS lacks lymphatic drainage and this contributes to the so-called 'immune-privilege' status. It is now realised that dendritic cells are able to migrate from the CNS to cervical lymph nodes (Hatterer et al. 2006) or indeed 'lymphatic structures' in the CNS where antigen presenting cells can come in contact with T cells (Serafini et al. 2006). In MS and EAE, myelin antigens (de Vos et al. 2002) and axonal antigens (van Zwam et al. 2006) are present in the cervical lymph node. However, whether this results in pathogenic autoimmunity or a mechanism by which the CNS limits 'pathogenic responses' is still unclear. Alternatively, axonal antigens, released in soluble form upon CNS damage (Galea et al. 2007), may reach the regional lymph nodes although the exact pathways require further study. Harling-Berg et al. (1999) showed indeed that injection of proteins in the ventricles or the brain parenchyma drained to the CLN and this route was very effective for mounting a humoral immune response.

As discussed in this review pathogenic autoimmunity to neuronal structures are present in patients and the question is 'what are the mechanisms by which such responses cause injury to neurons?' One such way is by interfering with neuronal function. Neurofilaments are synthesised and assembled in neuronal cell bodies, transported along axons and degraded in the synapse. In several pathological diseases such as ALS, diabetic neuropathy and Parkinson's disease, where NF aggregates form Lewy bodies, and in neurofibrillary tangles in Alzheimer's disease, neuronal filaments aggregate in the cell bodies and axons. In peripheral disease such as Charcot-Marie-Tooth syndrome disease (Brownlees et al. 2002) abnormalities in neurofilaments assembly and axonal transport is due to mutations in the protein. Such abnormalities in alph-internexin as well as NF have also been identified in neuronal intermediate filament inclusion disease (Momeni et al. 2006). Aggregation of NF proteins may be due to mutations in the proteins themselves, or alternatively immunological mechanisms may induce abnormal function leading to aggregation for example by cross-linking of antibodies recognising neuronal structures. Microinjection of antibodies to kinesin and dynein - proteins involved in axonal transport of NF - in the DRG in which green fluorescent protein was used to tag NF impaired anterograde and retrograde NF transport (Theiss et al. 2005).

Receptors for Fc (FcR) of immunoglobulin facilitate uptake of immunoglobulin by cells. This mechanism aids the uptake and clearance of, for example, bacteria coated or 'opsonised' with antibodies. Immunoglobulin bound to FcR trigger numerous biological activities in effector cells depending on whether they activate immunoresponsive tyrosine activating motifs (ITAMS) or inhibitory motifs (ITIMs), which are phosphorylated by tyrosine kinases during signal transduction. In the peripheral nervous system FcR are expressed by Schwann cells (Vedeler et al. 1991) and in the CNS FcR are widely expressed by microglia. Few studies have described such expression on neurons in vivo (Andoh and Kuraishi 2004) although expression of FcR is observed on a neuronal cell line in vitro (Gorini et al. 1992). The high affinity receptor IgG receptor FcgRI is expressed on primary sensory neurons and is activated by Ig-antigen complex which leads to increased intracellular calcium, and release of neurotransmitters. Excessive release is associated with neuronal damage and disease. As described above Ig from ALS patients is taken up by neurons and may enhance neuronal damage by exacerbating neurotransmitter release. Mohamed and colleagues (2002) elegantly showed that F(ab')2 fragments of Ig from ALS patients are not taken up by neurons and thus does not induce neurotransmitter release. Likewise neurons in mice lacking the gamma subunit of the FcR, fail to take up ALS IgG and the acetylcholine release were markedly reduced. Thus targeting this pathway may help in the treatments of ALS but also spasticity and neuronal damage in other neurodegenerative disorders such as MS.

For several disorders such as MG and paraneoplastic disorders, removing the source of antibody (tumor) or blocking activity with for example IVIg results in improvement of the clinical disease. IVIg has slight but detectable beneficial effects on diabetic patients presenting with axonal damage and is a recognised therapy in MS. It is unclear whether IVIg is beneficial in MS patients with axonal damage. IVIg is able to enter the CNS only when BBB function is compromised such as during EAE. In MS autoimmunity to myelin proteins have prompted therapeutic regimens such a tolerance strategies to re-establish immunological tolerance to self-antigens and regulate autoimmunity. Tolerance strategies to CNS antigens are highly effective in regulating EAE in particular chronic relapsing EAE (Heijmans et al. 2005, Pryce et al. 2005 Smith et al. 2005). Since antibodies to neuronal and axonal antigens may have a pathogenic role in neurological diseases, tolerance strategies should also target axonal antigens.

## Conclusion

Although MS has long-been considered an autoimmune disorder in which aberrant immune responses attack and damage myelin it is also probable that autoimmunity to neuronal antigens plays a role in the neurodegeneration observed in disease. Similar to other neurodegenerative disorders, such as ALS, AD and PD, antibodies to axonal and neuronal proteins are present in sera and CSF of MS patients on axons in the lesions. It remains to be determined whether neuronal protein specific antibodies augment or exacerbate axonal damage in MS as has been shown with antibodies to myelin. In any case, the draining cervical lymph nodes may play a crucial role, either by mounting a humoral response to neuronal antigens or by suppression of pathogenic autoimmunity. If indeed autoimmunity to neuronal antigens plays a role in the axonal damage seen in MS, or other neurodegenerative disorders, therapeutic strategies designed to inhibit such pathogenic antibodies may be key to the treatment of the destructive progressive disease and axonal damage associated with cognitive changes in chronic MS and neurodegenerative disorders.

## References

Adamus, G. 2003. Autoantibody-induced apoptosis as a possible mechanism of autoimmune retinopathy. *Autoimmun. Rev.* 2:63-68.

Almeras, L., Lefranc, D., Drobecq, H., de Seze, J., Dubucquoi, S., Vermersch, P., and Prin, L. 2004. New antigenic candidates in multiple sclerosis: identification by serological proteome analysis. *Proteomics* 4:2184-2194.

Amor, S., Smith, P.A., Hart, B, Baker, D. 2005. Biozzi mice: of mice and human neurological diseases. *J. Neuroimmunol.* 165:1-10.

Andoh, T., Kuraishi, Y. 2004. Expression of Fc epsilon receptor I on primary sensory neurons in mice. *Neuroreport.* 15:2029-2031.

Ankeny DP, Lucin KM, Sanders VM, McGaughy VM, Popovich PG. 2006 Spinal cord injury triggers systemic autoimmunity: evidence for chronic B lymphocyte activation and lupus-like autoantibody synthesis. *J. Neurochem.* 99:1073-87.

Annunziata P, Maimone D, Guazzi GC 1995 Association of polyclonal anti-GM1 IgM and anti-neurofilament antibodies with CSF oligoclonal bands in a young with amyotrophic lateral sclerosis. *Acta. Neurol. Scand.* 92:387-93.

Appel, S.H., Engelhardt, J.I., Garcia, J., Stefani, E. 1991. Immunoglobulins from animal models of motor neuron disease and from human amyotrophic lateral sclerosis patients passively transfer physiological abnormalities to the neuromuscular junction. *Proc. Natl. Acad. Sci. USA*. 88:647-51.

Appel, S.H., Le, W.D., Tajti, J., Haverkamp, L.J., Engelhardt, J.I. 1992 Nigral damage and dopaminergic hypofunction in mesencephalon-immunized guinea pigs. *Ann. Neurol.* 32(4):494-501.

Bae JS, Kim BJ 2005 Cerebellar ataxia and acute motor axonal neuropathy associated with Anti GD1b and Anti GM1 antibodies. *J. Clin. Neurosci.* 12:808-10.

Ballok, D.A., Earls, A.M., Krasnik, C., Hoffman, S.A., Sakic, B. 2004 Autoimmune-induced damage of the midbrain dopaminergic system in lupus-prone mice. *J. Neuroimmunol.* 152:83-97.

Ballok, D.A. 2006 Neuroimmunopathology in a murine model of neuropsychiatric lupus. *Brain Res. Rev.* (ahead of print).

Berghs S, Ferracci F, Maksimova E, Gleason S, Leszczynski N, Butler M, De Camilli P, Solimena M 2001 Autoimmunity to beta IV spectrin in paraneoplastic lower motor neuron syndrome. *Proc. Natl. Acad. Sci. USA*. 98:6945-50.

Bernal F, Shams'ili S, Rojas I, Sanchez-Valle R, Saiz A, Dalmau J, Honnorat J, Sillevis Smitt P, Graus F 2003 Anti-Tr antibodies as markers of paraneoplastic cerebellar degeneration and Hodgkin's disease. *Neurology*. 60:230-4.

Bour-Jordan, H., Thompson, H.L., Bluestone, J.A. 2005 Distinct effector mechanisms in the development of autoimmune neuropathy versus diabetes in nonobese diabetic mice. *J. Immunol.* 175:5649-5655.

Brok, H.P., Bauer, J., Jonker, M., Blezer, E., Amor, S., Bontrop, R.E., Laman, J.D., 't Hart, B.A. 2001. Non-human primate models of MS. *Immunol. Rev*. 183:173-185.

Brownlees J, Ackerley S, Grierson AJ, Jacobsen NJ, Shea K, Anderton BH, Leigh PN, Shaw CE, Miller CC 2002 Charcot-Marie-Tooth disease neurofilament mutations disrupt neurofilament assembly and axonal transport. *Hum. Mol. Genet.* 11:2837-44

Calcutt, N.A. 2002. Future treatments for diabetic neuropathy: clues from exper.imental neuropathy. *Curr. Diab. Rep.* 2:482-488.

Candler PM, Dale RC, Griffin S, Church AJ, Wait R, Chapman MD, Keir G, Giovannoni G, Rees JH 2006 Post-streptococcal opsoclonus-myoclonus syndrome associated with anti-neuroleukin antibodies *J. Neuro.l Neurosurg. Psychiatry*. 77:507-12.

Caporale, C.M., Capasso, M., Luciani, M., Prencipe, V., Creati, B., Gandolfi, P., De Angelis, M.V., Di Muzio, A., Caporale, V., Uncini, A. 2006. Experimental axonopathy induced by immunization with Campylobacter jejuni lipopolysaccharide from a patient with Guillain-Barre syndrome. *J. Neuroimmunol.* 174:12-20.

Carpentier, A.F., Rosenfeld, M.R., Delattre, J.Y., Whalen, R.G., Posner, J.B., Dalmau, J.D.N.A. 1998. Vaccination with HuD inhibits growth of a neuroblastoma in mice. *Clin. Cancer. Res*. 4:2819-2824.

Chan, K.H., Vernino, S., Lennon, V.,A. 2001. ANNA-3 anti-neuronal nuclear antibody: marker of lung cancer-related autoimmunity. *Ann. Neurol.* 50:301-311.

Chapman J, Feldon J, Alroy G, Michaelson DM 1989 Immunization of rats with cholinergic neurons induces behavioral deficits. *J. Neural Transplant.* 1:63-76.

Church AJ, Cardoso F, Dale RC, Lees AJ, Thompson EJ, Giovannoni G 2002 Anti-basal ganglia antibodies in acute and persistent Sydenham's chorea. *Neurology*. 59:227-31.

Church AJ, Dale RC, Cardoso F, Candler PM, Chapman MD, Allen ML, Klein NJ, Lees AJ, Giovannoni G 2003 CSF and serum immune parameters in Sydenham's chorea: evidence of an autoimmune syndrome? *J. Neuroimmunol.*136:149-53.

Christadoss, P., Poussin, M., Deng, C. 2000. Animal models of myasthenia gravis. *Clin. Immunol.* 94:75-87.

Coesmans, M., Smitt, P.A., Linden, D.J., Shigemoto, R., Hirano, T., Yamakawa, Y., van Alphen, A.M., Luo, C., van der Geest, J.N., Kros, J.M., Gaillard, C.A., Frens, M.A., de Zeeuw, C.I. 2003. Mechanisms underlying cerebellar motor deficits due to mGluR1-autoantibodies. *Ann. Neurol.* 53:325-336.

Couratier P, Yi FH, Preud'homme JL, Clavelou P, White A, Sindou P, Vallat JM, Jauberteau MO 1998 Serum autoantibodies to neurofilament proteins in sporadic amyotrophic lateral sclerosis. *J. Neurol. Sci.* 154:137-45.

Cohly HH, Panja A Immunological findings in autism 2005 *Int .Rev. Neurobiol.* 71:317-41.

Cox AL, Coles AJ, Nortje J, Bradley PG, Chatfield DA, Thompson SJ, Menon DK 2006 An investigation of auto-reactivity after head injury. *J. Neuroimmunol.* 174:180-6.

Dale RC, Church AJ, Surtees RA, Lees AJ, Adcock JE, Harding B, Neville BG, Giovannoni G 2004 Encephalitis lethargica syndrome: 20 new cases and evidence of basal ganglia autoimmunity. *Brain.* 127:21-33.

Dale RC, Candler PM, Church AJ, Wait R, Pocock JM, Giovannoni G 2006 Neuronal surface glycolytic enzymes are autoantigen targets in post-streptococcal autoimmune CNS disease. *J. Neuroimmunol.* 172:187-97.

Dahlstrom A, Wigander A, Lundmark K, Gottfries CG, Carvey PM, McRae A. 1990. Investigations on auto-antibodies in Alzheimer's and Parkinson's diseases, using defined neuronal cultures. *J. Neural. Transm. Suppl.* 29:195-206.

D'Andrea MR. 2005 Add Alzheimer's disease to the list of autoimmune diseases. *Med. Hypotheses.* 64:458-63.

Defazio G, Dal Toso R, Benvegnu D, Minozzi MC, Cananzi AR, Leon A 1994 Parkinsonian serum carries complement-dependent toxicity for rat mesencephalic dopaminergic neurons in culture. *Brain Res.* 633:206-12.

DeGiorgio LA, Konstantinov KN, Lee SC, Hardin JA, Volpe BT, Diamond B. 2001 A subset of lupus anti-DNA antibodies cross-reacts with the NR2 glutamate receptor in systemic lupus erythematosus. *Nat. Med.* 7:1189-93.

DeVries GH. 2004 Cryptic axonal antigens and axonal loss in multiple sclerosis. *Neurochem. Res.* 29:1999-2006.

de Vos AF, van Meurs M, Brok HP, Boven LA, Hintzen RQ, van der Valk P, Ravid R, Rensing S, Boon L, 't Hart BA, Laman JD 2002 Transfer of central nervous system autoantigens and presentation in secondary lymphoid organs. *J. Immunol.* 169:5415-23.

De Santis ML, Roth GA, Cumar FA 1992 Cellular immune crossreactivity between myelin basic protein and synapsin in rats with experimental allergic encephalomyelitis. *J. Neurosci. Res.* 31:46-51.

Dinkel, K., Meinck, H.M., Jury, K.M., Karges, W., Richter, W. 1998 Inhibition of gamma-aminobutyric acid synthesis by glutamic acid decarboxylase autoantibodies in stiff-man syndrome. *Ann. Neurol.* 44:194-201.

Drachman, D.B., Kuncl, R.W. 1989. Amyotrophic lateral sclerosis: an unconventional autoimmune disease? *Ann. Neurol.* 26:269-74.

Drachman D.B, McIntosh KR, Yang B. 1998. Factors that determine the severity of experimental myasthenia gravis. *Ann. NY Acad. Sci.* 841:262-82.

Duhaime AC 2006 Large animal models of traumatic injury to the immature brain. *Dev. Neurosci.* 28:380-7.

Ehling, R., Lutterotti, A., Wanschitz, J., Khalil, M., Gneiss, C., Deisenhammer, F., Reindl, M., and Berger, T. 2004. Increased frequencies of serum antibodies to neurofilament light in patients with primary chronic progressive multiple sclerosis. *Mult. Scler.* 10:601-606.

Eikelenboom, M.J, Petzold, A., Lazeron, R.H., Silber, E., Sharief, M., Thompson, E.J., Barkhof, F., Giovannoni, G., Polman, C.H., Uitdehaag, B.M. 2003 Multiple sclerosis: Neurofilament light chain antibodies are correlated to cerebral atrophy. *Neurology.* 60:219-223.

El-Fawal H A, Waterman S J, De Feo A, and Shamy M Y 1999 Neuroimmunotoxicology: humoral assessment of neurotoxicity and autoimmune mechanisms. *Environ. Health Perspect.* 107(Suppl 5): 767–775.

Engelhardt JI, Appel SH, Killian JM. 1990 Motor neuron destruction in guinea pigs immunized with bovine spinal cord ventral horn homogenate: experimental autoimmune gray matter disease. *J. Neuroimmunol.* 27:21-31.

Engelhardt, J.I., Siklos, L., Appel, S.H. 1997. Immunization of guinea pigs with human choline acetyltransferase induces selective lower motoneuron destruction. *J. Neuroimmunol.* 78:57-68.

Engelhardt, J.I., Soos, J., Obal, I., Vigh, L., Siklos, L. 2005. Subcellular localization of IgG from the sera of ALS patients in the nervous system. *Acta. Neurol. Scand.* 112:126-133.

Eslamboli, A. 2005. Marmoset monkey models of Parkinson's disease: which model, when and why? *Brain Res. Bull.* 68:140-149.

Fadare, O., Hart, H.J. 2004 Anti-Ri antibodies associated with short-term memory deficits and a mature cystic teratoma of the ovary. *Int. Semin. Surg. Oncol.* 1:11.

Fernandez-Shaw C, Marina A, Cazorla P, Valdivieso F, Vazquez J 1997Anti-brain spectrin immunoreactivity in Alzheimer's disease: degradation of spectrin in an animal model of cholinergic degeneration. *J. Neuroimmunol.* 77:91-8.

Flink, M.T., Atchison, W.D. 2003. Ca2+ channels as targets of neurological disease: Lambert-Eaton Syndrome and other Ca2+ channelopathies. *J. Bioenerg. Biomembr.* 35:697-718.

Fishman PS, Drachman DB 1995 Internalization of IgG in motoneurons of patients with ALS: selective or nonselective. *Neurology.* 45:1551-4.

Fiszer U, Mix E, Fredrikson S, Kostulas V, Olsson T, Link H 1994. Gamma delta+ T cells are increased in patients with Parkinson's disease. *J. Neurol. Sci.* 121:39-4.

Folli F, Solimena M, Cofiell R, Austoni M, Tallini G, Fassetta G, Bates D, Cartlidge N, Bottazzo GF, Piccolo G, de Camilli P 1993 Autoantibodies to a 128-kd synaptic protein in three women with the stiff-man syndrome and breast cancer. *N. Engl. J. Med.* 328:546-51.

Furlan R, Brambilla E, Sanvito F, Roccatagliata L, Olivieri S, Bergami A, Pluchino S, Uccelli A, Comi G, Martino G 2003 Vaccination with amyloid-beta peptide induces autoimmune encephalomyelitis in C57/BL6 mice. *Brain.* 126:285-91.

Galea I, Bechmann I, Perry VH 2007 What is immune privilege (not)? *Trends Immunol.* 28:12-8.

Gajdusek DC. 1985. Hypothesis: interference with axonal transport of neurofilament as a common pathogenetic mechanism in certain diseases of the central nervous system. *N. Engl. J. Med.* 312:714-9.

Gimsa U, Peter SV, Lehmann K, Bechmann I, Nitsch R 2000 Axonal damage induced by invading T cells in organotypic central nervous system tissue in vitro: involvement of microglial cells. *Brain Pathol.* 10:365-7.

Giuliani, F., Goodyer, C.G., Antel, J.P., Yong, V.W. 2003 Vulnerability of human neurons to T cell-mediated cytotoxicity. *J. Immunol.* 171:368-379.

Gorini G, Ciotti MT, Starace G, Vigneti E, Raschella G. 1992 Fc gamma receptors are expressed on human neuroblastoma cell lines: lack of correlation with N-myc oncogene activity. *Int. J. Neurosci.* 62:287-97.

Grady MS, McLaughlin MR, Christman CW, Valadka AB, Fligner CL, Povlishock JT 1993 The use of antibodies targeted against the neurofilament subunits for the detection of diffuse axonal injury in humans. *J. Neuropathol. Exp. Neurol.* 52:143-52.

Greenlee JE, Burns JB, Rose JW, Jaeckle KA, Clawson S 1995Uptake of systemically administered human anticerebellar antibody by rat Purkinje cells following blood-brain barrier disruption. *Acta. Neuropathol.* (Berl).89:341-5.

Gultekin, S.H., Rosenfeld, M.R., Voltz, R., Eichen, J., Posner, J.B., Dalmau, J. 2000. Paraneoplastic limbic encephalitis: neurological symptoms, immunological findings and tumour association in 50 patients 123:1481-1494.

Ha, G.K., Huang, Z., Streit, W.J., Petitto, J.M. 2006 Endogenous T lymphocytes and microglial reactivity in the axotomized facial motor nucleus of mice: effect of genetic background and the RAG2 gene. *J. Neuroimmunol.* 172:1-8.

Hallett, J.J., Harling-Berg, C.J., Knopf, P.M., Stopa, E.G., Kiessling, L.S. 2000 Anti-striatal antibodies in Tourette syndrome cause neuronal dysfunction. *J. Neuroimmunol.* 111:195-202.

Halstead, S.K., O'Hanlon, G.M., Humphreys, P.D., Morrison, D.B., Morgan, B.P., Todd, A.J., Plomp, J.J., Willison, H.J. 2004. Anti-disialoside antibodies kill perisynaptic Schwann cells and damage motor nerve terminals via membrane attack complex in a murine model of neuropathy. *Brain.* 127:2109-2123.

Harling-Berg CJ, Park JT, Knopf PM 1999 Role of cervical lymphatics in the Th2-type hierarchy of CNS immune regulation. *J. Neuroimmunol.* 101:111-127.

Hart IK, Maddison P, Newsom-Davis J, Vincent A, Mills KR 2002 Phenotypic variants of autoimmune peripheral nerve hyperexcitability. *Brain.* 125:1887-95.

Hassin-Baer, S., Wertman, E., Raphael, M., Stark, V., Chapman, J., Michaelson, D.M. 1992. Antibodies from Down's syndrome patients bind to the same cholinergic neurofilament protein recognized by Alzheimer's disease antibodies. *Neurology.* 42:551-555.

Hatterer E, Davoust N, Didier-Bazes M, Vuaillat C, Malcus C, Belin MF, Nataf S. 2006 How to drain without lymphatics? Dendritic cells migrate from the cerebrospinal fluid to the B-cell follicles of cervical lymph nodes. *Blood.* 107:806-12.

He, Y., Le, W.D., Appel, S.H. 2002. Role of Fcgamma receptors in nigral cell injury induced by Parkinson disease immunoglobulin injection into mouse substantia nigra. *Exp. Neurol.* 176:322-327.

Hikawa, N., Kiuchi, Y., Maruyama, T., Takenaka, T. 1997. Delayed neurite regeneration and its improvement by nerve growth factor (NGF) in dorsal root ganglia from MRL-lpr/lpr mice in vitro. *J. Neurol. Sci.* 149:13-7.

Hoeldtke RD, Bryner KD, Hobbs GR, Horvath GG, Riggs JE, Christie I, Ganser G, Marcovina SM, Lernmark A 2000 Antibodies to glutamic acid decarboxylase and peripheral nerve function in type 1 diabetes. *J. Clin. Endocrinol. Metab.* 85:3297-308.

Huerta PT, Kowal C, DeGiorgio LA, Volpe BT, Diamond B Huerta PT, Kowal C, DeGiorgio LA, Volpe BT, Diamond B 2006 Immunity and behavior: antibodies alter emotion. *Proc. Natl. Acad. Sci. USA.* 103:678-83.

Huizinga R., Heijmans N., Schubert P., Gschmeissner S., 't Hart BA., Herrmann H., Amor S. 2007. Immunization with neurofilament light protein induces spastic paresis and axonal degeneration in Biozzi ABH mice. *J. Neuropathol. Exp. Neurol. in press.*

Huber VC, Mondal T, Factor SA, Seegal RF, Lawrence DA. 2006 Serum antibodies from Parkinson's disease patients react with neuronal membrane proteins from a mouse dopaminergic cell line and affect its dopamine expression. *J. Neuroinflammation.* 20;3:1.

Hoshino S, Kobayashi S, Nakazawa S. 1996 Prolonged and extensive IgG immunoreactivity after severe fluid-percussion injury in rat brain. *Brain Res.* 711:73-83.

Hoffman, K.L., Hornig, M., Yaddanapudi, K., Jabado, O., Lipkin, W.I. 2004. A murine model for neuropsychiatric disorders associated with group A beta-hemolytic streptococcal infection. *J. Neurosci.* 24:1780-91.

Hoftberger, R., Aboul-Enein, F., Brueck, W., Lucchinetti, C., Rodriguez, M., Schmidbauer, M., Jellinger, K., Lassmann, H. 2004 Expression of major histocompatibility complex class I molecules on the different cell types in MS lesions. *Brain Pathol.* 14:43-50.

Hughes RA, Cornblath DR 2005 Guillain-Barre syndrome. *Lancet.* 366:1653-66.

Heijmans, N., Smith PA. Morris-Downes MM., Pryce G., Baker D., Donaldson AVJ., 't Hart B., Amor S. 2005 Encephalitogenic and Tolerogenic potential of altered peptide ligands of MOG and PLP in Biozzi ABH mice. *J. Neuroimmunol.* 167:23-33.

Ishida, K., Mitoma, H., Wada, Y., Oka, T., Shibahara, J., Saito, Y., Murayama, S, Mizusawa, H. 2007. Selective loss of Purkinje cells in a patient with anti-glutamic acid decarboxylase antibody-associated cerebellar ataxia. *J. Neurol. Neurosurg. Psychiatry.* 78:190-2.

Jha, S., Xu, K., Maruta, T., Oshima, M., Mosier, D.R., Atassi, M.Z., Hoch, W. 2006 Myasthenia gravis induced in mice by immunization with the recombinant extracellular domain of rat muscle-specific kinase (MuSK). *J. Neuroimmunol.* 175:107-117.

Jones, T.B., Hart, R.P., Popovich, P.G. 2005 Molecular control of physiological and pathological T-cell recruitment after mouse spinal cord injury. *J. Neurosci.* 25:6576-6583.

Kalman J, Engelhardt JI, Le WD, Xie W, Kovacs I, Kasa P, Appel SH 1997Experimental immune-mediated damage of septal cholinergic neurons. *J. Neuroimmunol.* 77:63-74.

Kirvan CA, Swedo SE, Kurahara D, Cunningham MW 2006 Streptococcal mimicry and antibody-mediated cell signaling in the pathogenesis of Sydenham's.chorea. *Autoimmunity*. 39:21-9.

Kleopa KA, Elman LB, Lang B, Vincent A, Scherer SS Neuromyotonia and limbic encephalitis sera target mature Shaker-type K+ channels: subunit specificity correlates with clinical manifestations. *Brain*. 2006 129:1570-84.

Kowal, C., Degiorgio, L.A., Lee, J.Y., Edgar, M.A., Huerta, P.T., Volpe, B.T., Diamond, B., 2006 Human lupus autoantibodies against NMDA receptors mediate cognitive impairment. *Proc. Natl. Acad. Sci. USA*. 103:19854-19859.

Kolln J, Ren HM, Da RR, Zhang Y, Spillner E, Olek M, Hermanowicz N, Hilgenberg LG, Smith MA, van den Noort S, Qin Y 2006. Triosephosphate isomerase- and glyceraldehyde-3-phosphate dehydrogenase-reactive autoantibodies in the cerebrospinal fluid of patients with multiple sclerosis. *J. Immunol.* 177:5652-8.

Krampfl K, Mohammadi B, Buchwald B, Jahn K, Dengler R, Toyka KV, Bufler J. 2003 IgG from patients with Guillain-Barre syndrome interact with nicotinic acetylcholine receptor channels. *Muscle Nerve*. 27:435-41.

Kusunoki, S., Shimizu, J., Chiba, A., Ugawa, Y., Hitoshi, S., Kanazawa, I. 1996 Experimental sensory neuropathy induced by sensitization with ganglioside GD1b. A*nn. Neurol.* 39:424-431.

Kusunoki, S., Hitoshi, S., Kaida, K., Arita, M., Kanazawa, I. 1999. Monospecific anti-GD1b IgG is required to induce rabbit ataxic neuropathy. *Ann. Neurol.* 45:400-403.

Kwidzinski, E., Mutlu, L.K., Kovac, A.D., Bunse, J., Goldmann, J., Mahlo, J., Aktas, O., Zipp, F., Kamradt, T., Nitsch, R., Bechmann, I. 2003 .Self-tolerance in the immune privileged CNS: lessons from the entorhinal cortex lesion model. *J. Neural. Transm. Suppl.* 65:29-49.

Le WD, Engelhardt J, Xie WJ, Schneider L, Smith RG, Appel SH 1995 Experimental autoimmune nigral damage in guinea pigs. *J. Neuroimmunol.* 57:45-53.

Le, W., Rowe, D., Xie, W., Ortiz, I., He, Y., Appel, S.H., 2001 Microglial activation and dopaminergic cell injury: an in vitro model relevant to Parkinson's disease. *J. Neurosci.* 21:8447-55.

Lefranc, D., Almeras, L., Dubucquoi, S., de Seze, J., Vermersch, P., and Prin, L. 2004. Distortion of the self-reactive IgG antibody repertoire in multiple sclerosis as a new diagnostic tool. *J. Immunol.* 172:669-678.

Levin MC, Lee SM, Kalume F, Morcos Y, Dohan FC Jr, Hasty KA, Callaway JC, Zunt J, Desiderio D, Stuart JM 2002. Autoimmunity due to molecular mimicry as a cause of neurological disease. *Nat. Med.* 8:509-13.

Levite. M., Fleidervish. I.A., Schwarz. A., Pelled. D., Futerman. A.H. 1999. Autoantibodies to the glutamate receptor kill neurons via activation of the receptor ion channel. *J. Autoimmun*. 13:61-72.

Levite, M, Hermelin, A., 1999 Autoimmunity to the glutamate receptor in mice--a model for Rasmussen's encephalitis? *J. Autoimmun*. 13:73-82.

Lim MJ, Beake J, Bible E, Curran TM, Ramirez-Montealegre D, Pearce DA, Cooper JD 2006 Distinct patterns of serum immunoreactivity as evidence for multiple brain-directed autoantibodies in juvenile neuronal ceroid lipofuscinosis. *Neuropathol. Appl. Neurobiol.* 32:469-82.

Lopez-Escribano, H., Minambres, E., Labrador, M., Bartolome, M.J., Lopez-Hoyos, M. 2002. Induction of cell death by sera from patients with acute brain injury as a mechanism of production of autoantibodies. *Arthritis. Rheum.* 46:3290-3300.

Margutti P, Delunardo F, Ortona E 2006 Autoantibodies associated with psychiatric disorders. *Curr. Neurovasc. Res.* 3:149-57.

Martino D, Giovannoni G 2004 Antibasal ganglia antibodies and their relevance to movement disorders. *Curr. Opin. Neurol.* 17:425-32.

Medana I, Martinic MA, Wekerle H, Neumann H 2001 Transection of major histocompatibility complex class I-induced neurites by cytotoxic T lymphocytes. *Am. J. Pathol.* 159:809-15.

Michaelson DM, Kadar T, Weiss Z, Chapman J, Feldon J. 1990 Immunization with cholinergic cell bodies induces histopathological changes in rat brains. *Mol. Chem. Neuropathol.*13:71-80.

Mitoma H, Ishida K, Shizuka-Ikeda M, Mizusawa H. 2003 Dual impairment of GABAA- and GABAB-receptor-mediated synaptic responses by autoantibodies to glutamic acid decarboxylase. *J. Neurol. Sci.* 208:51-6.

Momeni P, Cairns NJ, Perry RH, Bigio EH, Gearing M, Singleton AB, Hardy J. 2006 Mutation analysis of patients with neuronal intermediate filament inclusion disease (NIFID). *Neurobiol. Aging.* 27:1-778.

Morales, D.M., Marklund, N., Lebold, D., Thompson, H.J., Pitkanen, A., Maxwell, W.L., Longhi, L., Laurer, H., Maegele, M., Neugebauer, E., Graham, D.I., Stocchetti, N., McIntosh, T.K. 2005. Experimental models of traumatic brain injury: do we really need to build a better mousetrap? *Neuroscience* 36:971-989.

Mor F, Quintana F, Mimran A, Cohen IR. 2003 Autoimmune encephalomyelitis and uveitis induced by T cell immunity to self beta-synuclein. *J. Immunol.* Jan 1;170(1):628-34.

Mor F, Izak M, Cohen IR 2005 Identification of aldolase as a target antigen in Alzheimer's disease. *J. Immunol.* 175:3439-45.

Neumann, H., Cavalie, A., Jenne, D.E., Wekerle, H. 1995. Induction of MHC class I genes in neurons. *Science.* 269:549-52.

Newcombe J, Gahan S, Cuzner ML. 1985 Serum antibodies against central nervous system proteins in human demyelinating disease. *Clin. Exp. Immunol.* 59:383-90.

Niebroj-Dobosz, I., Janik, P., Kwiecinski, H. 2004. Serum IgM anti-GM1 ganglioside antibodies in lower motor neuron syndromes. *Eur. J. Neurol.* 11:13-16.

Niebroj-Dobosz, I., Dziewulska, D., Janik, P. 2006. Auto-antibodies against proteins of spinal cord cells in cerebrospinal fluid of patients with amyotrophic lateral sclerosis (ALS). *Folia Neuropathol.* 44:191-196.

Nemni R, Feltri ML, Fazio R, Quattrini A, Lorenzetti I, Corbo M, Canal N 1990 Axonal neuropathy with monoclonal IgG kappa that binds to a neurofilament protein. *Ann. Neurol.* 28:361-4.

Nicoll JA, Wilkinson D, Holmes C, Steart P, Markham H, Weller RO 2003 Neuropathology of human Alzheimer disease after immunization with amyloid-beta peptide: a case report. *Nat. Med.* 9:448-52.

Nitsch, R., Pohl, E.E., Smorodchenko, A., Infante-Duarte, C., Aktas, O., Zipp, F. 2004. Direct impact of T cells on neurons revealed by two-photon microscopy in living brain tissue. *J. Neurosci.* 24:2458-64.

Norgren N, Edelstam A, Stigbrand T 2005 Cerebrospinal fluid levels of neurofilament light in chronic experimental autoimmune encephalomyelitis. *Brain Res. Bull.* 67:264-8.

Offen, D., Halevi, S., Orion, D., Mosberg, R., Stern-Goldberg, H., Melamed, E., Atlas, D. 1998 Antibodies from ALS patients inhibit dopamine release mediated by L-type calcium channels. *Neurology*. 51:1100-1103.

Oron L, Dubovik V, Novitsky L, Eilam D, Michaelson DM 1997 Animal model and in vitro studies of anti neurofilament antibodies mediated neurodegeneration in Alzheimer's disease. *J. Neural. Transm. Suppl.*; 49:77-84.

Orr, C.F., Rowe, D..B, Mizuno, Y., Mori, H., Halliday, G.M. 2005. A possible role for humoral immunity in the pathogenesis of Parkinson's disease. *Brain.* 128:2665-2674.

Pellkofer, H., Schubart, A.S., Hoftberger, R., Schutze, N., Pagany, M., Schuller, M., Lassmann, H., Hohlfeld, R., Voltz, R., Linington, C. 2004. Modelling paraneoplastic CNS disease: T-cells specific for the onconeuronal antigen PNMA1 mediate autoimmune encephalomyelitis in the rat. *Brain*. 2004 127:1822-1830.

Philippens, I.H., Melchers, B.P., Roeling, T.A., Bruijnzeel, P.L. 2000. Behavioral test systems in marmoset monkeys. *Behav. Res. Methods Instrum. Comput*. 32:173-179.

Plomp JJ, Molenaar PC, O'Hanlon GM, Jacobs BC, Veitch J, Daha MR, van Doorn PA, van der Meche FG, Vincent A, Morgan BP, Willison HJ 1999 Miller Fisher anti-GQ1b antibodies: alpha-latrotoxin-like effects on motor end plates. *Ann. Neurol.* 45:189-99.

Polak T, Schlaf G, Scholl U, Krome-Cesar C, Mader M, Felgenhauer K, Weber F 2001 Characterization of the human T cell response against the neuronal protein synapsin in patients with multiple sclerosis. *J. Neuroimmunol.* 115:176-81

Posner JB 2003 Immunology of paraneoplastic syndromes: overview *Ann. NY Acad. Sci.* 998:178-86.

Pryce G, O'Neill JK, Croxford JL, Amor S, Hankey DJ, East E, Giovannoni G, Baker D. 2005 Autoimmune tolerance eliminates relapses but fails to halt progression in a model of multiple sclerosis. *J. Neuroimmunol.* 165:41-52.

Pullen AH, Humphreys P 2000 Ultrastructural analysis of spinal motoneurones from mice treated with IgG from ALS patients, healthy individuals, or disease controls. *J. Neurol. Sci.* 180:35-45.

Raju, R., Rakocevic, G., Chen, Z., Hoehn, G., Semino-Mora, C., Shi, W., Olsen, R., Dalakas, M.C. 2006 Autoimmunity to GABAA-receptor-associated protein in stiff-person syndrome. *Brain*. 129:3270-3276.

Ramirez-Montealegre D, Chattopadhyay S, Curran TM, Wasserfall C, Pritchard L, Schatz D, Petitto J, Hopkins D, She JX, Rothberg PG, Atkinson M, Pearce DA 2005 Autoimmunity to glutamic acid decarboxylase in the neurodegenerative disorder Batten disease. *Neurology*. 64:743-5.

Redwine JM, Buchmeier MJ, Evans CF 2001 In vivo expression of major histocompatibility complex molecules on oligodendrocytes and neurons during viral infection. *Am. J. Pathol.* 159:1219-24.

Resnick, S.M., Pham, D.L., Kraut, M.A., Zonderman, A.B., and Davatzikos, C. 2003. Longitudinal magnetic resonance imaging studies of older adults: a shrinking brain. *J. Neurosci.* 23:3295-3301.

Roberts WK, Darnell RB 2004 Neuroimmunology of the paraneoplastic neurological degenerations. *Curr. Opin. Immunol.* 16:616-22.

Rohn, T.T., Ivins, K.J., Bahr, B.A., Cotman, C.W., Cribbs, D.H. 2000. A monoclonal antibody to amyloid precursor protein induces neuronal apoptosis. *J. Neurochem.* 74:2331-2342.

Rose, N.R, Bona, C. 1993. Defining criteria for autoimmune diseases (Witebsky's postulates revisited) *Immunol. Today*. 14:426-30.

Rosenmann, H., Meiner, Z., Geylis, V., Abramsky, O., Steinitz, M. 2006a Detection of circulating antibodies against tau protein in its unphosphorylated and in its neurofibrillary tangles-related phosphorylated state in Alzheimer's disease and healthy subjects. *Neurosci. Lett.* 410:90-93.

Rosenmann, H., Grigoriadis, N., Karussis, D., Boimel, M., Touloumi, O., Ovadia, H., Abramsky, O. 2006b. Tauopathy-like abnormalities and neurologic deficits in mice immunized with neuronal tau protein. *Arch. Neurol.* 63:1459-1467.

Rousseau, A., Benyahia, B., Dalmau, J., Connan, F., Guillet, J.G., Delattre, J.Y., Choppin, J. 2005. T cell response to Hu-D peptides in patients with anti-Hu syndrome. *J. Neurooncol.* 71:231-236.

Rudehill S, Muhallab S, Wennersten A, von Gertten C, Al Nimer F, Sandberg-Nordqvist AC, Holmin S, Mathiesen T 2006 Autoreactive antibodies against neurons and basal lamina found in serum following experimental brain contusion in rats. *Acta. Neurochir.* (Wien). 148:199-205.

Sakai, K., Shirakawa, T., Kitagawa, Y., Li, Y., Hirose, G. 2001. Induction of cytotoxic T lymphocytes specific for paraneoplastic cerebellar degeneration-associated antigen in vivo by DNA immunization. *J. Autoimmun.* 17:297-302.

Sakic, B., Kirkham, D.L., Ballok, D.A., Mwanjewe, J., Fearon, I.M., Macri, J., Yu, G, Sidor, M.M., Denburg, J.A., Szechtman, H., Lau, J., Ball, A.K, Doering, L.C. 2005 Proliferating brain cells are a target of neurotoxic CSF in systemic autoimmune disease. *J. Neuroimmunol.* 169:68-85.

Saida, T., Saida, K., Silberberg, D.H., Brown, M.J. 1981. Experimental allergic neuritis induced by galactocerebroside. *Ann. Neurol.* 9:87-101.

Salih AM, Nixon NB, Dawes PT, Mattey DL 1998 Prevalence of antibodies to neurofilament polypeptides in patients with rheumatoid arthritis complicated by peripheral neuropathy. *Clin. Exp. Rheumatol.*16:689-94.

Schloot, N.C., Batstra, M.C., Duinkerken, G., De Vries, R.R., Dyrberg, T., Chaudhuri, A., Behan P.O., Roep, B.O. 1999 GAD65-Reactive T cells in a non-diabetic stiff-man syndrome patient. *J. Autoimmun.* 12:289-96.

Schmidt RE, Dorsey DA, Beaudet LN, Peterson RG. 2003 Analysis of the Zucker Diabetic Fatty (ZDF) type 2 diabetic rat model suggests a neurotrophic role for insulin/IGF-I in diabetic autonomic neuropathy. *Am. J. Pathol.* 163:21-8.

Slavin DA, Bucher AE, Degano AL, Soria NW, Roth GA 1996 Time course of biochemical and immunohistological alterations during experimental allergic encephalomyelitis. *Neurochem. Int.* 29:597-605.

Semra YK, Seidi OA, Sharief MK 2002 Heightened intrathecal release of axonal cytoskeletal proteins in multiple sclerosis is associated with progressive disease and clinical disability. *J. Neuroimmunol.* 122:132-9.

Serafini B, Rosicarelli B, Magliozzi R, Stigliano E, Capello E, Mancardi GL, Aloisi F 2006 Dendritic cells in multiple sclerosis lesions: maturation stage, myelin uptake, and interaction with proliferating T cells. *J. Neuropathol. Exp. Neurol.* 65(2):124-41.

Sheikh, K.A., Zhang, G., Gong, Y., Schnaar, R.L., Griffin, J.W. 2004 An anti-ganglioside antibody-secreting hybridoma induces neuropathy in mice. *Ann. Neurol.* 56:228-39.

Shigemoto, K., Kubo, S., Maruyama, N., Hato, N., Yamada, H., Jie C., Kobayashi, N., Mominoki, K., Abe, Y., Ueda, N., Matsuda, S. 2006. Induction of myasthenia by immunization against muscle-specific kinase. *J. Clin. Invest.* 116:1016-1024.

Shu XM, Cai FC, Zhang XP 2006Carbohydrate mimicry of Campylobacter jejuni lipooligosaccharide is critical for the induction of anti-GM1 antibody and neuropathy. *Muscle Nerve*. 33:225-31.

Sidor, M.M., Sakic, B., Malinowski, P.M., Ballok, D.A., Oleschuk, C.J., Macri, J. 2005. Elevated immunoglobulin levels in the cerebrospinal fluid from lupus-prone mice. *J. Neuroimmunol.* 65:104-113.

Silber, E., Semra, Y.K., Gregson, N.A., and Sharief, M.K. 2002. Patients with progressive multiple sclerosis have elevated antibodies to neurofilament subunit. *Neurology* 58:1372-1381.

Sillevis Smitt P, Manley G, Dalmau J, Posner J 1996 The HuD paraneoplastic protein shares immunogenic regions between PEM/PSN patients and several strains and species of experimental animals. *J. Neuroimmunol.* 71:199-206.

Singer HS, Morris CM, Williams PN, Yoon DY, Hong JJ, Zimmerman AW 2006 Antibrain antibodies in children with autism and their unaffected siblings. *J. Neuroimmunol.* 178:149-55.

Skoda D, Kranda K, Bojar M, Glosova L, Baurle J, Kenney J, Romportl D, Pelichovska M, Cvachovec K. 2006 Antibody formation against beta-tubulin class III in response to brain trauma. *Brain Res. Bull.* 68:213-6.

Smith PA. Morris-Downes MM., Heijmans, N., Pryce G., Arter E., O'Neill JK., Baker D., Amor S. 2005 Epitope Spread is not Critical for the relapse and progression of MOG 8-21 induced EAE in Biozzi ABH mice. *J. Neuroimmunol.* 164:76-84.

Smith, R.G., Alexianu, M.E., Crawford, G., Nyormoi, O., Stefani, E., Appel, S.H. 1994 Cytotoxicity of immunoglobulins from amyotrophic lateral sclerosis patients on a hybrid motoneuron cell line. *Proc. Natl. Acad. Sci.* 91:3393-3397.

Stein TD, Fedynyshyn JP, Kalil RE 2005 Circulating autoantibodies recognize and bind dying neurons following injury to the brain. *J. Neuropathol. Exp. Neurol.* 2002 61:1100-8.

Sommer C, Weishaupt A, Brinkhoff J, Biko L, Wessig C, Gold R, Toyka KV 2005 Paraneoplastic stiff-person syndrome: passive transfer to rats by means of IgG antibodies to amphiphysin. *Lancet.* 365:1406-11.

Soussan, L., Tchernakov, K., Bachar-Lavi, O., Yuvan, T., Wertman, E., Michaelson, D.M. 1994 Antibodies to different isoforms of the heavy neurofilament protein (NF-H) in normal aging and Alzheimer's disease. *Mol. Neurobiol.* 9:83-91.

Stubbs, E.B. Jr, Lawlor, M.W., Richards, M.P., Siddiqui, K., Fisher, M.A., Bhoopalam, N., Siegel, G. 2003Anti-neurofilament antibodies in neuropathy with monoclonal gammopathy of undetermined significance produce experimental motor nerve conduction block. *Acta. Neuropathol.* (Berl) 105:109-116.

Takahashi, Y., Mori, H., Mishina, M., Watanabe, M., Kondo, N., Shimomura, J., Kubota, Y., Matsuda, K., Fukushima, K., Shiroma, N., Akasaka, N., Nishida, H., Imamura, A., Watanabe H., Sugiyama N., Ikezawa M., Fujiwara T. 2005. Autoantibodies and cell-mediated autoimmunity to NMDA-type GluRepsilon2 in patients with Rasmussen's encephalitis and chronic progressive epilepsia partialis continua. *Epilepsia* 46; 5:152-158.

Tanaka, M., Tanaka, K., Shinozawa, K., Idezuka, J., Tsuji, S. 1998. Cytotoxic T cells react with recombinant Yo protein from a patient with paraneoplastic cerebellar degeneration and anti-Yo antibody. *J. Neurol. Sci.* 161:88-90.

Tanaka, K., Tanaka, M., Inuzuka, T., Nakano, R., Tsuji, S. 1999. Cytotoxic T lymphocyte-mediated cell death in paraneoplastic sensory neuronopathy with anti-Hu antibody. *J. Neurol. Sci.* 163:159-62.

Tanaka, K., Ding, X., Tanaka, M. 2004. Effects of antineuronal antibodies from patients with paraneoplastic neurological syndrome on primary-cultured neurons. *J. Neurol. Sci.* 217:25-30.

Takamori M, Hamada T, Komai K, Takahashi M, Yoshida A. 1994 Synaptotagmin can cause an immune-mediated model of Lambert-Eaton myasthenic syndrome in rats. *Ann. Neurol.* 35:74-80.

Takigawa, T., Yasuda, H., Kikkawa, R., Shigeta, Y., Saida, T., Kitasato, H. 1995 Antibodies against GM1 ganglioside affect K+ and Na+ currents in isolated rat myelinated nerve fibers. *Ann. Neurol.* 37:436-442.

Terryberry JW, Thor G, Peter JB 1998 Autoantibodies in neurodegenerative diseases: antigen-specific frequencies and intrathecal analysis. *Neurobiol. Aging.* 19:205-16.

Theiss, C., Napirei, M., Meller, K. 2005. Impairment of anterograde and retrograde neurofilament transport after anti-kinesin and anti-dynein antibody microinjection in chicken dorsal root ganglia. *Eur. J. Cell Biol.* 84:29-43.

Toro-Goyco, E., Cora, E.M., Kessler, M.J., Martinez-Carrion, M. 1986. Induction of experimental myasthenia gravis in rhesus monkeys: a model for the study of the human disease. P R Health. *Sci. J.* 5:13-18.

Towns R, Kabeya Y, Yoshimori T, Guo C, Shangguan Y, Hong S, Kaplan M, Klionsky DJ, Wiley JW 2005 Sera from patients with type 2 diabetes and neuropathy induce autophagy and colocalization with mitochondria in SY5Y cells. *Autophagy.* 1:163-70.

Toyka, K.V., Brachman, D.B., Pestronk, A., Kao, I. 1975 Myasthenia gravis: passive transfer from man to mouse. *Science.* 190:397-399.

Toyka KV, Drachman DB, Griffin DE, Pestronk A, Winkelstein JA, Fishbeck KH, Kao I 1977 Myasthenia gravis. Study of humoral immune mechanisms by passive transfer to mice. *N. Engl. J. Med.* 296:125-31.

Trapp, B.D., Peterson, J., Ransohoff, R.M., Rudick, R., Mork, S., Bo, L. 1998 Axonal transection in the lesions of multiple sclerosis. *N. Engl. J. Med.* 338:323-325.

Twyman RE, Gahring LC, Spiess J, Rogers SW. 1995 Glutamate receptor antibodies activate a subset of receptors and reveal an agonist binding site. *Neuron.* 14:755-62.

Van Geel WJ, Rosengren LE, Verbeek MM An enzyme immunoassay to quantify neurofilament light chain in cerebrospinal fluid. *J. Immunol. Methods.* 296:179-85.

Vedeler CA, Matre R, Kristoffersen EK, Ulvestad E 1991 IgG Fc receptor heterogeneity in human peripheral nerves. *Acta. Neurol. Scand.* 84:177-80.

Van Zwam M, Huizinga R, Wierenga,Wolf AF, Melief MJ, Van Meurs M, Voerman JS, Biber KPH, Boddeke HWGM, Hintzen RQ, 't Hart BA, Amor S, Laman JD, Boven LA 2006. Neuronal antigen-containing antigen presenting cells in cervical lymph nodes of multiple sclerosis patients and EAE animals are functionally distinct from myelin-containing cells. Congress abstract. *J. Neuroimmunol.* 178 (suppl 1):145.

Vincent A, Lily O, Palace J. 1999. Pathogenic autoantibodies to neuronal proteins in neurological disorders. *J. Neuroimmunol.* 100:169-80.

Vincent, A. 2006. Immunology of disorders of neuromuscular transmission. *Acta. Neurol. Scand. Suppl.* 183:1-7.

Vinik AI, Anandacoomaraswamy D, Ullal J 2005 Antibodies to neuronal structures: innocent bystanders or neurotoxins? *Diabetes Care.* 28:2067-72.

Wang ZY, Karachunski PI, Howard JF Jr, Conti-Fine BM. 1999. Myasthenia in SCID mice grafted with myasthenic patient lymphocytes: role of CD4+ and CD8+ cells. *Neurology.* 52:484-497.

Watanabe, K., Kim, S., Nishiguchi, M., Suzuki, H., Watarai, M., 2005. Brucella melitensis infection associated with Guillain-Barre syndrome through molecular mimicry of host structures. *FEMS Immunol. Med. Microbiol.* 45:121-127.

Williams, R.C. Jr, Sugiura, K., Tan, E.M. 2004. Antibodies to microtubule-associated protein 2 in patients with neuropsychiatric systemic lupus erythematosus. *Arthritis. Rheum.* 50:1239-1247.

Willison, H.J. 2005. The immunobiology of Guillain-Barre syndromes. *J. Peripher. Nerv. Syst.* 10:94-112.

Yang R, Puranam RS, Butler LS, Qian WH, He XP, Moyer MB, Blackburn K, Andrews PI, McNamara JO 2000 Autoimmunity to munc-18 in Rasmussen's encephalitis. *Neuron.* 28:375-83.

Zimmerman AW, Jyonouchi H, Comi AM, Connors SL, Milstien S, Varsou A, Heyes MP 2005 Cerebrospinal fluid and serum markers of inflammation in autism. *Pediatr Neurol.* 33:195-201.

Zanone MM, Petersen JS, Peakman M, Mathias CJ, Watkins PJ, Dyrberg T, Vergani D 1994 High prevalence of autoantibodies to glutamic acid decarboxylase in long-standing IDDM is not a marker of symptomatic autonomic neuropathy. *Diabetes.* 43:1146-51.

Zhang G, Lopez PH, Li CY, Mehta NR, Griffin JW, Schnaar RL, Sheikh KA. 2004. Anti-ganglioside antibody-mediated neuronal cytotoxicity and its protection by intravenous immunoglobulin: implications for immune neuropathies. *Brain.* 127:1085-100.

Zhang Y, Da RR, Hilgenberg LG, Tourtellotte WW, Sobel RA, Smith MA, Olek M, Nagra R, Gupta S, Van den Noort S, Qin Y 2005a. Clonal expansion of IgA-positive plasma cells and axon-reactive antibodies in MS lesions. *J. Neuroimmunol.* 167: 120-130.

Zhang Y, Da RR, Guo W, Ren HM, Hilgenberg LG, Sobel RA, Tourtellotte WW, Smith MA, Olek M, Gupta S, Robertson RT, Nagra R, Van den Noort S, Qin Y 2005b. Axon reactive B cells clonally expanded in the cerebrospinal fluid of patients with multiple sclerosis. *J. Clin. Immunol.* 25: 254-264.

Zhu, Y., Antony, J., Liu, S., Martinez, J.A., Giuliani, F., Zochodne, D., Power, C. 2006. CD8+ lymphocyte-mediated injury of dorsal root ganglion neurons during lentivirus infection: CD154-dependent cell contact neurotoxicity. *J. Neurosci.* 26:3396-3403.

In: New Immunology Research Developments
Editor: Gunter V. Müller

ISBN 978-1-60021-701-2


*Chapter 6*

# Neurologic Manifestations of West Nile Virus Infection

***Ronen Spiegel* and Yoseph Horovitz***
Pediatric Department A, HaEmek Medical Center, Afula,
Rappaport School of Medicine, Technion, Haifa

## Abstract

West Nile virus (WNV) infection is a zoonotic disease. The virus belongs to the family Flaviviridae. Wild birds serve as the reservoir of the virus in nature and mosquitoes mainly from the culex species serve as the vector for its replication cycle.

Humans as well as horses and other domestic animals are incidental hosts.

Until recently, WNV infections were traditionally considered to be a mild self-limited disease. When symptomatic it usually manifested with fever, headache, myalgia, generalized lymphadenopathy and rash. Central nervous system (CNS) involvement was infrequent. In the last decade, several epidemics of WNV have occurred in several areas in Europe, in Israel and, for the first time, in the Western Hemisphere, accounting for a large outbreak in New York. These epidemics were characterized by an exceptionally high rate of neurological morbidity and mortality.

The most common neurological involvement are encephalitis/meningoencephalitis followed by aseptic meningitis and flaccid paralysis. Other less common neurological presentations include Guillain-Barre syndrome, rhombencephalitis, optic neuritis and aphasia. The cause for this clinical evolution from a mild flu-like illness to a severe neuroinvasive disease is not fully understood and is thought in part to be related to the emergence of more neurovirulent WNV strains.

This article will discuss the wide range of neurologic manifestations of WNV infections, as well as the pathogenesis of WNV nervous system involvement and current and future therapeutic strategies.

* Tel: 972-4-6494316, Fax: 972-4-6495251, E-mail: spiegelr@zahav.net.il

# West Nile Virus (WNV)

This virus was first isolated from the blood of a febrile woman in the West Nile district of Uganda in 1937 [1]. The virus is a member of the genus Flavivirus, family Flaviviridae which also includes Japanese encephalitis, St. Louis encephalitis, Murray Valley encephalitis and Kunjin viruses [2]. WNV is a small spherical single stranded positive sense RNA virus of approximately 11,000 nucleotides associated with a core protein (nucleocapsid) and wrapped by a viral envelope which contains several proteins (of most importance is the envelope (E) protein), thought to be responsible for tissue tropism, attachment and entry into host cells and stimulation of host immune responses [3].

Phylogenetic studies demonstrated two distinct lineages of the virus. Strains belonging to lineage I have a worldwide distribution and are responsible for all the outbreaks occurring during the last decade including the 1996 Romania, 1999 Rusian (Volvograd), 1999 and 2000 United States and 2000 Israel. Lineage II strains are distributed mostly in Africa [4].

# Transmission and Replication

WNV is an arthropod-borne virus (arbovirus) which means it is transmitted between vertebrate hosts by mosquitoes serving as vectors. In nature, the virus has two replication cycles. The first is in mosquitoes, mainly from the culex species, and the second (amplifying) cycle occurs in wild birds particularly crows. Infected mosquitoes carry the virus in their gut and salivary glands and infect susceptible birds by biting them. The infected birds demonstrate a prolonged period and high level viremia enabling an amplification cycle with every new mosquito bite [5]. Humans as well as other domestic animals exhibit a shorter, low level, viremia period preventing the creation of a new transmission cycle and therefore serve as a dead-end hosts.

Despite this axiomatic hypothesis, several novel modes of transmission were reported including vertical infection from mothers to babies through breastfeeding, in utero transplacental infection, via transplanted infected organ or tissue, and percutaneous exposure from infected blood by laboratory and hospital workers [59].

This avian-mosquito-human interplay is considered to be the mode of introduction of this virus to the American continent at the end of the last century, either by migratory birds, imported infected birds or viremic humans. This global expansion of the virus is responsible for the 1999 New York West Nile outbreak [6,7].

# Clinical Features of the Non-Neurological West Nile Fever

The incubation period of WNV in humans usually range from 2-6 days, but may extend to 14 days [8]. When clinically symptomatic, West Nile fever is characterized by a flu-like illness beginning with an abrupt onset of high fever that may be accompanied by chills usually lasting 3-5 days. Other non specific symptoms may include general malaise, headache, myalgia, arthralgia, backache, vomiting, nausea, abdominal pain, diarrhea, maculopapular rash, conjunctivitis, and lymphadenopathy [8-10]. The later was thought to be more prevalent in symptomatic patients in previous outbreaks, but is uncommon in recent reports (less than 5%) [11].

Other less common manifestations may present in more severe cases and include hepatosplenomegaly [10], hepatitis, myocarditis [12] and pancreatitis [13].

Abnormal laboratory findings are usually mild and nonspecific and include either mild leukocytosis in less than 50% of the patients or mild leukopenia in less than 10% of the patients [11], mild anemia, mild thrombocytopenia, mild elevation of liver transaminases, and mild hypokalemia [11,14].

## Neurologic Manifestations

West Nile (WN) infection predominantly affects the nervous system. Involvement of the central nervous system (CNS) is associated with significant morbidity and mortality rates. In earlier WN epidemics neurologic involvement was considered to be a rare complication and therefore excellent prognosis was the rule in general [8-10]. By contrast, in recent epidemics neurologic manifestations predominated especially in the hospitalized cases [11,14,15].

In general, neurologic symptomatology may be divided into the following three main groups depending on the anatomic location of the nervous system part damaged:

1. Aseptic meningitis – when involving mainly the meninges.
2. Encepalitis or meningoencephalitis – when most of the inflammatory process involves the brain parenchyma with or without the meninges.
3. Myelitis – characterized by predominant spinal cord inflammation.

In some cases two or even three of these manifestations may coexist in the same patient.

Our discussion will concentrate on these three major neurologic presentations. We will also describe in brief other less common central nervous manifestations reported in the literature.

## Encephalitis

In several recent wide range WN epidemics, encephalitis was the most common presentation among hospitalized patients accounting for about 60% of hospital admissions [11,14,15]. Still, results of a household based seroepidemiological survey estimated that the 1999 New York epidemic consisted of about 8200 WNV human infections and since there were 59 cases of WN encephalitis (WNE), less than 1% of WNV infections suffered severe neurological disease [16]. The clinical course of WNE is usually abrupt with the triad of fever, headach and altered level of consciousness. This may resemble the clinical features of other causes of viral encephalitis including arthropod-borne viruses, enteroviruses etc. This similar nonspecific features makes it difficult to identify the offending pathogen in viral encephalitis based on clinical base [17]. Seizures were reported to occur more frequently in early reports of WN encephalitis but were uncommon in later outbreaks [11,14]. The cause for this change is not completely understood. The lack of convulsions is in contrast with Japanese encephalitis infections where seizures play a major role in the presentation of the disease [18].

Ataxia and extrapyramidal signs were reported in 17% of the cases in one report [15] but were uncommon in others [11,14]. Cranial nerve abnormalities were relatively rare and when they did occur were associated with high mortality rate [19].

The laboratory findings typical for WN encephalitis include cerebrospinal fluid (CSF) pleocytosis (mean 38-308 cells/mm$^3$, range 0-1750 cells/$^3$) with mild lymphocytic predominance, elevated CSF protein concentration (mean 85-110 mg/dL, range 18-1900 mg/dL) and normal glucose concentration. This CSF indices are nonspecific to the etiologic pathogen of the encephalitis and may be found in most other causes of viral encephalitis [17]. As a rule, when tested, CSF immunoglobulin M (IgM) -capture enzyme immunoassay (EIA) to WNV are usually found during the first week of illness. In the New York/New Jersey 2000 epidemic, almost all patients (18 out of 19) had positive CSF IgM-capture EIA and 9 of them had >four-fold serial change in plaque-reduction neutralizing antibody titer (PRNT) to WNV in paired, appropriately timed CSF samples [19]. By definition demonstration of IgM antibodies to WNV in the CSF by EIA or by >four-fold rise in PRNT antibodies are diagnostic for recent WNV infection with CNS involvement [20]. Detection of WNV in the CSF by either PCR techniques or by virus isolation is diagnostic for current CNS infection, however its utility in clinical practice is of limited value. In a study of patients serologically diagnosed as WNV meningoencephalitis using TaqMan reversed transcript (RT)-PCR on CSF samples the sensitivity was only 57% [21]. The sensitivity of RT-PCR for detection of WNV nucleic acids from the CSF was even lower during the New York/New Jersey 2000 epidemic as only 1 out of 13 confirmed meningoencephalitis patients was tested positive making this assay non reliable in daily non research practice [19].

Electroencephalogram (EEG) studies performed on encephalitic patients usually reveal generalized slow waves without convulsive tendency consistent with nonspecific encephalitis. No specific pattern for WNV infection was reported [11].

Brain computerized tomography (CT) performed in the acute encephalitic phase is normal in most cases and may reveal preexisting chronic lesions such as old infarcts, cortical atrophy and old hemorrhages and therefore this imaging technique is of no diagnostic value in these patients [11,14,19]. Initial brain magnetic resonance imaging (MRI) revealed nonspecific leptomeningeal and periventricular enhancement in 30% of the patients tested consistent with acute inflammatory process. However, this findings are non specific for WN infection [14].

Histologic features of WN encephalitis as demonstrated from autopsies of four patients in the 1999 New York epidemic showed minimal non specific evidence of viral inflammation in brain tissue. This included microglial nodules, perivascular cuffing, neuronal degeneration, neurophagia and focal inflammation involving mainly the medulla and the thalamus and less frequently the cerebellum and cerebrum. WNV was identified in autopsy brain tissue by either PCR and immunohistochemical stain [22,23].

In a search for risk factors associated with the development of WNE, the only independent risk factor found was an advanced age. This age related susceptibility was clearly demonstrated by the correlation of patients age groups versus symptomatic infection in general and versus CNS involvement in specific [15]. This unique age distribution is completely opposite to the age distribution of Japanese encephalitis virus infections where most of the CNS morbidity occurs among the pediatric group sparing the elderly group [18]. Although WN infection in the pediatric group usually carries a mild course with low CNS morbidity, children with immune deficiency states such as patients receiving chemotherapy, are at increased risk for severe CNS WN infection [24]. Immunocompromised patients were more vulnerable to severe WNV infection in all age groups. We found two case reports of HIV infected patients with CD4 counts below 200 cells/mm$^3$ who developed severe encephalitis [60]. Other case reports of immune deficient patients included two patients with lymphoma who developed WN encephalitis while receiving chemotherapy treatment. In both patients reported, the encephalitis evolved during the neutropenic phase [24,59]. This apparent relation was reinforced by the findings found during the 2000 Israeli outbreak where immunocompromised patients experienced statistically significant higher mortality rates compared with immunocompetent patients (31% vs. 13%) [11].

Apart from old age and the probable consequential immune deficiency, no underlying medical condition such as hypertension, chronic lung disease, or diabetes mellitus was statistically correlated with the development of encephalitis. However, encephalitic patients were found on a case control study to spend more time outdoors daily during the epidemic period. The authors speculated that this association is related to exposure to more bites of infected mosquitoes which increase the viral inoculum sufficient to invade the neural system to create a clinically significant infection [25].

The outcome of WN encephalitis is not favorable. As a rule all the fatalities reported were patients initially presenting with encephalitis that had a further clinical deterioration. Overall mortality/case ratio ranged from 4.3% [14,15] to 14% [11]. Among encephalitic patients alone the fatality rate was even higher reaching 19% in New York 1999 epidemic and 24% in the Israeli 2000 epidemic [11,14]. Among encephalitic patients over 75 years the prognosis was the poorest [14]. Recovery rates of WNE from one epidemic found that 37% recovered completely and 53% recovered partially 26% were ambulatory with assistance and 11% were bedridden. 26% required outpatient physical therapy, 16% required speech therapy, and 11% required occupational therapy after hospital discharge [19].

## Aseptic Meningitis

WN aseptic meningitis is clinically similar to all other etiologic viral meningitis [26]. Its clinical features include fever, headache, vomiting and signs of meningeal irritation (stiff neck, Brudjinski sign, Kernig sign). The lack of mental status change differentiates it from WN meningoencephalitis.

During the recent WN epidemics aseptic meningitis comprised 16%, 29% and 42% of all documented WN cases [11,14,19]. The clinical course is milder than that of encephalitis/meningoencephalitis and complete recovery without neurologic sequels should be expected. Typical CSF indices include pleocytosis with lymphocytic predominance, although some reports described a polymorphonuclear predominance most probably due to the early stage of the disease the lumbar puncture was performed [27], elevated protein concentration, normal glucose concentration and negative culture results.

In general patients presenting with aseptic meningitis tend to be younger than patients presenting with encephalitis. This age related clinical difference proved to be statistically significant during the Israeli 2000 epidemic [11].

## Acute Myelitis

Encephalomyelitis epidemics were reported previously in horses and birds following an infection with WNV. These reports described the concomitant expression of meningoencephalitis and acute myelitis (polio-like and non polio-like syndromes) in these animals [28-30].

The first report of acute anterior myelitis complicating WN fever in humans appeared in 1979. In their report Gadoth et al described a 22-year-old Israeli scuba diver who presented with an acute febrile illness and developed flaccid paresis of the lower left extremity with loss of deep tendon reflexes but without mental changes or sensory changes. Initial lumbar puncture revealed 94 cells/$mm^3$ and elevated protein concentration of 63 mg/dL. Subsequent spinal taps showed decrease in the WBC count and increase in the protein concentration. His disease natural course was of gradual recovery with resolution of muscle strength and deep tendon reflexes but mild diminution of the muscle strength of the affected limb remained [31].

Since this report no other WN cases of acute myelitis were documented until the epidemics in Romania and Russia during the last decade of the former century. In these reports 15-20% of the patients demonstrated variable degree of muscle weakness as well as lower extremities paresis or paralysis as part of their WN infection [32,33]. During the recent wide epidemics of WN in the United States and in Israel muscular and peripheral nervous involvement became a prominent neurological manifestation presenting as either non specific muscle weakness or flaccid paralysis. The New York 1999 epidemic reached the highest rate in this respect when according to Nash et al 27% of the patients experienced decreased muscle strength, 32% of the patients had hyporeflexia or afeflexia, and 10% of the patients had "true" flaccid paralysis without ascending or descending pattern of progression [14]. The clinical variability is wide and may range from muscle weakness alone involving the lower limbs without tendon reflex changes on the one hand, to quadriplegia with urinary retention due to bladder dysfunction, dysphagia and respiratory distress necessitating mechanical ventilation, on the other hand. The paresis may be symmetric or asymmetric and may involve either the upper limbs, lower limbs or both. Sensory function is usually spared. Laboratory findings in WN myelitis are similar to those found in central nervous WN infection (encephalitis/aseptic meningitis). When obtained the CSF reveals mild to moderate pleocytosis with lymphocyte predominance, elevated protein concentration, normal glucose concentration and negative culture results. When subsequent spinal taps are performed the WBC count tend to decrease concomitantly with increase in the protein concentration

[14,22]. When obtained WNV specific IgM capture antibodies were detected in the CSF by EIA [14,22].

MRI of the complete spinal cord was normal in the few patients it was performed and therefore is usually unnecessary if the diagnosis of WNV myelitis is definite [34,35]. Electromyography (EMG) and nerve conduction velocity (NCV) are the laboratory procedures most informative in these cases. In the New York 1999 epidemic 80% of the patients who underwent EMG and NCV studies demonstrated abnormal findings. This included reduced compound muscle potentials and fibrillation potentials, and reduced motor amplitudes with either normal or slightly decreased nerve conduction velocities[14,22]. These results were consistent with axonal type polyneuropathy with sparing of the sensory fibers and differed from the findings usually found in Guillain-Barre syndrome where nerve conduction studies usually reveal prolonged motor and sensory conduction rates due to demyelination [36].

In the last year two brief reports were published describing a specific poliomyelitis-like syndrome typical to WN infection in four different patients [37,38]. Polio virus infection produces a well-defined specific clinical entity characterized by the triad of asymmetric flaccid paralysis, diminished or absent tendon reflexes of the affected limbs and no paresthesias or sensory loss. This clinical syndrome is the result of the virus ability to attach to receptors in the anterior horn of the spinal cord. Laboratory findings typical to polio infection include CSF pleocytosis and elevated protein concentration [39]. Since the almost global eradication of polio virus from the developed countries with the aid of the combined inactivated polio vaccine (IPV) and the live attenuated oral polio vaccine (OPV), paralytic polio-like syndrome are caused by other RNA viruses including enteroviruses, echoviruses and coxsackiviruses [40]. Several case reports have associated poliomyelitis-like syndrome to other flaviviruses including Japanese encephalitis virus and dengue fever [41,42]. In 2003 Sejvar et al reported the greatest group of patients ever published with poliomyelitis-like syndrome due to WN infection. This report included a detailed clinical description, laboratory, and electrodiagnostic workup of seven patients who underwent a thorough evaluation. All patients present with acute asymmetric flaccid paralysis, decreased or absent tendon reflexes in the affected limb, and typical electrophysiologic findings suggesting anterior horn damage without sensory abnormalities [34].

All the patients were from Mississippi and Louisiana and were ill within a two-month period (July-August 2002). The age range of the patients was 39 to 69 years (mean 53 years old). This age group is significantly younger than the age group of WNE. Three of the seven patients reported had nuchal rigidity consistent with meningitis and three of the seven had mental status changes consistent with encephalitis. 5 of the patients had asymmetric upper limb involvement and 3 had asymmetric lower limb involvement. Electrodiagnostic studies showed reduced compound muscle action potentials of the affected extremity, widespread denervation and normal sensory nerve action potentials. These findings are consistent with severe asymmetric process affecting the anterior horn. Myopathy, demyelinating polyneuropathy and diffuse axonal polyneuropathy were not evident [34,43].

We found only one report of autopsy examination of the spinal cord in a patient with WN meningoencephalitis and polio-like paralysis. The macroscopic examination of the spinal cord was non remarkable. The microscopic examination showed a non specific chronic inflammatory infiltrate throughout the length of the spinal cord more prominent in the lumbar region [44].

The prognosis of WN myelitis depends on several factors. Bad prognostic factors include the presence of encephalitis, elderly patients, and severe spinal cord dysfunction. Death was either the result of severe encephalitis or the consequence of respiratory failure due to paralysis and malfunction of the respiratory muscles.

Mild cases (only muscle weakness) usually achieved complete recovery but in most cases of moderate to severe paralysis certain degree of weakness remained [14,19,34,36]. In the subgroup of polio-like syndrome most of the patients remained with a certain degree of limb weakness [37,38].

In general WN encephalitic patients accompanied by muscle weakness were more likely to bear a poorer prognosis compared with encephalitic patients with preserved muscle strength. In the first group the case fatality rate reached 30% [14].

In summary, WNV infection is associated with a heterogenous neurologic manifestations that include muscle weakness, flaccid paralysis and a well defined poliomyelitis-like syndrome. A strict detailed clinical documentation along with laboratory tests, electrophysiologic studies and neuroimaging should be conducted in order to better define and understand the etiology and pathogenesis of this WN flaccid paralysis clinical spectrum.

## Rare Neurological Manifestations

Aside from the three main neurologic manifestations of WNV infection i.e encephalitis, aseptic meningitis and acute myelitis (poliomelitis-like and non poliomyelitis-like) other rare neurologic manifestations were reported in the recent epidemics mainly as isolated case reports.

*Guillain-Barre syndrome (GBS)* – During the 1999 New York WN epidemic Ahmed et al described a 65-year-old man who presented with decreased muscle strength of upper and lower limbs associated with areflexia numbness and sensory changes in his hands and feet. During his hospital stay he developed bilateral peripheral facial nerve palsy, his weakness progressed and he became bedridden and as a result of a further respiratory distress he required mechanical ventilation. CSF sample revealed elevated protein concentration without WBC. EMG and NCV studies revealed prolonged distal motor and sensory latencies, reduced compound motor action potentials (CMAP), and unobtainable F and H waves. These findings were consistent with demyelinating polyneuropathy with secondary motor axon degeneration. WNV-PCR and WNV specific IgM-capture antibodies from the CSF were both positive. The patient was diagnosed as GBS secondary to WN infection. Despite 5 courses of plasmapheresis and two courses of intravenous gammaglobulins he experienced only slight improvement of muscle strength [45].

GBS is an autoimmune disorder of the peripheral nervous system resulting in inflammation and demyelination hence it is often termed acute demyelinating polyradiculoneuropathy (AIDP). GBS patients typically present with symmetric muscle weakness initially affecting the lower limbs and progressing in an ascending form to involve upper limbs and respiratory muscles [46]. Classically, abnormal sensation such as tingling and numbness in the hands and face accompany the motor deficits. Tendon reflexes are either reduced or absent. The CSF protein concentration is elevated with a paucity of WBC. This phenomenon was termed albuminocytologic dissociation. Several infectious pathogens are associated with preceding the development of the syndrome by a mechanism of molecular mimicry in which the immune response to specific antigens or infectious organisms attack similar epitopes in the peripheral nervous system of the host. In this respect the most common pathogens known to cause GBS are cytomegalo virus (CMV), Epstein-Barr virus (EBV), campylobacter jejuni, mycoplasma pneumonia, several herpes viruses, etc [36]. The precise mechanism in which WNV causes GBS is yet to be discovered. We assume that WNV induced GBS is a unique clearly defined presentation that might be included within the heterogenous group of WN myelitis.

*Optic neuritis* – During the Israeli 2000 WN outbreak Vaispapir et al. described a 55-year-old woman who was admitted with clinical symptoms symptoms consistent with meningoencephalitis. Her CSF contained 400 WBC/mm$^3$, elevated protein concentration, normal glucose concentration and a negative culture. During her hospitalization she experienced neurologic deterioration with the development of right abducens and facial cranial nerve palsies, blurred vision with progressive worsening of visual acuity and severe cerebellar ataxia. Ophthalmologic examination revealed bilateral optic disk swelling more prominent on the right side, constriction of visual field, and relative afferent pupillary defect (ARPD). Diagnosis of acute WNV infection was made by positive serum specific WNV-IgM antibodies. She gradually recovered on conservative treatment and was discharged after 30 days. Mild ataxia, blurred vision and right optic disc swelling were still present on discharge and long-term follow up was not reported [47].

Optic neuritis is a self limited condition characterized by unilateral or bilateral blurring of vision which may progress to almost complete loss of vision over days to weeks. Other clinical features include pain in the affected eye, loss of colour vision, visual field defects, and RAPD on ophthalmologic examination [48]. The most common underlying cause of optic neuritis is multiple sclerosis. Viral infections may cause optic neuritis by two mechanisms. This includes viral induced optic neuritis as part of a CNS infection most commonly by neurovirulent pathogens. The second mechanism is a postinfectious inflammatory optic neuritis. In the latter, the patient usually presents with bilateral and simultaneous eye involvement. Based on the case report described above, it appears that WNV may cause optic neuritis by direct inflammation of the optic nerve as well as other cranial nerves (abducens and facial nerves).

Although systemic steroids may hasten the speed of visual recovery it does not improve the ultimate visual outcome [48]. Therefore in WNV associated optic neuritis there seems to be no additional role for steroid treatment at present and expectant approach should be preferred by the physician in charge. One should also weigh the potential risk of exacerbating the disease course by using steroids.

*Rhombencephalitis* – During the 1999 New York outbreak Nichter et al described a 15-year-old boy who was hospitalized because of fever, headache, and acute confusion. The CSF examination on admission revealed pleocytocis with lymphocytic predominance and elevated protein concentration. During his stay he developed difficulties in swallowing due to depressed gag reflex which necessitated the insertion of nasogastric tube for feeding, truncal ataxia and bilateral facial weakness. The boy experienced a gradual course of recovery, with the use of auxiliary supportive treatment, which lasted six months. Positive CSF specific IgM antibodies to WNV confirmed the etiologic cause of his disease [49].

Rhombencephalitis is the term used to define specific encephalitis involving the brain stem. In most cases the cause of rhomencephalitis is infectious. The most common etiologic pathogens are: Listeria monocytogenes, Micoplasme pneumonia, herpes simplex viruses, EBV, influenza A virus, varicella, adenovirus, echoviruses and enteroviruses [50-52]. Perhaps, the most important etiologic pathogen associated with this relatively rare complication is enterovirus 71. In 1998 a wide epidemic of this virus was reported in Taiwan, accompanied by a high rate of morbidity and mortality due to rhombencephalitis [40]. Among the flaviviruses only Japanese encephalitis virus was reported previously to cause rhombencephalitis although this manifestation is rare in the clinical spectrum of this virus [18].

MRI studies performed in patients with rhombencephalitis showed that the majority of lesions are located in the pontine tegmentum followed by the medulla oblongata, midbrain, and dentate nuclei in decreased order [40,53]. The prognosis depends on the severity of rhombencepalitis. Grade I lesions are associated with cranial nerve palsies and ataxia and have a milder self limited course in most cases. Grade III lesions are associated by cardiopulmonary failure and significant morbidity and mortality [40].

Unfortunately, in the WN patient described by Nichter MRI was not performed during the acute stage of the illness. Late image during the convalescent stage was unremarkable [49].

*Aphasia* – During the 2000 Israeli WN epidemic we reported a 4-year-old boy with Hodgkin's lymphoma receiving chemotherapy treatment who was admitted with acute febrile illness. During his stay he became neutropenic in parallel to the development of meningoencephalitis. His serum WNV-IgM specific antibodies were positive. His disease course was predominated by generalized seizures and global aphasia. He was treated with oral ribavirin and intensive supportive care including speech therapy. Complete recovery was achieved within months with motor aphasia being the last to recover [24].

Aphasia is a defined neurological entity characterized by the loss of comprehension and formulation of language. Aphasia is usually the result of lesions located in the left hemisphere of the brain. The most common insults known to cause aphasia are stroke, head injury, cerebral tumors, degenerative CNS diseases and CNS infections. There are several types of aphasia defined by their clinical typical features and the exact anatomic location of the offending cerebral lesion. The classic aphasia variants include Broca's aphasia, Wernicke's aphasia, conduction aphasia, global aphasia and transcortical aphasia [54,55].

The child we described presented with features compatible most with the global aphasia variant. The cerebral part known to be affected in global aphasia are the frontal and temporoparietal left hemisphere [55]. Unfortunately, MRI study was not conducted in this patient and therefore there was no imaging correlation with the clinical symptoms.

## Pathogenesis of WNV Neural Damage

Following an infected mosquito bite an initial replication develops at the bite site (skin and regional lymph nodes) which produces the primary viremia. The virus then seeds the reticuloendothelial system (RES) where it replicates to produce the second viremia. During this viremia the virus may be isolated from the blood (usually within two days before the beginning of clinical symptoms to four days during the disease course). Isolation of the virus depends on the duration and the level of the viremia with the latter being more important [56,57]. Following the second viremia the virus may reach any organ including the nervous system. Virus replication occurs in monocytes/macrophages and in peripheral tissues mainly the RES. At this point the course of the disease, its severity and the target organs involved depends on both host and viral factors. Host factors include the immune system (humoral and cell mediated), the efficacy of the blood brain barrier (BBB) in preventing invasion to the CNS and other factors such as age, medications, pre morbid state etc. Viral factors include tissue tropism (for example WNV has nervous system tropism), virulence elements, and its ability to change its nucleic acid composition. Perhaps the most important factor in WNV virulence is the E protein which mediates cell attachment and neuroinvasiveness [56]. Finally, intracellular viral-host cell interactions play a major role in the ability of WNV to replicate and to successfully assemble virion particles to exit the infected host cell [57]. Recent study in this field demonstrated in inbred mice an allele termed *Oas 1b* that confers resistance to flaviviruses in mice. A truncated protein product due to a stop codon confers these mutated mice susceptible to flavivirus infection [58]. Expression of the resistant allele of *Oas1b* in susceptible embryo fibroblasts resulted in partial inhibition of the replication of a flavivirus [58]. There is no homologous *Oas 1b* mouse gene in the human genome but this knowledge may play a role in future antiviral medication.

WNV is a neurotropic virus. Evidence of its presence in neural tissues was demonstrated by several techniques. Only recently, the virus was successfully isolated for the first time from the CSF of a patient with WNE [59]. Former molecular studies in patients with WNE detected viral nucleic acids in the CSF using TaqMan RT-PCR technique [14]. Finally, autopsy studies in patients who died from WNE demonstrated by using immunohistochemical staining the presence of viral antigens in neurons, neuronal processes, and areas of necrosis [22,24]. In order to cause nervous system infection WNV should cross the BBB. The port of entry into the CNS is probably via hematogenous spread. The virus may produce a third replication cycle in the endothelial cells at the BBB. Another proposed mechanism of invading the nervous system is by neuronal transport via axons and nerve processes.

By knowing the factors that influence viral entry into the CNS, we are now able to undestand more precisely some of the risk factors related to severe neurologic presentations:

1. Immune deficiency states –We mentioned earlier the high rate of WN encephalitis among patients with certain degree of immunosupression such as HIV [60], malignant diseases with chemotherapy induced myelosupression [24,59], etc. Earlier reports emphasized that in immunocompromised patients there is higher magnitude and duration of viremia [61]. This may promote the virus ability to invade the BBB.

2. Elderly – The association between older age and higher rates of hypertension and vascular diseases such as diabetes mellitus is well documented. These vascular, age related lesions may disrupt cerebral endothelium enabling higher proportion of viral entry into the CNS.

Pathologic studies in WN patients with brain parenchimal disease (encephalitis) and spinal cord disease (myelitis) demonstrated two mechanisms of neural tissue damage. The presence of viral antigens within damaged neuronal and glial cells suggests direct viral induced cytolysis. The second mechanism is an inflammatory neuronal damage demonstrated by perivascular cuffing, microglial nodules, and leukocyte infiltration. Microglial nodules are composed of lymphocytes and histiocytes and represent host inflammatory reaction to neuronal damage [22,24].

Parenchimal damage was more prominent in the brain stem, medulla cerebrum especially the temporal lobes and the proximal spinal cord especially the anterior horn [22,24]. This anatomic predilection of WNV in humans is in correlation with the clinical manifestations described above and may suggest targeted neurotropism. The factors that influence this targeted neurotropism are presently unknown. Further studies are needed to reveal them.

WNV infection in humans elicit both humoral and cell mediated immune response. WNV specific neutralizing antibodies are produced against viral epitopes especially against the E protein which provides viral attachment properties. These antibodies have a significant role in host defense during the acute infection and may be found in the serum of infected patients during the first week of infection (IgM antibodies). The switch to an IgG antibody response occurs after 4-5 days on average [62]. The presence of WNV-IgM antibodies in the CSF reflects CNS involvement since IgM antibodies are unable to cross the BBB. Another evidence for the autonomic WN antibody local production in the CNS was suggested by Tardei et al. These researchers showed that in several WNE patients when recurrent paired serum and CSF samples were taken simultaneously during disease course IgM antibodies appeared in the CSF before they were found in the serum [62]. CSF WNV specific antibodies protect brain parenchyma by reducing viral replication and by interfering with viral attachment to neuronal cells surface. It is believed that after recovery WNV IgG specific antibodies confer long-term immunity against reinfection [63].

We learn about the importance of cell-mediated immunity in host defense against WNV infections from indirect data. For example the higher prevalence of CNS involvement in patients with cell-mediated immune deficiency states such as HIV patients [60], and patients receiving chemotherapy [24,59]. Yet, its exact role and the complex interplay it has with humoral immunity is not understood and further studies are needed to disclose them.

Animal histologic studies in monkeys and hamsters confirmed persistent CNS infection [64,65]. Similar studies were not performed in humans and, therefore, it is not known whether the mechanism for permanent neurological damage is persistent inflammatory process in the brain parenchyma, or irreversible neurologic damage that was caused during the acute infection. We believe, clinical complete recovery after WNE or WN myelitis is correlated with compatible histologic complete resolution.

# Treatment of Neural WN Infection

In non neurologic WN infections the treatment is symptomatic. Self limited course is expected in most uncomplicated cases [56].

Treatment in neurologic WN cases is divided into general supportive treatment and specific antiviral therapy. Supportive care includes anticonvulsive medications in cases where seizure activity predominates the clinical course. The most frequent cause of death in WNE is cerebral edema [66]. Early diagnosis of this life-threatening condition should be followed by immediate initiation of mannitol. Steroids also may be used to reduce cerebral edema although their beneficial use should be carefully weighed against their potential risk of exacerbating the viral infection. WNE may require intensive care setup in severe complicated cases including mechanical ventilation, nasogastic feeding etc. During the recovery stage patients may benefit from physical therapy, occupational therapy, and speech therapy depending on their degree of disability [19,66].

There is no established antiviral treatment for WNE or other flavivirus infection. Several antiviral agents were studied in-vitro and in vivo. For most agents we found only anecdotal case reports. Double blind placebo controlled studies are therefore needed to confirm efficacy of all the proposed medications.

Antiviral therapy for WN encephalitis may be divided into three categories: 1. Purine and pyramidine analogues (ribavirin); 2. Interferon α 2b; and 3. Intravenous immunoglobulins.

Ribavirin is a synthetic guanosine analogue that inhibits replication of DNA and RNA viruses [67]. Ribavirin is effective against hepatitis C virus which also belongs to the flaviviridae family. This evidence raised the hypothesis that it also may be effective against other flaviviruses such as WNV, Japanese encephalitis virus and St Louis encephalitis virus. In vitro studies on incubated human neural cells demonstrated that high doses of ribavirin are effective in inhibiting WNV replication as measured by RT-PCR, and in decreasing the cytopathic effect of WNV on neural cells [68] Based on these data several case descriptions of ribavirin treatment in WNE were reported with variable degrees of success [11,24,69]. Controlled studies are still needed to confirm its efficacy. Wide range epidemics such as the 1996 Romanian, 1999 New York, and 2000 Israeli may serve as population base for this kind of study, but strict inclusion criteria should be defined ahead. Another nucleoside analogue pyridazine nucleoside was found to be effective in preventing WN replication in in-vitro studies.

Interferon α 2b is a known antiviral agent in routine use for hepatitis C infection. Open clinical trials using this agent in other flaviviruses (St. Louis encephalitis and Japanese encephalitis viruses) have shown promising results thus far [70,71]. Several case reports of the use of interferon alpha in WN patients were reported with variable degree of success [69]. Based on these data an open randomized clinical trial of the efficacy of interferon alpha in WN patients is conducted by Rahal. Eligible criteria for entering the study include age above 50 years and initiation of therapy within the first four days of hospitalization (in order to prevent irreversible CNS damage in this high risk age group) [72].

Intravenous immunoglobulin preparation was shown to be dramatically effective in an Israeli 70-year-old WNE patient who was in a coma on initiation of treatment. When checked for the content of specific WNV antibodies this preparation was found to have a high content of the specific antibodies. This is most probably a reflection of the endemic character of this virus in Israel [73]. The protective role of specific WNV antibodies in host immunity was comprehensively discussed above. We conclude that specific WNV immunoglobulin preparations may be useful in severe cases.

Regardless of antiviral agent used, our aim is to begin treatment early in the course of the disease in order to prevent the development of encephalitis. To be able to initiate early therapy one must have rapid, widely available, and highly reliable diagnostic tests.

Finally, at present no specific WNV immunization is available although research in this field is active [74,75]. The development of effective formalin inactivated vaccine for Japanese encephalitis virus [17] is encouraging that similar vaccination for WNV will be available in the future.

In the absence of such reliable vaccine prevention of WNV, infections will continue to depend on public education, national vector (mosquito) control programs, and prospective surveillance of infected mosquitoes, birds and horses [76-78].

## References


[1] Smithburn KC, Hughes TP, Burke AW, Paul JH. A neurotropic virus isolated from the blood of a native Uganda. *Am. J. Trop. Med.* 1940; 20:471-492.

[2] Gubler DJ, Roehring JT. Togaviruses and Flaviviridae. In: CollierL, Balows A, Sussman M, editors. *Topley and Wilson's microbiology and microbial infections*. London: Arnold Publishing; 1999 p. 579-600.

[3] Heinz FX, Collett MS, Purcell RH, Gould EA, Howard CR, Houghton M et al. Family: Flaviviridae. In: Van Regenmortel MHV, Fauquet CM, Bishop DHL,Carstens EB, Estes MK, Lemon SM et al, editors. Virus taxonomy: classification and nomenclature of viruses. *7th Report of the International Committee on Taxonomy of Viruses*. San Diego: Academy Press; 1999. p. 859-878.

[4] Lanciotti RS, Ebel GD, Deubel V, et al. Complete genome sequences and phylogenetic analysis of West Nile virus strains isolated from United States, Europe, and the Middle East. *Virology* 2002; 298: 96-105.

[5] Rappole JH, Derrickson SR, Hubalek Z. Migratory birds and spread of West Nile virus in Western Hemisphere. *Emerg. Infect. Dis.* 2000; 6:319-328.

[6] Turell MJ, Sardelis MR, Dohm DJ, O'guinn ML. Potential North American vectors of West Nile virus. *Ann.. NY Acad. Sci.* 2001; 951:317-324.

[7] Lanciotti RS, Roering JT, Deubel V, et al. Origin of West Nile virus responsible for an outbreak of encephalitis in the northeastern United States. *Science* 1999; 286:2333-2337.

[8] Goldblum N, Sterk VM, Paderski B. The clinical features of the disease and theisolation of West Nile virus from the blood nine human cases. *Am. J. Hygiene* 1954; 59:89-103.

[9] Spingland I, Jasinska-Klingberg W, Hofshi E, Goldblum N. Clinical and laboratory observations in the outbreak of West Nile fever in Israel in 1957. *Harefuah* 1958; 54:275-281.

[10] Marberg K, Goldblum K, Sterk VV, Jasinska-Klingberg W, Klingberg MA. The natural history of West Nile fever. I. Clinical observations during an epidemic in Israel. *Am. J. Hygiene* 1956; 64:259-269.

[11] Chowers MY, Lang R, Nassar F, et al. Clinical characteristics of the West Nile fever outbreak, Israel, 2000. *Emerg. Infect. Dis*. 2001; 7:675-678.

[12] Solomon T, Vaughn DW, Clinical features and pathophysiology of Japanese encephalitis and West Nile virus infections. In: Mackenzie JS, Barrett AD, Deubel V, eds. Current topics in microbiology and immunology: *Japanese encephalitis and West Nile virus infections*. Berlin: Springer-Verlag, 2002:171-194.

[13] Perelman A, Stern J. Acute pancreatitis in West Nile fever. *Am. J. Trop. Med. Hyg.* 1974; 23:1150-1152.

[14] Nash D, Mostashari F, Fine A, et al. The outbreak of West Nile infection in the New York city area in 1999. *N. Eng. J. Med*. 2001; 344:1807-1814.

[15] Tsai TF, Popovici F, Cernescu C, Campbell GL, Nedelcu NI. West Nile encephalitis epidemic in southeastern Romania. *Lancet* 1998; 352:767-771.

[16] Mostashari F, Bunning ML, Kitsutani PT, et al. Epidemic West Nile encephalitis, New York, 1999: results of a household-based seroepidemiological survey. *Lancet* 2001; 358:261-264.

[17] Whitlley RJ, Gnann JW. Viral encephalitis: familiar infections and emerging pathogens. *Lancet* 2002; 359:507-514.

[18] Solomon T, Dung NM, Kneen R, Gainsborough M, Vaughn DW, Khanh VT. Japanese encephalitis. *J. Neurol. Neurosurg. Psychiatry* 2000; 68:405-415.

[19] Weiss D, Carr D, Kellachan J et al. Clinical findings of West Nile virus infection in hospitalized patients, New York and New Jersey, 2000. *Emerg. Infect. Dis*. 2001; 7:654-8.

[20] Cennters for Disease Control and Prevention. Case definitions for infectious conditions under public health surveillance. *MMWR Morb. Mortal. Wkly. Rep*. 1997; 46:1-55.

[21] Lanciotti RS, Kerst AJ, Nasci RS, et al. Rapid detection of West Nile virus from human clinical specimens, field collected mosquitoes, andd avian samples by a Taqman reverse transcriptase-PCR assay. *J. Clin. Microbiol*. 2000; 38:4066-4071.

[22] Asnis DS, Conetta R, Teixeira AA, Waldman G, Sampson BA. The West Nile virus outbreak of 1999 in New York: The Flushing hospital experience. *Clin. Infect. Dis*. 2000; 30:413-418.

[23] Shieh WJ, Guarner J, Layton M et al. The role of pathology in an investigation of an outbreak of West Nile encephalitis in New York, 1999. *Emerg. Infect. Dis*. 2000; 6:370-372.

[24] Spiegel R, Miron D, Gavriel H, Horovitz Y. West Nile meningoencephalitis complicated by motor aphasia in hodgkin's lymphoma. *Arch. Dis. Child* 2002; 86:441-442.

[25] Han LL, Popovici F, Alexander JP, et al. Risk factors for West Nile virus infection and meningoencephalitis, Romania, 1996. *J. Infect. Dis*. 1999; 179:230-233.

[26] Rotbart H. Viral meningitis and the aseptic meningitis syndrome. In: Scheld W, Whitley R, Durack D, editors. Infections of the central nervous system. Philadelphia: *Lippincot-Raven Publishers*; 1997. p. 239-263.

[27] Flatau E, Kohn D, Daher O, Varsano N. West Nile fever encephalitis. *Isr. J. Med. Sci.* 1981; 17:1057-1059.

[28] Cantile C, Di Guardo G, Eleni C, Arispici M. Clinical and neuropathological features of West Nile virus equine encephalomyelitis in Italy. *Equine Vet. J.* 2000; 32:31-35.

[29] Cantile C, Del Piero F, Di Guardo G, Arispici M. Pathologic and immunohistochemical findings in naturally occurring West Nile virus infection in horses. *Vet. Pathol.* 2001; 38:414-421.

[30] Steele KE, Linn MJ, Schoepp RJ et al. Pathology of fatal West Nile virus infections in native and exotic birds during the 1999 outbreak in New York City, New York. *Vet. Pathol.* 2000; 37:208-224.

[31] Gadoth N, Weitzman S, Lehmann E. Acute anterior myelitis complicating West Nile fever. *Arch. Neurol.* 1979; 36:172-173.

[32] Platonov AE, Shipulin GA, Shipulina OY. Outbreak of West Nile infection, Volvograd region, Russia, 1999. *Emerg. Infect. Dis.* 2001; 7:128-132.

[33] Cenescu C, Ruta SM, Tardei G, et al. A high number of severe neurologic clinical forms during an epidemic of West Nile virus infection. *Rom. J. Virol.* 1997; 48:13-25.

[34] Sejvar JJ, Leis AA, Stokic DS, et al. *Acute flaccid paralysis and West Nile virus infection*. 2003; 7:788-793.

[35] Ohry A, Kaprin H, Yoeli D, Lazari A, Lerman Y. West Nile virus melitis. *Spinal Cord* 2001; 39:662-663.

[36] Joseph SA, Tsao CY. Guillain Barre syndrome. *Adolesc. Med.* 2002; 3:487-494.

[37] Leis AA, Stokic DS, Polk JL, Dostrow V, Winkelmann M. A poliomyelitis-like syndrome from West Nile virus infection. *N. Eng. J. Med.* 2002; 347:1279-1280.

[38] Glass JD, Samuels O, Rich MM. Poliomyelitis due to West Nile virus. *N. Eng. J. Med.* 2002; 347:1280-1281.

[39] Ohka S, Nomoto A. Recent insights into poliovirus pathogenesis. *Trends Microbiol.* 2001;9:501-506.

[40] Huang C, Liu C, Chang Y. Neurologic complications in children with enterovirus 71 infection. *N. Eng. J. Med.* 1999; 341:936-942.

[41] Solomon T, Kneen R, Dung N et al. Poliomyelitis-like illness due to Japanese encephalitis virus. *Lancet* 1998; 351:1094-1097.

[42] Sumarmo W, Jahja E, Gubler D, Suharyono W, Sorenson K. Clinical observations on virologically confirmed fatal dengue infections in Jakarta, Indonesia. *Bull World Health Organ* 1983; 61:693-701.

[43] Centers for Disease Control and Prevention. Acute flaccid paralysis syndrome associated with West Nile virus infection Mississippi and Louisiana, July-August 2002. *MMWR Morb. Mortal Wkly. Rep.* 2002; 51:825-828.

[44] Kelley TW, Prayson RA, Ruiz AI, Isada CM, Gordon SM. The neuropathology of West Nile virus meningoencephalitis: A report of two cases and review of the literature. *Am. J. Clin. Pathol.* 2003; 119:749-753.

[45] Ahmed S, Libman R, Wesson K, Ahmed F, Einberg K. Guillain Barre syndrome: An unusual presentation of West Nile virus infection. *Neurology* 2000; 55:144-146.

[46] Asbury AK, Cornblath DR. Assesment of current diagnostic criteria for the diagnosis of Guillain Barre syndrome. *Ann. Neurol.* 1990; 27(suppl):S21-S24.

[47] Vaispapir V, Blum A, Soboh, S, Ashkenazi H. West Nile virus meningoencephalitis with optic neuritis. *Arch. Intern. Med.* 2002; 162:606-607.

[48] Hickman SJ, Dalton CM, Miller DH, Plant GT. Management of optic neuritis. *Lancet* 2002; 360:1953-1962.

[49] Nichter CA, Pavlakis SG, Shaikh U. Rhombencephalitis caused by west Nile fever virus. *Neurology* 2002; 55:153.

[50] Armstrong RW, Pung PC. Braistem encephalitis (rhombencephalitis) due to Listeria monocytogenes: case report and review. *Clin. Infect. Dis.* 1993; 16:689-702.

[51] Hurst DL, Mehta S. Acute cerebellar swelling in varicella encephalitis. *Pediatr. Neurol.* 1988; 4:122-123.

[52] Shian WJ, Chi CS. Fatal brainstem encephalitis caused by Epstein-Barr virus. *Pediatr. Radiol.* 1994; 24:596-597.

[53] Protheroe SM, Mellor DH. Imaging in influenza A encephalitis. *Arch. Dis. Child* 1991; 66:702-705.

[54] Damasio AR. Aphasia. *N. Eng. J. Med.* 1992; 326:531-539.

[55] Kreisler A, Godefroy O, Delmaire C. The anatomy of aphasia revisited. *Neurology* 2000; 54:1117-1123.

[56] Campbell GL, Marfin AA, Lanciotti RS, Gubler DJ. West Nile virus. *Lancet Infect. Dis.* 2002; 2:519-529.

[57] Marfin AA, Gubler DJ. West Nile encephalitis: an emerging disease in the United States. *Clin. Infect. Dis.* 2001; 33:1713-1719.

[58] Perelygin AA, Scherbik SV, Zhulin IB, Stockman BM, Li Y, Brinton MA. Positional cloning of the murine flavivirus resistance gene. *Proc. Natl. Acad. Sci. USA* 2002; 9:9322-9327.

[59] Huang C, Slater B, Rudd R, et al. First isolation of West Nile virus from a patient with encephalitis in the United States. *Emerg. Infect. Dis.* 2002; 8:1367-1371.

[60] Rimland D, Koplan J, Stephen DS. Conference summary: West Nile virus southeast conference *Emerg. Infect. Dis.* 2003; 9:897-898.

[61] Southam CM, Moore AE. Clinical studies of viruses as antineoplastic agents, with particular reference to Egypt 101 virus. *Cancer* 1952; 5:1025-1034.

[62] Tardei G, Ruta S, Chitu V, Rossi C, Tsai TF, Cerenscu C. Evaluation of immunoglobulin M (IgM) and IgG enzyme immunoassays in serologic diagnosis of West Nile virus infection. *J. Clin. Microbiol.* 2000; 38:2232-2239.

[63] Hubalek Z. Comparative symptomatology of West Nile fever. *Lancet* 2001; 358:254-255.

[64] Pogodina VV, Frolova MP, Malenko GV, et al. Study on West Nile virus persistence in monkeys. *Arch. Virol.* 1983; 75:71-86.

[65] Xiao SY, Guzman H, Zhang H, et al. West Nile virus infection in the golden hamster (Mesocricetus auratus): a model for west Nile encephalitis. *Emerg. Infect. Dis.* 2001; 714-721.

[66] Solomon T, Ooi MH, Beasley DWC, Mallewa M. West Nile encephalitis. *BMJ* 2003; 326:865-869.

[67] Hayden FG. Ribavirin. In: Mandell GL, Bennet JE, Dalin ,R, eds. *Principles and practice of infectious diseases,* 5$^{th}$ ed. Churchill Livingston Inc, 2000; p. 477-9.

[68] Jordan I, Briese T, Fischr N, Lau JYN, Lipkin WI. Ribavirin inhibits West Nile virus replication and cytopathic effect in neural cells. *J. Infect. Dis.* 2000; 182:1214-1217.

[69] Anderson JF, Rahal JJ. Efficacy of interferon α-2b and ribavirin against West Nile virus in vitro. *Emerg. Infect. Dis.* 2002; 8:107-108.

[70] Rahal J, Anderson J, Rosenberg C, Reagan T, Thompson L. Effect of interferon alpha-2b on St Louis (SL) virus meningoencephalitis: clinical and laboratory results. *Infectious Diseases Society of America*, 40$^{th}$ Meeting 2002, Chicago, II:A823.

[71] Solomon T, Dung NM, Wills B et al. A double blind placebo controlled trial of interferon alpha in Japanese encephalitis. *Lancet* 2003; 361:821-826.

[72] Quick M. First treatment trial for West Nile infection begins. *Lancet Infect. Dis.* 2002; 2:589.

[73] Shimoni Z, Niven MJ, Pitlick S, Bulvik S. Treatment of West Nile virus encephalitis with intravenous immunoglobulin. *Emerg. Infect. Dis.* 2001; 7:759.

[74] Monath TP, Arroyo J, Miller C, Guirakhoo F. West Nile virus vaccine. *Curr. Drug. Targets Infect. Dsord.* 2001 1:37-50.

[75] Lustig S, Halevy M, Fuchs P, et al. Can West Nile virus outbreaks can be controlled? *Isr. Med. Assoc. J.* 2000; 2:733-737.

[76] Komar N, Panella NA, Boyce E. Exposure of domestic mammals to West Nile virus during an outbreak of human encephalitis, New York city, 1999. *Emerg. Infect. Dis.* 2001; 7:736-738.

[77] Kulasekera VL, Kramer L, Nasci RS, et al. West Nile infection in mosquitoes, birds, horses, and humans, staten island, New York, 2000 *Emerg. Infect. Dis.* 2001; 7:722-725.

[78] Petersen LR, Roering JT. West Nile virus: A reemerging global pathogen. *Emerg. Infect. Dis.* 2001; 7:611-614.

In: New Immunology Research Developments
Editor: Gunter V. Müller

ISBN 978-1-60021-701-2


*Chapter 7*

# Evidence Suggesting a Neuroimmunomodulatory Role of Nerve Growth Factor in Airways Inflammation

***Barbara Stampachiacchiere[1], Alessandra Micera[1] and Luigi Aloe*[2]***

[1]CIR Laboratory of Ophthalmology,
University Campus Bio-Medico and G.B.Bietti,
Foundation, Rome, Italy

[2]Institute of Neurobiology and Molecular Medicine,
National Research Council (INMM-CNR), Rome, Italy

## Abstract

Nerve growth factor (NGF) is a pleiotropic factor implicated in several physiological and pathological processes. Originally linked to the nervous system, NGF has been recently associated with many immune related disorders (chronic inflammatory, autoimmune allergy). NGF is produced by several cells belonging to the nervous, endocrine, immune and visual systems. In particular, NGF is produced by and acts on immune (T and B lymphocytes, mast cells (MCs), eosinophils (EOs), neutrophils, monocytes/macrophages) as well as structural cells (epithelial cells [ECs], fibroblast [FBs], endothelial cells). The specific response to NGF is mediated by the expression of both tyrosin kinase $trkA^{NGFR}$ and pan-neurotrophin $p75^{NTR}$ receptors. Being constitutively expressed by structural and immune cells, NGF represents a molecule potentially responsible for modulating the crosstalk between the immune and peripheral nervous system.

Increased circulating and tissutal NGF levels have been reported in chronic allergic inflammatory condition such as allergic rhinitis, rhino-conjunctivitis and allergic asthma. The role of NGF during these process is actually controversial: NGF might exert pro-

* Tel.: 39 06 501 703 240, Fax : 39 06 501 703 311, E-mail: aloe@inmm.cnr.it

inflammatory or anti-inflammatory effect as well as acts as a "modulator" of the local immune and inflammatory responses.

Studies of the last decade suggest that NGF takes part in the development of allergic asthma. The process is characterized by a chronic Th2 mediated inflammation, airway hyper-responsiveness, goblet cell hyperplasia, mucus hyper-production and thickening of the sub-epithelial zone. Positively correlated with the severity of asthma, airway hyper-responsiveness appears to be mediated by multiple independent and additive pathways working in concert and leading to recurrent reversible bronco-obstruction. During chronic inflammatory responses, the up-regulation of Substance P (SP) has been reported, to be associated with increased NGF, indicating a link between NGF/SP and respiratory symptoms. Experimentally induced models of asthma indicate a clear role of NGF in chronic inflammatory response, though a number of unresolved questions regarding the mechanism(s) through which NGF exerts its action remains to be address. In this review we will present and discuss findings and hypotheses indicating the neuroimmunododulatory contribution of NGF in airway inflammations.

**Keywords**: allergy, eosinophils, inflammation, mast cells, NGF, neurotrophins, asthma.

# 1. Introduction

Neurotrophins (NTs) are a family of homologous proteins showing similarities in receptor utility and physiologic activities. NGF is the first and best characterized member of the neurotrophin family, which includes Brain Derived Neurotrophic Factor (BDNF) and neurothophins (NTs) 3, 4 and 5 [Barde, 1990]. NTs were originally identified as essential factors for the development of the vertebrate nervous system, regulate the survival, death, or differentiation of neurons in the embryonic and postnatal stages, as well as neuronal maintenance in adult-hood. All members of this family of growth factors exhibit partial overlap as well as distinct patterns of expression and target cells. Particularly, Nerve Growth Factor (NGF) is up-regulated in chronic inflammatory diseases often associated with tissue remodelling. NGF seems to modulate both allergic inflammation and tissue remodelling, through binding to its receptors trkA$^{NGFR}$ tyrosine kinase and p75$^{NTR}$ glycoprotein.

Based on previous findings coming from literature, it is possible to hypothesize that NGF might exert a main role during chronic inflammation and tissue repair/remodelling in allergic diseases.

# 2. Nerve Growth Factor (NGF)

NGF is essential for the growth, differentiation, survival/apoptosis and functional activity of neuronal cells in the central and peripheral nervous system. In addition to its classical nervous system domain [Levi-Montalcini, 1987], NGF acts on a variety of immune cells [Aloe and Levi-Montalcini, 1977; Levi-Montalcini, 1998; Bracci-Laudiero et al., 2003; Lambiase et al., 2004). NGF is physiologically present in the bloodstream and tissues of mammals, humans included [Sofroniew et al., 2001], and undergoes significant changes during neuro- and immuno-inflammatory disorders [Aloe, 2004; Micera et al., 2003; Micera et al., 2004]. According to its wide-spread action encompassing nervous, endocrine, immune and visual systems, NGF is currently recognised as a pleiotrophic factor [Aloe et al., 1998] (Figure 1). The biological activity of NGF is mediated by specific binding to trkA$^{NGFR}$ and p75$^{NTR}$ receptors [Sofroniew et al., 2001].

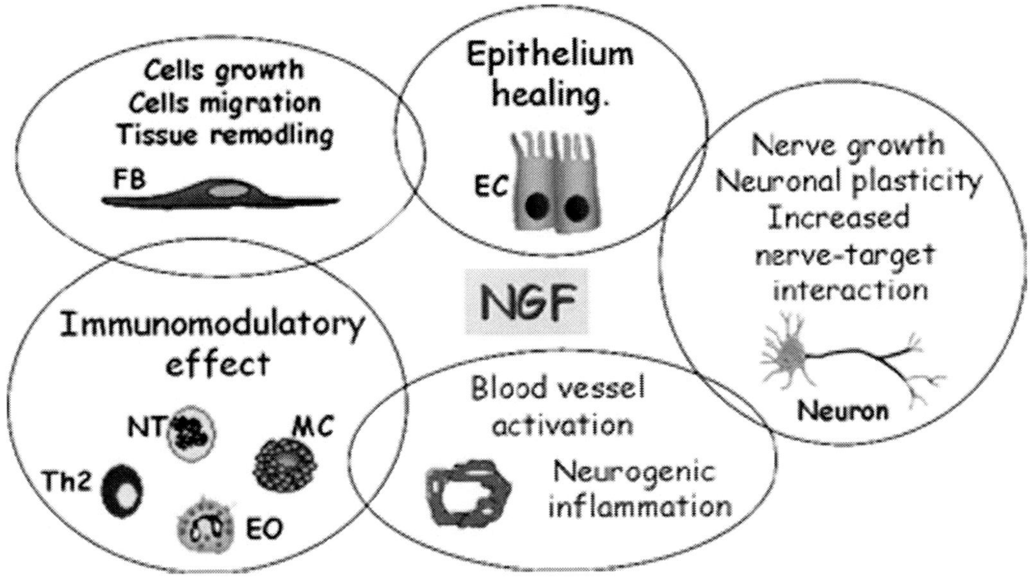


Figure 1. Schematic representation of NGF involvement in a number of different cell growth, differention, and function, within and outside the immune system. FBs: fibroblasts, ECs: epithelial cells, Th2: Th2-type lymphocytes, EOs: eosinophils, MCs: mast cells, NTs: neutrophils.

## A. Structure and Signalling: The Role of trka$^{NGFR}$ and P75$^{NTR}$

A highly conserved molecule among different species, NGF is a protein of 118 aminoacids, consisting of three sub-units ($\alpha 2,\beta,\gamma 2$; molecular weight 130kD).

The signal transduction pathway of NGF has been extensively investigated in the Pheochromocytoma 12 (PC12) cell model [Green et al., 1986]. NGF binds independently to two distinct receptors: the trkA tyrosine kinase receptor (termed p140trkA$^{NGFR}$, and shorted as trkA$^{NGFR}$) and the pan-neurotrophin receptor p75 (named p75$^{NTR}$), whose transduction signal has not been completely elucidated yet [Green et al., 1986; Meakin and Shooter, 1992; Chao and Hempstead, 1995]. While p75$^{NTR}$ binds all NTs with equal affinity (1nM Kd), trkA$^{NGFR}$ is very specific in its binding (10pM Kd). Both receptors contribute to the high-affinity receptor binding sites [Hempstead et al., 1991]. The duration and magnitude of NGF signalling depends on the ratio of p75$^{NTR}$ and trkA$^{NGFR}$ [Yoon et al., 1998].

Most of the NGF-mediated biological activities (from differentiation/activation to proliferation/survival) are due to ligand-dependent trkA$^{NGFR}$ tyrosine kinase autophosphorylation and subsequent activation of several signal transduction cascades, including the MAPK-Ras-Erk pathway, phospholipase Cy1, P3I kinase and SNT proteins (*suc* associated neurotrophic factor-induced tyrosine-phosphorylated target) [Sofroniew et al.,

2001; Esposito et al., 2001]. TrkA$^{NGFR}$ mediated cell rescue involves either the activation of survival signals or the suppression of death signals mediated by p75$^{NTR}$ [Smith et al., 1994].

Even thought lacking intrinsic tyrosine domains, p75$^{NTR}$, a member of the tumor necrosis factor receptor superfamily, is functional through a specific transduction pathway involving NF-kB (Rel/NF-kB transcription factors) and c-Jun kinase (JNK), as well as through increased production of ceramide, leading to gene transcription or programmed cell death [Wooten et al., 2001; Culmsee et al., 2002; Frade et al., 1996].

## B. An Overview of NGF in the Immune System

Increasing evidence shows that NGF plays a role in the complex and fascinating linkage between the nervous and the immune systems, due to NGF ability to modulate functions of inflammatory cells. NGF is produced by several immune cell types, accumulated in different tissues and in the peripheral blood [Levi-Montalcini et al.,1998; Bracci-Laudiero et al., 2003]. The mechanisms regulating NGF synthesis and release have not been yet clarified.

In 1977, the discovery of NGF effects on MCs prompt to several in vitro/exvivo studies on NGF in the immune system [Aloe and Levi-Montalcini, 1977; Lambiase et al., 2004]. From these studies, NGF treatment on newborn rats induced an increase in the number of MCs in several compartments of the body [Aloe and Levi-Montalcini, 1977]. The administration of neutralizing anti-NGF antibodies reduced the number of MCs in hepatic granulomas of Schistosoma mansoni-infected rats [Aloe and Tuveri, 1997]. In vitro, NGF induced MC development from mouse bone marrow cells in the presence of IL-3, promoted human and cell line MC maturation (chymase expression) and finally increased rat peritoneal MC survival by inhibiting in vitro their apoptosis [Aloe et al., 2000].

Besides MCs, NGF activates human peripheral blood EOs, from subjects with mild eosinophilia, to selectively release inflammatory mediators [Solomon et al., 1998]. EOs store and release NGF [Kobayashi et al., 2002], suggesting a possible role for NGF in conditions associated with eosinophilia, including allergic disease.

In 1997, Lambiase and co-workers investigated the trkA$^{NGFR}$, NGF expression, NGF production and release by human CD4+ cell clones, which have primary relevance in regulating inflammatory events through their different subsets of functional phenotypes suggesting a possible functional role of NGF in modulating the immune and inflammatory network [Lambiase et al., 1997; Lambiase et al., 2004].

The involvement of NGF in allergic disorders was postulated when in 1995 high NGF plasma levels were detected in patients with vernal keratoconjunctivitis (VKC), a Th2-driven ocular inflammatory disorder [Lambiase et al., 1995]. Increased levels of NGF were correlated with increased total IgE levels, and with an increased number of MCs and EOs in the tarsal conjunctiva of these VKC patients. In 1996, Bonini and co-workers confirmed the NGF contribution in allergy after the observation of high circulating NGF levels in patients suffering from allergic asthma, urticaria-angioedema and allergic rhinoconjunctivitis [Bonini et al., 1996; Bonini et al., 2000].

# 3. Chronic Allergic Asthma

Allergy shows increasing incidence in industrialized countries, with an high social impact in terms of patient discomfort and working day loss. Conventional treatments (steroids, anti-histamine drugs, β2-agonists, etc) are not always able to stabilize the disease. Allergy represents the most significant risk factor for development of childhood asthma. Asthma process is characterized by a chronic inflammatory state, airway hyper-responsiveness, goblet cell (GCs) hyperplasia, mucus hyper-production and thickening of the sub-epithelial zone [Rogers, 2002]. The asthma process comprises an early phase, driven by sensitized MCs, and by a late phase, the result of EOs recruitment in the airway tissue. MCs and EOs contribute to the pathogenesis of the entire process, through the release of different cytokines, growth factors and cytotoxic mediators. Asthma process is also characterized by development of hyper-reactivity (AHR), recurrent reversible airway obstruction and airway remodelling. Temporally, the early-phase develops within few second after allergen exposure, while the late-phase develops within few hours. Besides MCs and EOs, early and late phases are characterized by the presence and activation of types both inflammatory (T lymphocytes, neutrophils and macrophages) and structural (ECs, FBs, endothelial cells, smooth muscle cells) cells. If the asthmatic subject is continuously exposed to the allergen and/or develops a viral or bacterial infection, the inflammatory process may become chronic [Martin, 2006].

## A. The Immune-Mediated Process: Role of Mast Cells and Eosinophils

The allergic early-phase reaction is caused by the binding of the allergen with the immunoglobulin (IgE) bound to the high affinity IgE receptor of MCs, bone-marrow-derived tissue dwelling cell. MCs have a determinant key role in allergy, since MCs elicit the early stages of the allergic inflammatory response. IgE-bearing MCs (also known as primed-MCs) bind the antigen and release several preformed and newly synthesized mediators [Williams and Galli, 2000]. The release of chemotactic factors, cytokines and chemokines, from activated MCs, induces the onset of the late-phase reaction, characterized by tissue infiltration and activation of various inflammatory cells such as EOs. Cytokines/chemokines/growth factors, detected in human MCs include interleukin (IL)-3, IL-4, IL-5, IL-6, IL-8, IL-10, IL-13, IL-16, Tumor Necrosis Factor-α (TNF-α), RANTES/Eotaxin, Vascular Endothelial Growth Factor (VEGF), Granulocyte Macrophage-Colony Stimulating Factor (GM-CSF), Stem Cell Factor (SCF), NGF, β-Fibroblast Growth Factor (β-FGF) and Macrophage Inhibitory Protein-1α (MIP-1α) [Williams and Galli, 2000]. By specific release of IL-5, GM-CSF, TNF-α and tryptase, MCs promote recruitment, activation and survival of EOs inside the tissue [Williams and Galli, 2000]. The subsequent synthesis and release of cytokines and chemokines from MCs induces both onset and perpetuation of the late-phase reaction, characterized by tissue infiltration and activation of several inflammatory cells as EOs, that persist throughout the allergic response [Smith and Levi-Schaffer, 2000].

Derived from bone-marrow via IL-3/ IL-5/GM-CSF specific environment, peripheral blood EOs infiltrate the tissues in several pathological conditions, such as parasitic infections, allergic inflammation and neoplastic states [Simon et al., 2000].

EOs contain in their cytoplasmic granules characteristically preformed basic proteins (eosinophil peroxidase (EPO), eosinophil-derived neurotoxin (EDN), major basic protein (MBP), eosinophil cationic protein (ECP)) [Simon et al., 2000]. Their granules also contain several preformed cytokines (GM-CSF, TNF-$\alpha$, IL-2, IL-6, IL-4, IL-5) and growth factors (TGF-$\beta$1 and NGF). [Kobayashi al., 2002]. It is now a statement that a cross-talk between MCs and EOs exists and might regulate/amplify the local allergic inflammatory response, once established [Smith and Levi-Schaffer, 2000]. MC-derived TNF-$\alpha$ and tryptase enhance survival and functional activity of in vitro EOs [Temkin and Levi-Schaffer, 2001; Temkin et al., 2002], while EO-derived MBP and SCF cause release of histamine, GM-CSF and Prostaglandin $D_2$ from cultured MCs [Piliponsky et al., 2001; Piliponsky et al., 2003].

## B. The *Neurogenic* Inflammation: Role of Substance P

The inflammation induces an airway hyperresponsiveness showing similarities to hyperalgesia. Hyperalgesia can be defined as a decrease in the threshold for painful stimuli and heightened reflex pathways in sensory neurons [Carr and Undem, 2001]. NTs play an key role in inflammation induced hyperalgesia [Safieh-Garabedian et al., 1995; Woolf et al., 1997]. Even though the inflammatory response results from the coordinated action of specific immune cells (Th2 lymphocytes, MCs and EOs), also structural/neuronal cell types (fibroblast, epithelial cells and neurons) play a crucial role in the ongoing process.

Structurally, the lung and airways possess a complex network of small diameter axons that course through the parenchyma and in particular within the epithelium. This loose network drives dysfunction/disregulation that might contribute to the pathogenesis of asthma. In fact, the development of acute symptoms including broncho-obstruction and airway inflammation can be triggered under certain circumstances, via stimulation of local sensory and motor neurons, also named as "neurogenic inflammation" [Braun et al., 2002]. When an insult (pathogen, allergen, chemical or mechanical injury) occurs in the lung mucose, neurogenic inflammation develops through the release of neuromodulators (substance P (SP), calcitonin-gene related peptide (CGRP), tachyninins (TNK)), leading to tissue blood barrier breakdown, edema formation and release of polymorphonuclear cells (PMNs). Neurogenic inflammation takes part at both the onset and chronicity of lung disorders. Neuropeptides and growth factors have been extensively studied for their influence on both inflammatory and structural cells, in terms of functional activities. In particular, NTs have been identified as important mediators of inflammatory signals regarding the bronchial nervous system. Either resident or infiltrating the lung, immune cells (macrophages, lymphocytes, PMNs, MCs and EOs) are common sources of neuropeptides during allergic inflammation. Increased SP and CGRP levels have been detected in the lung of patients with allergic asthma, as well as in the murine model of allergic airway inflammation [Baumgarten et al., 1996; Kaltreider et al., 1997]. SP is a proinflammatory neuropeptides, belonging to the family of tachykinins, widely described to trigger the typical features of symptoms of bronchial asthma, including airway smooth muscle constriction and acute inflammation (neurogenic inflammation) [Cheung et al., 1994; Barnes et al., 1998]. MC-derived SP can amplify the inflammatory process by releasing an array of proinflammatory cytokines (IL-1, IL-8 and TNF-alpha) [Ansel et al., 1997; Zhao and Pothoulakis, 2003] and trigger the proliferation of lymphocytes [Bienenstock et al., 1989].

Besides several finding, it is actually debated if neurogenic inflammation is a direct effect or a cause of chronic inflammation. By the way, any efforts to understand mechanisms in underling between nervous system and immune system may provide additional tools for new therapeutic approaches.

## C. The Process of Tissue Remodeling: Role of Epithelial Cells and Fibroblasts

As a consequence of the chronic airway inflammation, the Goblet cell (GC) hyperplasia develops as feature of mild, moderate and severe asthma [Fahy, 2002]. Increase in GC number is accompanied by changes in stored/secreted mucins (MUC1-4; MUC5AC; MUC5B; MUC7) [Fahy, 2002] The functional consequences of mucin changes is represented by the accelerated loss in lung function. CD4(+) T cells and their T-helper type-2 derived cytokines are important mediators of GC hyperplasia. In asthmatic patients MUC5AC is the dominant MUC gene in GC, 60% expressed over healthy subjects [Fahy, 2002]. In particular, MUC5AC and Gob5, a calcium-activated chloride channel, are frequently associated with increased surface mucus/GCs in asthmatic airways [Komiya et al., 1999; Zhou et al., 2001]. In cultured airway epithelial cells Gob5 overexpression induces mucus cell metaplasia [Nakanishi et al., 2001; Zhou et al., 2001]. Recently, it has been found that gob5mRNA is induced by Th2 cytokine stimulation of airway ECs and likewise the up-regulation of MUC5AC in these cells is the critical first event leading to cell differentiation to GCs [Temann et al,1997]. Among all pro-inflammatory cytokines involved in the allergic process, IL-9, IL-4 and IL-13 have been described as, either direct or indirect, regulatory molecules in mucus production [Longphre et al., 1999; Fahy, 2002].

The role of NGF in GC hyperplasia and mucus production is actually an open field. It has been recently reported an NGF-mediated MUC1 up-regulation in a human mammalian epithelial line cells [Canbay, 2003]. In an other study, carried out on primary cells, NGF primed the conjunctival ECs differentiation by up-regulation of MUC5ACmRNA [Pellegrini et al., 2006]. By the way, these interesting data need further investigation in order to better clarity the role of NGF in the epithelial-stromal interaction during physiological and pathological states.

Any insult (allergen, virus, bacteria ecc.) lead to EC activation, which in turn might regulate remodelling process, mainly driven by FBs. Allergic asthma is a chronic inflammatory process often associated with tissue-remodeling and over-fibrosis, characterized by accumulation of extracellular matrix collagen in the alveolar interstitium, as a consequence of increased proliferation of activated lung FBs and the developing of myofibroblast (myoFBs). Lung remodelling/fibrosis is associated with organ function decline (Figure 2).

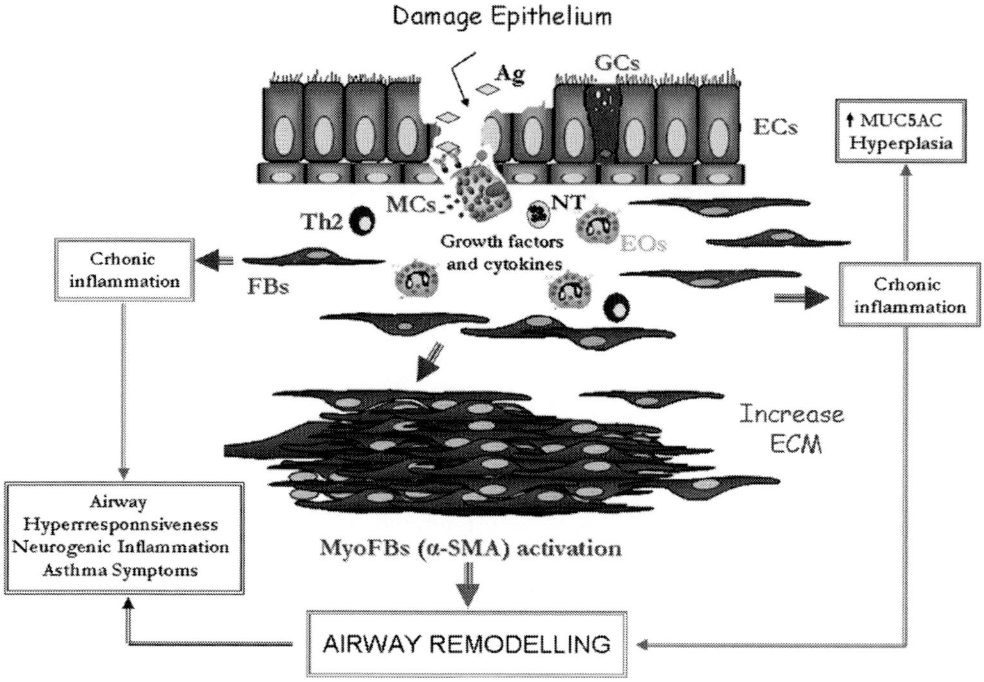


Figure 2. Epithelial-stroma interaction during chronic asthma. The scheme summering all cellular events leading to the chronic inflammatory, tissue remodelling process and the related airway dysfunction observed in asthma. Th2 cytokines and growth factors generated are involved in these process. FBs: fibroblasts, myoFBs: myofibroblasts, ECs: epithelial cells, GCs: goblet cells, Th2: Th2-type lymphocytes, EOs: eosinophils, MCs: mast cells, NTs: neutrophils, Ag: allergen.

FBs represent the main target and effector cells in the tissue remodelling/fibrosis. Activated FBs migrate to the injured area, proliferate, produce extracellular matrix (ECM), differentiate into myoFBs and finally contract the wound [Desmouliere et al., 2005]. MyoFB phenotype is responsible for wound contraction and their loss (via apoptosis or their phenotypical reversion to FBs) is necessary to terminate successfully the repair process [Ramm et al., 2000; Nedelec et al., 2001; Phan, 2002]. It is a recent concept that prolonged myoFB survival might contribute to the abnormal ECM deposition and therefore fibrosis [Zhang and Phan, 1999].

Indeed, FBs are viewed as "regulatory" cells driving tissue homeostasis, since they can produce cytokines and several growth factors with autocrine and paracrine activities [Levi-Schaffer et al., 2001; Smith and Levi-Schaffer, 2000]. Together with MCs and EOs, FBs are known to play a major role in the pathogenesis of allergic bronchial asthma. MCs and EOs seem to influence the functional activity of FBs [Smith and Levi-Schaffer, 2000] and viceversa since FBs influence MCs and EOs survival and activity, probably by SCF and GM-CSF respectively [Smith and Levi-Schaffer, 2000]. Both EOs and MCs participate in the development of tissue repair and fibrosis by modulating the proliferation of FBs and the ECM metabolism [Smith and Levi-Schaffer, 2000] through production of different mediators, such as histamine, tryptase [Smith and Levi-Schaffer, 2000; Garbuzenko et al., 2002], TGF-β1 [Levi-Schaffer et al., 1999) and most probably NGF [Solomon et al., 1998; Kobayaschi et al., 2002; Leon et al., 1994; Levi-Schaffer et al., 2002].

The presence of EOs in chronic allergic inflammation has been recognized as "critical" element, inducing the inflammatory process and causing tissue damage. EO-derived cytokines, such as TGF-α, TGF-β1, GM-CSF, IL-3, IL-5, and IL-6, may also promote EC proliferation, metaplasia, angiogenesis, FB proliferation, ECM generation and tissue remodelling [Martin et al., 1996; Rubbia-Brandt et al., 1991; Finotto et al., 1994]. However, lung FBs contribute to the process of EOs recruitment by releasing chemokines such as RANTES, eotaxin, which prime specifically EOs through CCR3 receptor, upon Th2 cytokines stimuli [Teran et al., 1999].

Cytokines and several growth factors influence and are produced by FBs. One of the most important factors is TGF-β1, the prototype of the TGF-β superfamily, which is found largely involved in wound repair process [Gabbiani et al., 1971]. Compelling in vitro and in vivo evidence shows that FBs are one of the sources/targets of NGF [Micera et al., 2001; Micera et al., 2003; Micera et al., 2005], actively involved in the healing process [Matsuda et al., 1998].

At present, NGF might be viewed as a cross-talking factor between all these cells and more investigations are needed to define its role in allergic inflammatory conditions.

## 4. NGF and Chronic Allergic Asthma

In 1996, Bonini and co-workers described for the first time an increased NGF levels in the blood of allergic asthma patients. Within the lung, the increase in NTs expression parallels the influx of inflammatory cells into the airway tissue, showing a direct relationship between NTs production and immune response. The lymphocytes, MCs and EOs are influenced by NT signalling and it has been recently shown that these cells express NGF and its receptors. Many data make interesting the NGF role in the pathogenesis of the asthma.

### A. An Historical Overview of NGF in Allergic Disorders: From Human Evidences to Experimental Models

The discovery of NGF occurred in the early 1950s, when Rita Levi-Montalcini (Nobel Prize in 1985) observed for the first time the ability of NGF to stimulate growth and differentiation of peripheral sensory and sympathetic neurons [Levi-Montalcini, 1987]. In 1977, Aloe and co-workers showed that MCs increase in tissues of neonatal rats injected with the NGF, suggesting a pivotal NGF role in native immunity [Aloe and Levi-Montalcini, 1977]. The relationship between NGF and allergic disorders is strengthen by increased NGF plasma levels in vernal keratoconjunctivitis (VKC) [Lambiase et al., 1995]. To support, the highest circulating NGF levels were found in patients with severe allergic asthma [Bonini et al., 1996]. In 1996, Bonini and co-workers measured the NGF serum levels in patients with asthma and/or rhinoconjunctivitis and/or urticaria-angioedema. This study showed that allergic asthma patients had elevated NGF serum levels compared with nonallergic asthma patients, accompanied with a high degree of bronchial hyperreactivity, high total IgE and eosinophil cationic protein [Bonini et al., 1996]. These data represent the first observation that NGF is increased in human allergic inflammatory diseases and asthma. Increasing NGF levels have been later on detected in the bronchoalveolar lavage fluids (BALF) after experimental segmental allergen challenges [Virchow et al., 1998]. Recent evidence shows NGF down-regulation in the superficial nasal scraping and NGF up-regulation in the nasal fluids of patients with symptomatic allergic rhinitis [Sanico et al., 2000; Kassel et al., 2001; Renz, 2001]. Kassel and co-workers in 2001 reported that the increased number of MC and expression of NGF, induced by allergen exposure in the bronchus of asthmatic patients, is occurring before the onset of symptoms [Kassel et al., 2001]. After allergen exposure, increased MC number and NGF expression occurred before the onset of symptoms in the bronchus of asthmatic patients, suggesting the potential NGF role in the early stage of the allergic inflammation in asthma. The presence of $trkA^{NGFR}$ in respiratory MCs and EOs [Solomon et al., 1998] provided some evidence of MCs/EOS as target for the activity of increased NGF. All the same, it is unclear how NGF acts in allergic inflammation. It is feasible to hypothesize that NGF have either an immuno-modulatory role on inflammatory cells acts on the pathological process of fibrosis and/or remodelling following tissue damage induced by inflammatory reaction.

Studying the allergic inflammatory diseases of the upper airways, in 2000, Sanico and coworkers observed that high NGF release was involved in the Hyperalgesia associated with reflex symptoms [Sanico et al., 2000]. Neurons are target for NGF released in the airways and NGF might be involved in the ''nerve hyperalgesia''. Since this discovery, it has been demonstrated the role of NGF in tissue remodelling, modulation of the inflammatory response, neurogenic inflammation and its influence on cellular differentiation, both in human and animal models.

In the early phase, NGF might trigger bronchial hyperresponsiveness, through a direct effect on the peripheral nervous system leading to an increased production of numerous neuropeptides, such as SP, known to be up-regulated during asthma exacerbation [Renz, 2001]. In a guinea-pig model the increase of SP and neurokininA in the lung in response to allergen challenge is due to an induction of these neuropeptides in neurons of the nodose ganglion [Fischer et al., 1996]. Furthermore, it has shown that high SP levels was enhanced by NGF [Lindsay and Harmar , 1989; Donnerer et al., 1992; Vedder et al., 1993; Hunter et al., 2000], who was shown to up regulate neuropeptide production in sensory neurons and contribute to inflammatory hypersensitivity [Donnerer et al., 1992]. In addition to NGF, other NTs such as BDNF have been associated in allergic asthma. Braun and coworkers have show that BDNF was increased in BALF from mice after allergen challeng and that many infiltrating immune cells were responsible of the enhanced BDNF in allergic inflammation [Braun et al., 1999]. These studies designate new pathways of the NTs role in the allergic asthma.

## B. NGF Treatment in Experimental Models of Asthma

In allergic airway asthma, the role of NGF is still controversial. Despite these experimental reports, no evidence yet provides a direct link between increased levels of NGF and bronchial hyper-responsiveness in asthmatic patients.

To further understand the critical role of NGF in asthma other studies have been done on animal models. In ovalbumin-sensitized guinea pigs NGF has been reported to evoke airway hyperresponsiveness [de Vries et al., 1999], while neutralising anti-NGF antibodies inhibited the acute broncho-constriction due to allergen challenge [de Vries et al., 2002]. Treatment of sensitized and aerosol challenged BALB/c mice with neutralising anti-NGF antibodies inhibited allergen-induced early-phase reaction and suppressed airway inflammation [Path et al., 2002], while NGF transgenic mice (overexpressing NGF in the airway) sensitized and challenged showed increased serotonin levels, whereas IgE levels remained unchanged, when compared with wild-type mice [Path et al., 2002]. In anti-NGF treated mice, EOs airway recruitment was significantly reduced, as well as IL-4 and IL-5 production, providing evidence for the functional role of NGF in the development of allergic early phase responses in the airways and the lung. These results demonstrates the involvement of NGF in the early phase of the allergic reaction via increased release of MC mediators. Indeed, NGF seems to promotes allergic inflammation in terms of EOs and lymphocyte infiltration as well as production of IL-4 and IL-5.

It is actually unclear how NGF participates in the allergic inflammation and which cells, other than activated MCs and EOs, are responsible for the increase of NGF in allergic responses.

Therefore, we used an animal model of allergic bronchial inflammation with low (NGF-deprived rats) or high levels of NGF, to understand the role of NGF in the inflammatory disorders. The rationale behind this novel experimental approach was that low circulating levels of NGF would reduce inflammatory responses, the number of immune cells of the immune system, and the concentration of cytokines that are critically important in the development of asthma-related symptoms, while high levels would exacerbate these responses.

We found that ovalbumin-sensitized (OVA) rats developed asthma-like responses, characterized by increased levels of circolating IgE and TNF-$\alpha$, and were characterized by an increase in EOs in the BALF. Both EOs and MCs were also found increased in the lung tissues (Figure 3). However, when bronchial inflammation was induced in NGF-deprived rats, a reduction of NGF in the serum and BALF was observed, but not in the levels of IgE, TNF-$\alpha$ and EOs, while exogenous injection of NGF in control and OVA rats did not enhance the IgE levels. In this study, no changes in the BDNF levels in the lungs and BALF of OVA rats were found.

This study showed that specific NGF deprivation did not affect the allergic inflammatory response observed in OVA rats (Figure 4), suggesting that NGF does not exert a direct role in allergic inflammatory events. Other NTs, via $p75^{NTR}$, may be responsible of many tissue structural changes in allergic bronchial asthma fenomens [Stampachiacchiere et al., 2006]. One of these NTs could be BDNF. BDNF is known to induce neuropeptide synthesis in neurons [Zhang et al., 1995].

BDNF modulates neuronal activity and enhances tachykinin neuropeptide production [Lewin and Barde, 1996]. Even though not specific for BDNF, $p75^{NTR}$ plays a central role in cellular signalling of BDNF.

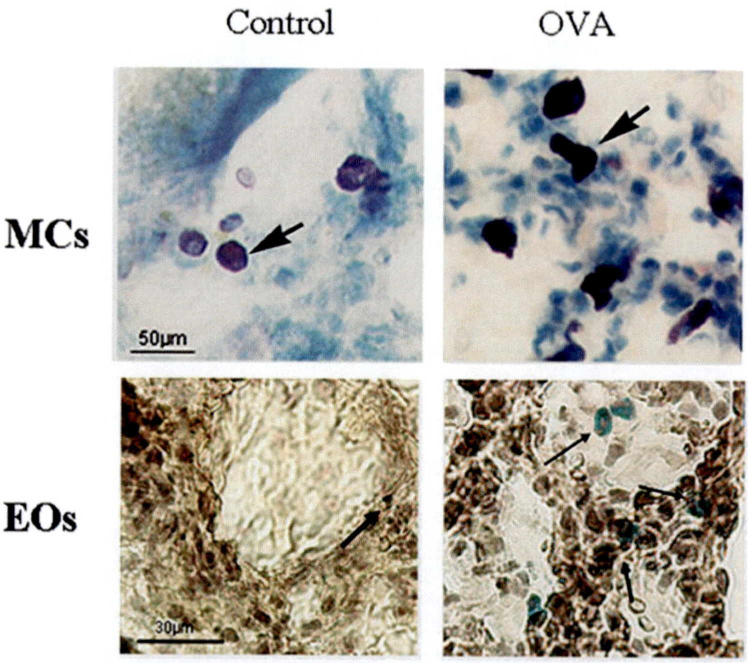


Figure 3. Mast cells and eosinophils are involved in the pathogenesis of asthma. Both mast cells and eosinophils are increased in lung tissue upon asthma induction (OVA) as compared to untreated rats (control). Mast cell are stained with toluidine blue, magnification, X-250; eosinophils stained with Luxol fast blue, magnification, X-400.

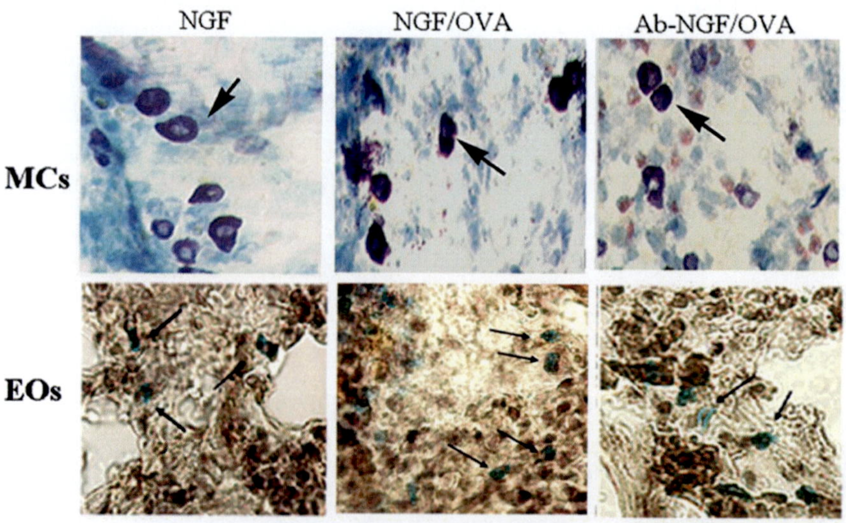


Figure 4. Lung tissues of rats treated with NGF, NGF/OVA and Ab-NGF/OVA showing the distribution of mast cell and eosinophil distribution. Mast cell number increases in the lung of OVA/NGF and Ab-NGF/OVA rats as compared to NGF rats, toluidine blue stained sections, magnification, X-250. The number of eosinophils increased in the lung of NGF treated rats, while circulating Ab-NGF antibodies in rats was unable to reduce significantly the presence of eosinophils in the lung, luxol fast blue, magnification, X-400. These observations suggest that the increase of eosinophils is not directly associated with the elevated presence of NGF.

### C. A Suggested Role of p75 $^{NTR}$ in Experimental Models of Allergic Asthma

NGF acts by trkA$^{NGFR}$/p75$^{NTR}$ receptors: while the trkA$^{NGFR}$ has been extensively studied, how p75$^{NTR}$ takes part in many physio-pathological processes is actually controversial and requiring elucidations.

Recently, Renz and co-workers highlighted the role of p75$^{NTR}$ in asthma models. Analysis of p75$^{NTR-/-}$ mice revealed that airway inflammation is to a large extent dependent upon this pan-neurotrophin receptor, suggesting a new molecular pathway in the neuro-immune pathogenesis of the asthma [Renz et al., 2004]. p75$^{NTR}$ is required for the development of several characteristic features of bronchial asthma [Renz et al., 2004]. After Deactivating p75$^{NTR}$ in mice, a marked reduction of allergic airway inflammation, characterized by the lowered influx of EOs and lymphocytes was observed [Kerzel et al., 2003].

These data were supported by the observations of Tokuoka and coworkers [Tokuoka et al., 2001], who found that the numbers of EOs and IL-5 levels in p75$^{NTR-/-}$ mice BALF decreased, showing for the first time a role for p75$^{NTR}$ as a link between non-immune and immune cells.

## Conclusion

NGF has a marked effect on the cells of the immune system, many of which have an important function in the development of pulmonary inflammation and asthma-related symptoms [Bonini et al., 1996; Renz, 2001; de Vries et al., 2002; Path et al., 2002]. However, the functional significance of such an increase has not yet been clearly established, since the evidence obtained both with humans and animals indicate that NGF can exert both a pro-inflammatory [Renz et al., 2001; Braun et al., 2002; Quarcoo et al., 2004; Blasing et al., 2005] and an anti-inflammatory role [Banks et al., 1984 ; Lambiase et al., 1998a; Lambiase et al., 1998b; Micera et al., 1998; Villoslada et al., 2000; Lambiase et al., 2000; Sanico et al., 2000; Flugel et al., 2001; Villoslada and Genain, 2004; Bracci-Laudiero et al., 2005; Stampachiacchiere and Aloe, 2005; Micera et al., 2006; Stampachiacchiere et al., 2006] (Figure 5).

Data obtained from animal models and humans showed that NGF increases after allergic inflammatory responses [Lambiase et al., 1995; Bonini et al., 1996; Virchow et al., 1998]. The cellular origin of the increased levels of NGF in allergic diseases is not clear, though the available evidence suggests that MCs, migrated EOs, local FBs and ECs might be some of the main sources of NGF [Kobayashi et al., 2002; Micera et al., 2003; Noga et al., 2003; Lambiase et al., 2004; Micera et al., 2006; Hahn et al., 2006].

It has been hypothesized that the elevated amount of NGF, observed in the fluids and tissues, might be the result of a reduced number and/or capacity of NGF receptive cells localized in the respiratory system [Hu et al., 2002]. It is therefore possible that NGF has different effects on a number of cells, such as neurons, smooth muscle and immune cells [Micera et al., 2003]. An hystorical overwiew (1950-2006) on the role of NGF in allergic disorders is depicted in Figure 6.

Findings reported by Kohjama and Micera have shown that NGF can modulate the speed of and intensity of repair by increasing the rate at which FBs migrate in response to chemoattractants [Kohyama et al., 2002; Micera et al., 2003].

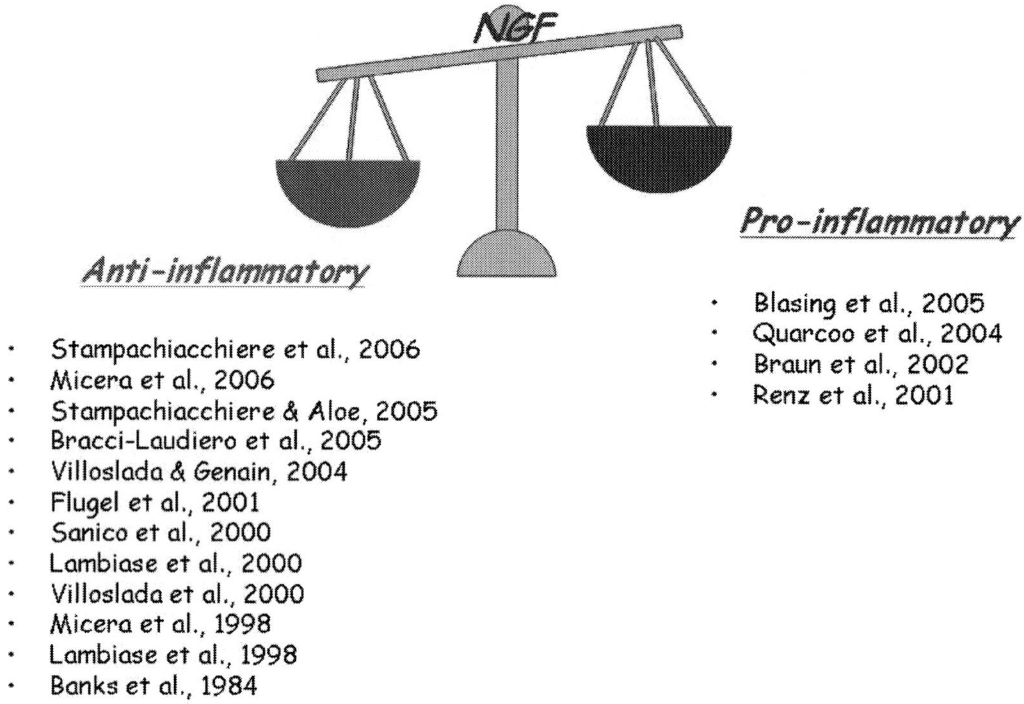


Figure 5. Historic overview of NGF discovery and early and recent evidence regarding the effect of NGF on cells of the immune system and the hypothesis on the role of NGF as pro and/or anti-inflammatory action of the NGF in animal models and in humans.

It is therefore possible that NGF, even in the presence of other cytokines, can be considered a positive and negative mediator and that the balance of these two effects could have a pro-inflammatory or anti-inflammatory action. Moreover it should be taken into consideration that NGF, through its regulatory action on peripheral sympathetic and sensory nerves, can decrease the associated damaging effects of inflammation on peripheral nerve endings and on specific subpopulation of immune cells.

Thus, to establish whether NGF promotes, exacerbates or decreases bronchial airway inflammation, further biochemical, pharmacological and molecular experimental strategies remain to be done with this animal model. One possible experimental strategy to address this question would be to treat the animal model of airway inflammation with specific agonist or antagonist involved in inflammatory responses and monitor the biochemical and molecular changes of endogenous NGF determinants.

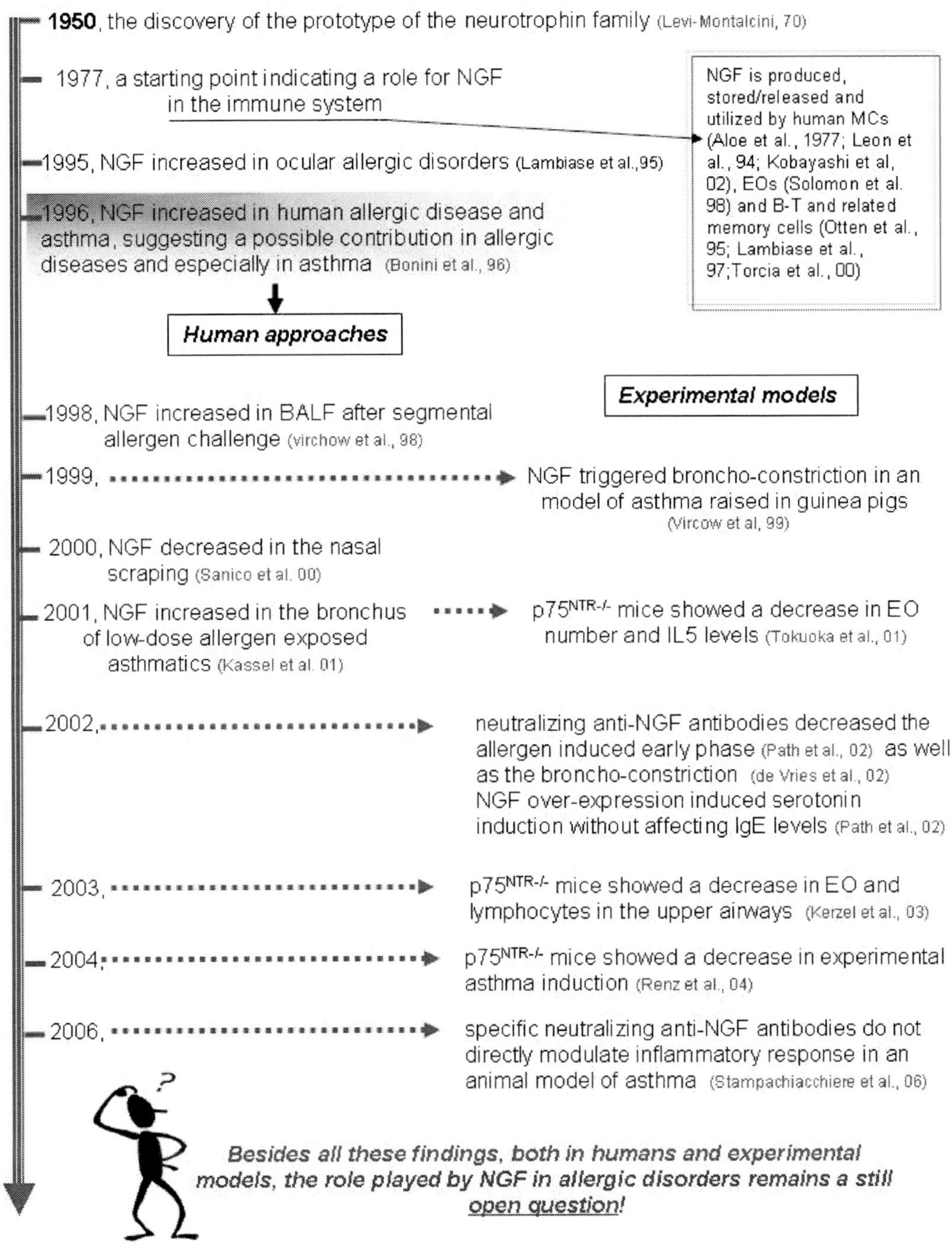


Figure 6. This figure reports previous and recent findings indicating the involvement of NGF in anti-inflammatory or pro-inflammatory mechanisms, including the mechanisms leading to acute or chronic allergic asthma.

# References

Aloe, L. and Levi-Montalcini, R. Mast cells increase in tissues of neonatal rats injected with the nerve growth factor. *Brain Res.* 1977; 133:358-366.

Aloe, L. and Tuveri, MA. Nerve growth factor and autoimmune rheumatic diseases. *Clin. Exp. Rheum.* 1997; 15: 433-438.

Aloe L., Bracci-Laudiero L., Bonini Se., Manni L. The expanding role of nerve growth factor: from neurotrophic activity to immunologic diseases. *Allergy.* 1998; 52: 883-994.

Aloe L., Micera A., Bonini Se. Nerve growth factor, mast cells, and allergic inflammation. In: Mast cells and basophils. Edited by: Marone G., Lichtenstein LM. and Galli SJ. *Academic Press Harcourt Publishers*. 2000; Chapter 21, pgs 325-339.

Aloe L. Nerve growth factor, human skin ulcers and vascularization. Our experience. *Prog. Brain Res*. 2004; 146:515-22.

Ansel JC., Armstrong CA., Song I., Quinlan KL., Olerud JE., Caughman SW., Bunnett NW. Interactions of the skin and nervous system. *J. Investig. Dermatol. Symp. Proc*. 1997; 2: 23-6.

Banks BE., Vernon CA., Warner JA. Nerve growth factor has anti-inflammatory activity in the rat hindpaw oedema test. *Neurosci. Lett*. 1984; 47:41-5.

Barde YA. The nerve growth factor family. *Prog. Growth Factor Res.* 1990; 2: 237-248.

Barnes PJ., Chung KF., Page CP. Inflammatory mediators of asthma: an update. *Pharmacol. Rev*. 1998; 50:515-96.

Baumgarten CR., Witzel A., Kleine-Tebbe J., Kunkel G. Substance P enhances antigen-evoked mediator release from human nasal mucosa. *Peptides.* 1996; 17:25-30.

Bienenstock J., Croitoru K., Ernst PB., Stead RH., Stanisz A. Neuroendocrine regulation of mucosal immunity. *Immunol. Invest*. 1989; 18:69-76.

Blasing H., Hendrix S., Paus R. Pro-inflammatory cytokines upregulate the skin immunoreactivity for NGF, NT-3, NT-4 and their receptor, p75NTR in vivo: a preliminary report. *Arch. Dermatol. Res*. 2005; 296:580-4.

Bonini S., Lambiase A., Bonini S., Angelucci F., Magrini L., Manni L., Aloe L. Circulating nerve growth factor levels are increased in humans with allergic diseases and asthma. *Proc. Natl. Acad. Sci. USA* 1996; 93: 10955-10960.

Bonini St., Lambiase A., Rama P., Caprioglio G., Aloe L. Topical treatment with nerve growth factor for neurotrophic keratitis. *Ophthalmology.* 2000; 107: 1347-1352.

Bracci-Laudiero L., Celestino D., Starace G., Antonelli A., Lambiase A., Propoli A., Rumi C., Lai M., Picardi A., Ballatore G., Bonini S., Aloe L. CD34-positive cells in human umbilical cord blood express nerve growth factor and its specific receptor TrkA. *J. Neuroimmunol*. 2003; 136: 130-9.

Bracci-Laudiero L., Aloe L., Caroleo MC., Buanne P., Costa N., Starace G., Lundeberg T. Endogenous NGF regulates CGRP expression in human monocytes, and affects HLA-DR and CD86 expression and IL-10 production. *Blood.* 2005; 106:3507-14.

Braun A., Lommatzsch M., Mannsfeldt A., Neuhaus-Steinmetz U., Fischer A., Schnoy N., Lewin GR., Renz H. Cellular sources of enhanced brain-derived neurotrophic factor production in a mouse model of allergic inflammation. *Am. J. Respir. Cell Mol. Biol.* 1999; 21:537-46.

Braun A., Nockher WA., Renz H. Control of nerve growth and plasticity *Cur.r Opin. Pharmacol.* 2002; 2:229-34.

Canbay E. Erb-B2 homodimerization inhibits MUC1 transcription in cultured human mammary epithelial cells. *Cell Biol. Int.* 2003; 27:477-81.

Carr MJ. and Undem BJ. Inflammation-induced plasticity of the afferent innervation of the airways. *Environ Health Perspect.* 2001;4:567-71.

Chao MV. and Hempstead BL. p75 and Trk: a two-receptor system.*Trends Neurosci.* 1995; 18:321-326.

Cheung D., van der Veen H., den Hartigh J., Dijkman JH., Sterk PJ. Effects of inhaled substance P on airway responsiveness to methacholine in asthmatic subjects in vivo. *J. Appl. Physiol.* 1994; 77:1325-32.

Culmsee C., Gerling N., Lehmann M., Nikolova-Karakashian M., Prehn JH., Mattson MP., Krieglstein J. Nerve growth factor survival signaling in cultured hippocampal neurons is mediated through TrkA and requires the common neurotrophin receptor p75. *Neuroscience.* 2002; 115:1089-1108.

Desmouliere A., Chaponnier C., Gabbiani G. Tissue repair, contraction, and the myofibroblast. *Wound Repair Regen.* 2005; 13:7-12.

de Vries A., Dessing MC., Engels F., Henricks PAJ., Nijkamp FP. Nerve growth factor induces a neurokinin-1 receptor-mediated airway hyperresponsiveness in guinea pigs. *Am. J. Respi.r Crit. Care Med.* 1999; 159: 1541-1544.

de Vries A., Engels F., Henricks PAJ., Leusnk-Muis T., Fischer A., Nijkamp FP. Antibodies directed against nerve growth factor inhibit the acute bronhocostriction due to allergen challenge in guinea pig. *Clin. Exp. Allergy.* 2002; 32: 325-328.

Donnerer J., Schuligoi R., Stein C. Increased content and transport of substance P and calcitonin gene-related peptide in sensory nerves innervating inflamed tissue: evidence for a regulatory function of nerve growth factor in vivo. *Neuroscience.* 1992; 49:693-8.

Esposito D., Patel P., Stephens RM., Perez P, Chao MV, Kaplan DR, Hempstead BL. The cytoplasmic and transmembrane domains of the p75 and trkA receptors regulate high affinity binding to nerve growth factor. *J. Biol. Chem.* 2001; 276:32687-32695.

Fahy JV. Goblet cell and mucin gene abnormalities in asthma. *Chest.* 2002; 122:320-326.

Finotto S., Ohno I., Marshall JS., Gauldie J., Denburg JA., Dolovich J., Clark DA., Jordana M. TNF-alpha production by eosinophils in upper airways inflammation (nasal polyposis). *J. Immunol.* 1994; 153:2278-89.

Fischer A., McGregor GP., Saria A., Philippin B., Kummer W. Induction of tachykinin gene and peptide expression in guinea pig nodose primary afferent neurons by allergic airway inflammation. *J. Clin. Invest.* 1996; 98:2284-91.

Flugel A., Matsumuro K., Neumann H., Klinkert WE., Birnbacher R., Lassmann H., Otten U., Wekerle H. Anti-inflammatory activity of nerve growth factor in experimental autoimmunen encephalomyelitis: inhibition of monocyte transendothelial migration. *Eur. J. Immunol.* 2001; 31:11-22.

Frade JM., Rodriguez-Tebar A., Barde YA.. Induction of cell death by endogenous nerve growth factor through its p75 receptor. *Nature.* 1996; 383:166-168.

Gabbiani G., Ryan GB., Majne G. Presence of modified fibroblasts in granulation tissue and their possible role in wound contraction. *Experientia.* 1971; 27:549-50.

Garbuzenko E., Nagler A., Pickholz D., Gillery P., Reich R., Maquart FAX., Levi-Schaffer F. Human mast cells stimulate fibroblast proliferation, collagen synthesis and lattice contraction: a direct role for mast cells in skin fibrosis. *Clin. Exp. Allergy.* 2002; 32: 237-246.

Green SH., Rydel RE., Connolly JL., Green LA. PC12 cell mutants that possess low- but not high-affinity nerve growth factor receptors neither respond to nor internalize nerve growth factor. *J. Cell Biol.* 1986; 102:830-843.

Hahn C., Islamian AP., Renz H., Nockher WA. Airway epithelial cells produce neurotrophins and promote the survival of eosinophils during allergic airway inflammation. *J. Allergy Clin. Immunol.* 2006; 117:787-94.

Hempstead BL., Martin-Zanca D., Kaplan DR., Parada LF., Chao MV. High-affinity NGF binding requires coexpression of the trk proto-oncogene and the low-affinity NGF receptor. *Nature.* 1991; 350: 678-683.

Hu C., Wedde-Beer K., Auais A., Rodriguez MM., Piedimonte G. Nerve growth factor and nerve growth factor receptors in respiratory syncytial virus-infected lungs. *Am. J. Physiol. Lung Cell Mol. Physiol.* 2002; 283:494-502.

Hunter DD., Myers AC., Undem BJ. Nerve growth factor-induced phenotypic switch in guinea pig airway sensory neurons. *Am. J. Respir. Crit. Care Med.* 2000; 161:1985-90.

Kaltreider HB., Ichikawa S., Byrd PK., Ingram DA., Kishiyama JL., Sreedharan SP., Warnock ML., Beck JM., Goetzl EJ. Upregulation of neuropeptides and neuropeptide receptors in a murine model of immune inflammation in lung parenchyma. *Am. J. Respir. Cell Mol. Biol.* 1997; 16:133-44.

Kassel O., de Blay F., Duvernelle C., Olgart C, Israel-Biet D, Krieger P, Moreau L, Muller C, Pauli G, Frossard N. Local increase in the number of mast cells and expression of nerve growth factor in the bronchus of asthmatic patients after repeated inhalation of allergen at low-dose. *Clin. Exp. Allergy.* 2001; 31:1432-1440.

Kerzel S, Path G, Nockher WA, Quarcoo D, Raap U, Groneberg DA, Dinh QT, Fischer A, Braun A, Renz H. Pan-neurotrophin receptor p75 contributes to neuronal hyperreactivity and airway inflammation in a murine model of experimental asthma. *Am. J. Respir. Cell Mol. Biol.* 2003;28:170-8.

Kobayashi H., Gleich GJ., Butterfield JH., Kita H. Human eosinophils produce neurotrophins and screte nerve growth factor on immunologic stimuli. *Blood.* 2002; 99: 2214-2220.

Kohyama T., Liu X., Wen FQ., Kobayashi T., Abe S., Ertl R., Rennard SI. Nerve growth factor stimulates fibronectin-induced fibroblast migration. *J. Lab. Clin. Med.* 2002; 140:329-35.

Komiya T., Tanigawa Y., Hirohashi S. Cloning and identification of the gene gob-5, which is expressed in intestinal goblet cells in mice. *Biochem. Biophys. Res. Commun.* 1999; 255:347-51.

Lambiase A., Bonini St., Bonini Se., Micera A., Magrini L., Bracci-Laudiero L., Aloe L. Increased plasma levels of nerve growth factor in Vernal Keratoconjunctivitis and relationship to conjunctival mast cells. *Invest Ophthalmol Vis Sci.* 1995; 36: 2127-2132.

Lambiase A., Bracci-Laudiero L., Bonini S., Bonini S., Storace G., D'Elios MM., De Carli M., Aloe L. Human CD4+ T cell clones produce and release nerve growth factor and express high-affinity nerve growth factor receptors. *J. Allergy Clin. Immunol.* 1997; 100:408-414.

Lambiase A., Bonini S., Micera A., Rama P., Bonini S., Aloe L. Expression of nerve growth factor receptors on the ocular surface in healthy subjects and during manifestation of inflammatory diseases. *Invest Ophthalmol. Vis. Sci.* 1998a; 39:1272-5.

Lambiase A., Rama P., Bonini S., Caprioglio G., Aloe L. Topical treatment with nerve growth factor for corneal neurotrophic ulcers. *N. Engl. J. Med.* 1998b; 338:1174-80.

Lambiase A., Bonini S., Aloe L., Rama P., Bonini S. Anti-inflammatory and healing properties of nerve growth factor in immune corneal ulcers with stromal melting. *Arch. Ophthalmol.* 2000; 118:1446-9.

Lambiase A, Micera A, Sgrulletta R, Bonini S, Bonini S. Nerve growth factor and the immune system: old and new concepts in the cross-talk between immune and resident cells during pathophysiological conditions. *Curr. Opin. Allergy Clin. Immunol.* 2004; 4: 425-30.

Leon A., Buriani A., dal Toso R., Fabris M., Romanello S., Aloe L., Levi-Montalcini R. Mast cells synthesize, store, and release nerve growth factor. *Proc. Natl. Acad. Sci. USA.* 1994; 9:3739-43.

Levi-Montalcini R. The nerve growth factor 35 years later. *Science.* 1987; 237:1154-1162.

Levi-Montalcini R. The saga of the nerve growth factor. *Neuroreport.* 1998; 16:71-83.

Levi-Schaffer F., Garbuzenko E., Rubin A., Reich R., Pickholz D., Gillery P., Emonard H., Nagler A., Maquart FAX. Human eosinophils regulate human lung- and skin- derived fibroblast properties in vitro: a role for transforming growth factor β (TGF-β). *Proc. Natl. Acad. Sci. USA.* 1999; 96: 9660-9665.

Levi-Schaffer F., Micera A., Maquart FX., Aloe L. Nerve growth factor is produced by human fibroblasts and modulates them: role of nerve growth factor in tissue repair. *Int. Arch. Allergy Immunol.* 2001; 124: 279-281.

Levi-Schaffer F., Micera A., Zamir E., Mechoulam H., Puxeddu I., Piliponsky AM., Aloe L., Pe'er J. Nerve growth factor and eosinophils in inflamed juvenile conjunctival nevus. *Invest. Ophthalmol. Vis. Sci.* 2002; 43:1850-6.

Lewin GR. and Barde YA. Physiology of the neurotrophins. *Annu. Rev. Neurosci.* 1996; 19:289-317.

Lindsay RM. and Harmar AJ. Nerve growth factor regulates expression of neuropeptide genes in adult sensory neurons. *Nature.* 1989; 337:362-4.

Longphre M., Li D., Gallup M., Drori E., Ordonez CL., Redman T., Wenzel S., Bice DE., Fahy JV., Basbaum C. Allergen-induced IL-9 directly stimulates mucin transcription in respiratory epithelial cells. *J. Clin. Invest.* 1999; 104:1375-82.

Martin LB., Kita H., Leiferman KM., Gleich GJ. Eosinophils in allergy: role in disease, degranulation, and cytokines. *Int. Arch. Allergy Immunol.* 1996; 109:207-15.

Martin RJ. Infections and asthma. *Clin. Chest. Med.* 2006; 27:87-98.

Matsuda H., Koyama H., Sato H., Sawada J., Itakura A., Tanaka A., Matsumoto M., Konno K., Ushio H., Matsuda K. Role of nerve growth factor in cutaneous wound-healing: accelerating effects in normal and healing-impaired diabetic mice. *J. Exp. Med.* 1998; 187:297-306.

Meakin SO. and Shooter EM. The nerve growth factor family of receptors. *Trends Neurosci.* 1992; 15:323-331.

Micera A., Vigneti E., Aloe L. Changes of NGF presence in nonneuronal cells in response to experimental allergic encephalomyelitis in Lewis rats. *Exp. Neurol.* 1998; 154:41-6.

Micera A., Vigneti E., Pickholtz D., Reich R., Pappo O., Bonini S., Maquart FX., Aloe L., Levi-Schaffer F. Nerve growth factor displays stimulatory effects on human skin and lung fibroblasts, demonstrating a direct role for this factor in tissue repair. *Proc. Natl. Acad. Sci. USA*. 2001. 22; 98:6162-7.

Micera A., Puxeddu I., Aloe L., Levi-Shaffer F. New Insight on the involvement of nerve growth factor in allergic inflammation and fibrosis. *Cytokine and Growth Factor Rev.* 2003; 14:369-374.

Micera A., Lambiase A., Aloe L., Bonini S., Levi-Schaffer F., Bonini S. Nerve growth factor involvement in the visual system: implications in allergic and neurodegenerative diseases. *Cytokine Growth Factor Rev*. 2004; 15: 411-7.

Micera A., Puxeddu I., Lambiase A., Antonelli A., Bonini S., Bonini S., Aloe L., Pe'er J, Levi-Schaffer F. The pro-fibrogenic effect of nerve growth factor on conjunctival fibroblasts is mediated by transforming growth factor-beta. *Clin. Exp. Allergy*. 2005; 35:650-6.

Micera A., Lambiase A., Puxeddu I., Aloe L., Stampachiacchiere B., Levi-Schaffer F., Bonini S., Bonini S. Nerve growth factor effect on human primary fibroblastic-keratocytes: possible mechanism during corneal healing. *Exp. Eye Res*. 2006; 83:747-57.

Nakanishi A., Morita S., Iwashita H., Sagiya Y., Ashida Y., Shirafuji H., Fujisawa Y., Nishimura O., Fujino M. Role of gob-5 in mucus overproduction and airway hyperresponsiveness in asthma. *Proc. Natl. Acad. Sci. USA*. 2001; 98:5175-80.

Nedelec B., Shankowsky H., Scott PG., Ghahary A., Tredget EE. Myofibroblasts and apoptosis in human hypertrophic scars: the effect of interferon $\alpha 2\beta$. *Surgery.* 2001; 130: 798-808.

Noga O., Englmann C., Hanf G., Grutzkau A., Seybold J., Kunkel G. The production, storage and release of the neurotrophins nerve growth factor, brain-derived neurotrophic factor and neurotrophin-3 by human peripheral eosinophils in allergics and non-allergics. *Clin. Exp. Allergy*. 2003; 33:649-54.

Path G., Braun A., Meents N., Kerzel S., Quarcoo D., Raap U., Hoyle GW., Nockher WA., Renz H. Augmentation of allergic early-phase-reaction by nerve growth factor. *Am. J. Respir. Crit. Med.* 2002; 166:818-826.

Pellegrini G., Barbaro V., Merlo D., de Luca M., Bonini S., Lambiase A. *NGF effect on epithelial cell cultures*. Abstract ARVO 2006.

Phan SH. The myofibroblast in pulmonary fibrosis. *Chest*. 2002; 122:286S-289S.

Piliponsky AM., Gleich GJ., Nagler A., Bar I., Levi-Schaffer F. Non-IgE-dependent activation of human lung- and cord blood-derived mast cells is induced by eosinophil major basic protein and modulated by the membrane form of stem cell factor. *Blood.* 2003; 101:1898-1904.

Piliponsky AM., Pickholtz D., Gleich GJ., Levi-Schaffer F. Human eosinophils induce histamine release from antigen-activated rat peritoneal mast cells: a possible role for mast cells in late-phase allergic reactions. *J. Allergy Clin. Immunol.* 2001; 107: 993-1000.

Quarcoo D., Schulte-Herbruggen O., Lommatzsch M., Schierhorn K., Hoyle GW., Renz H., Braun A. Nerve growth factor induces increased airway inflammation via a neuropeptide-dependent mechanism in a transgenic animal model of allergic airway inflammation. *Clin. Exp. Allergy*. 2004; 34:1146-51.

Ramm GA., Carr SC., Bridle KR., Li L., Britton RS., Crawford DHG., Vogler CA., Bacon BR. Tracy Jr TF. Morphology of liver repair following cholestatic liver injury: resolution of ductal hyperplasia,matrix deposition and regression of myofibroblasts. *Liver*. 2000; 20: 387-396.

Renz H. The role of neurotrophins in bronchial asthma. *Eur. J. Pharmacol.* 2001; 429: 231-237.

Renz H., Kerzel S., Nockher WA. The role of neurotrophins in bronchial asthma: contribution of the pan-neurotrophin receptor p75. *Prog. Brain Res.* 2004; 146:325-33.

Rogers DF. Airway goblet cell hyperplasia in asthma: hypersecretory and anti-inflammatory? *Clin. Exp. Allergy*. 2002; 32:1124-7.

Rubbia-Brandt L., Sappino AP., Gabbiani G. Locally applied GM-CSF induces the accumulation of alpha-smooth muscle actin containing myofibroblasts. *Virchows Arch. B Cell Pathol. Incl. Mol. Pathol.* 1991; 60:73-82.

Safieh-Garabedian B., Poole S., Allchorne A., Winter J., Woolf CJ. Contribution of interleukin-1 beta to the inflammation-induced increase in nerve growth factor levels and inflammatory hyperalgesia. *Br. J. Pharmacol.* 1995; 115:1265-75.

Sanico AM., Stanisz AM., Gleeson TD., Bora S., Proud D., Bienenstock J., Koliatsos VE., Togias A. Nerve growth factor expression and release in allergic inflammatory disease of the upper airways. *Am. J. Respir. Crit. Care Med.* 2000; 161:1631-1635.

Simon HU., Weber M., Becker E., Zilberman Y., Blaser K., Levi-Schaffer F. Eosinophils Maintain Their Capacity to Signal and Release Eosinophil Cationic Protein Upon Repetitive Stimulation with the Same Agonist. *J. Immunol.* 2000; 165: 4069-4075.

Smith CA., Farrah T., Goodwin RG. The TNF receptor superfamily of cellular and viral proteins: activation, costimulation, and death. *Cell.* 1994; 76:959-962.

Smith S. and Levi-Schaffer F. Cross-talk between eosinophils, mast cells and fibroblasts. *Chem. Immunol.* 2000; 78: 81-92.

Sofroniew MV., Howe CL., Mobley WC. Nerve growth factor signaling, neuroprotection, and neural repair. *Annu. Rev. Neurosci.* 2001; 24: 1217-1281.

Solomon A., Aloe L., Pe'er J., Frucht-Pery J., Bonini S., Bonini S., Levi-Schaffer F. Nerve growth factor is preformed in and activates human peripheral blood eosinophils. *J. Allergy Clin. Immunol.* 1998; 102: 454-460.

Stampachiacchiere B. and Aloe L. Differential modulatory effect of NGF on MHC class I and class II expression in spinal cord cells of EAE rats. *J. Neuroimmunol.* 2005; 169:20-30.

Stampachiacchiere B., Aloe L., Micera A., Bonini S. Allergic bronchial airway inflammation in nerve growth factor (ngf)-deprived rats: evidence suggesting a neuroimmunomodulatory role of NGF. *Exp. Lung Res.* 2006; 32: 305-20.

Temkin V. and Levi-Schaffer F. Mechanism of tumor necrosis factor alpha mediated eosinophil survival. *Cytokine.* 2001; 15:20-26.

Temkin V., Kantor B., Weg V., Hartman ML., Levi-Schaffer F. Tryptase activates the mitogen-activated protein kinase/activator protein-1 pathway in human peripheral blood eosinophils, causing cytokine production and release. *J. Immunol.* 2002; 169:2662-9.

Temann UA., Prasad B., Gallup MW., Basbaum C., Ho SB., Flavell RA., Rankin JA. A novel role for murine IL-4 in vivo: induction of MUC5AC gene expression and mucin hypersecretion. *Am. J. Respir. Cell Mol. Biol.* 1997; 16:471-8.

Teran LM., Mochizuki M., Bartels J., Valencia EL., Nakajima T., Hirai K., Schroder JM. Th1- and Th2-type cytokines regulate the expression and production of eotaxin and RANTES by human lung fibroblasts. *Am. J. Respir. Cell Mol. Biol.* 1999; 20:777-86.

Tokuoka S., Takahashi Y., Masuda T., Tanaka H., Furukawa S., Nagai H. Disruption of antigen-induced airway inflammation and airway hyper-responsiveness in low affinity neurotrophin receptor p75 gene deficient mice. *Br. J. Pharmacol.* 2001; 134:1580-6.

Vedder H., Affolter HU., Otten U. Nerve growth factor (NGF) regulates tachykinin gene expression and biosynthesis in rat sensory neurons during early postnatal development. *Neuropeptides*. 1993; 24:351-7.

Villoslada P., Hauser SL., Bartke I., Unger J., Heald N., Rosenberg D., Cheung SW., Mobley WC., Fisher S., Genain CP. Human nerve growth factor protects common marmosets against autoimmune encephalomyelitis by switching the balance of T helper cell type 1 and 2 cytokines within the central nervous system. *J. Exp. Med.* 2000; 191:1625-30.

Villoslada P. and Genain CP. Role of nerve growth factor and other trophic factors in brain inflammation. *Prog. Brain Res*. 2004; 146:403-14.

Virchow JC., Julius P., Lommatzsch M., Luttmann W., Renz H., Braun A. Neurotrophins are increased in bronchoalveolar lavage fluid after segmental allergen provocation. *Am. J. Respir. Crit. Care Med.* 1998; 158: 150-153.

Wooten MW, Seibenhener ML, Mamidipudi V, Diaz-Meco MT, Barker PA, Moscat J. The Atypical Protein Kinase C-interacting Protein p62 is a Scaffold for NF-kB Activation by Nerve Growth Factor. *J. Biol. Chem.* 2001; 276:7709-7712.

Williams CM. and Galli SJ. The diverse potential effector and immunoregulatory roles of mast cells in allergic disease. *J. Allergy Clin. Immunol.* 2000; 105:847-59.

Woolf CJ., Allchorne A., Safieh-Garabedian B., Poole S. Cytokines, nerve growth factor and inflammatory hyperalgesia: the contribution of tumour necrosis factor alpha. *Br. J. Pharmacol.* 1997; 121:417-24.

Yoon SO., Casaccia-Bonnefil P., Carter B., Chao MV. Competitive Signaling Between TrkA and p75 Nerve Growth Factor Receptors Determines Cell Survival. *J. Neurosci.* 1998; 18:3273-3281.

Zhang Q., Ji RR., Lindsay R., Hokfelt T. Effect of growth factors on substance P mRNA expression in axotomized dorsal root ganglia. *Neuroreport*. 1995; 6:1309-12.

Zhang HY. and Phan SH. Inhibition of myofibroblast apoptosis by transforming growth factor β1. *Am. J. Respir. Cell Mol. Biol.* 1999; 21: 658-665.

Zhao D. and Pothoulakis C. Rho GTPases as therapeutic targets for the treatment of inflammatory diseases. *Expert. Opin. Ther. Targets*. 2003; 7: 583-92.

Zhou Y., Dong Q., Louahed J., Dragwa C., Savio D., Huang M., Weiss C., Tomer Y., McLane MP., Nicolaides NC., Levitt RC. Characterization of a calcium-activated chloride channel as a shared target of Th2 cytokine pathways and its potential involvement in asthma. *Am. J. Respir. Cell Mol. Biol.* 2001; 25:486–491.

In: New Immunology Research Developments
Editor: Gunter V. Müller
ISBN 978-1-60021-701-2


*Chapter 8*

# Immunotherapeutic Efficacy of DNA Vaccine Combination with Antiviral Drugs in the Chronic Duck Hepatitis B Virus Infection Model

***Alexandre Thermet[1,2], Thierry Buronfosse[1,2,3], Franck Le Guerhier[1,2], Pierre Pradat[4], Christian Trepo[1,2,4], Fabien Zoulim[1,2,4] and Lucyna Cova*[1,2]***

[1]INSERM, Unit 871, Lyon F-69424, France
[2]Université Lyon 1, IFR62, Lyon F-69008, France
[3]Ecole Nationale Vétérinaire, Marcy l'Etoile F-69280, France
[4]Hospices Civiles de Lyon, Department of Hepatology, Hotel-Dieu, Lyon F-69002, France

## Abstract

Design of novel treatment options for chronic hepatitis B virus (HBV) infections is actually of particular importance, since current therapies based on IFNα and nucleoside analogues (lamivudine, adefovir) are limited by the emergence of drug–resistant mutants and the persistence of intranuclear covalently closed circular viral DNA (cccDNA) responsible for persistence of infection. Increasing number of recent data suggest that rationale therapy of hepatitis B may combine the use of antiviral drugs and immunotherapeutic approaches. In this regard, DNA-based immunization appears as a pertinent new approach, inducing rapid, potent and specific immune responses to hepadnavirus structural proteins as demonstrated in naïve chimpanzees, woodchuck and duck models. However, the therapeutic DNA vaccination against chronic hepatitis B was less investigated.

Our aim was to explore in the chronic duck HBV (DHBV) infection model, whether DNA vaccine-based immunotherapy in combination or not with an antiviral drug

* Phone: (33) 4 72 68 19 81, Fax: (33) 4 72 68 19 71; E-mail address: lucyna.cova@inserm.fr

(adefovir, lamivudine) treatment is able to enhance cccDNA clearance and break humoral immune tolerance in chronic DHBV carriers. We have first realized a study associating adefovir with DNA vaccine against DHBV envelope and compared herein its therapeutic efficacy with our recent study combining lamivudine with DNA vaccine against viral envelope and/or core proteins.

In an adefovir-DNA study, a group of DHBV-infected ducks received adefovir treatment (weeks 6-10 p.i.) in combination or not with DNA immunization to DHBV preS/S protein (weeks 6, 9, 12 and 22). A marked drop in viremia titres (97%), reaching the limit of detection of the assay, was observed during the 4 weeks of drug administration in all adefovir-treated as compared with untreated ducks, although it was followed by a rebound of viral replication after drug withdrawal. At the end of follow-up, analysis of intrahepatic DHBV DNA revealed a more pronounced decrease in viral DNA in combination therapy group as compared with DNA or adefovir monotherapy groups suggesting a trend to an additive effect of drug and DNA vaccine. However only few animals eliminated liver viral DNA and no correlation with humoral anti-preS response restoration was observed.

In lamivudine-DNA study, lamivudine was administrated alone or in combination with DNA vaccine to DHBV envelope and/or core proteins. DHBV-carrier ducks received lamivudine treatment earlier (weeks 1-8), with higher number of DNA immunizations (weeks 6,10,14,28,35), shorter overlap with DNA vaccination (2 weeks), larger amounts of plasmid and a longer follow-up in larger animal groups. A decrease in viremia titers (70%) was observed in all lamivudine-treated compared to untreated animals, although it was limited to only the first 3 weeks of lamivudine treatment and was followed by a rapid rebound in viral replication. Interestingly, about 30% of the animals, which received DNA vaccine alone or in association with lamivudine, had cccDNA levels that were at or under the lower real-time PCR detection limit and was associated for majority of them with restoration of anti-preS response.

In conclusion, our comparison of two combination therapy studies associating DNA vaccine-based immunotherapy with either adefovir or lamivudine indicates a better efficacy of the lamivudine-DNA protocol. In the adefovir-DNA study, only modest effect in term of viral cccDNA clearance and seroconversion was observed, in spite of the higher antiviral potency of the drug. By contrast, data obtained in lamivudine-DNA study provided a first demonstration that DNA vaccine alone and associated with drug treatment was able to induce drastic and sustained suppression of viremia and enhance viral cccDNA clearance in DHBV carriers, which was tightly associated with a break of immune tolerance. Because both studies differed not only by the choice of drug but, importantly, by the design of DNA immunization protocol, a number of factors known to determine the success of genetic vaccination such as plasmid construct, amount of plasmid DNA, number of DNA injections and immunization schedule may play an important role in better therapeutic efficacy of lamivudine-DNA study. Further investigations aiming to increase the potency of DNA vaccine–based immunotherapeutics need to be performed in animal models with the goal of acheiving a complete and sustained recovery from chronic hepatitis B.

**Keywords**: Hepatitis B, duck HBV (DHBV), hepatitis B, lamivudine; adefovir, DNA vaccine, combination therapy, immunotherapy, closed circular viral DNA (cccDNA), animal model.

# Introduction

Chronic hepatitis B virus (HBV) infection remains a major public health problem with 350 million virus carriers who are of a high risk of cirrhosis and hepatocellular carcinoma [7]. HBV-infected patients are currently treated with interferon (IFN)–$\alpha$ and nucleotide analogues such as lamivudine, adefovir or entacavir. Lamivudine (2',3'-dideoxy-3'-thiacytidine or 3-TC) is a potent and the most widely anti-HBV drug actually used, known to induce a rapid decline in viral load by 3-5 log10copies/ml after a year therapy [30]. However, long-term lamivudine therapy led to the emergence of drug-resistant mutants, which results in viral breakthrough. [15,30,47]. Adefovir dipivoxil (PMEA), a recently developed antiviral compound appeared initially of particular interest since it inhibited both wild-type and lamivudine-resistant HBV mutants, however a long-term adefovir treatment also results in drug-resistance [2,33,43,47]. Thus, the efficacy of current treatments is limited by the emergence of drug–resistant mutants and the persistence of covalently closed circular viral DNA (cccDNA) in the nucleus of infected cells, which is responsible for viral relapse after treatment withdrawal [2,39,45,47].

Interestingly, studies in lamivudine-treated chronic HBV-carrier patients clearly demonstrated that the marked reduction in viremia during antiviral treatment is followed by a break of T cell nonresponsiveness resulting in the transient restoration of HBV-specific CD4+ T cell activity followed, by cytotoxic T cell activity and the CD8+ T cell proliferation [3-5]. Therefore, a concept of combination therapy has been proposed that is based on association of nucleoside analogues treatment, able to transiently restore antiviral immune responses, with immune therapeutics aiming to stimulate these responses in a sustained manner [5].

Recent studies have investigated such combination therapies in the chronic woodchuck HBV (WHV)-carrier woodchucks and showed that the association of clevudine (L-FMAU) treatment with WHsAg alum-adjuvanted vaccine led to the inhibition of chronic hepatitis and delay in onset of hepatocellular carcinoma [14]. These promising results have been strengthened by a recent clinical study in HBV carriers showing a benefit of lamivudine combination with HBsAg vaccine in terms of serum HBV DNA negativity and absence of variants emergence as compared with lamivudine monotherapy treated patients group [13].

Within the actual immunotherapeutic strategies, DNA-based vaccine appears as a pertinent new approach, inducing rapid, strong and specific immune responses to HBV, WHV and DHBV structural proteins in naïve animals as documented by several studies [9,11,22,27,34,35,36,40,42,44]. However, the therapeutic DNA vaccination against chronic HBV infection was less investigated. The ability of a DNA vaccine to HBV envelope to decrease viral replication was first demonstrated in the transgenic mouse lineage, E36 [23,28], although viral cccDNA clearance cannot be analyzed in this model. The DNA vaccine-based therapy of chronic DHBV-carrier ducks resulted in variable efficacy. We have previously reported that DNA immunization of carriers with plasmid expressing viral large envelope protein induced a marked decrease in DHBV replication, although the number of animals included in that study was small and no correlation with a break of humoral immune tolerance was observed [34]. Treatment of DHBV-carrier ducks with combination of entecavir (ETV) with DNA vaccine to virus envelope and core showed a potent antiviral effect of ETV, although DNA vaccination alone or combined with ETV have not resulted in reduction of viral replication [10].

We report here the results of two independent studies conducted in our laboratory which allowed us to compare the efficacy and safety of such chemo-immunotherapy associating either DNA vaccine with adefovir [18] or lamivudine [41]. We have chosen the DHBV-infected duck model for these studies, since it is a pivotal model for evaluation of novel anti-HBV approaches and appreciation of their impact on intranuclear cccDNA clearance [1,8,19,26]. The comparison of both studies has highlighted the importance of different factors such as choice of drug, plasmid constructs, amount of plasmid DNA and therapeutic protocol design, in the antiviral efficacy of such DNA-vaccine-based immunotherapies.

# Materials and Methods

## Drug

The 9-(2-phosphomethoxyethyl) adenine (adefovir (PMEA), a generous gift of Gilead Sciences, and the β-L(-)-2',3'-dideoxy-3'thia-cytidine (3TC, lamivudine), generously provided by J. Rhodes (GlaxoSmithKline), were dissolved in phosphate buffered saline (pH 7.2).

## Plasmid Expression Vectors

DHBV large envelope (preS/S) and core (C) genes were previously cloned in pCI vector under the control of CMV promoter and are referred to pCI-preS/S [34] and pCI-C [40] respectively. Plasmids were purified by Endotoxin-Free Giga prep (Qiagen, Hilden, Germany). The ability of these plasmids constructs to express DHBV large envelope and core protein has been previously demonstrated [34,40] and was re-confirmed before their use in immunotherapeutic protocols.

## Animals

DHBV-carrier Pekin ducks (*Anas domesticus*) ducks were obtained by intravenous inoculation of 3-day-old ducklings with a viremic serum pool ($2x10^8$ viral genome equivalent (vge)/animal) as previously described [8,16]. Ducks were housed at the facilities of the National Veterinary School of Lyon (ENVL, Marcy l'Etoile, France) Animal experimentation was performed in accordance with guidelines for animal care of the ethics committee of ENVL.

## Therapeutic Protocols

In adefovir-DNA protocol DHBV-carrier ducks were assigned into four groups (6-9 animals/group) (Table 1): group 1 (untreated or empty vector-treated controls), group 2 (DNA monotherapy with pCI-preS/S), group 3 (adefovir monotherapy), group 4 (combination therapy with adefovir and pCI-preS/S) (Table 1A). Adefovir administration started at week 6 post-hatch at 15 mg/kg per day, via intraperitoneal (i.p.) route as previously described [32], and was followed by drug administration for 5 days/week during 4 consecutive weeks. DNA immunization began at week 6 p.i. and was followed by 3 boosts (weeks 9, 12 and 22) (Figure 1). Ducks received a total of 150 μg of pCI-preS/S or pCI plasmid/animal/boost at three injection sites as described in detail previously [34].

**Table 1. Summary of protocols and effects on intrahepatic viral DNA clearance of two DNA vaccine-based immunotherapeutic studies**

*(A) Adefovir-DNA vaccine study*

| Treatment | Group | Adefovir | Plasmid DNA immunization | Undetectable[b] DHBV DNA | cccDNA[c] Clearance |
|---|---|---|---|---|---|
| Controls | 1 | - | pCI or none | 1/7 (0) | NT |
| DNA Monotherapy | 2 | - | pCI-preS/S | 1/5 (1) | NT |
| Adefovir Monotherapy | 3 | + | none | 0/5 (0) | NT |
| Combination Therapy | 4 | + | pCI-preS/S | 2/5 (1) | NT |

*(B) Lamivudine-DNA vaccine study*

| Treatment | Group | Lamivudine | Plasmid DNA immunization | Undetectable[b] DHBV DNA | cccDNA[c] clearance |
|---|---|---|---|---|---|
| Controls | 1 | - | pCI or none | 1/5 | 0/5 (0) |
| DNA Monotherapy | 2<br>3<br>4 | - | pCI-preS/S<br>pCI-preS/S & pCI-C<br>pCI-C | 0/4<br>2/4<br>3/7 | 0/4 (1)<br>1/4 (1)<br>3/7 (2) |
| Lamivudine Monotherapy | 5 | + | pCI or none | 0/7 | 0/7 (0) |
| Combination Therapy | 6<br>7<br>8 | + | pCI-preS/S<br>pCI-preS/S & pCI-C<br>pCI-C | 4/8<br>2/3<br>0/4 | 3/8 (3)<br>2/3 (0)<br>0/4 (0) |

[a] DHBV-carrier ducks were assigned into following groups : controls (untreated or empty vector-treated); DNA vaccine monotherapy with plasmids encoding either viral envelope (pCI-preS/S) and/or core (pCI-C); antiviral drug (adefovir or lamivudine) monotherapy; combination therapy with antiviral drug and DNA vaccine as detailed in Materials and Methods.

[b]number of ducks presenting undetectable liver DHBV DNA/number of treated ducks as assessed by Southern blot analysis of autopsy liver samples at the end of follow-up;

[c]cccDNA clearance was defined as cccDNA levels at or below real-time PCR detection limit (0.04 ccc-DHBV DNA copies/cell); number of animals which seroconverted is indicated in parentheses. NT-not tested.

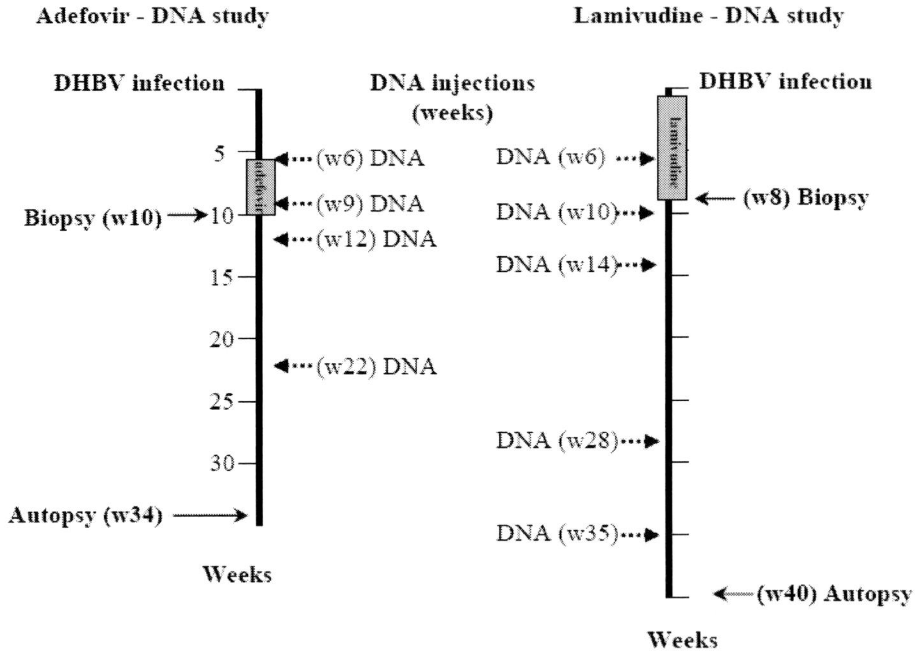


Figure 1. Design of therapeutic protocols for adefovir-DNA and lamivudine-DNA studies. DHBV-carriers ducks were obtained by i.v. inoculation of 3-day old ducklings with viremic DHBV serum pool. The antiviral treatment (grey bar) consisted in either adefovir or lamivudine administration, which was associated or not with DNA-based immunizations against DHBV envelope and/or capsid proteins (dotted arrows) at different weeks p.i. as specified in brackets (w). Arrows symbolize biopsy and autopsy.

In lamivudine-DNA protocol, chronically infected ducks were randomly assigned into 8 groups (6-9 animals/group): group 1 (untreated or empty vector-treated controls), groups 2-4 (DNA monotherapy with pCI-preS/S or pCI-preS/S and pCI-C or pCI-C respectively), group 5 (lamivudine monotherapy), groups 6-8 (combination therapy with lamivudine and pCI-preS/S or pCI-preS/S and pCI-C or pCI-C respectively) as detailed in Table 1B. Lamivudine was administrated (groups 5-8) at 25 mg/kg/day via i.p. route during 5 consecutive days of the 1$^{st}$ week post infection (p.i.) and thereafter 3 times/week during 7 following weeks. DNA immunization consisted in multiple intramuscular (i.m.) injections of 300 µg endotoxin-free plasmid DNA per animal (weeks 6,10,14,28,35) as described [34,35,40] (Figure 1).

In both protocols blood samples were collected three times a week during the first 5 weeks p.i. and once a week thereafter until the end of the of follow-up i.e. week 34 and 40 for adefovir-DNA and lamivudine-DNA protocols respectively. Monitoring of animal weight was performed throughout the entire follow-up.

## Duck Liver Biopsy and Autopsy

Liver biopsies were performed under general anaesthesia with 15 mg/kg of tiletamin and 15 mg/kg of zolazepam (Zoletil; Virbac, Carros, France) at the end of each antiviral treatment *i.e.* at week 10$^{th}$ and 8$^{th}$ p.i. for adefovir-DNA and lamivudine-DNA study respectively in randomly selected 2 or 3 ducks from different groups. At week 40 and 34 respectively all animals from adefovir-DNA and lamivudine-DNA study were euthanized by pentobarbital injection (Dolethal; Vetoquinol, Lure, France).

## ELISA Analysis of Anti-Pre-S Response

The humoral anti-preS response of ducks was determined in a direct ELISA using the recombinant preS protein as detailed previously [6, 35]. The end-point titres were taken as the reciprocal of the highest serum dilution which gave an $OD_{405}$ above the mean signal of 2 replicates of control sera [6, 35].

## Analysis of Viremia

Viremia was assessed by serum DHBV DNA detection using a previously described dot blot hybridization assay [8]. Filters were scanned by PhosphorImager (Amersham Pharmacia Biotech) and counted by the ImageQuant software as described [8]. The limit of DHBV DNA detection was 0.5 pg.

## Analysis of Intrahepatic Viral DNA

Total viral DNA was extracted from biopsy or autopsy liver samples according to procedures previously described [8, 18]. In addition, a specific extraction of non-protein bound cccDNA was performed as described [17, 18]. Ten micrograms of total DNA or cccDNA preparation were then subjected to electrophoresis through 0.9% agarose gel, transferred by blotting to a nylon membrane (Hybond $N^+$, Amersham Pharmacia Biotech), and viral DNA was detected by hybridization with a radiolabelled probe followed autoradiography as described previously [8].

### *Quantification of Liver cccDNA by Real-Time PCR*

The selective quantification of intrahepatic DHBV cccDNA was similar to that previously described by Werle-Lapostolle *et al.* [45] for HBV cccDNA quantification. Briefly, selective primers for DHBV cccDNA amplification (targeted to opposite sides of the single-stranded gap region of relaxed circular DHBV DNA) were designed using Oligo 5 software (MedProbe, Olso, Norway). To enhance specificity of cccDNA detection, Plasmide-safe DNase (Epicentre, Madison, WI) was used, which efficiently degraded single stranded and relaxed circular forms of viral DNA prior to PCR, but not cccDNA [45]. Thus, 500 ng of extracted DNA were digested for 1 hour at 37°C in a 20 µl volume containing 2.5 mM ATP, 1X Plasmid-safe DNase reaction buffer, and 2 units of Plasmid-safe DNase, followed by subsequent DNase inactivation at 70°C for 30 minutes. Real-time PCR was performed in a Light Cycler (Roche, Grenoble, France) using 4 µl of this reaction volume in the presence of 0.5 mM of the following primers used for amplification: forward 5'-

GCTGCTTGCCAAGGTATC-3' (cccDS1 nt 2554-2571) and reverse primer 5'-CCCTGTGTAGTCTGCCAG-3' (cccDAS1 nt 2826-2843) and 0.2 µM and 0.4 µM of 3'-labelled fluorescein probe DHBV FL and 5'-labelled Red 640 DHBV LC probe respectively (TibMolBiol, Berlin, Germany), whose sequences were described elsewhere [31]. Amplification of 272 bp cccDNA product occurred after denaturation at 95°C for 10 minutes, followed by 45 cycles of denaturation at 95°C for 10 seconds, fluorescence acquisition at 58°C for 3 seconds, annealing for 10 seconds at 61°C and extension at 72°C for 15 seconds. All samples were analyzed in duplicate. GAPDH gene amplification, used for normalization, was performed on extracted DNA as previously described [31,38]. Detection limit was estimated as $4 \times 10^{-2}$ copies of cccDNA per cell, after spiking of intrahepatic DNA from DHBV-negative duck livers with serial dilutions of plasmid containing DHBV monomer used as quantification standards.

### Histological Analysis of Liver Samples

Three micrometers thickness formalin-fixed liver tissue sections were stained with hematoxylin-eosin-safran (HES) stain and examined, under code, with a light microscope.

### Statistical Analysis

Mann-Whitney tests were used to compare the efficiency of therapies on viremia. The Bliss Independence model was used to determine the potential additive effect of the adefovir-DNA combination therapy [12]. The association between DNA vaccination and cccDNA clearance or between cccDNA clearance and seroconversion was analyzed using the Fisher exact test. The $p<0.05$ was considered as statistically significant.

## Results

### Decrease in Viremia during Antiviral Drug Administration

In the adefovir-DNA study, a marked drop in viremia titres (97%), reaching the limit of detection of the assay, was observed during the 4 weeks of drug administration in all adefovir-treated as compared with untreated ducks (group 3, adefovir monotherapy and group 4, combination therapy) (see Figure 2). However, the rebound of viremia was observed in almost all animals every week during the 2 days off treatment. The long-term follow-up showed low and fluctuating viremia in the control groups (group1, empty vector-treated and untreated). In DNA monotherapy group 2, the viremia fluctuated with the titres comparable to that of controls (groups 1), during the first 27 weeks of follow-up, although at week 29, an important drop in viremia titers was observed which was transient and was followed by a rebound at week 30. Interestingly the median serum DHBV DNA in the combination therapy group, which received DNA vaccine and adefovir, was the lowest compared with other groups, and was maintained until the end of follow-up *i.e.* week 34 without additional DNA boosts. Analysis of individual viremia titres showed that several animals have undetectable viremia and this contributed to the lower mean viremia titres in this group. However the differences observed in the viremia medians (Figure 2), did not reach statistical significance.

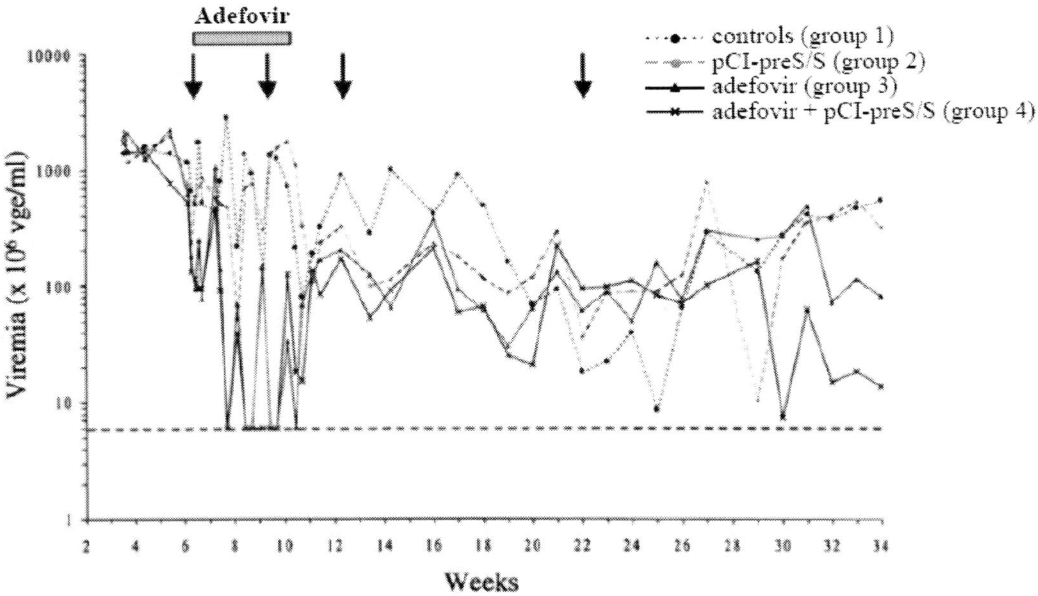


Figure 2. Effect of adefovir-DNA therapy on viremia. Viremia was monitored throughout the study period i.e. 34 weeks by DHBV DNA quantification using a dot-blot hybridization assay. The median viremia levels for each group (1-4) are plotted on the graph (logarithmic scale). Grey bar represents the adefovir treatment period (weeks 6-10 p.i.). Arrows indicate DNA injections at weeks 6, 9, 12 and 22. The cut-off of the assay is indicated by a dotted line.

In the lamivudine-DNA study, a marked decrease in viremia was observed in all drug-treated (groups 5-8) compared to untreated (groups 1-4) animals, although it was limited to only the first 3 out of 8 weeks of lamivudine treatment (Figure 3). Analysis of median viremia levels during following weeks showed a decrease and fluctuations, which were observed without significant differences between duck groups (Figure 3 and data not shown). However the review of individual viremia levels revealed that a total of 11 out of 30 animals, which received specific DNA immunization in association or not with lamivudine presented undetectable viremia starting from the 4$^{th}$ DNA immunization and up to the end of follow up (week 40) (data not shown).

The comparison of antiviral effect of adefovir versus lamivudine suggests a more potent antiviral efficacy of adefovir on viremia, which reached undetectable levels during the drug administration period and the better efficacy of a combination therapy associating adefovir with DNA vaccine. However in both studies the drop in viremia following DNA vaccine immunotherapy alone or in association with antiviral drug treatment did not reach a statistical significance. This may be due to the large individual variations in viremia within each duck group, which included as well non-responders with high viremia titers and responders animals with low or undetectable viremia.

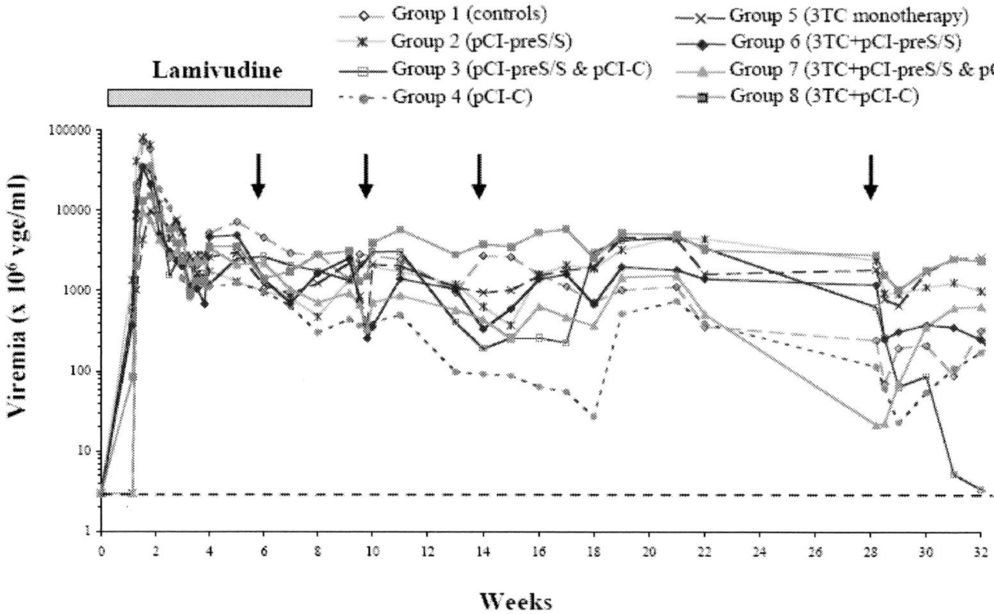


Figure 3. Effect of lamivudine-DNA therapy on viremia. Follow-up of viremia during weeks 1-34 is represented. Viremia was monitored using a dot-blot hybridization assay. The median viremia levels for each group (1-8) are plotted on the graph (logarithmic scale). Grey bar represents the lamivudine (3TC) treatment period (weeks 1-8 p.i.). Arrows indicate DNA injections at weeks 6, 10, 14, 28 and 35. The cut-off of the assay is indicated by a dotted line.

## Impact of DNA-Based Immunotherapy on Intrahepatic Viral Replication

At the end of adefovir and lamivudine treatment (week 10 and 8 respectively), randomly selected biopsy specimens (2-3 ducks) have been performed to assess the impact of antiviral drug treatment on intrahepatic viral replication. However, Southern blot analysis of these liver biopsies revealed high amounts of intrahepatic DHBV DNA replicative intermediates, including cccDNA, in ducks from different groups with or without DNA immunization irrespectively of antiviral drug (lamivudine or adefovir) and therapeutic protocol used (data not shown).

In the adefovir-DNA study, analysis of autopsy liver samples at the end of the follow-up (week 34) showed the presence of viral DNA replicative intermediates for all controls (group 1), except one duck consistently with the absence of detectable viremia in this animal. In DNA monotherapy (group 2), 1 out of 5 ducks had undetectable viral DNA and another one presented a dramatic decrease but no clearance of viral replication (Table 1A and data not shown). No DHBV DNA clearance was observed in 5 out of 5 adefovir monotherapy-treated (group 3). By contrast within the combination therapy (group 4), 2 out of 5 ducks had undetectable DHBV DNA in their livers (Table 1A) consistent with their undetectable viremia during the 4 last follow-up weeks. PhosphorImager quantification of Southern blots revealed a greater than 51% decrease in intrahepatic DHBV DNA in the combination therapy treated group, whereas adefovir or DNA monotherapy alone decreased viral DNA by 14 and 38%, respectively, compared to controls, suggesting a trend to an additive effect of both protocols in the decrease in intrahepatic viral replication levels (51% inhibition instead of 47% expected) (data not shown). However the impact of DNA therapy alone or in combination with adefovir on DHBV DNA clearance did not reach a statistical significance.

In the lamivudine-DNA study, a similar analysis of autopsy liver samples (week 40) revealed viral DNA presence in 4 out of 5 controls (group 1). Amongst animals on DNA monotherapy (groups 2-4) viral DNA clearance was observed in a total of 5 out of 15 (30%) ducks : 2/4 (50%) receiving co-immunization against envelope and core (group 3) and 3/7 (43%) immunized against core alone (group 4) (Table 1B). Interestingly none of 7 ducks on lamivudine monotherapy (group 5) eliminated DHBV DNA, whereas a total of 6 of 15 (40%) ducks on combination therapy (groups 6-8) presented undetectable viral DNA. Within those, 4 of 8 (50%) ducks on combination of lamivudine with DNA vaccine against envelope (group 6), showed undetectable viral DNA, including cccDNA, compared to 0 of 7 on lamivudine monotherapy (group 5), suggesting a trend for a beneficial effect of such combination, which was just above significance ($p$=0.07) (Table 1B). This benefit became significant if groups 6 and 7 receiving lamivudine and DNA immunization against envelope alone and in co-immunization against core protein were pooled together since 6 out of 11 (55%) animals responded to therapy having undetectable liver DHBV DNA compared to 0 out of 7 on lamivudine monotherapy ($p$=0.038). PhosphorImager quantification of Southern blots revealed no significant difference between different treatment groups 2-8 as compared with the controls and this may be related to the relatively low mean DHBV DNA levels in the controls and individual variations in DHBV DNA each treatment group, which included as well animals with high and undetectable viral DNA (data not shown).

Collectively these results suggest a better efficacy of lamivudine-DNA study since higher percentage of DHBV-carriers presented undetectable liver DHBV DNA in southern blot analysis as compared with adefovir-DNA study.

## Clearance of cccDNA Following DNA-Based Immunotherapy

In the adefovir-DNA study the Southern blot analysis following a specific cccDNA extraction confirmed undetectable cccDNA in only 4 liver samples: 2 belonging to DNA combination therapy group, 1 to DNA monotherapy and 1 to controls (Table 1A and data not shown).

In the lamivudine-DNA study we searched for persistence of residual cccDNA by a real-time PCR for cccDHBV DNA detection in liver samples showing undetectable DHBV DNA in Southern blot analysis. Out of 12 liver samples presenting undetectable cccDNA in Southern blotting, 3 presented detectable cccDNA levels between 0.2–0.7 ccc-DHBV DNA copies/cell, including a control animal (group 1), receiving empty plasmid immunization (Table 1B and data not shown). Importantly, 9 out of 30 (30%) ducks from DNA monotherapy (groups 2-4) and combination therapy (groups 6-8), showed cccDNA levels at or under the lowed detection limit of real-time PCR (0.04 ccc-DHBV DNA copies/cell) *i.e.* at least 1000-fold lower as compared with the controls or lamivudine monotherapy treated ducks, which had about 35 to 45 (mean 40) cccDNA copies/cell (Table 1B and data not shown). These results were reproducibly observed in three independent experiments.

Therefore DNA vaccine-based immunotherapy alone and combined with lamivudine resulted in a sustained suppression of DHBV replication in about one third of carriers.

Correlation between virus clearance and restoration of huomoral immune responses Before use of pCI-preS/S and pCI-C plasmids for therapeutic DNA vaccination of chronic DHBV-carriers ducks, using either adefovir-DNA or lamivudine-DNA protocol, we have first tested their ability to induce anti-preS and anti-C humoral response in naïve ducks. Significant and specific anti-preS and anti-C antibody response that reached a plateau level after 2$^{nd}$ DNA boost was observed in naïves animals immunized either with preS/S or with pCI-C respectively. No difference was found in magnitude and kinetics of anti-preS response following pCI-preS/S immunization alone or in association with pCI-C plasmid (data not shown).

Next, we investigated whether humoral immune tolerance could be broken in DHBV carriers by a DNA vaccine and whether it could be correlated with viral cccDNA clearance. In the adefovir-DNA study only 2 out of 10 (20%) DHBV-carriers which received DNA mono- or combination therapy mounted a detectable anti-preS response. The presence of anti-preS antibodies was associated with low or undetectable levels of intrahepatic DHBV DNA (Table 1A and data not shown). However, anti-preS antibodies were undetectable in two other animals, one belonging to DNA monotherapy and another one to combination therapy group, which had either cleared or had dramatically lowered liver DHBV DNA (data not shown). Thus no clear correlation could be established between DHBV DNA clearance following DNA vaccine based immunotherapy and induction or restoration of anti-preS response in this study.

This contrasts with the results observed in the lamivudine-DNA study. No anti-preS antibody response was detected in untreated or empty vector-immunized controls (group 1), including one duck having undetectable viral DNA in Southern blotting but clearly detectable in real-time PCR (data not shown). Only 1 duck (group 2) mounted anti-preS response within a total of 28 ducks, which have not shown serum and liver DHBV DNA clearance (Table 1B and data not shown). Interestingly, seroconversion to anti-preS was observed in 6 out of 9 (66%) ducks which cleared cccDNA as assessed by real-time PCR. Within these 6 animals, 3 belonged to combination therapy (group 6) and 3 to DNA monotherapy (groups 3-4) (Table 1B).

As illustrated in Figure 4 for one representative duck (no 175) from combination therapy group 6, the seroconversion to anti-preS was observed after 1$^{st}$ or 2$^{nd}$ DNA boost. Therefore, in lamivudine-DNA study the seroconversion to anti-preS was observed in 6 out of 9 (66%) ducks with cccDNA clearance defined as cccDNA levels at or below real-time PCR detection limit, compared to seroconversion of only 1 out of 28 (3.6%) ducks without clearance whatever treatment group ($p<0.001$), suggesting a significant correlation between viral cccDNA clearance and restoration of humoral response in these animals.

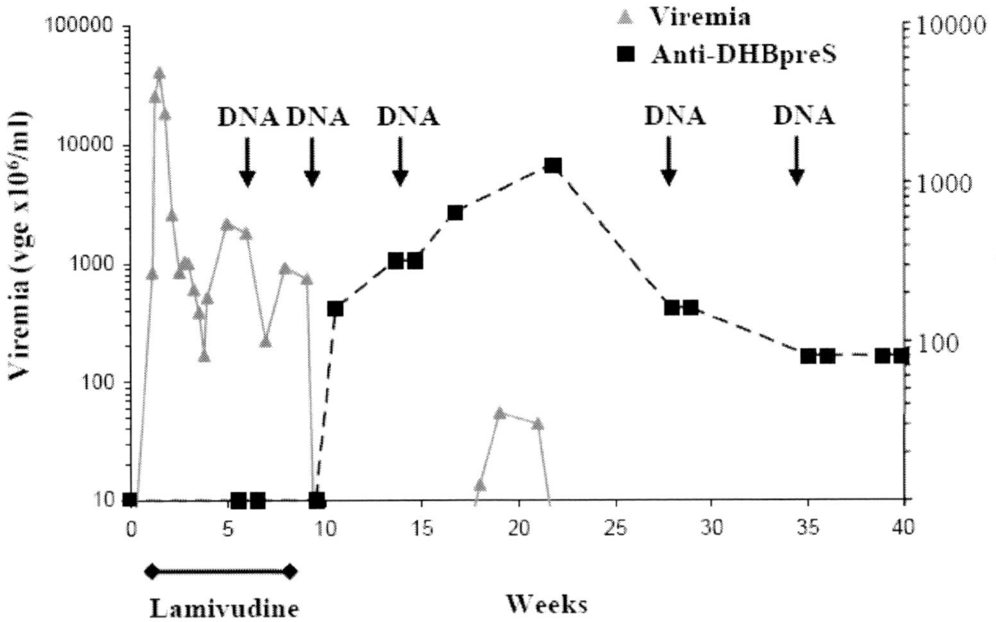


Figure 4. Individual evolution of viremia in correlation with seroconversion during DHBV infection clearance. Evolution of viremia and anti-preS humoral response (logarithmic scale) for one duck (no 175, group 6) belonging to lamivudine-DNA study. This DHBV-carrier duck received combination therapy associating lamivudine with pCI-preS/S plasmid and cleared cccDNA in its liver as assessed by real-time PCR (see also Table 1B). The anti-preS titers, determined by a direct ELISA test and viremia were monitored throughout the study. Black arrows show DNA injections. Black bar represents the lamivudine treatment period.

### Absence of Adverse Effects of Therapy

In both adefovir-DNA and lamivudine-DNA studies no significant variations in animal weight were observed indicating that treatments were well-tolerated. Several death occurred within follow-up, although they were accidental and occurred within all animal groups whatever the protocol used. Liver histology analysis showed occasional presence of steatosis, amyloidosis and mild to moderate inflammatory infiltrates in duck livers without marked differences between different treatment groups from both studies (data not shown).

## Discussion

We investigated here whether DNA vaccine-based immunotherapy in combination or not with an antiviral drug (adefovir, lamivudine) treatment is able to enhance cccDNA clearance and break humoral immune tolerance in chronic DHBV carriers. We have first realized a study associating adefovir with DNA vaccine against DHBV envelope [18] and compared herein its therapeutic efficacy with our recent study combining lamivudine with DNA vaccine against viral envelope and/or core proteins [41]. We report herein a better efficacy of lamivudine-DNA study since DNA vaccine alone and after treatment with lamivudine was able to eliminate viremia and intrahepatic cccDNA in about 30% of carriers, which was tightly correlated with the restoration of specific humoral immune responses. This is of particular interest, since in term of antiviral efficacy lamivudine was less potent as compared with adefovir. Thus, in adefovir-DNA study the viremia analysis showed the potent antiviral effect of adefovir during the 4 weeks of drug administration consistent with the observations of Nicoll et al. [32]. In addition, adefovir-treated DHBV-carrier ducks exhibited undetectable viremia levels during the drug administration period. This contrasts with the lamivudine-DNA study in which the drop of viremia was less pronounced and viremia remained detectable during the entire antiviral treatment. However, despite a marked decrease in viremia peak, adefovir or lamivudine treatments have not significantly decreased liver DHBV replication as assessed by biopsies examination from randomly chosen animals at the end of drug treatment. In addition, the decrease in viremia was transient and was followed by a rebound after drug cessation in all animals as well from lamivudine monotherapy as adefovir monotherapy groups. This is not surprising, since in both studies at the end follow-up (week 34 and 40), the intrahepatic viral cccDNA form responsible for chronicity of infection was still detectable in all ducks from adefovir or lamivudine monotherapy groups respectively. Thus, neither adefovir nor lamivudine alone had exhibited a sustained antiviral pressure during the 4 or 8 weeks respectively of drug administration in this model.

By contrast, the analysis of DHBV DNA in autopsy liver samples revealed that DNA vaccine-based immunotherapy alone and combined with antiviral drug treatment was able in both studies to considerable decrease and even eliminate the replicative DHBV DNA intermediates, including the cccDNA. Thus in adefovir-DNA study, 3 out of 10 animals (30%) which received DNA vaccine alone or combined with adefovir had undetectable viral DNA in their livers, including the cccDNA. In addition, combination therapy with adefovir led to a more pronounced decrease (51%) in the total intrahepatic viral load as compared with DNA monotherapy (38%). In spite of relatively small number of animals in this study, Bliss independence analysis [12] suggested a trend to an additive antiviral effect of therapy combining adefovir with DNA immunization against the hepadnaviral envelope protein [18]. In the lamivudine-DNA study we have also observed that elimination of replicative DHBV DNA intermediates occurred in DNA vaccine-treated groups only and was more pronounced in animals on combination (40%) as compared with those on DNA monotherapy (30%), suggesting a benefit of antiviral drug association with DNA vaccine, although this effect was relatively modest and did not reach statistical significance. It is of interest to note that if groups receiving lamivudine and DNA vaccine against envelope alone and in co-immunization against core were pooled together a significant benefit of combination therapy compared to lamivudine monotherapy was observed, suggesting a role of DNA immunization against envelope protein in therapeutic efficiency of such combination therapy.

In recent years it become increasingly apparent that intranuclear hepadnaviral cccDNA pool plays a crucial role in persistence and reactivation of viral replication as documented by studies in animal models and in chronically infected patients [1,19,25,29,45,47]. Another important issue of our studies was therefore the search for residual cccDNA presence in ducks, which apparently resolved infection following DNA mono- or combination therapy. To address this issue we designed a highly sensitive quantitative real-time PCR for DHBV cccDNA detection similar to the assay recently developed for human HBV cccDNA quantification [45]. We have not analyzed by this assay the presence of residual cccDNA in duck livers from adefovir-DNA study, since all but 3 liver samples presented detectable cccDNA in Southern blot analysis. However, analysis of 12 duck livers from lamivudine study presenting undetectable DHBV DNA in Southern blotting, revealed that 9 (30%) of carriers receiving DNA vaccine alone or combined with lamivudine had cccDNA levels that were at or under the lower limit of detection (0.04 cccDNA copies/cell) of this assay. By contrast no cccDNA clearance was observed in lamivudine monotherapy-treated animals presenting about 40 cccDNA copies/cell, consistently with reported estimates of cccDNA copy number from 30 to 50/cell in chronically DHBV-infected duck livers [1]. Whether the residual cccDNA, which was undetectable by us using the real-time PCR, may act as a template for viral replication or alternatively may be inert and non replicative, as suggested recently in a study analyzing cccDNA in ducks that resolved transient DHBV infection [19], remains an open question which deserves further investigations. In this regard our data are promising, since the viremia and cccDNA remained undetectable at week 40 in 30% of ducks indicating already no rebound in viral replication during the 5 weeks following immunotherapy cessation.

The optimal DNA vaccine-based immunotherapy would break immunologic tolerance in virus carriers. In the adefovir-DNA study, the analysis of the anti-preS response in chronically infected ducks on DNA mono-or combination therapy showed no clear correlation between antibody response and viral clearance. By contrast, in the lamivudine-DNA study viral elimination was tightly associated with seroconversion, since 66% of ducks that cleared serum and liver DHBV DNA, including the cccDNA pool undetectable by real-time PCR, developed an anti-preS response compared to only 3% of ducks which seroconverted without viral elimination. These data indicate a significant ($p<0.001$) correlation between viral cccDNA clearance following DNA-based immunotherapy and restoration or activation of specific humoral responses. This is an important finding of our study, since data accumulated in HBV-transgenic mice [23,28] and in patients [24,46] showed the ability of DNA vaccine to decrease intrahepatic hepadnaviral replication and to break immune tolerance, although the correlation with cccDNA clearance has not yet been demonstrated. However, in the lamivudine-DNA study not all carriers, which cleared viral replication, have mounted a detectable anti-preS response. This can be related to the immune complexes presence in serum of these animals, which masked circulating anti-preS antibodies and hampered their detection in our ELISA test. In both adefovir and lamivudine-DNA studies we were unable to analyze the role of T cell response in viral clearance, since the tools for duck cellular response analysis are still lacking and need to be developped. The ongoing characterization of these responses and in particular recent development by us of duck IFN-γ RNA monitoring [31], should allow a better understanding of immunity modulation during DHBV infection clearance.

It is important to note that DNA vaccine–based immunotherapy in association with adefovir or lamivudine was safe and well tolerated. Thus, in spite of accidental deaths which occurred during these long-term studies, liver histology revealed occasional presence of changes, which are frequently observed in DHBV-infected adult Pekin ducks [34], in animals from both adefovir and lamivudine-DNA study regardless of treatment group.

Altogether our results indicate a better therapeutic efficacy of the lamivudine-DNA protocol as compared with adefovir-DNA protocol in which only modest effect in term of viral cccDNA clearance and seroconversion was observed in spite of higher antiviral efficacy of the drug. Foster et al. [10] investigated entacavir (ETV) treatment combination with DNA vaccination to DHBV envelope and core and showed a potent antiviral effect of ETV on serum and liver viral DNA, however DNA vaccine was ineffective in reduction or clearance of viral cccDNA. The above-mentioned studies differed not only by the choice of antiviral drug but, importantly, by the design of DNA immunization protocol, which may play a key role in the better efficacy of DNA-lamivudine study. Thus, the lamivudine-DNA differs by a number of factors from adefovir-DNA protocol such as: i/ larger amounts of plasmid DNA (300 versus 150 μgDNA/animal/boost), ii/ higher number of DNA boosts (5 versus 4) including two delayed boosts (weeks 28, 35) versus one (week 22), iii/ and longer DNA immunization schedule. In both studies the same pCI-preS/S plasmid was used for immunization against viral envelope, although in the lamivudine-DNA study we have added core as an additional target for DNA vaccine, since genetic immunization against DHBV core has been recently set up by us and demonstrated to induce potent and specific humoral responses in naïve ducks [41]. Moreover, the schedule of combination therapy and in particular drug-DNA immunizations overlap was different in both studies as illustrated in Figure 1. Finally, a larger number of animals and a longer follow-up period allowed us to appreciate a sustained antiviral effect of DNA-vaccine based immunotherapy in the lamivudine-DNA study.

In conclusion, we have analyzed two pre-clinical combination therapy studies associating a DNA vaccine with two different antiviral drugs in the chronic DHBV infection model. We showed a higher potency of lamivudine-DNA protocol, conducted in a large group of chronic DHBV-carriers ducks, which provided a first demonstration that DNA vaccine-based immunotherapy alone and associated with antiviral drug treatment was able to induce drastic and sustained suppression of viremia and to enhance intrahepatic viral cccDNA clearance, which, importantly, was tightly correlated with restoration of specific humoral responses. A number of factors known to determine the success of genetic vaccination such as plasmid construct, amounts of plasmid DNA delivered, number of DNA injections and immunization schedule [20] may play an important role in better therapeutic efficacy of lamivudine-DNA protocol described herein as compared with studies previously published by us and others [10,18,34]. The development of a therapeutic DNA vaccine has been recently accelerated with first clinical trials showing its safety and ability to activate T-cell responses in some HBV infected patients [24,46]. Further studies aiming to increase the potency of DNA vaccine–based immunotherapeutics need to be performed in animal models in view to obtain a complete and sustain recovery from chronic hepatitis B. In this view, genetic immunization with plasmid constructs encoding hepadnaviral proteins and gamma interferon has been recently demonstrated as particularly effective in immune responses stimulation [37,44] suggesting a therapeutic potential of such novel DNA vaccine that deserve further exploration in woodchuck and duck models of chronic hepatitis B.

## Acknowledgments

We are grateful to Craig S. Gibbs (Gilead Sciences) to provide us with adefovir and to John Rhodes (GlaxoSmithKline) to provide us with lamivudine. This work was supported by grant from ARC and GlaxoSmithKline, AT was recipient of a fellowship from Mérieux Foundation and ARC. The authors are grateful to Catherine Jamard, for expert assistance with animals.

## References

[1] Addison, WR; Walters, KA; Wong, WWS; Wilson, JS; Madej, D; Jewell, LD; Tyrrell, DL. Half-life of the Duck Hepatitis B Virus covalently closed circular DNA pool *in vivo* following inhibition of viral replication. *J. Virol.*, 2002, 76, 6356-6363.

[2] Angus, PR; Vaughan, S; Xiong, H; Yang, W; Delaney, C; Gibbs, C; Brosgart, C; Colledge, D; Edwards, R; Ayres, A; Bartholomeusz, A; Locarnini, S. Resistance to adefovir dipivoxil therapy associated with the selection of a novel mutation in the HBV polymerase. *Gastroenterology*, 2003,125, 292-297.

[3] Boni, C; Bertoletti, A; Penna, A; Cavalli, A; Pilli, M; Urbani, S; Scognamiglio, P; Boehme, R; Panebianco, R; Fiaccadori, F; Ferrari, C. Lamivudine treatment can restore T cell responsiveness in chronic hepatitis B. *J. Clin. Invest.*, 1998,102, 968-975.

[4] Boni C; Penna A; Ogg GS; Bertoletti A; Pilli M; Cavallo C; Cavalli, A; Urbani, S; Boehme, R; Panebianco, R; Fiaccadori, F; Ferrari, C. Lamivudine treatment can overcome cytotoxic T-cell hyporesponsiveness in chronic hepatitis B: new perspectives for immune therapy. *Hepatology*, 2001, 33, 963-971.

[5] Boni C; Penna A; Bertoletti A; Lamonaca V; Rapti I; Missale G; Pilli, M; Urbani, S; Cavalli, A; Cerioni, S; Panebianco, R; Jenkins, J; Ferrari, C. Transient restoration of anti-viral T cell responses induced by lamivudine therapy in chronic hepatitis B. *J. Hepatol.* 2003, 39, 595-605.

[6] Chassot, S; Lambert, V; Kay, A; Godinot, C; Trépo, C; Cova, L. Identification of major antigenic domains of duck hepatitis B virus pre-S protein by peptide scanning. *Virology* 1994, 200, 72-78.

[7] Chisari, FV. Rous-Whipple Award Lecture. Viruses, immunity, and cancer: lessons from hepatitis B. *Am. J. Pathol.*, 2000, 156, 1117-1132.

[8] Cova, L; Zoulim, F. Duck hepatitis B virus model in the study of hepatitis B virus. *Methods Mol. Med*, 2004, 96, 261-268.

[9] Davis, HL; McCluskie, MJ; Gerin, JL; Purcell, RH. DNA vaccine for hepatitis B: evidence for immunogenicity in chimpanzees and comparison with other vaccines. *Proc. Natl. Acad. Sci. USA*, 1996, 93, 7213-7218.

[10] Foster, WK; Miller, D; Marion, PL; Colonno, RJ; Kotlarski, I; Jilbert, AR. Entecavir therapy combined with DNA vaccination for persistent duck hepatitis B virus infection. *Antimicrob Agents Chemother*, 2003, 47, 2624-2635.

[11] Garcia-Navarro, R; Blanco-Urgoiti, B; Berraondo, P; Sanchez de la Rosa, R; Vales, A; Hervas-Stubbs, S; Lasarte, JJ; Borras, F; Ruiz, J; Prieto, J. Protection against

woodchuck hepatitis virus (WHV) infection by gene gun co-immunization with WHV core and interleukin-12. *J. Virol.*, 2001, 75, 9068-9076.

[12] Greco, WR; Bravo, G; Parsons, JC. The search for synergy: a critical review from a response surface perspective. *Pharmacol. Rev.*, 1995, 47 (2), 331-385.

[13] Horiike, N; Fazle Akbar, SM; Michitaka, K; Joukou, K; Yamamoto, K; Kojima, N; Hiasa, Y; Abe, M; Onji, M. *In vivo* immunization by vaccine therapy following virus suppression by lamivudine: a novel approach for treating patients with chronic hepatitis B. *J. Clin. Virol.*, 2005, 32, 156-161.

[14] Korba, BE; Cote, PJ; Menne, S; Toshkov, I; Baldwin, BH; Wells, FV; Tennant, BC; Gerin, JL. Clevudine therapy with vaccine inhibits progression of chronic hepatitis and delays onset of hepatocellular carcinoma in chronic woodchuck hepatitis virus infection. *Antivir. Ther.*, 2004, 9**,** 937-52.

[15] Lai, CL; Dienstag, J; Schiff, E; Leung, NW; Atkins, M; Hunt, C; Brown, N; Woessner, M; Boehme, R; Condreay, L. Prevalence and clinical correlates of YMDD variants during lamivudine therapy for patients with chronic hepatitis B. *Clin. Infect. Dis.*, 2003, 36, 687-696.

[16] Le Guerhier, F; Pichoud, C; Guerret, S; Chevallier, M; Jamard, C; Hantz, O; Li, XY; Chen, SH; King, I; Trepo, C; Cheng, YC; Zoulim, F. Characterization of the antiviral effect of 2',3'-dideoxy-2', 3'-didehydro-beta-L-5-fluorocytidine in the duck hepatitis B virus infection model. *Antimicrob Agents Chemother*, 2000, 44, 111-122.

[17] Le Guerhier, F; Pichoud, C; Jamard, C; Guerret, S; Chevallier, M; Peyrol, S; Hantz, O; King, I; Trepo, C; Cheng, YC; Zoulim, F. Antiviral activity of beta-L-2',3'-dideoxy-2',3'-didehydro-5-fluorocytidine in woodchucks chronically infected with woodchuck hepatitis virus. *Antimicrob Agents Chemother*, 2001, 45, 1065-1077.

[18] Le Guerhier, F; Thermet, A; Guerret, S; Chevallier, M; Jamard, C; Gibbs, CS; Trepo, C; Cova, L; Zoulim, F. Antiviral effect of adefovir in combination with a DNA vaccine in the duck hepatitis B virus infection model. *J. Hepatol.*, 2003, 38, 328-334.

[19] Le Mire, MF; Miller, DS; Foster, WK; Burrell, CJ; Jilbert, A. Covalently closed circular DNA is the predominant form of duck hepatitis B virus DNA that persists following transient infection. *J. Virol.*, 2005, 79, 12242-12252.

[20] Leitner, WW; Ying, H; Restifo, NP. DNA and RNA-based vaccines: principles, progress and prospects. *Vaccine*, 2000, 18, 765-777.

[21] Leung, NW; Lai, CL; Chang, TT; Guan, R; Lee, CM; Ng, KY; Lim, SG; Wu, PC; Dent, JC; Edmundson, S; Condreay, LD; Chien, RN. Extended lamivudine treatment in patients with chronic hepatitis B enhances hepatitis B e antigen seroconversion rates: results after 3 years of therapy. *Hepatology*, 2001, 33, 1527-1532.

[22] Lu, MJ; Hilken, G; Kruppenbacher, J; Kemper, T; Schirmbeck, R; Reimann, J; Roggendorf, M. Immunization of woodchucks with plasmids expressing woodchuck hepatitis virus (WHV) core antigen and surface antigen suppresses WHV infection. *J. Virol.*, 1999, 73, 281-289.

[23] Mancini, M; Hadchouel, M; Davis, HL; Whalen, RG; Tiollais, P; Michel, ML. DNA-mediated immunization in a transgenic mouse model of the hepatitis B surface antigen chronic carrier state. *Proc. Natl. Acad. Sci. USA*, 1996, 93, 12496-12501.

[24] Mancini-Bourgine, M; Fontaine, H; Scott-Algara, D; Pol, S; Brechot, C; Michel, ML. Induction or expansion of T-cell responses by a hepatitis B DNA vaccine administered to chronic HBV carriers. *Hepatology*, 2004, 40, 874-882.

[25] Mason, WS; Cullen, J; Moraleda, G; Saputelli, J; Aldrich, CE; Miller, DS; Tennant, B; Frick, L; Averett, D; Condreay, LD; Jilbert, AR. Lamivudine therapy of WHV-infected woodchucks. *Virology*, 1998, 245, 18-32.

[26] Mason, WS; Cullen, J; Saputelli, J; Wu, TT; Liu, C; London, WT; Lustbader, E; Schaffer, P; O'Connell, AP; Fourel, I; *et al.* Characterization of the antiviral effects of 2'-carbodeoxyguanosine in ducks chronically infected with duck hepatitis B virus. *Hepatology* 1994, 19, 398-411.

[27] Michel, ML; Davis, HL; Schleef, M; Mancini, M; Tiollais, P; Whalen, RG. DNA-mediated immunization to the hepatitis B surface antigen in mice: aspects of the humoral response mimic hepatitis B viral infection in humans. *Proc. Natl. Acad. Sci. USA*, 1995, 92, 5307-5311.

[28] Michel ML. Towards immunotherapy for chronic hepatitis B virus infections. *Vaccine*, 2002, 19, 83-88.

[29] Moraleda, G; Saputelli, J; Adrich, CE; Averett, D; Condreay, L; Mason, WS. Lack of effect of antiviral therapy in nondividing hepatocyte cultures on the closed circular DNA of woodchuck hepatitis virus. *J. Virol.*, 1997, 71, 9392-9399.

[30] Nafa, S; Ahmed, S; Tavan, D; Pichoud, C; Berby, F; Stuyver, L; Johnson, M; Merle, P; Abidi, H; Trepo, C; Zoulim, F. Early detection of viral resistance by determination of hepatitis B virus polymerase mutations in patients treated by lamivudine for chronic hepatitis B. *Hepatology*, 2000, 32, 1078-1088.

[31] Narayan, R; Buronfosse, T; Schultz, U; Chevallier-Gueyron, P; Guerre, S; Chevalier, M; Saade, F; Ndeboko, B; Trepo, C; Zoulim, F; Cova, L. Rise in interferon gamma expression during resolution of Duck Hepatitis B Virus infection. *J. Gen. Virol.*, 2006, 87, 3225-3232.

[32] Nicoll, AJ; Colledge, DL; Toole, JJ; Angus, W; Smallwood, R A; Locarnini, SA.. Inhibition of duck hepatitis B virus replication by 9-(2-phosphonylmethoxyethyl)adenine, an acyclic phosphonate nucleoside analogue. *Antimicrob Agents Chemother*. 1998, 42, 3130-3135.

[33] Perrillo, R; Schiff, E; Yoshida, E; Statler, A; Hirsch, K; Wright, T; Gutfreund, K; Lamy, P; Murray A. Adefovir dipivoxil for the treatment of lamivudine-resistant hepatitis B mutants. *Hepatology*, 2000, 32(1),129-134.

[34] Rollier, C; Sunyach, C; Barraud, L; Madani, N; Jamard, C; Trepo, C; Cova, L. Protective and therapeutic effect of DNA-based immunization against hepadnavirus large envelope protein. *Gastroenterology*, 1999, 116, 658-665.

[35] Rollier, C; Charollois, C; Jamard, C; Tepo, C; Cova, L. Early life humoral response of ducks to DNA immunization against hepadnavirus large envelope protein. *Vaccine*, 2000, 18, 3091-3096.

[36] Rollier, C; Charollois, C; Jamard, C; Tepo, C; Cova, L. Maternally transferred antibodies from DNA-immunized avians protect offspring against hepadnavirus infection. *J. Virol.*, 2000, 74, 4908-4911.

[37] Saade, F; Buronfosse, T; Narayan, R; Schultz, U; Zoulim, F; Trepo, C; Cova, L. Codelivery of cytokines genes DNA vaccine to ducks hepatitis B virus improves its therapeutic efficacy. *J. Clin. Virol.*, 2006, 36, S31.

[38] Seigneres, B; Martin, P; Werle, B; Schorr, O; Jamard, C; Rimsky, L; Trepo, C; Zoulim, F. Effects of pyrimidine and purine analog combinations in the duck hepatitis B virus infection model. *Antimicrob Agents Chemother*, 2003, 47, 1842-1852.

[39] Tenney, DJ; Levine, SM; Rose, RE; Walsh, AW; Weinheimer, SP; Discotto, L; Plym, M; Pokornowski, K; Yu, CF; Angus, P; Ayres, A; Bartholomeusz, A; Sievert, W; Thompson, G; Warner, N; Locarnini, S; Colonno, RJ. Clinical emergence of entecavir-resistant hepatitis B virus requires additional substitutions in virus already resistant to Lamivudine. *Antimicrob Agents Chemother*, 2004, 48, 3498-3507.

[40] Thermet, A; Robaczewska, M; Rollier, C; Hantz, O; Trepo, C; Deleage, G; Cova, L. Identification of antigenic regions of duck hepatitis B virus core protein with antibodies elicited by DNA immunization and chronic infection. *J. Virol.*, 2004, 78, 1945-1953.

[41] Thermet, A; Buronfosse, T; Werle-Lapostolle, W; Chevallier, M; Pradat, P; Trepo, C; Zoulim, F; Cova, L. DNA vaccination in combination or not with lamivudine treatment breaks humoral immune tolerance and enhances cccDNA clearance in the ducks model of chronic hepatitis B virus infection. *J.Gen.Virol., 2008, 89,1192-1201.*

[42] Triyatni, M; Jilbert, AR; Qiao, M; Miller, DS; Burrell, CJ. Protective efficacy of DNA vaccines against duck hepatitis B virus infection. *J. Virol.*, 1998, 1, 84-94.

[43] Villeneuve, JP; Durantel, D; Durantel, S; Westland, C; Xiong, S; Brosgart, CL; Gibbs, CS; Parvaz, P; Werle, B; Trepo, C; Zoulim, F. Selection of a hepatitis B virus strain resistant to adefovir in a liver transplantation patient. *J. Hepatol.*, 2003, 39, 1085-1089.

[44] Wang, J; Gujar, SA; Cova, L; Michalak, TI. Bicistronic woodchuck hepatitis virus core and gamma interferon DNA vaccine can protect from hepatitis but does not elicit sterilizing antiviral immunity. *J. Virol.*, 2007, 2, 903-916.

[45] Werle-Lapostolle, B; Bowden, S; Locarnini, S; Wursthorn, K; Petersen, J; Lau, G; Trepo, C; Marcellin, P; Goodman, Z; Delaney, WE; Xiong, S; Brosgart, CL; Chen, SS; Gibbs, CS; Zoulim, F. Persistence of cccDNA during the natural history of chronic hepatitis B and decline during adefovir dipivoxil therapy. *Gastroenterology*, 2004, 126, 1750-1758.

[46] Yang, SH; Lee, CG; Park, SH; Im, SJ; Kim, YM; Son, JM; Wang, JS; Yoon, SK; Song, MK; Ambrozaitis, A; Kharchenko, N; Yun, YD; Kim, CM; Kim, CY; Lee, SH; Kim, BM; Kim, WB; Sung, YC. Correlation of antiviral T-cell responses with suppression of viral rebound in chronic hepatitis B carriers: a proof-of-concept study. *Gene. Ther.*, 2006, 13, 1110-1117.

[47] Zoulim F. Antiviral therapy of chronic hepatitis B: can we clear the virus and prevent drug resistance ? *Antivir. Chem. Chemother*, 2004, 15, 299-305.

In: New Immunology Research Developments
Editor: Gunter V. Müller

ISBN 978-1-60021-701-2


*Chapter 9*

# Omega-3 Fatty Acids in Early Life and Links to Immune Development and Allergy Prevention

***Janet Dunstan and Susan L. Prescott***
School Paediatrics and Child Health Research,
University of Western Australia, Perth, Western Australia
PO Box D184, Princess Margaret Hospital, Perth WA 6001, Australia

## Abstract

Environmental changes over the last 40-50 years have been associated with an epidemic increase in many immune-mediated diseases, particularly allergic diseases. Changing dietary habits are among a number of Western lifestyle changes implicated in the increasing susceptibility to inflammatory disease, including a decline in omega-3 polyunsaturated fatty acids (n-3 PUFA), which have well described anti-inflammatory properties. There has been growing speculation that reduced exposure to these protective dietary factors may adversely influence patterns of immune responsiveness, particularly in during critical stages of "immune programming" in early life. This chapter reviews the anti-inflammatory properties of n-3 PUFA in the context of allergic disease. It also examines epidemiological links between dietary n-3 PUFA and the risk of inflammatory symptomatology, particularly in early life. Associations between immunomodulatory dietary nutrients and allergic disease may not only help define mechanisms of disease pathogenesis, but also offer avenues to prevent disease. Thus, we also review recent intervention studies that explore a potential role of n-3 fish oil supplementation in modifying immune development and reducing disease risk in early life. As escalating rates of allergic disease begin to also affect the developing world, these kinds of simple, cost-effective strategies are of growing relevance and enormous potential benefit.

**Keywords:** omega 3 polyunstarated fatty acids (n-3 PUFA), allergy, cord blood, cytokines, disease prevention, asthma, children, immune development

# Introduction

With rising numbers of infants with early signs of allergic disease there has been more intense interest in the effects of environmental changes on immune development. This chapter will address the role of a major candidate factor in this epidemic rise in allergic disease, namely the effects of dietary fatty acids and their effects on the developing human immune system. We will also explore how these nutrients might be used to modify early immune responses and reduce the risk of allergic diseases.

Allergic disease appears to be the culmination of both epithelial dysfunction in local tissues where disease is manifest and more generalised immune dysregulation which results in the predisposition for allergic T helper type 2 (Th2) responses. As major components of all cell membranes n-3 PUFA have enormous potential to influence cell function in many aspects of local and systemic immune networks. Although earlier research focused on the role of the polarity of T helper cell signalling as the defining factor in immune responses, it is now recognised that other cells with regulatory properties have a more key role. It has been recently proposed that allergic disease may result from an inappropriate balance between impaired regulatory cell function (including but not limited to CD4+CD25+ T regulatory cells) and excessive Th2 effector cell responses, which promote production of allergic IgE antibodies. In the airways, a number of other cells also have important regulatory effects on local immune responses, including epithelial cells and airway dendritic cells (DC). This review examines potential effects on n-3 PUFA on different aspects of these immune pathways, as well as the clinical relevance.

# 1. The Allergy Epidemic

The dramatic increase in asthma and allergic disease over the last half century has highlighted an urgent need to identify causal pathways. Approximately 40% of young children in Western countries develop allergic sensitisation and many of these go on to develop disease. Concern is mounting as developing countries begin to show the same trends. It is virtually axiomatic that environmental as opposed to genetic factors must be primarily responsible for this epidemic rise disease, and there is an urgent search for causal factors that may also be logical targets for disease prevention. Although this is certain to be multifactorial, one significant change during this period has been a progressive decline in the intake of dietary anti-inflammatory "n-3" polyunsaturated fatty acids (PUFA) in Western diets, with a corresponding increase in n-6 PUFA fatty acids. Both epidemiological and experimental data also provide a plausible link between these dietary changes and allergic diseases (as discussed further below).

## 2. Current Concepts of Immune Development and Dysregulation in Allergic Disease

The remarkable increase in many immune-mediated diseases includes not only Type 2 T helper (Th2) cell mediated allergic diseases but also Type 1 T helper (Th1) cell mediated autoimmune diseases such as type 1 diabetes, Crohns disease, multiple sclerosis [1]. The common theme appears to be a breakdown in immune regulation, which allows the expression of inappropriate immune responses (to allergens or self antigens, depending on genetic predisposition [2]. The high rate of allergic diseases indicates that a high percentage of the population is susceptible under certain environmental conditions.

Thus although early research focused on the role of Th2 polarity of T cell signalling as a key factor in the pathogenesis of allergic responses, it is now recognised that "regulatory" cells have a more key role in initiating this process. Many cells have regulatory activity (including but not limited to CD4+CD25+T regulatory cells, CD8+ T cells, epithelial cells, dendritic cells [DC] and other antigen presenting cells [APC]) (reviewed in detail by [2]). Although these cells have different functions they all promote appropriate protective host responses to noxious agents, while limiting excessive or inappropriate responses which can be equally harmful to the host. These cells provide regulatory signals by direct cell contact (in the case of CD4+CD25+T regulatory cells) [3,4] or by the production of key regulatory cytokines (IL-10 and TGFβ) [5-7]. It has been proposed that "normal" exposure to allergen results in development of regulatory T cells and subsequent tolerance, but that inadequate production of regulatory IL-10 (or excessive IL-4 or IL-13 production) may instead result in the production of aberrant Th2 clones [8].

This model also challenges the notion that modern environmental changes are having a "Th2 skewing effect" by specifically promoting Th2 responses or inhibiting Th1 responses. Indeed, any potential beneficial effects of n-3 PUFAs in preventing or modifying allergic immune responses (discussed further below) do not appear to be operating through "skewing" T cell responses. Rather, these anti-inflammatory fatty acids appear to be associated with suppression of both Th1 and Th2 cytokine responses (reviewed in [9]). Thus, understanding the origins of allergic inflammation and identifying strategies for its prevention need to go beyond the original Th1/Th2 paradigm.

## 3. The Role of Environmental Changes in the Allergy Epidemic, Including a Role for Dietary n-3 Fatty Acids

One significant change during this period of rising asthma and allergic disease has been a progressive decline in the intake of dietary anti-inflammatory n-3 PUFA in Western diets, and a corresponding increase in "pro-inflammatory" n-6 PUFA fatty acids [10]. Today, in Western diets, the ratio of n-6 to n-3 fatty acids ranges from approximately 20-30:1 instead of the traditional range of 1-2:1[11]. These dietary changes are also reflected in the changing content of breast milk, which has similarly shown falling n-3 PUFA content and increasing n-

6 PUFA levels over the last 20 years [12]. This, coupled with inadequate supplementation of milk formulae, has led to falling intake of anti-inflammatory n-3 PUFA during early life during the critical period of immune maturation.

Both epidemiological and experimental data provide a plausible link between these dietary changes and allergic diseases (reviewed in [10,13]), and are consistent with numerous experimental studies demonstrating the immunological effects of dietary PUFA (below). However, despite this there is no definitive evidence of a causal link. The inherent difficulty of performing studies to establish causality makes it very difficult to prove. Associations between dietary exposures and immune development are of greatest interest in childhood when immune responses are developing. The major dietary source of long chain n-3 PUFAs is oily fish. Perhaps the best known study to address this [14] observed that children who regularly consumed oily fish were significantly less likely to develop asthma (odds ratio 0.26), but there have been relatively few other studies to confirm this association. In general, because of the limitations of these population-based studies, attention is turning to well controlled intervention studies to examine potential effects of n-3 PUFAs in a more controlled manner (below).

## 4. The Importance of Early Life Events in the Development of Allergic Disease

Clinical features of allergic disease are frequently manifest within months of life, usually as food allergies or atopic eczema. Although these conditions generally improve with age a high proportion go on to develop persistent aeroallergen sensitisation and associated respiratory tract disease, often by school age. This increasing manifestation of the allergic propensity earlier in life highlights the importance of understanding the role of early events, including those in the uterine environment (reviewed in [15]).

Variations in early immune function appear to influence susceptibility to early airway inflammation and the risk of subsequent chronic allergic diseases such as asthma (reviewed in [16]). Thus, factors that may have functional influences on the developing immune system are therefore of prime interest, particularly in the first year of life. Accordingly, it is logical that dietary exposures with immunomodulatory potential (such as n-3 PUFA) also have greater effects during early development than once immune responses are established. Furthermore, these dietary factors may provide non-invasive avenues of preventing disease, and this has become a research priority [17]. If such strategies reduce the risk or the severity of disease expression (even slightly) it could have enormous impact in this global context at relatively little cost.

From the moment of conception n-3 PUFA play a vital role in many aspects of neonatal development. Many complex physiological changes occur during gestation to ensure survival of a healthy fetus. Harmful immune reactions between mother and fetus are inhibited by reduced expression of fetal MHC class II antigens, enhanced T suppressor function, and the hormonal changes which favour Th2 responses. DHA (n-3), which is concentrated in the fetal circulation at 10-15 times maternal levels (by its high affinity for fetal carrier protein $\alpha$-fetoprotein), plays an important role in immune tolerance by suppressing fetal MHC Class II expression [18]. These important mechanisms for modulating T-cell activity during early development emphasize the potential effect of maternal dietary DHA on developing immune responses to many proteins, including allergens.

# 5. Presymptomatic Immunological Differences in Allergic Infants, and Links with Dietary n-3 Fatty Acids

Although the aetiological factors are still not well defined, there is mounting evidence of *presymptomatic* differences in the immune function of newborns who later develop allergic disease, suggesting that events during fetal life are of crucial interest (reviewed in [15]). These differences seem to affect a number of different "read outs" of immune activity at birth, including the magnitude [19-21] and pattern on cellular responses *in vitro* [20,22-26], circulating neonatal levels of cytokines [27] or cytokine producing cells [28] *in vivo*, and activity of progenitors that give rise to pro-allergic inflammatory cells (eosinophil progenitors) [29].

Consistent observations (by many groups) that subsequent allergic disease (or atopic risk) is associated with T less mature helper Type 1 (Th1) function at birth has lead to speculation that allergic disease is the result of less efficient Th1 maturation. It has not been clear if these perinatal differences are merely a detectable measure of increased genetic predisposition, or whether they are indicative of early (*in utero*) environmental influences that are already promoting the development of the allergic phenotype. It seems increasingly likely that both are true, particularly as some antenatal exposures (such as infection [30], maternal diet [31] and smoking [32]) are known to modify neonatal Th1 function.

As central components of cell structure and function, dietary fatty acids play an important role in the developing immune system. Thus, variation in early dietary exposures (including maternal diet in pregnancy), represent a major environmental influence. There is wide regional variation in maternal n-3/n-6 PUFA intake and neonatal serum PUFA levels [33] which reflect the changes in industrialised countries (as above). Earlier studies observed that higher breast milk n-3 PUFA levels protected from infant atopy [34]. However more recent studies [35] have reported significantly higher maternal colostrum levels of docosapentaenoic acid (DPA; 22:5n-3) and DHA in infants sensitised to food at 6 months ($P=0.001$; $P=0.007$ respectively) compared to non-sensitised infants. Though conflicting, these findings do suggest an association between maternal PUFA status and allergy predisposition, and further research is clearly required to delineate this further. A number of studies have also linked disturbances in the cord blood n-3/n-6 PUFA profiles with later allergy (or a family history of allergy), but these cord blood abnormalities are variable and not predictive ([36,37] and others).

Although some have proposed that altered fatty acid levels noted in atopy may be due to abnormalities of (delta-6-desaturase) lipid metabolism [38,39] other studies do not support this [40] and suggest that in dietary variation is more likely to be implicated. It remains possible that functional genetic polymorphisms in these pathways could alter dietary effects on immune function but more studies are needed to assess this.

# 6. The Effects of n-3 PUFA on Immune Function and Immune Development

Classified by different positions of their double bonds, n-3 and n-6 PUFA have different biological effects. The cell membrane PUFA composition alters with dietary intake, and affects membrane fluidity, surface receptor expression, prostaglandin metabolism and immunological responses (reviewed in [41]). N-6 PUFA (linoleic acid [LA] and arachadonic acid [AA]) promote allergic inflammation, by enhancing mononuclear proliferation, prostaglandin production (particularly PGE2), and potentiate "pro-allergic" Th2 differentiation [13], as summarized on Table 1. In contrast, n-3 fatty acids (including DHA docosahexanoic acid [DHA] and eicosapentanoic acid [EPA]) inhibit allergic immune responses through a number of anti-inflammatory properties, including inhibition of PGE2 [42] which normally enhances IgE production.

**Table 1. Summary of reported immunological effects of n-3 and n-6 PUFA (effects observed in some but not all studies)**

| n-6 PUFA | n-3 PUFA |
|---|---|
| General pro-inflammatory responses | General anti-inflammatory responses |
| Favour production of 2-series prostaglandins and 4 series leukotriences (more inflammatory) | Favour production of 3-series prostaglandins and 5 series leukotriences (less inflammatory) |
| Favour IL-1 and IL-6 inflammatory responses | Inhibit IL-1b, IL-2, IL-6, TNFa |
| No major effect in IL-2 responses | Inhibit in vivo delayed (type 4) hypersensitivity (DTH) |
| No inhibition of antigen presentation or class II MHC | Inhibit class II HLA expression |
| | Reduced antigen presentation |
| No major effects on lymphoproliferation | Inhibition of lymphoproliferation |
| Favour production of PGE2 and other pro-inflammatory eicosanoids, which favours Th-2 differentiation | Inhibit PGE2 synthesis, which inhibits Th-2 differentiation |
| | Decreased monocyte adherence |
| | Reduced adhesion molecule expression after activation (VCAM, ICAM, CD36) |
| | Reduced natural killer cell activity |
| | Reduced chemotaxis |
| | Reduced nitric oxide production |
| | Reduced expression of activation markers (CD69) |
| Possible mechanism of these effects: modified cellular physiology by altered lipid rafts (with modified intracellular signal transduction and modified downstream events) | |

### a) Inhibition of PGE2 by n-3 PUFA Inhibits Allergic Th2 Differentiation

Many of the anti-inflammatory properties of n-3 PUFA appear to be mediated through the competitive inhibition of $PGE_2$ synthesis. Higher proportions of EPA (20:5n-3) and DHA (22:6n-3) in cell membranes as a result of dietary fish oil decrease the proportion of AA (20:4n-6) as a for the synthesis of the pro-inflammatory 2-series prostaglandins (such as $PGE_2$) and the 4 series leukotrienes [43] [44] [45,46] [47]. $PGE_2$ is a powerful regulator of the inflammatory immune response, inhibiting T cell proliferation and production of Th1 cytokines (IL-2 and IFNγ) [48] [49] [50], as well as production of pro-Th1 cytokines by antigen presenting cells (APC), such as IL-12 [51]. $PGE_2$ also synergises with IL-4 to promote immunoglobulin IgE-isotype switching in B cells [52]. Together these properties promote "pro-allergic" Th2 differentiation [13,49,53]. Unlike the arachidonic derivatives, eicosanoids produced from n-3 PUFA are far less potent than oxidative derivatives of n-6 PUFA [54], and although they have have some inflammatory activity the efficiency of this is very low [11,55]. Our *in vitro* studies suggest that n-3 PUFA inhibit both Th1 (IFNγ) and Th2 (IL-4) responses (Figure 1). Although inhibition of Th2 responses appear to greater than inhibition of Th1 responses the significance of this is not clear. In our *in vivo* studies we also observed that oral fish oil supplementation was associated with inhibition of both Th1 and Th2 responses [31], as discussed further below.

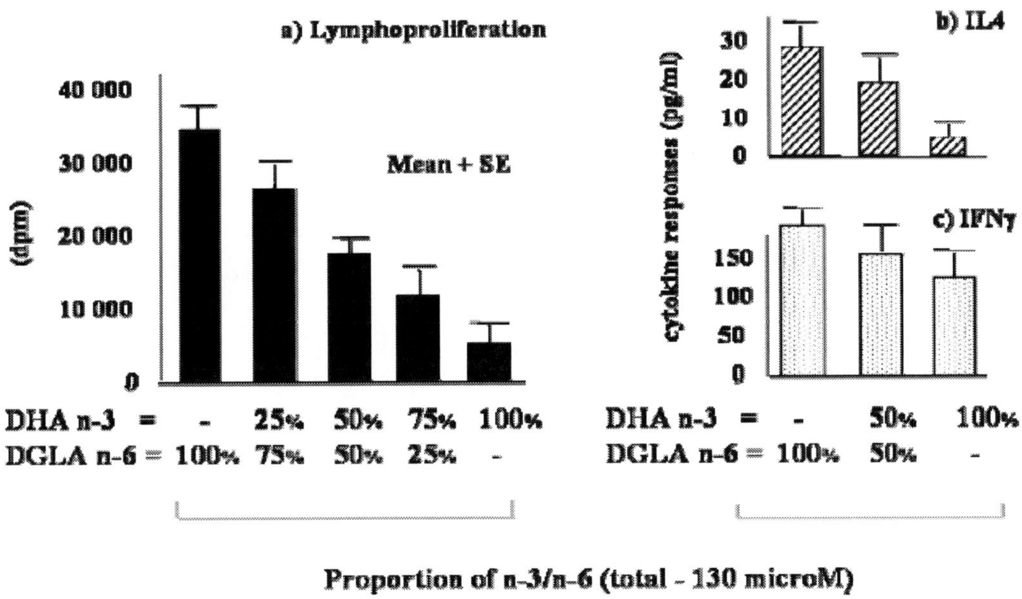


Figure 1. Effects of changing the composition of n-3/n-6 PUFA in culture median on peripheral blood mononuclear cell responses to mitogen stimulation (PHA) The a) lymphoproliferation b) IL-4 and c) IFNγ responses are shown for parallel cultures incubated for 6 days (lymphoproliferation) or 48 hours (cytokine responses) with different ratios of n-3/n-6 in the culture medium (n=6). The total amount of fatty acids remained constant (130nM) and the percentage of n-3 (DHA) and n-6 (DGLA) are shown on the x-axis. All cultures were incubated at 37 degrees C and 5% carbon dioxide, and human albumin was used as the carrier protein. Levels are shown as the mean and standard deviation.

### b) Modulation of Cell Signalling and Gene Expression by n-3 PUFA

In addition to effects on production of prostaglandins, n-3 PUFAs can regulate T cell function directly through effects on cell membrane fluidity and consequent cell signalling and gene transcription (reviewed in [9]). Recently, it has been shown that n-3 PUFA can inhibit T cell signal transduction by displacing lipid rafts [56], which provide a mechanism for laterally sorting membrane proteins [56-58] and are important in the initiation of T cell activation. Formation and function of the immunological synapse is also suppressed by n-3 PUFA (mainly DHA; 22:6n-3) through effects on the co-stimulatory CD28 receptor [59], adhesion molecules (ICAM 1 and LFA-1) [60] and either CD8 [61] [62] or CD4 [63] [64]. N-3 PUFA also have effects on the T cell signalling pathway by altering intracellular calcium (Ca2+) levels [65]. The subsequent activation of protein kinase C (PKC) is also suppressed [66]. All of these effects impact on the release of calcineurin and the activation of transcription factors (nuclear factor [NF]-κβ and NF-AT). Collectively these factors result in reduced production of IL-2 [67,68] and inhibited lymphocyte proliferation [67].

### c) Effects of n-3 PUFA on T Cell Function (Lymphoproliferation and Cytokine Production)

Many studies have demonstrated that dietary n-3 PUFA supplementation in both humans [46] [69] [43] [70] and rodents [71] [72] [68] significantly reduces lymphocyte proliferation to mitogens. *In vitro* studies in which peripheral blood mononuclear cells (PBMC) are incubated with fatty acids, have also generally shown a decrease in T cell responses to mitogens [73] [74] [75]. We have also shown that proportional increases in the ratio of n-3/n-6 PUFA are associated with an almost ten-fold suppression of mitogen induced lymphoproliferation (Figure 1a). To date, there have been few studies that have examined the effect of PUFA on allergen-specific responses (with the exception of our preliminary results in neonates, below).

To assess effects of dietary n-3 PUFA supplementation on T cell cytokine responses most human studies have been limited to the measurement IL-2 in mitogen-stimulated cultures. IL-2 production is generally inhibited by n-3 PUFA but the effect appears to depend on the dose, gender and age of the subjects [43] [76] [77] [46] [69]. An in vitro study with human cells reported that n-6 and n-3 PUFA (LA, AA, ALA, EPA and DHA) all inhibit the production of IL-2 by mitogen [67]. In this study, EPA had the most marked effect, resulting in 90% inhibition of IL-2 response.

### d) The Effects of n-3 PUFA on Antigen Presenting Cells (APC) and Other Regulatory Cells

PUFA may also modify T cell effector function through effects on regulatory cell populations. Increasing the content of n-3 PUFAs in cell membranes reduces the capacity of APC to present antigen to T cells (by inhibiting the upregulation of HLA class II receptors) [78]. These fatty acids also decrease production of cytokines by APCs, including the synthesis of IL-12, an important pro-Th1 cytokine [53]. These effects of n-3 PUFA are generally related to the reduced capacity for T cell responses. However, there have been no studies to directly address the specific effects of n-3 PUFAs on IL-10- and TGFβ associated regulatory pathways. If anything, n-3 PUFA supplementation appears to be associated with decreased IL-10 production in some [31,79,80] but not all [81] studies. This is also associated with decreases in the production of cytokines including tumor necrosis actor (TNF)α and IL-1 ([45] [44] and others), but effects on other cytokines are still not well documented. Clearly a better understanding of the effects of n-3 PUFAs is necessary to explore both causal and/or therapeutic pathways. Specific effects on T regulatory cells also still need to be defined.

As indicated above, n-3 PUFA also appear to effect the production of pro-inflammatory cytokines (IL-1, TNFα and IL-6) by human APC, although reports are inconsistent. Some studies have reported decreased IL-1 and TNFα response by PBMC to LPS [45] [43] [44], however, other studies have found no effect [82] [83] [84]. Reports in rodents fed n-3 PUFA are also conflicting. Some studies report enhanced TNFα production [85] [86] [87], some show decreased production [88] and others show no effect [89]. Decreased IL-1 and IL-6 production [90] in LPS stimulated murine macrophages have also been reported. APC derived nitric oxide (NO) also appears to play a key role in inflammatory responses, however, the effects of n-3 PUFA supplementation on this pathway are also unclear, with some studies showing an increase in NO production [91] and others a decrease [88] [92-94]. However *in vitro* studies have shown that n-3 DHA inhibits NO production [95], as well as the accumulation of iNOS, mRNA, and iNOS transcription in murine macrophages [95] [93].

### e) The Effects of n-3 PUFA on Neutrophil Function

Numerous studies have shown that human supplementation with fish oil attenuates some aspects of neutrophil function, particularly the production of $LTB_4$, a potent inflammatory mediator which plays an important role in the immediate phase of the allergic hypersensitivity reaction. N-3 PUFA supplementation reduces $LTB_4$ production, in favour of $LTB_5$ (the EPA eicosanoid derivative) [96,97] which is 10 to 30 times less potent than $LTB_4$ in causing aggregation, chemotaxis, and degranulation of neutrophils [98]. This has not been associated with impaired ability to phagocytose or internalise bacteria, or in the respiratory burst activity [99].

### f) Effects of n-3 PUFA on Other Aspects of Immune Function

Suppression of Th1-delayed type hypersensitivity and natural killer cell activity [100] have also been reported in rodents treated with n-3 PUFA. N-3 PUFA inhibit migration of inflammatory cells into local tissues by down-regulating adhesion molecule expression (VCAM-1, ICAM-1 and E-selectin) and monocyte adherence to vascular endothelium ([78] and others). These n-3 PUFA associated alterations in immune responses do not result in obvious clinical vulnerability to infection. Moreover, the effects vary with the activating stimulus. DHA differentially inhibits proliferative responses to mitogens, while it promotes responses to self antigens [101], suggesting important added immunomodulatory effects.

### g) Potential Effects of n-3 PUFA on Developing Immune Function

Preliminary data suggests that variation in n-3 PUFA exposure is associated with variation in immune function in very early life. This includes both observational studies [36,37] and intervention studies ([31] discussed further below), which support the notion that n-3 PUFA have an important influence on the developing immune system.

This has lead to growing interest in how these effects may be mediated at the molecular level, including effects on mitogen activated protein [MAP] kinases, c-Jun N-terminal kinase [JNK], extracellular signal related kinase [ERK] and p38 MAP kinase. MAP kinases, ERK and JNK, which are important in cytokine production, are poorly activated in neonatal (cord blood) T lymphocytes than adults T cells [102]. This is a very likely explanation for the impaired ability of neonatal T cell to produce cytokines [103]. These studies also noted a large variation in neonatal T cell expression in PKC isozymes between individuals. Research from our group indicates that differences in expression may lead to corresponding differences in disease susceptibility. In our study [31] (discussed further below) neonatal T-cell PKCzeta expression was lower in children who had evidence of allergic disease ($P = 0.001$) or sensitization (positive skin prick test) at ($P = 0.02$) at 1 year of age (104). Because increased neonatal PKC expression can be induced by stimulation *in vitro*, it is possible that *in vivo* factors also influence expression in this early period and raises the interesting question of whether n-3 PUFA supplementation pre-natally or peri-natally alters the expression of PKC in T lymphocytes. In the same study [104] we found that fish oil supplementation in pregnancy was associated with significantly higher neonatal PKCzeta expression ($P = 0.014$), whereas most other isozymes were reduced by fish oil supplementation. Because n-3 PUFA are known to alter signalling through PKC [105,106] [107], we may also speculate that these fatty acids may influence developing patterns of cytokine response possibly through activation of JNK expression which is associated with Th1 development [108].

## 7. Using n-3 PUFA to Modify Immune Responses in Inflammatory Diseases

### a) General Use of n-3 PUFA in Inflammatory Diseases

Interest in n-3 PUFA and their potential health benefits in chronic disease resulted from epidemiological observations in the 1970's, that populations who consumed diet rich in fat from seals, whales and fish had very low rates of cardiovascular disease (reviewed in [109]). Subsequently, there has been convincing evidence for the role of n-3 PUFA in the prevention or treatment of a number of inflammatory diseases including coronary heart disease [110-112], autoimmune disorders (such as rheumatoid arthritis [113,114] and inflammatory bowel disease [115]), cancers (breast, colon and prostate) [116], cystic fibrosis [117], and asthma [118,119].

### b) n-3 PUFA Supplementation in Allergic Disease

Despite the theoretical beneficial effects of fish oil for the treatment of asthma, evidence from clinical trials in adults with established disease is controversial. A recent Cochrane systematic review of nine randomised controlled studies compared n-3 PUFA supplementation with placebo [120] [121] [122] [123] [124] [125][126] or with n-6 PUFA supplementation [127] and found no evidence to support the use of marine n-3 PUFA in the treatment of asthma [118]. Seven of the studies were conducted in adults and only two [126,127] in children. Outcomes measured included asthma symptoms, medication usage, bronchial hyperactivity, and measures of lung function. Although the review concluded that there was no evidence of consistent benefit of n-3 PUFAs in the management of asthma, two of the studies reported an improvement in lung function [120,128] and one study reported an improvement in asthma symptoms [122]. Conversely, none of the studies reported any exacerbation of asthma symptoms.

Of the two of the studies that were conducted in children, one [126] reported that fish oil supplementation was associated with improved asthma symptom scores and reduced medication usage. The authors of the other study [127] provided additional information for the Cochrane review, which indicated a significant improvement in peak expiratory flow and asthma medication use after concurrent dietary manipulation and n-3 PUFA supplementation. While inconclusive, these observations highlight the need for further studies particularly in children with asthma.

It is also worth noting that a number of the studies not included in this Cochrane review have demonstrated clinical benefits for asthma [129] [130] [131] [132] [133] [134] [135][136]. They were excluded from the review for varying reasons including: not randomised controlled trials, supplementation period less than 4 weeks, and/or n-3 PUFA not of marine origin. Masuev et al [133] [134] reported benefits of n-3 rich "eiconol' supplementation in individuals with atopic disease. In these placebo controlled studies, n-3 supplemented individuals demonstrated less frequent attacks of asphyxia and reduced medication dosage [133] and significant attenuation of late allergic response in provocative tests with allergen [134]. A further controlled trial by Machura et al [130] examined the effect of fish oil on the clinical progress of asthma in children. After the eighth week of supplementation, there was slight improvement in cases with mild asthma but not severe asthma.

Very few studies have reported on the effects of n-3 PUFA supplementation on allergic skin disease. In 1877, it was recommended that severe itching should be "treated with liberal doses of cod liver oil" (cited in [119]). More recently Bjorneboe et al [137] reported that dietary supplementation with fish oil improved itch, scaling and subjective severity of atopic dermatitis in adults. However other studies have found no effect on clinical severity [138] or the cutaneous late phase response in affected individuals [139]. Using a more radical method of delivery, intravenous administration of n-3 fatty acid has been shown to improve severe atopic dermatitis [140].

Although trials of fish oil supplementation for the treatment of established allergic disease have been disappointing, it is possible that the immunomodulatory benefits of n-3 PUFAs may be greater during earlier critical stages of immune development before allergic responses are established. Thus, there remains considerable interest in the role of these fatty acids in early life for the prevention of disease.

# 8. Using n-3 PUFA to Modify Early Immune Development

It has been postulated that higher levels of n-6 (and relative deficiency of n-3) PUFA during gestation may enhance T cell activation during early immune development, and thereby favour immunological reactivity to antigens (both self antigens, and environmental allergens) [31]. This dietary profile also appears to favour Th2 differentiation (as above). Although allergen-specific responses are normally Th2-skewed in the milieu of pregnancy, this appears to be down-regulated in the postnatal period in favour of Th1 differentiation. Diets rich in n-6 (and relative deficient in n-3) PUFA could, forseeably, alter normal immune maturation and favor subsequent Th2 development.

Dietary supplementation with n-3 rich fish oil in pregnancy increases neonatal DHA levels (by up to 45%) and is associated with inhibition of neonatal prostaglandin synthesis [42] and improved pregnancy outcome [141]. There is currently only one study (by our own group) to examine the effects of n-3 PUFA supplementation in pregnancy on fetal immune development [31], and studies of effects on early postnatal immune development are still ongoing. We examined the effects of giving fish oil (3.7g n-3 PUFA/ day) or a placebo to allergic women (n=98) for the final 20 weeks of pregnancy [31,142,143]. Fish oil supplementation achieved significantly higher proportions of n-3 PUFAs in neonatal erythrocyte membranes compared to the control group ($P < 0.001$) [31,142]. The average concentration of the Th2 cytokine IL-13 in umbilical cord plasma was 65% lower in the fish oil group and there was an inverse relationship between the concentration of IL-13 and the DHA content of neonatal erythrocytes [143]. Neonatal mononuclear cell responses to all allergens tested also showed a consistent trend for all cytokines studied (IL-5, IL-13, IL-10, IFN-γ) to be lower in the fish oil group (although this was statistically significant only for IL-10 responses to cat allergen) [31]. There were statistically significant inverse relationships between the n-3 PUFA content of neonatal erthrocytes and cytokine responses [31]. Although these relationships were most evident for IFN-γ and IL-10 responses, the same trends were seen for most other Th2 cytokines. Conversely, there were significant positive relationships between the n-6 PUFA content of neonatal erythrocytes and the cytokine responses [31]. These observations suggest that n-3 PUFAs in pregnancy have effects on neonatal immune function. Furthermore neutrophil production of proinflammatory leukotriene (LT) B4 was significantly lower in the neonates whose mothers had received fish oil compared to those who had not [144]. We also observed for the first time that n-3 PUFA supplementation was associated with alterations in numbers and function of myeloid precursors [145]. CD34+

progenitors were increased in cord blood in the supplement group. There were also significantly more IL-5 (but not IL-3 or GM-CSF) responsive cells in cord blood from the fish oil supplemented group [145]. Although the significance of this is not clear, this area clearly warrants further study; these cells give rise to eosinophils (and basophils) and effects on their function have obvious implications for the development of allergic inflammation. Clinical studies (below) are still needed to confirm the clinical relevance of these observations.

## 9. The Role of n-3 PUFA in Prevention of Allergic Disease

Although our study (described above)[31] was not designed to examine clinical effects or allergy prevention specifically, it was noted that infants in the fish oil group were consistently less likely to develop clinical features including food allergy, recurrent wheeze, persistent cough, diagnosed asthma, angioedema, or anaphylaxis, compared to the control group [31]. Although there was no difference in the frequency of atopic dermatitis at 1 year of age, infants in the fish oil group had significantly less severe disease (OR 0.09; 95% CI, 0.01-0.94; $P = 0.045$), (Figure 2a). Children in the fish oil group were also three times less likely to have a positive skin prick test to egg at 1 year of age (OR 0.34; 95% CI, 0.11-1.02; $P = 0.055$) (Figure 2c). Since 37.8% of infants in the control group and 17.1% in the fish oil group were sensitised to egg, this represents an absolute reduction of 20.7%, and in this population a relative risk reduction of 54.6% [31]. These differences were not statistically significant because of the study size (the study was "powered" to look at immunologic rather than clinical outcomes). Nevertheless, this study provides useful justification for larger long term studies.

The only other study to examine the preventative effects of early fish oil supplementation in high risk infants with parent/sibling atopy (n = 616), commenced fish oil (500 mg day) at weaning or at 6 months of age if still breastfed [146]. At 18 months (n = 543), the authors reported that fish oil supplementation was associated with 9.8% absolute reduction (95% CI, 1.5-18.1; $P = 0.02$) in the prevalence of any wheeze and a 7.8% absolute reduction (95% CI, 0.5-15.1, $P = 0.04$) in prevalence of wheeze [146]. At 3 years of age (n=526) there was a significant 10.0% (95% CI, 3.7-16.4) reduction in the prevalence of cough in atopic children in the group who received fish oil (p = 0.003; number needed to treat, 10) but a negligible 1.1% (95% CI, -7.1 to 9.5) reduction cough among nonatopic children [147]. No significant difference in wheeze was found in the 3 year follow up [147]. Although this suggests subtle immunomodulatory effects of n-3 PUFA on inflammatory airway events, there was no effect on sensitization to foods or atopic dermatitis, which are common manifestations of allergy in earlier infancy. At age 5 years there was no association between omega-3 or omega-6 fatty acids and any allergic outcomes [148]. It is of interest that our study [31] which used a much earlier intervention did suggest effects on these early markers of infant allergic disease (sensitisation to foods and atopic dermatitis). This may indicate that earlier interventions could be more effective in preventing early sensitisation (and possibly the processes which lead on to aeroallergen sensitivity). We are currently conduction further studies to explore earlier postnatal interventions (from birth) that may potentially have greater effects prior to the establishment of the "atopic march".

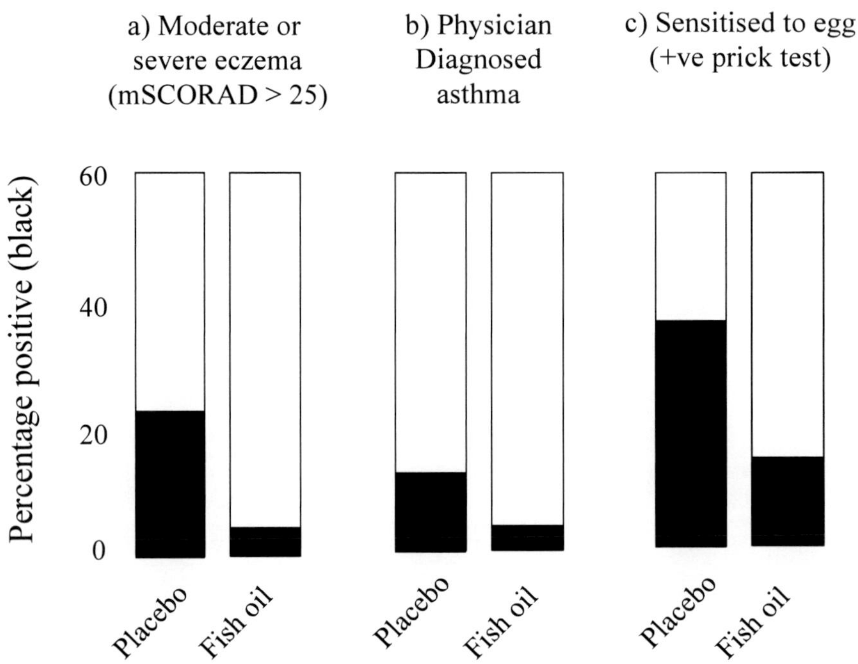


Figure 2. Effects of fish oil supplementation in pregnancy on early symptoms of allergic disease (1 year of age) This compares the clinical outcomes of a) moderate to severe dermatitis (modified SCORAD index > 25), b) physician diagnosed asthma (responsive to bronchodilators) and c) sensitisation to food allergens (egg) at 1 year of age, in high risk children (with maternal allergy) whose mothers were supplemented with either fish oil (3.7g n-3 PUFA/d; n=40) or a placebo (olive oil; n=43) from 20 weeks of gestation. The shaded boxes indicate the percentage of each group affected in each category.

The only other study to examine the preventative effects of early fish oil supplementation in high risk infants with parent/sibling atopy (n = 616), commenced fish oil (500 mg day) at weaning or at 6 months of age if still breastfed [146]. At 18 months (n = 543), the authors reported that fish oil supplementation was associated with 9.8% absolute reduction (95% CI, 1.5-18.1; $P = 0.02$) in the prevalence of any wheeze and a 7.8% absolute reduction (95% CI, 0.5-15.1, $P = 0.04$) in prevalence of wheeze [146]. At 3 years of age (n=526) there was a significant 10.0% (95% CI, 3.7-16.4) reduction in the prevalence of cough in atopic children in the group who received fish oil (p = 0.003; number needed to treat, 10) but a negligible 1.1% (95% CI, -7.1 to 9.5) reduction cough among nonatopic children [147]. No significant difference in wheeze was found in the 3 year follow up [147]. Although this suggests subtle immunomodulatory effects of n-3 PUFA on inflammatory airway events, there was no effect on sensitization to foods or atopic dermatitis, which are common manifestations of allergy in earlier infancy. At age 5 years there was no association between omega-3 or omega-6 fatty acids and any allergic outcomes [148]. It is of interest that our study [31] which used a much earlier intervention did suggest effects on these early markers of infant allergic disease (sensitisation to foods and atopic dermatitis). This may indicate that earlier interventions could be more effective in preventing early sensitisation (and possibly the processes which lead on to aeroallergen sensitivity). We are currently conduction further studies to explore earlier postnatal interventions (from birth) that may potentially have greater effects prior to the establishment of the "atopic march".

## Conclusion

In summary, the existing literature provides epidemiologic and biologic evidence that alterations in the composition of essential dietary fatty acids in cell membranes have a plausible role in the recent rise in allergic diseases and other inflammatory disorders. Further studies are needed to determine how this significant environmental exposure could influence fetal immune system ontogeny and contribute to the development of allergic disease and its prevention. Preliminary data from our group [31] and others [146] suggest that improving n-3 PUFA status in very early life has the potential to modify immune responses and clinical symptoms of allergy. This clearly needs further investigation in terms of both larger clinical studies and mechanistic studies, before this can be proposed for allergy prevention. Future studies also need to address the reol o potential functional genetic polymorphisms that could alter individuals susceptibility to dietary exposures.

## References


[1] Bach JF. The effect of infections on susceptibility to autoimmune and allergic diseases. *N. Engl. J. Med.* 2002; 347:911-20.

[2] Wills-Karp M, Santeliz J, Karp CL. The germless theory of allergic disease: revisiting the hygiene hypothesis. *Nat. Rev. Immunol.* 2001; 1:69-75.

[3] Shevach EM. CD4+ CD25+ suppressor T cells: more questions than answers. *Nat. Rev. Immunol.* 2002; 2:389-400.

[4] Shevach EM. Certified professionals: CD4(+)CD25(+) suppressor T cells. *J. Exp. Med.* 2001; 193:F41-6.

[5] Levings MK, Roncarolo MG. T-regulatory 1 cells: a novel subset of CD4 T cells with immunoregulatory properties. *J. Allergy Clin. Immunol.* 2000; 106:S109-12.

[6] Gilliet M, Liu YJ. Generation of human CD8 T regulatory cells by CD40 ligand-activated plasmacytoid dendritic cells. *J. Exp. Med.* 2002; 195:695-704.

[7] Horwitz DA, Zheng SG, Gray JD. The role of the combination of IL-2 and TGF-beta or IL-10 in the generation and function of CD4+ CD25+ and CD8+ regulatory T cell subsets. *J. Leukoc. Biol.* 2003; 74:471-8.

[8] Akbari O, Stock P, DeKruyff RH, Umetsu DT. Role of regulatory T cells in allergy and asthma. *Curr. Opin. Immunol.* 2003; 15:627-33.

[9] Calder PC, Yaqoob P, Thies F, Wallace FA, Miles EA. Fatty acids and lymphocyte functions. *Br. J. Nutr.* 2002; 87 Suppl 1:S31-48.

[10] Weiss S. *Diet as a risk factor for asthma.* in *CIBA Foundation Symposium*. 1997. New York: Wiley.

[11] Simopoulos AP. Essential fatty acids in health and chronic disease. *Am. J. Clin. Nutr.* 1999; 70:560S-569S.

[12] Makrides M, Simmer K, Neumann M, Gibson R. Changes in the polyunsaturated fatty acids of breast milk from mothers of full-term infants over 30 wk of lactation. *Am. J. Clin. Nutr.* 1995; 61:1231-3.

[13] Black P, Sharpe S. Dietary fat and asthma: Is there a connection? *Eur. Respir. J.* 1997; 10:6-12.

[14] Hodge L, Salome C, Peat J, Haby M, Xuan W, Woolcock A. Consumption of oily fish and childhood asthma risk. *Med. J. Aust.* 1996; 164:137-140.

[15] Prescott SL. Early origins of allergic disease: a review of processes and influences during early immune development. *Curr. Opin. Allergy Clin. Immunol.* 2003; 3:125-32.

[16] Holt PG, Sly PD. Interactions between respiratory tract infections and atopy in the aetiology of asthma. *Eur Respir J* 2002; 19:538-45.

[17] Johansson SGO, Haahtela T. *Prevention of Allergy and Asthma.* in *World Allergy Organisation (WAO).* 2002. Geneva: World Health Organisation (WHO).

[18] Khair-el-Din TA, Sicher SC, Vazquez MA, Wright WJ, Lu CY. Docosahexaenoic acid, a major constituent of fetal serum and fish oil diets, inhibits IFN gamma-induced Ia-expression by murine macrophages in vitro. *Journal of Immunology* 1995; 154:1296-306.

[19] Piastra M, Stabile A, Fioravanti G, Castagnola M, Pani G, Ria F. Cord blood mononuclear cell responsiveness to beta-lactoglobulin: T-cell acitivity in "atopy-prone" and "non-atopy-prone" newborns. *Int. Arch. Allergy Immunol.* 1994; 104:358-365.

[20] Warner JA, Miles EA, Jones AC, Quint DJ, Colwell BM, Warner JO. Is deficiency of interferon gamma production by allergen triggered cord blood cells a predictor of atopic eczema? *Clin. Exp. Allergy* 1994; 24:423-430.

[21] Miles EA, Warner JA, Jones AC, Colwell BM, Bryant TN, Warner JO. Peripheral blood mononuclear cell proliferative responses in the first year of life in babies born to atopic parents. *Clin. Exp. Allergy* 1996; 26:780-788.

[22] Rinas U, Horneff G, Wahn V. Interferon gamma production by cord blood mononuclear cells is reduced in newborns with a family history of atopic disease and is independant from cord blood IgE levels. *Ped. Allergy Immunol.* 1993; 4:60-64.

[23] Tang MLK, Kemp AS, Thorburn J, Hill D. Reduced interferon gamma secretion in neonates and subsequent atopy. *Lancet* 1994; 344:983-85.

[24] Liao S, Liao T, Chiang B, Huang M, Chen C, Chou C, Hsieh K. Decreased production of IFNg and decreased production of IL-6 by cord blood mononuclear cells of newborns with a high risk of allergy. *Clin. Exp. Allergy* 1996; 26:397-405.

[25] Martinez F, Stern D, Wright A, Holberg C, Taussig L, Halonen M. Association of interleukin-2 and interferon-g production by blood mononuclear cells in infancy with parental allergy skin tests and with subsequent development of atopy. *J. Allergy Clin. Immunol.* 1995; 96:652-60.

[26] Prescott SL, Macaubas C, Smallacombe T, Holt BJ, Sly PD, Loh R, Holt PG. Reciprocal age-related patterns of allergen-specific T-cell immunity in normal vs. atopic infants. *Clin. Exp. Allergy* 1998; 28 Suppl 5:39-44; discussion 50-1.

[27] Macaubas C, de Klerk NH, Holt BJ, Wee C, Kendall G, Firth M, Sly PD, Holt PG. Association between antenatal cytokine production and the development of atopy and asthma at age 6 years. *Lancet* 2003; 362:1192-7.

[28] Spinozzi F, Agea E, Russano A, Bistoni O, Minelli L, Bologni D, Bertotto A, de Benedictis FM. CD4+IL13+ T lymphocytes at birth and the development of wheezing and/or asthma during the 1st year of life. *Int. Arch. Allergy Immunol.* 2001; 124:497-501.

[29] Upham JW, Hayes LM, Lundahl J, Sehmi R, Denburg JA. Reduced expression of hemopoietic cytokine receptors on cord blood progenitor cells in neonates at risk for atopy. *J. Allergy Clin. Immunol.* 1999; 104:370-5.

[30] Matsuoka T, Matsubara T, Katayama K, Takeda K, Koga M, Furukawa S. Increase of cord blood cytokine-producing T cells in intrauterine infection. *Pediatr. Int.* 2001; 43:453-7.

[31] Dunstan J, Mori TA, Barden A, Beilin LJ, Taylor A, Holt PG, Prescott SL. Fish oil supplementation in pregnancy modifies neonatal allergen-specific immune responses and clinical outcomes in infants at high risk of atopy: a randomised controlled trial. *J. Allergy Clin. Immunol.* 2003; 112:1178-84.

[32] Noakes PS, Holt PG, Prescott SL. Maternal smoking in pregnancy alters neonatal cytokine responses. *Allergy* 2003; 58:1053-8.

[33] Otto SJ, Houwelingen AC, Antal M, Manninen A, Godfrey K, Lopez-Jaramillo P, Hornstra G. Maternal and neonatal essential fatty acid status in phospholipids: an international comparative study. *Eur. J. Clin. Nutr.* 1997; 51:232-42.

[34] Duchen K, Yu G, Bjorksten B. Atopic sensitization during the first year of life in relation to long chain polyunsaturated fatty acid levels in human milk. *Pediatr. Res.* 1998; 44(4):478-84.

[35] Stoney RM, Woods RK, Hosking CS, Hill DJ, Abramson MJ, Thien FC. Maternal breast milk long-chain n-3 fatty acids are associated with increased risk of atopy in breastfed infants. *Clin. Exp. Allergy* 2004; 34:194-200.

[36] Galli E, Picardo M, Chini L, Passi S, Moschese V, Terminali O, Paone F, Fraioli G, Rossi P. Analysis of polyunsaturated fatty acids in newborn sera: a screening tool for atopic disease? *Br. J. Dermatol.* 1994; 130:752-6.

[37] Yu G, Bjorksten B. Serum levels of phospholipid fatty acids in mothers and their babies in relation to allergic disease. *Eur. J. Pediatr.* 1998; 157:298-303.

[38] Horrobin DF. Fatty acid metabolism in health and disease: the role of delta-6-desaturase. *Am. J. Clin. Nutr.* 1993; 57:732S-736S; discussion 736S-737S.

[39] Wright S. Atopic dermatitis and essential fatty acids: a biochemical basis for atopy? *Acta. Derm. Venereol. Suppl. (Stockh)* 1985; 114:143-5.

[40] Yu G, Bjorksten B. Polyunsaturated fatty acids in school children in relation to allergy and serum IgE levels. *Pediatr. Allergy Immunol.* 1998; 9:133-8.

[41] Grimble RF. Nutritional modulation of cytokine biology. *Nutrition* 1998; 14:634-40.

[42] Sorensen JD, Olsen SF, Pedersen AK, Boris J, Secher NJ, FitzGerald GA. Effects of fish oil supplementation in the third trimester of pregnancy on prostacyclin and thromboxane production. *American Journal of Obstetrics & Gynecology* 1993; 168:915-22.

[43] Meydani SN, Dinarello CA. Influence of dietary fatty acids on cytokine production and its clinical implications. *Nutr. Clin. Pract.* 1993; 8:65-72.

[44] Caughey GE, Mantzioris E, Gibson RA, Cleland LG, James MJ. The effect on human tumor necrosis factor alpha and interleukin 1 beta production of diets enriched in n-3 fatty acids from vegetable oil or fish oil. *Am. J. Clin. Nutr.* 1996; 63:116-22.

[45] Endres S, Ghorbani R, Kelley VE, Georgilis K, Lonnemann G, van der Meer JW, Cannon JG, Rogers TS, Klempner MS, Weber PC. The effect of dietary supplementation with n-3 polyunsaturated fatty acids on the synthesis of interleukin-1 and tumor necrosis factor by mononuclear cells. *N. Engl. J. Med.* 1989; 320:265-71.

[46] Endres S, Meydani SN, Ghorbani R, Schindler R, Dinarello CA. Dietary supplementation with n-3 fatty acids suppresses interleukin-2 production and mononuclear cell proliferation. *J. Leukoc. Biol.* 1993; 54:599-603.

[47] Sperling RI, Benincaso AI, Knoell CT, Larkin JK, Austen KF, Robinson DR. Dietary omega-3 polyunsaturated fatty acids inhibit phosphoinositide formation and chemotaxis in neutrophils. *J. Clin. Invest.* 1993; 91:651-60.

[48] Snijdewint F, Kalinski P, Wieringa E, Bos J, Kapsenberg M. Prostaglandin E2 differentially modulates cytokine secretion profiles of human T-helper lymphocytes. *J. Immunol.* 1993; 150:5321-5329.

[49] Gold K, Weyand C, Goronzy J. Modulation of helper T cell function by prostaglandins. *Arthritis. Rheum.* 1994; 37:925-933.

[50] Kinsella JE, Lokesh B, Broughton S, Whelan J. Dietary polyunsaturated fatty acids and eicosanoids: potential effects on the modulation of inflammatory and immune cells: an overview. *Nutrition* 1990; 6:24-44; discussion 59-62.

[51] van der Pouw Kraan TC, Boeije LC, Smeenk RJ, Wijdenes J, Aarden LA. Prostaglandin-E2 is a potent inhibitor of human interleukin 12 production. *J. Exp. Med.* 1995; 181:775-9.

[52] Roper RL, Brown DM, Phipps RP. Prostaglandin E2 promotes B lymphocyte Ig isotype switching to IgE. *J. Immunol.* 1995; 154:162-70.

[53] Kalinski P, Hilkens C, Snijders A, Snijdewint G, Kapsenburg M. IL-12 deficient dendritic cells, generated in the presence of PGE2 promote type 2 cytokine production in maturing human naive T helper cells. *J. Immunol.* 1997; 159:28-35.

[54] von Schacky C. Prophylaxis of atherosclerosis with marine omega-3 fatty acids. A comprehensive strategy. *Ann. Intern. Med.* 1987; 107:890-9.

[55] James MJ, Gibson RA, Cleland LG. Dietary polyunsaturated fatty acids and inflammatory mediator production. *Am. J. Clin. Nutr.* 2000; 71:343S-8S.

[56] Stulnig TM, Huber J, Leitinger N, Imre EM, Angelisova P, Nowotny P, Waldhausl W. Polyunsaturated eicosapentaenoic acid displaces proteins from membrane rafts by altering raft lipid composition. *J. Biol. Chem.* 2001; 276:37335-40.

[57] Simons K, Ikonen E. Functional rafts in cell membranes. *Nature* 1997; 387:569-72.

[58] Stulnig TM, Berger M, Sigmund T, Raederstorff D, Stockinger H, Waldhausl W. Polyunsaturated fatty acids inhibit T cell signal transduction by modification of detergent-insoluble membrane domains. *J. Cell Biol.* 1998; 143:637-44.

[59] Arrington JL, McMurray DN, Switzer KC, Fan YY, Chapkin RS. Docosahexaenoic acid suppresses function of the CD28 costimulatory membrane receptor in primary murine and Jurkat T cells. *J. Nutr.* 2001; 131:1147-53.

[60] Hughes DA, Pinder AC. Influence of n-3 polyunsaturated fatty acids (PUFA) on the antigen- presenting function of human monocytes. *Biochem. Soc. Trans.* 1996; 24:389S.

[61] Jenski LJ, Bowker GM, Johnson MA, Ehringer WD, Fetterhoff T, Stillwell W. Docosahexaenoic acid-induced alteration of Thy-1 and CD8 expression on murine splenocytes. *Biochim. Biophys. Acta.* 1995; 1236:39-50.

[62] Sasaki T, Kanke Y, Nagahashi M, Toyokawa M, Matsuda M, Shimizu J, Misawa Y, Takita T. Dietary docosahexaenoic acid can alter the surface expression of CD4 and CD8 on T cells in peripheral blood. *J. Agric. Food Chem.* 2000; 48:1047-9.

[63] Sasaki T, Kanke Y, Kudoh K, Misawa Y, Shimizu J, Takita T. Effects of dietary docosahexaenoic acid on surface molecules involved in T cell proliferation. *Biochim. Biophys. Acta.* 1999; 1436:519-30.

[64] Grakoui A, Bromley SK, Sumen C, Davis MM, Shaw AS, Allen PM, Dustin ML. The immunological synapse: a molecular machine controlling T cell activation. *Science* 1999; 285:221-7.

[65] Chow SC, Sisfontes L, Jondal M, Bjorkhem I. Modification of membrane phospholipid fatty acyl composition in a leukemic T cell line: effects on receptor mediated intracellular Ca2+ increase. *Biochim. Biophys. Acta.* 1991; 1092:358-66.

[66] May CL, Southworth AJ, Calder PC. Inhibition of lymphocyte protein kinase C by unsaturated fatty acids. *Biochem. Biophys. Res. Commun.* 1993; 195:823-8.

[67] Calder PC, Newsholme EA. Polyunsaturated fatty acids suppress human peripheral blood lymphocyte proliferation and interleukin-2 production. *Clin. Sci. (Colch)* 1992; 82:695-700.

[68] Jolly CA, Jiang YH, Chapkin RS, McMurray DN. Dietary (n-3) polyunsaturated fatty acids suppress murine lymphoproliferation, interleukin-2 secretion, and the formation of diacylglycerol and ceramide. *J. Nutr.* 1997; 127:37-43.

[69] Thies F, Nebe-von-Caron G, Powell JR, Yaqoob P, Newsholme EA, Calder PC. Dietary supplementation with gamma-linolenic acid or fish oil decreases T lymphocyte proliferation in healthy older humans. *J. Nutr.* 2001; 131:1918-27.

[70] Kelley DS, Branch LB, Love JE, Taylor PC, Rivera YM, Iacono JM. Dietary alpha-linolenic acid and immunocompetence in humans. *Am. J. Clin. Nutr.* 1991; 53:40-6.

[71] Alexander NJ, Smythe NL. Dietary fat modulation of in vitro lymphocyte function. *Ann. Nutr. Metab.* 1988; 32:192-9.

[72] Kumar GS, Das UN. Effect of prostaglandins and their precursors on the proliferation of human lymphocytes and their secretion of tumor necrosis factor and various interleukins. *Prostaglandins. Leukot. Essent. Fatty Acids* 1994; 50:331-4.

[73] Soyland E, Nenseter MS, Braathen L, Drevon CA. Very long chain n-3 and n-6 polyunsaturated fatty acids inhibit proliferation of human T-lymphocytes in vitro. *Eur. J. Clin. Invest.* 1993; 23:112-21.

[74] Khalfoun B, Lacord M, Bardos P, Lebranchu Y. Effects of docosahexaenoic and eicosapentaenoic acids on in vitro- induced human lymphoproliferative responses. *Transplant Proc.* 1996; 28:2913-4.

[75] Purasiri P, McKechnie A, Heys SD, Eremin O. Modulation in vitro of human natural cytotoxicity, lymphocyte proliferative response to mitogens and cytokine production by essential fatty acids. *Immunology* 1997; 92:166-72.

[76] Meydani SN, Endres S, Woods MM, Goldin BR, Soo C, Morrill-Labrode A, Dinarello CA, Gorbach SL. Effect of oral n-3 fatty acid supplementation on the immune response of young and older women. *Adv. Prostaglandin. Thromboxane Leukot. Res.* 1991; 21A:245-8.

[77] Gallai V, Sarchielli P, Trequattrini A, Franceschini M, Floridi A, Firenze C, Alberti A, Di Benedetto D, Stragliotto E. Cytokine secretion and eicosanoid production in the peripheral blood mononuclear cells of MS patients undergoing dietary supplementation with n-3 polyunsaturated fatty acids. *J. Neuroimmunol.* 1995; 56:143-53.

[78] Hughes DA, Southon S, Pinder AC. (n-3) Polyunsaturated fatty acids modulate the expression of functionally associated molecules on human monocytes in vitro. *J. Nutr.* 1996; 126:603-10.

[79] Dunstan J, Mori TA, Barden A, Beilin LJ, Taylor A, Holt PG, Prescott SL. The Effect of Maternal Fish Oil Supplementation on Neonatal Immune Responses. In: Marone, G, ed. *Clinical Immunology and Allergy in Medicine*. Naples:JGC Editions, 2003: 409-412.

[80] Petursdottir DH, Olafsdottir I, Hardardottir I. Dietary fish oil increases tumor necrosis factor secretion but decreases interleukin-10 secretion by murine peritoneal macrophages. *J Nutr* 2002; 132:3740-3.

[81] Foitzik T, Eibl G, Schneider P, Wenger FA, Jacobi CA, Buhr HJ. Omega-3 fatty acid supplementation increases anti-inflammatory cytokines and attenuates systemic disease sequelae in experimental pancreatitis. *JPEN J. Parenter. Enteral. Nutre.* 2002; 26:351-6.

[82] Molvig J, Pociot F, Worsaae H, Wogensen LD, Baek L, Christensen P, Mandrup-Poulsen T, Andersen K, Madsen P, Dyerberg J. Dietary supplementation with omega-3-polyunsaturated fatty acids decreases mononuclear cell proliferation and interleukin-1 beta content but not monokine secretion in healthy and insulin-dependent diabetic individuals. *Scand. J. Immunol.* 1991; 34:399-410.

[83] Cannon JG, Fiatarone MA, Meydani M, Gong J, Scott L, Blumberg JB, Evans WJ. Aging and dietary modulation of elastase and interleukin-1 beta secretion. *Am. J. Physiol.* 1995; 268:R208-13.

[84] Schmidt EB, Varming K, Moller JM, Bulow Pedersen I, Madsen P, Dyerberg J. No effect of a very low dose of n-3 fatty acids on monocyte function in healthy humans. *Scand. J. Clin. Lab. Invest.* 1996; 56:87-92.

[85] Lokesh BR, Sayers TJ, Kinsella JE. Interleukin-1 and tumor necrosis factor synthesis by mouse peritoneal macrophages is enhanced by dietary n-3 polyunsaturated fatty acids. *Immunol. Lett.* 1990; 23:281-5.

[86] Chang HR, Arsenijevic D, Pechere JC, Piguet PF, Mensi N, Girardier L, Dulloo AG. Dietary supplementation with fish oil enhances in vivo synthesis of tumor necrosis factor. *Immunol Lett* 1992; 34:13-7.
[87] Erickson KL, Hubbard NE. Dietary fish oil modulation of macrophage tumoricidal activity. *Nutrition* 1996; 12:S34-8.
[88] Boutard V, Fouqueray B, Philippe C, Perez J, Baud L. Fish oil supplementation and essential fatty acid deficiency reduce nitric oxide synthesis by rat macrophages. *Kidney Int.* 1994; 46:1280-6.
[89] Tappia PS, Grimble RF. Complex modulation of cytokine induction by endotoxin and tumour necrosis factor from peritoneal macrophages of rats by diets containing fats of different saturated, monounsaturated and polyunsaturated fatty acid composition. *Clin. Sci. (Colch)* 1994; 87:173-8.
[90] Yaqoob P, Calder P. Effects of dietary lipid manipulation upon inflammatory mediator production by murine macrophages. *Cell Immunol.* 1995; 163:120-8.
[91] Yaqoob P, Knapper JA, Webb DH, Williams CM, Newsholme EA, Calder PC. Effect of olive oil on immune function in middle-aged men. *Am. J. Clin. Nutr.* 1998; 67:129-35.
[92] Joe B, Lokesh B. Role of capsaicin, curcumin and dietary n-3 fatty acids in lowereing the generation of reactive oxygen species in rat peritoneal macrophages. *Biochim. Biophys. Acta.* 1994; 1224:255-263.
[93] Lu CY, Penfield JG, Khair-el-Din TA, Sicher SC, Kielar ML, Vazquez MA, Che L. Docosahexaenoic acid, a constituent of fetal and neonatal serum, inhibits nitric oxide production by murine macrophages stimulated by IFN gamma plus LPS, or by IFN gamma plus Listeria monocytogenes. *Journal of Reproductive Immunology* 1998; 38:31-53.
[94] Jeyarajah DR, Kielar M, Penfield J, Lu CY. Docosahexaenoic acid, a component of fish oil, inhibits nitric oxide production in vitro [In Process Citation]. *J. Surg. Res.* 1999; 83:147-50.
[95] Khair-el-Din TA, Sicher SC, Vazquez MA, Lu CY. Inhibition of macrophage nitric-oxide production and Ia-expression by docosahexaenoic acid, a constituent of fetal and neonatal serum. *American Journal of Reproductive Immunology* 1996; 36:1-10.
[96] Strasser T, Fischer S, Weber PC. Inhibition of leukotriene B4 formation in human neutrophils after oral nafazatrom (Bay g 6575). *Biochem. Pharmacol.* 1985; 34:1891-4.
[97] Croft KD, Codde JP, Barden A, Vandongen R, Beilin LJ. Effect of dietary fish oils on the formation of leukotriene B4 and B5, thromboxane and platelet activating factor by rat leukocytes. *Clin. Exp. Pharmacol. Physiol.* 1988; 15:517-25.
[98] Strasser T, Fischer S, Weber PC. Leukotriene B5 is formed in human neutrophils after dietary supplementation with icosapentaenoic acid. *Proc. Natl. Acad. Sci. USA* 1985; 82:1540-3.
[99] Halvorsen DS, Hansen JB, Grimsgaard S, Bonaa KH, Kierulf P, Nordoy A. The effect of highly purified eicosapentaenoic and docosahexaenoic acids on monocyte phagocytosis in man. *Lipids* 1997; 32:935-42.

[100] Taki H, Morinaga S, Yamazaki K, Hamazaki T, Suzuki H, Nakamura N. Reduction of delayed-type hypersensitivity by the injection of n-3 polyunsaturated fatty acids in mice. *Transplantation* 1992; 54:511-4.

[101] Jenski L, Scherer J, Caldwell L, Ney V, W S. The triggering signal dictates the effect of docosahexaenoic acid on lymphocyte function in vitro. *Lipids* 1998; 33(9):869-78.

[102] Hii CS, Costabile M, Mayne GC, Der CJ, Murray AW, Ferrante A. Selective deficiency in protein kinase C isoenzyme expression and inadequacy in mitogen-activated protein kinase activation in cord blood T cells. *Biochem. J.* 2003; 370:497-503.

[103] Adkins B, Williamson T, Guevara P, Bu Y. Murine neonatal lymphocytes show rapid early cell cycle entry and cell division. *J. Immunol.* 2003; 4548-56.

[104] Prescott SL, Irvine J, Dunstan JA, Hi C, and Ferrante. Protein kinase Czeta: a novel protective neonatal T-cell marker that can be upregulated by allergy prevention strategies. J Allergy Clin Immunology 2007 120(1):200-6

[105] Hii CS, Moghadammi N, Dunbar A, Ferrante A. Activation of the phosphatidylinositol 3-kinase-Akt/protein kinase B signaling pathway in arachidonic acid-stimulated human myeloid and endothelial cells: involvement of the ErbB receptor family. *J. Biol. Chem.* 2001; 276:27246-55.

[106] Murakami K, Routtenberg A. Direct activation of purified protein kinase C by unsaturated fatty acids (oleate and arachidonate) in the absence of phospholipids and Ca2+. *FEBS Lett.* 1985; 192:189-93.

[107] McPhail LC, Clayton CC, Snyderman R. A potential second messenger role for unsaturated fatty acids: activation of Ca2+-dependent protein kinase. *Science* 1984; 224:622-5.

[108] Rincon M, Flavell RA, Davis RA. The JNK and P38 MAP kinase signaling pathways in T cell-mediated immune responses. *Free Radic. Biol. Med.* 2000; 28:1328-37.

[109] O'Keefe JH, Jr., Harris WS. From Inuit to implementation: omega-3 fatty acids come of age. *Mayo. Clin. Proc.* 2000; 75:607-14.

[110] Nestel PJ. Fish oil and cardiovascular disease: lipids and arterial function. *Am. J. Clin. Nutr.* 2000; 71:228S-31S.

[111] Weber P, Raederstorff D. Triglyceride-lowering effect of omega-3 LC-polyunsaturated fatty acids-- a review. *Nutr. Metab. Cardiovasc. Dis.* 2000; 10:28-37.

[112] Hu FB, Manson JE, Willett WC. Types of dietary fat and risk of coronary heart disease: a critical review. *J. Am. Coll Nutr.* 2001; 20:5-19.

[113] James MJ, Cleland LG. Dietary n-3 fatty acids and therapy for rheumatoid arthritis. Semin *Arthritis. Rheum.* 1997; 27:85-97.

[114] Tidow-Kebritchi S, Mobarhan S. Effects of diets containing fish oil and vitamin E on rheumatoid arthritis. *Nutr. Rev.* 2001; 59:335-8.

[115] Belluzzi A, Boschi S, Brignola C, Munarini A, Cariani G, Miglio F. Polyunsaturated fatty acids and inflammatory bowel disease. *Am. J. Clin. Nutr.* 2000; 71:339S-42S.

[116] Hardman WE. Omega-3 fatty acids to augment cancer therapy. *J. Nutr.* 2002; 132:3508S-3512S.

[117] Beckles Willson N, Elliott TM, Everard ML. Omega-3 fatty acids (from fish oils) for cystic fibrosis. *Cochrane Database Syst. Rev.* 2002; CD002201.

[118] Woods RK, Thien FC, Abramson MJ, *Dietary marine fatty acids (fish oil) for asthma in adults and children (Cochrane Review)*, in The Cochrane Library. 2003, Oxford: Updated Software.

[119] Calder PC, Miles EA. Fatty acids and atopic disease. *Pediatr. Allergy Immunol.* 2000; 11(Suppl 13):29-36.

[120] Arm JP, Horton CE, Mencia-Huerta JM, House F, Eiser NM, Clark TJ, Spur BW, Lee TH. Effect of dietary supplementation with fish oil lipids on mild asthma. *Thorax* 1988; 43:84-92.

[121] Kirsch CM, Payan DG, Wong MY, Dohlman JG, Blake VA, Petri MA, Offenberger J, Goetzl EJ, Gold WM. The 1988 report of the Joint National Committee on Detection, Evaluation, and Treatment of High Blood Pressure [see comments] Effect of eicosapentaenoic acid in asthma. *Arch. Intern. Med.* 1988; 148:1023-38.

[122] Stenius-Aarniala B, Aro A, Hakulinen A, Ahola I, Seppala E, Vapaatalo H. Evening primose oil and fish oil are ineffective as supplementary treatment of bronchial asthma. *Ann. Allergy* 1989; 62:534-7.

[123] McDonald CF, Vecchie L, Pierce RJ, Strauss BJG, *Effect of fish-oil derived omega-3 fatty acid supplements on asthma control.* 1990, Deakin University: Melbourne, Australia. p. 526.

[124] Dry J, Vincene D. Interest of fish oil in asthma: results of a 1 year double blind study. *Int. Arch. Allergy Appl. Immunol.* 1991; 95:156-157.

[125] Thien F, Mencia-Huerta J, Lee T. Dietary fish oil effects on seasonal hay fever and asthma in pollen sensitive subjects. *Am. Rev. Respir. Dis.* 1993; 147:1138-1143.

[126] Nagakura T, Matsuda S, Shichijyo K, Sugimoto H, Hata K. Dietary supplementation with fish oil rich in omega-3 polyunsaturated fatty acids in children with bronchial asthma.[In Process Citation]. *Eur. Respir. J.* 2000; 16:861-5.

[127] Hodge L, Salome CM, Hughes JM, Liu-Brennan D, Rimmer J, Allman M, Pang D, Armour C, Woolcock AJ. Effect of dietary intake of omega-3 and omega-6 fatty acids on severity of asthma in children. *Eur. Respir. J.* 1998; 11:361-5.

[128] Arm JP, Lee TH. The use of fish oil in bronchial asthma. *Allergy Proc.* 1989; 10:185-7.

[129] Sakakibara H, Hirose K, Matsushita K, Nakamura S, Sato M, Kako K, Suetsugu S. [Effect of supplementation with eicosapentaenoic acid ethyl ester, MND- 21, on generation of leukotrienes by calcium ionophore-activated leukocytes in bronchial asthma]. *Nihon. Kyobu. Shikkan. Gakkai. Zasshi.* 1995; 33:395-402.

[130] Machura E, Brus R, Kalacinnski W, Lacheta M. [The effect of dietary fish oil supplementation on the clinical course of asthma in children]. *Pediatr. Pol.* 1996; 71:97-102.

[131] Broughton KS, Johnson CS, Pace BK, Liebman M, Kleppinger KM. Reduced asthma symptoms with n-3 fatty acid ingestion are related to 5-series leukotriene production. *American Journal of Clinical Nutrition* 1997; 65:1011-7.

[132] Hashimoto N, Majima T, Ichimura K, Iwata T, Suguro H, Horie T. Effects of eicosapentaenoic acid in patients with bronchial asthma (abstract only). *Nihon. Kyobu. Shikkan. Gakkai. Zasshi.* 1997; 35:634-40.

[133] Masuev KA. The effect of polyunsaturated fatty acids of the omega-3 class on the late phase of the allergic reaction in bronchial asthma patients (abstract only). *Ter. Arkh.* 1997; 69:31-3.

[134] Masuev KA. The effect of polyunsaturated fatty acids of the omega-3 class on the late phase of the allergic reaction in bronchial asthma patients (abstract only). *Ter. Arkh.* 1997; 69:31-3.

[135] Villani F, Comazzi R, De Maria P, Galimberti M. Effect of dietary supplementation with polyunsaturated fatty acids on bronchial hyperreactivity in subjects with seasonal asthma. *Respiration* 1998; 65:265-9.

[136] Gorelova Z, Ladodo KS, Levachev MM, Lupinovich VL, Mamonova LG, Orlova SV, Balabolkin, II, Zadkova GF, Arutiunova MB. [Role of polyunsaturated fatty acids in diet therapy of children with allergic diseases]. *Vopr. Pitan.* 1999; 68:31-5.

[137] Bjorneboe A, Soyland E, Bjorneboe GE, Rajka G, Drevon CA. Effect of dietary supplementation with eicosapentaenoic acid in the treatment of atopic dermatitis. *Br. J. Dermatol.* 1987; 117:463-9.

[138] Berth-Jones J, Graham-Brown RA. Placebo-controlled trial of essential fatty acid supplementation in atopic dermatitis. *Lancet* 1993; 341:1557-60.

[139] Thien FC, Atkinson BA, Khan A, Mencia-Huerta JM, Lee TH. Effect of dietary fish oil supplementation on the antigen-induced late- phase response in the skin. *J Allergy Clin Immunol* 1992; 89:829-35.

[140] Mayser P, Mayer K, Mahloudjian M, Benzing S, Kramer HJ, Schill WB, Seeger W, Grimminger F. A double-blind, randomized, placebo-controlled trial of n-3 versus n-6 fatty acid-based lipid infusion in atopic dermatitis. *JPEN J. Parenter. Enteral. Nutre.* 2002; 26:151-8.

[141] Olsen S, Sorenson J, Secher N, Hedegaard M, Henriksen T. Randomised controlled trial of effect of fish oil supplementation on pregnancy duration. *Lancet* 1992; 339:1003-7.

[142] Dunstan JA, Mori TA, Barden A, Beilin LJ, Holt PG, Calder PC, Taylor AL, Prescott SL. Effects of n-3 polyunsaturated fatty acid supplementation in pregnancy on maternal and fetal erythrocyte fatty acid composition. *Eur. J. Clin. Nutr.* 2004; 58:429-37.

[143] Dunstan JA, Mori TA, Barden A, Beilin LJ, Taylor AL, Holt PG, Prescott SL. Maternal fish oil supplementation in pregnancy reduces interleukin-13 levels in cord blood of infants at high risk of atopy. *Clin. Exp. Allergy* 2003; 33:442-8.

[144] Prescott SL, Barden A, Mori TA, Dunstan JA. Maternal fish oil supplementation in pregnancy modifies neonatal leukotriene production in cord blood derived neutrophils. Clinical Science (London) 2007 113(10): 409-16.

[145] Hatfield HM, Dunstan JA, Holt PG, Hayes L, Sehmi R, Denburg J, Prescott SL. Fish oil supplementation in pregnancy modifies neonatal progenitor numbers and responsiveness to IL-5 in infants at risk of atopy. *Pediatr. Res.* (accepted July 2004):

[146] Mihrshahi S, Peat JK, Marks GB, Mellis CM, Tovey ER, Webb K, Britton WJ, Leeder SR. Eighteen-month outcomes of house dust mite avoidance and dietary fatty acid modification in the Childhood Asthma Prevention Study (CAPS). *J. Allergy Clin. Immunol* 2003; 111:162-8.

[147] Peat JK, Mihrshahi S, Kemp AS, Marks GB, Tovey ER, Webb K, Mellis CM, Leeder SR. Three-year outcomes of dietary fatty acid modification and house dust mite reduction in the Childhood Asthma Prevention Study. *J. Allergy Clin. Immunol.* 2004; 114:807-13.

[148] Almqvist C, Garden F, Xuan W, Mihrshahi S, Leeder SR, Oddy W, Webb K, Marks GB; CAPS team. Omega-3 and omega-6 fatty acid exposure from early life does not affect atopy and asthma at age 5 years. J Allergy Clin Immunol. 2007;119(6):1438-44.

In: New Immunology Research Developments
Editor: Gunter V. Müller
ISBN 978-1-60021-701-2


Chapter 10

# Hemorrhagic Cystitis after Bone Marrow Transplantation Is Neither Quantitatively nor Qualitatively Correlated to the Urinary Excretion of Polyomaviruses

***Stefan S. Biel*[*1,2], *Barbara Chmielewicz*[1] *and Andreas Nitsche*[1,3]**
[1]Robert Koch-Institut, Berlin, Germany
[2]Beiersdorf AG, Hamburg, Germany
[3]Klinik für Innere Medizin m.S. Hämatologie und Onkologie,
Charité Campus Virchow-Klinikum,
Humboldt Universität zu Berlin, Germany

## Abstract

Hemorrhagic cystitis, a common complication after bone marrow transplantation (BMT), has often been attributed to polyomavirus reactivation. However, this link is still being controversially discussed and needs to be further examined.

In a prospective study, 571 urine samples from 101 patients undergoing BMT were examined for the presence of human polyomaviruses BK (BKV) and JC (JCV) using electron microscopy, qualitative and quantitative PCR. The urine samples were also screened for adenoviruses, cytomegalovirus, and polyomavirus SV 40. The degree of hematuria as a marker for hemorrhagic cystitis was determined using semi-quantitative dipstick analysis.

Polyomaviruria was observed in 49 % of the patients. Thirty-three percent excreted only BKV, 9 % were found positive only for JCV, and in 7 % of the patients both viruses were detected. Hematuria occurred in 29 % of the patients. No urine was positive for other viral agents. Statistical analysis showed that neither sex, disease, conditioning, thrombocytopenia, nor acute graft-versus-host-disease correlated significantly with the

[*] Phone: +49 (0)40 4909-6671, Fax: +49 (0)40 4909-4882, Email: Stefan.Biel@.Beiersdorf.com

development of polyomaviruria or hematuria. For patients undergoing *allogeneic* BMT, the incidence was significantly higher for both hematuria ($p = 0.002$) and BKV excretion ($p = 0.0002$), but not for JCV excretion. However, stratified analysis revealed no significant correlation between polyomaviruria and hematuria; for patients with parallel hematuria and viruria, the degree of hematuria did not correlate with the viral load anyway.

Based on these data we presume that hemorrhagic cystitis after BMT cannot easily be linked to single episodes of polyomaviruria; it rather seems to depend on individually varying and independent factors.

## Introduction

Reactivation of latent viruses is a common phenomenon occurring in immuno-suppressed individuals and has been described for different virus families, e.g. herpesviruses, polyomaviruses and adenoviruses. In immuno-suppressed patients undergoing transplantation, the reactivation of latent viruses can lead to complications ranging from mild to life-threatening disease, and therefore has to be carefully monitored. For some viral agents, the association between the reactivation of a distinct virus and the respective complications has been clearly demonstrated [1, 2, 3], for others, the link to disease is still an open area of research. Unfortunately, there is a huge number of factors influencing the patients' state after transplantation, and the development of a certain disease cannot always be correlated to a singular factor or infection.

Hemorrhagic cystitis (HC) is a common complication following high-dose chemotherapy and bone marrow transplantation [4]. Although seldom life-threatening, HC may cause significant morbidity. Its occurrence has been attributed to a number of different causes, e.g. to the use of drugs such as oxazaphosphorines and busulfan [4] as well as the reactivation of human polyomaviruses [5, 6]. However, especially the link to polyomaviral reactivation is still being controversially discussed. While some studies show a significant correlation between hemorrhagic cystitis and the shedding of human polyomaviruses in urine [5, 6, 7, 8, 9, 10, 11], other studies present data showing no significant link between hematuria and polyomaviruria [12, 13, 14, 15]. Furthermore, HC has also been linked to infection with adenoviruses [10, 13, 16] or cytomegalovirus [17].

The aim of the study presented here was to clarify the question whether polyomaviral reactivation is responsible for the development of HC, using new sensitive polyomavirus type-specific and quantitative technology. For this purpose, we used two different PCR assays allowing not only for the qualitative detection of both subtypes of human polyomaviruses BKV and JCV, but also for the quantification of the polyomaviral and adenoviral load in urine of BMT patients. In addition, we investigated the presence of viral particles using negative staining EM. The degree of hematuria was monitored as a marker for hemorrhagic cystitis.

# Material and Methods

## Patient Collective

101 patients (71 male, 30 female) with a median age of 35 years (range <1 – 60 years) undergoing allogeneic (n = 56) or autologous (n = 45) BMT at the Charité Campus Virchow-Klinikum, Berlin, from January 1997 to July 1998, were included in this study. Samples were collected over a period of 1-38 weeks (median 4 weeks); detailed patient data are given in Table 1.

**Table 1. Clinical data for 101 patients undergoing BMT at the Charité Campus Virchow-Klinikum, Berlin, from January 1997 to July 1998. Data are given in absolute numbers and percentages according to subgroups.**

| | | |
|---|---|---|
| Age | | |
| Range | 0-60 y | |
| Median | 35 y | |
| Sex | | |
| Male | 71 | (70 %) |
| Female | 30 | (30 %) |
| Primary disease | | |
| chronic myelogenous leukemia | 19 | (19 %) |
| chronic lymphocytic leukemia | 2 | (2 %) |
| acute myelogenous leukemia | 9 | (9 %) |
| acute lymphoblastic leukemia | 12 | (12 %) |
| Hodgkin's disease | 5 | (5 %) |
| non-Hodgkin's lymphoma | 15 | (15 %) |
| multiple myeloma | 8 | (8 %) |
| germ cell tumor | 9 | (9 %) |
| solid tumor, other | 9 | (9 %) |
| others | 13 | (13 %) |
| Type of BMT | | |
| allogeneic | 56 | (55 %) |
| autologous | 45 | (45 %) |
| Preparative regimen | | |
| Busulfan only | 6 | ( 6 %) |
| Cyclophosphamide only | 16 | (16 %) |
| Ifosfamide | 10 | (10 %) |
| Busulfan / Cyclophosphamide | 33 | (33 %) |
| Others | 36 | (36 %) |
| Acute graft-versus-host disease | | |
| $< °II$ | 76 | (75 %) |
| $\geq °II$ | 25 | (25 %) |

## Sample Collection

A total number of 571 mid-stream urine samples was obtained weekly from patients prior to and after BMT (n = 101) and also from healthy control persons (n = 15). Urine was transported at room temperature and stored at 4 °C; to protect the urine from bacterial growth, sodium azide was added to a final concentration of 0.02 % (w/v).

## Dipstick Analysis

Hematuria was monitored with urine dipsticks according to the manufacturer's directions (Multistix, Bayer Diagnostics). The erythrocyte concentration was assessed semi-quantitatively in four categories: *0* = no hematuria, *1* = 10-25 erythrocytes/µL, *2* = 25-80 erythrocytes/µL, *3* = 80-200 erythrocytes/µL.

## Electron Microscopy (EM)

Urine samples were analyzed by negative staining electron microscopy as described elsewhere [18]. Briefly, the samples were adsorbed to 400 mesh copper grids covered with Pioloform F and carbon. Afterwards they were negatively contrasted using 2 % uranyl acetate and examined in a transmission EM (Zeiss EM 10A) for at least 15 min. For virus enrichment by sedimentation, prior to EM preparation ultracentrifugation was performed with 5 mL urine for 60 min at 100,000 xg in a Beckman centrifuge. The supernatant was discarded and the pellet was resuspended in 50 µL sterile double-distilled water.

## Polymerase Chain Reaction (PCR)

### *Polyomaviruses BK and JC*

Polyomavirus PCR was performed as recently described [19]. Untreated urine (5 µL, 1:10 diluted) was examined with a quantitative TaqMan-PCR assay (TM-PCR) detecting BKV as well as JCV. Each 50 µL-PCR assay contained 5 µL of template, 500 nM concentrations of each primer, 100 nM exonuclease probe, 100 µM of each dNTP (Gibco), 5 µL 10x amplification buffer, 1 µM ROX and 2 U Platinum Taq DNA polymerase (Gibco). After initial denaturation for 3 min, the sample was subjected to 45 cycles of 94 °C for 30 s and 62 °C for 30 s. Fluorescence intensity was read automatically during PCR cycling in an ABI Prism 7700 SDS.

Polyomavirus-positive urine samples were subjected to a semi-nested PCR (snPCR) in order to differentiate between BKV and JCV. Each 30 µL-PCR mixture contained 5 µL of template, 333 nM concentrations of each primer, 50 µM of each dNTP (Gibco), 3 µL 10x amplification buffer and 1 U Platinum Taq DNA polymerase (Gibco). After initial denaturation for 3 min, the sample was subjected to 30 cycles of 94 °C for 20 s and 53 °C for 20 s and a final extension for 5 min at 72 °C for the first amplification round. 1 µL of the resulting PCR product was used as template in a second amplification round under the same conditions, merely increasing the annealing temperature to 58 °C.

### *Adenovirus*

Adenoviral load was examined using a real-time PCR targeting the viral DNA-Polymerase gene [20]. The 25µl reaction volume contained 1x PCR Buffer, 6mM $MgCl_2$, 1mM dNTP (200µM each), 1µM ROX, 0.5U Platinum Taq Polymerase (Invitrogen), all primers at a concentration of 100nM and two different adenovirus probes (each 50nM). Reaction conditions were 5 minutes at 95°C for activation of Taq Polymerase and denaturation of the DNA, followed by 40 cycles consisting of denaturation at 95°C for 15 seconds, annealing at 60°C for 20 seconds and primer extension at 72°C for 30 seconds.

### *SV40, Cytomegalovirus*

The screening for other infectious agents was performed with DNA preparations from urine pools. Each pool contained equal amounts of 20 different urine samples; commercial kits (QIAGEN, Hilden, Germany) were used for DNA preparation following the manufacturer's rules. Sensitivity of the pool analyses is in the same order of magnitude as for the polyoma assays of individual samples (dilution factor 1: 20 for pools vs. 1: 10 for untreated urine).

The presence of polyomavirus SV 40 was examined using a nested PCR-assay (nPCR). Each 30 µL-PCR mixture contained 5 µL of template, 333 nM concentrations of each primer (1st PCR: *SVFout* CTC CAC Agg CCT ATg CTg TgA T, *SVBOut* AAA CCT TgC CAA ACT gTC CC; 2nd PCR: *SVFIn* CTg CAA ACT gTg ACT ggT gTg A, *SVBIn* CTT TCA AgC Tgg TgT gAg gTg A), 50 µM of each dNTP (Gibco), 10 µL 10x amplification buffer and 1 U Platinum Taq DNA polymerase (Gibco). After initial denaturation for 3 min, the sample was subjected to 30 cycles of 94 °C, 60 °C, and 72 °C for 30 s each, and a final extension for 5 min at 72 °C for the first amplification round. 1 µL of the resulting PCR product was used as template in a second amplification round under the same conditions, merely increasing the annealing temperature to 61 °C.

Cytomegalovirus PCR was performed with 1: 10 diluted urine using a recently described TM-PCR assay [21]. Each 50 µL-PCR assay contained 5 µL of template, 800 nM concentrations of each primer, 50 nM exonuclease probe, 200 µM of each dNTP (Gibco), 5 µL 10x amplification buffer, 1 µM ROX and 1 U Platinum Taq DNA polymerase (Gibco). After initial denaturation for 3 min, the sample was subjected to 45 cycles of 94 °C for 10 s, 64 °C for 10 s, and 72 °C for 30 s. Fluorescence intensity was read automatically during PCR cycling in an ABI Prism 7700 SDS. All PCR analyses were performed at least in duplicates; questionable results were re-evaluated for clarification.

## Statistics

Statistical analysis was performed using EpiInfo 6.04a (Centers for Disease Control and Prevention, Atlanta GA, USA). Mantel-Haenszel's and Yates corrected Chi-square test, Fisher's exact test, and Mann-Whitney test were chosen for analysis as appropriate.

# Results

## Virus Detection

Polyomaviruria was detected in a total number of 149 samples from 49/101 patients (49 %); the different diagnostic assays welche genau? for the detection of polyomaviruses showed an excellent correlation. Typing with the snPCR assay revealed that 33/101 patients (33 %) excreted only BKV, while 9 patients (9 %) were found positive exclusively for JCV; in 7 patients (7 %) both viruses were detected either simultaneously or at different time points. To differentiate from sporadic events, the duration of viral shedding was examined: excretion of polyomaviruses over a period of at least 1 week (i.e. in two consecutive urine samples) was shown for 19 (BKV, 19 %), 3 (JCV, 3 %), and 2 (BKV/JCV, 2 %) patients. In EM diagnosis only urine samples revealed particles that were also PCR-positive for BKV; in the JCV PCR-positive samples no viral particles could be detected. Interestingly, the amount of virus particles as detected by EM is not correlated to the amount of viral genomes measured by quantitative PCR (see e.g. Figure 2a).

All tested urine samples were negative for herpesvirus (e.g. cytomegalovirus) or adenovirus by electron microscopy. All urine samples were negative for adenovirus by quantitative PCR; moreover, PCR of urine pools was negative for polyomavirus SV 40, cytomegalovirus, kann das weg?

Dipstick analysis revealed hematuria in 29 patients (29 %) after transplantation; 19 patients (19 %) had episodes of hematuria for longer than 1 week (median duration 2 weeks). Onset of hematuria was at least 3 days after transplantation.

## Risk Factors for the Development of Hemorrhagic Cystitis and/or Polyomaviruria

Statistical analysis revealed that patients after allogeneic BMT have a significantly higher risk for developing non-sporadic hematuria (27 % allogeneic BMT vs. 2 % autologous BMT, $p = 0.002$) and non-sporadic BK viruria (67 % allogeneic BMT vs. 18 % autologous BMT, $p = 0.0009$), but not for JC viruria (Table 2a); moreover, 94 % (15/16) of the patients with non-sporadic hematuria and 92 % (22/24) of the patients with non-sporadic BK viruria were within the allogeneic BMT group.

The apparent correlation between hematuria and polyomaviruria for the whole patient collective could be put down to dissimilar data distribution among the transplantation types; a significant correlation between hematuria and polyomaviruria could not be detected neither in the allogeneic BMT group nor in the autologous BMT group (Table 2b). Likewise, the correlation between hematuria/viruria and acute lymphoblastic leukemia or thrombocytopenia could be put down to dissimilar data distribution.

**Table 2a. Analysis of selected factors possibly influencing the development of non-sporadic polyomaviruria and/or hematuria for 101 patients (median age: 35 years) undergoing BMT at the Charité Campus Virchow-Klinikum, Berlin, from January 1997 to July 1998. Data given in the table are number of patients and the respective percentages in parenthesis, and p-values according to Chi²-test statistics.**

| | Total | Hematuria > 1 week | | BKV excretion > 1 week | |
|---|---|---|---|---|---|
| Sex male<br>female | n = 71<br>n = 30 | 9 (13 %)<br>7 (23 %) | p = 0.324 | 19 (27 %)<br>5 (17 %) | p = 0.404 |
| Age ≤ 20 years<br>> 20 years | n = 34<br>n = 67 | 8 (14 %)<br>8 (12 %) | p = 0.217 | 16 (47 %)<br>8 (12 %) | p < 0.001 |
| aGvHD ≥ °II<br>< °II | n = 25<br>n = 76 | 7 (28 %)<br>9 (11 %) | p = 0.911 | 11 (44 %)<br>13 (15 %) | p = 0.701 |
| Disease ALL<br>other | n = 12<br>n = 89 | 4 (33 %)<br>12 (13 %) | p = 0.009 | 8 (67 %)<br>8 (18 %) | p < 0.001 |
| Graft allogeneic<br>autologous | n = 56<br>n = 45 | 15 (27 %)<br>1 ( 2 %) | p = 0.002 | 22 (39 %)<br>2 ( 4 %) | p < 0.001 |
| Thrombozytopenia > 1 week<br>0 – 1 week | n = 45<br>n = 56 | 9 (20 %)<br>7 (13 %) | p = 0.182 | 18 (40 %)<br>6 (11 %) | p = 0.187 |
| Hematuria > 1 week<br>0 – 1 week | n = 16<br>n = 85 | - | - | 8 (50 %)<br>16 (19 %) | p = 0.021 |
| BKV excretion > 1 week<br>0 – 1 week | n = 24<br>n = 77 | 8 (33 %)<br>8 (10 %) | p = 0.021 | - | - |

**Table 2b. Analysis of selected factors possibly influencing the development of non-sporadic polyomaviruria and/or hematuria for 56 patients (median age: 26 years) undergoing *allogeneic* BMT at the Charité Campus Virchow-Klinikum, Berlin, from January 1997 to July 1998. Data given in the table are number of patients and the respective percentages in parenthesis, and p-values according to Chi²-test statistics.**

| | Total | Hematuria > 1 week | | BKV excretion > 1 week | |
|---|---|---|---|---|---|
| Age ≤ 20 years<br>> 20 years | n = 25<br>n = 31 | 8 (32 %)<br>7 (23 %) | p = 0.632 | 15 (60 %)<br>7 (23 %) | p = 0.010 |
| aGvHD ≥ °II<br>< °II | n = 25<br>n = 76 | 7 (28 %)<br>8 (11 %) | p = 0.912 | 11 (44 %)<br>11 (15 %) | p = 0.697 |
| Disease ALL<br>other | n = 11<br>n = 45 | 4 (36 %)<br>11 (24 %) | p = 0.459 | 7 (64 %)<br>15 (33 %) | p = 0.071 |
| Thrombozytopenia > 1 week<br>0 – 1 week | n = 34<br>n = 22 | 9 (26 %)<br>6 (27 %) | p = 0.807 | 16 (47 %)<br>6 (27 %) | p = 0.232 |
| Hematuria > 1 week<br>0 – 1 week | n = 15<br>n = 41 | - | - | 8 (53 %)<br>14 (34 %) | p = 0.316 |
| BKV excretion > 1 week<br>0 – 1 week | n = 22<br>n = 34 | 8 (36 %)<br>7 (21 %) | p = 0.316 | - | - |

Patients younger than 20 years significantly more often show BK viruria than elder patients (47 % vs. 12 %, $p = 0.0002$ for all patients; 60 % vs. 23 %, $p = 0.01$ for patients after allogeneic BMT). Other possible risk factors, e.g. sex, disease other than acute lymphoblastic leukemia, conditioning, aGvHD ≥ °II could not be significantly correlated to the development of viruria or hematuria.

## Correlation of Polyomaviruria and Hemorrhagic Cystitis

Viral load and degree of hematuria did not show any significant correlation as shown in Figure 1. A total number of 17 patients (17 %) had overlapping episodes of hematuria and BK-viruria. Figure 2 shows time courses for viral load and erythrocyte content in the urine of 4 representative patients. While 6 patients (6 %) developed hematuria after onset of BK-viruria (Figure 2a, 2c), in 11 patients (11 %) hematuria started before onset of BK-viruria (see Figure 2b). For some patients the course of hematuria and viral load is similar (Figure 2c), for others, however, there is no correlation (Figure 2b). The development of hematuria was neither associated with the maximum value nor with maximum gradient of the viral load (Figure 2c). No overlapping between episodes of JC-viruria and hematuria could be detected (Figure 2d).

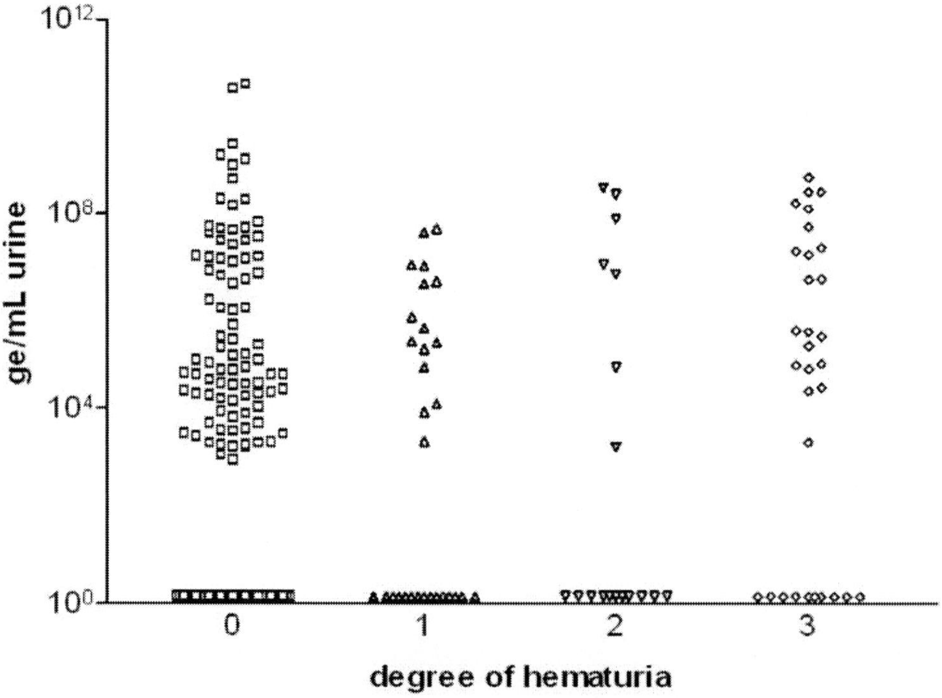


Figure 1. Correlation of hematuria and viral load in urineFollowing the results from the dipstick analysis, the urine samples were divided into four categories: 0 = no hematuria, 1 = 10-25 erythrocytes/µL, 2 = 25-80 erythrocytes/µL, 3 = 80-200 erythrocytes/µL. The viral load is given in ge/mL as determined by TaqMan PCR and is plotted against the respective category; the median viral load for all 4 categories is 0 ge/mL.

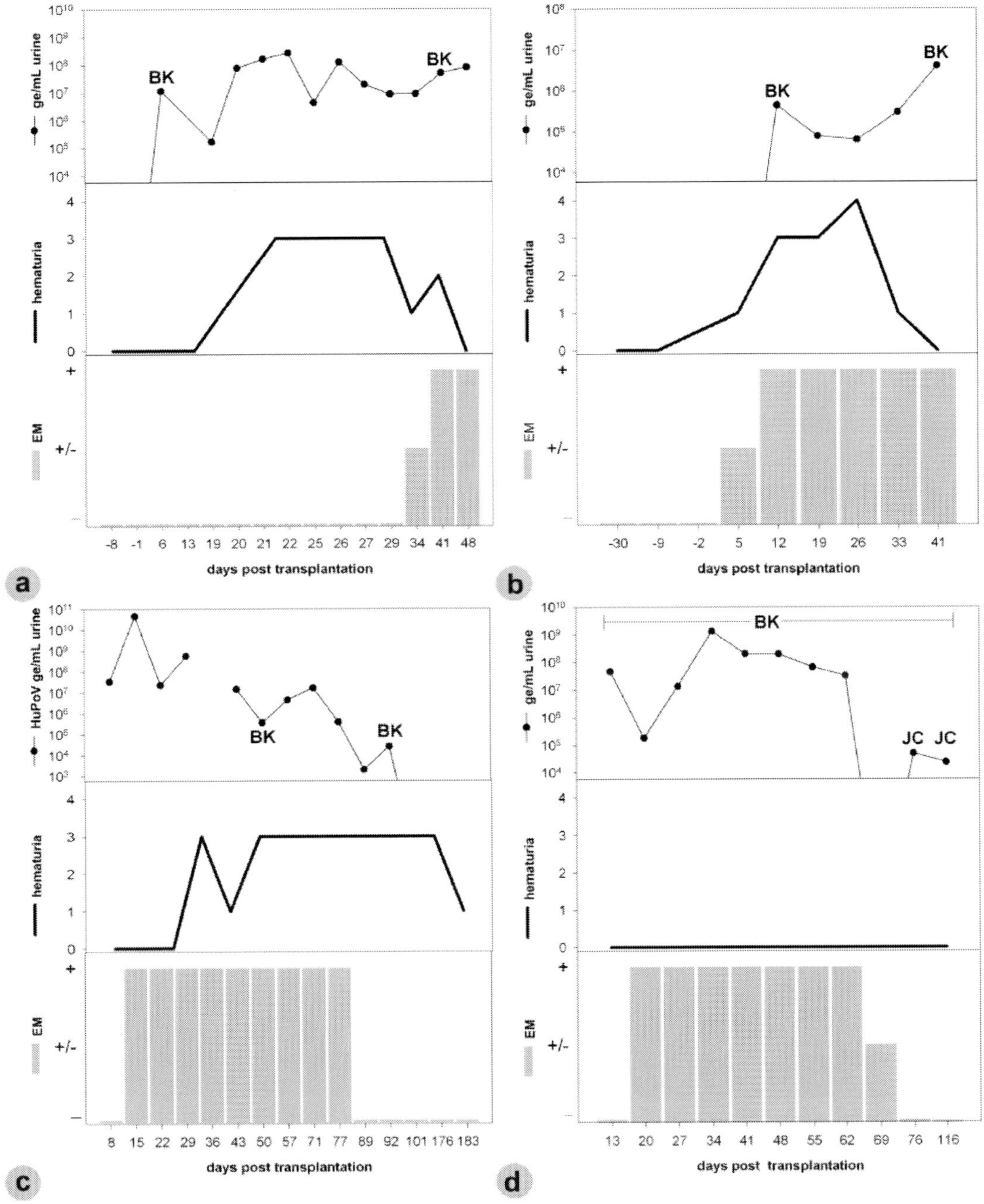


Figure 2. Time course of polyomaviruria and hematuria of 4 representative patients The top panel shows the concentration of polyomaviral DNA in the urine, as well as the result of viral subtyping at separate time-points (BK = BKV positive, JC = JCV positive). The middle panel gives the degree of hematuria as determined by dip-stick analysis. The lower panel shows the results of electron microscopy (- = no virus particles detected; +/- = questionable; + = virus particles detected).

# Conclusion

While many of the up-to-date studies published on the correlation between hematuria and polyomaviruria examined only parts of the viral etiology, our data represent a more complete view: All BMT patients were monitored for the excretion of polyomaviruses during the whole time of hospitalization; monitoring was performed on a quantitative basis and followed by determination of the respective subtype. Additionally, attention was given not only to one specific agent, but also to other viruses possibly correlated to hematuria.

Stratified statistical analysis of our data clearly revealed that there is no association between polyomaviruria and hematuria. Thus we presume that polyomaviruses are not causative for hemorrhagic cystitis. An apparent link between both could be deduced from the fact that the incidence for both events is significantly elevated in patients after allogeneic BMT than in those after autologous BMT, especially for non-sporadic episodes. Moreover, these findings correlate well with results from other studies [12, 13].

The missing statistical link between polyomaviruria and hematuria is further supported by the fact that no uniform time course for viral load and erythrocyte content could be detected in the urine of individual patients with both polyomaviruria and hematuria: neither the onset of viruria and hematuria show any interdependence, nor can the amount of viral load be correlated to the erythrocyte content. However, although there is no significant statistic correlation, both events are apparently closely associated. They are both favored by the same risk factor (i.e. allogeneic BMT), and additionally, the highest incidence of both events in our patient group is nearly at the same time (20 days post BMT; data not shown). This close association may in part have been misinterpreted as a causal link in earlier studies.

The differences between reactivation of BKV and JCV match closely with the literature: Generally, BKV is known to play the more important role in transplant patients compared to JCV [22, 23] and the prevalence of BKV in children is known to be much higher than for JCV [7]. Our observations also support the hypothesis that polyomaviruria after BMT is more likely to be caused by reactivation of latent viruses than by recent infection [24], as JCV viruria is almost exclusively shown for adults. However, the fact that all urine samples PCR positive for JCV did not show viral particles should be further examined.

Although our statistical data are clear-cut, we cannot exclude a correlation between hemorrhagic cystitis and polyomaviruria in single individuals, as we have published before [25]. In addition, it has recently been shown that polyoma*viremia* in transplant patients seems to be a very reliable indicator for serious reactivation of polyomaviruses [26, 27, 28]. However, in this study the post-examination of 100 urine samples from 20 patients with severe polyomaviruria was negative for both, BKV or JCV DNA (data not shown).

In summary, hemorrhagic cystitis after BMT cannot easily be linked to single episodes of viral shedding, as shown here in detail for polyomaviruses and also in part for adenoviruses or cytomegalovirus. The development of hemorrhagic cystitis seems to depend on many varying and independent factors, which are still not well understood. In this study, we identified allogeneic BMT as one important influencing factor, which has also found to be relevant in other studies [29]. It should, however, be taken into account, that BMT accompanied by intense pharmaceutical treatment is a major intervention to the patient's physiology, resulting in many different reactions which have, so far, only been partly described.

The previously described link of hemorrhagic cystitis to adenovirus reactivation could not be confirmed in this study since none of the 571 urine samples contained viral DNA. However, patient collectives without adenovirus positive urine sample have also been described before [29, 30], and it should be further examined whether the incidence of adenovirus shedding after BMT might be also influenced by seasonal or regional phenomena.

Our results imply that a prospective viral monitoring for suspicious agents is not too helpful in BMT units; in addition, positive findings for polyomaviruses or other agents in patients with hematuria cannot be taken as clinical relevant. Also the use of quantitative instead of qualitative PCR assays as recently described by us and several other groups [19, 31 32, 28] does not necessarily lead to a better understanding of the possible role of polyomavirus reactivation for the emergence of hematuria. While some studies show a quantitative dependence of clinical symptoms from the viral load in urine [31], this study as well as others do not show a clear correlation between polyomavirus load in urine and hematuria or hemorrhagic cystitis [30].

In figure 2, some evidence is shown that the combination of two different diagnostic techniques targeting to different stages of the viral life cycle might lead to a better understanding of the events after polyomavirus reactivation [18]. This is a very time consuming approach and suitable rather for research than for day-by-day diagnostic purposes. However, the question concerning the link between polyomaviruria and hematuria can finally be answered only by combining urine diagnostics with histopathological and virological examination of bladder and kidney biopsies.

## Acknowledgments

The authors are grateful to N. Steuer and D. Barz, Charité Campus Virchow-Klinikum, and to L. Briedigkeit, Charité, for their help with the PCR, to J. Beyersmann, Beiersdorf AG, and R. Hartmann, Charité Campus Virchow-Klinikum, for their advice on statistics, and to W. Siegert, Charité Campus Virchow-Klinikum, and G. Pauli, Robert Koch-Institute, for helpful discussions. Finally, this study would have been impossible without the kind support of the staff from the Klinik für Innere Medizin m.S. Hämatologie und Onkologie and the Otto-Heubner-Centrum für Kinder- und Jugendmedizin, Charité Campus Virchow-Klinikum.

## References

[1] Barber S. Allogeneic bone marrow transplantation: implications of herpesvirus screening and diagnosis. *Br. J. Biomed. Sci.* 1998; 55:281-286.

[2] Salomon N, Perlman DC. Cytomegalovirus pneumonia. *Semin. Respir. Infect.* 1999; 14:353-358.

[3] Liang R, Lau GK, Kwong YL. Chemotherapy and bone marrow transplantation for cancer patients who are also chronic hepatitis B carriers: a review of the problem. *J. Clin. Oncol.* 1999; 17:394-398.

[4] deVries CR, Freiha FS. Hemorrhagic cystitis: a review. *J. Urol.* 1990; 143:1-9.

[5] Apperley JF, Rice SJ, Bishop JA, Chia YC, Krausz T, Gardner SD, et al. Late-onset hemorrhagic cystitis associated with urinary excretion of polyomaviruses after bone marrow transplantation. *Transplantation* 1987; 43:108-112.

[6] Arthur RR, Shah KV, Baust SJ, Santos GW, Saral R. Association of BK viruria with hemorrhagic cystitis in recipients of bone marrow transplants. *N. Engl. J. Med.* 1986; 315:230-234.

[7] Arthur RR, Shah KV. Occurrence and significance of papovaviruses BK and JC in the urine. *Prog. Med. Virol.* 1989; 36:42-61.

[8] Bedi A, Miller CB, Hanson JL, Goodman S, Ambinder RF, Charache P, et al. Association of BK virus with failure of prophylaxis against hemorrhagic cystitis following bone marrow transplantation. *J. Clin. Oncol.* 1995; 13:1103-1109.

[9] Chan PK, Ip KW, Shiu SY, Chiu EK, Wong MP, Yuen KY. Association between polyomaviruria and microscopic haematuria in bone marrow transplant recipients. *J. Infect* 1994; 29:139-146.

[10] Childs R, Sanchez C, Engler H, Preuss J, Rosenfeld S, Dunbar C, et al. High incidence of adeno- and polyomavirus-induced hemorrhagic cystitis in bone marrow allotransplantation for hematological malignancy following T cell depletion and cyclosporine. *Bone Marrow Transplant* 1998; 22:889-893.

[11] Fioriti D, Degener AM, Mischitelli M, Videtta M, Arancio A, Sica S, Sora F, Pietropaolo V. BKV infection and hemorrhagic cystitis after allogeneic bone marrow transplant. *Int. J. Immunopathol. Pharmacol.* 2005; 18: 309-316.

[12] Saitoh K, Sugae N, Koike N, Akiyama Y, Iwamura Y, Kimura H. Diagnosis of childhood BK virus cystitis by electron microscopy and *PCR. J. Clin. Pathol.* 1993; 46:773-775.

[13] Kondo M, Kojima S, Kato K, Matsuyama T. Late-onset hemorrhagic cystitis after hematopoietic stem cell transplantation in children. *Bone Marrow Transplant* 1998; 22:995-998.

[14] Sencer SF, Haake RJ, Weisdorf DJ. Hemorrhagic cystitis after bone marrow transplantation. Risk factors and complications. *Transplantation* 1993; 56:875-879.

[15] Rabenau HF, Preiser W, Franck S, Schwerdtfeger S, Doerr HW. Polyomavirus viruria in bone marrow transplant recipients: lack of correlation with clinical symptoms. *Infection* 2002; 30: 91-93.

[16] Echavarria MS, Ray SC, Ambinder R, Dumler JS, Charache P. PCR detection of adenovirus in a bone marrow transplant recipient: hemorrhagic cystitis as a presenting manifestation of disseminated disease. *J. Clin. Microbiol.* 1999; 37:686-689.

[17] Russell SJ, Vowels MR, Vale T. Haemorrhagic cystitis in paediatric bone marrow transplant patients: an association with infective agents, GVHD and prior cyclophosphamide. *Bone Marrow Transplant* 1994; 13:533-539.

[18] Biel SS, Nitsche A, Kurth A, Siegert W, Özel M, Gelderblom HR. Diagnosis of human polyomaviruses in urine from bone marrow transplant patients: a comparison of electron microscopy with PCR. *Clin. Chem.* 2004; 50:306-312.

[19] Biel SS, Held TK, Landt O, Niedrig M, Gelderblom HR, Siegert W, et al. Rapid quantification and differentiation of human polyomavirus DNA in undiluted urine from patients after bone marrow transplantation. *J. Clin. Microbiol.* 2000; 38:3689-3695.

[20] Chmielewicz B, Ellerbrok H, Nitsche A. Development of a PCR-based assay for the detection, quantification and genotyping of human adenovirus. *Clin. Chem.* 2005; 51:1365-73.

[21] Nitsche A, Steuer N, Schmidt CA, Landt O, Siegert W. Different real-time PCR formats compared for the quantitative detection of human cytomegalovirus DNA. *Clin. Chem.* 1999; 45:1932-1937.

[22] Arthur RR, Shah KV, Charache P, Saral R. BK and JC virus infections in recipients of bone marrow transplants. *J. Infect. Dis.* 1988; 158:563-569.

[23] O'Reilly RJ, Lee FK, Grossbard E, Kapoor N, Kirkpatrick D, Dinsmore R, et al. Papovavirus excretion following marrow transplantation: incidence and association with hepatic dysfunction. *Transplant Proc.* 1981; 13:262-266.

[24] Bogdanovic G, Priftakis P, Taemmeraes B, Gustafsson A, Flaegstad T, Winiarski J, et al. Primary BK virus (BKV) infection due to possible BKV transmission during bone marrow transplantation is not the major cause of hemorrhagic cystitis in transplanted children. *Pediatr Transplant* 1998; 2:288-293.

[25] Held TK, Biel SS, Nitsche A, Kurth A, Chen S, Gelderblom HR, et al. Treatment of BK virus-associated hemorrhagic cystitis and simultaneous CMV reactivation with cidofovir. *Bone Marrow Transplant* 2000; 26:347-350.

[26] Nickeleit V, Klimkait T, Binet IF, Dalquen P, Del Z, V, Thiel G, et al. Testing for polyomavirus type BK DNA in plasma to identify renal-allograft recipients with viral nephropathy. *N. Engl. J. Med.* 2000; 342: 1309-1315.

[27] Boeckh M, Erard V, Zerr D, Engylund J. Emerging viral infections after hematopoietic cell transplantation. Pediatr. *Transplant.* 2005; 9 Suppl 7: 48-54.

[28] Erard V, Kim HW, Corey L, Limaye A, Huang ML, Myerson D, Davis C, Boeckh M. BK DNA viral load in plasma: evidence for an association with hemorrhagic cystitis in allogeneic hematopoietic cell transplant recipients. *Blood* 2005; 106: 1130-1132.

[29] Leung AY, Mak R, Lie AK, Yuen KY, Cheng VC, Liang R, Kwong YL. Clinicopathological features and risk factors of clinically overt haemorrhagic cystitis complicating bone marrow transplantation. *Bone Marrow Transplant.* 2002; 29: 509-513.

[30] Priftakis P, Bogdanovic G, Kokhaei P, Mellstedt H, Dalianis T. BK virus (BKV) quantification in urine samples of bone marrow transplanted patients is helpful for diagnosis of hemorrhagic cystitis, although wide individual variations exist. *J. Clin. Virol.* 2003; 26: 71-77.

[31] Leung AY, Suen CK, Lie AK, Liang RH, Yuen KY, Kwong YL. Quantification of polyoma BK viruria in hemorrhagic cystitis complicating bone marrow transplantation. *Blood* 2001; 98: 1971-1978.

[32] McNees AL, White ZS, Zanwar P, Vilchez RA, Butel JS. Specific and quantitative detection of human polyomaviruses BKV, JCV, and SV40 by real time PCR. *J. Clin. Virol.* 2005; 34: 52-62.

In: New Immunology Research Developments
Editor: Gunter V. Müller

ISBN 978-1-60021-701-2


*Chapter 11*

# Antiphospholipid Antibodies and the Antiphospholipid Syndrome

***Olga Amengual, Tatsuya Atsumi* and Takao Koike***
Department of Medicine II
Hokkaido University Graduate School of Medicine
Sapporo, Japan

## Abstract

The association of persistent presence of circulating antiphospholipid antibodies (aPL) and recurrent vascular thrombosis, pregnancy morbidity or a combination of these events is termed antiphospholipid syndrome (APS). The dominant antigenic targets in APS are phospholipid (PL)-binding plasma proteins such as β2glycoprotein I (β2GPI) and prothrombin.

In the last few years, great interest has arisen concerning the binding of aPL to endothelial cells or other pro-coagulant cells, and how this binding mediates cell dysfunctions that potentially induce the clinical manifestations of APS. Pro-coagulant cells, exposed by aPL in the presence of PL -binding proteins, produce thrombophilic molecules such as tissue factor, adhesion molecules and tumor necrosis factor α. It is now recognized that the p38 mitogen activated protein kinase (MAPK) pathway plays an important role in aPL-mediated cell activation. Moreover, the role of annexin II as receptor for β2GPI and the interaction of β2GPI with different members of the low density lipoprotein receptor family have been reported.

In this chapter we review the new research relating to the pathophysiological mechanisms that may contribute to the manifestations of APS, focusing on the pro-coagulant cell scenario.

* Telephone: + 81 - 11 - 706 - 5915; Fax: + 81 - 11 – 706 –7710; E-mail address: at3tat@med.hokudai.ac.jp

**Keywords:** antiβ2glycoprotein I antibodies, antiprothrombin antibodies, thrombosis, p38 MAPK

# Introduction

Antiphospholipid antibodies (aPL) are a heterogeneous group of circulating immunoglobulins associated with the antiphospholipid syndrome (APS) [1]. The APS, also known as Hughes' syndrome, is an autoimmune disorder in which vascular thrombosis or pregnancy morbidity occur in patients having persistent laboratory evidence for aPL, anticardiolipin antibodies (aCL) and/or lupus anticoagulant (LA) [2].

Although the original concept of aPL considers that those antibodies were directed against anionic phospholipids (PL), evidence shows that PL-binding plasma proteins such as β2glycoprotein I (β2GPI) [3-5] and prothrombin [6] are the dominant antigenic targets recognized by aPL in patients with APS.

Antiphospholipid antibodies have been shown to enhance thrombus formation, and numerous mechanisms have been proposed to explain the thrombotic tendency of patients with aPL, but the precise mechanisms still remain unclear [7-14] (Table 1). It is not yet possible to assert whether one dominant mechanism is responsible for some specific clinical manifestations of APS or whether different antibodies acting together may predispose to thrombosis [15].

In the last few years, increasing interest has arisen concerning the binding of aPL to pro-coagulant cells and how this binding facilitates cell dysfunctions that potentially induce the clinical events characteristic of the APS. Pro-coagulant cells, exposed by aPL in the presence of PL-binding proteins, produce thrombophilic molecules such as tissue factor (TF), tumor necrosis factor α ( TNFα) or adhesion molecules.

The cell membrane receptors and the signal transduction pathways involved in the pro-coagulant cell activation mediated by aPL have been the focus of intensive investigations. As a result of those studies, the p38 mitogen activated protein kinase (MAPK) pathway has been revealed as a an important player in aPL-mediated cell activation [16-18]. Moreover, cell surface receptors for β2GPI, including annexin II and apolipoprotein E receptor 2' (Apo ER2') have been suggested to mediate the activation of platelets or endothelial cells by aPL

This chapter reviews some of the major pathophysiological mechanisms that may contribute to the manifestations of APS, specially focused in the pro-coagulant cell scenario.

**Table 1. Proposed mechanism of antiphospholipid antibody-mediated thrombosis**

| | |
|---|---|
| 1. | Inhibition of endothelial cell prostacyclin production |
| 2. | Pro-coagulant effects on platelets |
| 3. | Impairment of intrinsic and extrinsic fibrinolysis |
| 4. | Interference with the thrombomodulin-protein S-protein C pathway |
| 5. | Induction of pro-coagulant activity on cells (endothelial cells or monocytes) |
| 6. | Increased thrombin generation |

# β2Glycoprotein I: Molecule and Immunological Characteristics

## 1. Antigenic Target

β2Glycoprotein I, also recognized as apolipoprotein H was first described in 1961 [19], but it was not until the early 1990s that clear evidence emerged of the major role of β2GPI in the binding of aCL to PL in patients with APS. β2GPI is a single-chain (50-kDa) plasma protein of 326 amino acid residues containing a high proportion of proline and cysteine [20], and present in normal human plasma at approximately 200 μg/ml.

β2GPI is a member of the complement control protein repeat or short consensus repeat (SCR) superfamily, and it is composed of five homologous motifs of approximately 60 amino acids designated as SCR or as sushi domains. Each motif contains four conserved half cysteine residues, related to the formation of two internal disulfide bridges. While the first four domains are typical, the fifth domain is a modified form containing 82 amino acid residues and six half cysteines (Figure 1)

Human β2GPI was crystallized in 1999, and its tertiary structure revealed a highly glycosylated protein with an elongated fishhook-like arrangement of the globular SCR domains [21, 22]. β2GPI binds to solid phase PL through a major PL binding site located in the fifth domain, Cys 281-Cys 288 close to the hydrophobic loop [23, 24] and the PL binding property is significantly reduced by cleavage of one particular site (Lys317 -Thr318) on the domain V of β2GPI (nicked β2GPI). This cleavage is generated by activated plasmin [25].

Figure 1. Amino acid sequence and location of disulfide bonds in human β2Glycoprotein I.

**Table 2. The *in vitro* properties of β2Glycoprotein I**

| |
|---|
| Anticoagulant |
| 1. Inhibition of prothrombinase activity (thrombin generation) |
| 2. Inhibition of Factor X activation |
| 3. Inhibition of Factor XI activation |
| 4. Inhibition of Factor XII activation |
| 5. Inhibition of platelets aggregation |
| Procoagulant |
| 1. Inhibition of protein C activation |
| 2. Inhibition of inactivation of Factor Va by activated protein C |
| 3. Inhibition of protein Z anticoagulant pathway. |

## 2. Properties and Functions of β2Glycoprotein I

The physiological functions of β2GPI in coagulation are not completely elucidated, but the *in vitro* properties of β2GPI as a natural regulator of coagulation have been proposed in a large number of reports [26-29] (Table 2).

β2GPI may act as an anticoagulant by binding to the PL on platelet surfaces and inhibiting the contact pathway.

This protein plays a major role in thrombin generation as demonstrated by the significant reduction of *in vitro* ability to generate thrombin observed in plasma from β2GPI–null mice [30]. β2GPI binds directly to factor XI and inhibits activation of factor XI by a combination of thrombin and activated FXII; this inhibition attenuates thrombin generation, being the domain V of β2GPI essential [31, 32]

Recently, Rahgozar et al. demonstrate that β2GPI is able to bind exosites I and II on thrombin, and that domain V of β2GPI is crucial for this interaction [33]. The interaction between β2GPI and thrombin may interfere with the coagulation system, as well as with many of the biological functions in which thrombin participates. In addition, the same authors [33] showed that antiβ2GPI antibodies enhance the inhibition of factor XI activation by β2GPI and thrombin complex, leading to a decreased generation of thrombin. It is apparently paradoxical that antiβ2GPI antibodies enhance one function of the antigen, similar to the effect seen in the β2GPI, antiβ2GPI antibodies and protein C scenario [29]. Antiβ2GPI antibodies enhanced the inhibitory effect of β2GPI on activated protein C, which proteolyzes activated factorV/activated factor VIII and reduced thrombin generation. The direct effect of antiβ2GPI antibodies on thrombin-dependent factor XI activation may, in part, explain why antiβ2GPI antibodies have LA activity, but does not lead straightforward to the elevated thrombin generation found in patients with APS.

Apart from specific haemostatic functions, β2GPI activates lipoprotein lipase [34], lowers the triglyceride levels [35], binds to oxidized low-density lipoprotein[36], and binds to non-self particles or apoptotic bodies to allow their clearance [37, 38] Despite the regulatory functions of β2GPI in the coagulation cascade *in vitro* familial deficiency of β2GPI does not represent a risk factor for thrombosis [39, 40] In addition, plasma levels of β2GPI were found either normal or elevated in patients with APS [41, 42]. Therefore, aCL associated thrombosis cannot be explained as a result of a secondary β2GPI deficiency, but it is likely that antiβ2GPI antibodies modify the roles of β2GPI.

Our group showed that nicked β2GPI further suppresses plasmin generation by binding Glu-plasminogen via domain V, representing a negative feedback loop controlling in extrinsic fibrinolysis [43].

## 3. Epitopes Recognized by Antiβ2Glycoprotein I Antibodies

It is widely recognized that aCL found in patients with APS recognize the cardiolipin-β2GPI complex, and that the epitope locates on β2GPI molecule. Therefore, both aCL and antiβ2GPI antibodies represent the autoantibodies that bind to PL-β2GPI complex. However, the mechanisms by which antiβ2GPI antibodies bind to β2GPI are still a matter of discussion. It has been proposed that binding of β2GPI to anionic PL enhances the local concentration of β2GPI, thus promoting an increase in the intrinsic affinity and binding of the autoantibodies to β2GPI [44, 45]. Other theory is based on the recognition of cryptic epitope (s) on β2GPI by antiβ2GPI antibodies. Those cryptic epitope(s) are only exposed when β2GPI interacts with lipid membranes containing negatively charged PL, such as cardiolipin, or also when adsorbed on a polyoxygenated polystyrene surface [46, 47].

The location of the exact epitopic sites for antiβ2GPI antibodies on β2GPI molecule has been focus of intensive debate. Antiβ2GPI antibodies have been shown to recognize different epitopes located in all five domains of β2GPI. Domain IV or I were reported as candidates for epitopic location by using a series of deletion mutant proteins of β2GPI [48]. Wang et al. [49] found antiβ2GPI antibodies directed to domain V, and domain IV has been revelaed as one of the major epitopic location for monoclonal aCL raised from APS patients [50].

In contrast, Iverson et al [51] demonstrated that antiβ2GPI antibodies, in the major population of APS patients, bind to a particular structure in domain I of β2GP I, and that single amino acid substitution of full-length β2GPI disrupt antibody binding to β2GPI. However, some particular mutations made in domain IV also affected to antibody binding to β2GPI in the antiβ2GPI antibody enzyme-linked immunosorbent assay (ELISA) [52].

Recently, de Laat et al showed that pathogenic aCL bind a cryptic epitope on domain I of β2GPI which is accessible for aCL only after conformational change, and is induced by the binding of β2GPI to a negatively charged surface via a positive-charge patch in domain V [53, 54]. Moreover, our group demonstrated that epitopic structures recognized by antiβ2GPI antibodies are cryptic and that three electrostatic interactions between domain IV and V ($D^{193}$-$K^{246}$, $D^{222}$-$K^{317}$ and $E^{228}$-$K^{308}$) are involved in their exposure [55]. Binding of antiβ2GPI antibodies to solid phase β2GPI was significantly diminished by L replacement of $W^{235}$, an amino acid residue partly located in an inner region on domain IV and commonly found in the epitopic structures. Thus, cryptic epitopes in domain IV might by recognized by antiβ2GPI antibodies found in patients with APS and epitope spreading may occur in the region surrounding $W^{235}$. This hypothesis is also supported by our previous data showing that replacement of one single amino acid at position 247 of β2GPI, which is important for the interaction between domain IV and V, can alter the antigenicity of β2GPI for pathogenic autoantibodies [56, 57].

The mechanisms eliciting pathogenic autoreactive T cells responses in APS have also been investigated. Hattori et al [58] identified $CD4^+$ T cells autoreactive against β2GPI that promote antiβ2GPI antibodies production in patients with APS These β2GPI-specific $CD4^+$ T cells recognize a cryptic peptide encompassing amino acid residues 276-290 in the context of DRB4 *0103 (DR53); this epitope is located in domain V and contains the major PL-binding site. The binding of β2GPI to anionic PL facilitates processing and presentation of a cryptic epitope that activated pathogenic autoreactive T cells [59]. The exposure of the cryptic epitope to the immune system may be critical for inducing APS by triggering the activation of β2GPI-reactive $CD4^+$ T cells, which subsequently would stimulate B cells to produce pathogenic antiβ2GPI antibodies through the expression of CD40 and interleukin 6 (IL-6) [60].

## Prothrombin and Antiprothrombin Antibodies

### 1. Antigenic Target

Prothrombin, the other major PL-binding protein, is a vitamin K-dependent single chain glycoprotein of 579 amino acid residues with a molecular weight of 72kDa and present at a concentration of approximately 100 μg/ml in normal plasma [61]. Prothrombin undergoes γ-carboxylation during its liver biosynthesis. These γ-carboxyglutamic residues, known as the GLA domain, are located on fragment 1 of the prothrombin molecule. The GLA domain is essential for the calcium-dependent binding of PL to prothrombin. A kringle domain containing two kringle structures and a carboxyl-terminal serine protease follows the GLA domain.

Prothrombin is physiologically activated by the prothrombinase complex (activated factor X, factor V, calcium and PL). Once negatively charged PL bind prothrombin, prothrombinase complex converts prothrombin to thrombin, which triggers fibrinogen polymerization into fibrin [62]. Thrombin binds thrombomodulin on the surface of endothelial cells and activates protein C, which then exerts its anticoagulant activity by digesting activated factor V and depriving the prothrombinase complex of its most important cofactor. Because of this negative feedback pathway, prothrombin/thrombin behaves as "indirect" anticoagulant.

The involvement of prothrombin as a cofactor for a circulating anticoagulant was first considered in 1959 by Loeliger [63]. Twenty years later, Bajaj et al [64] were the first to ascertain the presence of prothrombin-binding antibodies in patients with LA and severe hypoprothrombinemia. They postulated that hypoprothrombinemia results from the rapid clearance of prothrombin-antiprothombin complexes from the circulation. Then, prothrombin-antiprothombin complexes were detected by crossed-immunoelectrophoresis (CIE) in the plasma of patients with LA but without severe hypoprothrombinemia [65]. These finding were confirmed and extended by Fleck et al who showed that antiprothrombin antibodies had LA activity [66]. Subsequently, circulating prothrombin-antiprothrombin antibodies complexes were also observed in patients with LA with normal prothrombin levels. In 1991, Bevers et al [6] highlighted the importance of antiprothrombin antibodies in causing LA activity and Oosting et al [10] showed that LA inhibited endothelial cell-mediated prothrombinase activity and the IgG fraction containing LA activity bound to PL-prothrombin complex.

### 2. Prothrombin-Antiprothrombin Antibody Interaction

Unlike β2GPI, prothrombin requires calcium ions for its binding to anionic PL. Antiprothrombin antibodies may be directed against cryptic or neoepitopes exposed when prothrombin binds to those PL In the presence of calcium, the N-terminal region of prothrombin undergoes a conformational change that results in the exposure of a hydrophobic patch though to be crucial for functional PL binding [67, 68]. It has been also proposed that a second conformational change creates a surface-exposed hydrophilic cleft that may be complementary in shape and charge to that of the polar group [69].

On the other hand, antiprothrombin antibodies may be low affinity antibodies recognised more efficiently when the prothrombin is bound to phosphatidylserine coated on ELISA plates [70], or may bind bivalently to immobilized prothrombin [71]. Thus, prothrombin complexed with phosphatidylserine could allow clustering and better orientation of the antigen, offering optimal conditions for antibody recognition

It is still not defined which is the epitope(s) recognized by antiprothrombin antibodies. Rao et al [72] showed binding of antiprothrombin antibodies to prethrombin 1 and fragment 1, as well as to the whole prothrombin molecule, but none of the antibodies reacted with immobilised thrombin. Therefore the dominant epitopes are likely to be located near the PL-binding site of prothrombin, although they may have heterogeneous distribution. Morevoer, Akimoto et al [73] found that around 62% of antiprothrombin antibodies dominantly directed to the fragment-1 of prothrombin and 38 % to the prethrombin site (the fragment 2 plus □-thrombin).

## Antiphospholipid Syndrome: Clinical Manifestations and Diagnosis

### 1. Clinical Manifestations

The APS, first described in 1983, is a clinical disorder characterized by vascular thrombosis and pregnancy morbidity associated to the persitent presence of aPL [1]. APS can occur without any other autoimmune disease or may coexist with other autoimmune diseases, particularly systemic lupus erythematosus (SLE) [74].

The most common manifestation in patients with APS is venous thrombosis, particularly deep vein thrombosis in the lower extremities, occasionally complicated by pulmonary embolism [75]. In the arterial circulation, the involvement of intracranial arteries, leading to cerebral infarction or transient ischemic attacks, is the most frequent feature, being the APS one of the most important risk factor for ischaemic cerebral events in young people without congenital atherosclerotic diseases [75]

Recurrent fetal losses are one of the most consistent complications of the APS, and aPL may be found in up to 20% of woman with recurrent pregnancy losses [76, 77] [78]. aPL-related fetal losses can occur at any stage of pregnancy, although are strikingly frequent during the second and third trimester. APS patients are susceptible to early onset of pregnancy complications such as severe pre-eclampsia and hemolysis, elevated liver enzymes, low platelet count (HELLP) syndrome [79, 80].

Since the first description of APS, the range of abnormalities associated with aPL has considerably broaden with recognition of other manifestations such as livedo reticularis, non-thrombotic neurological syndromes, psychiatric manifestations, skin ulcers, haemolytic anemia, thrombocytopenia, pulmonary hypertension, nephropaty, heart valve abnormalities and atherosclerosis [75].

The term "catastrophic" was added to the APS in order to highlight an accelerated form of this syndrome with multiorgan failure, severe thrombocytopenia and adult respiratory distress syndrome. Catastrophic APS is a rare but life-threatening condition with poor prognosis and a high rate of mortality [81].

**Table 3. Revised classification criteria for the antiphospholipid syndrome [79]**

Clinical Criteria

1. Vascular thrombosis

   $\geq$ 1 clinical episodes of arterial, venous, or small vessel thrombosis, in any tissue or organ confirmed by objective validated criteria by imaging or histopathology in the absence of significant evidence of inflammation in the vessel wall.

2. Pregnancy morbidity
   a) $\geq$ 1 unexplained deaths of a morphological normal fetus at or beyond the 10th week of gestation, or
   b) $\geq$ 1 premature deaths of a morphological normal neonate before the 34th week of gestation, due to eclampsia, severe pre-eclampsia or placental insufficiency, or
   c) $\geq$ 3 unexplained consecutive spontaneous abortions before the 10th week of gestation (maternal anatomic or hormonal abnormalities and paternal and maternal chromosomal causes excluded).

Laboratory Criteria

a) Lupus anticoagulant present in plasma, on $\geq$ 2 occasions at least 12 weeks apart, detected according to the guidelines of the International Society on Thrombosis and Haemostasis [83, 184]
b) IgG and/or IgM anticardiolipin antibodies present in medium or high titer in serum or plasma, on $\geq$ 2 occasions at least 12 weeks apart, measured by a standardized ELISA [185]
c) IgG and/or IgM antiβ2glycoprotein I antibodies present in >$99^{th}$ percentile titer, in serum or plasma, on $\geq$ 2 occasions at least 12 weeks apart, measured by a standardized ELISA [186]

Antiphospholipid syndrome is present if at least one of the clinical criteria and one of the laboratory criteria are met. ELISA: enzyme-linked immunosorbent assay.

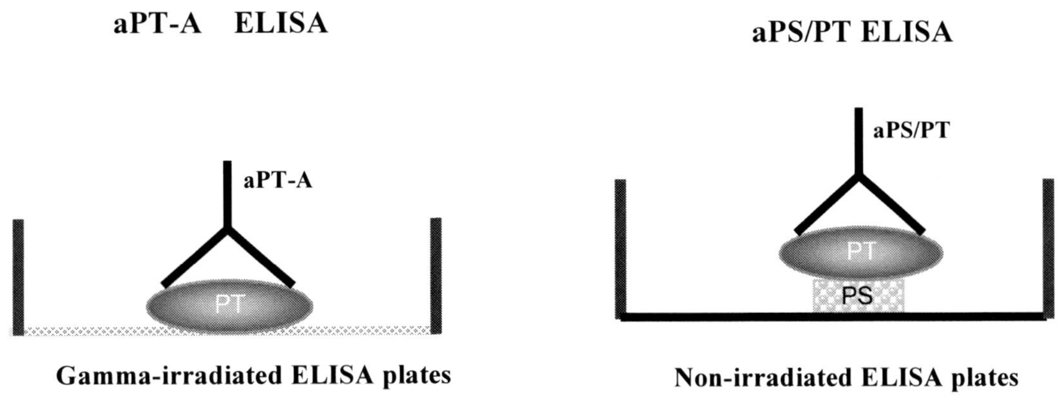


Figure 2. Enzyme-linked immunosorbent assays for antiprothrombin antibodies detection. Two types of antiprothrombin antibodies may be detected by enzyme-linked immunosorbent assay (ELISA). 1) Antiprothrombin antibodies directed against prothrombin alone coated on gamma-irradiated ELISA plates (aPT-A ELISA); 2) antiprothrombin antibodies directed against phosphatidylserine-bound prothrombin complexes coated on non-irradiated ELISA plates (aPS/PT ELISA). PT: prothrombin, PS: phosphatidylserine.

## 2. Diagnosis of Antiphospholipid Syndrome

Antiphospholipid antibodies are usually detected by their binding to immobilized anionic PL in solid phase ELISA, termed anticardiolipin antibodies (aCL) [82], or by their ability to prolong the clotting time of PL-dependent coagulant assays, called LA [83].

New assays have been developed for the detection of antibodies directed against PL-binding protein complexes, including antiβ2GPI and antiprothrombin antibodies.

Several studies have highlighted the significance of using antiβ2GPI antibodies as an alternative ELISA method that has higher specificity for the diagnosis of APS than does the conventional aCL ELISA [84-86].

Antiprothrombin antibodies, detected by ELISA, are a heterogeneous population which comprise antibodies directed against prothrombin alone coated on gamma irradiated or activated polyvinylchloride ELISA plates (aPT-A) [70, 87, 88], and antibodies to the phosphatidylserine-prothrombin complex (aPS/PT) [70, 89] (Figure 2). Moreover antiprothrombin antibodies have been detected against prothrombin bound hexagonal (II) phase phosphatidylethanolamine [90].

An international consensus statement on classification criteria for definite APS was published in 1999 [91] and revised in 2006 [79]. The diagnosis of APS can be made when venous and/or arterial thrombosis and/or pregnancy morbidity occurs in a patient whose laboratory tests for aPL are positive A patient with APS must meet at least one of the clinical criteria (vascular thrombosis or pregnancy morbidity) and one of the laboratory criteria (LA, aCL or antiβ2GPI antibodies) Table 3.

# Clinical Significance of Antiphospholipid Antibodies

Antiβ2GPI antibodies represent an independent risk factor for thrombosis and pregnancy morbididty [92-95]. The detection of IgG and IgM antiβ2GPI antibodies are listed in the criteria for the classification of APS with a threshold for positive antiβ2GPI antibodies > 99th percentile of controls. The interpretation of antiβ2GPI antibody results has some limitations mainly due to the difference of methodology used among laboratories and the lack of standardization. Further, the possible interference of cryoglobulins and rheumatoid factor should be considered in the interpretation of IgM antiβ2GPI antibodies [79].

Data on clinical significance of aPT-A are contradictory implying low sensitivity of these antibodies for the diagnosis of APS APT-A are found in 60% of APS patients, but less than two-third of those antibodies had LA activity [70, 87, 96, 97]. No association between the presence of antiprothrombin antibodies and the risk of thrombosis was found in a systematic review [92]. In contrast, aPS/PT strongly correlate with the presence of LA and both, sensitivity and specificity of aPS/PT for the diagnosis of APS, were demonstrated to be higher than those for aPT-A Therefore, the aPS/PT may serve as a confirmatory assay for LA and APS [89].

# Pathogenicity of Antiphospholipid Antibodies

The association between aPL and the occurrence of thrombosis and pregnancy loss is widely recognized. Some of the proposed mechanisms to explain this thrombotic tendency include the inhibition of the natural anticoagulant systems, the impairment of fibrinolytic activity and the direct effect of those antibodies on cell functions

## 1. Interference with the Coagulation Pathway

### *a) Protein C System*

The protein C system is one of the most important anti-thrombotic pathways mediated by the vessel wall which impairment may result in the development of thrombosis. Thrombin-thrombomodulin complex activates protein C leading to the clotting inhibition by proteolytic cleavage of activated factors V and VIII in the presence of protein S. Protein C and its cofactor protein S are PL-binding plasma proteins making this system one of the most likely to be involved in the pathogenesis of thrombosis in patients with APS.

Antiphospholipid antibodies might inhibit PL-dependent reactions of the protein C pathway in different ways. First, purified aPL can interfere with the activation of protein C by the thrombin/thrombomodulin complex [98] Inhibition of thrombin formation by aPL could paradoxically cause a prothrombotic tendency due to insufficient protein C activation.

Second, the proteolytic effect of activated protein C on activated factor V/activated factor VIII may be inhibited by aPL. A reduction of activated factor V degradation was detected in plasma of patients with LA [99] Malia et al [100] confirmed the inhibitory effect of IgG purified from patients with aPL on activated factor V degradation by activated protein C. In addition, purified IgG/M from aPL positive patients disturbed the anticoagulant activity of activated protein C on human endothelial cells [101]. Our group demonstrated that human monoclonal antiβ2GPI antibodies inhibit activated protein C function, confirming the effect of autoimmune aPL on this system [29] We also showed that aCL may bind to protein C in the presence of both PL and antiβ2GPI antibodies, and that binding activities strongly correlated with antiβ2GPI antibody titers, thus protein C could be a target of aCL leading to protein C dysfunction [102]

Furthermore, Galli et al [103] reported that most prothrombin/antiprothrombin antibodies immune complexes may predispose to thrombosis by interfering with the inactivation of activated Factor V by the activated protein C in the presence of protein S. Those data were confirmed and extended by Field et al [104] who showed this inhibitory effect of antiprothrombin antibodies on the activated protein C activity in the absence of protein S.

Finally, the cofactor effect of protein S in the protein C pathway can be affected by aPL. Decreased plasma levels of protein S have been found in patients with APS [9, 105], and it was shown that some of the IgG which inhibit activated factor V degradation were not directed only against PL-bound protein C but also against PL-bound protein S [10]

### *b) Protein Z*

The inhibition of protein Z, a natural anticoagulant pathway, has been suggested as an additional thrombotic mechanism in APS. However, the physiological relation between low plasma protein Z and the thrombotic tendency risk has not yet been elucidated.

Protein Z is a vitamin K dependent protein which functions as a natural anticoagulant by acting as cofactor for a plasma protease inhibitor for the inhibition of activated factor X [106]. Deficiency in protein Z levels was observed in patients with aPL [107, 108] and associated with arterial thrombosis and fetal loss [109-112].

Forastiero et al [113] showed that aPL greatly impair the inhibition of activated factor X by protein Z-dependent protease inhibitor in the presence of β2GPI. β2GPI-antiβ2GPI antibody complexes might compete with protein Z-protease inhibitor-activated factor X for the same PL-binding site, thus interfering with the activation of factor X.

## 2. Impairment of Fibrinolysis

Fibrinolytic reactions involve the formation of plasmin and the hydrolytic cleavage of fibrin to fibrin degradation products by plasmin. Plasmin is one of the most potent enzymes, thus the regulation of plasmin generation and activity is highly important to maintain the homeostatic balance *in vivo.* Plasmin formation from plasminogen by tPA is a key event in extrinsic fibrinolysis for the thrombolysis against intravascular blood clots. Endothelial cells, when activated, secrete the inhibitor of plasminogen activator-1 (PAI-1), as well as tPA, to depress fibrinolysis by blocking tPA activity.

The effect of aPL in the fibrinolytic system has been evaluated with controversial results probably due to the small size of the cohorts and heterogeneity of subjects. Jurado et al [114] proposed a hypofibrinolytic condition in patients with connective tissue diseases, including

APS, mainly related to increased PAI-1 levels. PAI-1 release by endothelial cell stimulation after venous occlusion, was greatly increased in patients compared with healthy controls, but no difference was found in tPA release. To avoid the influence of the acute phase nature of PAI-1, Ames et al [9] focused in patients with aPL without underlying rheumatic diseases and confirmed the up-regulation of PAI-I levels in female patients with APS. They further showed reduction in tPA release by endothelial cell stimulation in those subjects, suggesting that tPA/PAI-1 balance was crucial to develop thrombosis in some APS patients.

Several other reports pointed toward a hypofibrinolytic state in APS characterized by elevated PAI-1 indicating a perturbation of endothelial cells with consequent fibrinolytic impairment, but no direct evidence was reported in the induction of PAI-1 by aPL [115-117]. Hypofibrinolysis might be related to antibodies which specifically interact with the catalytic domain of tPA which have been found in patients with APS [118].

Factor XII is a protein of the contact activation system with a key role in intrinsic fibrinolyis, as well as intrinsic coagulation. Deficiencies in contact proteins have been found in patients with unexplained recurrent abortions [119]. Our group showed that β2GPI and monoclonal antiβ2GPI antibody suppress intrinsic fibrinolytic activities [120], and this inhibition was attributed to a reduced contact activation reaction initiated by activated factor XII. Carmona et al [121] found impaired activated factor XII-dependent activation of fibrinolysis in pregnant woman with APS which developed late-pregnancies complications.

Lipoprotein a [Lp(a)] is an apoprotein which shares some sequence homology with plasminogen. Lp(a) inhibits fibrinolytic activity not only by acting as an uncompetitive inhibitor of tPA [122], but also by increasing PAI-1 expression in endothelial cells [123]. This behaviour confers Lp(a) a prothrombotic potential. APS patients had high plasma Lp(a) levels [124, 125]. In addition, lower plasma D-dimer but higher PAI-1 levels were detected in patients with elevated plasma Lp(a) [124] indicating that deranged fibrinolysis was related to Lp(a) in patients with APS. Plasma Lp(a) is genetically determined, an it is possible that high LP(a) levels in APS patients might account for the impairment of fibrinolysis independently of the presence of aPL.

## Antiphosphopholipid Antibody-Cell Interaction

### 1. Antiphospholipid Antibody-Endothelial Cell/Monocyte Interactions

Activated and /or injured endothelial cells or monocytes may be a predominant target of aPL [11, 12, 14, 126-129]. Cultured endothelial cells incubated with aPL express high levels of adhesion molecules such as intercellular cell adhesion molecule-1 (ICAM-1), vascular cell adhesion molecule (VCAM-1) and P-Selectin [130, 131]. This effect is mediated by β2GPI and may promote inflammation and thrombosis [129, 132].

aPL also induce TF antigen, activity or mRNA on endothelial cells and monocytes [8, 11, 12, 14]. Furthermore, markedly enhanced levels of endothelin-1 (ET-1), the most potent endothelium derived contracting factor modulating vascular smooth muscle tone, were found in plasma of patients with APS with arterial thrombosis [133] Human monoclonal aCL induced prepro ET-1 mRNA levels, confirming the direct effect of aPL on endothelium regarding ET-1 production. Thus, the production of ET-1 induced by aPL may play an important role in altering arterial tone and probably contributing to arterial occlusion [133].

Several *in vivo* studies supported the hypothesis that assembly of β2GPI/ antiβ2GPI antibodies complex on the endothelial cell surface cannot induce thrombosis without a priming factor. The priming factor might lead to some structural modifications or regulate the expression of cell receptors, potentially increasing the probability the β2GPI/antiβ2GPI antibodies complex interact with them [134-136].

A human monoclonal IgG antiprothrombin antibody (IS6), raised from one patient with primary APS that possesses LA activity, was reported to enhance prothrombin binding to damaged endothelial cells and to shorten plasma coagulation times [137] Moreover, Vega-Ostertag et al demonstrated that IS6 is thrombogenic *in vivo* and up-regulates expression of TF and E-selectin on endothelial cells [138].

Microparticle production is a hallmark of cell activation and aPL have been shown to stimulate the release of microparticles from endothelial cells which may represent a new pathogenic mechanism for the thrombotic complications of APS [139-141]. Finally, some aPL that recognizes annexin-V are able to induce apoptosis on endothelial cells [142].

## 2. Antiphospholipid Antibody-Platelet Interaction

Antiphospholipid antibodies can stimulate platelet agglutination and aggregation [143-145] and activated platelets are found in patients with APS [146, 147].

The importance of platelet activation in the pathogenesis of thrombosis is supported *in vivo*. The thrombi resulting from the infusion of antiβ2GPI antibodies in hamsters, which carotid arteries were primed with a photochemical injury, were shown to be rich in platelets [135].

Membranes of activated platelets are an important source of negatively charged PL providing a catalytic surface for blood coagulation, and β2GPI bind to surface membranes of activated platelets [148-150]. Activated factor X and thrombin are generated by the tenase and prothrombinase complexes, respectively, via the catalytic surface of activated platelets and procoagulant microparticles shed by platelet activation. β2GPI inhibits the generation of activated factor X by activated platelets, and antiβ2GPI antibodies interfered with this inhibition [149].

## 3. Cell Receptors for Antiphosphospholipid Antibody Interactions

Antiβ2GPI antibodies activate monocytes, endothelial cells and platelets in a β2GPI–dependent manner, and this cell activation might require an interaction between β2GPI and a specific cell receptor.

Annexin II, also known as Annexin A2, is an endothelial cell receptor for tPA and plasminogen. Annexin II has been suggested to interact with the β2GPI/antiβ2GPI antibody complex on the endothelial cell surface mediating cell activation [151, 152]. However, it is still unclear whether such a putative receptor is actually involved in cell activation because annexin II does not span the cell membrane and the presence of an unknown "adaptor" was proposed to induce activation. This receptor can also be directly targeted on endothelial cell activated by anti-annexin II antibodies [153].

The Toll-like receptor (TLR) family may also mediate a role in the interaction of the β2GPI/antiβ2GPI antibody complex on the endothelial cell surface [154] Antiβ2GPI antibodies might cross-link β2GPI molecules likely together with TLR, eventually favoring the receptor polymerization and the activation of the signaling cascade. TLR2 and TLR4 might be the responsible receptors in this family [155, 156].

The ApoER2', the only member of the low-density lipoprotein receptor present on platelets, has been suggested to be involved in the activation of platelets. The blockage of ApoER2' receptor on platelets using a receptor associated protein leads to a loss of the increased adhesion of platelets to collagen induced by β2GPI/antiβ2GPI antibody complex [157]. Moreover, dimeric β2GPI interacts with ApoER2' and it has been hypothesized that the β2GPI/antiβ2GPI antibody complex initially has to form on the exposed phosphatidylserine on cell surfaces before interacting with ApoER2' [157]. This procedure requires an initial independent priming stimulus to lead the platelets to the surface exposure of phosphatidylserine. The same authors further demonstrated that the binding site on β2GPI molecule for ApoER2' on platelets is located in domain V which does not overlap with the PL-binding site [158].

β2GPI has been also shown to directly bind to glycoprotein (GP) Ibα subunit of the platelet adhesion receptor GPIb/IX/V *in vitro* [159, 160] GPIb□ subunit is located on platelets, being von Willebrand factor the most important ligand, and also serves to localize factor XI and thrombin on the platelet surfaces [161]. Binding of β2GPI to GPIbα enables antiβ2GPI antibodies directed against domain I to activate platelets, leading to thromboxane production and to the activation of the phosphoinositol-3 kinase (PI3-kinase)/Akt pathway [159]. The PI3-kinases/Akt pathway is involved in the signaling downstream of GPIb□contributing to the platelet adhesion and aggregation.

The involvement of Fcγ receptor on cellular activation has been investigated *in vivo* [135] and *in vitro* studies on platelets [157, 162], monocytes [163] and endothelial cells [152, 154] indicating that this receptor is not strictly necessary for cellular activation.

## 4. Signaling Pathways of Cell Activation

Recently, research has focused on the signal transduction mechanisms implicated in the increased expression of pro-coagulants substances in response to aPL. The adapter molecule myeloid differentiation protein (MyD88)-dependent signaling pathway and the nuclear factor kappa B (NFkB) have been involved in endothelial cell activation by aPL [154, 164-166]. IgG purified from patients with APS induced the nuclear translocation of NFkB leading to the transcription of a large number of genes that have a NFkB-responsive element in their promoter. This nuclear translocation of NFkB mediates, at least in part, the increased expression of TF and adhesion molecules by endothelial cells.

Several groups revealed the essential role of p38 MAPK pathway in aPL-mediated cell activation. We [16] demonstrated that stimulation of monocytes by monoclonal antiβ2GPI antibodies derived from APS patients induce phosphorylation of p38MAPK, locational shift of NFkB into the nucleus and up-regulation of TF expression. The TF expression occurs only in the presence of β2GPI, suggesting that perturbation of monocyte by antiβ2GPI antibodies is initiated by interaction between the cell and the autoantibody-bound β2GPI (Figure 3).

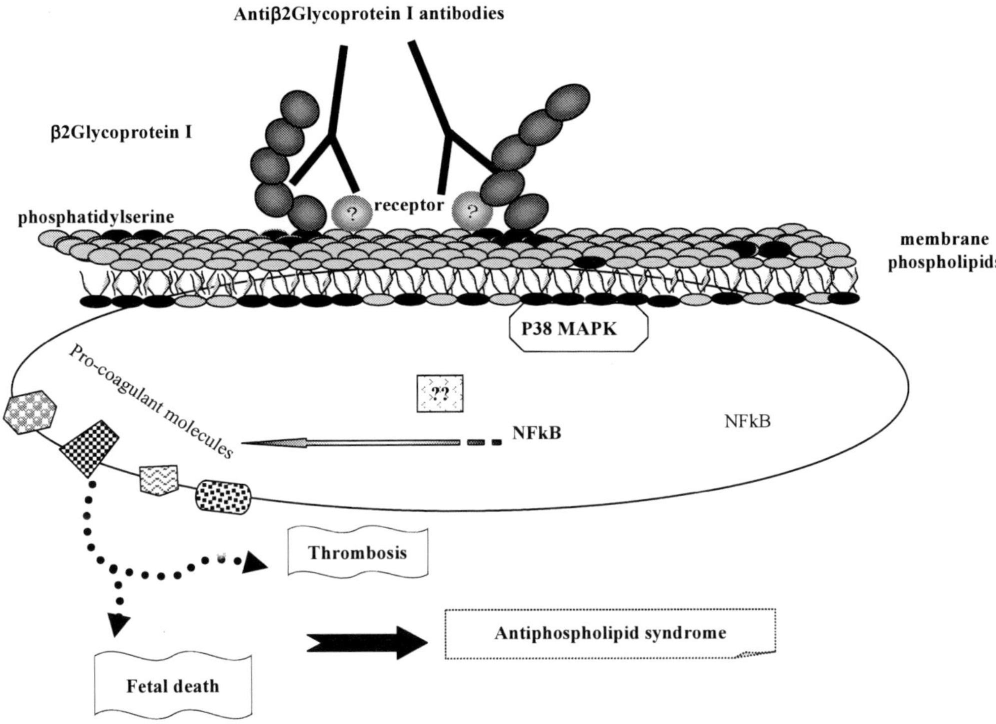


Figure 3. Proposed effects of antiphospholipid antibodies on pro-coagulant cells. Stimulation of pro-coagulant cells (monocytes or endothelial cells) by antiβ2 glycoprotein I antibodies induce phosphorylation of p38 MAPK which leads to the nuclear translocation of NFkB, and to the transcription of procoagulant substances. The production of those pro-coagulant molecules (tissue factor, endothelin-1, tumor necrosis alpha and plasminogen activator inhibitor-1) leads to thrombosis and fetal death, the antiphosphospholipid syndrome. p38 MAPK: p38 mitogen activated protein kinase; NFkB: nuclear factor Kappa B.

Almost simultaneously, Vega-Ostertag et al reported that phosphorylation of p38 MAPK is involved in aPL-mediated production of thromboxane B2 by platelets [167]. Pre-treatment of platelets with a p38 MAPK specific inhibitor, SB203580, completely abrogated aPL-mediated platelet aggregation. These authors also demonstrated the involvement of p38 MAPK in the up-regulation of TF in endothelial cells [17]. Activation of p38 MAPK pathway increases activities of inflammatory cytokines such as TNF-α and IL-1β [168].

Up-regulation of TNF-α, IL-1β and macrophage inflammatory protein 3β (MIP3β) on monocytes treated with aPL have been also reported by our group [16]. Downstream of activated p38, MAPK-activated protein kinase 2/3 (MAPKAPK 2/3) is a substrate for p38 that undergoes post-transcriptional regulation of TNF-α. P38 also activates transcriptional factors such as activating transcriptional factor-2 (ATF2) which form a heterodimer with JUN family transcriptional factors and associated with activator protein-1 (AP-1) binding site.

After stimulation of dendritic cells with lipopolisaccharide, NH2-termini of histone H3 undergoes structural alteration in a p38 dependent pathway, which results in enhancement of accessibility of the cryptic NFkB binding sites [169]. The promoter region of the TF gene contains two AP-1 binding sites and one NFkB binding site, and these transcription factors are proven required for maximal induction of TF gene transcription.

Furthermore, p38 MAPK pathway had been involved in the regulation of TF expression in monocyte, endothelial cells and smooth muscle cells [170-174].

## Complement and Antiphospholipid Antibodies

Complement is part of the innate immune system and represents one of the effector arms of antibody-mediated immunity [175].

Complement activation has been associated with the pathogenesis of pregnancy loss in patients with APS [176, 177]. Throphoblast cells of the placenta may be a target for aPL resulting in activation of the complement cascade through the classical pathway. The complement cascade is initiated with activation of C3, and subsequently, C5. Generated C5a recruits and activates polymorphonuclear leukocytes and monocytes and stimulates the release of mediators of inflammation which ultimately leads to thrombosis and fetal injury [178].

Increased levels of C3 and C4 have been shown to predict subsequent miscarriages in patients with unexplained recurrent miscarriages [179]. Moreover, elevated complement activation products were detected in the plasma of APS patients with cerebral ischemic events compared with patients with non-APS-related cerebral ischemia [180].

Using a murine model of surgically induced thrombosis, Pierangeli et al [136] showed that activation of complement C3 and C5 by aPL mediates the activation of endothelial cells and the induction of thrombosis. Furthermore, Fischetti et al [134] demonstrated the involvement of complement activation in the pathogenesis of thrombosis in an animal model in which polyconal IgG aPL from APS patients were transfer to rats pre-treated with lipopolisaccharide. Rats receiving IgG aPL developed thrombus but those receiving polyclonal IgG antibodies from healthy volunteers did not.

The IgG isotype of aPL is the most frequently found in patients with APS, and the IgG2 subclass the most prevalent [181, 182]. IgG2 and IgG4 subclasses have a relatively weak ability to fix the complement via the classical pathways, which suggested that additional mechanism should be involved in the enhancement of complement activation in patients with aPL.

Our group showed that hypocomplementemia, related with complement overactivation, is common in patients with primary APS. The complement activation was correlated with LA activity and TNFα levels in patients' plasma, suggesting that aPL-induced complement activation may be involved in the thrombophilic state in patients with APS [183]. The recognition of this cross-link between complement activation and prothrombotic status highlights an important role for the complement system in the physiopathology of the APS

Figure 4 shows the possible mechanisms involved in the complement mediated-pathogenicity of aPL on fetal and placental injury.

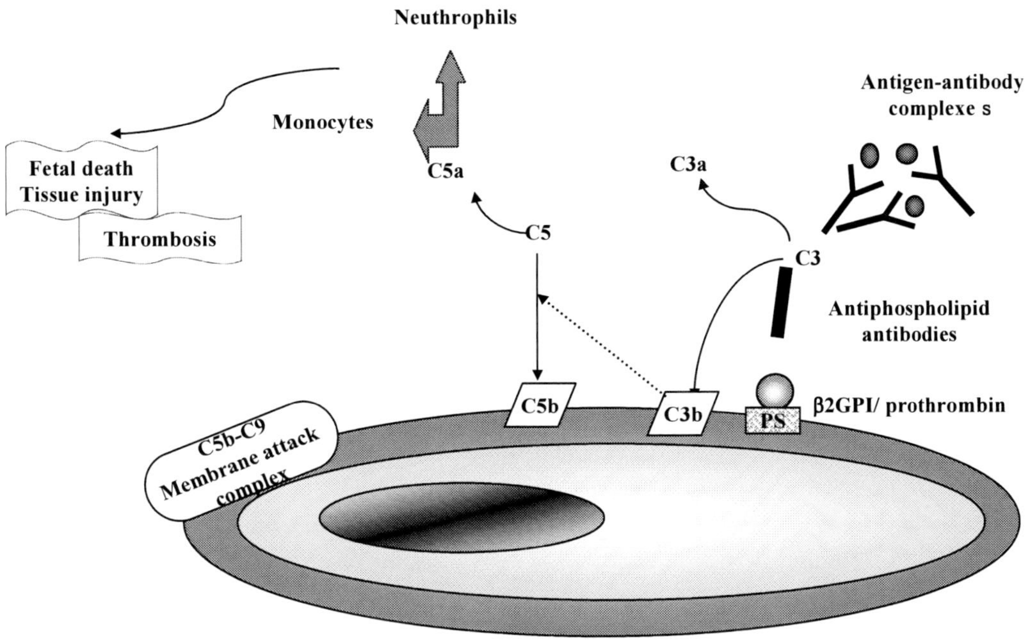


Figure 4. Potential mechanisms involved in complement-mediated pathogenicity of antiphospholipid antibodies. Placenta throphoblast cells are targeted by phospholipid-binding proteins/antiphospholipid antibodies complexes leading to the activation of the complement cascade through the classical pathway. C3, and subsequently, C5 are activated. Generated C5a recruits and activates neutrophils and monocytes and stimulates the release of mediators of inflammation which ultimately, results in thrombosis, fetal death and tissue injury. β2GPI: β2Glycoprotein I.

## Conclusion

The intensive research focused on the thrombotic mechanisms mediated by aPL, performed in the last few years, has significantly advanced our understanding of the pathophysiology of the APS. Those findings have opened new insights in the therapeutical approach of patients with APS leading to the investigation of a specific target therapy.

## Acknowledgments

This work was supported by the Japanese Ministry of Health, Labour and Welfare, and the Japanese Ministry of Education, Culture, Sports, Science and Technology.

## References

[1] Hughes GR. Thrombosis, abortion, cerebral disease, and the lupus anticoagulant. *Br Med. J. (Clin Res Ed)*, 1983, 287, 1088-9.

[2] Khamashta MA: Hughes syndrome: history. In Khamashta MA, editor: Hughes Syndrome: Antiphospholipid syndrome. London, Springer-Verlag 2006: 3-8.

[3] Galli M, Comfurius P, Maassen C *et al.* Anticardiolipin antibodies (ACA) directed not to cardiolipin but to a plasma protein cofactor. *Lancet*, 1990, 335, 952-3.

[4] Matsuura E, Igarashi Y, Fujimoto M, Ichikawa K and Koike T. Anticardiolipin cofactor(s) and differential diagnosis of autoimmune disease. *Lancet*, 1990, 336, 177-8.

[5] McNeil HP, Simpson RJ, Chesterman CN and Krilis SA. Anti-phospholipid antibodies are directed against a complex antigen that induces a lipid-binding inhibitor of coagulation: β2-glycoprotein I (apolipoprotein H). *Proc. Natl. Acad. Sci. USA*, 1990, 87, 4120-4.

[6] Bevers EM, Galli M, Barbui T, Comfurius P and Zwaal RF. Lupus anticoagulant IgG's (LA) are not directed to phospholipids only, but to a complex of lipid-bound human prothrombin. *Thromb. Haemost.*, 1991, 66, 629-32.

[7] Schorer AE, Wickham NW and Watson KV. Lupus anticoagulant induces a selective defect in thrombin-mediated endothelial prostacyclin release and platelet aggregation. *Br. J. Haematol.*, 1989, 71, 399-407.

[8] Reverter JC, Tassies D, Font J *et al.* Effects of human monoclonal anticardiolipin antibodies on platelet function and on tissue factor expression on monocytes. *Arthritis. Rheum.*, 1998, 41, 1420-7.

[9] Ames PR, Tommasino C, Iannaccone L, Brillante M, Cimino R and Brancaccio V. Coagulation activation and fibrinolytic imbalance in subjects with idopathic antiphospholipid antibodies - a crucial role for acquired free protein S deficiency. *Thromb. Haemost.*, 1996, 76, 190-4.

[10] Oosting JD, Derksen RHWM, Bobbink IWG, Hackeng TM, Bouma BN and de Groot PG. Antiphospholipid antibodies directed against a combination of phospholipids with prothrombin, protein C, or protein S: An explanation for their pathogenic mechanism. *Blood*, 1993, 81, 2618-25.

[11] Kornberg A, Blank M, Kaufman S and Shoenfeld Y. Induction of tissue factor-like activity in monocytes by anti-cardiolipin antibodies. *J. Immunol.*, 1994, 153, 1328-32.

[12] Amengual O, Atsumi T, Khamashta MA and Hughes GRV. The role of the tissue factor pathway in the hypercoagulable state in patients with the antiphospholipid syndrome. *Thromb. Haemost.*, 1998, 79, 276-81.

[13] Tannenbaum SH, Finko R and Cines DB. Antibody and immune complexes induce tissue factor production by human endothelial cells. *J. Immunol.*, 1986, 137, 1532-7.

[14] Branch DW and Rodgers GM. Induction of endothelial cell tissue factor activity by sera from patients with antiphospholipid syndrome: a possible mechanism of thrombosis. *Am. J. Obstet. Gynecol.*, 1993, 168, 206-10.

[15] Giannakopoulos B, Passam F, Rahgozar S and Krilis SA. Current concepts on the pathogenesis of the antiphospholipid syndrome. *Blood*, 2007, 109, 422-30.

[16] Bohgaki M, Atsumi T, Yamashita Y *et al.* The p38 mitogen-activated protein kinase (MAPK) pathway mediates induction of the tissue factor gene in monocytes stimulated with human monoclonal anti-beta2Glycoprotein I antibodies. *Int. Immunol.*, 2004, 16, 1633-41.

[17] Vega-Ostertag M, Casper K, Swerlick R, Ferrara D, Harris EN and Pierangeli SS. Involvement of p38 MAPK in the up-regulation of tissue factor on endothelial cells by antiphospholipid antibodies. *Artritis. Rheum.*, 2005, 52, 1545-54.

[18] Lopez-Pedrera C, Buendia P, Cuadrado MJ *et al.* Antiphospholipid antibodies from patients with the antiphospholipid syndrome induce monocyte tissue factor expression through the simultaneous activation of NF-kappaB/Rel proteins via the p38 mitogen-activated protein kinase pathway, and of the MEK-1/ERK pathway. *Arthritis. Rheum.*, 2006, 54, 301-11.

[19] Schultze HE, Heide K and Haput H. Uber ein bisher ubekanntes niedermolekulars β2-Globulin des Humanserums. *Naturwissenschaften*, 1961, 48, 719.

[20] Lozier J, Takahashi N and Putnam FW. Complete amino acid sequence of human plasma β2-glycoprotein I. *Proc. Natl. Acad. Sci. USA.*, 1984, 81, 3640-4.

[21] Bouma B, de Groot PG, van den Elsen JM *et al.* Adhesion mechanism of human β(2)-glycoprotein I to phospholipids based on its crystal structure. *EMBO J.*, 1999, 18, 5166-74.

[22] Schwarzenbacher R, Zeth K, Diederichs K *et al.* Crystal structure of human beta2-glycoprotein I: implications for phospholipid binding and the antiphospholipid syndrome. *EMBO J.*, 1999, 18, 6228-39.

[23] Hunt JE, Simpson RJ and Krilis SA. Identification of a region of β2-glycoprotein I critical for lipid binding and anti-cardiolipin antibody cofactor activity. *Proc. Natl. Acad. Sci. USA.*, 1993, 90, 2141-5.

[24] Hunt J and Krilis S. The fifth domain of β2-glycoprotein I contains a phospholipid binding site (Cys281-Cys288) and a region recognized by anticardiolipin antibodies. *J. Immunol.*, 1994, 152, 653-9.

[25] Ohkura N, Hagihara Y, Yoshimura T, Goto Y and Kato H. Plasmin can reduce the function of human beta2 glycoprotein I by cleaving domain V into a nicked form. *Blood*, 1998, 91, 4173-9.

[26] Shi W, Chong B, Hogg P and Chesterman C. Anticardiolipin antibodies block the inhibition by β2-glycoprotein I of the factor Xa generating activity of platelets. *Thromb. Haemost.*, 1993, 70, 342-5.

[27] Schousboe I and Rasmussen MS. Synchronized inhibition of the phospholipid mediated autoactivation of Factor XII in plasma by β2-glycoprotein I and anti-β2-glycoprotein I. *Thromb. Haemost.*, 1995, 73, 798-804.

[28] Nimpf J, Wurm H and Kostner GM. b2-glycoprotein-I (apo-H) inhibits the release reaction of human platelets during ADP-induced aggregation. *Atherosclerosis*, 1987, 63, 109-14.

[29] Ieko M, Ichikawa K, Triplett DA *et al.* Beta2-glycoprotein I is necessary to inhibit protein C activity by monoclonal anticardiolipin antibodies. *Arthritis. Rheum.*, 1999, 42, 167-74.

[30] Sheng Y, Reddel SW, Herzog H *et al.* Impaired thrombin generation in β2-glycoprotein I null mice. *J. Biol. Chem.*, 2001, 276, 13817-21.

[31] Shi T, Iverson GM, Qi JC *et al.* Beta 2-Glycoprotein I binds factor XI and inhibits its activation by thrombin and factor XIIa: loss of inhibition by clipped beta 2-glycoprotein I. *Proc. Natl. Acad. Sci. USA*, 2004, 101, 3939-44.

[32] Shi T, Giannakopoulos B, Iverson GM, Cockerill KA, Linnik MD and Krilis SA. Domain V of beta2-glycoprotein I binds factor XI/XIa and is cleaved at Lys317-Thr318. *J. Biol. Chem.*, 2005, 280, 907-12.

[33] Rahgozar S, Yang Q, Giannakopoulos B, Yan X, Miyakis S and Krilis S. b2-glycoprotein I binds to thrombin via exotise I and exotise II; anti-b2GPI antibodies potentiate the inhibitory effect of b2GPI on thrombin medaited FXa generation. *Arthritis. Rheum.*, 2006, 2006.

[34] Nakaya Y, Schaefer EJ and Brewer HB, Jr. Activation of human post heparin lipoprotein lipase by apolipoprotein H (beta 2-glycoprotein I). *Biochem. Biophys. Res. Commun.*, 1980, 95, 1168-72.

[35] Wurm H, Beubler E, Polz E, Holasek A and Kostner G. Studies on the possible function of beta 2-glycoprotein-I: influence in the triglyceride metabolism in the rat. *Metabolism*, 1982, 31, 484-6.

[36] Kobayashi K, Matsuura E, Liu Q *et al.* A specific ligand for beta(2)-glycoprotein I mediates autoantibody-dependent uptake of oxidized low density lipoprotein by macrophages. *J. Lipid. Res.*, 2001, 42, 697-709.

[37] Manfredi AA, Rovere P, Galati G *et al.* Apoptotic cell clearance in systemic lupus erythematosus. I. Opsonization by antiphospholipid antibodies. *Arthritis. Rheum.*, 1998, 41, 205-14.

[38] Manfredi AA, Rovere P, Heltai S *et al.* Apoptotic cell clearance in systemic lupus erythematosus. II. Role of beta2-glycoprotein I. *Arthritis. Rheum.*, 1998, 41, 215-23.

[39] Bancsi LF, van der Linden IK and Bertina RM. β2-glycoprotein I deficiency and the risk of thrombosis. *Thromb. Haemost.*, 1992, 67, 649-53.

[40] Takeuchi R, Atsumi T, Ieko M *et al.* Coagulation and fibrinolytic activities in 2 siblings with beta (2)-glycoprotein I deficiency. *Blood*, 2000, 96, 1594-5.

[41] de Benedetti E, Reber G, Miescher PA and de Moerloose P. No increase of β2-glycoprotein I levels in patients with antiphospholipid antibodies. *Thromb. Haemost.*, 1992, 68, 624.

[42] Galli M, Cortelazzo S, Daldossi M and Barbui T. Increased levels of beta 2-glycoprotein I (aca-Cofactor) in patients with lupus anticoagulant. *Thromb Haemost*, 1992, 67, 386.

[43] Yasuda S, Atsumi T, Ieko M *et al.* Nicked beta2-glycoprotein I: a marker of cerebral infarct and a novel role in the negative feedback pathway of extrinsic fibrinolysis. *Blood*, 2004, 103, 3766-72.

[44] Roubey RAS. Immunology of the antiphospholipid antibody syndrome. *Arthritis. Rheum.*, 1996, 39, 1444-54.

[45] Sheng Y, Kandiah DA and Krilis SA. Anti-b2-glycoprotein I autoantibodies from patients with the "antiphospholipid" syndrome bind to b2-glycoprotein I with low affinity: dimerization of b2-glycoprotein I induces a significant increase in anti-b2-glycoprotein I antibody affinity. *J. Immunol.*, 1998, 161, 2038-43.

[46] Matsuura E, Igarashi Y, Fujimoto M *et al.* Heterogeneity of anticardiolipin antibodies defined by the anticardiolipin cofactor. *J. Immunol.*, 1992, 148, 3885-91.

[47] Matsuura E, Igarashi Y, Yasuda T, Triplett DA and Koike T. Anticardiolipin antibodies recognize β2-glycoprotein I structure altered by interacting with an oxygen modified solid phase surface. *J. Exp. Med.*, 1994, 179, 457-62.

[48] Igarashi M, Matsuura E, Igarashi Y *et al.* Human β2-glycoprotein I as an anticardiolipin cofactor determined using deleted mutants expressed by a Baculovirus system. *Blood*, 1996, 87, 3262-70.

[49] Wang MX, Kandiah DA, Ichikawa K *et al.* Epitope specificity of monoclonal anti β2-glycoprotien I antibodies derived from patients with the antiphospholipid syndrome. *J. Immunol.*, 1995, 155, 1629-36.

[50] George J, Gilburd B, Hojnik M *et al.* Target recognition of b2-glycoprotein I (b2GPI)-dependent anticardiolipin antibodies: evidence for involvement of the fourth domain of b2GPI in antibody binding. *J. Immunol.*, 1998, 150, 3917-23.

[51] Iverson GM, Reddel S, Victoria EJ *et al.* Use of single point mutations in domain I of beta 2-glycoprotein I to determine fine antigenic specificity of antiphospholipid autoantibodies. *J. Immunol.*, 2002, 169, 7097-103.

[52] Koike T, Ichikawa K, Atsumi T, Kasahara H and Matsuura E. β2-glycoprotein I-anti-β2-glycoprotein I interaction. *J. Autoimmun.*, 2000, 15, 97-100.

[53] de Laat B, Derksen RH, Urbanus RT and de Groot PG. IgG antibodies that recognize epitope Gly40-Arg43 in domain I of beta 2-glycoprotein I cause LAC, and their presence correlates strongly with thrombosis. *Blood*, 2005, 105, 1540-5.

[54] de Laat B, Derksen RH, van Lummel M, Pennings MT and de Groot PG. Pathogenic anti-beta2-glycoprotein I antibodies recognize domain I of beta2-glycoprotein I only after a conformational change. *Blood*, 2006, 107, 1916-24.

[55] Kasahara H, Matsuura E, Kaihara K *et al.* Antigenic structures recognized by anti-beta2-glycoprotein I auto-antibodies. *Int. Immunol.*, 2005, 17, 1533-42.

[56] Atsumi T, Tsutsumi A, Amengual O *et al.* Correlation between beta2-glycoprotein I valine/leucine247 polymorphism and anti-beta2-glycoprotein I antibodies in patients with primary antiphospholipid syndrome. *Rheumatology*, 1999, 38, 721-3.

[57] Yasuda S, Atsumi T, Matsuura E *et al.* Significance of valine/leucine247 polymorphism of beta2-glycoprotein I in antiphospholipid syndrome: increased reactivity of anti-beta2-glycoprotein I autoantibodies to the valine247 beta2-glycoprotein I variant. *Arthritis. Rheum.*, 2005, 52, 212-8.

[58] Hattori N, Kuwana M, Kaburaki J, Mimori T, Ikeda Y and Kawakami Y. T cells that are autoreactive to beta2-glycoprotein I in patients with antiphospholipid syndrome and healthy individuals. *Arthritis. Rheum.*, 2000, 43, 65-75.

[59] Kuwana M, Matsuura E, Kobayashi K *et al.* Binding of beta 2-glycoprotein I to anionic phospholipids facilitates processing and presentation of a cryptic epitope that activates pathogenic autoreactive T cells. *Blood*, 2005, 105, 1552-7.

[60] Arai T, Yoshida K, Kaburaki J *et al.* Autoreactive CD4(+) T-cell clones to beta2-glycoprotein I in patients with antiphospholipid syndrome: preferential recognition of the major phospholipid-binding site. *Blood*, 2001, 98, 1889-96.

[61] Chow BK, Ting V, Tufaro F and MacGillivray RT. Characterization of a novel liver-specific enhancer in the human prothrombin gene. *J. Biol. Chem.*, 1991, 1991, 18927-33.

[62] Mann KG, Nesheim ME, Church WR, Haley P and Krishnaswamy S. Surface-dependent reactions of the vitamin K-dependent enzyme complex. *Blood*, 1990, 76, 1-16.

[63] Loeliger A. Prothrombin as a co-factor of the circulating anticoagulant in systemic lupus erythematosus? *Thromb. Diath. Haemorrh.*, 1959, 3, 237-56.

[64] Bajaj SP, Rapaport SI, Fierer DS, Herbst KD and Schwartz DB. A mechanism for the hypoprothrombinemia of the acquired hypoprothrombinemia-lupus anticoagulant syndrome. *Blood*, 1983, 61, 684-92.

[65] Edson JR, Vogt JM and Hasegawa DK. Abnormal prothrombin crossed-immunoelectrophoresis in patients with lupus inhibitors. *Blood*, 1984, 64, 807-16.

[66] Fleck RA, Rapaport SI and Rao LVM. Anti-prothrombin antibodies and the lupus anticoagulant. *Blood*, 1988, 72, 512-9.

[67] Wu JR and Lentz BR. Phospholipid-specific conformational changes in human prothrombin upon binding to procoagulant acidic lipid membranes. *Thromb. Haemost.*, 1994, 71, 596-604.

[68] Zwaal RF, Comfurius P and Bevers EM. Lipid-protein interactions in blood coagulation. *Biochim. Biophys. Acta.*, 1998, 1376, 433-53.

[69] McDonald JF, Shah AM, Schwalbe RA, Kisiel W, Dahlback B and Nelsestuen GL. Comparison of naturally occurring vitamin K-dependent proteins: correlation of amino acid sequences and membrane binding properties suggests a membrane contact site. *Biochemistry*, 1997, 36, 5120-7.

[70] Galli M, Beretta G, Daldossi M, Bevers EM and Barbui T. Different anticoagulant and immunological properties of anti-prothrombin antibodies in patients with antiphospholipid antibodies. *Thromb. Haemost.*, 1997, 77, 486-91.

[71] Bevers EM, Zwaal RF and Willems GM. The effect of phospholipids on the formation of immune complexes between autoantibodies and beta2-glycoprotein I or prothrombin. *Clin. Immunol.*, 2004, 112, 150-60.

[72] Rao L, Hoang A and Rapaport S. Mechanism and effects of the binding of lupus anticoagulant IgG and prothrombin to surface phospholipid. *Blood*, 1996, 88, 4173-82.

[73] Akimoto T, Akama T, Kono I and Sumida T. Relationship between clinical features and binding domains of anti-prothrombin autoantibodies in patients with systemic lupus erythematosus and antiphospholipid syndrome. *Lupus*, 1999, 8, 761-6.

[74] Vianna JL, Khamashta MA, Ordi-Ros J *et al.* Comparison of the primary and secondary antiphospholipid syndrome: A European multicenter study of 114 patients. *Am. J. Med*, 1994, 96, 3-9.

[75] Cervera R, Piette JC, Font J *et al.* Antiphospholipid syndrome: clinical and immunologic manifestations and patterns of disease expression in a cohort of 1,000 patients. *Arthritis. Rheum.*, 2002, 46, 1019-27.

[76] Parke AL, Wilson D and Maier D. The prevalence of antiphospholipid antibodies in women with recurrent spontaneous abortion, women with successful pregnancies, and women who have never been pregnant. *Arthritis. Rheum.*, 1991, 34, 1231-5.

[77] MacLean MA, Cumming GP, McCall F, Walker ID and Walker JJ. The prevalence of lupus anticoagulant and anticardiolipin antibodies in women with a history of first trimester miscarriages. *Br. J. Obstet. Gynaecol.*, 1994, 101, 103-6.

[78] Branch DW, Silver R, Pierangeli S, van Leeuwen I and Harris EN. Antiphospholipid antibodies other than lupus anticoagulant and anticardiolipin antibodies in women with recurrent pregnancy loss, fertile controls, and antiphospholipid syndrome. *Obstet. Gynecol.*, 1997, 89, 549-55.

[79] Miyakis S, Lockshin MD, Atsumi T *et al.* International consensus statement on an update of the classification criteria for definite antiphospholipid syndrome (APS). *J Thromb. Haemost.*, 2006, 4, 295-306.

[80] Le Thi Thuong D, Tieulie N, Costedoat N *et al.* The HELLP syndrome in the antiphospholipid syndrome: retrospective study of 16 cases in 15 women. *Ann. Rheum. Dis.*, 2005, 64, 273-8.

[81] Asherson RA. The catastrophic antiphospholipid syndrome. *J. Rheumatol.*, 1992, 19, 508-12.

[82] Harris EN, Gharavi AE, Boey ML *et al.* Anti-cardiolipin antibodies: Detection by radioimmunoassay and association with thrombosis in systemic lupus erythematosus. *Lancet*, 1983, ii, 1211-4.

[83] Brandt JT, Triplett DA, Alving B and Scharrer I. Criteria for the diagnosis of lupus anticoagulants: an update. On behalf of the Subcommittee on Lupus Anticoagulant/Antiphospholipid Antibody of the Scientific and Standardisation Committee of the ISTH. *Thromb. Haemost.*, 1995, 74, 1185-90.

[84] Roubey RA, Maldonado MA and Byrd SN. Comparison of an enzyme-linked immunosorbent assay for antibodies to beta 2-glycoprotein I and a conventional anticardiolipin immunoassay. *Arthritis. Rheum.*, 1996, 39, 1606-7.

[85] McNally T, Mackie IJ, Machin SJ and Isenberg DA. Increased level of β2 glycoprotein I antigen and β2 glycoprotein I binding antibodies are associated with a history of thromboembolic complications in patients with SLE and primary antiphospholipid syndrome. *Br. J. Rheumatol.*, 1995, 34, 1031-6.

[86] Amengual O, Atsumi T, Khamashta M, Koike T and Hughes GRV. Specificity of ELISA for antibody to β2-glycoprotein I in patients with antiphospholipid syndrome. *Br. J. Rheumatol.*, 1996, 35, 1239-43.

[87] Arvieux J, Darnige L, Caron C, Reber G, Bensa JC and Colomb MG. Development of an ELISA for autoantibodies to prothrombin showing their prevalence in patients with lupus anticoagulant. *Thromb. Haemost.*, 1995, 74, 1120-5.

[88] Pengo V, Biasiolo A, Brocco T, Tonetto S and Ruffatti A. Autoantibodies to phospholipid-binding plasma proteins in patients with thrombosis and phospholipid-reactive antibodies. *Thromb. Haemost.*, 1996, 75, 721-4.

[89] Atsumi T, Ieko M, Bertolaccini ML *et al.* Association of autoantibodies against the phosphatidylserine-prothrombin complex with manifestations of the antiphospholipid syndrome and with the presence of lupus anticoagulant. *Arthritis. Rheum.*, 2000, 43, 1982-93.

[90] Rauch J, Tannenbaum M, Neville C and Fortin PR. Inhibition of lupus anticoagulant activity by hexagonal phase phosphatidylethanolamine in the presence of prothrombin. *Thromb. Haemost.*, 1998, 80, 936-41.

[91] Wilson WA, Gharavi AE, Koike T *et al.* International consensus statement on preliminary classification criteria for definite antiphospholipid syndrome: report of an international workshop. *Arthritis. Rheum.*, 1999, 42, 1309-11.

[92] Galli M, Luciani D, Bertolini G and Barbui T. Anti-beta 2-glycoprotein I, antiprothrombin antibodies, and the risk of thrombosis in the antiphospholipid syndrome. *Blood*, 2003, 102, 2717-23.

[93] Reber G and de Moerloose P. Anti-beta2-glycoprotein I antibodies--when and how should they be measured? *Thromb. Res.*, 2004, 114, 527-31.

[94] Faden D, Tincani A, Tanzi P *et al.* Anti-beta 2 glycoprotein I antibodies in a general obstetric population: preliminary results on the prevalence and correlation with pregnancy outcome. Anti-beta2 glycoprotein I antibodies are associated with some obstetrical complications, mainly preeclampsia-eclampsia. *Eur. J. Obstet. Gynecol. Reprod. Biol.*, 1997, 73, 37-42.

[95] Lee RM, Branch DW and Silver RM. Immunoglobulin A anti-beta2-glycoprotein antibodies in women who experience unexplained recurrent spontaneous abortion and unexplained fetal death. *Am. J. Obstet. Gynecol.*, 2001, 185, 748-53.

[96] Horbach DA, van Oort E, Derksen RH and de Groot PG. The contribution of anti-prothrombin-antibodies to lupus anticoagulant activity--discrimination between functional and non-functional anti-prothrombin-antibodies. *Thromb. Haemost.*, 1998, 79, 790-5.

[97] Amengual O, Atsumi T and Koike T. Specificities, properties, and clinical significance of antiprothrombin antibodies. *Arthritis. Rheum.*, 2003, 48, 886-95.

[98] Cariou R, Tobelem G, Bellucci S *et al.* Effect of lupus anticoagulant on antithrombotic properties of endothelial cells - Inhibition of thrombomodulin-dependent protein C activation. *Thromb. Haemost.*, 1988, 60, 54-8.

[99] Marciniak E and Romond EH. Impaired catalytic function of activated protein C: a new in vitro manifestation of lupus anticoagulant. *Blood*, 1989, 71, 2426-32.

[100] Malia RG, Kitchen S, Greaves M and Preston FE. Inhibition of activated protein C and its cofactor protein S by antiphospholipid antibodies. *Br. J. Haematol.*, 1990, 76, 101-7.

[101] Borrell M, Sala N, de Castellarnau C, Lopez S, Gari M and Fontcuberta J. Immunoglobulin fractions isolated from patients with antiphospholipid antibodies prevent the inactivation of factor Va by activated protein C on human endothelial cells. *Thromb. Haemost.*, 1992, 68, 101-7.

[102] Atsumi T, Khamashta MA, Amengual O *et al.* Binding of anticardiolipin antibodies to protein C via β2-glycoprotein I (β2-GPI): a possible mechanism in the inhibitory effect of antiphospholipid antibodies on the protein C system. *Clin. Exp. Immunol.*, 1998, 112, 325-33.

[103] Galli M, Willems GM, Rosing J *et al.* Anti-prothrombin IgG from patients with anti-phospholipid antibodies inhibits the inactivation of factor Va by activated protein C. *Br. J. Haematol.*, 2005, 129, 240-7.

[104] Field SL, Chesterman CN and Hogg PJ. Dependence on prothrombin for inhibition of activated protein C activity by lupus antibodies. *Thromb. Haemost.*, 2000, 84, 1132-3.

[105] Ginsberg J, Demers C, Brill-Edwards P *et al.* Acquired free protein S deficiency is associated with antiphospholipid antibodies and increased thrombin generation in patients with systemic lupus erythematosus. *Am. J. Med.*, 1995, 98, 379-83.

[106] Broze GJJ. Protein Z-dependent regulation of coagulation. *Thromb. Haemost.*, 2001, 86, 8-13.

[107] Steffano B, Forastiero R, Martinuzzo M and Kordich L. Low plasma protein Z levels in patients with antiphospholipid antibodies. *Blood Coagul. Fibrinolysis.*, 2001, 12, 411-2.

[108] McColl MD, Deans A, Maclean P, Tait RC, Greer IA and Walker ID. Plasma protein Z deficiency is common in women with antiphospholipid antibodies. *Br. J. Haematol.*, 2003, 20, 913-4.

[109] Vasse M, Guegan-Massardier E, Borg JY, Woimant F and Soria C. Frequency of protein Z deficiency in patients with ischaemic stroke. *Lancet. Mar 24*, 2001, 357, 933-4.

[110] Ayoub N, Esposito G, Barete S, Soria C, Piette JC and Frances C. Protein Z deficiency in antiphospholipid-negative Sneddon's syndrome. *Stroke*, 2004, 35, 1329-32.

[111] Gris JC, Quere I, Dechaud H *et al.* High frequency of protein Z deficiency in patients with unexplained early fetal loss. *Blood*, 2002, 99, 2606-8.

[112] Gris JC, Mercier E, Quere I *et al.* Low-molecular-weight heparin versus low-dose aspirin in women with one fetal loss and a constitutional thrombophilic disorder. *Blood*, 2004, 103, 3695-9.

[113] Forastiero RR, Martinuzzo ME, Lu L and Broze GJ. Autoimmune antiphospholipid antibodies impair the inhibition of activated factor X by protein Z/protein Z-dependent protease inhibitor. *J. Thromb. Haemost.*, 2003, 1, 1764-70.

[114] Jurado M, Paramo JA, Gutierrez-Pimentel M and Rocha E. Fibrinolytic potential and antiphospholipid antibodies in systemic lupus erythematosus and other connective tissue disorders. *Thromb. Haemost.*, 1992, 68, 516-20.

[115] Francis RB, McGehee JA and Feinstein DI. Endothelial-dependent fibrinolysis in subjects with the lupus anticoagulant and thrombosis. *Thromb. Haemost.*, 1988, 59, 412-4.

[116] Violi F, Ferro D, Valesini G *et al.* Tissue plasminogen activator inhibitor in patients with systemic lupus erythematosus and thrombosis. *BMJ*, 1990, 300, 1099-102.

[117] Keeling DM, Campbell SJ, Mackie IJ, Machin SJ and Isenberg DA. The fibrinolytic response to venous occlusion and the natural anticoagulant in patients with antiphospholipid syndrome both with and without systemic lupus erythematosus. *Br. J. Haematol.*, 1991, 77, 354-9.

[118] Cugno M, Cabibbe M, Galli M *et al.* Antibodies to tissue-type plasminogen activator (tPA) in patients with antiphospholipid syndrome: evidence of interaction between the antibodies and the catalytic domain of tPA in 2 patients. *Blood*, 2004, 103, 2121-6.

[119] Sugi T and Makino T. Autoantibodies to contact proteins in patients with recurrent pregnancy losses. *J. Reprod. Immunol.*, 2002, 53, 269-77.

[120] Takeuchi R, Atsumi T, Ieko M, Amasaki Y, Ichikawa K and Koike T. Suppressed intrinsic fibrinolytic activity by monoclonal anti-beta-2 glycoprotein I autoantibodies: possible mechanism for thrombosis in patients with antiphospholipid syndrome. *Br. J. Haematol.*, 2002, 119, 781-8.

[121] Carmona F, Lazaro I, Reverter JC *et al.* Impaired factor XIIa-dependent activation of fibrinolysis in treated antiphospholipid syndrome gestations developing late-pregnancy complications. *Am. J. Obstet. Gynecol.*, 2006, 194, 457-65.

[122] Loscalzo J. Lipoprotein (a). A unique risk factor for atherothrombotic disease. *Arteriosclerosis*, 1990, 10, 672-9.

[123] Etingin OR, Hajjar DP, Hajjar KA, Harpel PC and Nachman RL. Lipoprotein (a) regulates plasminogen activator inhibitor-1 expression in endothelial cells. *J. Biol. Chem.*, 1991, 266, 2459-65.

[124] Atsumi T, Khamashta MA, Andujar C *et al.* Elevated plasma lipoprotein(a) level and its association with impaired fibrinolysis in patients with antiphospholipid syndrome. *J. Rheumatol.*, 1998, 25, 69-73.

[125] Yamazaki M, Asakura H, Jokaji H *et al.* Plasma levels of lipoprotein(a) are elevated in patients with the antiphospholipid antibody syndrome. *Thromb. Haemost.*, 1994, 71, 424-7.

[126] Le Tonqueze M, Salozhin K, Dueymes M *et al.* Role of beta 2-glycoprotein I in the antiphospholipid antibody binding to endothelial cells. *Lupus*, 1995, 4, 179-86.

[127] Del Papa N, Guidali L, Spatola L *et al.* Relationship between anti-phospholipid and anti-endothelial cell antibodies III: beta 2 glycoprotein I mediates the antibody binding to endothelial membranes and induces the expression of adhesion molecules. *Clin. Exp. Rheumatol.*, 1995, 13, 179-85.

[128] Del PaPa N, Guidali L, Sala A *et al.* Endothelial cells as target for antiphospholipid antibodies. *Arthritis. Rheum.*, 1997, 40, 551-61.

[129] Del Papa N, Sheng YH, Raschi E *et al.* Human beta 2-glycoprotein I binds to endothelial cells through a cluster of lysine residues that are critical for anionic phospholipid binding and offers epitopes for anti-beta 2-glycoprotein I antibodies. *J. Immunol.*, 1998, 160, 5572-8.

[130] Simantov R, LaSala JM, Lo SK *et al.* Activation of cultured vascular endothelial cells by antiphospholipid antibodies. *J. Clin. Invest.*, 1995, 96, 2211-9.

[131] Pierangeli SS, Espinola RG, Liu X and Harris EN. Thrombogenic effects of antiphospholipid antibodies are mediated by intercellular cell adhesion molecule-1, vascular cell adhesion molecule-1, and P-selectin. *Circ. Res.*, 2001, 88, 245-50.

[132] Meroni PL, Raschi E, Camera M *et al.* Endothelial activation by aPL: a potential pathogenetic mechanism for the clinical manifestations of the syndrome. *J. Autoimmun.*, 2000, 15, 237-40.

[133] Atsumi T, Khamashta MA, Haworth RS *et al.* Arterial disease and thrombosis in the antiphospholipid syndrome: a pathogenic role for endothelin 1. *Arthritis. Rheum.*, 1998, 41, 800-7.

[134] Fischetti F, Durigutto P, Pellis V *et al.* Thrombus formation induced by antibodies to beta2-glycoprotein I is complement dependent and requires a priming factor. *Blood*, 2005, 106, 2340-6.

[135] Jankowski M, Vreys I, Wittevrongel C *et al.* Thrombogenicity of beta 2-glycoprotein I-dependent antiphospholipid antibodies in a photochemically induced thrombosis model in the hamster. *Blood*, 2003, 101, 157-62.

[136] Pierangeli SS, Girardi G, Vega-Ostertag M, Liu X, Espinola RG and Salmon J. Requirement of activation of complement C3 and C5 for antiphospholipid antibody-mediated thrombophilia. *Arthritis. Rheum.*, 2005, 52, 2120-4.

[137] Zhao Y, Rumold R, Zhu M *et al.* An IgG antiprothrombin antibody enhances prothrombin binding to damaged endothelial cells and shortens plasma coagulation times. *Arthritis. Rheum.*, 1999, 42, 2132-8.

[138] Vega-Ostertag M, Liu X, Kwan-Ki H, Chen P and Pierangeli S. A human monoclonal antiprothrombin antibody is thrombogenic in vivo and upregulates expression of tissue factor and E-selectin on endothelial cells. *Br. J. Haematol.*, 2006, 135, 214-9.

[139] Combes V, Simon AC, Grau GE *et al.* In vitro generation of endothelial microparticles and possible prothrombotic activity in patients with lupus anticoagulant. *J. Clin. Invest.*, 1999, 104, 93-102.

[140] Dignat-George F, Camoin-Jau L, Sabatier F *et al.* Endothelial microparticles: a potential contribution to the thrombotic complications of the antiphospholipid syndrome. *Thromb. Haemost.*, 2004, 91, 667-73.

[141] Morel O, Jesel L, Freyssinet JM and Toti F. Elevated levels of procoagulant microparticles in a patient with myocardial infarction, antiphospholipid antibodies and multifocal cardiac thrombosis. *Thromb. J.*, 2005, 3, 15.

[142] Nakamura N, Ban T, Yamaji K, Yoneda Y and Wada Y. Localization of the apoptosis-inducing activity of lupus anticoagulant in an annexin V-binding antibody subset. *J. Clin. Invest.*, 1998, 101, 1951-9.

[143] Campbell AL, Pierangeli SS, Wellhausen S and Harris EN. Comparison of the effects of anticardiolipin antibodies from patients with the antiphospholipid syndrome and with syphilis on platelet activation and aggregation. *Thromb. Haemost.*, 1995, 73, 529-34.

[144] Nojima J, Suehisa E, Kuratsune H *et al.* Platelet activation induced by combined effects of anticardiolipin and lupus anticoagulant IgG antibodies in patients with systemic lupus erythematosus--possible association with thrombotic and thrombocytopenic complications. *Thromb. Haemost.*, 1999, 81, 436-4.

[145] Wiener MH, Burke M, Fried M and Yust I. Thromboagglutination by anticardiolipin antibody complex in the antiphospholipid syndrome: a possible mechanism of immune-mediated thrombosis. *Thromb. Res.*, 2001, 103, 193-9.

[146] Emmi L, Bergamini C, Spinelli A *et al.* Possible pathogenetic role of activated platelets in the primary antiphospholipid syndrome involving the central nervous system. *Ann. NY Acad. Sci.*, 1997, 823, 188-200.

[147] Forastiero R, Martinuzzo M, Carreras LO and Maclouf J. Anti-beta2 glycoprotein I antibodies and platelet activation in patients with antiphospholipid antibodies:

association with increased excretion of platelet-derived thromboxane urinary metabolites. *Thromb. Haemost.*, 1998, 79, 42-5.

[148] Nimpf J, Bevers EM, Bomans PH *et al.* Prothrombinase activity of human platelets is inhibited by beta 2-glycoprotein-I. *Biochim. Biophys. Acta.*, 1986, 884, 142-9.

[149] Shi W, Chong BH and Chesterman CN. β2-glycoprotein I is a requirement for anticardiolipin antibodies binding to activated platelets: differences with lupus anticoagulants. *Blood*, 1993, 81, 1255-62.

[150] Vazquez-Mellado J, Llorente L, Richaud-Patin Y and Alarcon-Segovia D. Exposure of anionic phospholipids upon platelet activation permits binding of beta 2 glycoprotein I and through it that of IgG antiphospholipid antibodies. Studies in platelets from patients with antiphospholipid syndrome and normal subjects. *J. Autoimmun.*, 1994, 7, 335-48.

[151] Ma K, Simantov R, Zhang JC, Silverstein R, Hajjar KA and McCrae KR. High affinity binding of beta 2-glycoprotein I to human endothelial cells is mediated by annexin II. *J. Biol. Chem.*, 2000, 275, 15541-8.

[152] Zhang J and McCrae KR. Annexin A2 mediates endothelial cell activation by antiphospholipid/anti-beta2 glycoprotein I antibodies. *Blood*, 2005, 105, 1964-9.

[153] Cesarman-Maus G, Rios-Luna NP, Deora AB *et al.* Autoantibodies against the fibrinolytic receptor, annexin 2, in antiphospholipid syndrome. *Blood*, 2006, 107, 4375-82.

[154] Raschi E, Testoni C, Bosisio D *et al.* Role of the MyD88 transduction signaling pathway in endothelial activation by antiphospholipid antibodies. *Blood*, 2003, 101, 3495-500.

[155] Satta N, Dunoyer-Geindre S, Reber G *et al.* The role of TLR2 in the inflammatory activation of mouse fibroblasts by human antiphospholipid antibodies. *Blood*, 2007, 109, 1507-14.

[156] Meroni PL, Raschi E, Testoni C, Parisio A and Borghi MO. Innate immunity in the antiphospholipid syndrome: role of toll-like receptors in endothelial cell activation by antiphospholipid antibodies. *Autoimmun. Rev.*, 2004, 3, 510-5.

[157] Lutters BC, Derksen RH, Tekelenburg WL, Lenting PJ, Arnout J and de Groot PG. Dimers of beta 2-glycoprotein I increase platelet deposition to collagen via interaction with phospholipids and the apolipoprotein E receptor 2'. *J. Biol. Chem.*, 2003, 278, 33831-8.

[158] van Lummel M, Pennings MT, Derksen RH *et al.* The binding site in β2-glycoprotein I for ApoER2' on platelets is located in domain V. *J. Biol. Chem.*, 2005, 280, 36729-36.

[159] Shi T, Giannakopoulos B, Yan X *et al.* Anti-beta2-glycoprotein I antibodies in complex with beta2-glycoprotein I can activate platelets in a dysregulated manner via glycoprotein Ib-IX-V. *Arthritis. Rheum.*, 2006, 54, 2558-67.

[160] Pennings MT, Derksen RH, van Lummel M *et al.* Platelet adhesion to dimeric beta-glycoprotein I under conditions of flow is mediated by at least two receptors: glycoprotein Ibalpha and apolipoprotein E receptor 2'. *J. Thromb. Haemost.*, 2007, 5, 369-77.

[161] Baglia FA, Shrimpton CN, Emsley J *et al.* Factor XI interacts with the leucine-rich repeats of glycoprotein Ibalpha on the activated platelet. *J. Biol. Chem.*, 2004, 279, 49323-9.

[162] Robbins DL, Leung S, Miller-Blair DJ and Ziboh V. Effect of anticardiolipin/beta2-glycoprotein I complexes on production of thromboxane A2 by platelets from patients with the antiphospholipid syndrome. *J. Rheumatol.*, 1998, 25, 51-6.

[163] Zhou H, Wolberg AS and Roubey RA. Characterization of monocyte tissue factor activity induced by IgG antiphospholipid antibodies and inhibition by dilazep. *Blood*, 2004, 104, 2353-8.

[164] Meroni PL, Raschi E, Testoni C *et al.* Statins prevent endothelial cell activation induced by antiphospholipid (anti-beta2-glycoprotein I) antibodies: effect on the proadhesive and proinflammatory phenotype. *Arthritis. Rheum.*, 2001, 44, 2870-8.

[165] Dunoyer-Geindre S, De Moerloose P, Galve-De Rochemonteix B, Reber G and Kruithof E. NFkappaB is an essential intermediate in the activation of endothelial cells by anti-beta(2) glycoprotein 1 antibodies. *Thromb. Haemost.*, 2002, 88, 851-7.

[166] Espinola RG, Liu X, Colden-Stanfield M, Hall J, Harris EN and Pierangeli SS. E-Selectin mediates pathogenic effects of antiphospholipid antibodies. *J. Thromb. Haemost.*, 2003, 1, 843-8.

[167] Vega-Ostertag M, Harris EN and Pierangeli SS. Intracellular events in platelet activation induced by antiphospholipid antibodies in the presence of low doses of thrombin. *Arthritis. Rheum.*, 2004, 50, 2911-9.

[168] Nakajima K, Tohyama Y, Kohsaka S and Kurihara T. Protein kinase C alpha requirement in the activation of p38 mitogen-activated protein kinase, which is linked to the induction of tumor necrosis factor alpha in lipopolysaccharide-stimulated microglia. *Neurochem. Int.*, 2004, 44, 205-14.

[169] Saccani S, Pantano S and Natoli G. p38-Dependent marking of inflammatory genes for increased NF-kappa B recruitment. *Nat. Immunol.*, 2002, 3, 69-75.

[170] McGilvray ID, Tsai V, Marshall JC, Dackiw AP and Rotstein OD. Monocyte adhesion and transmigration induce tissue factor expression: role of the mitogen-activated protein kinases. *Shock*, 2002, 18, 51-7.

[171] Ohsawa M, Koyama T, Nara N and Hirosawa S. Induction of tissue factor expression in human monocytic cells by protease inhibitors through activating activator protein-1 (AP-1) with phosphorylation of Jun-N-terminal kinase and p38. *Thromb. Res.*, 2003, 112, 313-20.

[172] Blum S, Issbruker K, Willuweit A *et al.* An inhibitory role of the phosphatidylinositol 3-kinase-signaling pathway in vascular endothelial growth factor-induced tissue factor expression. *J. Biol. Chem.*, 2001, 276, 33428-34.

[173] Eto M, Kozai T, Cosentino F, Joch H and Luscher TF. Statin prevents tissue factor expression in human endothelial cells: role of Rho/Rho-kinase and Akt pathways. *Circulation*, 2002, 105, 1756-9.

[174] Herkert O, Diebold I, Brandes RP, Hess J, Busse R and Gorlach A. NADPH oxidase mediates tissue factor-dependent surface procoagulant activity by thrombin in human vascular smooth muscle cells. *Circulation*, 2002, 105, 2030-6.

[175] Walport MJ. Complement. First of two parts. *N. Engl. J. Med.*, 2001, 344, 1058-66.

[176] Holers VM, Girardi G, Mo L *et al.* Complement C3 activation is required for antiphospholipid antibody-induced fetal loss. *J. Exp. Med.*, 2002, 195, 211-20.

[177] Girardi G, Redecha P and Salmon JE. Heparin prevents antiphospholipid antibody-induced fetal loss by inhibiting complement activation. *Nat. Med.*, 2004, 10, 1222-6.

[178] Salmon JE, Girardi G and Lockshin MD. The antiphospholipid syndrome as a disorder initiated by inflammation: implications for the therapy of pregnant patients. *Nat. Clin. Pract. Rheumatol.*, 2007, 3, 140-7; quiz 1 p following 87.

[179] Sugiura-Ogasawara M, Nozawa K, Nakanishi T, Hattori Y and Ozaki Y. Complement as a predictor of further miscarriage in couples with recurrent miscarriages. *Hum. Reprod.*, 2006, 21, 2711-4.

[180] Davis WD and Brey RL. Antiphospholipid antibodies and complement activation in patients with cerebral ischemia. *Clin. Exp. Rheumatol.*, 1992, 10, 455-60.

[181] Sammaritano LR, Ng S, Sobel R *et al.* Anticardiolipin IgG subclasses: association of IgG2 with arterial and/or venous thrombosis. *Arthritis. Rheum.*, 1997, 40, 1998-2006.

[182] Amengual O, Atsumi T, Khamashta MA, Bertolaccini ML and Hughes GR. IgG2 restriction of anti-beta2-glycoprotein I as the basis for the association between IgG2 anticardiolipin antibodies and thrombosis in the antiphospholipid syndrome: comment on the article by Sammaritano et al. *Arthritis. Rheum.*, 1998, 41, 1513-5.

[183] Oku K, Atsumi T, Sakai Y *et al.* Significance of hypocomplementemia in patients with antiphospholipid syndrome: a correlation to elevated plasma tumor necrosis factor alpha levels. *Arthritis. Rheum.*, 2006, 54, S796 (2029).

[184] Wisloff F, Jacobsen EM and Liestol S. Laboratory diagnosis of the antiphospholipid syndrome. *Thromb. Res.*, 2002, 108, 263-71.

[185] Harris EN and Pierangeli SS. Revisiting the anticardiolipin test and its standardization. *Lupus*, 2002, 11, 269-75.

[186] Reber G, Tincani A, Sanmarco M, de Moerloose P and Boffa MC. Proposals for the measurement of anti-beta2-glycoprotein I antibodies. Standardization group of the European Forum on Antiphospholipid Antibodies. *J. Thromb. Haemost.*, 2004, 2, 1860-2.

In: New Immunology Research Developments
Editor: Gunter V. Müller

ISBN 978-1-60021-701-2


*Chapter 12*

# Cholinergic System in Lymphocytes

***María del Carmen Esandi, María José De Rosa and Cecilia Bouzat****
Instituto de Investigaciones Bioquímicas de Bahía Blanca. UNS-CONICET.
8000 Bahía Blanca. Argentina

## Abstract

Acetylcholine (ACh) plays an important role as a neurotransmitter of the central and peripheral nervous systems. Interestingly, this molecule and its synthesizing enzyme, choline acetyltransferase, are also present in lymphocytes. In addition, several types of nicotinic (nAChR) and muscarinic (mAChR) receptors have been identified in these blood cells. These findings have provided evidence that lymphocytes have most of the essential components needed to constitute a non neuronal cholinergic system. However, the precise role of this extraneuronal cholinergic system is poorly understood. ACh may act as an immunomodulator. Activated immune cells may use the released ACh in self-modulating autocrine and paracrine loops.

Upon phytohemagglutinin (PHA) stimulation of human lymphocytes, an increment in the synthesis of ACh occurs, suggesting that the neurotransmitter modulates T-cell activation. Different subtypes of mAChRs are present in lymphocytes. mAChRs are involved in lymphocyte activation by enhancing T cell antigen receptor/CD3-induced IL-2 production. Different nAChR subtypes have been reported in blood cells, although their patterns of expression and function remain unknown. $\alpha$7 nAChR mRNA has been detected in peripheral human lymphocytes. Nicotine, probably acting through $\alpha$7 nAChRs, elicits transient increases in $Ca^{2+}$ in mononuclear leukocytes and human leukemic cell lines. Nicotine and the antagonist $\alpha$-bungarotoxin lead to up-regulation of $\alpha$7 and to a concomitant protection of lymphocytes from cortisol-induced apoptosis, suggesting that $\alpha$7 is involved in the modulation of this process. In summary, in addition to the recognized cytokine network, the extraneuronal cholinergic system plays a key role in the regulation of the immune function.

The extraneuronal cholinergic system could function independently or coordinated with the neural system. It is interesting to note that lymphocytes may reflect the

* E-mail: inbouzat@criba.edu.ar, cesandi@criba.edu.ar

metabolism of brain cells and this may be exploited as a neural and possible genetic probe in studies of psychiatric disorders.

# Introduction

Acetylcholine (ACh) plays an important role as a neurotransmitter of the central and peripheral nervous systems. There is increasing evidence that ACh is also widely expressed in a variety of extraneuronal tissues and organs including vascular endothelial cells, ammniotic fluid, placenta, epithelial cells within the respiratory and digestive systems, and blood cells [1, 2]. These findings suggest that ACh has also a non-neuronal function. Furthermore, ACh has been found in protozoa, bacteria as well as in plants, where it might be involved in the regulation of transport processes across the cell membrane. Apparently, this neurotransmitter represents a phylogenetically very old molecule with a primitive function as a modulator of cell processes and lately, after emergence of the nervous system, as a neurotransmitter [1].

Besides the ability of lymphocytes to synthesize ACh, the presence of both muscarinic (mAChR) and nicotinic (nAChR) receptors has been demonstrated in these cells [3-5]. However, little is known about their functional roles in these cells. Lymphocytes have a complete cholinergic system that could function independently or coordinated with the nervous system. In other words, since the nervous system is a major producer of ACh, the immune cholinergic system could mediate neuroimmune interactions, or it might serve as an internal regulator of immune responses.

# Detection of Components of the Non-Neuronal Cholinergic System

## Presence of the Neurotransmitter Acetylcholine in Lymphocytes

ACh is probably the oldest signaling molecule, and appeared very early in evolution before the nervous system. Similar to neurons, lymphocytes are able to synthesize and release the signaling molecule ACh, which might act locally as an auto/paracrine mediator through binding to cholinergic receptors.

ACh in blood has been determined in a variety of mammalian species, including human, despite the presence of cholinesterase [6]. However, the variability in the detected concentration of ACh is high, which probably results from the difficulties to develop a sensitive and specific procedure for measuring ACh in blood samples. Kawashima *et al.* [6] developed a radioimmunoassay (RIA) for ACh with adequate sensitivity and specificity. Using this method, it was determined that ACh levels in blood are higher than in plasma, suggesting that ACh originates from blood cells. Indeed, the ACh content of mononuclear leukocytes (MNLs), which consisted of 84% lymphocytes and 14% monocytes, was 5.01 ± 0.59 pmol/ml and it corresponded to about 60% of the level found in whole blood. No ACh was detected in polymorphonuclear leukocytes [6].

ACh in the central nervous system (CNS) is primarily synthesized by choline acetyltransferase (ChAT), whereas in the peripheral nervous system, carnitine acetyltransferase (CarAT) also contributes to its synthesis [7]. In T-cell lines, a correlation between the production of ACh and ChAT activity has been demonstrated. Using inhibitors for both enzymes, ChAT and CarAT, it has been determined that the synthesis of ACh in T-lymphocytes is catalized mainly by ChAT and to a lesser extent by CarAT [8]. The first attempt to conclusively demonstrate that ACh is synthesized by ChAT in T-lymphocytes was made by Fujii *et al.* [9], who showed that both the ChAT mRNA and the protein are present in human leukemic T-cell lines. Multiple ChAT mRNA species (R-, N0-, N1-, N2-, and M-types) exist in human brain and spinal cord. The type of ChAT expressed in T-lymphocytes remains to be elucidated. Ogawa *et al.* [10] showed that the major mRNA species in the human leukemic T-cell line CEM are N2- and M-type, while another cell line, MOLT-3, expresses only the N2-type.

In neurons, newly synthesized ACh is transported into storage vesicles by a vesicular ACh transporter (VAChT) system [11]. VAChT is a protein that by acting as a proton antiporter exchanges intravesicular protons for its cationic substrate ACh. Regarding the extraneuronal system, Fujii *et al.* [12] argue against vesicular storage of ACh in lymphocytes since they did not detect expression of VAChT in MNLs. They propose that, in contrast to the neuronal system, non-neuronal ACh may not necessarily be stored in specialized organelles from which it is released in response to propagated specific signals. They support the idea that ACh is constitutively synthesized by and released from lymphocytes. This means that these immune cells have developed mechanisms, different from those of neurons, to store and regulate the release of local ACh [1]. However, Tayebati *et al.*[13] have shown VAChT immunoreactivity in both T and B peripheral blood lymphocytes. Confocal laser microscopy pictures showing VAChT immunoreactivity in vesicle-like structures suggest that lymphocytes share with neurons the same storage system. There is no explanation for this discrepancy. Further investigation is needed to elucidate the mechanisms of storage and release of ACh in lymphocytes.

## Cholinergic Receptors in Lymphocytes

ACh activates muscarinic and nicotinic receptors, and both types of cholinergic receptors can be simultaneously present in lymphocytes. These two types of receptors are considerably different in both structure and function. The mAChR was first discovered by its ability to bind to the alkaloid, muscarine, derived from the mushroom *Amanita muscaria*. This receptor belongs to the family of G-protein-coupled receptors. The nAChR derives its name from its affinity for nicotine and belongs to the family of ligand-gated ion channels.

### *Muscarinic AChRs*

Muscarinic receptors belong to the seven-transmembrane (TM) G-protein-coupled receptors. They were among the earliest members to be defined pharmacologically [14]. The binding of ACh to these receptors leads to slow responses, which may be either excitatory or inhibitory.

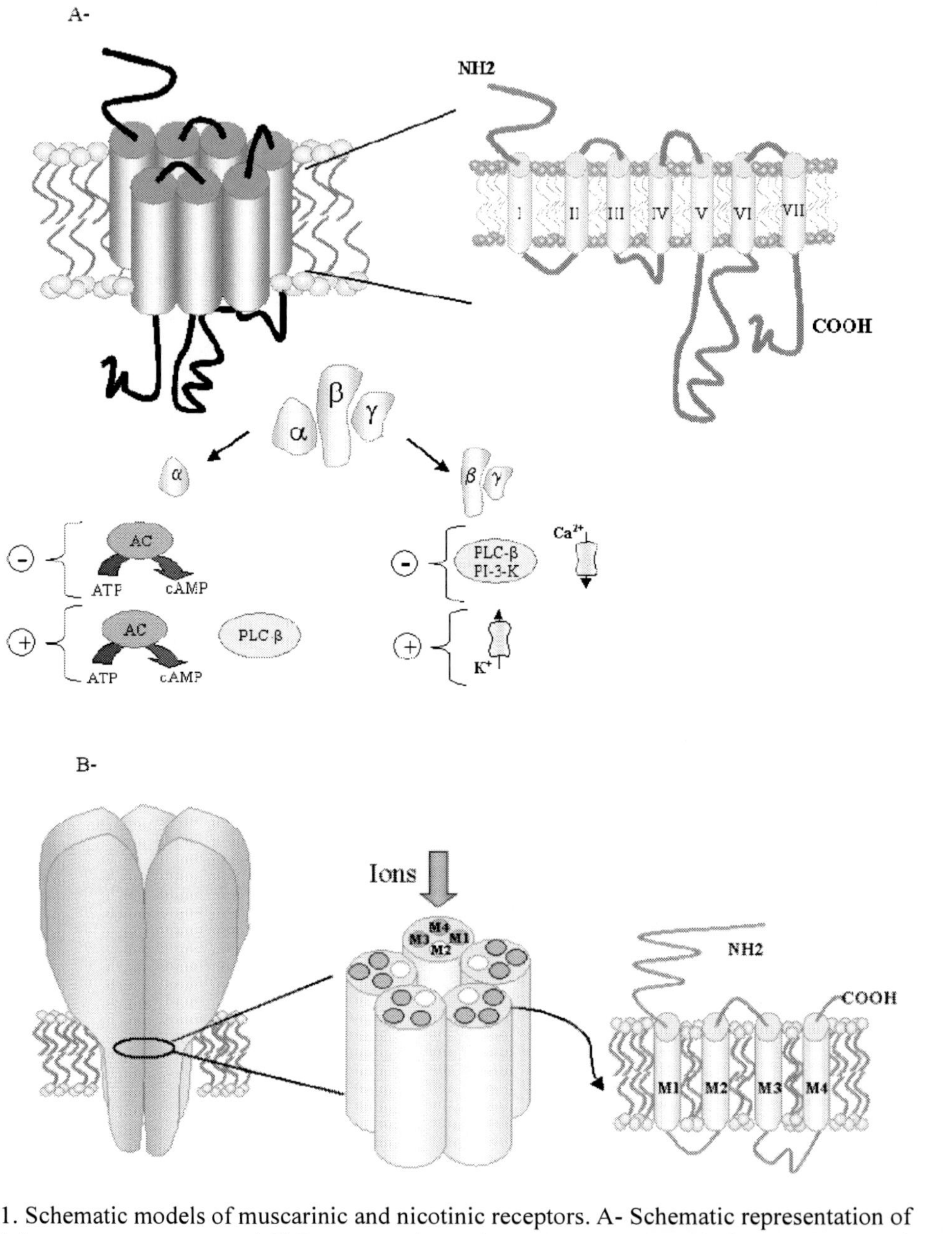


Figure 1. Schematic models of muscarinic and nicotinic receptors. A- Schematic representation of muscarinic receptor structure. mAChRs are metabotropic receptors composed of seven transmembrane domains (TM I-VII). Following agonist binding, the G-protein dissociates in Gα and Gβ/γ. Once dissociated, these subunits modulate different effectors. + indicates activation, and - indicates inhibition.AC: adenylyl cyclase; PLC-β: phospholipase C-β; PI-3K: phosphoinositide-3-kinase. B- Schematic representation of nicotinic receptor structure. nAChRs are ligand-activated ion channels composed of five homologous subunits. Each subunit contains an extracellular N-terminal, four transmembrane domains (M1-M4) and an extracellular C-terminal. The M2 domain of each subunit delineates the ion pore.

All members of the superfamily are characterized by a single protein molecule that spans the plasma membrane seven times, resulting in seven hydrophobic transmembrane segments

(TM) connected by three extracellular and three intracellular hydrophilic loops [15] (Figure 1A).

The N-terminal is located on the extracellular membrane side and contains potential glycosylation sites. The COOH terminus is located on the cytoplasmic side of the membrane and contains a cysteine residue highly conserved across the family members. An homology model of the M1 mAChR based on the rodopsin backbone shows that the transmembrane helices are arranged in an approximate ellipse that is buttressed by TM4, which crosses the outer surface of TM3 and TM2 [16].

Signal transduction is determined by structural elements of the receptor that allow it to bind selectively to ACh and to an appropriate G-protein.

Mutational data indicate that residues located on TM2, TM3, TM5, TM6 and TM7 are needed for agonist interactions [17]. Coupling of mAChR to G-protein occurs mainly through the second and third intracellular loops. By constructing chimeras between subtypes from the two functional classes of mAChRs, the third cytoplasmic loop has been shown to be the region that defines subtype specificity for distinct G-proteins [18-20]. Studies with hybrid M1 and beta-adrenergic receptors suggest that the second cytoplasmic loop may be also involved in coupling [21]. This loop may function as the switch enabling G-protein activation [22].

Five subtypes of mAChRs have been detected by molecular cloning, with different localizations and pharmacology. The different mAChR subtypes display unique, but not exclusive, expression patterns in the CNS and peripheral organs [23]. The amino acid sequence is highly conserved among the mAChR subtypes with at least 90% sequence similarity within their TM domains [24]. Less conservation is found in the hydrophilic cytoplasmic domains and extracellular loops and tails.

These receptors act by two distinctly different second messenger signaling systems: M1, M3 and M5 subtypes activate Gq/11 protein that is responsible for stimulation of phospholipase C activity. The increase of inositol-1,4,5-triphosphate causes release of intracellular calcium from the endoplasmatic reticulum. The increase of diacylglycerol activates protein kinase C that plays a role in the modulation of function (Figure 1A). In contrast, M2 and M4 receptors interact with a distinct group of G-proteins, in particular Gi and Go, resulting in the inhibition of adenylate cyclase and decreased cyclic AMP formation, activation of receptor-operated $K^+$ channels, and suppression of the activity of voltage-gated $Ca^{2+}$ channels (Figure 1A). Among a plethora of other possible responses, in a suitable cellular context, all of the mAChR subtypes can activate non-receptor tyrosine kinases, transactivate the epidermal growth factor receptor and activate extracellular signal-related protein kinase cascades [15]. In many cells, exposure to muscarinic agonists induces rapid desensitization and internalization of the cell surface mAChRs that is followed by a loss of total number of cellular receptors in the following hours. This process, also termed down-regulation, can only be overcome by de novo receptor synthesis. In contrast, chronic treatment with muscarinic antagonists, such as atropine, induces a dose-dependent increase in mAChRs in different tissues (review in Koppen and Kaiser [23]).

Several studies have shown the presence of mAChRs on lymphocytes. By using the muscarinic antagonist [$^3$H] quinuclidinyl benzilate (QNB), mAChRs have been detected in splenic, nod, thymic, and blood lymphocytes (see review in Kawashima and Fujii [2]).

RT-PCR and Northern blot analysis have allowed the identification of mAChR subtypes expressed in lymphocytes. The results show that although all subtypes may be present in lymphocytes, there is a great variability among individual subjects and cell lines. In a systematic study using RT-PCR, Sato *et al.* [4] showed that the M4 and M5 subtypes are always present in human MNLs and leukemic cell lines. In contrast, M1, M2 and M3 subtypes show high variability, suggesting that their expression may be regulated by environmental factors, such as infection.

mRNAs for the M3, M4 and M5 subtypes were also detected in mononuclear cells and purified T cells while M1 and M2 mRNAs were not detected in these cells [25]. No M1-M5 mRNA was detected in B cells, indicating the absence of mAChRs in these cells [25]. More recently, Tayebati *et al.* [13] showed by Western blot analysis that peripheral blood lymphocytes express M2–M5 mAChRs. They also showed by immunocytochemistry that peripheral blood lymphocytes display immunoreactivity when exposed to anti M2–M5 mAChR antibodies. The immune reaction was more intense for M3 followed by M5, M4 and M2 receptors [13].

### *Nicotinic AChRs*

Nicotinic receptors are ligand-gated ion channels, members of the Cys-loop receptor superfamily. They are expressed in many regions of the central and peripheral nervous system. In muscle, nAChR plays a major role in neuromuscular transmission, initiating the action potential which ends in muscle contraction. In neuronal tissues, nAChRs contribute to a wide range of brain activities and influence a number of physiological functions [26, 27].

Cys-loop receptors are composed of five identical (homopentamers) or different (heteropentamers) subunits arranged around an axis perpendicular to the membrane (Figure 1B). The analysis of the evolutionary relationships within the superfamily suggests that the ancestor receptor was probably homo-oligomeric and appeared 2500 million years ago [28, 29]. The $\alpha7$ neuronal receptor is the nicotinic homomeric receptor.

Subunits are classified as $\alpha$ or non-$\alpha$, with the $\alpha$ subunits containing a CC motif in the binding site. A wide number of $\alpha$ and non-$\alpha$ subunits have been cloned for all members of the superfamily (Ligand-gated ion channel database, http://www.ebi.ac.uk/compneur-srv/LGICdb/cys-loop.php). Homomeric receptors are composed of five identical $\alpha$ subunits. To date, several AChR $\alpha$ ($\alpha1$ to $\alpha10$) and non-$\alpha$ subunits ($\beta1$-$\beta4$, $\delta$, $\varepsilon$, $\gamma$) have been identified in vertebrates (reviewed in Gotti and Clementi,[27]). The muscle-type nAChR is formed by a combination of four different subunits in a stoichiometry that depends on the developmental stage of the muscle: $\alpha1_2\beta1\gamma\delta$ in embryonic muscle and $\alpha1_2\beta1\varepsilon\delta$ in adult muscle. Neuronal nAChRs can be formed by the combination of several $\alpha$ ($\alpha2$-$\alpha6$) and $\beta$ ($\beta2$-$\beta4$) subunits. There is evidence supporting the existence of neuronal receptors containing one, two, three, or even four different subunits (reviewed in Gotti *et al.*; McGehee and Role [26, 30]). The $\alpha9$ and $\alpha10$ subunits assemble to form the nAChR that mediates synaptic transmission between efferent olivocochlear fibers and hair cells of the cochlea [31].

The subunits of this gene superfamily are built on a modular basis. The extracellular domain forms the agonist binding sites. The transmembrane domain contains the pore and the channel gate, the structure that prevents ion flow in the absence of agonist and swings open to allow flow in its presence [32]. The junction between binding and pore domains has recently emerged as crucial for coupling binding to gating [33-36].

The large N-terminal domain is located extracellularly, bearing the neurotransmitter binding sites. This model was confirmed by the crystallographic structure of the acetylcholine binding protein (AChBP) from *L. stagnalis* [37], which resembles the extracellular portion of nAChRs. The ligand binding sites are located at the interfaces between subunits [37-41]. The transmembrane region is formed by four transmembrane segments (TM1-TM4) per subunit. TM2 from each subunit forms the wall of the ion channel. It also forms a hydrophobic girdle that constitutes the gate, which in the activated (open) state allows the passage of ions through the channel.

The cytoplasmic loop between TM3 and TM4 contains the greatest sequence divergence among the members of this receptor superfamily. This region is important for receptor modulation by phosphorylation-dephosphorylation processes [42-44]. The anchorage of certain receptors to the cytoskeleton is also mediated by the interaction of non-receptor proteins, such as rapsyn, with the cytoplasmic domain.

The complete atomic-resolution structure of any fast synaptic receptor channel has not been resolved yet. However, a refined model of the membrane-associated *Torpedo* nAChR in the closed state obtained from electron images at 4 Å resolution has been recently presented [45]. The five subunits are arranged pseudo-symmetrically around an axis that passes through the ion pore, perpendicular to the plane of the lipid membrane.

The nAChR may exist in a minimum of three interconvertible states [46-50]. In the absence of the neurotransmitter ACh, most receptors are in a closed, agonist-activatable state (i.e., resting state). This state has low affinity for agonists. Upon neurotransmitter binding, the receptor is activated in the microsecond to millisecond range, reaching the open state with high affinity for agonists. The intrinsically-coupled ion channel opens and allows ions to cross the lipid membrane to finally depolarize the membrane. In the prolonged presence of agonist, the activated receptor converts to a desensitized state in the second to minute timeframe. In this state, which shows high affinity for agonist, the ion channel remains closed. The physiological role of the desensitization process in the Cys-loop receptor superfamily has not been fully elucidated. However, under some pathological conditions its importance becomes apparent (reviewed in Jones and Westbrook [51]). Desensitization might be very important in the prevention of citotoxicity, in the process of nicotine addiction, or in other pathological states (reviewed in Quick and Lester [52]).

The nAChR family is implicated in several important physiological functions throughout the nervous system, such as cognition, reward, motor activity, analgesia [26, 53]. Their role in lymphocytes is less understood. nAChRs are also involved in different neurological disorders including Alzheimer's disease (AD) and Parkinson's disease (PD), schizophrenia, epilepsy, drug addiction, Tourette's syndrome, myasthenia gravis and myasthenic syndromes, depression, anxiety, ulcerative colitis, attention-deficit hyperactivity disorder, and neuroinflammation [26, 43, 54-56].

The $\alpha7$ gene (CHRNA7) is located on chromosome 15q13-14, a region which has been linked with schizophrenia in several studies [57]. CHRNA7 has a partial duplication of exons that constitute the $\alpha7$-like receptor subunit gene or CHRFAM7A. The CHRFAM7A transcript may have a regulatory function on CHRNA7. This gene is transcribed in human brain and immortalized lymphocytes, but it is not known whether it is translated.

The presence of nAChRs has been shown in rat, mouse, rabbit and human lymphocytes (See Kawashima and Fujii [2]). Different nAChR subunits have been reported in blood cells although their patterns of expression and function remain unclear. A high variability in the expression pattern among individuals and within the same individual at different times has been observed [58]. Such variability suggests that the level of expression may be regulated by environmental factors and it probably explains the controversial results about the type of nAChR subunits expressed in blood cells that can be found throughout the literature [4, 59-61].

Controversial results either showing [3, 62] or discarding [4] the presence of muscle nAChR subunits in lymphocytes have been reported. We have also observed the expression of muscle nAChR subunits in freshly isolated lymphocytes [58]. However, the four different muscle subunits are not expressed simultaneously. In addition, we only detected the presence of the ε subunit, and not the γ subunit. In muscle, the γ subunit is expressed only in embryonic and denervated muscle. After maturation of the end plate, the γ subunit is replaced by the ε subunit. It seems likely that the lack of this subunit in lymphocytes is due to the fact that our study was restricted to adult blood cells. However, a direct correlation between muscle and blood cells cannot be established, since nerve-dependent trophic factors have been described as regulators of the expression of γ and ε subunits in the muscle junction [63]. An alternative explanation can be related to the high variability observed in the nAChRs expression, as it occurs for other subunits. Muscle nAChR subunits also appear to be expressed in incomplete sets in the thymus [64]. The reason why some but not all subunits are transcribed in a given sample remains intriguing given that the four different subunits are necessary for surface expression of the muscle nAChR.

Peng *et al.* [65] demonstrated by a combination of techniques (including RT-PCR, single-cell RT-PCR, Northern and Western blot analysis and immunofluorescence) the expression of both α9 and α10 in purified populations of T-cells (CD3+,CD4+, CD8+ and the Jurkat, MT2 and CEM T-cell lines). Despite the strong evidence about the expression of α9 and α10 in these cells, these authors were unable to demonstrate functionality of the α9-α10 receptor using single-cell electrophysiological techniques [65]. In addition, Peng *et al.* and Lustig *et al.* using different techniques demonstrated production of α9 and α10 mRNA in immortalized B-cells [65, 66].

Different neuronal nAChR subunits have been also detected in lymphocytes and their expression also shows variability among individuals. When Sato *et al.* [4] analyzed the expression, all donor MNLs expressed α2, α5 and α7 subunits, whereas no MNLs expressed α3, α4, β3 and β4 subunits. In contrast, α4 was detected in myeloma X63-Ag8 and hybridoma 1D6 cell lines [5]. Expression of α6 and β2 was observed in some samples (see review in Kawashima and Fujii [2]).

Many authors have reported the presence of α7 in lymphocytes and related cell lines. α7 was detected in murine B cell-derived myeloma X63-Ag8 and hybridoma 1D6 cell lines [5], in both B and T lymphocyte-derived leukemic cell lines [4]. The presence of both α4 and α7 subunits were demonstrated in B lymphocyte-derived cell lines, myeloma and hybridoma, with subunit-specific antibodies [5, 67]. These receptors may be involved in regulating cell proliferation and antibody production [5]. In agreement with these results, we have detected α7 subunit in most of the tested samples of peripheric human lymphocytes. In contrast to human cells, no α7 mRNA was detected in peripheric and splenic rat lymphocytes [58].

# Role of the Cholinergic System in the Modulation of Lymphocyte Function

## Synthesis of ACh after Phytohemagglutinin (PHA) Stimulation

Several reports have shown an increment of ACh released in PHA-stimulated lymphocytes. The increase in the neurotransmitter is demonstrated by the transcription induction of the enzyme responsible of its synthesis, ChAT [8, 12, 68]. It was also established that PHA activation increases α7 nAChR and M5 mAChR expression in lymphocytes [69, 70]. Up-regulation of M5 mAChR has been also observed in B-cell lines activated by *Staphylococcus aureus* [69]. These results suggest that the immunological stimulation acts as inductor of the ACh synthesis, and supports the idea that this neurotransmitter is also an immunoregulator through binding to cholinergic receptors.

## Role of Muscarinic Receptors in Lymphocyte Function

Fujino *et al.* [71] have shown that pretreatment of human peripheral blood lymphocytes (PBL) with oxotremorine (Oxo-M), a non-selective muscarinic receptor agonist, or ACh enhances PHA-induced interleukine-2 (IL-2) production. Interestingly, this effect is not observed when cells are incubated with nicotine, excluding that nAChR activation is directly involved in cytokine production. The authors reported that mAChRs are present in both CD4- and CD8-positive lymphocytes and that activation of these receptors enhances mRNA expression of IL-2 and IL-2 receptor subunits, production of IL-2, and cell proliferation of activated lymphocytes. More recently, it was shown that the M1 mAChR subtype is involved in the up-regulation of the IL-2 and IL-2 receptor in PBL and Jurkat cells [72]. IL-2 has a pivotal role in the generation and regulation of immune responses. It induces T cell proliferation, enhances activity of natural killer (NK) cells and supports long-term growth of antigen-specific T-cell clones [73]. It has been proposed that activation of muscarinic receptors (M1, M3 and M5) produces an increase in the intracellular $Ca^{2+}$ concentration that induces the expression of *c-fos*, a transcriptional regulator involved in cell proliferation [2].

Another effect on lymphocytes upon mAChR activation is the stimulation of nitric oxide (NO) synthase. Kamimura *et al.* [74] showed that this effect is probably mediated by M1 and M3 mAChRs. Little is known about the physiological role of NO in lymphocytes [2]. It has been postulated that NO has the capacity to assume the polarization of activated T cells to the type 2 profile, inhibiting the synthesis of Interferon-γ (IFN-γ) and enhancing IL-10 and IL-4 production [75]. In a recent study, it has been proposed that NO potentiates T-cell receptor signaling to antigen at the immunological synapse [76].

## Nicotinic Receptors Are Involved in Lymphocyte Functions

α7 nAChRs are involved in the modulation of cortisol-induced apoptosis. Incubation of human PBL with nicotine increases α7 gene expression [58]. Up-regulation of nAChRs due to long exposure to nicotine has been described in detail in many neuronal cells [77, 78]. In addition to the up-regulation of α7, nicotine exposure leads to a concentration-dependent protection of lymphocyte to cortisol-induced apoptosis (Figure 2). This observation is in accordance with the neuroprotective effect associated with the presence of the α7 nAChR in primary hippocampal cultures and in the rat pheochromocytoma cell line, PC12 [78-81].

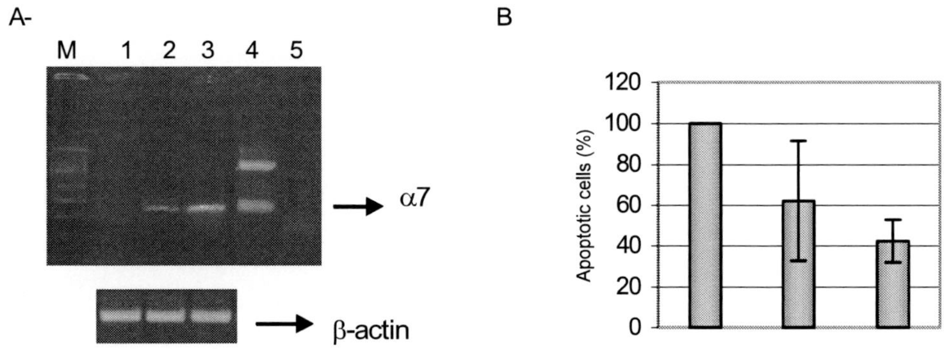


Figure 2. Nicotine incubation produces α7 up-regulation and apoptosis protection. A- Up-regulation of α7 in human lymphocytes by nicotine. Agarose gel electrophoresis of the semiquantitative RT-PCR reaction products from total RNA isolated from human lymphocytes. Total RNA was isolated from freshly human lymphocytes and from lymphocytes incubated in the presence and absence of nicotine (100 μM). Transcripts of the α7 nAChR (190 bp) were detected using RT-PCR. Samples were compared using β-actin mRNA expression as an internal standard. Sample 1: freshly isolated lymphocytes; sample 2: 48 h incubation without nicotine; sample 3: 48 h incubation with 100 μM nicotine; sample 4: PCR positive control (human α7 cDNA PCR product); sample 5: PCR negative control. M: DNA marker (100 bp ladder). The results are representative of 3 different experiments. B- Dose-dependent inhibition of cortisol-induced apoptosis by nicotine. Lymphocytes were incubated 24 h in the presence of different nicotine concentrations (10 and 100 μM) and then exposed to 10 μM cortisol. Twenty-four h later, cells were stained with DAPI. The degree of apoptosis for each condition was related to that achieved in the presence of cortisol alone, which was considered 100% apoptosis for the entire experiment. Results are expressed as mean ± SD of 4 independent experiments. Taken from De Rosa et al.[58] with permission.

Interestingly, we have also observed α7 up-regulation as well as apoptosis protection after incubation with α-bungarotoxin (α-BTX), a specific antagonist of α7, α9 and muscle nAChR [58]. These findings are different from reports on neurons, showing up-regulation of α7 but not protection from trophic factor withdrawal toxicity upon exposure to α-BTX [78, 82]. The explanation for this controversy can relay on the capacity of lymphocytes to synthesize ACh [83]. One possibility is that the new nAChRs induced after α-BTX incubation can be activated by the endogenous ACh before being blocked by α-BTX. This activation could be the starting point for the apoptosis inhibition. Under this hypothesis, activation of α7 would be related to its protective effect. However, it is more feasible that newly expressed nAChRs may be instantly blocked by α-BTX present in the medium.

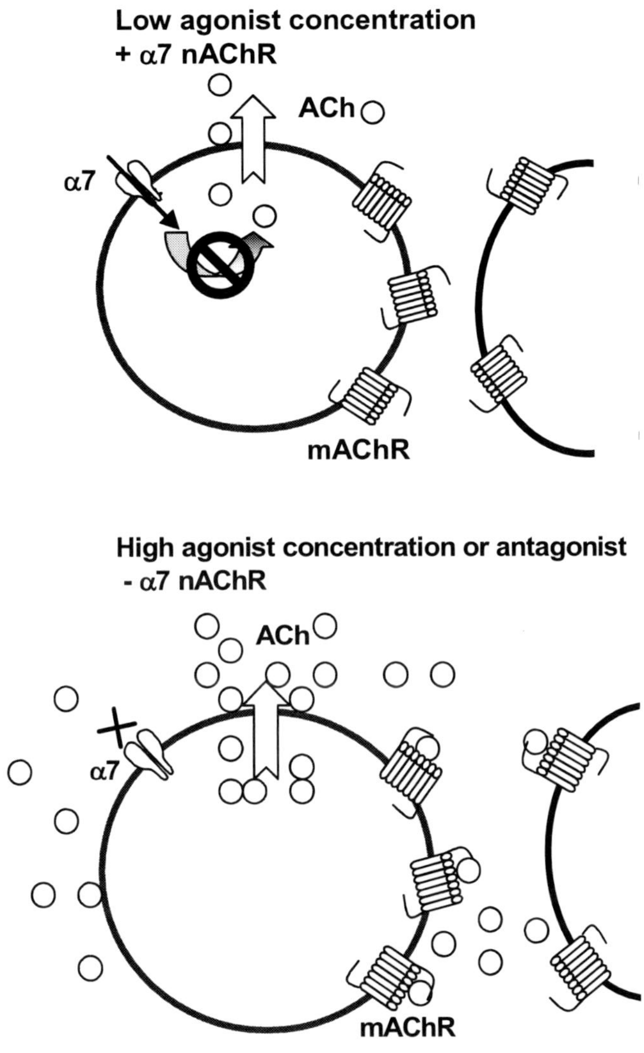


Figure 3. Hypothetical mechanism of the protection of cortisol-induced apoptosis in lymphocyte involving the α7 nAChRs The incubation with nicotine or α-BTX protects lymphocytes from cortisol-induced apoptosis by an unknown mechanism. The α7 nAChRs might be involved in this process by modulating ACh synthesis. Under this hypothesis, when α7 nAChRs are activated (+), the synthesis of ACh is inhibited. On the other hand, α7 inactivation (-), caused by long-term exposure to nicotine (desensitization) or α-BTX (blockade), blocks the inhibition and elevation of the ACh secretion occurs. Finally, secreted ACh activates mAChRs, which in turn may regulate the apoptosis process.

Therefore, another explanation can be that long term exposure to nicotine induces desensitization of α7 nAChRs, thus resulting in the same final effect as that exerted by incubation with an antagonist. Under this hypothesis, the blockade of α7 would be involved in the apoptosis protection. α7 nAChRs might act as modulators of the secretion of ACh, which in turn, may have an effect on apoptosis by acting through mAChRs or other types of nAChRs (Figure 3). Regarding this, stimulation of mAChRs induces $Ca^{2+}$ oscillations and up-regulates *c-fos* gene expression in lymphocytes [84]. It has been shown that *c-fos* is degraded by the multicatalytic proteasome in the early steps of cortisol-induced apoptosis [85]. Therefore, its up-regulation could be involved in the apoptosis protection.

These results suggest that α7 nAChRs in lymphocytes are involved in apoptosis modulation. Apoptosis is a process of high importance in maintaining homeostasis, especially in the immune system where cells are continually being generated and destroyed.

Other lines of experimental evidence support the anti-inflammatory activity mediated by the cholinergic system, specifically by ACh and α7 nAChRs. Recently, Nizri *et al.*[70] reported suppression of lymphocyte proliferation and production of pro-inflammatory cytokines (Tumor Necrosis Factor (TNF), IL-1β) upon treatment with inhibitors of acetylcholinesterase (AChEI). They attributed this effect to nAChRs since inhibition of T cell proliferation was observed after treatment with the agonist nicotine. Previous investigations have shown the anti-inflammatory effect of nicotine or α7 nAChR stimulation on the production of the pro-inflammatory cytokines in macrophages and microglia [86, 87].

Functional nicotinic α4β2 and α7 receptors have been detected in B-lymphocytes [5]. It has been shown that mice lacking nicotinic receptor subunits α4, β2 or α7 have less serum IgG and IgG-producing cells in the spleen, but show stronger immune response to both protein antigen *in vivo* and CD40 specific antibody *in vitro* than wild type mice [67]. Signalling through nAChR affects both the pre-immune state and activation of B lymphocytes in the immune response, possibly via CD40-dependent pathway. Skok *et al.*[67] suggested that T lymphocyte produces endogenous ACh and therefore, signalling through nicotinic receptors may mediate the neuro-immune interactions and it may be an additional pathway for the cross talk between B and T lymphocytes. The results from knock out mice studies reveal that the absence of a nAChR subunit had only moderate effects on immune response, indicating that signalling through nicotinic receptors is likely to exert a modulating, "tunning" effect on B lymphocyte-dependent immune processes. Recently, Skok *et al.*[88] have shown that both α4β2 and α7 nAChRs are involved in B lymphocyte development in the bone marrow, affecting the survival/expansion of developing B cells. In the spleen, the signal through α7 nAChRs favors both B and T cell expansion.

## Cross-Talk between the Cholinergic System of Immune and Neuronal Cells

There is an increasing body of evidence pointing to a close integration between the central nervous system and immunological functions with lymphocytes playing therein a central role. Hormones, cytokines and neurotransmitters are the main communicators between the nervous and immune systems. Many cytokines receptors have been localized in the CNS. These include receptors for IL-1, IL-2, IL-3, IL-4, IL-5, IL-6, IL-7, IL-10, Granulocyte Macrophage-Colony Stimulating Factor (GM-CSF), IFN, TNF [89, 90]. The existence of cytokine receptors on neurons indicates that cytokines have direct influence on neuronal function. In addition, lymphocytes can release neurotransmitters such as ACh and also express a number of cholinergic receptors, albeit further characterization is needed. Via these structures, lymphocytes and neurons are able to interact directly. For example, cytokine secretion in the CNS can be stimulated by neurotransmitter released.

Although the etiology and pathology of mental disorders are not well established, recent investigations have shown that there is a close association between the state of the immune system, particularly of lymphocytes, and major psychiatric disorders such as depression, stress, anxiety, schizophrenia, Alzheimer and Parkinson diseases [91]. Moreover, an immune-based neurodevelopmental hypothesis, in which autoimmune-T-cell deficiency is suggested to cause onset or progression of schizophrenia has been proposed [92]. Kipnis *et al.* [93] postulated that T-cell-mediated autoimmunity participates in physiological defense, maintenance and repair of the adult brain. However, unless such autoimmune responses to injury are rigorously controlled, they might lead to an autoimmune disease, where destructive activity overcomes the beneficial effect. In the case of schizophrenia, it has been proposed that brain damage occurring *in utero* or maternal immune activation during pregnancy can lead to release of fetal brain antigens to the periphery. These proteins enter the thymus of the fetus or neonate, and are presented by thymic epithelial cells to developing T cells. This causes deletion of or tolerance to T-cell clones reactive to these brain proteins, which will act as neuroprotective autoimmune T-cells. According to this theory, patients with schizophrenia lack the neuroprotective T-cells due to either prenatal deletion of these cells or acquisition of immune tolerance to them.

Lately, several studies revealed a comparable gene expression between lymphocytes and brain [91, 94]. Moreover, comparable gene expression was demonstrated in these tissues in patients with mental disorders. The availability of an accessible tissue whose gene expression profile is similar to more inaccessible CNS tissues has the potential to advance research in neuropsychiatric disorders, as well as the development of new peripheral biological markers for these diseases.

In schizophrenia, decreased levels of α7 nAChRs in postmortem brains of patients have been reported. By measuring mRNA levels in postmortem prefrontal cortex, it has been recently determined that the ratios of α7 to α7-like mRNA levels in bipolar disorder and schizophrenia are lower than in controls, with bipolar subjects showing the greatest magnitude of alteration [57]. On the other hand, Perl *et al.* detected decreased α7 mRNA levels in peripheral blood lymphocytes of schizophrenic patients [95]. Finally, the same investigators found negative correlation between the severity of the illness and the level of α7 mRNA in human lymphocytes [96]. These data substantiates the involvement of α7 nAChRs in the pathophysiology of schizophrenia and propose the assay of α7 nAChRs mRNA levels in PBLs as a potential peripheral biological marker for this illness.

A decrease in proteasome activity, possibly related to caspase activation, is detectable in PBLs of patients with Parkinson disease. These changes were disease related but also modulated by the pharmacological treatment, which confirms the potential role of apoptosis in PD pathogenesis and the modulatory influence of dopaminergic agents [97, 98].

Taken together, these observations suggest that lymphocytes could reflect the metabolism of brain cells and may be exploited as a neural and possible genetic probe in studies of psychiatric disorders. Candidate genes are the ones that encode proteins of the cholinergic system.

## Conclusion

Lymphocytes possess a complete cholinergic system: T cells contain ACh and express ChAT, an ACh synthesizing enzyme. Both T and B cells express mAChRs and nAChRs as well as AChE. The specific functions of the lymphoid cholinergic system are not precisely defined yet. Although several lines of new experimental evidence suggest that it may serve as an internal regulator of immune responses and it can mediate neuro-immune interactions.

The endogenous ACh synthesized by lymphocytes regulates cellular viability through binding to nicotinic receptors. In this respect, incubation of human lymphocytes with nicotine protects the cells from cortisol induced-apoptosis. During T cell activation, up-regulation of $\alpha 7$ and mAChRs as well as ACh synthesis have been reported.

It is probable that mAChRs act as effector receptors since their activation promotes directly IL-2 production and T cell proliferation. On the other hand, $\alpha 7$ receptors may act as modulators. Their action might be somewhat indirect since they affect the amount of neurotransmitter released available to interact with other receptors, such as the mAChRs.

Finally, it is very interesting to note that lymphocytes may reflect the metabolism of brain cells and this may be exploited as a neural and possible genetic probe in studies of psychiatric disorders. One candidate for these biological markers is the $\alpha 7$ receptor. Decreased levels of this receptor have been described in the brain as well as in lymphocytes of schizophrenic patients. Furthermore, studies comparing gene expression in neurons and leukocytes may help to identify responsible genes that underlie the processes of mental diseases. Lymphocytes may therefore serve as an easily accessible model to investigate alterations in immune neuroendocrine interactions observed in psychiatric disorders.

Concluding, a detailed understanding of the cross-talk between cholinergic system of lymphocytes and nervous system will be rewarded with many novel therapeutic strategies.

## Acknowledgments

This work was supported by grants from CONICET, Universidad Nacional del Sur, FONCYT and a fellowship from John Simon Guggenheim Memorial Foundation to CB and grants from Universidad Nacional del Sur to MCE.

## References

[1] Wessler I., Kirkpatrick C., and Racke C. (1998). Non-neuronal acetylcholine, a locally acting molecule, widely distributed in biological systems: expression and function in humans. *Pharmacol. Ther*. 77:59-79.

[2] Kawashima K., and Fujii T. (2000). Extraneuronal cholinergic system in lymphocytes. *Pharmacol. Ther*. 86:29-48.

[3] Toyabe S., Hai T., Fukuda M., Kawamura T., Susuki S., Uchiyama M., and Abo T. (1997). Identification of nicotinic receptors on lymphocytes in the periphery as well as thymus in mice. *Immunol.* 92:201-205.

[4] Sato K., Fujii T., Watanabe Y., Yamada S., Ando T., Kazuko F., and Kawashima K. (1999). Diversity of mRNA expression for muscarinic acetylcholine receptor subtypes and neuronal nicotinic acetylcholine receptor subunits in human mononuclear leukocytes and leukemic cell lines. *Neurosci. letter*. 266:17-20.

[5] Skok M., Kalashnik E., Koval L., Tsetlin V., Utkin Y., Changeaux J-P., and Grailhe R. (2003). Functional nicotinic acetylcholine receptors are expressed in B-lymphocytes-derived cell lines. *Mol. Pharmacol*. 64:885-889.

[6] Kawashima K., Kajiyama K., Susuki T., and Fujimoto K. (1993). Presence of acetylcholine in blood and its localization in circulating mononuclear leukocytes of human. *Biog. Amines*. 9:251-258.

[7] Tucek, S. (1988). Choline acetyltransferase and the synthesis of acetylcholine. *In* Handbook of experimental pharmacology. 86: 125-165. V. Whittaker, editor. Springer Verlag, Berlin. 125-165.

[8] Fujii T., Tsuchiya T., Yamada S., Fujimoto K., Susuki T., Kasahara T., and Kawashima, K. (1996). Localization and synthesis of acetylcholine in human leukemic T-cell lines. *J. Neurosci.* 44:66-72.

[9] Fujii T., Yamada S., Misawa H., Tajima S., Fujimoto K., Susuki T., and Kawashima K. (1995). Expression of choline acetyltransferase mRNA and protein in T-lymphocytes. *Proc. Jpn. Acad.* 71B.

[10] Ogawa H., Fujii T., Watanabe Y., and Kawashima K. (2003). Expression of multiple mRNA species for choline acetyltransferase in human T-lymphocytes. *Life Sci.* 72:2127-2130.

[11] Parsons S., Prior C., and Marshall T. (1993). Acetylcholine transport, storage and release. *Int. Rev. Neurobiol.* 35:279-390.

[12] Fujii, T., Yamada S., Watanabe Y., Misawa H., Tajima S., Fujimoto K., Kasahara T., and Kawashima K. (1998). Induction of choline acetyltransferase mRNA in human mononuclear leukocytes stimulated by phytohemagglutinin, a T-cell activator. *J. Neuroimmunol.* 82:101-107.

[13] Tayebati S., El-Assouad D., Ricci A., and Amenta F. (2002). Immunochemical and immunocytochemical characterization of cholinergic markers in human peripheral blood lymphocytes. *J. Neuroimmunol.* 132:147-155.

[14] Hulme E., Birdsall N., and Buckley N. (1990). Muscarinic receptor subtypes. *Annu. Rev. Pharmacol. Toxicol.* 30:633-673.

[15] Felder C. (1995). Muscarinic acetylcholine receptors: signal transduction through multiple effectors. *FASEB J.* 8:619-625.

[16] Hulme E., Lu Z., and Bee M. (2003). Scanning mutagenesis studies of the M1 muscarinic acetylcholine receptor. *Receptors. Channels*. 9:215-228.

[17] Burstein E., Spalding T., and Brann M. (1998). The second intracellular loop of the m5 muscarinic receptor is the switch which enables G-protein coupling. *J. Biol. Chem.* 273:24322-24327.

[18] Kubo T., Bujo H., Akiba I., Nakai J., Mishina M., and Numa S. (1988). Location of a region of the muscarinic acetylcholine receptor involved in selective effector coupling. *FEBS Lett.* 241:119-125.

[19] Wess J., Bonner T., Dorje F., and Brann M. (1990). Delineation of muscarinic receptor domains conferring selectivity of coupling to guanine nucleotide-binding proteins and second messengers. *Mol. Pharmacol.* 38:517-523.

[20] Wess J., Brann M., and Bonner T. (1989). Identification of a small intracellular region of the muscarinic m3 receptor as a determinant of selective coupling to PI turnover. *FEBS Lett.* 258:133-136.

[21] Wong S., Parker E., and Ross E. (1990). Chimeric muscarinic cholinergic: beta-adrenergic receptors that activate Gs in response to muscarinic agonists. *J. Biol. Chem.* 265:6219-6224.

[22] Burstein E., Spalding T., and Brann M. (1998). The second intracellular loop of the m5 muscarinic receptor is the switch which enables G-protein coupling. *J. Biol. Chem.* 273:24322-24327.

[23] Koppen C., and Kaiser B. (2003). Regulation of muscarinic acetylcholine receptor signaling. *Pharmacol. Ther.* 98:197-220.

[24] Bonner T. (1989). The molecular basis of muscarinic receptor diversity. *Trends. Neurosci.* 12:148-151.

[25] Hellstrom-Lindahl E., and Nordberg A. (1996). Muscarinic receptor subtypes in subpopulations of human blood mononuclear cells as analyzed by RT-PCR technique. *J. Neuroimmunol.* 68:139-144.

[26] Gotti C., Zoli M., and Clementi, F. (2006). Brain nicotinic acetylcholine receptors: native subtypes and their relevance. *Trends. Pharmacol. Sci.* 27:482-491.

[27] Gotti C., and Clementi F. (2004). Neuronal nicotinic receptors: from structure to pathology. *Prog. Neurobiol.* 74:363-396.

[28] Le Novere N., and Changeux J. (1995). Molecular evolution of the nicotinic acetylcholine receptor: an example of multigene family in excitable cells. *J. Mol. Evol.* 40:155-172.

[29] Ortells M., and Lunt G. (1995). Evolutionary history of the ligand-gated ion-channel superfamily of receptors. *Trends. Neurosci.* 118:121-127.

[30] McGehee D., and Role L. (1996). Presynaptic ionotropic receptors. *Curr. Opin. Neurobiol.* 6:342-349.

[31] Elgoyhen A.B., Vetter D.E., Katz E., Rothlin C., Heinemann S., and Boulter J. (2001). Alpha10: a determinant of nicotinic cholinergic receptor function in mammalian vestibular and cochlear mechanosensory hair cells. *Proc. Natl. Acad. Sci. USA.* 98:3501-6.

[32] Lester H., Dibas M., Dahan D., Leite J., and Dougherty D. (2004). Cys-loop receptors: new twists and turns. *Trends. Neurosci.* 27:329-336.

[33] Chakrapani S., Bailey T., and Auerbach A. (2004). Gating dynamics of the acetylcholine receptor extracellular domain. *J. Gen. Physiol.* 123:341-356.

[34] Kash T., Jenkins A., Kelley J., Trudell J., and Harrison N. (2003). Coupling of agonist binding to channel gating in the GABA (A) receptor. *Nature.* 421:272-275.

[35] Miyazawa A., Fujiyoshi Y., and Unwin N. (2003). Structure and Gating Mechanism of the Acetylcholine Receptor Pore. *Nature.* 423: 944-955.

[36] Bouzat C., Gumilar F., Spitzmaul G., Wang H., Rayes D., Hansen S., Taylor P., and Sine S. (2004). Coupling of agonist binding to channel gating in an ACh-binding protein linked to an ion channel. *Nature*. 430:896-900.

[37] Brejc K., van Dijk W.J., Klaassen R.V., Schuurmans M., van Der O.J., Smit A.B., and Sixma T.K. (2001). Crystal Structure of an ACh-Binding Protein Reveals the Ligand-Binding Domain of Nicotinic Receptors. *Nature*. 411:269-276.

[38] Bourne Y., Talley T., Hansen S., Taylor P., and Marchot P. (2005). Crystal structure of a Cbtx-AChBP complex reveals essential interactions between snake alpha-neurotoxins and nicotinic receptors. *EMBO J*. 24:1512-1522.

[39] Celie P., van Rossum-Fikkert S., van Dijk W., Brejc K., Smit A., and Sixma T. (2004). Nicotine and carbamylcholine binding to nicotinic acetylcholine receptors as studied in AChBP crystal structures. *Neuron*. 41:907-914.

[40] Schapira M., Abagyan R., and Totrov M. (2002). Structural model of nicotinic acetylcholine receptor isotypes bound to acetylcholine and nicotine. *BMC Struct. Biol.* 2:1.

[41] Sixma T., and Smit A. (2003). Acetylcholine binding protein (AChBP): a secreted glial protein that provides a high-resolution model for the extracellular domain of pentameric ligand-gated ion channels. *Annu. Rev. Biophys. Biomol. Struct.* 32:311-334.

[42] Cascio M. (2004). Structure and function of the glycine receptor and related nicotinicoid receptors. *J. Biol. Chem*. 279:19383-19386.

[43] Hogg R., Raggenbass M., and Bertrand D. (2003). Nicotinic acetylcholine receptors: from structure to brain function. *Rev. Physiol. Biochem. Pharmacol.* 147:1-46.

[44] Swope S., Moss S., Raymond L., and Huganir R. (1999). Regulation of ligand-gated ion channels by protein phosphorylation. *Adv. Second Messenger Phosphoprotein Res.* 33:49-78.

[45] Unwin N. (2005). Refined structure of the nicotinic acetylcholine receptor at 4A resolution. *J. Mol. Biol.* 346:967-989.

[46] Arias H. (2000). Localization of agonist and competitive antagonist binding sites on nicotinic acetylcholine receptors. *Neurochem. Int*. 36:595-645.

[47] Arias H., McCardy E., and Blanton M. (2001). Characterization of the dizocilpine binding site on the nicotinic acetylcholine receptor. *Mol. Pharmacol.* 59:1051-1060.

[48] Arias H., McCardy E., Bayer E., Gallagher M., and Blanton M. (2002). Allosterically linked noncompetitive antagonist binding sites in the resting nicotinic acetylcholine receptor ion channel. *Arch. Biochem. Biophys.* 403:121-131.

[49] Changeux J., and Edelstein S. (1998). Allosteric Receptors after 30 Years. *Neuron*. 21:959-980.

[50] Corringer P., Le Novere N., and Changeux J. (2000). Nicotinic receptors at the amino acid level. *Annu. Rev. Pharmacol. Toxicol.* 40: 431-458.

[51] Jones M., and Westbrook G. (1996). The impact of receptor desensitization on fast synaptic transmission. *Trends. Neurosci*. 19:96-101.

[52] Quick M., and Lester R. (2002). Desensitization of neuronal nicotinic receptors. *J. Neurobiol.* 53:457-478.

[53] Arias H., Bhumireddy P., and Bouzat C. (2006). Molecular mechanisms and binding site locations for noncompetitive antagonists of nicotinic acetylcholine receptors. *Int. J. Biochem. Cell Biol.* 38:1254-1276.

[54] Tuppo E., and Arias H. (2005). The role of inflammation in Alzheimer's disease. *Int. J. Biochem. Cell Biol.* 37:289-305.

[55] Lloyd G., and Williams M. (2000). Neuronal nicotinic acetylcholine receptors as novel drug targets. *J. Pharmacol. Exp. Ther.* 292:461-467.

[56] Leonard S., and Bertrand D. (2001). Neuronal nicotinic receptors: from structure to function. *Nicotine Tob. Res.* 3:203-223.

[57] De Luca V., Likhodi O., Van Tol H., Kennedy J., and Wong A. (2006). Regulation of alpha7-nicotinic receptor subunit and alpha7-like gene expression in the prefrontal cortex of patients with bipolar disorder and schizophrenia. *Acta. Psychiatr. Scand.* 114:211-215.

[58] De Rosa M.J., Esandi M.C., Garelli A., Rayes D., and Bouzat C. (2005). Relationship between α7 nAChR and apoptosis in human lymphocytes. *J. Neuroimmunol.* 160:154-161.

[59] Kuo Y.-P., Lucero L., Michaels J., DeLuca D., and Lukas R. (2002). Differential expression of nicotinic acetylcholine receptor subunits in fetal and neonatal mouse thymus. *J. Neuroimmunol.* 130:140-154.

[60] Hiemke C., Stolp M., Reuss S., Wevers A., Reinhardt S., Maelicke A., Schlegel S., and Schroder H. (1996). Expression of alpha subunit genes of nicotinic acetylcholine receptors in human lymphocytes. *Neurosci. Lett.* 214:171-174.

[61] Navaneetham D., Penn A., Howard Jr J., and Conti-Fine B. (1997). Expression of the alpha 7 subunit of the nicotinic acetylcholine receptor in normal and myasthenic hum thymuses. *Cell Mol. Biol.* 43:433-442.

[62] Wakkach A., Guyon T., Bruand C., Tzartos S., Cohen-Kaminsky S., and Berrih-Aknin S. (1996). Expression of acetylcholine receptor genes in human thymic epithelial cells: implications for myasthenia gravis. *J. Immunol.* 157:3752-3760.

[63] Witzemann V., Schwarz H., Koenen M., Berberich C., Villaroel A., Werning A., Brenner H., and Sakmann B. (1996). Acetylcholine receptor epsilon subunit deletion causes muscle weakness and atrophy in juvenile and adult mice. *Proc. Natl. Acad. Sci. USA.* 96:13286-13291.

[64] Bruno R., Sabater L., Tolosa E., Sospedra M., Ferrer-Francesch X., Coll J., Foz M., Melms A., and Pujol-Borrell R. (2004). Different patterns of nicotinic acetylcholine receptor subunit transcription in human thymus. *J. Neuroimmunol.* 149:147-159.

[65] Peng H., Ferris R., Matthews T., Hiel H., Lopez-Albaitero A., and Lustig L. (2004). Characterization of the human nicotinic acetylcholine receptor subunit alpha (alpha) 9 (CHRNA9) and alpha (alpha) 10 (CHRNA10) in lymphocytes. *Life Sci.* 76:263-280.

[66] Lustig L., Peng H., Hiel H., Yamamoto T., and Fuchs P. (2001). Molecular cloning and mapping of the human nicotinic acetylcholine receptor α10 (CHRNA10). *Genomics.* 73:272-283.

[67] Skok M., Grailhe R., and Changeaux J.-P. (2005). Nicotinic receptors regulate B lymphocyte activation and immune response. *Eur. J. Pharmacol.* 517:246-251.

[68] Rinner I., and Schauenstein K. (1993). Detection of choline-acetyltransferase activity in lymphocytes. *J. Neurosci. Res.* 35:188-191.

[69] Fujii T., Watanabe Y., Inoue T., and Kawashima K. (2003). Upregulation of mRNA encoding the M5 muscarinic acetylcholine receptor in human T- and B-lymphocytes during immunological responses. *Neurochem. Res.* 3:423-429.

[70] Nizri E., Hamra-Amitay Y., Sicsic C., Lavon I., and Brenner T. (2006). Anti-inflammatory properties of cholinergic up-regulation: a new role for acetylcholinesterase inhibitors. *Neuropharmacol.* 50:540-547.

[71] Fujino H., Kitamura Y., Yada T., Uehara T., and Nomura Y. (1997). Stimulatory roles of muscarinic acethylcholine receptors on T cell antigen receptor/CD3 complex-mediated interleukin-2 production in human peripheral blood lymphocytes. *Mol. Pharmacol.* 51:1007-1014.

[72] Nomura J., Hosoi T., Okuma Y., and Nomura Y. (2003). The presence and functions of muscarinic receptors in human T cells: the involvement in IL-2 and IL-2 receptor system. *Life Sci.* 72:2121-2126.

[73] Kuby, J. (1994). Cytokines. *In* Immunology. 297-322. Second edition. Editor: Freeman, WH, New York.

[74] Kamimura Y., Fujii T., Kojima H., Nagano T., and Kawashima K. (2003). Nitric oxide (NO) synthase mRNA expression and NO production via muscarinic acetylcholine receptor-mediated pathways in the CEM, human leukemic T-cell line. *Life Sci.* 72:2152-2154.

[75] Benbernou N., Esnault S., Shin H., Fekkar H., and Guenounou M. (1997). Differential regulation of IFN-γ, IL-10 and inducible nitric oxide synthase in human T cells by cyclic AMP-dependent signal transduction pathways. *Immunol.* 91:361-368.

[76] Ibiza S., Victor V., Bosca I., Ortega A., Urzainqui A., O'Connor J., Sanchez-Madrid F., Esplugues J., and Serrador J. (2006). Endothelial nitric oxide synthase regulates T cell receptor signaling at the immunological synapse. *Immunity.* 24:753-765.

[77] Wonnacott S. (1990). The paradox of nicotinic acetylcholine receptor upregulation by nicotine. *Trends. Pharmacol. Sci.* 11:216-219.

[78] Jonnala R., and Buccafusco J. (2001). Relationship between the increased cell surface alpha 7 nicotinic receptor expression and neuroprotection induced by several nicotinic receptor agonists. *J. Neurosci. Res.* 66:565-572.

[79] Li Y., Papke R., He Y., Millard W., and Meyer E. (1999). Characterization of the neuroprotective and toxic effects of alpha 7 nicotinic receptor activation in PC12 cells. *Brain Res.* 830:218-225.

[80] Dajas-Bailador F., Lima P., and Wonnacott S. (2000). The α7 nicotinic acetylcholine receptor subtype mediates nicotine protection against NMDA excitotoxicity in primary hippocampal cultures through a Ca2+ dependent mechanism. *Neuropharmacol.* 39:2799-2807.

[81] Guan Z., Zhang X., Mousavi M., Tian J., Unger C., and Nordberg A. (2001). Reduced expression of neuronal nicotinic acetylcholine receptors during the early stages of damage by oxidative stress in PC12 cells. *J. Neurosci. Res.* 66:551-558.

[82] Hejmadi M., Dajas-Bailador F., Barns S., Jones B., and Wonnacott S. (2003). Neuroprotection by nicotine against hypoxia-induced apoptosis in cortical cultures

involves activation of multiple nicotinic acethylcholine receptor subtypes. *Neurosci.* 24:779-786.

[83] Kawashima K., Fujii T., Watanabe Y., and Misawa H. (1998). Acetylcholine synthesis and muscarinic receptor subtype mRNA expression in T-lymphocytes. *Life Sci.* 62:1701-1705.

[84] Fujii T., and Kawashima K. (2000). Calcium signaling and c-fos gene expression via M3 muscarinic acetylcholine receptors in human T- and B- cell lines. *Jpn. J. Pharmacol.* 84:124-132.

[85] Distelhorst C. (2002). Recent insights into the mechanism of glucocorticosteroid-induced apoptosis. *Cell death Diff.* 9:6-19.

[86] Wang H., Yu M., Ochani M., Amella C., Tanovic M., Susarla S., Li J., Yang H., Ulloa L., Al-Abed Y., Czura C., and Tracey K. (2003). Nicotinic acetylholine receptor alpha7 subunit is an essential regulator of inflammation. *Nature*. 421:384-388.

[87] Shytle R, Mori T, Townsend K., Vendrame M., Sun N., Zeng J., Ehrhart J., Silver A., Sanberg P., and Tan J. (2004). Cholinergic modulation of microglial activation by alpha 7 nicotinic receptors. *J. Neurochem*. 89:337-343.

[88] Skok M., Grailhe R., Agenes F., and Changeaux J.-P. (2006). The role of nicotinic acetylcholine receptors in lymphocyte. *J. Neuroimmunol.* 171:86-98.

[89] Sternberg F. (1997). Neural immune interaction in health and disease. *J. Clin. Invest.* 100:2641-2647.

[90] Turnbull A., and Rivier C. (1999). Regulation of the hypothalamic pituitary adrenal axis by cytokines action s and mechanism of action. *Physiol. Rev*. 79:1-71.

[91] Gladkevich A., Kauffman H., and Korl J. (2004). Lymphocyte as a neural probe: potential for studying psychiatric disorders. *Prog. Neuropsicopharmacol. Biol. Psychiatric*. 28:559-576.

[92] Kipnis J., Cardon M., Strous R., and Schwartz M. (2006). Loss of autoimmune T cells correlates with brain diseases: possible implications for schizophrenia? *Trends. Mol. Med*. 12:107-112.

[93] Kipnis J., Mizrahi T., Hauben E., Shaked I., Schevach E., and Schwartz M. (2002). Neuroprotective autoimmunity: Naturally occurring CD4+CD25+ regulatory T cells suppress the ability to withstand injury to the central nervous system. *Proc. Natl. Acad. Sci. USA*. 99:15620-15625.

[94] Sullivan P., Fan C., and Perou C. (2006). Evaluating the comparability of gene expression in blood and brain. *Am. J. Med. Genet. B Neuropsychiatr. Genet*. 141:261-268.

[95] Perl O., Ilani T., Strous R., Lapidus R., and Fuchs S. (2003). The $\alpha 7$ nicotinic acetylcholine receptor in shizophrenia: decreased mRNA levels in peripheral blood lymphocytes. *FASEB*. 17:1948-1950.

[96] Perl O., Strous R., Dranikov A., Chen R., Fuchs S., Perl O., Strous R., Dranikov A., Chen R., and Fuchs S. (2006). Low levels of alpha7-nicotinic acetylcholine receptor mRNA on peripheral blood lymphocytes in schizophrenia and its association with illness severity. *Neuropsychobiol*. 53:88-93.

[97] Blandini F., Mangiagalli A., Cosentino M., Marino F., Samuele A., Rasini E., Fancellu R., Martignoni E., Riboldazzi G., Calandrella D., Frigo G., and Nappi G. (2003).

Peripheral markers of apoptosis in Parkinson's disease: the effect of dopaminergic drugs. *Ann. NY Acad. Sci.* 1010:675-678.

[98] Blandini F., Sinforiani E., Paahetti C., Samuele A., Bazzini E., Zangaglia R., Nappi G., and Martignoni E. (2006). Peripheral proteasome and caspase activity in Parkinson disease and Alzheimer disease. *Neurology*. 66:529-534.

# Index

## #



## A

## B

## C

## E

## F

## G

## H

# I

## M

## N

## O

## P

## Q



## R

## S

## U

## V



## W

## Y



## Z